OXFORD CLASSICAL MONOGRAPHS

*Published under the supervision of a Committee of the
Faculty of Literae Humaniores in the University of Oxford.*

OXFORD CLASSICAL MONOGRAPHS

The aim of the Oxford Classical Monographs series (which replaces the Oxford Classical and Philosophical Monographs) is to publish outstanding theses on Greek and Latin literature, ancient history, and ancient philosophy examined by the faculty board of Literae Humaniores.

PROPHECY AND HISTORY
IN THE
CRISIS OF THE
ROMAN EMPIRE

A Historical Commentary on the
Thirteenth Sibylline Oracle

D. S. POTTER

CLARENDON PRESS · OXFORD
1990

Oxford University Press, Walton Street, Oxford OX2 6DP

Oxford New York Toronto
Delhi Bombay Calcutta Madras Karachi
Petaling Jaya Singapore Hong Kong Tokyo
Nairobi Dar es Salaam Cape Town
Melbourne Auckland

and associated companies in
Berlin Ibadan

Oxford is a trade mark of Oxford University Press

Published in the United States
by Oxford University Press, New York

British Library Cataloguing in Publication Data
Potter, D. S. (David S)
Prophecy and history in the crisis of the Roman Empire: a
historical commentary on the Thirteenth Sibylline Oracle.
1. Sibylline oracles
I. Title
292.32
ISBN 0–19–814483–0

Library of Congress Cataloging in Publication Data
Potter, D. S. (David Stone), 1957–
Prophecy and history in the crisis of the Roman Empire: a
historical commentary on the Thirteenth Sibylline Oracle
(Oxford classical monographs)
Based on author's thesis completed in 1984.
Includes bibliographical references and index.
1. Oracular Sibyllina. 2. Rome—History—Period of military
anarchy, 235–284. I. Title. II. Series.
DG305.P68 1990 937'.07—dc20 90–38880
ISBN 0–19–814483–0

Set by Joshua Associates Limited, Oxford
Printed in Great Britain by
Bookcraft (Bath) Ltd., Midsomer Norton, Somerset

D. M. S.

H. L. P. ET B. A. P.

Preface and Acknowledgements

THE authors of the *Thirteenth Sibylline Oracle* were neither great poets nor profound thinkers. Indeed, the principal compiler of this text was a person of extraordinarily literal mind: it was no doubt a matter of some comfort to him that it was possible to interpret the crises of these years through the medium of prophecy. By doing so, this author has provided us with a unique insight into the way that the political and military failure of the Roman state, its failure to protect its subjects from outside aggression, impinged upon the life of a very average member of the upper classes in the province of Syria. The oracle is not only the sole surviving contemporary narrative account of the years AD 240–60 from within the Roman empire, it is also one of the rare pictures that we have of Roman history in any period from the pen of a provincial who had no obvious connection with the government. *The Thirteenth Sibylline Oracle* is therefore an unusual example of 'popular history', history from the perspective of the man in the street. We are particularly fortunate that this man in the street was reflecting upon a time of great drama in the history of the empire, and that we can see how the emperors and their agents appeared to their subjects at a time in which they were under tremendous pressure. We can see the history of these years through the eyes of a victim of the campaigns of Sapor I, which shook the government of Rome to its core.

The obscurity and complexity of the oracle have dictated the form of this book. It seemed to me that no good purpose would be served without a detailed commentary, and, as a number of readers of earlier versions pointed out to me, the commentary was difficult to use without a substantial introduction. There is some repetition between the commentary and the introduction, but I hope that this may be excused in the interests of clarity: neither the period nor the text is straightforward.

I should also say a few words about the view of Roman history implied in the title of this book. I take the word 'crisis' to mean 'a time of acute difficulty or danger', and I believe that this is an accurate description of the period between the death of Alexander Severus and the establishment of the tetrarchy from the perspective of the governing class of the Roman empire (by governing class I mean the army and the members of the imperial bureaucracy). I do not take it to mean that every peasant perceived that his or her world was undergoing profound or sudden changes, or that the world was notably more insecure than that of his or her ancestors; the lot of the peasant was squalid in the second century, it remained squalid in the third century, and continued to be so for centuries to come. The death of Decius in 251 and the sack of Antioch in 252 had a direct impact only on the very tiny proportion of the population which happened to be in the vicinity, and I doubt that the vast majority of people in the empire much cared or noticed. I suspect that the reforms instigated by Diocletian after 284 had considerably more impact, especially after refinements introduced by Constantine: the foundation of Constantinople and the espousal of Christianity. It could be argued that these reforms were no more than the logical development and culmination of administrative changes which had been taking place in a haphazard way since the reign of Marcus Aurelius. The more we know about the third century, the less original Diocletian appears. By the time that Gallienus was murdered in 268, the western senatorial career was taking on the pattern with which we are familiar in the fourth century, and the emperor himself was surrounded by a select field army that already appears to have been described as the *comitatus* by the time of Aurelian, if it had not, indeed, received that name under Gallienus as well. Smaller provinces were being carved out of larger ones in western Asia Minor during the reign of Philip. The emperor Valerian had provided an eloquent model for the persecution of the Christians, Gallienus had provided a model for edicts of toleration, and Aurelian provided a model for imperial intervention in ecclesiastical disputes. When Aurelian was murdered in 275 the coinage and imperial budget were still in disarray (the legacy of errors made from the period between Gordian III and Gallienus as the emperors clung to an unworkable pattern of finance), but, with the exception of Dacia, the frontiers were roughly where they had been when Septimius Severus died in 211.

A list of third-century 'precedents' for the government of Diocletian does credit neither to the emperors of the third century, nor to Diocletian himself. When Philip the Arab created the province of Caria-Phrygia, appointed his brother Julius Priscus as *corrector totius orientis*, or, as we now know that he styled himself, 'governor of Mesopotamia exercising the highest power', and his kinsman Servianus to a comparable position in the Balkans, he was not looking ahead to the Diocletianic *dioceses* or to the tetrarchy. He was responding to the need for strong central direction on two volatile frontiers, and the need to improve the efficiency of his administration. Furthermore, he failed. He succumbed to a revolution which began among the Danubian legions and, at the same time, was faced by a substantial revolt raging in the east. This can hardly be described as an encouraging precedent for Diocletian, who was about twelve years old and growing up around Sirmium when the fatal revolt broke out in the wake of Philip's proclamation of the millennium. Diocletian would probably have been twenty-four and in the early stages of his military service in 260 when Valerian was captured by the Persians, and he would scarcely have regarded the subsequent splintering of the empire as an event presaging his own reforms: I suspect that he would have regarded it as a catastrophe. The actions that he took as emperor do indeed have precedents in the years during which Diocletian and his contemporaries grew to maturity; the events of those years showed them the range of options that were available to them, and the pitfalls to be avoided.

The justification for Roman government was simple: it was victory in war. During the middle years of the third century the emperors ceased to win, and the weaknesses that were inherent in the monarchy were laid bare. The army upon which the emperors based their power was insufficiently disciplined, the financial system which supported it was shaky, and its leaders were incapable of meeting the challenges posed by the extraordinarily capable Sapor I. Diocletian styled himself and his colleagues as the men who restored the order of the Roman empire through the favour of the gods as revealed through their own capacity to slaughter barbarians. But it was not the old order of the empire that they had renewed. They created a new order, built upon their experience of Rome's failures under the leaders of the older generation in 'a time of acute difficulty or danger'.

Personalities matter in the history of a tiny governing class. Personal experience and personal ability go a long way towards explaining specific developments in the history of the Roman empire. The development of the late Roman system of government through a series of pragmatic responses by a group of capable officers to the failures of their predecessors was to have a profound effect upon the social, cultural, and intellectual milieu of the Mediterranean world for centuries to come.

This work began when the Fellows of New College elected me to a Harold Salvesen Junior Research Fellowship in 1981. I am extremely grateful to the late Warden, Arthur Cooke, and the Fellows for giving me that opportunity. I am further grateful to the college for the continuing support that it has given to my work, providing me with a congenial and comfortable base on the many occasions I have returned to Oxford after the completion of the thesis, from which this book emerged, in 1984. The final work on the manuscript was completed in Michaelmas term of 1989 while I held a Visiting Research Fellowship there, with additional support from a research grant provided by the Horace H. Rackham Graduate School of the University of Michigan. I owe an especial debt in this regard to the Dean, John Cowan, and for his friendship throughout these years.

I also owe considerable debts to two other institutions. The members of the Departments of Latin and Greek at Bryn Mawr College provided me with unstinting assistance and a marvellous environment in which to work from 1984 to 1986. The same is now true of the Department of Classical Studies at the University of Michigan. This work has been considerably improved by my colleagues and students in both places.

I owe further debts to the many scholars who have helped me at various times, and who have offered suggestions to improve this work at different stages. P. M. Fraser and R. G. M. Nisbet oversaw the earliest phases of my research, and the examiners of the thesis, C. R. Whittaker and E. L. Bowie, were most thorough in their reading. I have taken account of a number of their suggestions in this book. C. J. Howgego gave me invaluable assistance with the plates and advice on numismatic matters; Dr A. Burnett of the Department of Coins and Medals at the British Museum also provided prompt and generous assistance with other plates. B. W. Frier has allowed me to make extensive use of his chapter on the demography of the Roman empire in advance of publication, D. O. Ross has helped with assorted problems, Ludwig Koenen has given me the benefit of his learning on many questions relating to oracular literature. John Dillery and Ann Hanson read the proofs and saved me from a number of errors. I am also deeply grateful to Dr J. Waś (copy-editor for the Press) for his careful and helpful reading of the manuscript. New College and the Craven Committee provided me with grants that enabled me to visit eastern Turkey and Syria in 1982; New College also provided grants for a trip to western Turkey in 1981 and to Rome in 1983, where I was able to collate Codex Vaticanus gr. 1120 and Codex Vaticanus gr. 743, the principal manuscripts for the oracle. Bryn Mawr College provided me with a generous grant which enabled me to return to Turkey in 1985.

Glen Bowersock first taught me the principles of historical investigation as an undergraduate, between 1975 and 1979. In subsequent years his firm friendship, support, and gentle criticism have done much to improve every aspect of the commentary. John Matthews was the supervisor of the original thesis. He made the process of composition a real pleasure, and I have been unstinting in my inquiries of him throughout the years since: his influence informs every page. The extraordinary collection of classicists which inhabits New College, Professor W. G. Forrest, G. E. M. de Ste Croix, J. B. Hainsworth, R. J. Lane Fox, and our colleague, Professor A. Andrewes, has given me more than I can possibly describe. No student of the ancient world could ask for more kindness or patience, or for better friends. I can only hope that this book does not fall too far short of the standards they have set—though I am conscious that despite all the help that I have received there remains much that I could say better.

Rowland Smith and Nick Stylianou, Robert George and Michael Makin have shared in every stage of this work; their friendship has sustained this project through many travails. My parents have offered constant support for a course which none of us could have imagined in 1979. Ellen Bauerle made the completion of this work possible. It is dedicated to the memory of my grandparents, Harold and Barbara Potter, in deep gratitude for all they did.

D.S.P.

Ann Arbor, Michigan, and Oxford

Contents

List of Illustrations

Nos. 1–7, 9–22, 24, and 26 are reproduced courtesy of the Ashmolean Museum, Oxford; Nos. 8, 23, 25, and 27 are reproduced courtesy of the British Museum, London.

Abbreviations

General

AAS	*Les Annales archéologiques de Syrie*
AAWW	*Anzeiger der Österreichischen Akademie der Wissenschaften in Wien*
AÉ	*L'Année épigraphique*
AJP	*American Journal of Philology*
ANRW	*Aufstieg und Niedergang der römischen Welt*, ed. H. Temporini *et al.* (Berlin, 1972–)
Ath. Mitt.	*Athenische Mitteilungen*
AW	*Ancient World*
BCH	*Bulletin de correspondance hellénique*
BÉ	*Bulletin épigraphique*
BHAC	*Bonner Historia Augusta Colloquium*
BICS	*Bulletin of the Institute of Classical Studies*
BSOAS	*Bulletin of the School of Oriental and African Studies*
BZ	*Byzantinische Zeitschrift*
CAH	*The Cambridge Ancient History* (Cambridge, 1923–)
CJ	*Classical Journal*
Collins	J. J. Collins, 'The Sibylline Oracles'
CP	*Classical Philology*
CQ	*Classical Quarterly*
CR	*Classical Review*
CRAI	*Comptes rendus de l'Académie des Inscriptions et Belles-Lettres*
CSEL	Corpus Scriptorum Ecclesiasticorum Latinorum
GGA	*Göttingische gelehrte Anzeigen*
GNP	gross national product
GRBS	*Greek, Roman and Byzantine Studies*
HSCP	*Harvard Studies in Classical Philology*
HTR	*Harvard Theological Review*
IEJ	*Israel Exploration Journal*
JA	*Journal asiatique*
JBL	*Journal of Biblical Literature*
JEA	*Journal of Egyptian Archaeology*

JHS	*Journal of Hellenic Studies*
JJS	*Journal of Jewish Studies*
JNES	*Journal of Near Eastern Studies*
JQR	*Jewish Quarterly Review*
JRA	*Journal of Roman Archaeology*
JRS	*Journal of Roman Studies*
JTS	*Journal of Theological Studies*
LCM	*Liverpool Classical Monthly*
MAAR	*Memoirs of the American Academy in Rome*
MÉFR	*Mélanges de l'École Française de Rome*
MH	*Museum Helveticum*
MRR	T. R. S. Broughton, *The Magistrates of the Roman Republic*
MUSJ	*Mélanges de l'Université St. Joseph*
NGG	*Nachrichten von der Gesellschaft der Wissenschaften zu Göttingen*
NJA	*Neue Jahrbücher für das klassische Altertum*
Num. Chron.	*Numismatic Chronicle*
PCPS	*Proceedings of the Cambridge Philological Society*
PIR	*Prosopographia Imperii Romani*
PL	Patrologia Latina
PLRE	*Prosopography of the Later Roman Empire*
PO	*Patrologia Orientalis*
PW	H. W. Parke and D. E. W. Wormell, *The Delphic Oracle*, ii. *The Oracular Responses*
RB	*Revue biblique*
RE	*Real-Encyclopädie der classischen Altertumswissenschaft*, ed. A. Fr. von Pauly, rev. G. Wissowa *et al.* (Stuttgart, 1894–1980)
RÉA	*Revue des études anciennes*
RÉ Arm.	*Revue des études arméniennes*
RÉG	*Revue des études grecques*
Rev. Num.	*Revue numismatique*
Rev. Phil.	*Revue de philologie, de littérature et d'histoire anciennes*
RM	*Rheinisches Museum*
RSCI	*Rivista di storia della chiesa in Italia*
SAWW	Sitzungsberichte der Österreichischen Akademie der Wissenschaft

SBAW	Sitzungsberichte der Bayerischen Akademie der Wissenschaften
SEG	*Supplementum Epigraphicum Graecum*
Studien	A. Alföldi, *Studien zur Geschichte der Weltkrise des 3. Jahrhunderts nach Christus*
TAPA	*Transactions of the American Philological Association*
WS	*Wiener Studien*
YCS	*Yale Classical Studies*
ZN	*Zeitschrift für Numismatik*
ZPE	*Zeitschrift für Papyrologie und Epigraphik*
ZRGG	*Zeitschrift für Religions- und Geistesgeschichte*
ZRVI	*Zbornik Radova Vizantološkog Instituta* (Belgrade)

Sources

Amm.	Ammianus Marcellinus, *Res Gestae*, ed. Seyfarth
Aphrodisias and Rome	J. Reynolds, *Aphrodisias and Rome*
Aurel. Vict.	Sextus Aurelius Victor, *Liber de Caesaribus*, ed. Pichlmayr
Blockley	R. C. Blockley, *The Fragmentary Classicising Historians* ..., ii. *Eunapius, Olympiodorus, Priscus and Malchus*
BMC	*A Catalogue of the Greek Coins in the British Museum* (London, 1873–1927)
CIS	*Corpus Inscriptionum Semiticarum*
Dio	Cassius Dio, *Historia Romana*, ed. Boissevain
E&J²	V. Ehrenberg and A. H. M. Jones, *Documents Illustrating the Reigns of Augustus and Tiberius*, 2nd edn.
Epit. de Caes.	Anon., *Epitome de Caesaribus*, ed. Pichlmayr
Eutrop.	Eutropius, *Breviarium ab urbe condita*, ed. Santini
Fest. Brev.	Festus, *Breviarium*, ed. Eadie
FGrH	F. Jacoby, *Die Fragmente der griechischen Historiker*
FHG	*Fragmenta Historicorum Graecorum*
George	George Syncellus, *Ecloga Chronographica*, ed. Mosshammer
HA	*Scriptores Historiae Augustae*, ed. Hohl
Herod.	Herodian, *Historia ab excessu divi Marci*, ed. Whittaker
IG	*Inscriptiones Graecae* (Berlin, 1973–)
IGBR	G. Mihailov, *Inscriptiones Graecae in Bulgaria Repertae*

IGLS	Inscriptions grecques et latines de la Syrie
IGR	R. Cagnat, *Inscriptiones Graecae ad Res Romanas pertinentes*
ILS	H. Dessau, *Inscriptiones Latinae Selectae*
Insc. Did.	T. Wiegand, *Didyma*, vol. ii
Insc. Eryth.	H. Engelmann and R. Merkelbach, *Die Inschriften von Erythrai und Klazomenai*
u. Klaz.	
Insc. Mag.	O. Kern, *Die Inschriften von Magnesia am Mäander*
Insc. Strat.	M. Ç. Sahin, *Die Inschriften von Stratonikeia*
Inv.	J. Cantineau, *Inventaire des inscriptions de Palmyre*
Jord. Get.	Jordanes, *Getica*, ed. Mommsen
Mal.	John Malalas, *Chronographia*, ed. Dindorf
MAMA	*Monumenta Asiae Minoris Antiqua*
OGIS	W. Dittenberger, *Orientis Graeci Inscriptiones Selectae*
Orac. Sib.	Sibylline Oracle [cited after Geffcken's edn. (1902), except for No. 13]
Oros. Hist.	Orosius, *Historiarum adversus paganos libri septem*, ed. Zangemeister
contra pag.	
PGM	K. Preisendanz, *Papyri Graecae Magicae*
RGDS	A. Maricq, 'Res Gestae Divi Saporis' [English translations of this document are based upon Maricq's French version]
RIC	*Roman Imperial Coinage*
RRC	M. H. Crawford, *Roman Republican Coinage*
S. Theos.	Θεοσοφία Σιβύλλης, in H. Erbse, *Fragmente griechischer Theosophien*
TS	*Tabula Siarensis*
T. Theos.	*Tübingen Theosophy*, in H. Erbse, *Fragmente griechischer Theosophien*
Zon.	John Zonaras, *Epitome Historiarum*, ed. Dindorf
Zos.	Zosimus, *Historia Nova*, ed. Paschoud

INTRODUCTION

The Economic and Political Situation of the Roman Empire in the Mid-Third Century AD

GENERAL THEMES

When the armies of Alexander Severus launched a three-pronged invasion of the Persian empire in 232, it must have appeared to most of the inhabitants of the empire that Roman power was at its height. There would probably have been few men like the distinguished consular Cassius Dio, who felt that in his lifetime the empire had passed from being a kingdom of gold under Marcus Aurelius to one of rust and iron under Septimius Severus and his successors.[1] To the casual observer in Lyons or Ephesus, in Carthage or Thessaloniki, the reign of Caracalla, which Dio regarded as a horror, would have appeared as one in which the barbarians were kept from the frontiers and the one in which most of the inhabitants of the empire had been granted Roman citizenship. The threat of barbarian violence such as that which had rocked the Balkans under Marcus seemed a dim, if horrible, memory. Macrinus, the equestrian praetorian prefect who had succeeded to the throne after engineering Caracalla's murder, would have been little more than a name to most and few would have shared the aversion of Dio or Marius Maximus to having an emperor of his ancestry.[2] Elagabalus appeared odd to his subjects; the personal

1 Dio 71. 36 περὶ οὗ ἤδη ῥητέον, ἀπὸ χρυσῆς τε βασιλείας ἐς σιδηρᾶν καὶ κατιωμένην. . . .

2 For aversion cf. HA V. Macr. 2. 1 'humili natus loco et animi atque oris inverecundi, seque nunc Severum nunc Antoninum, cum in odio esset omnium et hominum et militum, nuncupavit' (deriving from Marius). Dio, though more favourably inclined because

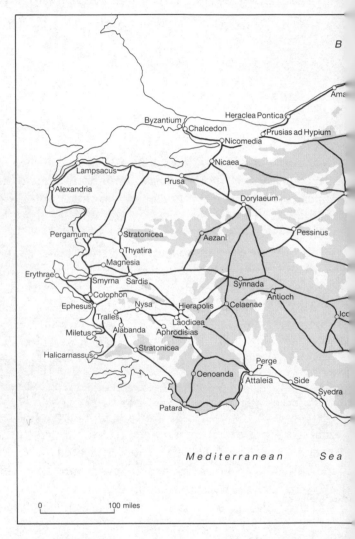

MAP I. The Eastern provinces in the third century AD

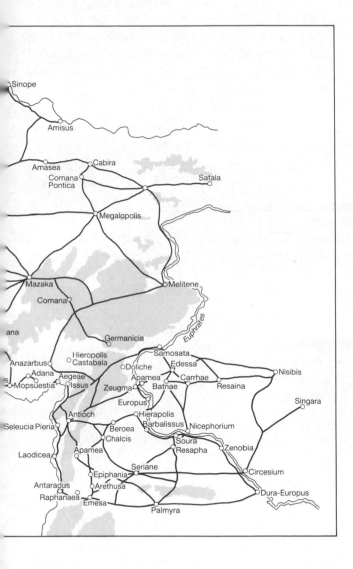

peculiarities of emperors tended to catch the imagination. But that was more than ten years in the past, and the empire had been reasonably administered even then.[3] So long as a person stayed clear of the capital where there were occasional riots by the garrison—in 223 a riot had caused the death of the prefect Ulpian, and another in 228 had forced Alexander to advise Dio that he should spend his second consulship away from Rome—everything must have seemed stable.[4]

This perception would have been deeply flawed; flawed for reasons that this hypothetical citizen, or even a man like Cassius Dio, could only begin to understand. In 232 the empire was facing new enemies in the east and, although it was greater than it had been a century earlier, the military power of Rome was insufficient to meet these new threats. Already the resources of the government seem to have been stretched to breaking-point. The generals who led the army were burdened with a rigid ideology and the political system itself was inherently unstable.[5]

of his hatred for Caracalla, still sees it as a great crime that he took the throne for himself rather than selecting a senator: cf. 78. 41; F. G. Millar, *A Study of Cassius Dio* (Oxford, 1964), 168. Herodian does not mention his birth and is generally favourable, though he blames him for his 'extravagance' in not dismissing the army and thereby giving the supporters of Elagabalus an opening: cf. Herod 5. 2. 2–6, 5. 4. 12.

[3] For popular perceptions of Elagabalus' quirks see ch. 3 nn. 135–6; on the administration see R. Syme, *Emperors and Biography* (Oxford, 1971), 145.

[4] For Ulpian's death see T. Honoré, *Ulpian* (Oxford, 1982), 40–1; on Dio see Dio 80. 5; for the Severan army in general see B. Campbell, *The Emperor and the Roman Army* (Oxford, 1984), 197. It should be noted that, despite his unpopularity, Dio was still able to retain control over his troops in *Pannonia Superior*. It was the antipathy of the praetorians at Rome that brought him down. The governorship of that province cannot be in 226–8 (as in Millar, *Cassius Dio*, p. 23) but in 223–4, during the period of Ulpian's prefecture: cf. Dio 80. 4. 2 καὶ τοὺς δορυφόρους πρὸς τῷ Οὐλπιανῷ καὶ ἐμὲ αἰτιάσαθαι . . . Cf. T. D. Barnes, 'The Composition of Cassius Dio's *Roman History*', *Phoenix*, 38 (1984), 244–5; Syme, *Emperors and Biography*, p. 144.

[5] Although I agree with M. Rostovtzeff, *The Social and Economic History of the Roman Empire*[2], ed. P. M. Fraser (Oxford, 1957), 392–502, that 'gradually there came to be one vital question, that of military defence' and, 'To solve this question, all available forces were concentrated on the one task of maintaining a strong army able to fight the enemy' (p. 466), I do not agree that what we see in this period is a war between the army, as supporters of the 'hereditary monarchy', and the educated classes for control of the state (p. 495). I do not think that the evidence will support his view that this was a century of revolution in which the army, drawn as it was from the countryside, overthrew the power

Although the Roman army in 232 was larger than it had been a century earlier, it was not as powerful in relative terms. It was over-extended, and its cost was fast exceeding the capacity of the state's inefficient tax system to support it.[6] The army had expanded by somewhat more than 10 per cent and its basic costs had increased by 66 per cent or more because of the pay increases that Septimius Severus and Caracalla had granted. These new costs were further inflated by the occasional distribution of huge donatives, which could double or triple the basic cost of the army (i.e. the amount that it cost in wages) for a given year. The empire's tax-base had not expanded to allow revenue easily to keep pace with expenditure; in fact, there is some reason to believe that it had contracted. This is because the economy of any pre-industrial state is based upon the size of its population. Economic growth in the absence of significant technological change is directly linked to the growth of the producing population. Now, while the expansion of the Roman army from the reign of Augustus to that of Antoninus Pius could have been supported by an increase in the population of the empire during that period,[7] the plague which began in 165 and raged intermittently for at least twenty-three years must have resulted in a serious decrease in the population by the end of the second century, and it is extremely unlikely that the population

of the cities, and I have therefore not adopted his model of class warfare. The model which I prefer to use is based upon the structures of government and their capacity to respond to changing circumstances. I think that the evidence does show that these administrative structures were profoundly shaken by the events of the 3rd cent. and that individual emperors tried to respond to specific dangers which threatened the stability of the political order. The scope of this introduction is not sufficient to explore the full implications of this approach through the reigns of Diocletian and Constantine. I hope to return to the problem elsewhere.

    [6] See Endnote 1 (end of chapter).
    [7] Prof. Frier suggests that the rate of increase might have been *c.* 35% between AD 14 and 164. He suggests that the total population would have been 61.4m. The total GNP might therefore have risen to *c.* 23,333m. HS. If the government's tax revenues amounted to 5% of this (see n. 18 below), imperial income may have been *c.* 1,666m. HS. It must be admitted that it is possible (although most unlikely) that there was no significant population increase during this period, just as there seems to have been no increase in the population of China in the first eight centuries AD and a rate of increase below 0.2% in India: cf. Goldsmith, 'Estimate of Size and Structure', p. 188.

recovered to any substantial degree by the time of Caracalla's death.[8] By that time five new legions had been formed, pay had been doubled, an expensive new province had been acquired in northern Mesopotamia, and large sums were expended as subsidies to keep the barbarians on the frontier quiet.[9]

These problems did not pass unnoticed. Dio complained about the state of imperial finances quite often in his history of his own time. He claimed the Severus was ruthless in extracting money from communities which had supported Niger in the civil war of 193–4, and he accused Caracalla of despoiling the rest of mankind in order to support his soldiers.[10] Herodian said that there was never an emperor as obsessed with money as Severus and that he used trumped-up charges against alleged supporters of his rivals to seize their estates.[11] Dio asserted that the *Constitutio Antoniniana* was no more than a ploy to increase his tax revenues.[12] He stated that northern Mesopotamia was a drain on the economy and that its formation had been a terrible mistake.[13] The excessive costs of the army by the end of Caracalla's life led Macrinus to attempt to reduce the pay of the legions to the level that it had been in the reign of Severus, apparently so that he would not have to rely on Caracalla's methods of raising money, which were extremely unpopular with the upper classes whose support he was trying to win.[14] His effort, however, was unsuccessful and may go a long way towards explaining the ease with which Elagabalus was able to gather support in the army. Severus himself had resorted to

---

[8] Prof. Frier observes that the plague may have reduced the population of the empire by *c.* 10%. The state's income might therefore have been reduced to *c.* 1,050m. HS. Again, it must be admitted that information on the plague is hard to quantify. On the basis of a careful examination of the surviving evidence from the period, J. F. Gilliam, 'The Plague under Marcus Aurelius', *AJP* 82 (1961), 225–51 = *Roman Army Papers* (Amsterdam, 1986), 227–54, shows that earlier discussions of the plague, which compared it with the Black Death, are excessive. R. J. Littman and M. L. Littman, 'Galen and the Antonine Plague', *AJP* 94 (1973), 243–55, identify the plague as smallpox on the basis of Galen's description of the symptoms and suggest that the mortality rate in the empire was *c.* 7–10% on the basis of comparison with later smallpox epidemics.

[9] Dio 78. 17. 3.   [10] Ibid. 74. 8. 4; 77. 9; see 78. 18.   [11] Herod. 3. 8. 6–7.

[12] Dio 77. 9. 5.   [13] Ibid. 75. 3.   [14] Ibid. 78. 12. 7, 36.

debasing the currency to meet his expenses, and the long period of peace at the end of his reign did enable him at his death to leave a substantial surplus in the treasury.[15] Unfortunately, this was probably exhausted by the enormous donative that Caracalla paid after his murder of Geta in 212, and he in turn had to resort to other means to meet his expenses.[16] In addition to his extra-ordinary impositions upon the rich, he took to manipulating the currency through the introduction of the antoninianus, sup-posedly struck to twice the weight of a denarius but in reality only one and a half times the original denarius, and by reducing the weight of the aureus.[17] But these were all stop-gap measures which could not solve the long-term problem, namely, the extremely inefficient tax structure of the empire.

It seems that the Roman state took in somewhere around 5 per cent of the GNP of the Roman empire in taxes.[18] This figure is comparable to states before the industrial revolution in western Europe, and suggests, as was also the case in early modern Europe, that the state's tax structure was not efficient. Indeed, the bulk of Rome's revenues derived from the *tributum soli*, the *tributum capitis* (both flat taxes), harbour dues, occasional other levies which might have been preserved in individual areas from pre-Roman governments, and the income from imperial estates. The collection of most taxes was based upon an estimate of what a community within a province should be able to pay the state from the revenues it received from these sources; it was then left up to the community to pass on its assessment.[19] It was therefore in the interest of local communities to under-represent their

---

[15] M. H. Crawford, 'Finance, Coinage and Money from the Severans to Constantine', *ANRW* ii/2. 562–3; D. Walker, *The Metrology of the Roman Silver Coinage*, iii. *From Pertinax to Uranius Antoninus* (BAR International Series, 40; Oxford, 1978), 106–9, for a valuable survey of Roman imperial attitudes towards money in terms of *avaritia*, *liberalitas*, and *parsimonia*, and pp. 129–30 for a summary of the policy of Severus.

[16] Walker, *Metrology*, p. 131.

[17] Ibid. 17–22, 130–2; for the antoninianus see pp. 32–4.

[18] See Endnote 2 (end of chapter).

[19] P. A. Brunt, 'The Revenues of Rome', *JRS* 71 (1981), 168–9, provides a valuable summary of the issues. Goldsmith, *Premodern Financial Systems*, pp. 51–6, suggests that 30–33% of the state revenue derived from the *tributum*, *c.* 25% from *vectigalia*.

worth, with the likely consequence that rich and powerful cities paid a smaller percentage of tax than lesser places. It was also inevitable that the greatest burden fell on the peasants and those least able to pay, and that the state had a difficult time tapping the vast accumulations of wealth in the hands of the upper classes. The problem is magnified by the fact that the greatest proportion of specie in an economy that may have been monetized to roughly 40 per cent was in the possession of these classes. Soldiers expected to receive their wages in coin, and it was precisely coin which the state would have had the most difficulty in extracting.[20]

Senators, the equestrian order, and the municipal aristocracy formed roughly the top 3 per cent of the population but controlled approximately 22 per cent of the empire's wealth. The imbalance was worsened by the state's considerable difficulty in acquiring any part of this resource.[21] This problem is perhaps best illustrated by the fact that during the crisis of the Marcomannic invasion of 168–9 Marcus Aurelius was forced to auction imperial properties in order to raise money for the war. His only other option in the emergency would have been to 'fall upon the rich like a torrent', devising various excuses for large-scale confiscation of property.[22] This expedient was open to Septimius

---

[20] Goldsmith, *Premodern Financial Systems*, pp. 36–42. For a detailed study of the late imperial budget, for which there is more direct evidence, see M. Hendy, *Studies in the Byzantine Monetary Economy c.300–1450* (Cambridge, 1985), 157–271. Although the empire of the 3rd cent. controlled greater resources from which to draw, there is no reason to believe that the overall picture was much different: the basic sources of revenue remained the same. Even though the methods of extraction changed somewhat, it was still very difficult indeed to raise money from the wealthy; see esp. Hendy, *Studies*, pp. 175–6, 237, esp. (p. 176) 'It is of course impossible to be certain of the accuracy of such figures, but the definite impression is gained that, although the major source of wealth may have been land, it was nevertheless effectively less harshly taxed than trade, and that the least severely taxed amongst the land-owners were precisely those who were in a position to contribute most: the senators.'

[21] Goldsmith, 'Estimate of Size and Structure', p. 285.

[22] Amm. 30. 8 'torrentis ritu ferabatur in divites'. The description is of Aurelian, when he was faced by a treasury emptied by Gallienus. Ammianus in fact suggests that his behaviour was justified by the emergency of the state, unlike the cruelty of Valentinian. Suetonius suggests that the cruelty of Caligula was partially motivated by his financial problems (*Cal.* 38. 1) and Tacitus observes that Tiberius was restrained towards the property of those condemned in the course during the early years of his reign (which is by

Severus after his defeats of Niger and Clodius Albinus (when the inquisition reached well beyond Rome into the provinces). Neither he nor Caracalla appears to have had any qualms about imposing heavy sentences upon the wealthy when they needed money; the charge of using the courts to fill the treasury was also levelled against Maximinus Thrax (possibly with less justification). But this was not always an option open to emperors. Macrinus, who felt that he needed to curry favour with the senate, could not adopt this course and it was not likely to be readily considered by the men who administered the state for Alexander Severus or Gordian III. In this period a 'good' emperor was also an emperor who kept his hands off the property of the rich. The failure to find an effective way to exploit the wealthy of the Roman world may help explain the fiscal difficulties encountered by the state in the third century.

The precarious nature of the empire's fiscal resources was one of the underlying causes of the problems which Rome encountered in the period covered by the extant portion of the *Thirteenth Sibylline Oracle* (*c.* 244–62). Financial constraints made it difficult for an emperor to muster the superiority of force that was necessary for a successful military operation. Another problem was that the Roman army in the second and third centuries was not organized for large-scale offensive or defensive actions.[23] Ever since fiscal shortages and military failure had put an end to an ambitious scheme of conquest under Augustus, the Roman army had adopted an increasingly fixed defensive posture.[24]

---

implication surprising given his basically cruel nature: see Tac. *Ann.* 1. 75. 4, 3. 18. 1, etc.); F. G. Millar, *The Emperor in the Roman World* (London, 1977), 163–74.

[23] E. Luttwak, *The Grand Strategy of the Roman Empire* (Baltimore, 1976), 126, 'It cannot be pretended that the expeditionary units extracted from an army that was everywhere based on static frontier positions could have as much combat power as the strategically mobile armies of the early principate.' Dio places a theory of fixed defence in the mouth of Maecenas (52. 27. 3 οὔτε γὰρ ἐπὶ τῶν καιρῶν βοηθείαις τισὶν ἔτι χρῆσθαι δυνάμεθα, αὐτοί τε τοσοῦτον ἀπὸ τῶν τῆς ἀρχῆς ἐσχατιῶν ἀπηρτημένοι καὶ πολεμίους ἑκασταχόθι προσοικοῦντας ἔχοντες) which reflects thinking in his own time.

[24] A. R. Birley, 'The Third Century Crisis in the Roman Empire', *Bulletin of the John Rylands University Library of Manchester*, 58 (1975), 265–7; Luttwak, *The Grand Strategy of the Roman Empire*, pp. 51–126.

Furthermore, Roman strategic thinking seems to have been dominated more and more by an obsessive desire to maintain control over every inch of land that had ever been brought under Roman control. This was a manifestation of the rigid code of military glory that was pervasive in the officer classes of the Roman army.[25] It may also have been a result of the fact that by the middle of the second century the legions had become firmly attached to their homes in the frontier zones. The first areas that the legions might have to abandon were those in which the legionaries grew up and where their families lived. When called away on campaign in other parts of the empire, soldiers knew that they were exposing their families to danger. Herodian says that one of the reasons for the troops' anger at Alexander Severus when they returned from the Persian campaign was that they had received reports about the destruction of their families by the Germans.[26] But even before this possessiveness had become deeply imbedded in the structure of military life, there had been clear antipathy to any withdrawal. Acts such as Hadrian's decision to evacuate the territory occupied by Trajan seem to have occasioned fierce debate.[27] As the attitude that the frontiers were 'walls' between the civilized and barbarian worlds developed, it took extraordinary courage, or desperation, for any emperor to admit that the state was incapable of defending any territory that it had formerly held.[28] A strategic withdrawal such as was included in Philip's treaty with Persia in 244 or Aurelian's retreat from Dacia was a matter for the utmost obfuscation. Philip's actions in the east were scarcely ever mentioned in the documents of the period; where they were, the reason may well be that someone made a mistake.[29] Aurelian covered his retreat from Dacia by creating new 'Dacian' provinces south of the Danube.[30] Gallienus' concentration of his resources in the Balkans and Italy, leaving the east under Odaenathus and Gaul to Postumus, was

---

[25] Campbell, *Emperor and Army*, pp. 358–62.
[26] Herod 6. 7. 3.
[27] Campbell, *Emperor and Army*, pp. 398–400.
[28] See on l. 105.   [29] See on l. 27.
[30] See below, pp. 61–2.

taken as a sign of his weak character.[31] The proper Roman response to any slight setback was revenge—a motive which had a long and glorious history in Roman military annals.[32] It may be that Decius was conscious of this tradition when he attacked the barbarians who were withdrawing after the sack of Philippopolis as soon as he could make contact—it is the best explanation why he led the army to destruction in the swamp at Abrittus in June 251.

Finance and rigid ideology were two problems, while the instability of the monarchy was a third. It has often been observed that there was no institutional way to select a new monarch.[33] The process could degenerate into chaos and civil war at any moment; and in the third century it quite often did for a number of reasons. One was the increased importance of the common soldiers. The emperor came to be seen as their companion, the man who had to lead them on major campaigns.[34] Even if the emperor were a boy like Elagabalus or Gordian III, his presence in the army was an important symbol: it served to remind the troops of their vital role in maintaining the empire. However, if something went wrong the emperor was the obvious focal point of the troops' dissatisfaction. A number of murders in the third century

---

[31] For a survey of the abuse of Gallienus in the later tradition see A. Alföldi, 'Zur Kenntnis der Zeit der römischen Soldatenkaiser, 2. Das Problem des "verweiblichten" Kaisers Gallienus', *ZN* 38 (1928), 156–74 = *Studien*, pp. 16–31. Alföldi attributes it to a subsequent 'militaristic reaction' against his 'philhellenism', which I doubt.

[32] For the motive of revenge see Caes. *BG* 1. 12. 7 'qua in re Caesar non solum publicas sed etiam privatas iniurias ultus est'; 3. 10. 2, 16. 4, 20. 1; 6. 9. 2; Tac. *Ann.* 1. 3. 6, 10. 2, 43. 2; *Tab. Siar.* 1. 12–15 'monum[entum . . . dedi]|casse memoriae Germanici Caesaris cum [i]is Germanis bello superatis [et . . .] | a Gallia summotis receptisque signis militaribus et vindicata frau[dulenta clade] | exercitus p.R.'; Hor. *Carm.* 3. 5; etc.

[33] Most succinctly discussed by R. Syme, 'Antonine Government and the Governing Class', *Roman Papers*, v (Oxford, 1988), 688–72. For the 3rd cent. in particular see F. Hartmann, *Herrscherwechsel und Reichskrise: Untersuchungen zu den Ursachen und Konsequenzen der Herrscherwechsel im Imperium Romanum der Soldatenkaiserzeit (3. Jahrhundert n. Chr.)* (Frankfurt am Main, 1982); Syme summarized the situation eloquently with the words 'Be he a boy, a buffoon, or a philosopher (a political scientist was less likely to be thrown up), the administration goes on unimpaired, being guided by the friends and agents of Caesar' ('History or Biography: The Case of Tiberius Caesar', *Historia*, 23 (1974), 481 = *Roman Papers*, iii (Oxford, 1984), 937).

[34] Campbell, *Emperor and Army*, p. 198.

appear not to have been planned to replace one person with another specific individual: the murder of Gordian III is a case in point. Gordian, who was nineteen at the time, can scarcely be considered the commander of his own army in 244, yet he was murdered after the army was defeated at Peroz-Shapor—in protest, so it would seem, against the overall bad management of the campaign.[35] The murder of Alexander Severus might be explained in the same way.[36] Philip the Arab may be held partially responsible for his own fate when he sent Decius to suppress the rebel Pacatianus in 249—the troops may have found his lack of interest insulting.

A second feature of the close association between the military and the emperor was that if a general was particularly successful, his troops might feel that he was better suited to command than the emperor himself, and raise him to the purple. They could also hope for greater financial rewards. Such considerations may lie behind the revolt of Aemilianus in 253, and of Macrianus in 260–1. It may also be one cause for that of Postumus in 260. Postumus, so the story goes, was asserting his men's claim to booty that they had won fairly, and this led to the murder of Gallienus' son.[37] Yet another factor was the rivalry between the great armies in the west, in the Balkans, and in the east.[38] This had been an important reason for the victory of Vespasian in 69, and there is no indication that the competitive instinct had weakened in the following century.[39] The armies that engaged in the civil wars after the murder of Commodus demonstrated a tremendous capacity for mutual slaughter.[40] A sense of bitterness could build among soldiers who felt that other troops were preferred to themselves; the army in the east seems to have resented excessive

---

[35] See on l. 20.

[36] For Alexander see below, pp. 22–3.

[37] J. F. Drinkwater, *The Gallic Empire: Separatism and Continuity in the North-Western Provinces of the Roman Empire A.D. 260–272* (Stuttgart, 1987), 25, 89.

[38] Hartmann, *Herrscherwechsel und Reichskrise*, pp. 89–94.

[39] See esp. Tac. *Hist.* 2. 85. 1; cf. 1. 51. 1–3, 3. 41. 2, for similar feelings in the Vitellian camp.

[40] See Dio 75. 6.

favour shown to the Danubian legions in the reign of Maximinus. There are also some indications in the third century that an army that had been defeated in civil war would be all the more likely to try again in order to regain its prestige. This may have been a contributing factor in the rise of Decius as well as in the revolt of Regalianus in 260.

The decline of army discipline was to contribute a great deal to the crisis of the mid-third century. So did the poor quality of leadership. Children such as Elagabalus (before his evident insanity made him unpalatable), Alexander Severus, and Gordian III were elevated to the throne because they were convenient. They would allow others to run the state for them, while their presence on the throne meant that the leading men of the time could avoid making one of their number emperor—jealousy may often have been a factor in a decision to allow a child to rule as nominal emperor, just as on other occasions the senate tended to select elderly candidates, deferring to age rather than capacity.[41] But this meant rule by committee, which was not always the best way to deal with new problems. In other instances it would appear that when they were faced with a crisis after the death or murder of an emperor, the marshals of the army might decide upon someone who was weak, again to act as a stop-gap or figure-head. This seems to be the reason why Philip was selected, and it may explain why Gallienus remained on the throne for eight years, surrounded by so many able men, such as the future emperors Claudius, Aurelian, and Probus. It is unfortunate that the sources do not explain why these men decided to take the throne for themselves in the second half of the third century, though it should be noted that in each case there was a threat of civil war: Claudius succeeded while Aureolus was still in rebellion at Milan and intervention from Postumus could be feared; Aurelian had to suppress Quintillus, Claudius' brother, and the empire was briefly divided between the forces of Probus and Florianus in 277. In 284 the old pattern seemed to reassert itself when the praetorian prefect Aper was passed over for the much

[41] Syme, *Emperors and Biography*, p. 166.

more junior Diocletian. The selection of a man of his enormous talent was the exception rather than the rule.

Rome's relative decline in the world was essentially the result of internal failings: an over-priced military establishment, flawed military doctrine, and inadequate leadership. But this was not all: the internal weakness of the Roman empire was all the more serious because of a slight shift in the balance of power. At the beginning of the century the army was barely able to restrain the tribes north of the Rhine and Danube, while the three legions of Britain seem to have been incapable of holding off a serious attack from the area north of Hadrian's Wall. The weakness of the empire's position had been amply demonstrated in the reign of Marcus Aurelius, when it had taken a decade of hard fighting to restore the frontier once it had been breached, and the result of the campaign had been inconclusive. The tribes and the frontier had remained where they were: the state found that it was easier to pay the barbarians large subsidies to stay on their side of the border than it was to fight them. Dio complained that subsidies for the barbarians cost as much as the army in the reign of Caracalla. This is an exaggeration, but it still reflects the importance that such payments had assumed.[42]

There is no evidence to suggest that the barbarians had become stronger. Roman restrictions on trade across the frontier were effective in maintaining a low level of development among the tribes—the warriors who fought at Adrianople appear to have been armed in the same way as those who fought Germanicus at Idistaviso or those depicted on the columns of Trajan and Marcus Aurelius.[43] New confederations, such as the Alamanni on the

---

[42] Dio 78. 17. 3; see also 77. 14. 4, asserting that Caracalla gave the barbarians good coins while he circulated debased coins within the empire.

[43] For the cultural level of the northern barbarians see E. Demougeot, *La Formation de l'Europe et les invasions barbares*, i. *Des origines germaniques à l'avènement de Dioclétien* (Paris, 1969), 293–315; J. F. Matthews, *The Roman Empire of Ammianus* (London, 1989), 306–32. F. Pitts, 'Relations between Rome and German "Kings" on the Middle Danube in the First to Fourth Centuries A.D.', *JRS* 79 (1989), 45–58, refines this picture, showing that there were areas of the frontier where Roman goods had spread more widely than others by the beginning of the 3rd cent.; but this does not seem to have had an impact on the military capacity of these tribes. Despite Vell. 2. 109. 1, Tac. *Ann.* 2. 45. 2, there is no sign that the

upper Rhine and the Goths, who began to move into the plains and hills above Moesia during the early third century, were no more effective than the Quadi, Marcomanni, and Sarmatians. But those tribes had been quite capable of holding their own, even to the extent that the Romans had found it was not worth the effort to attempt to occupy their underdeveloped lands.

The area where the balance of force changed was in the east. The Sassanian dynasty, which took power at Ctesiphon in 225, was far more effective than its Arsacid predecessor. This was a dynastic necessity. The first Sassanian king, Ardashir, was committed to an aggressive policy along his western frontier because the Arsacids had established dynastic links throughout that region. To ensure the safety of his line, Ardashir seems to have felt that he needed to replace the Arsacids in these areas. In the face of the threat that he posed, Ardashir's rivals sought the protection of Rome, and thus Ardashir was committed to war against the empire.[44] This was a very serious situation. Although the Romans had won striking victories against Persia under Trajan, Lucius Verus, and Septimius Severus, there were other times when the Persians proved that they were capable of inflicting severe defeats upon Roman armies. It should also be noted that the campaigns of both Trajan and Verus were lengthy affairs to which Rome committed all the resources at her disposal. On open terrain, such as the plain beyond Nisibis where Artabanus fought Macrinus to a standstill in 217, the two sides were evenly matched.[45] Indeed, Severus' occupation of northern Mesopotamia exposed two legions to the Persians under conditions which favoured the enemy. The new province would be the scene of several Roman disasters in the thirty-five years after the accession of Ardashir.

northern barbarians had adopted Roman military practice to any noticeable degree even by the 4th cent.: indeed, the fire-hardened stakes attested as a major element in Germanic armament in Tacitus' account of Germanicus' campaign in AD 16 (*Ann.* 2. 14. 3 'primam utcumque aciem hastatam, ceteris praecusta aut brevia tela') appear to have been important weapons for the Goths at the time of Adrianople: see Matthews, *The Roman Empire of Ammianus*, pp. 526–7 n. 29.

[44] See app. III, where this proposition is argued in detail.

[45] Dio 78. 27; Herod. 4. 15 with Whittaker ad loc.

The financial, ideological, political, and military problems sketched in the last few pages are all of importance for explaining the political crisis of the mid-third century. But they cannot explain everything. The personalities of individual emperors and commanders mattered a great deal, their mistakes and successes dictated the specific course of events. It was after all Decius who decided to lead his army into the swamp at Abrittus, and Valerian who decided to give battle to Sapor outside Edessa; just as it was Claudius II who was able to defeat the Goths at Naissus and Aurelian, *severissimus ultor noxarum*, who was able to overwhelm the armies of Zenobia.

THE POLITICAL CRISIS: 225–275

The rise of Sassanid Persia was the immediate cause of the political disorders in the mid-third century AD. It revealed the weakness of the frontier system in the east with disastrous consequences for the political stability of the empire as a whole. The situation remained in continual flux from the reign of Alexander Severus to that of Aurelian; or from the victory of Ardashir to the death of Sapor I in 270 or 273, when the Sassanid regime began to suffer from dynastic disorder so severe that Persia was not capable of posing a serious threat to the Roman frontier for nearly twenty-five years.[46] Indeed, the reigns of Ardashir and Sapor correspond very closely to the period which may be referred to as 'the crisis of the third century', the period between the murder of Alexander in 235 and Aurelian's re-unification of the empire.

Between 224 and 226 Ardashir overwhelmed the Arsacids,

---

[46] Sapor was succeeded by his son Hormizd, who reigned for about a year. Hormizd was succeeded by Bahram I, who seems to have been the son of Sapor by a lesser queen or concubine; he was succeeded in turn by his own son, Bahram II. Thus, Sapor's son Narses, who appears as king of the Sakas in the Naqsh-i Rustam inscription, was excluded from the succession. He did not become king until 293–4, when he deposed Bahram III. For discussion of this period see R. N. Frye, 'The Political History of Iran under the Sasanians', *The Cambridge History of Iran*, iii/1 (Cambridge, 1983), 127–9; id., *The History of Ancient Iran* (Munich, 1984), 241–96 (his appendices 4 and 5 provide translations of the *RGDS* and the inscription of Narses at Paikuli, describing his rise to power).

captured Ctesiphon, and was crowned King of Kings. But, despite his victory over Artabanus V, he still faced a number of serious threats to the security of his dynasty.[47] The sons of Artabanus had found protection in Armenia, and the king of Media was openly opposed to the new regime. Hatra, whose rulers appear to have had dynastic links with the Arsacids, was hostile and appears to have become much closer to Rome. This may have been a result of the pressure that Severus' new frontier arrangements placed on its trade routes, but that would not have been any comfort to Ardashir.[48] The Arab tribes of north-eastern Arabia appear to have remained loyal to the Arsacids, and Vologaeses V, the one-time rival of Artabanus, seems still to have been a force with whom Ardashir would have to reckon.

Obverse   *Reverse*

1. Silver drachm of Ardashir; *reverse*: fire-altar. 4.26 g. Ashmolean.

Ardashir moved rapidly to strengthen his position. Although he was defeated at Hatra, and was not completely successful in his initial effort to dislodge his rivals from Armenia and Media, he seems to have been able to keep pressure on them. He also began to put pressure on the Roman position in northern Mesopotamia.[49] He may well have sensed that Rome would move to strengthen the regime in Armenia, where Rome had always

[47] See app. III for further details.

[48] As argued by D. L. Kennedy, '"European" Soldiers and the Severan Siege of Hatra', in P. Freeman and D. L. Kennedy (eds.), *The Defense of the Roman and Byzantine East: Proceedings of a Colloquium Held at the University of Sheffield* (*BAR* International Series, 297; Oxford, 1986), 404.

[49] Dio 80. 3.2–3.

claimed an interest, and he may well have seen the empire as a refuge for his foes.[50] In the later 220s Persian pressure on the Roman frontier became acute, and it appears that there were serious problems with the discipline of the legions in Mesopotamia. Dio stated (somewhat optimistically, as it turned out) that, although Ardashir was of no great consequence himself, he could become a threat because the troops were disoloyal.[51] Some deserted to him and others mutinied, murdering the governor of Mesopotamia, Flavius Heracleo.[52] These events took place before Dio's retirement to Nicaea in 229. Shortly after this, Ardashir launched a massive attack across the Roman frontier. Nisibis was besieged, Cappadocia may have been raided, and Syria was threatened.[53] Ardashir may even have attempted to install a pretender on the throne of Oshroene, which had been vacant since the death of Abgar VIII in 212.[54] A usurper named Uranius is said to have been associated with the Persian invasion and to have been active around Edessa.[55]

[50] Herod. 6. 7. 8; at 7. 2. 1 he notes that Parthian deserters and mercenaries had joined the Roman army in some numbers during the reign of Alexander Severus.

[51] Dio 80. 4. 1 οὐχ ὅτι αὐτὸς λόγου τινὸς ἄξιος δοκεῖ, ἀλλ᾽ ὅτι οὕτω τὰ στρατιωτικὰ ἡμῖν διάκειται ὥστε τοὺς μὲν καὶ προστίθεσθαι αὐτῷ τοὺς δὲ οὐκ ἐθέλειν ἀμύνεσθαι.

[52] Dio 80. 3. 4; PRI² F 283 (nothing is known about him aside from this passage of Dio).

[53] Herod. 6. 2. 1 ἀλλὰ τὰς ὄχθας ὑπερβαίνων καὶ τοὺς τῆς Ῥωμαίων ἀρχῆς ὅρους Μεσοποταμίαν τε κατατρέχει καὶ Σύροις ἀπειλεῖ; George, p. 674 (= Mosshammer, p. 437) ἡνίκα καὶ Πέρσας καταδραμόντας Καππαδοκίαν καὶ Νίσιβιν πολιορκοῦντας; Zon. 12. 15 εἶτα Καππαδοκίαν ὁ Ἀρταξέρξης οὗτος σὺν τοῖς Πέρσαις κατέτρεχε, καὶ ἐπολιόρκει τὴν Νίσιβιν. The mention of the threat to Cappadocia and Nisibis in George and Zonaras comes in the midst of sections which were essentially derived from Herodian. There is no reason to suspect a corruption in the received text of Herodian at this point, so their information must reflect an insertion here on the part of their source. This source knew Dexippus' Chronika and may have taken the information from there. The insertion is not a close parallel to the similar information given at George, p. 681 (= Mosshammer, p. 443), and Zonaras at 12. 18, where it is recorded that Ardashir captured Carrhae and Nisibis, and is therefore not likely to be a doublet; it should also be noted that George and Zonaras do not say that Ardashir captured Nisibis (contra Whittaker, ed., Herodian, ii. 91 n. 2). See also A. Jardé, Études critiques sur la vie et le règne de Sévère Alexandre (Paris, 1925), 76–7.

[54] J. Teixidor, 'Les derniers rois d'Édesse d'après deux nouveaux documents syriaques', ZPE 76 (1989), 221.

[55] George, p. 674 (= Mosshammer, p. 437) Οὐράνιος δέ τις ἐν Ἐδέσσῃ τῆς Ὀσροϊνῆς αὐτοκράτωρ ἀναγορευθεὶς καὶ κατὰ Ἀλεξάνδρου τυραννήσας

The Persian attack appears to have come in 230, and the legions in the area were plainly incapable of handling the crisis without reinforcements. It was a scenario that would be repeated in 238 and 252, serving to illustrate the weakness of the Severan frontier system in the face of a determined adversary. Alexander and his advisers responded as well as they could. Preparations for a Persian expedition appear to have commenced immediately, but it took some time to assemble an adequate force and move it to the east. It is also possible that the legions had been allowed to drop well below their paper strength in the earlier years of the reign and that they had to be brought suddenly up to strength; however, it may be that the extraordinary levy which Herodian records on this occasion reflects the need to replace heavy losses sustained during the initial Persian offensive.[56]

The emperor did not leave Rome until the spring of 231. He crossed the Balkans, collecting vexillations from the garrisons along the way, and reached Antioch in the late summer or early autumn,[57] where there was a further delay to rest and train the newly arrived legions. There was also a mutiny among the men of *legio II Traiana* from Egypt and the local garrison.[58] The mutiny

διαφθείρεται ὑπ' αὐτοῦ, ἡνίκα καὶ Πέρσας καταδραμόντας Καππαδοκίαν καὶ Νίσιβιν πολιορκοῦντας Ἀλέξανδρος ἐξώθησεν; ibid. 675 (= Mosshammer, p. 439) καὶ Ἀλέξανδρος ὁ Μαμμαίας υἱὸς μετὰ τὴν ἀναίρεσιν Οὐρανίου τοῦ τυράννου καὶ τὴν κατὰ Περσῶν εὐδοκίμησιν . . .; Zos. 1. 12. 2 καὶ Οὐράνιος δέ τις ἐκ δουλείου γένους ἀναρρηθεὶς παραχρῆμα μετὰ τῆς ἀλουργίδος Ἀλεξάνδρῳ προσήχθη; Pol. Silv. *Chron.*, p. 521 'sub quo [i.e. Elagabalus] Marcellus Caesar, et Sallustius, Uranius, Seleucus atque Taurinus tyranni fuerunt'; *Epit. de Caes.* 24. 2 'sub hoc [i.e. Alexander] imperante Taurinus Augustus effectus ob timorem ipse se Euphrate fluvio abiecit'. Polemius' separation of Uranius and Taurinus suggests that they were not the same person (as suggested by F. Paschoud, ed., *Zosime*, i. 138–9 n. 35, H. R. Baldus, *Uranius Antoninus* (Bonn, 1971), 169–70; G. Barbieri, *L'albo senatorio da Settimio Severo a Carino (193–285)* (Rome, 1952), 400–1, conflates the Uranius under Alexander with Uranius Antoninus at Emesa). Indeed, there is room for both in these years. Uranius is associated with Edessa and it is possible that Taurinus was the usurper proclaimed in a mutiny after Alexander reached Antioch. If Uranius was not an ally of the Persians, he might be seen as precursor to Uranius Antoninus of Emesa in 253, a local noble who asserted himself in defence of his homeland when Rome proved incapable of defending it. The line between self-defence and usurpation was a very thin one in Roman eyes.

[56] Herod. 6. 3. 1. See Endnote 3 (end of chapter).
[57] For discussion of the date see Whittaker, *Herodian*, ii. 102–3 n. 2.
[58] Herod. 6. 4. 7 ἐγένοντό τινες καὶ ἀποστάσεις στρατιωτῶν, ἀπό τε Αἰγύπτου

appears to have been quickly suppressed, but it does suggest that the young emperor (who was accompanied in the camp by his mother) did not inspire confidence among his men. Subsequent events would justify any scepticism. The attack on Persia that began in 232 was a complicated affair, perhaps too complicated. It involved the simultaneous invasion of Persian territory by three columns in the face of a powerful enemy. One column was sent into Armenia and Media to draw the Persian army north and to succour Rome's allies in those regions. A second column moved down the Euphrates towards Ctesiphon while the third, accompanied by Alexander himself, invaded northern Mesopotamia.

The Roman plan of attack, like the very similar plan of Julian in 363, succeeded in confusing the Persians for a time: Ardashir is said to have led his main force north. But he soon realized his error (as Sapor II did in 363) and was able to concentrate his army in the south, where he won a crushing victory over the southern Roman column. Alexander seems to have succeeded in restoring control over the province of Mesopotamia, and the northern column returned with difficulty to Roman territory late in the year.[59] The result of the campaign was therefore indecisive. The Romans had recovered the territory that they had lost earlier, but Ardashir had also succeeded in defending his own lands and in doing what no Parthian monarch had done in the face of a determined Roman attack since the time of Trajan: he preserved Ctesiphon intact. According to Herodian, both sides suffered heavy losses, though it must be admitted that his statement about Persian casualties appears to be speculation based upon the fact that they did not launch a major attack upon the empire for several years after Alexander's departure.[60] Alexander's campaign did not compare well with those of Trajan, Lucius Verus, or Septimius Severus, and it seems to have severely damaged his reputation in the army. Loss of face before the troops, who

---

ἐληλυθότων, ἀλλὰ μὴν καὶ τῶν κατὰ Συρίαν, καινοτομῆσαί τινα ἐπιχειρησάντων περὶ τὴν βασιλείαν. This may be the revolt of Taurinus: see n. 55 above.

[59] Herod. 6. 5. 1–6. 3.   [60] Ibid. 6. 6. 5–6.

appear to have despised an emperor in his twenties dominated by the mother who travelled everywhere with him, would soon prove fatal to the regime. Contempt would overcome deep-seated loyalty to the dynasty.

2. Bronze Medallion of Alexander and Mamaea. *RIC* Alexander, 662. Ashmolean.

As Alexander led his army back from Persia, the Alamanni launched a raid across the Upper Rhine. According to Herodian this was considered a more serious threat than that posed by the Persians because the Germans were 'practically adjacent neighbours to the Italians'.[61] Despite these concerns, it appears to have taken Alexander a good deal of time to reach the new front. He returned to Rome first and appears to have celebrated a triumph over the Persians. This must have taken up the greater part of 233 and suggests that he did not take the field himself until the end of that year. By the end of 234 the Alamanni were driven back across the Rhine and a Roman army was concentrated at Mainz for an invasion of their territory. By this time the rank and file of the legions appear to have been deeply hostile: the invasion of Persia had not been a success, and when the western legions had returned to their bases they had discovered that their homes had been ravaged by the barbarians. It is not surprising, therefore, that they were unwilling to support Alexander when a distinguished warrior, C. Julius Verus Maximinus, raised the standard of revolt. The emperor and his mother were killed in late February or early March of 235.

Maximinus' name suggests that he might have been the descendant of Roman soldiers who settled in the Danubian

---

[61] Ibid. 6. 7. 4 παρὰ τοσοῦτον ὁμόρους καὶ γείτονας ποιεῖ Γερμανοὺς Ἰταλιώταις.

region during the early second century—veterans, perhaps, of Trajan's campaigns. The wild slanders reported by Herodian and other sources about his barbarous heritage are no more than that. His appearance on coins suggests that he might have been in his fifties when he assumed the throne, and therefore that he might have entered the service during the reign of Septimius Severus. It may be surmised that he rose through a series of equestrian posts during Severus' reign and then Caracalla's, and that by the time of his revolt he had obtained a high rank in the service.[62] Throughout his reign he advertised his military machismo, in stark contrast to his predecessor, whose soldiers had called him 'the cheap little girl' and 'the cowardly brat tied to his mother' as they killed him.[63]

3. Bronze Medallion of Maximinus Thrax. *RIC* Maximinus, 90. Ashmolean.

A number of serious difficulties confronted Maximinus the Thracian when he took the throne, and he does not seem to have handled them with a great deal of skill. One of these problems was his background. He was not the barbarian herdsman that his enemies made him out to be, but he was still an equestrian. Senators of the Severan aristocracy were apt to sneer at him or object to his pretensions, as Dio had once objected to those of Macrinus.[64] Maximinus had to work to build a consensus within the aristocracy, but this would take time and diplomacy; and he does not seem to have been well suited to the task. He appears to

[62] Syme, *Emperors and Biography*, pp. 179–93.
[63] Herod. 6. 9. 5 καὶ βοῶντες οἱ νεανίαι προυκαλοῦντο τοὺς συστρατιώτας καταλιπεῖν μὲν γύναιον μικρολόγον καὶ μειράκιον δειλὸν μητρὶ δουλεῦον; Campbell, *Emperor and Army*, pp. 68–9, on the image of Maximinus.
[64] See n. 2 above.

have been more comfortable on the battle-field, and even though he continued to employ members of the Severan aristocracy in the highest positions of government, he was not inclined to go to the lengths that Macrinus had to win support among the propertied classes at the expense of the soldiers. Instead, he tried to conciliate opinion by sending pictures of himself in combat with the enemies of Rome for public display in the capital.[65] A personal visit might have been more effective, but he might have felt that this would have been more dangerous than fighting the Germans. His fiscal policies made him extremely unpopular with the *plebs urbana*, who thought, quite rightly, that their money was being given to the soldiers.

Maximinus' most serious problem was probably financial. The soldiers who elevated him to the throne had complained that Alexander was cheap, as well as a coward.[66] Herodian says that when he addressed the recruits who first supported the revolution, Maximinus promised to double their pay and give them a large donative.[67] He then pictures him as a tyrant who fleeced the provinces to find money for the army with which he lived 'like a man in a citadel'.[68] This is not an entirely accurate picture.

Military pay had been raised to 600 denarii a year under Caracalla, and it would appear that it remained at that level until the reign of Diocletian.[69] It was once suggested that military pay had been reduced to the Severan level (400 denarii) under Alexander and that what Maximinus did was to raise it back to the Caracallan level,[70] but this is probably incorrect. In any event, the payment of donatives was probably a more serious issue than the regular pay of the army. In fact, the complaint of the soldiers

---

[65] Herod. 7. 2. 8.　　　　　　　　　　[66] Ibid. 6. 9. 4, 8. 4.
[67] Ibid. 6. 8. 8 ὡς δ᾽ αὐτοὺς ἐς εὔνοιαν καὶ προθυμίαν πάνυ προκαλέσαιτο, τά τε σιτηρέσια ἐπεδιπλασίασε, νόμας τε καὶ δόσεις μέγιστας ὑπέσχετο, τιμωρίας τε καὶ κηλῖδας πάσας αὐτοῖς ἀνῆκεν. . . .　　　[68] Ibid. 7. 1. 3, 3. 1–6.
[69] MacMullen, 'The Roman Emperor's Army Costs', pp. 572–3.
[70] A. von Domaszewski, 'Untersuchungen zur römischen Kaisergeschichte', *RM* 58 (1903), 383; but cf. A. Passerini, 'Gli aumenti del soldo militare da Commodo a Massimino', *Athenaeum*, 24 (1946), 158, who suggested that only the troops under Maximinus' command at the time of the mutiny were rewarded by becoming *duplicarii*; this might not be sufficient to explain Maximinus' needs.

against Julia Mamaea as they killed her and her son was that she was greedy and unwilling to distribute largess.[71] This is a clear reference to donatives.

Massive payments had become the order of the day at the end of the second century, and a new emperor would certainly have been expected to be generous.[72] An emperor might have been able to balance ordinary income and expenditure (with a certain surplus) in time of peace, but this does not mean that the treasury would always have the enormous reserves on hand to pay out a donative of the size that Macrinus had promised his men: 3,000 HS (over a year's pay) a man when he assumed the name 'Antoninus' and 20,000 HS when he learnt of the revolt of Elagabalus, of which he actually paid 4,000 HS. It may be assumed that Maximinus' promise to the men in 235 would have been on this scale and that there was not enough money in the treasury after four years of unremunerative warfare against Persia and the Alamanni to make good this promise. Indeed, the policies which Maximinus implemented after his accession appear to be no more than what was necessary to raise a substantial amount of money for a large single pay-out to the troops. They could not support a long-term pay increase. In the course of the lurid tales of judicial murder for money and the theft of temple treasures which Herodian sketches as Maximinus' policies there is one fact—that Maximinus reduced the amount of money for the *annona* and other distributions at Rome.[73]

Maximinus' financial problem was important. In his effort to keep the promise to his men he took a step that made him deeply unpopular at Rome, and the Roman *plebs* would prove to be one of the most important forces behind the revolt in 238. The

[71] Herod. 6. 9. 4 οἱ δὲ τὴν μητέρα ἐμέμφοντο ὡς φιλάργυρον καὶ τὰ χρήματα ἀποκλείουσαν, διά τε μικρολογίαν καὶ τὸ πρὸς τὰς ἐπιδόσεις ὀκνηρὸν τοῦ Ἀλεξάνδρου μεμισημένου. See Campbell, *Emperor and Army*, p. 197.

[72] Cf. Campbell, *Emperor and Army*, pp. 170–1; J.-P. Callu, *La Politique monétaire des empereurs romains de 238 à 311* (Paris, 1969), 310–11; also above, p. 9.

[73] Herod. 7. 3. 5 μετῆλθεν ἐπὶ τὰ δημόσια, καὶ εἴ τινα ἦν χρήματα πολιτικὰ ἐς εὐθηνίας ἢ νομὰς τῶν δημοτῶν ἀθροιζόμενα εἴτε θεάτροις ἢ πανηγύρεσιν ἀνακείμενα....

possibility that he promised a large donative which he could not pay immediately might also serve to explain why, despite his military virtues, Maximinus was not particularly popular in the army. Furthermore, the honorific title *Maximiniana* appears to have been restricted to units on the Rhine and Danubian frontiers before 238.[74] This would suggest that he showed particular favour to the troops under his immediate command, and it might explain why a number of eastern legions supported the revolution of 238. Indeed, the slow and uneven distribution of largess might even explain why he was not uniformly popular with the troops under his direct command. There were two serious plots against his life, the conspiracies of Magnus and Quartinus, even before the uprising in 238.[75]

Maximinus' campaigns on the northern frontier are not well documented. Herodian's description of them appears to have been based on the paintings that Maximinus sent to Rome, and other evidence is sparse.[76] But from what there is it is possible to see that in 235 he campaigned on the central Rhine and then moved east against the Alamanni in the Agri Decumantes. In 236 he seems to have moved east into Pannonia and Moesia, and to have remained in that area through the next year. The winter of 237–8 found him at Sirmium. It was there that he learnt of the rebellion of the Gordians in early January 238 and the subsequent defection of Italy to their cause at the end of that month or at the beginning of February.[77]

Herodian describes the extraordinary events of 238 in some

---

[74] X. Loriot, 'Les premières années de la grande crise du IIIe siècle: De l'avènement de Maximin le Thrace (235) à la mort de Gordian III (244)', *ANRW* ii/2. 673 with n. 131.

[75] For discussion cf. ibid., 672–3. See esp. Herod. 7. 1. 4, 9.

[76] Herod. 7. 2. 1–8 with Whittaker's n. (p. 166 n. 1); Loriot, 'De Maximin le Thrace', pp. 674–6.

[77] Loriot, 'De Maximin le Thrace', pp. 720–2. For a review of various chronologies see K. Kietz, *Senatus contra principem: Untersuchungen zur senatorischen Opposition gegen Kaiser Maximinus Thrax* (Munich, 1980), 345–7. The publication of a recently discovered inscription from Shaqqā in Syria appears to show that Gordian III was sole emperor on 27 May 238, and I have therefore given somewhat earlier dates than those suggested by Loriot. For discussion see M. Sartre, 'Le *Dies Imperii* de Gordien III: Une inscription inédite de Syrie', *Syria*, 61 (1984), 49–61.

detail, but he does not essay any explanation other than that the oppressive tactics of a procurator in *Africa proconsularis* led to a revolt by the young men in that province. They murdered him and elevated the elderly governor of their province, M. Antonius Gordianus Sempronianus Romanus Africanus, to the purple. He notified friends at Rome of his rebellion and they arranged for the murder of the Praetorian Prefect (or acting prefect) Vitalianus and for the senate's acclamation of Gordian. The future emperor Valerian, already a consular by that point, appears to have been his messenger.[78] The Senate then appointed a board of twenty to assist in the defence of the Republic against the 'tyrant' and to rally the provinces to their cause. Several of the eastern provinces responded favourably.[79] In March the governor of Numidia, Capelianus, who had a long-standing grudge against Gordian, led *legio III Augusta* to Carthage and crushed the revolt there.[80] Gordian's son died in battle and Gordian committed suicide. When the news of this disaster reached Rome, the Senate proclaimed a pair of elderly members of the board of twenty, Pupienus and Balbinus, as rulers in his place. This led to a riot, sparked by friends of the deceased Gordian, and Gordian's thirteen-year-old grandson was proclaimed as *Caesar* to the childless Pupienus and Balbinus.[81]

Maximinus invaded Italy at the end of February and came to a halt before the powerfully defended city of Aquileia. The siege dragged on for some time. Some people thought it was a miracle,[82] while Maximinus' troops became increasingly bored, sick, hungry, and discontented. In, as it now appears, April they murdered the emperor and his son.

It was once argued that a group of officials who had risen to high rank under Alexander Severus had been cast into obscurity by Maximinus and that they returned to power under Gordian

[78] Dietz, *Senatus contra principem*, pp. 171–81; Syme, *Emperors and Biography*, p. 165.

[79] Loriot, 'De Maximin le Thrace', pp. 699–700.

[80] Herod. 7. 9. 1–11. For discussion of these events and the identity of Capelianus, see Dietz, *Senatus contra principem*, pp. 109–20.

[81] Herod. 7. 10. 5–6.

[82] Ibid. 8. 3. 8–9.

III.[83] The revolt of 238 was thus a 'Severan' reaction against Maximinus. A careful investigation of all careers known from this period has shown that no such conclusions can be drawn. In fact, the reign of Maximinus shows remarkable continuity with that of his predecessor.[84] The adherence of many important men to the revolutionary cause in 238 has to be explained in other ways: snobbish contempt for Maximinus' background and a feeling that he was not suitably deferential to the senate, fear that property might be at risk, or simple opportunism and cold calculation that his army might not be particularly loyal. The career and actions of Maximinus suggest that he possessed a powerful and forceful personality. A firm hand may have been resented after years of committee rule in the time of Alexander Severus.[85] A more pliable monarch was to be preferred if the occasion offered. This was what the revolution in 238 provided.

4. Antoninianus of Gordian III. *RIC* Gordian, 83. Ashmolean.

Maximinus was replaced by another committee: first by the board of twenty which had been selected to guide the state in its time of crisis, and after the murder of Pupienus and Balbinus (some time in the first half of May) by the advisers to the young Gordian III. Like Alexander Severus before him, this Gordian was not noted for any personal eccentricity. He was probably an amiable adolescent who did what he was told. The effective day-

---

[83] H. G. Pflaum, *Le Marbre de Thorigny* (Bibliothèque de l'école des hautes études, 242; Paris, 1948), 49–52; see also the elaboration by P. W. Townsend, 'The Revolution of 238: The Leaders and their Aims', *YCS* 14 (1955), 49–105.

[84] Dietz, *Senatus contra principem*, pp. 290–300.

[85] Syme, *Emperors and Biography*, p. 178.

to-day administration of the state was in the hands of the praetorian prefects. Their power had been made increasingly clear in rescripts of the reign of Alexander, one of which stated that a procedure ordered by the praetorian prefect would have the force of law if the emperor did not later change it. In the reign of Gordian it was clearly stated that the praetorian prefects had the power to oversee the actions of provincial governors. A rescript of 243 stated that the praetorian prefects had the power to review the decisions made by governors in legal cases, and an inscription from the reign of Philip, which preserves a letter that he wrote as praetorian prefect, makes it clear that he was empowered to give orders to governors on other matters as well, in this case, as having the authority to aid the peasants on an imperial estate in Phrygia.[86]

In some ways the regime of Gordian III was a throw-back to the days of Alexander. An irrelevant emperor allowed the great men of his time to reach agreement among themselves as to how the state should be administered and to settle their differences. The civil war of 238 was blamed on the 'tyrant' and a number of his supporters remained men of considerable influence. Q. Petronius Melior, who was descended from a family of municipal dignitaries in Etruria, had been quaestor in 232, tribune of the plebs as *candidatus* of Caesar in 233, and praetor in 235. During the reign of Maximinus he had been *legatus* of *legio VIII Augusta* in *Germania superior* and thus must have been in close contact with the emperor, and then had been appointed *curator Pyrgensium et Ceretanorum*. In 238, or thereabouts, he was *legatus* of *legio XXX Valeria Victrix* in *Germania inferior*, around 242 he served as *praefectus frumenti dandi* and subsequently as *curator rei publicae Tarquiniensium et Graviscanorum*. In 244 or 245 he was consul *suffectus*.[87] D. Simonius Proculus Julianus, governor of Thrace in 236–7 and therefore a close associate of the emperor when he was on campaign in the Balkans, was then appointed governor of Arabia for 237–8, consul *suffectus* for 238, and then governor of

---

[86] *CJ* 1. 26. 2, 9. 2. 6 (on l. 8); *OGIS* 519; *IGR* iv. 598 (see on l. 21).
[87] Dietz, *Senatus contra principem*, pp. 197–9.

Dacia. He was *praefectus urbi* before 254.[88] These men do not seem to have fared any worse in their careers than did Valerius Claudius Acilius Priscilianus Maximus, a member of the board of twenty in 238, who was *praefectus urbi* in 255 and *consul ordinarius* in 256, or L. Caesonius Lucillus Macer Rufinianus, another member of the board of twenty, who had risen to the consulship by 222 and would rise to be *praefectus urbi* before 254.[89] The future emperors whose activity in 238 is recorded, Decius and Valerian, served on opposite sides. Decius held *Hispania Tarraconensis* for Maximinus, while Valerian carried the news of Gordian's revolt from Africa to Rome. The most important figure in the later years of Gordian's reign, C. Furius Sabinius Aquila Timesitheus, praetorian prefect from 241 to 243 and father-in-law of the emperor, appears to have been a loyal servant of Maximinus, as he had once been a loyal servant of Alexander. On the other hand, two of the most prominent leaders of the revolutionary cause, Rutilius Pudens Crispinus and Tullus Menophilus, the commanders of the defence of Aquileia, do not seem to have done particularly well in the reign of Gordian. Crispinus went on to be *legatus Augusti pro praetore Hispaniae citerioris et Gallaeciae*, *curator* of several cities in Italy, and *legatus Augusti pro praetore ad census acceptandos provinciae Lugduensis*. Menophilus, who was sent to govern Moesia, appears to have been executed for treason around 241.[90]

The advisers of Gordian were confronted by the same problems that had faced Maximinus: unstable frontiers and an expensive army of doubtful loyalty. Indeed, the problem of the army must have been the most pressing. The events of 235 and 238 had shown that the loyalty of the legions could not be guaranteed for any ruler. Alexander had been killed despite his connection with Septimius, thus illustrating the fact that whatever loyalty the soldiers might feel to a dynasty, it would not stand up against the pressure of defeat. Maximinus had been

---

[88] Ibid. 228–31; M. Sartre, *Trois études sur l'Arabie romaine et byzantine* (Brussels, 1982), 91.

[89] Dietz, *Senatus contra principem*, pp. 103–9, 245–6.

[90] Ibid. 210–26, 233–45.

killed because, despite all his efforts, he was not sufficiently trusted as a general. The army had to be carefully cultivated and paid for.

Enormous donatives had been promised in 238, first by Pupienus and Balbinus to rally support in Italy, and then to the armies after the murder of Maximinus.[91] They were certainly not going to resort to Maximinus' fatal expedient of cutting other expenditures to raise the money. Instead they resorted to the debasement of the currency.

Pupienus and Balbinus began to issue antoniniani soon after their election. This set in motion the rapid degeneration of the imperial silver coinage during the next thirty years, with dire consequences for other coinages throughout the empire.[92] The weight of the denarius had hovered around 3.10 g in the reign of Severus, it had remained about the same during the time of Caracalla, and averaged around 2.9–3.0 g in the reign of Alexander.[93] In the reign of Maximinus the weight was between 3.01 and 3.14 g. Under Gordian III the weight seems to have been around 3.00 g, in the reign of Philip it apparently declined to c. 2.80 g, and in the reign of Gallienus it fell to between 2.17 and 1.80 g.[94] The antoniniani which were issued by Caracalla, Macrinus, and Elagabalus between 215 and 219 varied in weight between 5.0 and 4.9 g.[95] The issues of Pupienus and Balbinus vary between 4.94 and 4.58 g; those of Gordian III have a mean between 4.46 (in

---

[91]   *HA V. Gord.* 10. 4; Herod. 8. 7. 7.

[92]   Crawford, 'Finance, Coinage and Money', pp. 569–70; for the disappearance of local coinage in the Greek east during the 260s cf. C. J. Howgego, *Greek Imperial Countermarks: Studies in the Provincial Coinage of the Roman Empire* (London, 1985), 65–73.

[93]   Callu, *Politique monétaire*, p. 237; Walker, *Metrology*, pp. 4–11 (in 194–5 Severus' denarii dipped to approximately 2.95 g, to 2.9 g in 196 and 2.7 g in 197; they reached c. 3.4 g in 200–1); pp. 17–19 for Caracalla; pp. 26–33 for Alexander.

[94]   For more specific measurements see Callu, *Politique monétaire*, p. 238; Walker, *Metrology*, pp. 3–51; Walker's figures are based upon better samples than those of Callu, and he provides convenient charts giving mean figures year by year; see also C. E. King, 'Denarii and Quinarii, A.D. 253–295', in R. A. G. Carson and C. M. Kraay (eds.), *Scripta Nummaria Romana: Essays Presented to Humphrey Sutherland* (London, 1978), 84, and her charts on pp. 98–104.

[95]   Callu, *Politique monétaire*, pp. 238–9; Walker, *Metrology*, pp. 19–22, 35–48, and pp. 49–51 for a valuable tabulation of his results.

240) and 4.06 (243–4) g, and those of Philip from 4.79 to 3.96 g. Under Decius the weight descended to just below 4 g (though the mean attained for eight coins from the mint at 'Milan' in 250–1 is 3.6) and under Gallus it descended to about 3.6–3.4 g. In the joint reign of Valerian and Gallienus, when there is substantial variation from mint to mint, the weights range from 3.78 to 3.09 g, and in the sole reign of Gallienus, when there was even greater variation according to mint and year, the range is between 4.04 and 2.45 g (at Antioch in the years 266–8).[96]

The decline of the silver content in these coins was even more impressive than the decline in their weight. In the reign of Marcus Aurelius the silver content of the denarius had been *c.*74–6 per cent. In the reigns of Septimius and Caracalla this had dropped to *c.*54–8 per cent (though issues just after Severus' arrival at Rome had reached 78.12–78.71 per cent and issues in 194/5–195/6 have a mean between 66.50 and 61.40 per cent). In the reign of Alexander Severus the percentage slipped slightly to around 44–46 per cent in most years (though the coinage of 227 seems to have had *c.*36 per cent and that of 230–5 *c.*51.1 per cent), and it remained at around 45 per cent throughout the reign of Gordian III. One coin in the reign of Gallienus contained only 8 per cent silver.[97] The antoniniani of Caracalla had varied between a high of *c.*59 per cent and a low of *c.*46 per cent silver. Those of Gordian varied between 47 and 37 per cent, those of Philip between 44 and 31 per cent, those of Decius between 49 and 26 per cent (at Antioch). There was even greater variation in the reign of Gallus, between a high of 49 per cent and a low of 17 per cent (also at Antioch). Aemilianus' antoniniani hovered between 37 and 36 per cent silver. The silver content virtually disappeared in the reigns of Valerian and Gallienus. The best coins that were minted in their time had a silver content of about 37 per cent, but it only reached that level at Rome in 253/4 (directly after Valerian took the throne) and at Cologne in 257/8. Ordinarily the antoniniani in these years contain between 10 and 15 per cent

[96] Callu, *Politique monétaire*, pp. 239–40.
[97] Ibid. 244–5; Walker, *Metrology*, pp. 49–50.

silver. Under Claudius the level descended to between 2 and 3 per cent (six coins from Cyzicus average as low as 1.55 per cent) and in the reign of Aurelian it ranges between 4 and 2.6 per cent before he undertook his reform of the coinage in 274.[98] The collapse of the imperial silver coinage, which was paralleled by a decline in the weight of the gold coinage and seems to have led to the virtual elimination of bronze coinage, reflects the imperial government's failure to adapt the tax structure of the empire to meet its necessary expenditures.[99] It is fair to place the beginning of this extraordinary decline in the reign of Gordian and to see it as the result of a short-sighted response to the fiscal exigencies caused by the civil war of 238. The impact of this action was increased by an explosion of pressure on the frontier, which increased costs and hampered the state's ability to collect revenue.

While the solution that Gordian's advisers adopted to their financial problems was not original—earlier emperors had also debased the coinage to meet extraordinary demands—it did set a trend for the next two decades which was to cause immense economic dislocation within the empire. But this possibility could scarcely have occurred to these men in the midst of their own immediate, pressing, concerns. The first priority must have been the pay of the army, but there were other areas where problems called for action. In north Africa *legio III Augusta*, which had been the main force employed for the suppression of the elder Gordians, was disbanded. Chaos seems to have ensued, and in 240 another governor of *Africa Proconsularis*, Sabinianus, was proclaimed emperor.[100] He was suppressed after a short time by Faltonius Restitutianus, the governor of *Mauretania Caesariensis*.[101] The fact that the rebellion of Sabinianus did not have the

[98] Callu, *Politique monétaire*, pp. 245–8, 323; Crawford, 'Finance, Coinage and Money', pp. 575–6; L. H. Cope, 'The Nadir of the Imperial Antoninianus in the Reign of Claudius II Gothicus A.D. 268–270', *Num. Chron.* 7 9 (1969), 145–61. For the first half of the 3rd cent. see Walker, *Metrology*, pp. 3–51.

[99] Callu, *Politique monétaire*, pp. 322–3.

[100] Loriot, 'De Maximin le Thrace', p. 734.

[101] H. G. Pflaum, *Les Carrières procuratoriennes équestres sous le haut-empire romain*, 3 vols. (Paris, 1960–1), No. 322.

same impact on the empire that the revolt of the Gordians did is a sign that the government of Gordian III was more effective in conciliating opinion than that of Maximinus had been, but the revolt still appears to have had serious consequences. One of them was the interruption of preparations for an offensive against the Persians. In 238 Ardashir had swept across northern Mesopotamia again, and this time he had succeeded in capturing both Nisibis and Carrhae. This had the effect of opening the southern route into the Arsamias basin to Persian attack and cutting off Hatra and *legio I Parthica* at Singara behind the Khabur and the Djebel Sindjar.[102]

Gordian was not able to react to this situation rapidly. It took a considerable amount of time to muster the forces necessary for a Persian war, and he had to contend with the north African revolt in 240 as well; it would be several years before effective action could be taken. In that time there would also be more trouble with the tribes against whom Maximinus had fought along the upper Rhine and Danube as well as a serious incursion by the Goths into *Moesia Inferior.*[103] Istria was destroyed and the garrison under the command of Tullus Menophilus was engaged in heavy fighting before it could drive the Goths back. In 241 it appears that a decision was made to remove Menophilus. His name was erased from inscriptions, which suggests that he was accused of conspiracy and executed. He was replaced by Sabinius Modestus, who may have been a relative of Timesitheus, who was emerging just then as the leading figure at Rome.[104] In 241 Gordian married Timesitheus' daughter, Sabinia Tranquillina.

Preparations for war with Persia began anew in the same year that Gordian was married, and by that time the situation was even worse than it had been in 238. At some point between April 240 and March 241 Hatra surrendered to the Persians.[105] In 242 the Roman army moved into northern Mesopotamia, defeated

---

[102] See on ll. 13–20.

[103] Loriot, 'De Maximin le Thrace', pp. 753–7 (with the correction noted on ll. 13–20).

[104] Dietz, *Senatus contra principem*, p. 227.

[105] See on ll. 13–20 for a full discussion of these events.

the Persians at Resaina, and recaptured Carrhae and Nisibis. This appears to have happened while Gordian was still on the march through the Balkans and Asia Minor. The kingdom of Osrhoene was briefly re-established and preparations were set in motion for the invasion of Persia. It was also at this time that Timesitheus died and was replaced by Julius Philippus, the brother of the surviving praetorian prefect, Julius Priscus.

The Persian campaign was to be a grand event, recalling the memory of Trajan and Alexander the Great. Reports were so encouraging that the young Plotinus left his studies at Alexandria to accompany the expedition in the hope that he would be able to meet the wise men of the east after the Roman victory. At the same time, but on the other side, another young philosopher, whose thought would prove to be even more influential than that of Plotinus, was experiencing the series of visions that would inspire his career. This was Mani.[106]

Obverse   *Reverse*

5. Silver drachm of Sapor I; *reverse*: fire-altar with two attendants. 4.33 g. Ashmolean.

Plotinus' hopes of visiting the east were shattered with the failure of Gordian's expedition. The army, which marched down the Euphrates in the winter, a very difficult time of year for campaigning in that part of the world, was defeated by Sapor at Misiche/Peroz-Sapor. The Romans fell back to the north, and in the region of Zaitha, just south of the Khabur, the troops rose in anger and murdered the young emperor.[107]

---

[106] It is possible that Mani was actually serving in the Persian army at this period: see L. Koenen, 'Manichäische Mission und Kloster in Ägypten', in *Das römisch-byzantinische Ägypten* (Mainz am Rhein, 1983), 97 n. 27.   [107] See on ll. 17, 20 for the circumstances.

Gordian was succeeded by one of the praetorian prefects, Julius Philippus, who had been born at Chahba in *Provincia Arabia*. At the time that he was promoted to the purple Julius Priscus was still praetorian prefect, and it seems that he had been responsible for Philip's elevation as his colleague in the prefecture. There is no way of knowing why Priscus was passed over, though it is possible that the fact that Philip had a son may have been a consideration.[108] In any event, it did not make much difference. Philip left Priscus in the east as *rector orientis* when he returned to Rome. Priscus was in effect the emperor of the east.[109]

6. Antoninianus of Philip I. *RIC* Philip, 2*b*. Ashmolean.

7. Bronze Medallion of Philip II. *RIC* Philip, 228. Ashmolean.

Philip's first priority was to end the war with Persia, and the terms that he accepted suggest that he was quite desperate.[110] He agreed to pay 500,000 aurei at once, and possibly a subsidy to the Persians thereafter. This was a tremendous drain on the treasury. He also agreed to abandon Roman territory that was still in Persian hands (or, less probably, the land between Singara and the

---

[108] See on l. 21. For further speculation on Philip's qualifications see below, p. 39.
[109] See on ll. 61–3.   [110] See on l. 27.

Euphrates) and not to give any further aid to the king of Armenia. After the defeat at Misiche it is very probable that Philip had no desire to fight another pitched battle with Sapor; it is also very probable that he had no desire to repeat the error of Maximinus by failing to visit Rome at the first opportunity. He headed back to Italy as fast as he could, and appears to have arrived by 23 July; but while he was in Antioch it appears that he stopped long enough to speak with Babylas, the bishop of that city. It is possible that he expressed polite interest in what Babylas had to say, and that this inspired Origen to write a letter explaining the faith to him and his wife (possibly hoping that he would have more success than he had once had with Julia Maesa).[111]

Peace did not last for long on the eastern frontier. The *Thirteenth Sibylline Oracle* confirms a report in Zonaras' *Epitome of the Histories* that Philip had to renounce the treaty after he arrived at Rome and suggests that hostilities began again in 245 or 246.[112] Shame over the territorial concessions that he made may explain why reference to Persia is rarely evident in Philip's titulature, and the fact that the war was resumed so soon suggests that such concessions were unacceptable to a substantial number of influential men at Rome. It might also explain why this renewal of hostilities was countenanced when there was serious trouble on another front. Jordanes records that the Goths invaded the empire because Philip ceased to pay them their regular subsidies.[113] After the payments that he had made to the Persians it is not surprising that Philip felt the need to cut his expenses elsewhere; there is also some evidence for changes in the administration of the provinces to enhance revenue collection. Papyri reveal the activity of two high officials, Marcellus and Saluteris, who appear in what seem to have been new roles, those of the *rationalis* and his assistant to oversee a programme of reform in the business of extracting money from the Egyptians. In Asia Minor a new province of Caria-Phrygia was created out of the old province of Asia. This looks like another step to

---

[111] For the legend of Philip's Christianity, see on l. 88.
[112] See on ll. 24, 25–7.   [113] See on l. 36.

increase the efficiency of the administration of the region.[114] Philip also cut subsidies to the northern tribes. The result was a raid in which the tribes breached the defences of Dacia on the Olt (the *limes transalutanus*) and the *Thirteenth Sibylline Oracle* suggests that there were also raids from the sea, precursors of the great Gothic expeditions of the 250s and 260s. The area as a whole had been left in the charge of another of Philip's relatives, a kinsman by marriage named Servianus.[115] The failures in this region were thus intimately linked to Philip's regime, and his evident desire to promote his relatives may have led people to question his judgement.

Philip himself does not seem to have been capable of decisive action (this may indeed have been a qualification for office). Priscus commanded during the war in the east, and Philip seems to have remained in Rome during the Gothic attack on the Balkan frontiers. Moreover, tension also seems to have been building in some areas as the thousandth anniversary of Rome's foundation approached.[116] In 248 Philip celebrated the millennium with lavish games at Rome. In Alexandria people wondered if this portended a great change. There were riots in the city in 247, and in 248 or 249 there was a pogrom against the Christians in the city.[117] There was open rebellion in the province of Syria and revolution broke out on the Danube.

The outbreak in the east is associated with the figure of Jotapianus. Aurelius Victor suggests that he was related to the Sampsigeramids of Emesa and Zosimus suggests that his revolt

---

[114] For the Egyptian evidence see P. J. Parsons, 'Philippus Arabs and Egypt', *JRS* 57 (1967), 134–41; J. D. Thomas, 'The Introduction of Dekaprotoi and Comarchs into Egypt in the Third Century A.D.', *ZPE* 19 (1975), 111–19, showing that the *dekaprotoi* replaced the *sitologoi c.* 242–6 and that the comarch replaced the *comogrammateus c.* 245–7/8; Dr T. Gagos (to whom I am grateful for discussion of the evidence) has also shown, in a forthcoming paper, that there was a change in the police structure, with the comarchs taking over from the *archephodos* in the same period. For Caria-Phrygia see S. Frei-Korsunsky, 'Meilensteine aus der Gegend von Eskişehir', *Epigraphica Anatolica*, 8 (1986), 1–5; Ch. Roueché, *Aphrodisias in Late Antiquity* (London, 1989), 1–2.

[115] Zos. 1. 19. 2; see Hartmann, *Herrscherwechsel und Reichskrise*, pp. 68, 186.

[116] See on ll. 46–9.

[117] See on ll. 50–3, 74–8.

was a response to the oppressive policies of Philip. He had spent a great deal of money on Bostra and in developing his birthplace, renamed Philippopolis in his honour. Some lines in the *Thirteenth Sibylline Oracle* reflect great antipathy towards the cities of Arabia, which may reflect hostility resulting from the iniquities of a regime which bore heavily on some provinces for the benefit of others.[118] But this did not matter much by comparison with events on the Danube.

Servianus' appointment on the Danube at the beginning of Philip's reign is mentioned only once in the sources, and it is impossible to know what happened to him in the next few years. He may no longer have been in the area when T. Claudius Marinus Pacatianus began his revolt late in 248 or early in 249.[119] One of Pacatianus' coins advertises the year 1001, and it may well

8. Antoninianus of Pacatianus. *RIC* Pacatianus, 4. British Museum.

be that he took advantage of the proclamation of the new millennium to promote revolution among his men, men who might anyway have been annoyed that Philip had shown so little personal interest in their struggle with the Goths. Nor did Philip move on this occasion. Instead, he sent a native of the region to put down the revolt. This was C. Messius Quintus Decius Valerianus, who appears to have come from an influential family in Sirmium. He had risen to the consulship in the reign of Alexander Severus and held *Hispania Tarraconensis* for Maximinus in 238.[120] The appointment of Decius proved to be a terrible mistake on Philip's part. He suppressed Pacatianus' revolt, but before 28 May the legions had risen and proclaimed him

[118] See on ll. 64–78, 68.   [119] See on ll. 79–80.   [120] See on l. 82.

emperor. He marched on Italy and defeated Philip near Verona between 29 August and 16 October 249.

The reason or reasons why events took this course can never be established with certainty, but this revolt does appear to be illustrative of two important trends in the third century. The first was the weakening of discipline in the army. There was a tendency for a mutiny to have a long-term unsettling effect on an army, and for troops who felt that they had not received what they should have in a previous uprising, or who felt that their position had been hurt by changes resulting from the preceding revolt, to rise again.[121] This appears to have been the case in the revolt of Quartinus during the reign of Maximinus, which is narrated in some detail by Herodian. Here the Osrhoenian archers who had been favoured by Alexander felt that they were snubbed by Maximinus (his difficulty in paying the donative he promised may have enhanced these feelings) and proclaimed as emperor a senior officer, Quartinus, whom Maximinus had dismissed.[122] Similar concerns may lie behind the revolt of Sabinianus under Gordian, the revolt of Regalianus after the suppression of Ingenuus in 260, and the civil wars in Gaul in 269–70.[123] The second trend appears to be the desire of the soldiers to have an emperor who understood their particular problem, who had a good knowledge of their local situation, and who was thought to be especially sympathetic to their specific demands. Decius' Sirmian background would therefore have provided a powerful impetus to the revolt.[124]

The emperor Decius was a curious figure. The evidence of his actions suggests that he was deeply conservative, that he was deeply pious, that he possessed a ferocious temper, and that he was quite stupid. He seems to have yearned for the days when the empire appeared to be invincible, and he appears to have cherished the memory of Trajan and the other emperors who

---

[121] See Zos. 1. 21. 3.　　　　　　　　　　　　　　　[122] Herod. 7. 1. 9–11.

[123] Drinkwater, *The Gallic Empire*, pp. 34–5; see also the interesting discussion of Hartmann, *Herrscherwechsel und Reichskrise*, pp. 106–9.

[124] See Hartmann, *Herrscherwechsel und Reichskrise*, pp. 158–69.

had made Rome great. Thus, one of his first acts after assuming
the throne was to take the name Trajan for himself and to issue
an edict ordering all the inhabitants of the empire to sacrifice to
the ancestral gods for the safety of the state.[125] His vision of the
empire may also be reflected in the remarkable series of antoniniani which were issued from the mint at Milan commemorating the deified emperors.[126]

9. Double sestertius of Decius. *RIC*
Decius, 126*a*. Ashmolean.

10. Sestertius of Herennius Etruscus.
RIC Decius, 167. Ashmolean.

11. Aureus of Hostilianus. *RIC* Decius,
181. Ashmolean.

Decius' edict on sacrifices is certainly the best known of his
actions, because it had the coincidental effect of causing serious
divisions within the Christian Church. The edict itself seems to
have been straightforward. All the inhabitants of the empire were

---

[125] See on ll. 82, 87.   [126] *RIC* Decius 117, 130–2.

required to sacrifice before the magistrates of their community 'for the safety of the empire' by a certain day (the date would vary from place to place and the order may have been that the sacrifice had to be completed within a specified period after a community received the edict). When they sacrificed they would obtain a certificate (*libellus*) recording the fact that they had complied with the order, just as they received a receipt from the tax-collectors whenever they paid their taxes: indeed, the procedure in this edict appears to parallel the process of tax collection very closely. Decius himself may have intended this act to reaffirm the *pax deorum*, and to reassure people throughout the empire that the empire was still secure after the passing of the millennium. For the Christian Church it caused a terrible crisis of authority as various bishops and their flocks reacted to it in different ways. Some Christians, such as Pionius in Smyrna, saw it as offering a splendid opportunity for martyrdom. Others thought that they should simply obey the order and obtain a *libellus*, others thought that they could evade the order by obtaining a false *libellus*, and still others thought that they should refuse to obey, but try to stay out of the way of local officials until the excitement died down. Decius himself may not have been conscious of any of this, and the notion that he issued a second edict strengthening the first when he discovered that some Christians were refusing to obey his order has been shown to be incorrect.[127] The edict reflects Decius' concern with tradition, but does not reflect a desire to eradicate Christianity, and by the time the edict was taking effect Decius had far more serious problems to worry about.

Jotapianus was still active in the east when Decius took the throne, and once Julius Priscus was removed (it is unfortunate that no details as to just how this was done have been preserved), Decius had to see to it that his revolt was brought to an end. This was duly accomplished, and Jotapianus was beheaded. But another figure emerged in his place. This was Mariades, and to judge from the *Thirteenth Sibylline Oracle* (as well as certain other,

---

[127] See on l. 87 for a full discussion.

scattered, evidence) he was a figure of considerable importance.[128] He seems to have been a native of Syria and to have assembled a large band of followers; there may even be some truth to the stories reported by John Malalas and the *Historia Augusta* that he was once a member of the curial class at Antioch. He appears to have had friends and admirers there in 252. Mariades' career as a raider began in the latter part of 250 and extended into 251. His depredations covered a broad area in Syria and Cappadocia, and he appears to have captured both Tyana and Mazaka. He evaded the Roman forces sent in pursuit of him and escaped into Persian territory, where he was generously received by Sapor.

While Mariades was ravaging the eastern provinces, the Goths once again invaded the empire. In the course of 250 the Carpi pierced the Dacian frontier and a large band of Goths, evidently under the command of a king named Cniva, attacked Moesia and laid siege to Marcianopolis.[129] They failed to take the city, but continued their invasion by moving into central Thrace and Macedonia. This probably took up a good part of the summer of 250, and the Roman situation soon got worse. Decius moved first against the invaders of Dacia, and then against Cniva and his followers. But when he caught up with them in the area of Beroea, he was heavily defeated.

News of Decius' defeat may have precipitated the short-lived revolt of Valens and the much more serious revolt of Priscus. This Priscus appears to have been the governor of Moesia, and he seized his chance to attack Decius by making an alliance with the Goths.[130] He handed the city of Philippopolis over to them to plunder in the spring of 251. After sacking Philippopolis, the Goths withdrew north through the Dobrudja (nothing is known about Priscus' fate) with Decius in pursuit. Decius caught up with them in late May or early June near Abrittus—possibly the modern Abtat Kalessi between Durosturum and Dionysopolis.[131]

---

[128] See on ll. 80–100, where the evidence is discussed in detail.
[129] Demougeot, *La Formation*, pp. 409–10.
[130] See on ll. 100–2 and below, p. 86.
[131] Demougeot, *La Formation*, pp. 411–12.

The Goths appear to have taken up a position around a marsh in the area, and when the Romans attacked they became entangled in this swamp. The result was a total disaster and Decius died on the field. His body was never recovered.

C. Vibius Trebonianus Gallus, who may have been governor of *Moesia Inferior* at the time, was elevated to the purple by the surviving Roman forces in the area. Rumour, which may be reflected in the *Thirteenth Sibylline Oracle* as well as the accounts preserved in the works of Zosimus and Zonaras, had it that Gallus had betrayed Decius to his death.[132] It is alleged that he advised the Goths to draw up their army in three divisions, two in front of the swamp and one behind it. When Decius drove back the first two divisions and entered the swamp, Gallus gave a signal to the enemy and they annihilated the force with Decius. There is no reason to believe that this is true: it is inconceivable that Roman soldiers would have supported a man who had sent their comrades to their death or that the surviving marshals could have supported him. But it is an interesting reflection of feeling towards a man whose reign would prove to be a disaster.

12. Sestertius of Gallus. *RIC* Gallus, 116*a*. Ashmolean.

13. Antoninianus of Volusianus, mint of Antioch. *RIC* Gallus, 214. Private collection in the Ashmolean.

---

[132] See on ll. 103, 104.

Gallus appears to have been in a desperate position after Decius' defeat, and he appears to have paid the barbarians an enormous bribe so that they would go home, and to have allowed them to take their plunder with them. This diplomacy put a temporary end to the Gothic invasion and Gallus went off to Rome to secure his position. The situation was complicated. Decius had two sons, Q. Herennius Etruscus Messius Decius and C. Valens Hostilianus Messius Quintus.[133] Herennius Etruscus had died in battle before the engagement at Abrittus, but Hostilianus, who appears to have been in his teens, was still alive and held the rank of *Augustus*. Gallus also had a son, Vibius Afinius Gallus Veldumianus Volusianus, who seems to have been in his twenties. After the defeat of Decius no one seems to have been interested in fighting a civil war to sort out the rival claims. Gallus therefore reached a compromise in which he would reign with Hostilianus as his fellow *Augustus* while Volusianus took the rank of *Caesar*. This arrangement lasted for a month or so in the summer of 251. But by the end of July Hostilianus had either been murdered or died of the plague.[134]

Gallus was soon confronted by an emergency in the east. In the course of 251 Sapor invaded Armenia, and drove the son of King Chosroes, Tiridates, from the country. This called for a serious Roman response, and preparations began for war with Persia in 252. But Sapor struck first. In the summer of 252 he moved up the Euphrates (an unusual route for a Persian army) to catch a major concentration of Roman troops near Barbalissos. Sapor won an overwhelming victory and effective Roman resistance in the area came to an end: before the summer was over he had captured the major legionary camps in Syria and sacked Antioch. To judge from the account in the *Thirteenth Sibylline Oracle*, Mariades played a major role in this campaign. It is even possible that he arranged for the capture of Antioch through treason. The oracle says that the city fell 'before the spear' through the folly of its citizens. This may confirm a story partially preserved by the

---

[133] Cf. on ll. 102, 142.   [134] See on l. 142.

anonymous Continuator of Cassius Dio that when Sapor and Mariades were encamped twenty stades from the city, the 'friends of Mariades' and other people who desired a revolution began to agitate. The fragment breaks off here, but it can be assumed that these people played some role in Sapor's subsequent capture of the city.[135] Nothing is known of Mariades' career after this. According to one tradition, which is surely fanciful, Sapor burnt him at the stake in Antioch. According to another tradition he was killed by his own men when Valerian came east in 254. He may simply have died from natural causes.[136]

As Sapor's armies were ravaging Syria, a new threat emerged in the Balkans. The Carpi attacked the central Danubian frontier once again, and a group of other tribes launched the first of a series of naval expeditions which broke out from the Black Sea and spread destruction along the coasts of Asia Minor as far south as Lycia.[137] The raiders from the sea appear to have returned home when they had their fill of plunder: there is no record that the Roman fleet was able to take any effective action against them. The situation was somewhat different on the Danube. In the early summer of 253 the Carpi were defeated in battle by Aemilius Aemilianus, the governor of one of the Pannonian provinces. He had promised a lavish distribution of booty after the victory; his men proclaimed him emperor and followed him in a march against Gallus. Gallus mustered what forces he could and sent P. Licinius Valerianus to rally support from the armies on the Rhine, perhaps hoping that he would be able to exploit the deep-seated rivalries between the garrisons of different parts of the empire. Aemilianus reached Italy before Valerian could return. Gallus was defeated and killed in battle near Interamna, but a few weeks later Valerian crossed the Alps and defeated Aemilianus at Spoletium.[138]

---

[135] For the Continuator of Dio see app. v, and for the circumstances of the campaign in general see on ll. 110, 111, 122–8, 131–3.

[136] See on ll. 89–100.   [137] See on l. 141.

[138] See on ll. 144–5. For discussion of rivalries between armies see Hartmann, *Herrscherwechsel und Reichskrise*, pp. 89–94. M. Christol, 'A propos de la politique extérieure de Trébonien Galle', *Rev. Num.* (1980), 68–74, suggests that resentment on the part of the

14. Antoninianus of Aemilianus. *RIC*
Aemilianus, 2. Ashmolean.

While civil war raged in the west, the Persians launched
another attack on the Syrian frontier. Although the details are
obscure, it appears that the dynast of Emesa, Lucius Julius
Aurelius Sulpicius Uranius Severus Antoninus, rallied what
forces he could and was able to drive the Persians back. There is
no way of knowing what he intended to do next. He issued a
series of coins in bronze, silver, and gold, but his actions do not
seem to indicate a desire to restore Emesene control of the central
government, or even to show 'the need for an emperor in the
area'.[139] They may only reflect a desire to illustrate his importance by adopting the symbols associated with power. Roman
symbols do not appear to have had the same specific meaning in
Syria which they had in Rome, and there was a long tradition in
Syria of adopting symbols associated with central power, such as
royal garb, to reflect purely local importance. A few years after
253 Paul of Samosata, the bishop of Antioch, would appear in
public with a retinue that was organized to resemble that of an
imperial procurator. When he did this he was not trying to claim
the power of a procurator. He was trying to impress people with
his importance as a bishop.[140] Uranius is best seen as a local

Danubian troops at Gallus' treaty with the Goths may have been a factor. He also suggests
that the troops in question had already been taken from their usual garrisons in preparation
for a Persian expedition. See also above, pp. 14–15.

[139] See on ll. 150–4. I hope to argue the proposition offered here at length in the near
future.

[140] Eus. *HE* 7. 30. 8; F. G. Millar, 'Paul of Samosata, Zenobia and Aurelian: The Church,
Local Culture and Political Allegiance in Third-Century Syria', *JRS* 61 (1971), 1–12. See
also *SEG* xvii. 759. The right to wear purple was still a privilege granted to local dignitaries
in the 3rd cent.: see L. Robert, 'Une vision de Pérpetue martyre', *CRAI* (1982), 258–9;
M. Wörrle, *Stadt und Fest im kaiserzeitlichen Kleinasien* (Munich, 1988), 186–93.

aristocrat doing his best to defend his city in the absence of effective defence by Rome.

The situation in the east began to stabilize after the summer of 253, and late in 254 Valerian himself arrived to take charge of the situation. Valerian had been born in the reign of Septimius Severus, or possibly that of Commodus; he had risen to the consulship in the reign of Alexander Severus. He was therefore an elderly man, like his immediate predecessors Decius and Gallus, and like Decius he seemed to be obsessed with the idea that he could return the empire to the condition it was in when he was a young man. His actions suggest that he was a man of tremendous energy and some imagination. Valerian's immediate promotion of his son, Gallienus, to the rank of *Augustus*, and the subsequent promotion of Gallienus' son Valerian to the same rank in the 250s, suggest that he felt that he could stabilize the situation on the frontiers if there was a member of the imperial family on hand to oversee important campaigns. This does indeed seem to foreshadow Diocletian's reorganization of the empire. It also appears that either he or Gallienus created the mobile field force of infantry and cavalry known as the *comitatus*.[141] His persecution edicts against the Christians of 257–8 (which were very similar to the first edict issued by Diocletian in February 304) may suggest that he also had an interest in purifying the empire of 'dangerous enemies' within as well as controlling her enemies beyond the frontiers.[142] But all his efforts were doomed to failure.

15. Antoninianus of Valerian. *RIC* Valerian, 46*d*. Ashmolean.

---

[141] See E. Ritterling, 'Zum römischen Heerwesen des ausgehenden dritten Jahrhunderts', *Beiträge zur alten Geschichte und griechisch–römischen Alterthumskunde: Festschrift zu Otto Hirschfelds sechzigstem Geburtstage* (Berlin, 1903), 345–9. See below, ch. 2 n. 49.

[142] See Endnote 4 (end of chapter).

16. Antoninianus of Valerian II. *RIC* Valerian II, 3. Ashmolean.

17. Aureus of Gallienus. *RIC* Gallienus, 446. Ashmolean.

18. Antoninianus of Saloninus. *RIC* Saloninus, 36. Ashmolean.

After seeing to the eastern frontier in 254, Valerian returned to the west. He reached Sirmium by the mid-summer of 255, and the recently discovered text of an imperial letter at Aphrodisias may place him at Mainz on 23 August 256. On 10 October of that year he seems to have been at Rome.[143] The evidence of coins and inscriptions suggests that he spent a great deal of time and energy setting the Rhenish and Danubian frontiers in order.[144] But in 257 and 258 the system began to fall apart. Dura Europus fell to the Persians in 257 (probably), and this may have been the event that called Valerian back to the east. In 258 Valerian II died

[143] See on ll. 158–61.   [144] Drinkwater, *The Gallic Empire*, pp. 22, 110.

on the Danube while Gallienus was still tied down in Gaul, which led to a weakening of control over that area.[145] In 259 Gothic raiders again landed in Asia Minor and swept east as far as Cappadocia. Valerian turned away from the Persian frontier to catch them. He failed to do so and his army seems to have been afflicted with the plague. In 260 Sapor swept across northern Mesopotamia and Valerian offered battle outside Emesa. The army was defeated and he was captured.[146]

It is difficult to know what happened in the next decade. The *Thirteenth Sibylline Oracle* is the one contemporary narrative account of the mid-third century, and it concludes with a brief notice of the events surrounding the emergence of Odaenathus as the pre-eminent figure in the east. The accounts of Zosimus and Zonaras are extremely impressionistic for these years, more so than usual, and there is no text with which to control their evidence save for the *Historia Augusta* biography of Gallienus, which provides four consular dates, and the biography of Claudius, which provides one more. Otherwise, there is an inscription from Asia Minor which confirms one of the dates in the *Vita Gallieni* (that of the Gothic raid on the coast of Asia Minor in 262).[147] There are papyri, coins, and inscriptions which combine to secure some dates in the east,[148] and coins and inscriptions in the west, especially from Gaul, which have recently been exploited to provide a convincing outline of events connected with the *imperium Galliarum.*[149]

The principal events between the capture of Valerian and the accession of Claudius appear to have unfolded as follows. In the

---

[145] See the discussion (summarizing earlier debate) ibid. 22–3.

[146] See on l. 161.

[147] *HA V. Gall.* 6. 2; L. Robert, 'Épitaphe de provenance inconnue faisant mention des barbares', *Hellenica*, vi (Paris, 1948), 117–22.

[148] In addition to the texts discussed by A. Stein, 'Zur Chronologie der römischen Kaiser von Decius bis Diocletian', *Archiv für Papyrusforschung*, 7 (1924), 30–51, see *P. Oxy.* 2710, which proves that Macrianus and Quietus held the consulship claimed for them in the summer of 260, and, most recently, the discussion by J. R. Rea, *P. Oxy.* xl. 15–26, for the chronology of the reigns of Claudius and Aurelian.

[149] I. König, *Die gallischen Usurpatoren von Postumus bis Tetricus* (Munich, 1981), and Drinkwater, *The Gallic Empire.*

east Macrianus, who may have been Valerian's *procurator summarum rationum*, and an officer named Callistus rallied the remnants of Roman armies in the region, and fell upon the army of Sapor after it had broken up into plundering expeditions throughout Cilicia and Cappadocia. They won a number of victories and were joined in their struggle by Odaenathus, the hereditary lord of Palmyra, as the Persians withdrew to their own territory.[150] The Persians took Valerian with them: later legend had it that after his death he was flayed and that his skin was stuffed for display in a temple. In Pannonia, where Valerian and Gallienus may have been losing control ever since the death of Valerian II in 258, the governor Ingenuus was proclaimed emperor. He was defeated in battle at Mursa.[151] His place was taken by another usurper, Regalianus, who was likewise suppressed within a few months.[152]

The revolt of Postumus broke out in Gaul during the late summer of 260 and led to the creation of the *imperium Galliarum*, which endured until 274. Marcus Cassianius Latinius Postumus may have been born on the Rhine frontier, and at the time of his revolt he appears to have been governor of *Germania Inferior*.[153] In that year there was a serious invasion across the Rhine; Postumus was only able to intercept a band of raiders as they were returning home. Silvanus, the official in overall control of the region with Saloninus, a young son of Gallienus who had been given the rank of *Caesar*, ordered him to turn over the plunder that he had recovered. He distributed it to his men instead; they proclaimed him emperor and marched on Cologne, where Silvanus and Saloninus were handed over to them and killed. Gallienus, who may have been involved with Ingenuus and Regalianus, or possibly

---

[150] See on ll. 161–3, 169; app. IV.

[151] Aur. Victor, *De Caes.* 33. 2; Zon. 12. 24; *PIR* ² i. 23; Drinkwater, *The Gallic Empire*, pp. 104–5.

[152] The circumstances are completely obscure: see A. Alföldi, 'The Numbering of the Victories of the Emperor Gallienus and the Loyalty of his Legions', *Num. Chron.* ⁵ 9(1929), 258 – *Studien*, p. 103; J. Fitz, *Ingenuus et Régalien* (Brussels, 1976), 38–71; M. Christol, 'Les règnes de Valérien et de Gallien (253–268), traveaux d'ensemble, questions chronologiques', *ANRW* ii/2. 820–1; Drinkwater, *The Gallic Empire*, p. 105.

[153] Drinkwater, *The Gallic Empire*, pp. 125–6.

with the serious Alamannic invasion of Italy which Zonaras records at the time of Valerian's capture, was not able to make an effective response to the revolt.[154] Postumus soon gained control over the provinces beyond the Alps with the exception of *Gallia Narbonensis.*

There was also rebellion in the east. Macrianus and Callistus appear to have reached an agreement whereby the sons of Macrianus, Macrianus and Quietus, would be elevated to the purple. Within a few months the forces of the usurpers had acquired control over most of the east, including Egypt. In 261 Macrianus and his son of the same name invaded the Balkans while Callistus remained in the east with Quietus. It is possible, as Zonaras suggests, that he might have been under pressure to take this action from troops that Valerian had brought with him from the west.[155]

19. Antoninianus of Macrianus. *RIC* Macrianus II, 12. Ashmolean.

20. Antoninianus of Quietus. *RIC* Quietus, 5. Ashmolean.

The expedition of Macrianus ended in disaster at some point in the summer of 261, and shortly thereafter Odaenathus of Palmyra, responding to an invitation from Gallienus, destroyed

[154] For the Alamanni see Zon. 12. 24; Drinkwater, *The Gallic Empire*, p. 104.
[155] Zon. 12. 24; see on l. 169.

the remaining rebels in Syria. A naval expedition during the same year dealt with the continuing resistance of Aemilianus, the prefect of Egypt who had gone over to Macrianus. As a reward for his services, Odaenathus was recognized as *corrector totius orientis*; he was thus placed in charge of the eastern part of the empire, as Priscus had been in the reign of Philip.[156] It would appear that he was highly successful in this role. He recovered northern Mesopotamia from the Persians in 264–5, and even launched an attack on Ctesiphon.[157] Although there is no direct evidence for his dealings with provincial governors in the region,[158] Odaenathus' own understanding of his position may be reflected by the fact that he paired the title 'King of Kings' with that of *corrector totius orientis*: titles which reflected his eminence in both the Roman and Semitic worlds. The court at Palmyra attracted a number of intellectuals from Syria, and the oasis city may have appeared to have begun to rival Rome as a centre for artistic patronage: Callinicus of Petra went there, as did his rival Genethlius; the famous rhetor Longinus was there, and perhaps too the historian Nicostratus of Trebizond.[159] Paul of Samosata, who became bishop of Antioch in 262, seems to have been welcome at court, and there is a tradition that Zenobia also received proselytes of Mani. This befitted the capital of a man who had the power of an emperor. It is therefore not surprising that a Manichaean text, which reflects contemporary perception of Odaenathus' status rather than his actual titulature, should describe Zenobia as 'the wife of Caesar'.[160]

---

[156] See app. IV.

[157] Zos. 1. 39. 1–2; *HA V. Gall.* 10. 1–3, 12. 1 (with consular dates); George, p. 716 (= Mosshammer, p. 467).

[158] But cf. George, p. 717 (= Mosshammer, p. 467) ἀκούσας (Odaenathus) τὰς συμφορὰς τῆς Ἀσίας σπουδαίως ἐπὶ τὴν Ποντικὴν Ἡράκλειαν ἔρχεται διὰ Καππαδοκίας σὺν ταῖς δυνάμεσι τοὺς Σκύθας καταληψόμενος. καὶ ὁ μὲν αὐτόθι δολοφονεῖται πρός τινος Ὠδενάθου τοὔνομα αὐτοῦ. If this story is true, and the context in George's account suggests that it derives from Dexippus' *Chronika*, then it would reflect the fact that Odaenathus was recognized as the person responsible for keeping order in this area. Epigraphic evidence from *Provincia Arabia* suggests that Gallienus continued to appoint the governors of that province and thus of other areas over which Odaenathus was *corrector*. See H.-G. Pflaum, 'La fortification de la ville d'Adraha d'Arabic', *Syria*, 29 (1952), 322–4.

[159] See below, pp. 71–2.   [160] Koenen, 'Manichäische Mission', p. 97 n. 27.

Odaenathus remained in power until 267/8, when he was murdered either. while on campaign in Cappadocia or in Emesa.[161] His victories over the Persians made it appear to at least one inhabitant of Syria that the peace and unity of the Roman empire had been restored.[162] The world would not have seemed so fortunate to inhabitants of the west. In the course of the 260s Gallienus made one or two expeditions against Postumus which appear to have failed after some initial success.[163] In 268 the Balkan tribes again surged across the frontier, and Gallienus had to face a revolt in his own army.[164] In the summer of that year Aureolus, who appears to have been in overall command of the *comitatus*, declared for Postumus. Postumus did not come to his aid, however, and he was besieged at Milan.[165] At this point the senior officers of the army seem to have tired of Gallienus and they arranged his murder between 20 August and 16 October 268.[166] Marcus Aurelius Valerius Claudius, a general from the Balkans who was probably in his early fifties, was made emperor.[167]

Claudius soon put an end to Aureolus, but that was to prove

---

[161] Zon. 12. 24 and Zos. 1. 39. 1 both say that he was killed at Emesa. George, p. 717 (= Mosshammer, p. 467) says that he was killed in Cappadocia while leading an army against Gothic raiders. Given the anecdotal nature of the first story, George's account is probably to be preferred. The date is secured by the regnal years of Vaballathus, whose year IV was 270/1; see Rea, *P. Oxy.* xl. 20; J.-P. Rey-Coquais, 'Syrie romaine de Pompée à Dioclétien', *JRS* 68 (1978), 59.

[162] H. Seyrig, 'Némésis et le temple de Maqam Er-Rabb', *MUSJ* 37 (1960–1), 261–7 = *Scripta Varia: Mélanges d'archéologie et d'histoire* (Paris, 1985), 145–53 = *BÉ* 1963, No. 278 (dedications by the priest Drusus to Kalos Kairos and Nemesis, dated Feb. 262).

[163] Drinkwater, *The Gallic Empire*, pp. 30, 105–6, 172.

[164] Demougeot, *La Formation*, pp. 422–5, dates this to 267; this seems to stem from the fact that he has accepted a date for the death of Gallienus in March, which is incorrect. The invasion can fit into 268 now that it is known that Gallienus died late in the summer. The sources do suggest that this invasion and Aureolus' revolt were closely connected.

[165] Alföldi, 'Zur Kenntnis der Zeit der römischen Soldatenkaiser, 1. Der Usurpator Aureolus und die Kavalleriereform des Gallienus', *ZN* 37 (1927), 198–212 = *Studien*, pp. 1–15; Christol, 'Les règnes de Valérien et de Gallien', p. 820; Drinkwater, *The Gallic Empire*, pp. 33, 145.

[166] Rea, *P. Oxy.* xl. 19.

[167] Syme, *Emperors and Biography*, pp. 209–11, for the circumstances and doubts as to the accuracy of the birthday reported for Claudius on 10 May 214 (cf. *PIR*² A 1626). The same year is given for Aurelian (cf. *PIR*² D 135) and may be a guess.

21. Aureus of Claudius II. *RIC* Claudius, 131. Ashmolean.

the least of his problems. A horde of Goths burst across the Danube and another barbarian fleet was ravaging the Aegean. Claudius, his senior officers, and very probably the majority of his troops were from the Balkans, and they hastened east to defend their homelands. Several names of Claudius' generals have been preserved, all of them men who moved into the upper echelons of command after the accession of Valerian. These are L. Domitius Aurelianus and M. Aurelius Probus, the future emperors, Trajan Mucianus, and the praetorian prefect Aurelius Heraclianus. Heraclianus' brother, Aurelius Apollinarius, was also a high official in the imperial service.[168] Claudius Tacitus, who succeeded Aurelian, may also have been a member of this group, as well as Annius Florianus (Tacitus' praetorian prefect and briefly his successor in 276), and so must have been Julius Placidianus, praetorian prefect in 269 and consul with Tacitus in 273.[169] With the exception of Tacitus and Placidianus, all of these men are firmly attested as being of Danubian origin, and it is likely that a Balkan province was also Tacitus' home. It is an impressive galaxy of talent; it was also a very different group indeed from the Severan aristocrats who had dominated the state into the 250s. The concentration of power in their hands may have been a fortuitous result of the dislocation of the army after 260. Although it is clear that there is no truth in Aurelius Victor's statements that Gallienus issued an edict barring senators from

[168] *IGBR* ii/2. 1568, 1569; M. Christol, 'La carrière de Traianus Mucianus et l'origine des *protectores*', *Chiron*, 7 (1977), 398–9.

[169] *PIR*² C 1046; ibid. A 649, casting doubt on statements that Florianus was Tacitus' brother; ibid. I 468; Syme, *Emperors and Biography*, pp. 246–7.

high commands,[170] it may be the case that his story reflects the increasing distinction between military and civilian careers, and between careers in the interior provinces and those on the frontier in this period. The praetorship ceased to be associated with the command of a legion or the government of a province, either public or imperial, in the years after 262; its holders are increasingly found holding posts associated with the government of Italy, as *curatores* of roads or *correctores* of districts. The general pattern appears to be along the lines of what has traditionally been associated with the senatorial career pattern of the post-Diocletianic period: senators governed in areas where they had personal connections, leaving less interesting areas to others.[171] A senatorial career in the direct service of the emperor increasingly appears to have begun with the consulship.[172] Even though they did not cause the total eclipse of the traditional aristocracy, the emergencies of the 250s and 260s were pushing the men from the frontier to the fore.[173]

Claudius encountered the Goths at Naissus in 269.[174] He

[170] Aur. Vict., *De Caes.* 33. 33, 37. 5.

[171] For the 4th cent. see J. F. Matthews, *Western Aristocracies and Imperial Court A.D. 364–425* (Oxford, 1975), 1–31.

[172] M. Christol, 'Les reformes de Gallien et la carrière sénatoriale', *Epigrafia e ordine senatorio*, i. *Tituli*, 4 (Rome, 1982), 143–66; id., *Essai sur l'évolution des carrières sénatoriales dans la 2ᶜ moitié du IIIᶜ s. ap. J.-C.* (Paris, 1986), for a discussion of this tendency.

[173] B. Malcus, 'Notes sur la révolution du système administratif romain au IIIᶜ siècle', *Opuscula Romana*, 7 (1969), 213–37, esp. pp. 220–6, 230–6; Christol, 'Les règnes de Valérien et de Gallien', p. 827; L. de Blois, *The Policy of the Emperor Gallienus* (Leiden, 1976), 55–87. I agree with G. Alföldy's summation of the issue in his commentary on Christol's discussion of senatorial careers (see last n.): 'Je crois que la réforme de Gallien ne fut pas une mesure rigide et bureaucratique: là où il y avait des sénateurs avec la qualification et la volonté de gouverner une province, même militaire, Gallien et ses successeurs ont utilisé aussi cette solution pour l'administration de l'Empire [*Epigrafia e ordine senatorio*, p. 165].' It certainly should not be thought that the limitation in areas where senators were active was unwelcome: the observation of Matthews, *Western Aristocracies*, p. 28, 'In those provinces which the senators governed most regularly, in Italy and Africa, the areas of their political, and of their social and their economic influence coincided precisely', appears to be true of the later 3rd cent. as well.

[174] The sources for this invasion are deeply confused. A. Alföldi, 'The Sources for the Gothic Invasions of the Years 260–270', *CAH* xii. 721–3 — *Studien*, pp. 436–9, has very properly suggested that the problem that arises with George's account (p. 717 — Mosshammer, p. 467), which puts all the details of the campaign in the reign of Gallienus, may

defeated them in battle, and drove them into the mountains to await their destruction through starvation and illness or their surrender.[175] It was a famous victory: its importance might best be reflected by the fact that, when he revised his family tree in 310, Constantine chose Claudius as ancestor. An orator of that year explained that Claudius was the first man to restore the pristine order of the Roman empire.[176]

The glory which Claudius won in battle with the Goths did not translate into a sudden restoration of unity to the empire. Although Autun may have been inspired to rebel against Postumus by the news, Claudius could still do nothing to help the city.[177] New problems were also developing in the east, where the young son of Odaenathus, Vaballathus, had been put on the throne under the regency of his mother Zenobia. Odaenathus had been recognized as *corrector totius orientis* by Gallienus, and it is clear that Zenobia claimed that Vaballathus had inherited both

---

be the result of the confusion about events which began under one emperor and ended under another. But he goes too far in his assertion that Gallienus was the emperor at the time of the great victory at Naissus (the place-name appears only at Zos. 1. 45. 1). His argument fails on technical grounds because he assumes that Zosimus' account was subject to the same sort of confusion at this point as George's. This is not the case, and it can be shown that Zosimus gets events in the proper order elsewhere (see on l. 141). There are two other considerations which militate against his argument. The first is that it is unlikely that Aureolus would have revolted after Gallienus had won a great victory. The second is the posthumous reputation of Claudius. When Constantine declared that Claudius was his ancestor, there were people alive who could remember the events of his reign. If he were not regarded as a great hero, there would have been no point in claiming him as a forefather. The legend that Constantine was born in Naissus suggests that this was the scene of the battle: there is no other obvious reason why his birthplace should have been moved from the eastern Balkans except to provide a closer link to the place of the great battle. For the problem of Constantine's birthplace see Syme, *Emperors and Biography*, p. 209. I date this battle to 269 because I do not see how Claudius, who can only have taken the throne in late August at the very earliest, could have defeated Aureolus, marched to Naissus, and defeated the Goths all before the end of the year. He first appears as *Germanicus Maximus* in 269 (*ILS* 569, 570).

[175] *HA V. Claud.* 11. 3; Zos. 1. 45. For this method of dealing with barbarian invasions compare *FGrH* 100 F 6. 14; Amm. 31. 8. 1–5.

[176] Pan. 6 (7). 2. 2 'ab illo enim divo Claudio manat in te avita cognatio qui Romani imperii solutam et perditam disciplinam primus reformavit'. For the circumstances see Syme, *Emperors and Biography*, p. 204.

[177] For the date see Drinkwater, *The Gallic Empire*, pp. 106, 178–80.

the title and the power that it implied. There seems to have been some confusion about this. Furthermore, Zenobia appears to have been trying to exert greater control over the tribes of northern Arabia in order to build up the power of her city.[178] Her actions may have caused problems with the governor of Arabia, who may have been disinclined to follow her orders. Thus, for one reason or another, relations between Palmyra and the central government began to sour and in 270–1 Zenobia decided to make good her claim by force of arms. Palmyrene armies overwhelmed *Provincia Arabia* and conquered Egypt.[179]

Claudius was no longer emperor when the Palmyrenes conquered Egypt. He died shortly before 28 August 270, and a brief struggle for power ensued between his brother Quintillus, who appears to have been in Italy, and Aurelian, who was with the army in the Balkans. The struggle ended with the death of Quintillus in the autumn.[180] The new emperor was immediately faced with a number of serious crises, which postponed any effort to deal with the eastern situation. It appears that the Alamanni burst through the Alps into Italy shortly after Aurelian took the throne. He defeated them at Placentia and drove them back to their own lands. A campaign against the Vandals followed almost immediately. A fragment from Dexippus' *Skythika* provides a picture of the emperor's dealings with these people.[181] After his victory over the Vandals in battle, Aurelian met their envoys and arranged a treaty by which they agreed to return home, to give hostages from the families of their leaders, to provide two thousand men for the Roman army, and to trade with the empire through a market established by the governor (of either *Pannonia Inferior* or Rhaetia). After the terms had been agreed, the emperor convened a meeting of the army to ask the troops their opinion on his negotiations. When they had shouted their approval the hostages could be exchanged, and the new

---

[178] Bowersock, *Roman Arabia* (Cambridge, 1983), 131–7.
[179] Rey-Coquais, 'Syrie romaine', pp. 59–60; M. J. Price, 'The Lost Year: Greek Light on a Problem of Roman Chronology', *Num. Chron.* 7 13 (1973), 84–5.
[180] Rea, *P. Oxy.* xl. 23–4.   [181] *FGrH* 100 F 7; below, pp. 87–8.

recruits could be selected. Aurelian then had to wait in the area until the barbarians had made good their promise to withdraw (which a number of them did not). Once this was done he was able to send the bulk of his army on to Italy while he made final arrangements for the care of the hostages. It was only then that he went to Italy himself to take charge of the campaign against the Juthungi. This is the best picture that has survived of a third-century emperor at work, and it provides admirable insight not only into the intellectual demands which the ruler faced, but also into the physical strain which he had to endure: it is very likely that these operations were carried out in the winter of 270–1.

22. Aureus of Aurelian. *RIC* Aurelian, 166. Ashmolean.

Aurelian appears to have settled his problems with the barbarians by the spring of 271, and he was free to turn his attention to the reunification of the empire. His first move was against Palmyra. The reason for this may well be that the empire of the Gauls was in a state of chaos such that it could pose no serious threat, while, on the other hand, the Palmyrenes controlled the grain supplies of Egypt. In February or March of 269 one of Postumus' officers, Ulpius Cornelius Laelianus, was proclaimed emperor at Mainz.[182] Postumus defeated him, but when he refused to allow his troops to sack Mainz they killed him. M. Aurelius Marius took his place for a few months, before he was killed in turn by M. Piavonius Victorinus, who seems to have come from a distinguished house in Trier, and to have served as Postumus' praetorian prefect.[183] When Victorinus died in 271 he

---

[182] Drinkwater, *The Gallic Empire*, pp. 34–5; König, *Die gallischen Usurpatoren*, pp. 132–6.

[183] Drinkwater, *The Gallic Empire*, pp. 31–2, 35–6; König, *Die gallischen Usurpatoren*, pp. 137–47.

was replaced by C. Pius Esuvius Tetricus, whose name suggests that he too was of Gallic extraction.[184] It is alleged that Victoria, the mother of Victorinus, played a major role in arranging his appointment.

Zenobia seems to have tried to negotiate with Aurelian ever since his accession, as is suggested by the fact that Vaballathus is not described as *Augustus* on public documents until 272, when all hope of accommodation with Aurelian had failed. Until that time he is ordinarily entitled *vir consularis rex dux Romanorum*, and Aurelian ordinarily appears as *Augustus* on coins and documents in the area under Palmyrene control.[185] In the summer of 272 a Roman army reoccupied Egypt,[186] and at roughly the same time Aurelian defeated the armies of Zenobia in two battles near Antioch. Palmyra was besieged, and surrendered at some point late in the year. Zenobia was spared and sent to Rome, where she seems to have enjoyed a comfortable retirement after appearing in Aurelian's triumph in 274. Her descendants apparently enjoyed a prominent position in Roman society into the late fourth century.[187]

Palmyra rose in revolt as Aurelian returned to the west in 273, and it may be presumed that whatever settlement he had made with the city had not been to the liking of the merchants who had dominated Palmyrene society. The final solution must have been even less to their liking. The city was so badly ruined by the Roman sack that it never recovered as a commercial centre.[188] Nor does Aurelian seem to have tried to put anything in its place.

[184] Drinkwater, *The Gallic Empire*, p. 39; König, *Die gallischen Usurpatoren*, pp. 158–67.
[185] Rey-Coquais, 'Syrie Romaine', p. 60.
[186] Rea, *P. Oxy.* xl. 25; Price, 'Lost Year', pp. 84–5.
[187] J. T. Milik, *Dédicaces faites par les dieux* (Paris, 1972), 320–1; G. W. Bowersock, 'Arabs and Saracens in the *Historia Augusta*', *BHAC 1984/5* (Bonn, 1987), 75–80.
[188] The Persians may also have been partially responsible for this. They had been at work to alter the tribal structure of northern Arabia in their own interests and to the detriment of Palmyra for some time. The fact that Dura also never recovered from the destruction of these years does suggest that there was a significant change in the trading pattern. This may also be reflected in the fact that Nisibis was made the official centre for trade between the two empires in Diocletian's treaty with Narses in 299. See Bowersock, *Roman Arabia*, pp. 131–3; J. F. Matthews, 'The Tax Law of Palmyra: Evidence for Economic History in a City of the Roman East', *JRS* 74 (1984), 169.

It was not until the reign of Diocletian that a significant effort was made to reconstruct a defensive line in the east, and it was Diocletian who placed a border camp at Palmyra in the course of his careful reorganization of the desert frontier.[189] This may reveal something about Aurelian's view of imperial defence—perhaps he had departed from the old ideal of defending a fixed frontier. Such lines were expensive, and the evidence of the last thirty years had shown that they could not withstand determined enemies. He understood that his resources were finite, that some effort had to be made to put the finances of the empire in better order: there was no point in wasting his resources here, and his decision with regard to Palmyra may be seen as a parallel to his earlier decision to abandon the Trajanic provinces of Dacia.[190] It may also be an indication of the fact that he was lucky. Sapor had died in Persia and the Sassanid regime may already have been on the brink of the troubles that would cripple its power during the next twenty years. The weakening of Persia should not be underestimated as a factor in Rome's recovery in the later third century any more than Persia's strength should be underestimated as a contributory cause of the disorders of the mid-third century.

Aurelian's final offensive was against Tetricus in Gaul. Early in 274 he led his army into the heart of the *imperium Galliarum*. Tetricus is said to have betrayed his own army by placing it in an indefensible position so that Aurelian could destroy it in return for a promise of a safe retirement at Rome. The final battle was fought at Châlons, the army of Gaul was defeated in a hard battle, and Tetricus was granted his life after he had graced Aurelian's triumph.[191]

Ammianus described Aurelian as the 'most severe avenger of

---

[189] Bowersock, *Roman Arabia*, pp. 138–45; D. van Berchem, *L'Armée de Dioclétien et la réforme constantinienne* (Paris, 1952), 15–20.

[190] No date is given in the sources for the decision to abandon Dacia (it was not the sort of thing that Aurelian would advertise), but it does seem possible that the process could have begun in 271 when Aurelian was taking troops from the Danube for the Palmyrene expedition; Demougeot, *La Formation*, pp. 452–8; A. Mócsy, *Pannonia and Upper Moesia*, trans. S. Frere (London, 1974), 211.

[191] Drinkwater, *The Gallic Empire*, pp. 41–3.

wrongs', and, like other late fourth-century writers, he pictured him as a man of great savagery.[192] This tradition may stem from Aurelian's willingness to exploit the wealth of individual senators, seized by him on various pretexts in order to fill the treasury. It also appears that he made a comprehensive effort to stabilize the currency, issuing reformed coinage in bronze, silver, and gold. Although the details of these reforms, especially that of the silver coinage in 274, remain open to debate, it does appear that this was part of a concerted effort to put the finances of the state on a firmer footing.[193]

When Aurelian was murdered in 275 the Roman empire once again stood firm against her external foes, but it was a very different empire from that which Septimius Severus had left to his sons. The old policies of static defence on the frontiers were being abandoned, and at the same time the army was already taking on the form that would be characteristic of the period after the accession of Diocletian. The principal strike-force was now the permanent *comitatus*, not an *ad hoc* army assembled for each important campaign by drawing troops from the frontiers. At the time of his death Aurelian appears to have been experimenting with ways to increase the revenues of the state, and the process of dividing the unwieldy provinces of the Antonine empire into smaller, more easily administered units was well under way.[194] There also seem to have been increasing distinctions between military and civilian careers. In the forty years between the death of Gordian and Diocletian's accession, these changes were the result of pragmatic responses to the problems which had beset the emperors, but, as yet, no new system had emerged, and political stability still eluded the grasp of the

[192] Amm. 31. 5. 17, 30. 8. 8; *HA V. Aurel.* 6–7; Aur. Vict. *De Caes.* 35. 12; *Epit. de Caes.* 35. 9 'fuit saevus et sanguinarius et trux omni tempore'; Eutr. *Brev.* 9. 13. 1, 14.

[193] Callu, *Politique monétaire*, pp. 323–30; Crawford, 'Finance, Coinage and Money', pp. 575–7.

[194] For the creation of the province of Phrygia and Caria out of Asia in the 250s see C. Roueché, 'Rome, Asia and Aphrodisias in the Third Century', *JRS* 71 (1981), 117, and above, n. 114; for the new provinces of Dacia and the division of Bithynia Pontus before the reign of Diocletian see T. D. Barnes, *The New Empire of Diocletian and Constantine* (Cambridge, 1982), 216, 223.

emperors. It is unfortunate that much of the detail that lies behind these changes remains obscure. This is in part a result of historiographic tendencies in the third century AD.

ENDNOTES TO CHAPTER I

1. For contemporary statements to the effect that the empire was as big as the emperors could afford in the 2nd and 3rd cents. cf. App. *Praef.* 7; Dio 75. 3. See also the provocative study of S. Mitchell, 'Imperial Building in the Eastern Roman Provinces', *HSCP* 91 (1987), 333–65, esp. p. 365: 'the names of Commodus and his successors up to the time of the Tetrarchy have hardly figured at all', among those of emperors who funded building projects, suggesting that the travails of the reign of Marcus were a watershed in the history of imperial finance.

As for the army, A. R. Birley, 'The Economic Effects of Roman Frontier Policy', in A. King and M. Henig (eds.), *The Roman West in the Third Century* (*BAR* International Series, 109; Oxford, 1981), 40–2, suggests that *c.*150 the army numbered approximately 405,500 (or 433,500) and under Severus 415,500 (or 445,500); Campbell, *Emperor and Army*, pp. 4–5, proposed 450,000. On the whole I feel that the lower figures are more likely to represent the actual size of the army; Campbell's estimate is based on its paper strength.

It is hard to know what the army meant in terms of the overall finances of the empire, but a reasonable approximation may be made on the basis of an estimate of the minimum GNP of the empire calculated according to the formula *total population* × *minimum net consumption* (estimated at *c.*380 HS per person: see R. Goldsmith, 'An Estimate of the Size and Structure of the National Product of the Early Roman Empire', *Review of Income and Wealth*, 30 (1984), 273; K. Hopkins, 'Taxes and Trade in the Roman Empire (200 B.C.–400 A.D.), *JRS* 70 (1980), 116–20). In the 1st century Hopkins ('Taxes and Trade', p. 119) estimates that the population of the empire was *c.*54m., that the tax rate was *c.*10%, and that the total tax revenue of the empire was *c.*824m. HS. He suggests that the army pay would have taken up over half of this: 454m. HS (p. 125 for his estimate of army cost, which may be inflated by the acceptance of too high a figure for the pay of auxiliaries). Goldsmith, 'Estimate of Size and Structure', pp. 263–88, calculates a gross national product of 'slightly over 20 billion' HS on the basis of a population of *c.*55m. His figure for the empire's population is probably too high; B. W. Frier suggests that a figure around 45m. might be closer to the mark in the Augustan period (I am grateful to Prof. Frier for allowing me to use his chapter on demography in the early empire in advance of publication in *CAH*). This would yield a GNP of *c.*17,100m. HS for the time of Augustus. Tax revenue at that time may have amounted to *c.*855m. HS (using Frier's figure for the population and estimating the tax rate at around 5%). Expenditure on the army would have taken up *c.*45–58% of this: see R. Goldsmith, *Premodern Financial Systems: A Historical Comparative Study* (Cambridge, 1987), 55. It is clear from Tacitus' account of the mutinies in AD 14 that the state could not afford to pay more for the military than it already was at that time (*Ann.* 1. 78. 2).

In the late 2nd and early 3rd cents. R. MacMullen, 'The Roman Emperor's Army Cost', *Latomus*, 43 (1984), 580, shows that peacetime pay for the pre-Severan army would have cost *c.*315m. HS, and 432m. HS after Severus; after Caracalla the basic pay of the army would have been *c.*500m. HS. Campbell, *Emperor and Army*, p. 162, suggests *c.*800m. HS, based upon a higher estimate of the soldiers' pay. The cost of the army in time of war, when transport costs were greatly increased, would have been much more; see above, n. 56. For changes in population and GNP by the middle of the 2nd cent. see above, n. 7.

2. Goldsmith, 'Estimate of Size and Structure', p. 283: 'the share of the expenditures of central and local government was very low, probably not above three percent for the imperial government and on the order of eight percent for all governmental units'. A figure of *c.*8% would be comparable with England before 1688 and the United States or France before 1820. I have arrived at the figure of 5% for the imperial government's share of tax revenue because it yields a figure for the emperor's revenue that is in line with the military budget from Augustus to Marcus Aurelius and then Severus, though I should stress that I suspect that army pay accounted for roughly half of the total military budget (see Endnote 3) in time of war. A lower figure, of 3%, would yield a figure for revenues that would be too low. The figures, using

Frier's estimate of population, which work well in this context, are as follows:

Population (m.)	GNP (нsm.)	Tax rate	Total revenue (нsm.)	Army pay (нsm.)
45	17,100	5%	855,000	311
61	23,332	5%	1,166,600	315
55	20,998	5%	1,049,000	˙432

The figures based upon a higher initial estimate of population in the time of Augustus (the figure of 54m. used by Hopkins), and assuming the same growth-rate (34.9%) to arrive at the figure for population in the reign of Marcus Aurelius, show that it is still necessary to assume a rate of 5% to arrive at figures which would be in line with army pay:

Population (m.)	GNP (нsm.)	Tax rate	Total revenue (нsm.)	Army pay (нsm.)
54	20,520	5%	1,026	311
72	27,680	5%	1,384	315
65	24,910	5%	1,245	432

In the case of Severus, my figures in both cases may be low, as I have not taken account of a possible rise in prices at the end of the 2nd cent., but the evidence for prices is so slight that it is impossible to tell if this was a significant factor, and the rate of increase between the end of the 1st cent. and the death of Commodus would appear to be no more than 25%, which would not change the figures that I offer in a significant way. For discussion of the evidence of Egyptian wheat prices see R. P. Duncan-Jones, 'The Price of Wheat in Roman Egypt under the Principate', *Chiron*, 6 (1976), 241–62; id., *The Economy of the Roman Empire: Quantitative Studies* [2] (Cambridge, 1982), 365. On the other hand, I have not taken into account the possibility that productivity declined, the result of the increased cultivation of marginal land and insufficient capital expenditure of the sort described by Pliny in *Epp.* 3. 19; it is unwise to generalize from individual cases of this sort, though it can be argued that the state recognized that insufficient capital formation made the expansion of agriculture difficult and adopted a form of share-cropping in response: on this point see the important study of

D. Kehoe, *The Economics of Agriculture on Roman Imperial Estates in North Africa* (Göttingen, 1988), esp. p. 186. Furthermore, an increase in population would naturally mean that more marginal land would be brought under cultivation, thus causing a decline in productivity per worker. See in general F. Braudel, *The Structures of Everyday Life: Civilization and Capitalism, 15th–18th Century*, rev. edn., i (New York, 1981).

The figures, assuming a 3% rate, are as follows for both sets of population figures (*a*), (*b*):

Population (m.)	GNP (нsm.)	Tax rate	Total revenue (нsm.)	Army pay (нsm.)
(*a*) 45.0	17,100	3%	513	311
(*b*) 54.0	20,250	3%	615	311
(*a*) 61.0	23,332	3%	700	315
(*b*) 72.8	27,681	3%	830	315
(*a*) 55.0	20,998	3%	630	432
(*b*) 65.0	24,910	3%	747	432

3. Herod. 6. 3. 1. The other evidence is not conclusive either way; E. Ritterling, 'Legio', *RE* xii. 1329–30, argues that *legio IV Italica* or *Parthica* could have been raised at this time, though he notes that the reign of Gordian III is also a possibility (ibid. 1337, 1549). This is the one passage that Crawford ('Finance, Coinage and Money', p. 591) adduces to support his suggestion that units of the army were kept under strength in time of peace in order to explain Cassius Dio's observations that the army cost more in time of war (Dio 52. 28. 5; see also 75. 3. 3, 11. 1). The papyrus texts which he also adduces (*P. Fayum* 105 = J. Y. Fink, *Roman Military Records on Papyri* (Ann Arbor, 1971), Nos. 73; *BGU* 696 (misprinted as 6866) = Fink, No. 64; P. Genev. Lat. 1 = Fink, Nos. 9, 10, 37, 58, 68) do not support the suggestion that there was any difference in unit strength between peace and war. They only show that these units were not up to their notional strength. *British Museum Pap.* 2851 = Fink, No. 63 reveals that a cohort in a war zone would have a substantial number of men on detached service, which makes it clear that conclusions such as Crawford's cannot be based on this sort of evidence. On the other hand, Tacitus' account of Vespasian's revolt in 69 does suggest that one of the first acts of a new campaign

was to hold a levy (*Hist.* 2. 82. 1 'prima belli cura agere dilectus, revocare veteranos'), and his account of Corbulo's campaigns suggests that a general might find it necessary to replace men who were deemed to be unfit for warfare, even if they were adequate for garrison duty (*Ann.* 13. 35. 1–2). The additional cost of transport as well as items such as boats for bridges, and the need to replace arms lost on campaign as well as additional drafts to replace battle casualties, should explain the added expenses; see also Tac. *Ann.* 1. 71. 2; *Hist.* 2. 82. The need to bring the army into fighting trim and to support it when it was operating at a distance from its bases was therefore the reason why it cost more in wartime. For a very much later period (when resources were admittedly less abundant), Hendy, *Studies*, pp. 221–3, shows that the cost of mounting a major overseas expedition (e.g. supplying transport) could equal the budget for a year. Furthermore, it appears that soldiers were entitled to higher rations while on campaign. The *expeditionalis annona*, which should be greater than the regular *annona*, is attested in the reign of Julian as something established by custom (*C. Th.* 7. 4. 4–6). A. H. M. Jones, *The Later Roman Empire* (Oxford, 1964), 628–9 with n. 44, observes that the quantities involved (3 pounds of bread and a pound of meat per day) were 'positively gargantuan'. It is not possible to know when this began as a form of 'hazardous service pay', but, if it was not Augustan, I suspect that it might well have been Severan.

4. The first edict (issued in 257) appears to have ordered the arrest of high-ranking members of the Church and included a provision that they be asked to sacrifice. If they did so, they could go free; if not, they would be imprisoned or exiled. Furthermore, if the leader of a Christian community refused to comply with the order to honour the gods, the presiding magistrate would forbid Christian meetings and the use of cemeteries. If the local Christian leader did comply, that could be the end of the affair. Valerian's edict was therefore not an order that Christians should forswear their ways, only that they recognize the standing of the gods of the state. The second measure appears to have been issued in the form of a rescript to the senate at Rome, possibly in answer to an inquiry about what to do with recalcitrant Christians who were already in custody. For the first edict see *Acta Proc.* 1. 1 'sacratissimi imperatores Valerianus et Gallienus literas ad me dare dignitati sunt quibus praeceperunt

eos, qui Romanam religionem non colunt, debere Romanas caere-
monias recognoscere'; 1. 4 'poteris ergo secundam praeceptum
Valeriani et Gallieni exul ad urbem Curubitanam proficisci'; 1. 7
'praeceperunt etiam ne in aliquibus locis conciliabula faciant nec
coemeteria ingrediantur'. Cf. Eus. *HE* 7. 11. 10 ὁρῶ ὑμᾶς ὁμοῦ
καὶ ἀχαρίστους ὄντας καὶ ἀναισθήτους τῆς πρᾳότητος τῶν
Σεβαστῶν ἡμῶν· δι' ὅπερ οὐκ ἔσεσθε ἐν τῇ πόλει ταύτῃ,
ἀλλὰ ἀποσταλήσεσθε εἰς τὰ μέρη τῆς Λιβύης καὶ ἐν τόπῳ
λεγομένῳ Κεφρώ· τοῦτον γὰρ τὸν τόπον ἐξελεξάμην ἐκ τῆς
κελεύσεως τῶν Σεβαστῶν ἡμῶν. οὐδαμῶς δὲ ἐξέσται οὔτε
ὑμῖν οὔτε ἄλλοις τισὶν ἢ συνόδους ποιεῖσθαι ἢ εἰς τὰ
καλούμενα κοιμητήρια εἰσιέναι. See C. Saumagne, *Saint
Cyprien évêque de Carthage 'pape' d'Afrique* (Paris, 1975), 145–8; M. M.
Sage, 'The Persecution of Valerian and the Peace of Gallienus', *WS*,
NS 17 (1983), 140–1, refining Saumagne's observations. For the
rescript of 258 see Cyp. *Epp.* 80. 1. 2 'quae autem sunt in vero ita se
habent, rescripsisse Valerianum ad senatum ut episcopi et presby-
teri et diacones in continenti animadvertantur, senatores vero et
egregii viri et equites Romani dignitate amissa etiam bonis
spolientur et si ademptis facultatibus christiani esse perseveraverint,
capite quoque multentur, matronae vero ademptis bonis in exilium
relegentur, Caesariani autem quicumque vel prius confessi fuerant
vel nunc confessi fuerint confiscentur et vincti in Caesarianas
possessiones descripti mittantur'. See Millar, *The Emperor in the
Roman World*, pp. 569–70. For points of contact between Valerian's
first edict and Diocletian see D. S. Potter, 'The Persecution of the
Early Church', in *The Anchor Bible Dictionary* (forthcoming);
G. E. M. de Ste Croix, 'Aspects of the Great Persecution', *HTR* 47
(1954), 73–113; S. Mitchell, 'Maximinus and the Christians', *JRS* 78
(1988), 105–24, for details of the Diocletianic actions. For more on
Valerian's persecution see D. S. Potter, 'Martyrdom as Spectacle'
(forthcoming).

2

Historiography in the Third Century AD

Although the only contemporary accounts of Roman political history to survive from the period between the civil war of 238 and the reign of Constantine are the *Thirteenth Sibylline Oracle* and the great inscription of Sapor at Naqsh-i-Rustam, it is not true that there was a hiatus in the writing of traditional history during these years—at least not in Greek. Serious historical writing in Latin seems to have given way to imperial biography in the reign of Hadrian, and it would appear that there was no historian of note who wrote in Latin to cover the period after AD 96. The 'canon' of historical writers in the late fourth century ended with Tacitus, and the author of a Latin account of Roman history in the third century appears to have relied upon the work of two Greeks for his history of that period.[1] He appears to have had no Latin source which could provide him with a chronological account of these years. On the other hand, the names of a number of Greek historians who treated the period after Maximinus have survived. Nicostratus of Trebizond composed a history of the period from the reign of Philip to the capture of Valerian and the victory of Odaenathus.[2] A historian named Eusebius composed a history of Rome from the time of Octavian to that of Carus, and a historian from Cyme named Ephorus, styled Ephorus the younger, treated the reign of Gallienus in twenty-seven books.[3] It is possible that Onasimus of Sparta or Cyprus, who wrote about Constantine, also wrote about the period after Gallienus.[4]

---

[1] For details of the connections between the extant sources for this period see app. II.

[2] *FGrH* 98.　　　　　　　　　　　　　　　　　　[3] *FGrH* 101, 212.

[4] *FGrH* 216 T 1 Ὀνάσιμος· Κύπριος ἢ Σπαρτιάτης· ἱστορικὸς καὶ σοφιστής, τῶν ἐπὶ Κωνσταντίνου γενομένων. ἔγραψε Στάσεων διαιρέσεις· Τέχνην δικανικὴν πρὸς Ἀψίνην· Περὶ ἀντιρρητικῆς τέχνης· Προγυμνάσματα·

Only one fragment of Eusebius, describing a siege of Thessaloniki by the Goths in the reign of Gallienus, survives.[5] The excerptor states that it came from the ninth book of his history. This may suggest that, as Ammianus would later do, he gave scanty treatment to the period before his own time, and discussed the events of his lifetime at length. Another possibility is that he only discussed wars between Rome and the Balkan tribes.[6] Certainty is impossible, and he seems to have had no influence on the tradition that is preserved in later authors.

There is not much that can be said about Nicostratus of Trebizond, save that his choice of period reflects a view of the time which may be described as 'eastern'. He began his work with Philip and brought it to a conclusion with the victory of Odaenathus. At the start of his work was the treaty that Philip made with Sapor, one in which Philip made a number of concessions to the Persian king and which the author of some lines preserved in the *Thirteenth Sibylline Oracle* regarded as harmful to the people of the eastern provinces.[7] The history ended, as does the oracle, with the disaster that Valerian suffered outside of Edessa, the wide-ranging Persian raids in its aftermath, the rise of Macrianus and his sons, and the final triumph of Odaenathus over the usurpers and the Persians. He may even have treated Odaenathus' campaigns against Mesopotamia in the 260s and, again like the compiler of the oracle, concluded his work before Odaenathus' murder in 267. The scope of his history suggests that it was intended to glorify Odaenathus and to demonstrate that as a ruler he was superior to the Roman emperors (Philip, Decius, Gallus, Aemilianus, and Valerian) whose reigns had been a disaster for the region. He may therefore

Μελέτας· Ἐγκώμια· καὶ ἄλλα πλεῖστα. An Onesimus is cited among authorities for the life of Probus. This may be coincidence.

[5] For the dating cf. Jacoby ad loc.

[6] For this possibility see Jacoby ad loc. Jacoby suggests that the *Parthica* of Arrian and that of Asinius Quadratus could provide models. Evagrius' description of the work—καὶ Εὐσέβιος δὲ ἀπὸ Ὀκταβιανοῦ καὶ Τραιανοῦ καὶ Μάρκου λαβὼν ἕως τῆς τελευτῆς Κάρου κατήντησεν—does suggest that he concentrated on reigns during which there was a great deal of fighting in the Balkans.

[7] See on ll. 28–30.

have been one of the intellectuals who were attracted to the court at Palmyra—men such as Longinus and the sophists Callinicus and Genathlius, both of Petra.[8] Nothing can be said about Onasimus. The two historians Philostratus and P. Herennius Dexippus of Athens, whose works provide the basis for the later Greek tradition, can be discussed in more detail. The earliest of the three principal representatives of this later tradition is Zosimus, a committed pagan who composed his *New History* in the fifth or sixth century, tracing the decline of the Roman empire from the third century to the reign of Honorius.[9] The second is George, a Palestinian monk who became the private secretary (*syncellos*) to the popular iconophile patriarch of Constantinople, Tarausius (784–806). He completed his *Ekloge Chronographias*, which covered the period from Adam to Diocletian, shortly after 810, and appears to have left the greater part of another chronicle which extended down to his own lifetime to be completed as the *Chronicle of Theophanes*.[10] The third is John Zonaras, scion of one of the leading court families of his time, author of numerous ecclesiastical works and a lexicon; he was also an officer of the imperial guard and head of the imperial chancery in the later part of the eleventh century. He retired or was exiled to the monastery at Hagia Glykera, where he composed his *Epitome of the Histories* from the Creation to 1118.[11] Both Philostratus and Dexippus were also read by the author of the reasonably extensive Latin history that was the source of the *Historia Augusta* biographies after Alexander Severus.[12]

The only detail preserved about Philostratus is the fact that he

---

[8] For the intellectual milieu of the Palmyrene court see Bowersock, *Roman Arabia*, p. 135.

[9] F. Paschoud, ed., *Zosime*, vol. i, pp. ix–xx.

[10] K. Krumbacher, *Geschichte der byzantinischen Literatur*[2] i (Munich, 1896), 339–42; H. Hunger, *Die hochsprachliche profane Literatur der Byzantiner* (Handbuch der Altertumswissenschaft, 12/5. 1; Munich, 1978), 331–2. C. Mango, 'Who Wrote the Chronicle of Theophanes?', *ZRVI* 18 (1978), 9–18, shows that George was probably the author.

[11] Krumbacher, *Geschichte*, i. 370–6; Hunger, *Literatur der Byzantiner*, pp. 416–18.

[12] See app. ii for further details.

was an Athenian.[13] This comes from George. Dexippus, however, was a member of one of the most important families in Athens during the third century, and he played a major role in the life of his city.[14] His ancestors and his own deeds are recorded by a number of inscriptions, while his views are preserved by a useful selection of fragments in the various Constantinian epitomes.

The family of Dexippus appears to have acquired considerable prestige in the arts and in Attic society. The historian's grandfather, Publius Herennius, who appears on prytany lists in the time of Commodus, was *hierokerux* of the Eleusinian mysteries and was the first member of the family to obtain the franchise.[15] He was the son of Apollonius the sophist, son of Eudemos.[16] This Publius Herennius had two sons, P. Herennius Ptolemaeus, who was described as 'the sophist' and served as *kerux* of the Areopagus, polemarch and agonothete,[17] and Herennius Hermaios, *hierokerux* at Eleusis. Dexippus was Ptolemaeus' son, and, as other members of his family had done, he held high office in his native city. He was *strategos*, he held three archonships (one of them the eponymous), was panygerarch and agonothete of the great Panathenaea at his own expense, and was sacred panygerist at Eleusis. There is some possibility that he played a role in the unsuccessful defence of Athens during the Herulian attack in 268, but the tradition relating this is not reliable.[18] He had at least

---

[13] FGrH 99 T 1. For possible identifications see Jacoby ad loc.

[14] F. G. Millar, 'P. Herennius Dexippus: The Greek World and the Third Century Invasions', *JRS* 59 (1969), 12–29, remains the basic study of Dexippus and his times.

[15] Millar, 'Dexippus', p. 20, suggests that the family obtained the franchise through L. Herennius Saturninus, proconsul of Achaea in 98 (*PIR*² H 126). This is extremely unlikely. Herennius the *hierokerux*, the first member of the family to hold the franchise, would not have been alive in 98, and his father might have been an infant at best. A better candidate is P. Herennius Severus, Arrian's probable consular colleague in 129, who is known to have had literary interests as the patron of Philo of Byblos and to have thought it a 'great thing' to decorate his library with the *imagines* of famous writers (Plin. *Epp.* 4. 28). The use of the praenomen Publius in Dexippus' family may also argue in his favour. See also *PIR*² H 130; for the date of the consulship see R. Syme, 'The Career of Arrian', *HSCP* 86 (1982), 199 = *Roman Papers*, iv (Oxford, 1988), 38.

[16] *IG* ii/iii². 3665; see also ibid. 1788. 39, 1792. 39, 1798. 16.   [17] Ibid. 3667, 3668.

[18] *HA Gallienus* 13. 8 'atque inde Cyzicum et Asiam, deinceps Achaiam omnem vastavarunt et ab Atheniensibus duce Dexippo, scriptore horum temporum, victi sunt, unde pulsi per Epirum Macedoniam Boeotiam pervagati sunt'. It was generally assumed

two sons, Herennius Ptolemaeus and Herennius Dexippus, and a daughter; he died in the reign of Probus. It is notable that Dexippus, like a number of other men of local eminence, did not enter the imperial service. He seems to have regarded it as sufficient to bring honour to his city through the way that he performed his liturgies and held its magistracies, and through the works of literature that he produced. He thus stands in the tradition of Plutarch and his own contemporary, the rhetor and philosopher Minucianus, rather than in that of Arrian.[19]

In 270 or thereabouts the sons of Dexippus erected a statue in his honour. The inscription on the base provides a useful summary of his accomplishments to that point and of the ideals to which he aspired:

According to the decree of the *boule* of the Areopagus and the *boule* of the seven hundred and fifty and the demos of the Athenians, his sons have erected this in honour of the *archon basileus*, the thesmothete and eponymous archon, the panygerarch and agonothete of the great Panathenaea at his own expense and sacred panygerist, Publius Herennius Dexippus Hermaios, son of Ptolemaeus, the rhetor and historian:

> The land of Cecrops has produced many men worthy of fame who are powerful in virtue, word, and council, and one of them is Dexippus. Revering history, he set out the long span of time accurately. Some events he saw for himself, others he gathered from books and composed an all-embracing history. Verily a great and famous man who, casting the scope of his mind back across long ages, learnt by heart the events of the past. Widespread in Hellas is the recent fame that his history has given Dexippus. For this reason his sons jointly erect this statue, formed from stone, for their father.[20]

that he was the speaker of *FGrH* 100 F 28–9 (Millar, 'Dexippus', pp. 26–8). This is probably wrong: cf. de Ste Croix, *The Class Struggle in the Ancient Greek World* (London, 1981), 654–5 n. 42, who shows that there is little reason to trust the *HA* here, especially as *IG* ii/iii². 3669 does not mention the exploit, and it is unknown to the Greek tradition.

[19] Millar, 'Dexippus', pp. 16–19; C. P. Jones, *Plutarch and Rome* (Oxford, 1971), 3–12.

[20] *IG* ii/iii². 3669 κατὰ τὸ ἐπερώτημα τῆς ἐξ Ἀρίου πάγου βουλῆς καὶ | τῆς βουλῆς τῶν ⸌ψν⸍ καὶ τοῦ δήμου τοῦ Ἀθηναίων τὸν | ἄρξαντα τὴν τοῦ βασιλέως

This text, which commemorates the completion of Dexippus' *Chronika*,[21] one of three historical works that he composed, stands as an admirable illustration of the way this man of affairs was also a man of letters in the finest tradition of the Greek east, and the way that literary accomplishment helped to enhance the reputation of a city's leading citizen.[22] It serves to place Dexippus himself in the tradition of great figures of the past; it serves to illustrate the way that the achievements of the past were generally considered the ones against which the present ought to measure itself.[23] A further examination of Dexippus' histories will show just how he viewed the past and sought to place his own age in the context of history. It will also reveal something of the skill with which he composed his histories, and offer some insight into the practice of historiography during his own time. His work will also offer a point of comparison with that of his contemporary, Philostratus.

In addition to the *Chronika*, Dexippus wrote a *Skythika* and a work on the Diadochoi entitled *The Events after Alexander*. The inscription just quoted refers only to the *Chronika*, which suggests that it was completed before both the *Skythika* and *The Events after Alexander*.[24] Each work is interesting in its own right, and an evaluation of Dexippus' insight must be based upon consideration of the complete corpus.

ἐν θεσμοθέταις ἀρχὴν καὶ | ἄρξαντα τὴν ἐπώνυμον ἀρχὴν καὶ πανηγυριαρ-
χήσαντα | καὶ ἀγωνοθετήσαντα τῶν μεγάλων Παναθηναίων οἴκο|θεν ἱερέα
παναγῆ ›Πό‹ Ἑρέν‹ Δέξιππον Πτολεμαίου | Ἕρμειον τὸν ῥήτορα καὶ
συνγραφέα ἀρετῆς ἕνεκα υἱ παῖδ[ες]. | *vacat* | ἀλκῇ καὶ μύθοισι καὶ ἐν βουλαῖσι
κρατίστους | ἄνδρας ἀγακλείτους γείνατο Κεκροπίη, | ὧν ἕνα καὶ Δέξιππον, ὃς
ἱστορίην ἐσαθρήσας | αἰῶνος δολιχὴν ἀτρεκέως ἔφρασεν· | καὶ τὰ μὲν αὐτὸς
ἐσεῖδε, τὰ δ' ἐκ βύβλων ἀναλέξας | εὕρατο παντοίην ἱστορίης ἀτραπόν. | ἡ
μέγα κλεινὸς ἀνήρ, ὃς νοῦ ἀπὸ μυρίον ὄμμα | ἐκτείνας χρονίους πρήξιας
ἐξέμαθεν. | φήμη μὲν περίβωτος ἀν' Ἑλλάδα, τὴν ὁ νεανθὴς | αἶνος Δεξίππῳ
δῶκεν ἐφ' ἱστορίῃ. | τοὔνεκα δὲ καὶ παῖδες ἀγάκλειτον γενετῆρα | μορφάεντα
λίθου θῆκαν ἀμειβόμενοι.

21 Millar, 'Dexippus', p. 21.
22 See G. W. Bowersock, *Greek Sophists in the Roman Empire* (Oxford, 1969), 17–58; E. L. Bowie, 'The Importance of Sophists', *YCS* 27 (1982), 29–59.
23 See in general L. Robert, 'Une épigramme d'Automédon et Athènes au début de l'empire', *RÉG* (1981), 348–61.
24 Millar, 'Dexippus', pp. 21–2. Millar notes that *The Events after Alexander* could have been composed 'at any time in Dexippus' adulthood', though he favours an early date.

Although it is not directly relevant to the history of the third century, *The Events after Alexander* is of considerable interest because of the oddity of the theme. A great number of writers composed works on the life of Alexander the Great, who remained a figure of enduring interest and emulation throughout the imperial period. Trajan recalled his campaigns as he gazed out on the Persian Gulf, Caracalla tried to appear as Alexander, and Julian included him among the emperors in his *Caesares*. The authors of the *Fifth* and *Twelfth Sibylline Oracles* begin their accounts of Roman history with his deeds, as if the Romans were successors of Alexander.[25] But no one seems to have been very interested in the Diadochoi for their own sake. Aside from Dexippus, the only author who is known to have devoted a work to them in the imperial period was Arrian; he seems to have done this as a continuation of his *Anabasis* of Alexander and, possibly, to describe the period before the beginning of his *Bithyniaka*.[26] The usual pattern for a Greek historian who wrote Roman history of any sort was to write local history as well. The fact that Dexippus did not adhere to this might suggest that he thought that the period between the death of Alexander and Antipater's return to Europe after Triparadeisos in 320,[27] the period which this history covered, had some relevance to his own time. These years in the history of the Greek world did raise issues that were particularly relevant to the later third century. The period after Alexander's death was a time of transition in which a great empire was broken up, and during which the struggle between Perdiccas and those who sought their own kingdoms took place. During these years the army made the most important political decisions of the day. This was also a time in which the cities of Greece sought to assert their independence, with disastrous consequences. There was much here for a man to ponder, especially after the reign of Gallienus. The descriptions of

---

[25] *Orac. Sib.* 5. 4–7, 12. 4–7.

[26] P. A. Stadter, *Arrian of Nicomedia* (Chapel Hill, 1980), 151–2.

[27] For the date see R. M. Errington, 'From Babylon to Triparadeisos: 323–320 B.C.', *JHS* 90 (1970), 49–77. His conclusions have been confirmed by E. M. Anson, 'Diodorus and the Date of Triparadeisus', *AJP* 107 (1986), 208–17.

Dexippus' literary career provided by Eunapius and the *Suda* suggest that all of his works fall at the end of his life, and, as has already been noted, the inscription on the statue erected by his sons mentions only the *Chronika*.[28]

The history itself was not nearly so full as Arrian's, which appears to have been Dexippus' principal source (there is no reason to believe that he read the boring Hieronymus of Cardia or any other contemporary historian).[29] Arrian wrote in ten books, Dexippus in four; the material that was omitted was probably narrative detail. There was no need to clutter the picture with irrelevant facts which might obscure the main issues. These issues were fully explored in long speeches, such as that of Hyperides before the Lamian war or that of his opponent (fragments are preserved in the *Excerpta de sententiis*).[30] On the other hand, he does seem to have reproduced the details which he excerpted from Arrian with some care. He may have been an epitomator, but he was a careful one.

Dexippus' earlier work, the *Chronika*, was a very different matter, though here too his tendency to eschew narrative detail is evident. The *Chronika* was a history of the world from earlier times to the end of the 261st Olympiad in twelve books.[31] In the preface to his own history Eunapius described the achievement as follows:[32]

Dexippus of Athens organizes his History under Athenian archons, from the date when archons were instituted, adding also the names of Roman consuls, although the work begins before the institution of either archons or consuls. The guiding principle of this History is to avoid the earlier material and that which is more congenial to poets,

---

[28] *FGrH* 100 T 1 γεγονὼς ἐπὶ Βαληριανοῦ καὶ Γαλιήνου καὶ Κλαυδίου δευτέρου καὶ Αὐρηλιανοῦ τῶν βασιλέων Ῥωμαίων (from the *Suda*); T 2 τοὺς δὲ χρόνους εἰς Γαλλίηνον καὶ Κλαύδιον ⟨προ⟩βιβάζειν συνέβαινεν (Porphyry) Τάκιτόν τε καὶ Αὐρηλιανὸν καὶ Πρόβον, καθ' οὓς ἦν καὶ Δέξιππος ὁ τὴν Χρονικὴν Ἱστορίαν συγγράψας. . . .

[29] *FGrH* 100 F 8. For the reputation of Hieronymus and his contemporaries see also ibid. 154 T 12.

[30] Ibid. 100 F 32–3, with Jacoby ad loc.

[31] Ibid. 100 F 2.

[32] Ibid. 100 F 1. 3–4 = Eunapius 1. 1 (Blockley's trans.).

leaving it to those plausible writers who are more inclined to persuade the reader as to what happened. Dexippus himself brings together the later, better evidenced events and organizes them with an accuracy appropriate for history and with a reliability of judgement. He gives his narrative shape by dividing it up by Olympiads and archons within each Olympiad. He provides his History with a preface full of beauty and, as he proceeds, he imparts great stateliness to the body of the work by omitting material which is mythological or excessively ancient, returning it like an old and discredited medicine to those who mixed it. As he surveys the Egyptian period and presses on to the foundation and major achievements of the states amongst each people, he notes the leaders and fathers of history, making it clear and almost producing evidence to prove that every unhistorical event had been set down before him by another writer. He draws his history from many, varied sources, making a compact and coherent narrative which is like a perfumery store that carries a variety of useful goods. All events which men regard as important or which are connected with a particularly distinguished person are rapidly surveyed and arranged in the text.

Dexippus closes his history with the reign of the emperor Claudius, his first year in which he both ascended the throne and died (he thus ruled for one year though others give him a second.) Then he tabulates such-and-such a number of Olympiads and coordinates with them the consuls and archons. He even indicates the years by the thousand, as if he were in agony unless he set before his readers a catalogue comprising an enormous number of years.

Eunapius goes on from here to quote some lines from Dexippus' preface which would appear to reflect Dexippus' principal concerns:[33]

Dexippus himself points out [that] while all or the majority of chronologies are discrepant, there is absolute agreement over the famous events that are of more than local importance. For who is so well known to all readers and producers of literature as Lycurgus the Lacedaemonian? For everyone can tell of the testimony of the god to him, declaring him divine on account of his work in legislation. Yet who, when he has recited this, agrees upon the date of that legislation?

---

[33] *FGrH* 100 F 1. 7 = Eunapius 1. 1 (Blockley's trans.).

Dexippus himself admitted that the dating of any event was often uncertain and that in following the method that he did he created a work that was like a meeting without a chairman, riddled with errors and contradictions.[34] Eunapius' description and the phrases which he drew from the preface suggest a number of points about the *Chronika* as a whole. The first is that the bulk of the work was derived from earlier chronographers—this is surely what is meant by the statement that Dexippus followed 'plausible writers'. The second is that he began with the Egyptians; the work must therefore have begun around three thousand years before the first Olympiad, so that the total number of years that he surveyed must have been nearly four thousand. Indeed, Dexippus' disclaimer that he did his best with intractable material suggests that he spent the bulk of his work comparing the accounts of earlier chronographers. He only reached his own time in the twelfth book, which was presumably the penultimate.[35] The final book contained a comprehensive chronological table.[36] Thus, each book must have contained an average of 350 years. Even though it is likely that there were more years in the earlier books and fewer in the later, it is probable that he had to include around 200 years in books treating the historical periods.

The extent of the early history in the *Chronika* is revealed by two fragments from the tenth book. One of these states that 'they took the great and famous city of the Macedonians of Macedonia once known as Epidamnus, later known as Dyrrachium, by force'.[37] Jacoby suggested that this referred to an otherwise unattested event in the third century.[38] But that is not likely. The information provided here should come at the first point at

---

[34] Ibid. 100 F 1. 6 ὅτι ταῦτα οὐκ ἔστιν ἀληθῆ κατὰ τοὺς χρόνους, ἀλλὰ τῷ μὲν οὕτως τῷ δὲ ἑτέρως ἔδοξε, καὶ περιφανῶς ἑαυτοῦ κατηγορεῖν, ὥσπερ ἐκεῖνος, ὅτι χρονικὴν ἱστορίαν γράφων πλανωμένην τινὰ καὶ μεστὴν τῶν ἀντιλεγόντων ὥσπερ ἀπρόεδρον ἐκκλησίαν ἐκτίθησι τὴν γραφήν . . .

[35] Ibid. 100 F 5.

[36] Ibid. 100 F 1, with Jacoby ad loc.

[37] Ibid. 100 F 3 Δέξιππος δὲ ἐν Χρονικῶν ῑ φησὶν οὕτως· καὶ Μακεδόνων τὴν ⟨πρότερον⟩ μὲν Ἐπίδαμνον, ἐς ὕστερον δὲ Δυρράχιον μετονομασθεῖσαν, πόλιν τῆς Μακεδονίας μεγάλην καὶ εὐδαίμονα, κατὰ κράτος αἱροῦσιν.

[38] See Jacoby ad loc. This is accepted by Millar, 'Dexippus', p. 23.

which Epidamnus was mentioned in the *Chronika*, and it would have been very difficult indeed to omit the place in any account of Caesar's war against Pompey. But this cannot come from a note on 48 BC, because Caesar did not capture the city by force. Another possibility would be a mention of the operations by Teuta's Illyrians before the Roman intervention in 229 (surely an event of sufficient importance for a Greek to warrant comment) or even an account of the events leading up to the Peloponnesian war in 435. Of these two prospects the former is marginally preferable because another fragment from book 10 mentions an African tribe called the Σουκχαῖοι.[39] This might come from an account of the Punic wars.

The early books would have been structured according to lists of kings, and no doubt included discussion of the best synchronisms, as well as the great events that occurred under each king. This is what Eunapius must mean when he says that Dexippus began with the Egyptians and pressed on to the events of the states of each people and 'almost' produced evidence to prove 'that every unhistorical event has been set down before him by an earlier writer'. Dexippus' technique may be illustrated by a fragment in which the return of the Heracleidae and the foundation of Rhodes are placed at the same time.[40] When he reached the period after the first Olympiad he could adopt another format, one which seems to have been similar to that which appears in the fragment of the papyrus chronicle from Oxyrhyncus attributed to Phlegon of Tralles and in the more concise *Olympic Chronicle* from the same site.[41] A list of Olympic victors would open each section. A list of the archons and consuls who served within that Olympiad might then follow, and events would be listed by year as follows—'in the first year the Romans fought the Samnites and were defeated'; or, more probably, the archons and consuls for each year would be given, followed by the events in their year. This seems to have been the practice of the chronographer used by Diodorus.[42] Dexippus could also have included

[39] *FGrH* 100 F 4.   [40] Ibid. 100 F 9.   [41] Ibid. 255, 257 A.
[42] E. Schwartz, 'Diodorus', *RE*, v. 665–6.

remarks on cultural events and the careers of cultural figures at the end of each year or of each Olympiad. An Olympiad entry might appear on the page as follows:

Olympiad 108

Polycles of Cyrene won the stadion. Theophilus was archon at Athens; M. Valerius Corvus and M. Popillius Laenas were consuls at Rome. In this year Philip, whose aim was to seize the cities of the Hellespont, aquired Mecyberna and Torone through treason. He defeated the people of Olynthus ... In this year Plato died and Speusippus succeeded as head of the school.[43]

The amount of material recorded under each year could vary in accordance with Dexippus' interest. There was occasion for editorial comment, such as an explanation of why the Roman empire was greater than the previous three world empires (those of the Assyrians, Medes, and Macedonians).[44] But it would appear that no single entry could be longer than perhaps ten or twenty lines, and many must have been shorter (presuming that each book contained about 1,000 lines, which may be an excessively high estimate). As a whole, the *Chronika* would have provided a useful summary of the main events of classical history, without too many details. It may not in fact have been very different in scope or content from the text attributed to Phlegon.[45] This sort of brief historical summary appears to have been popular during the third century, and indeed had a respectable pedigree extending back for centuries.[46]

Several extensive fragments from Dexippus' third work, the *Skythika*, have been preserved in the Constantinian *Excerpta*. It would appear that the *Skythika* was composed of three books.

---

[43] Cf. Diod. 16. 53; *FGrH* 255. 3. The consular dates given in the *Historia Augusta*, which appear to derive from Dexippus, suggest that the organization within the Olympiad was by archon and consular year; see also *HA V. Gordian*, 23. 4, 5; 26. 3; 29. 1; *HA V. Gall.* 1. 2; 5. 2; 10. 1; 12. 1; *HA V. Tyr. trig.* 9. 1; *HA V. Claud.* 11. 3; Syme, *Emperors and Biography*, p. 210 n. 4, pp. 235–6.   [44] *FGrH* 100 F 12.

[45] See R. C. Blockley, 'Dexippus of Athens and Eunapius of Sardis', *Latomus*, 30 (1971), 710–15, *contra* D. Buck, 'A Reconstruction of Dexippus' *Chronika*', *Latomus*, 43 (1984), 596–7; Jacoby, in his note on F 1, suggested that the *Chronika* might have resembled Diodorus.   [46] Millar, 'Dexippus', p. 15.

A long fragment (fr. 6) preserved in the *Excerpta de legationibus* describes a meeting between Aurelian and ambassadors from the Juthungi, a tribe that lived north of Raetia. It comes from book 3, and there is no evidence that he treated any event later than the time of Aurelian. The fragments preserved in the *Excerpta* come to just over 450 lines in Jacoby's closely printed text. If Dexippus' books were as long as those of Herodian, which average about 780 lines in the less closely printed Teubner, it would appear that the extant fragments account for somewhat more than one half a book, or between 16 and 20 per cent of the whole. This is a large enough sample upon which to base some general conclusions about the work.

There are eight fragments in the *Excerpta*. They include two legations, the extensive account of Aurelian's negotiations with the Juthungi alluded to above, and a discussion of a treaty with the Vandals (fr. 7; both events are datable to 270), three sieges (fr. 25, 27, 29), a long letter from Decius to the city of Philippopolis (fr. 26), two long extracts from a speech which appears to have been given by a leader of the defence of Athens against the Herulians (fr. 28), and a fragment which may come from the preface (fr. 24). A further fragment is preserved in Jordanes' *Getica*, which describes the origins of the Goths and their journey from the southern shore of the Baltic to the Danube (fr. 30). Taken as a whole, the Constantinian fragments confirm the impression of Dexippus' skills that may be derived from *The Events after Alexander* and the *Chronika*. He was a man with an interest in the dramatic and not much interest in extensive narrative detail, though he would take care in reporting the details that he thought were important in his source. The fragments also suggest a great deal about his sources of information and, along with information that can be gleaned from the other representatives of his tradition such as George and Zonaras, they cast an important light on the history provided by the *Thirteenth Sibylline Oracle*. They reveal that Dexippus was little, if at all, better informed than the writers whose work is preserved in the oracle about the events of his own time.

The most important fragment is the description of Aurelian's negotiations with the Juthungi. This is because it reflects what Dexippus had to say in the surrounding narrative and is therefore extremely revealing about his sources and overall technique. He says that the Juthungi came to Aurelian after they had been defeated in a battle by the Danube.[47] They hoped to renew their treaty with Rome and retain the subsidies that they had received before the outbreak of hostilities.[48] When he learnt that the embassy had arrived, Aurelian told the ambassadors that he would hear them on the next day and arranged an imposing spectacle for them. He received them in his purple robe from a high tribunal that was located in the midst of the *comitatus*[49] drawn up in battle array in a semicircle with the officers in the

[47] In 270, as shown by A. Alföldi, 'Über die Juthungeneinfälle unter Aurelian', *Bull. de l'Inst. Arch. Bulg.* 16 (1950), 21–4 = *Studien*, pp. 427–30.

[48] *FGrH* 100 F 6. 1 τὴν δὲ αἴτησιν τῆς εἰρήνης ἐδόκει μὴ σὺν τῷ ἄγαν περιδεεῖ καὶ καταπεπληγότι ἐκ τῆς ἥττης ποιεῖσθαι, ὡς ἂν ὑπάρχοι σφίσιν καὶ τῶν πρόσθεν φοιτώντων χρημάτων παρὰ Ῥωμαίων ἡ ἀποδοχή. . . .

[49] Ibid. 100 F 6. 2 κατόπιν δὲ βασιλέως τὰ σημεῖα ἦν τῆς ἐπιλέκτου στρατιᾶς. Millar, 'Dexippus', p. 25, noted that this was contemporary evidence for the formation of the later *comitatus* (for this use of ἐπιλέκτος see Eus. *MP* 11. 21). Much clearer evidence is provided by *FGrH* 100 F 7. 4 τήν τε ἀμφ' αὑτὸν τάξιν ἑταιρικὴν καὶ ὅση δορυφορία τοῦ ἄρχοντος τῶν τε συμμάχων ὅσοι ἦσαν Βανδήλων . . ., where σύμμαχος must mean *comes*, as in an inscription from Oenoanda which dates from the reign of Valerian, *IGR* iii. 481. 1–6 Οὐαλέριον Στατεί|λιον Κᾶστον, τὸν | κράτιστον σύμμα|χον τῶν Σεβαστῶν | πραιπόσιτον Βιξιλα|τιώνων; see also H. von Soden, *Urkunden zur Enstehungsgeschichte des Donatismus* (Kleine Texte für Vorlesungen und Übungen, 122; Bonn, 1913), No. 28 = J. L. Maier, *Le Dossier du donatisme*, i (Texte und Untersuchungen, 134; Berlin, 1987), No. 29 'inducto et applicato Victore grammatico, assistente etiam Nundinario diacono, Zenophilus vir clarissimus consularis dixit: "Quis vocaris?" Respondit: "Victor." Zenophilus vir clarissimus consularis dixit: "Cuius condicionis es?" Victor dixit: "Professor sum Romanarum litterarum, grammaticus latinus." Zenophilus vir clarissimus consularis dixit: "Cuius dignitatis es?" Victor dixit: "Patre decurione Constantiniensium avo milite; in comitatu militaverat: nam origo nostra de sanguine Mauro descendit."' The hearing at which Victor made this appearance was in Dec. 320. The grandfather must therefore have served in the mid-third century (*contra* Maier, who suggests that he served under Maximian). This suggests that Gallienus' cavalry corps, in which North African cavalry had an important place (M. P. Speidel, 'The Rise of Ethnic Cavalry Units in the Roman Army', *ANRW* ii/3. 212–13, 221 = *Roman Army Studies* (Amsterdam, 1984), 127–8, 136), was part of an organization referred to as the *comitatus*. The τάξιν ἑταιρικήν in the same fragment is probably a reference to the *protectores* (as Millar suggests); the existence of the *protectores* in this period is confirmed by *ILS* 569, 9479; see further Christol, 'La carrière de Traianus Mucianus', pp. 393–408.

front and the standards and *imagines* of the deified emperors behind him. The barbarians were duly impressed, but presented their original demands anyway in a long speech that is replete with echoes of several Thucydidean orations.[50] The ambassadors expatiate upon the mutability of fortune and warn the emperor that he should not become arrogant through his success, for the arrogant soon fall. They were able to field 40,000 horsemen and 80,000 foot from their tribe alone, and they had proved their courage through their invasion of Italy.[51] They would be valuable allies of Rome in the future if they were allowed to withdraw to their territory unmolested (they do concede that they would not raid extensively in their retreat and that they would take only what was in their path). The Romans should remember that they were victorious in battle by the Ister through good luck rather than courage. They would be fortunate to have allies such as the Juthungi and should continue to pay them subsidies. If the Romans would not accept this final condition the Juthungi would continue to fight. Aurelian answered in measured terms. He said that their demands were outrageous, that they had proved faithless in the past, and that the Romans were worthy victors: they had not only defeated the Juthungi, but had also warded off earlier attacks by the Alamanni and 300,000 'Skyths'.[52] They were cut off in Roman territory and the Romans did not even need to risk battle against them in the future—they could hold off and wait for famine to take its toll.[53] The

---

[50] For discussion of Thucydidean elements in Dexippus' style see F. J. Stein, *Dexippus et Herodianus: Rerum scriptores quatenus Thucydidem secuti sint* (Bonn, 1957), 4–71; for this passage see esp. pp. 48–55.

[51] *FGrH* 100 F 6. 4 ὥστε μέρει ἐλαχίστῳ τὰς πρὸς Ἴστρῳ πόλεις ἐπελθόντες Ἰταλίαν μικροῦ πᾶσαν κατειλήφαμεν, ἱππικῷ μὲν στρατεύσαντες ἐς μυριάδας δ᾽, καὶ τούτων οὐ μιγάδων οὐδὲ ἀσθενῶν ἀλλὰ Ἰουθούγγων καθαρῶς, ὧν πολὺς ἐφ᾽ ἱππομαχίᾳ λόγος. ἀσπίδα δὲ ἄγομεν διπλασίαν δυνάμεως τῆς ἱππικῆς, οὐδὲ ἐν τούτοις ταῖς ἑτέρων ἐπιμιξίαις ἐπισκιάζοντες τοῦ σφετέρου στρατοῦ τὸ ἀν⟨αν⟩ταγώνιστον.

[52] Ibid. F 6. 11; see also Zon. 12. 24, where the same number is given for a raid by the Alamanni during the reign of Gallienus, an event which is distinct from the one referred to here, which is the invasion of 268–9.

[53] *FGrH* 100 F 6. 14 τὸ γὰρ δὴ πλῆθος ὑμῶν σώμασί τε ἥκιστα ἰσχύει καὶ φρονήμασιν. ἀπείληπται γὰρ †Ῥοδανοῦ† μὲν εἴσω καὶ τῶν ἡμετέρων ὁρίων,

barbarians realized that their demands would not be met and went away dispirited.

There is enough here to suggest not only that the negotiations are a rhetorical construct, but that the description of the entire campaign was fanciful. There are two serious objections to information in the speeches which must reflect information that was also in the main narrative. The first is geographical. The Juthungi lived north of Raetia, and if there was a battle on the Danube they would not be cut off in the middle of Roman territory—they would have been on the edge of their own lands.[54] The second has to do with the numbers: 120,000 is an absurd figure for a single barbarian tribe, and the number 300,000 given for the 'Skyths' who were defeated in Epirus is a similar fantasy. Only the bare outline of events can be believed: that the barbarians invaded Italy and were defeated. The coincidental details which Dexippus gives about the army are no more than could be gleaned from one of the captioned pictures that were used to advertise imperial victories, and in fact the scene that he paints resembles several on the columns of Marcus and Trajan in which the emperor addresses defeated tribesmen.

Serious problems can be detected elsewhere. The three siege sequences comprise 113 lines in Jacoby's text, and they contain a fair amount of material about the stratagems employed by both sides, with a fair amount of Thucydidean colouring for literary effect.[55] But they offer few of the items which Lucian suggested

σπανίῳ δὲ ἀγορᾷ συνεχόμενον καὶ τῇ ἄλλῃ ταλαιπωρήσει τοῖς ἀλγεινοῖς τοῖς μὲν ἤδη σύνεστι, τοῖς δὲ μέλλει, καὶ προκαμὸν ἐν τῷ ἀεὶ μοχθεῖν ἀτολμότερον ἔσται καὶ χρῆσθαι αὐτῷ παρέξει ἀμαχεὶ ὅ τι ἂν βουλώμεθα, ὡς ἂν πρὸς τὴν χρόνιον διατριβὴν ἀπειρηκότι.

[54] For the history of the Juthungi see M. Schönfield, 'Iuthungi', *RE* x. 1347–8; Demougeot, *La Formation*, ii. 294–6.

[55] R. C. Blockley, 'Dexippus and Priscus and the Thucydidean Account of the Siege of Plataea', *Phoenix*, 26 (1972), 18–22, shows that Dexippus did not simply copy his account of the siege of Philippopolis from Thucydides. He concludes (p. 22), 'It is unreasonable to impugn Dexippus' account solely on the grounds of verbal imitation of Thucydides, and, unless his material can be shown to be unhistorical on other grounds, it should be accepted that he has merely used Thucydidean expressions to communicate authentic material.' His point is fair, but I suggest that Dexippus' account can be impugned on the grounds that he elsewhere shows little knowledge of detail.

were essential for understanding a battle.[56] Dexippus does not name the commanders, nor does he give the numbers involved, the length of the sieges, or the casualties. There is only one name given in the three accounts, that of the philosopher Maximus, who is said to have inspired the defence of Marcianopolis. This complete omission of relevant detail in the body of the fragments cannot be attributed to the carelessness of the excerptors, whose tendency is to make mistakes at the beginning and end of the sections they reproduce and to retain the details in between with reasonable accuracy.[57] These battle-scenes are no more than artful arrangements of *strategemata*, just as the speeches are no more than artful collections of topoi which serve the time-honoured function of underlining the points that the author thought were important, of adding dramatic effect and pathos to the narrative. Thus, the long letter of Decius to the city of Philippopolis is a notably ironic piece. He advises the people to stay behind the walls and not to engage the enemy in the field. Such a course would be disastrous for untried troops against experienced foes. Whatever happened they should endure the destruction of their property outside the walls and keep their faith in him, for he would soon come with his experienced army to their rescue. He would make good the damage that was done. The letter itself sums up the dilemma of people in many cities throughout the empire, people whose only protection lay in their walls, and its message would have been underscored by the context. It is addressed to the Priscus who would be proclaimed emperor and betray the city to the Goths.[58]

There is no evidence to suggest that Dexippus made a con-

---

[56] Lucian, *Quomodo hist. consc.* 49.

[57] P. A. Brunt, 'On Historical Fragments and Epitomes', *CQ*, NS 30 (1980), 483–4.

[58] *FGrH* 100 F 26; see on ll. 100–2 below. F. Hartmann's objection (*Herrscherwechsel und Reichskrise*, p. 162 n. 2) that the addressee of this letter cannot be identified with the Priscus who later rebelled against Decius is not cogent. Even if it is allowed that the scenario proposed by G. Walzer is correct, viz. that Priscus was elevated to the purple by Gothic auxiliaries (this option is favoured by Hartmann, *Herrscherwechsel und Reichskrise*, pp. 111–12) and handed the city over to them as a reward, this Priscus is clearly a high imperial official. Economy of hypothesis dictates that there was only one man named Priscus in a high position of authority in this region in 250–1.

scientious effort to interview witnesses or consult a wide range of documents. But this does not mean that he was completely incompetent. It means that he was at the mercy of whatever sources were readily available and that these varied enormously in quality. In some places there are signs of better-informed sources than in others. The fragment describing the negotiations between Aurelian and the Vandals is a case in point. The quality of information here is very much better than that provided in the description of the negotiations with the Juthungi. The excerptor says that after a severe defeat the Vandals came to Aurelian to discuss terms and that there was an extended conversation between the barbarians and the emperor (which seems to have been given at length in the original, though he did not choose to copy it out) and a treaty was made. On the next day Aurelian assembled the troops, and when he asked them if they approved of the peace—a remarkable example of the role of the rank and file in decision-making—they shouted their approbation.[59] Dexippus described the way that the treaty was enacted in some detail: the 'kings and leaders' of the barbarians gave hostages, and two thousand Vandal cavalry were selected to serve with the Romans.[60] Some of these men were chosen by the Romans, the others were volunteers. The rest of the Vandals were to return home and the governor was to supply them with a market on the Danube. Most of the Vandals accepted these terms and headed for home, but there were some who broke away from the main body and began looting. The '*hegemon* of the foreign soldiers' rounded them up and killed them—the number was about 500.[61]

---

[59] FGrH 100 F 7. 1 τῇ δὲ ὑστεραίᾳ τό τε πλῆθος τῶν Ῥωμαίων στρατιωτῶν αὖθις ἠθροίσθη καὶ ἐρομένου βασιλέως ὅ τι σφίσι περὶ τῶν παρόντων λῶον εἶναι δοκεῖ, κρίνοντες τὴν εὐτυχίαν τὴν ὑπάρχουσαν προμηθείᾳ τῆς ὑπὲρ τῶν ὄντων ἀσφαλείας διασώσασθαι καὶ βοῇ τὸ βουλόμενον σημαίνοντες σύμπαντες ἐς τὴν κατάλυσιν τοῦ πολέμου ἐχώρησαν.

[60] Ibid. 100 F 7. 2 συνεμάχουν δὲ ἀπὸ τῆσδε Ῥωμαίοις Βανδήλων ἱππεῖς εἰς δισχιλίους, οἱ μέν τινες αἱρετοὶ ἐκ τοῦ πλήθους ἐς τὴν συμμαχίαν καταλεχθέντες, οἱ δὲ καὶ ἐθέλοντες ἑκούσιον στρατείαν ὑποδυόμενοι.

[61] Ibid. 100 F 7. 3 ὅσοι δὲ παραβάσει τῶν σπονδῶν ἐπὶ λείας συλλογὴν ἀφθόνως ἀπεσκεδάσθησαν, ἀνῃρέθησαν σύμπαντες ὑπὸ τοῦ ἡγεμόνος τῶν ξενικῶν στρατοπέδων οὐ μείους γενόμενοι πεντακοσίων.

On their way home some other Vandals, thinking that they were protected by the treaty, also began to raid. Their fate is lost in a textual corruption. After the treaty had been made Aurelian had sent the main body of the army on ahead to Italy, and he followed a few days later with the *protectores* (?) and two thousand of the *comitatus*.[62] Unlike the account of the negotiations with the Juthungi, there is nothing in this fragment that is inherently improbable: the terms imposed upon the Vandals (that they surrender hostages, provide troops for the army, and trade through a specific location) are in line with standard Roman practice, and the numbers are reasonable. The coincidental details about the workings of the army are also plausible, though they cannot be checked. It would therefore appear that Dexippus had a reliable informant here and reproduced the information that he received accurately—albeit with some embellishment, if he did indeed, as the excerptor suggests, include a long dialogue between the emperor and the ambassadors. This appears to conform with his practice in *The Events after Alexander* and the *Chronika*. The variation in the accuracy of the *Skythika* reflects the fact that information was very difficult to obtain.

There are a number of places where the later tradition also suggests that Dexippus' contemporary history was of variable quality. Zonaras and Zosimus have an account of the murder of Gordian III which appears to derive from the *Chronika* and which is clearly inadequate, though it does seem to reflect the same sort of gossip that informed the author of some lines in the *Thirteenth Sibylline Oracle*.[63] A fragment which George preserves from the *Chronika* shows that Dexippus was uncertain of the details of Decius' family: he thought that Gallus' son, Volusianus, was a son of Decius.[64] This is understandable in so far as other writers had similar problems with details of Decius' family (including, it seems, the author of lines in the *Thirteenth Sibylline Oracle*), and

---

[62] FGrH 100 F 7. 4 καὶ διαλιπόντων οὐ μάλα συχνῶν ἡμερῶν τήν τε ἀμφ' αὑτὸν τάξιν ἑταιρικὴν καὶ ὅση δορυφορία τοῦ ἄρχοντος τῶν τε συμμάχων ὅσοι ἦσαν Βανδήλων . . . ; see also n. 49 above.

[63] See on l. 20 below.   [64] FGrH 100 F 22; see on ll. 141–4.

parallels may be adduced in earlier writers.[65] Dexippus also seems to have thought that Antioch was captured by the Persians after the defeat of Valerian in 260. This may have been a natural assumption on the part of anyone who heard of a great disaster in the east, though the *Res Gestae* of Sapor show that it would have been an incorrect assumption, and it might have been the result of confusion between Antioch on the Orontes and Antioch ad Cragum.[66] There is a difficulty of another sort with all western accounts of the Persian invasion in 252: none of them mentions the Roman defeat at Barbalissos, which is recorded in Sapor's great inscription.[67] These errors and omissions may be further indications of the difficulty which anyone living in the mid-third century would have had in gathering information unless he was particularly dedicated, which Dexippus was not.

On the other hand, it should be noted that Dexippus did get some things right. He has Decius' defeat in the right place, on the Abrittus, and his relative chronology for the Gothic invasions appears to be reliable (even though some of the details might be invented). He is probably the source for the loss of the province of Mesopotamia to the Persians in 238, and, as has already been seen, he appears to be a reliable source for Aurelian's dealings with the Vandals. If the picture of his skills as a historian is uneven, this is because it would have taken a man of extraordinary energy and access to the highest levels of government to get better information. Like most of his contemporaries, Dexippus had to rely on imperial communiqués and visitors to his home city. Even a man as well connected as Cassius Dio found it hard to get at the truth. Dexippus was an elderly man when he turned to the writing of history (he was about 70 when he completed the *Chronika*), and he did the best that he could with what came to hand. If he accepted some things as fact when he should not have,

---

[65] Dio is in error about Diadumenianus, saying that he was proclaimed when news of his father's accession reached Rome, rather than a year later (Dio 78. 17. 1; see Millar, *Cassius Dio*, p. 163), and about the ancestry of Elagabalus (Dio 78. 30. 2; see G. W. Bowersock, 'Herodian and Elagabalus', *YCS* 24 (1975), 231–4).

[66] See on ll. 161–3.

[67] See on l. 110.

he was being no more gullible than many of his contemporaries, including the person who compiled the *Thirteenth Sibylline Oracle*.

Philostratus, who appears to have been the source for Petrus Patricius' account of the third century, is a more shadowy figure;[68] the tentative conclusions which may be drawn about his history do suggest that he had interests which were somewhat different from those of Dexippus, and that he had very different sources of information. The long summary of his history concerning the reign of Gallienus that Zonaras appears to have taken from Petrus provides a good indication of the sort of things that caught his attention. The incidents which he records are as follows:

1. The origins of Aureolus. He was a man from Dacia. He was a valiant soldier and Gallienus put him in charge of his cavalry. When Ingenuus revolted at Sirmium, he defeated him. The Moorish cavalry (who were descended from the Medes) were particularly important in the battle and Ingenuus was killed, while fleeing, by his guards.

2. Postumus rebelled against Gallienus. Gallienus left his son, Gallienus, at Cologne under the tutelage of Albinus while the barbarians were invading Gaul. Postumus, who was in command on the Rhine, intercepted some barbarians while they were returning from a raid and defeated them. He divided the plunder which they had taken, and he had taken from them, among his troops. Albinus demanded that the plunder be delivered to himself and the younger Gallienus. Postumus gathered his troops together to give them this news, thinking that it would cause them to revolt. It did and they attacked Cologne; the people in the city handed Gallienus II and Albinus over and they were killed.

3. Gallienus attacked Postumus; he was defeated in one battle, but won the second. Postumus escaped because Aureolus did not press the pursuit hard enough. Gallienus defeated Postumus again and besieged him, but was forced to abandon the siege after he suffered an arrow-wound.[69]

---

[68] The case for the identification of Philostratus as the source of Petrus is argued in app. II.

[69] For a thorough discussion of these and other accounts see Drinkwater, *The Gallic Empire*, pp. 24–30, 54–60.

4. Macrianus revolted against Gallienus. He had two sons, Macrianus and Quietus, whom he proclaimed emperor. He did not take the throne himself because he was physically deformed. After making a few assaults upon the Persians he marched against Gallienus with the younger Macrianus. Quietus remained in the east with the cavalry commander Ballista. Gallienus sent Aureolus against him. Aureolus captured some prisoners and spared them in the hope that Macrianus' troops would desert. They did not, but when battle was joined a standard-bearer tripped and lowered his standard. When they saw the standard lowered, the other standard-bearers did the same; the army surrendered and proclaimed Gallienus emperor. Macrianus and his son escaped with some Pannonian troops, but when they saw that the men were thinking of handing them over they surrendered and the Pannonians followed suit.

5. Gallienus sent Odaenathus of Palmyra against Quietus and Ballista. When news of the defeat of the Macriani in Pannonia arrived many cities deserted Quietus and Ballista. Odaenathus defeated them outside Emesa and killed Ballista; the Emesenes killed Quietus. Gallienus made Odaenathus ruler of the east.[70]

6. Odaenathus proved to be a great warrior and defeated many peoples in battle, including the Persians. He was killed by a nephew. Odaenathus had reprimanded this nephew for killing animals before he had in the course of a hunt, but he kept on doing so. Odaenathus became angry and took his horse away, which was a 'great insult among barbarians'. He was rude to Odaenathus and Odaenathus cast him in prison, but Odaenathus' eldest son asked that he release him. Odaenathus did and the nephew killed both him and his son at a banquet to which he had been invited.

7. Aureolus revolted against Gallienus, but Gallienus defeated him in battle and besieged him in Milan. Gallienus' wife had accompanied him on the campaign and while he was engaging some of the enemy she fell into great danger. The enemy saw that the camp was weakly held and made an attack on it, hoping to

[70] For discussion of this account and its connection to others see on l. 169.

seize the queen. She was saved through the bravery of one of the men left in the camp.

8. The murder of Gallienus. Aurelian arrived with his cavalry at the siege of Milan with some men who were planning a coup. When they thought that the plan had been discovered they decided to speed up its execution. They sent someone to tell Gallienus that the enemy was approaching. He leapt on his horse to meet them. He saw some men coming towards him and when they did not show proper respect he asked what they wanted, and they replied that they wanted to end his reign. He fled on his horse and would have escaped if he had not run into a ditch. One of his pursuers threw a spear at him which hit the mark and he died.[71]

Two fragments of Petrus, preserved in the *Excerpta de legationibus gentium ad Romanos*, describe events in the east. One narrates an embassy from Odaenathus to Sapor. Odaenathus wanted to cultivate Sapor because he saw that he was far more powerful than the Romans, and sent him letters along with a train of camels loaded with gifts for the Persians. Sapor had the gifts thrown into the river and asked who it was that dared write to his lord. If Odaenathus wished a lighter penalty he ought to deliver himself to Sapor with his hands bound behind him; if he did not do that, then Sapor would destroy him and his country.[72] Another fragment describes a retreat by Sapor past Edessa, in which he bribed the garrison not to attack him as he went past.[73] It is also possible that a fragment from the anonymous Continuator of Dio,[74] which describes the fall of Antioch in 252, derives from Petrus.[75] It contains information that may be confirmed by the *Thirteenth Sibylline Oracle* and which, therefore, may be derived from a contemporary author.

In places where fragments of Petrus derive from Dio, it

---

[71] Zonaras reports that there were several traditions concerning his death, and records one in which the prefect Heraclianus, plotting with Claudius, killed Gallienus (12. 25) in his tent. Zosimus' account of the murder seems to be derived from the same source (1. 40. 3). *HA V. Gall.* 14 makes Marcianus and Cecropius the plotters.

[72] *FHG* iv, F 10; see also *FGrH* 99 F 2 (this is the episode which links Petrus' account with Philostratus); see Bowersock, *Roman Arabia*, p. 130.   [73] *FHG* iv, F 11.

[74] See app. v.   [75] *FHG* iv, p. 192 F 1; see on ll. 89–100.

appears that he retained the general tenor of the account which he found in his sources, and at times that he copied them almost verbatim.[76] For this reason it is likely that the account of the reign of Gallienus that is found in Zonaras reflects the general tenor of the account which Petrus found in his source, and so it is possible to see that this writer was very different from Dexippus.

Dexippus does not seem to have been greatly interested in personalities. He seems to have been interested in events as illustrations of principles. The Lamian War raised the issue of Athens' place in a world dominated by kings. The negotiations between Aurelian and the Juthungi suggested a parallel with Sparta's appeal to Athens in 425, which failed. Decius' letter to Philippopolis is a disquisition upon the way that a city ought to behave in the face of a barbarian invasion. The speech after the capture of Athens discusses the stratagems which men ought to employ under the circumstances and exhorts the Athenians to recall the glories of the past, to fight for the honour of the city. It has been proposed that 'With Dexippus, it may be suggested tentatively that we are approaching a "Byzantine" viewpoint, with the inhabitants of the principal Greek areas—the Balkans, Greece and Asia Minor—embattled against the barbarian threat.'[77] This does not seem likely. When the citizens of Greek cities are presented as the defenders of their homelands this is no more than a reflection of the facts. The regular army was far away or in disarray. This meant that men had to fall back on their traditions to find hope in the present danger.[78] As Aelius Aristides once dreamt that he was delivering Demosthenes' *De corona* before appearing in court to defend his immunities,[79] so too might a man like Dexippus recall the repulse of the Persians in 480, and try to set the bewildering circumstances of the present in the context of the past to explain them. His history may be full of rhetorical topoi, but these were meaningful. They provided the

---

[76] *FHG* iv, p. 184 F 2.

[77] Millar, 'Dexippus', p. 25. He suggests that this is supported by the formulaic nature of the siege accounts.

[78] Hartmann, *Herrscherwechsel und Reichskrise*, p. 171.

[79] Ael. Arist. 50. 97.

standard for the interpretation of contemporary history. Philostratus seems to have been different. He saw his history, if the
impression which Zonaras gives is correct, in terms of the deeds
of the great men of his time. He was apparently fond of anecdote.
It is notable that Zonaras' account moves from one important
individual to another, and describes each event in terms of the
way that it affected the principal actor; the significance lies in
what the incident revealed about a man's character or fortune.

The final verdict has to be that neither Dexippus nor Philostratus has much of value to say about imperial politics or the
details of foreign affairs. They set down what they could learn
and tried to give this information significance in their own ways.
They do not seem to have had consistent access to good information: Philostratus may have known more about events on the
eastern frontier than Dexippus did (Zonaras suggests that his
source was interested in Odaenathus), and Dexippus may have
been more interested in the northern tribes. Both appear to have
been highly idiosyncratic, and were thus worthy heirs to Cassius
Dio and Herodian, who set down the history of their own times
as it came to them and as it interested them.[80] The quality of Dio
and Herodian as accurate reporters of events varies tremendously
according to their sources, perceptions, and prejudices. Neither is
wholly satisfactory nor is either wholly unsatisfactory. Both
reflect their own interests and, to a certain extent, those of their
audiences. The same is true of Dexippus and Philostratus, and
while this means that it is impossible to know much about
imperial politics in the third century, it is possible to see how
people reacted to what they could learn. This is the same perspective that the *Thirteenth Sibylline Oracle* presents.

---

[80] For a cogent discussion of Dio see Millar, *Cassius Dio*, pp. 119–73, esp. pp. 172–3,
'The basic stuff of his contemporary history was the general knowledge of affairs and
incidents which any man in public life would possess.' For Herodian see Whittaker, ed.,
Herodian, vol. i, pp. xxxvi–lxxxii. On p. xxxvii Whittaker makes the important point that
Herodian was highly regarded as a historian by other writers. See also Z. Rubin, *Civil War
Propaganda and Historiography* (Brussels, 1980).

3

The Sibylline Oracles

THE EXTANT COLLECTIONS

The surviving corpus of Sibylline Oracles consists of two collections, of which one (henceforth collection A) may have been
compiled after the late fifth century AD by the redactor of the
'Sibylline Preface'. This preface opens with an exhortation to read
the oracles and provides some further information about Sibyls.[1]
It gives the 'Sibylline Canon', the list of ten Sibyls which Lactantius derived from Varro,[2] and the story of Tarquinius Priscus'
dealings with the Cumaean Sibyl, and it assures the reader that
Sibyls knew the truth about the Christian God. The information
which the author provides appears to be taken from the *Sibylline
Theosophy*, a work which must be earlier than the end of the fifth
century because it was the source of an account of Sibyls in the
tenth book of a work entitled *On True Belief* which was
composed in the reign of the emperor Zeno.[3] There is no way of
knowing how long after the composition of the *Sibylline Theosophy* this collection was assembled: the earliest manuscripts date
from the fifteenth century, and it is not quoted by an extant
author.

The collection once contained eight oracles or λόγοι, some
of which appear to have been subdivided into τόμοι. The
manuscripts themselves fall into two classes, Φ (containing six

---

[1] The preface is preserved in only three MSS in Φ; see J. Geffcken (ed.), *Die Oracula
Sibyllina* (Leipzig, 1902), p. xxii.

[2] For discussion of this list see H. W. Parke, *Sibyls and Sibylline Prophecy in Classical
Antiquity* (London, 1988), 30–5; H. Erbse, *Fragmente griechischer Theosophien: Herausgegeben
und quellenkritisch untersucht* (Hamburg, 1941), 30–40.

[3] Rzach, *RE* iiA. 2120; Erbse, *Fragmente*, pp. 30, 40; E. Schürer, *The History of the Jewish
People in the Age of Jesus Christ*², iii, ed. G. Vermes, F. G. Millar, and M. Goodman (Edinburgh, 1986), 623–4.

manuscripts) and Ψ (which has four). Φ gives the oracles in the order in which they appear in modern editions. Ψ gives them in the order 8, 1–7, though two of the manuscripts break off part of the way through book 5.[4] In both families there is great confusion over the division of books 1–3. At the beginning of book 3 (as the text is now printed) the manuscripts indicate that these lines are from the third τόμος of the second λόγος of the Sibyl concerning God. At line 92 Ψ notes that there is a lacuna in which the end of the second λόγος and the beginning of the third have been lost. Two of the manuscripts in Φ note that something is missing here as well.[5] Therefore, the present books 1 and 2 and the first 92 lines of book 3 are the remains of two oracles (λόγοι) that were divided into three volumes (τόμοι). The other oracles appear all to have been in one τόμος.

The oracles vary widely in content. The remains of books 1 and 2 provide a history of the world from the Creation to the Last Judgement, organized in a very rough approximation to a scheme of ten generations.[6] The *First Oracle* describes the first seven generations and the life of Christ, and concludes with an attack on the Jews. The *Second Oracle* opens with the tenth generation, and moves on to describe events connected with the Day of

[4] Geffcken, *Oracula Sibyllina*, pp. xxii–xxiv, for details.

[5] Ibid., pp. l–li; see also the lucid discussion in Schürer, *Jewish People in the Age of Jesus Christ* [2], iii. 630–1.

[6] Geffcken, *Comp. u. Ent.*, pp. 47–53; J. J. Collins, 'The Development of the Sibylline Tradition', *ANRW* ii/20. 1. 441–6 for more detailed discussion. These discussions are, however, severely hampered by an obsessive desire to isolate specific 'Christian', 'Jewish', and 'Pagan' elements in the poems and then to date them. As far as the contents of 1–8 go, I feel that it may indeed be possible to date individual passages which make overt references to historical events, but no more. Given the composite nature of these texts, I am extremely sceptical of any effort to isolate and date 'Sibylline doctrines'. The texts have passed through too many stages before they reach the form in which they appear in the present collection for us to be sure of anything: as we have them they all date from the 6th cent. or later. In this I find that I am in complete agreement with J. G. Gager's discussion of these problems in 'Some Attempts to Label the *Oracula Sibyllina*, Book 7', *HTR* 65 (1972), 96–7. For the methodological problems inherent in dealing with texts which must change their meaning in the eyes of their readers across the centuries, or be lost, see L. Koenen, 'Die Prophezeiungen des Topfers', *ZPE* 2 (1968), 178–209; id., 'The Prophecies of a Potter: A Prophecy of World Renewal Becomes an Apocalypse', in D. Samuel (ed.), *Proceedings of the Twelfth International Congress of Papyrology* (Toronto, 1970), 249–54.

Judgement. It also contains a long extract of hexameter *sententiae* of pseudo-Phocylides. The *Third Sibylline Oracle* (as it is now printed) is the longest in the collection, and is very much a composite work. It contains some Ptolemaic material and some that can be dated to the period after Actium, as well as some matter—such as an extraordinary account of the war between the gods and the Titans (ll. 105–55) and numerous prophecies against various nations—which cannot be dated with any hope of precision.[7] It concludes with a Sibylline biography that identifies the prophetess as the daughter of Noah who will be incorrectly identified as the daughter of Circe and Gnostos in the course of her prophetic wanderings. The preservation of such diverse material serves to indicate that texts with overtly Jewish content were still acceptable to Christians on the grounds that they provided Old Testament material which dated the Sibyl to deepest antiquity, and thus illustrated the truth of Christian doctrine. A great number of lines appearing in this oracle are also cited by early Christian authors, especially by Lactantius in his *Divine Institutes*, but it cannot be shown that these quotations come from a text directly connected with this one.[8]

The *Fourth*, *Fifth*, *Seventh*, and *Eighth Sibylline Oracles* are eschatological texts. The *Fourth Oracle* provides a history of the world in accordance with two quite distinct patterns: one is that of ten generations, with the world ending in the tenth, while the

[7] Geffcken, *Comp. u. Ent.*, pp. 1–17; J. J. Collins, *The Sibylline Oracles of Egyptian Judaism* (Missoula, 1974), 21–41; id., 'Development', pp. 430–6; V. Nikiprowetzky, *La Troisiéme Sibylle* (Paris, 1970) for more optimistic views. The most reasonable summary of the problems with this text appears in Schürer, *Jewish People in the Age of Jesus Christ*[2], iii. 632–9.

[8] B. Thompson, 'The Patristic Use of the Sibylline Oracles', *Review of Religion*, 16 (1952), 115–36. He points out that around 800 lines are quoted in 22 patristic writings. By far the most extensive quotations appear in Lactantius' *Divine Institutes*. For a useful list of quotations see Thompson's pp. 130–6. For an excellent treatment of the development of the Sibylline tradition in the Christian Middle Ages see B. McGinn, '*Teste David cum Sibylla*: The Significance of The Sibylline Tradition in the Middle Ages', in J. Kirshner and S. F. Wemple (eds.), *Women of the Medieval World: Essays in Honor of John H. Mundy* (Oxford, 1985), 7–35. A. Momigliano, 'Dalla Sibilla pagana alla Sibilla cristiana: Profezia come storia della religione', *ASNP* 17 (1987), 407–28, discusses the value of the Sibylline format to Christians and Jews looking for a form in which to present their apocalyptic visions, after a valuable survey of the early tradition.

other is that of four empires, with the world ending during the rule of a fifth. The two patterns are not reconciled in this text with any ease. The first four empires, those of the Assyrians, the Medes, the Persians, and the Macedonians, take up all ten generations; the Assyrians get six, the Medes two, the Persians and the Macedonians get one each. There is nothing left for the fifth kingdom, which is Rome. The eschatological pattern is further complicated when the end of the world is placed after the destruction of an allegorical Jerusalem, itself placed in the context of the return of Nero.[9] In addition to these confusions, lines 97–8 repeat two lines (with a minor variation) which are mentioned as 'oracular' in two different places by Strabo,[10] and there is no reason to believe that the text Strabo knew had a direct link with this one. The doctrinal confusion which is evident in this oracle provides a very good example of the way in which material could be transferred from one context to another by various compilers who did not have a thorough understanding of the contents. The main appeal of this oracle in its final version may well have been no more than that it contained a number of recognizable eschatological motifs. As will be seen shortly, the mere appearance of 'true' oracular inspiration, which was guaranteed by the reader's awareness that a prophet had said something similar to what appeared in the text before him, might be enough to assure the acceptance of a text as genuine.

The *Fifth Oracle* opens with a 51-line précis of world history from the end of the Pharaohs to the reign of Hadrian. The rest of the text is taken up with a long series of prophecies against various nations, the return of Nero, the coming of a saviour, and the destruction of the world.[11] The historical prologue is of some

---

[9] Geffcken, *Comp. u. Ent.*, pp. 18–21; Collins, 'Development', pp. 427–9.

[10] *Orac. Sib.* 4. 97–8 ἔσσεται ἐσσομένοις, ὅτε Πύραμος ἀργυροδίνης | ἠιόνα προχέων ἱερήν ἐς νῆσον ἵκηται. Cf. Strabo 1. 3. 7, 12. 2. 4 ὥστε ἐπ' αὐτῷ καὶ χρησμὸς ἐκπεπτωκὼς φέρεται τοιοῦτος· ἔσσεται ἐσσομένοις, ὅτε Πύραμος ἀργυροδίνης | ἠιόνα προχόων ἱερὴν ἐς Κύπρον ἵκηται.

[11] Geffcken, *Comp. u. Ent.*, pp. 25–30; Collins, *The Sibylline Oracles*, pp. 73–95; id., 'Development', pp. 436–8; Schürer, *Jewish People in the Age of Jesus Christ* [2], iii. 641–3. I am not confident that the 'consensus' that this text is Jewish and that it should be dated to c. AD 80 is correct, though I would agree that no elements in this composition can be shown to be later than that date.

interest because it is very similar to the opening of the *Twelfth Oracle*, and because it presents Rome as the successor to Alexander the Great. The opening twelve lines run as follows:[12]

Come hear my mournful history of the Latins. First after the ruined kings of Egypt, all of whom the even-handed earth took away and after the man of Pella, to whom the whole east and the wealthy west bowed down, whom Babylon tested and gave as a corpse to Philip, the man who was wrongly said to be the son of Zeus, who was wrongly said to be the son of Ammon, and after the man of the race of the blood of Assaracus, who came from Troy, who split the onslaught of fire, and after many kings and many warlike men, after the bastards, the children of the flock-destroying beast, there will be the very first king, who will give twice the number ten from his first letter, and he will be victorious for a long time in war.

The *Seventh Oracle* contains a number of prophecies of world destruction (1–28, 40–63, 96–149), suggestions on the form of prayer (76–91), a prophecy of the coming of the Messiah (29–39) and a prophecy of the baptism of Christ (64–75). It concludes with an autobiographical statement by the Sibyl (150–62).[13] The *Eighth Oracle* opens with 216 lines which predict the end of the world in the middle of the second century AD.[14] The end of line 216 is lost in a lacuna, and there is a sudden change of matter in

---

[12] *Orac. Sib.* 5. 1–3, cf. 12. 1–13, 5. 12–13 are ἔσσετ᾽ ἄναξ πρώτιστος, ὅ τις δέκα δὶς κορυφώσει | γράμματος ἀρχομένου· πολέμων δ᾽ ἐπὶ πουλὺ κρατήσει and 12. 12–13 are καὶ μετὰ τὰς ἐτέων ἑκατοντάδας ἐξ διαβῆναι | καὶ δισσὰς δεκάδας Ῥώμης δικτάτορος οὔσης. The first 11 lines are exactly parallel in the two texts. This sort of variation is typical of the extant oracles, where a number of similar passages are integrated into different contexts. See pp. 119–20, 125–32 below.

[13] Geffcken, *Comp. u. Ent.*, pp. 33–7; Collins, 'Development', pp. 449–51; Gager, 'Some Attempts to Label', pp. 91–7.

[14] Ll. 65–7 refer to Antoninus Pius, Marcus Aurelius, and Lucius Verus. Ll. 68–72 εἰς μὲν πρέσβυς ἐὼν σκήπτρων ἐπὶ πουλὺ κρατήσει, | οἰκτρότατος βασιλεύς, ὃς χρήματα κόσμου ἅπαντα | δώμασιν ἐγκλείσει τηρῶν, ἵν᾽, ὅταν γ᾽ ἐπανέλθῃ | ἐκ περάτων γαίης ὁ φυγὰς μητροκτόνος αἴθων, | ταῦτα ἅπασι διδοὺς πλοῦτον μέγαν Ἀσίδι θήσει may also refer to Marcus (as Geffcken suggests, *Comp. u. Ent.*, pp. 39–40) or, given the description of the emperor as an old man, to Antoninus Pius. Ll. 131–8 also suggest that the return to Nero which presages the end of the empire in ll. 139–59 is to fall in the reign of Pius. The fact that no emperor after Pius (or Marcus) is mentioned in this text may suggest that the prophecies in the opening section came into something like their present form during the 2nd cent.

line 217 to the exposition of Christian doctrine. Lines 217–50 provide an acrostic on the words Ἰησοῦς Χρειστὸς Θεοῦ υἱὸς σωτὴρ σταυρός which is also known from a slightly different version in Constantine's *Oratio ad sanctos* and from a Latin translation of a shorter and even more different version in Augustine's *Civitas Dei*.[15] The rest of the oracle contains a long poem on Christ (251–336), a further description of eschatological disturbances (337–58), a speech by God on the evils of idolatry (containing two echoes of the Delphic oracle's first response to Croesus: 357–428),[16] a hymn to God (429–55), and a discussion of the incarnation (456–79). It concludes with a general exhortation to ethical and ritual purity (480–500).[17] The *Sixth Oracle* is a short hymn to Christ.

The second collection (henceforth collection B) appears to

[15] *Civ. Dei* 18. 23. Augustine's text lacked the last six lines which are in *Orac. Sib.* 8 (245–50), and in two places his translation bears no relationship to the Greek texts. In his l. 22 he offers 'sic pariter fontes torrentur fluminaque igni', *Orac. Sib.* 8. 238 reads σὺν πηγαῖς, ποταμοί τε καχλάζοντες λείψουσιν; Augustine's l. 24 is 'Orbe, gemens facinus miserum variosque labores'; *Orac. Sib.* 8. 240 reads ὠρύουσα μύσος. μελέων καὶ πήματα κόσμου. The variations between Constantine's acrostic and that in the oracle are on the whole minor; see *Orac. Sib.* 8. 217 ἱδρώσει δὲ χθών – 1 ἱδρώσει γὰρ χθών; 222 σαρκοφόρων δ' ἀνδρῶν ψυχὰς – 6 σαρκοφόρων ψυχὰς δ' ἀνδρῶν; 224 ῥίψουσιν δ' – 8 ῥίψωσί τ'; 225 ἐκκαύσει – 9 ἐκκαύσῃ; 228 τῶν ἁγίων· ἀνόμους δέ – 12 τοὺς ἁγίους ἀνόμους τε; 231 θρῆνος δ' – 14 θρῆνος τ'; 237 οὐκέτι πλοῦν ἕξει. γῆ γὰρ φρυχθεῖσα τότ' ἔσται – 21 οὐκ εἰς πλοῦν ἕξει. γῆ γὰρ φρυχθεῖσα κεραυνῷ (κεραυνῷ is read by Φ and Ψ); 240 ὠρύουσα μύσος μελέων – 24 ὠρύουσα μύσος μέλλον; 242 – 26 ἥξουσιν δ' ἐπὶ βῆμα θεοῦ βασιλῆες ἅπαντες (but cf. the line cited by Lactantius at *DI* 7. 20. 3, which also reads βασιλῆος, a reading which Geffcken prints in his text to bring the oracle into line with Augustine's *reges*); 244 σφρηγὶς ἐπίσημος – 28 ἀριδείκετον, οἷον; 246 πρόσκομμα δέ – 30 πρόσκομμά τε. For a summary of the discussions of the connection between these texts see M.-L. Guillaumin, 'L'exploitation des "oracles sibyllins" par Lactance et par le "discours à l'assemblée des saints"', in J. Fontaine and M. Perrin (eds.), *Lactance et son temps* (Paris, 1978), 189–200. These discussions are on the whole vitiated by the incorrect assumption that Lactantius and Constantine had access to the present collection of the oracles in an 'earlier edition'. There is no evidence to suggest that the present collection A existed before the end of the 5th cent. It should also be noted that Constantine and Augustine thought that they were dealing with the work of the Erythraean Sibyl; there is no suggestion of this identification in *Orac. Sib.* 8. To judge from the way that Augustine described the text, these lines were not known to him as part of a longer poem.

[16] See n. 72 below on the Apollinine echoes in ll. 361 and 373.

[17] For further discussion see Geffcken, *Comp. u. Ent.*, pp. 34–46; Collins, 'Development', pp. 446–8.

have been assembled after the final Arab conquest of Egypt in 646.[18] It is in extremely fragmentary shape and sections of only seven texts (numbered 9–15) out of an original containing at least fifteen have survived. The *Ninth Oracle* contains material which is paralleled in the other collection as the *Sixth Oracle* and as lines 218–428 in the *Eighth*. The *Tenth Oracle* is parallel to the *Fourth Oracle* while the *Fifteenth Oracle*, which is found in only one manuscript, contains nine lines parallel to lines 1–9 in the *Eighth*. The *Eleventh* to *Fourteenth Oracles* contain dynastic prophecies of a very different sort from the eschatological and ethical texts in the other collection. The *Eleventh* gives an account of the history of the world to the fall of the Ptolemies, the *Twelfth* and *Thirteenth* give the history of Rome from Augustus to the victory of Odaenathus, and the *Fourteenth* appears to contain a number of dynastic oracles which were compiled to provide background for a prophecy of the Arab conquest. It is possible that the second collection represents a continuation of collection A, but the close connection between three of these texts and texts in that collation suggests that this is not the case. Although there is a great deal of repetition in the oracles, it would be very surprising indeed if so much material that was so similar appeared in separate oracles within the same collection.

Despite the presence of a great number of lines in books 1–8 that are also quoted in earlier Christian writers, there is no way to connect any one of these texts directly with any text that was cited by an earlier writer.[19] Nor is it possible to assign a date to any of the oracles in this first collection. While it is clear that they contain many individual passages which can be dated quite closely, each text as a whole represents too complex a fusion of earlier material to be assigned to any period before the final compilation of the collection in which it was included. The best that can be said is that the collection may give 'a very fair picture

[18] For the date of *Orac. Sib.* 14, showing that it is the latest oracle in the collection as it stands, see W. Scott, 'The Last Sibylline Oracle of Alexandria', *CQ* 9 (1915), 144–66, 207–28; ibid. 10 (1916), 7–16; Rzach, *RE* iiA. 2164.

[19] Parke, *Sibyls and Sibylline Prophecy*, pp. 1–4.

of Sibylline prophecy as accepted into the Christian tradition in the third and fourth centuries'.[20] This is not the case with two texts in the second collection. These are the *Twelfth* and *Thirteenth Oracles*, which can be shown to have been composed in the mid-third century and to have come into the collection virtually intact. This is because their subject-matter, the history of the Roman empire, made them valuable for their own sakes.[21]

SIBYLLINE ORACLES IN THE ROMAN EMPIRE

It is probably incorrect to speak of a 'Sibylline tradition' in antiquity. As was also the case with works attributed to the inspiration of Orpheus, the oracles attributed to Sibyls are too varied in content, and beliefs about the lives of Sibyls are too confused.[22] It is, however, possible to draw some general

23. Drachma of Erythrae depicting the Sibyl Herophile. *BMC Ionia*, 'Erythrae', 273. British Museum.

conclusions about the way that the oracles were read and about what audiences expected from oracular texts. The fact that oracular texts were encoded with a wide range of meanings by their readers, and that there was an enormous fluctuation in what an individual text could signify, accounts for the survival of the disparate passages included in the surviving collection. Audience reaction and expectation are therefore points of central importance for evaluating the information given by the oracles about historical events. But before discussing these issues, it will be

---

[20] Parke, *Sibyls and Sibylline Prophecy*, p. 4.   [21] See below, pp. 154–7.
[22] M. L. West, *The Orphic Poems* (Oxford, 1983), esp. pp. 1–38, for the problems of the Orphic tradition.

useful to review some of the developments in beliefs about Sibyls, and the texts they were believed to have produced, even though this can only be done in very general terms.

In the late fifth century BC it does appear that 'Sibylla' was the name given to a single inspired prophetess.[23] It would also appear that her words were circulated as books of prophecy and that her name was inserted in these books. This may also have been the case with books attributed to other early prophets such as Orpheus, Epimenides, Bacis, or Musaeus, and the inclusion of a name served to differentiate her utterances from those of the prophets and prophetesses at oracular shrines who spoke only as the mouthpiece of a god, and who did not include details of their lives in their responses.[24] The circulation of such collections in Greece may be traced back to at least the sixth century, the time when the activity of chresmologists, 'oracle-collectors', is first attested. The earliest story concerns Hipparchus, the son of Pisistratus, who is said to have expelled Onomacritus the chresmologue for inserting a false prophecy into his collection of the works of Musaeus to the effect that Lemnos would disappear under the sea.[25] Aside from this, all that can be said is that 'Sibylla' appears to have been less interesting to people in mainland Greece than other prophets, such as Bacis or Epimenides, until the end of the fourth century. This may well be the case because the areas that seem to be connected with her activity in the earliest period, Erythrae and Marpessus in the Troad, were in Asia Minor. Like other wandering prophets, she was not

---

[23] Rzach, *RE* iiA. 2074–5; Parke, *Sibyls and Sibylline Prophecy*, p. 23. E. Rohde, *Psyche: Seelencult und Unsterblichkeitsglaube der Griechen*⁴, ii (Tübingen, 1907), 64 n. 1, believed that it was a generic term for prophetess, but this does not conform with the usage of the word in the earliest testimonia. These are Heracleitus B 92 DK "Σίβυλλα δὲ μαινομένῳ στόματι" καθ᾽ Ἡράκλειτον ἀγέλαστα καὶ ἀκαλλώπιστα καὶ ἀμύριστα φθεγγομένη χιλίων ἐτῶν ἐξικνεῖται τῇ φωνῇ διὰ τὸν θεόν (it is not clear how much of this should be attributed to Heracleitus; see M. Marcovich, ed., *Heracleitus* (Merida, 1967), 405–6); Ar. *Eq.* 61; *Pax* 1095 οὐ γὰρ ταῦτ᾽ εἶπε Σίβυλλα, 1115–16. Rohde was correct when he pointed out that the name later came to be a generic term for an inspired prophetess, as Bacis came to be a generic name for prophets.

[24] Parke, *Sibyls and Sibylline Prophecy*, p. 9.

[25] Hdt. 7. 6. 3; Parke, *Sibyls and Sibylline Prophecy*, pp. 9, 184–9; West, *The Orphic Poems*, p. 40.

associated with a specific shrine and was thought to produce her oracles because she had some sort of special divine knowledge. The form of her prophecies may have been much like that of the surviving books: a series of conditional and final clauses saying that 'when certain conditions obtain, something will happen'. It does not seem to be the case that her books had any unity other than that they were supposed to contain the utterances of a single prophetess.

It is impossible to know how this form of prophetic behaviour developed. It has been argued that the Sibylline tradition developed because there was in fact a famous prophetess of that name who was a representative of an indigenous tradition in the Troad.[26] This may be true (it is impossible to prove), but it does not explain the currency of the style of prophecy with which the Sibyl is associated. She was just one of a number of mythical and semi-mythical characters to whom such books were attributed. The format, a long collection of prophecies uttered by a single prophet, has obvious earlier parallels in Palestine, Mesopotamia, and the wisdom literature of Egypt.[27] Therefore the most likely explanation for the spread of this form of presentation in archaic Greece is that it was borrowed from the east. What does not seem to be paralleled—though it must be emphasized that many of the surviving texts from Mesopotamia are broken in such a way that it is not possible to know who the prophet was—is the association of a woman with this sort of book. But this is not a serious problem. Both men and women had an important role as prophets in the Greek world, and even if the form was 'borrowed' from another culture, it is entirely to be expected that it would be interpreted within the spectrum of Greek activity. Hence, both men and women could be imagined as producing such books.

The number of Sibyls proliferated in the wake of Alexander's

---

[26] Parke, *Sibyls and Sibylline Prophecy*, pp. 51–67.

[27] For another view, discounting the impact of eastern prophecy on the grounds that women are not found as prophets of the 'Sibylline' sort in eastern texts, see Parke, *Sibyls and Sibylline Prophecy*, pp. 216–20.

conquest of the east. According to Varro, who composed a list of them for his work on the *Antiquities of Human and Divine Matters*, there were ten of them: the Babylonian, the Libyan, the Delphic, the Cimmerian, the Erythraean, the Samian, the Cumaean, the Hellespontine, the Phrygian, and the Tiburtine.[28] The Libyan Sibyl may be a creation of Varro, or an earlier scholar, based on Euripides' *Busiris*.[29] The Babylonian Sibyl was reported by Nicanor, the author of a history of Alexander (and possibly a member of his staff),[30] the Delphic Sibyl was discussed by Chrysippus in his work on divination, and the Cimmerian was the invention of Naevius. The Erythraean appeared in the work of Apollodorus of Erythrae, the Samian was uncovered by Eratosthenes, and the Hellespontine was discussed by Heracleides Ponticus. Heracleides is known from other sources to have mentioned the Phrygian Sibyl, and he may be the source for

---

[28] Lact. *DI* 1. 6. 8–12 'primam fuisse de Persis, cuius mentionem fecerit Nicanor, qui res gestas Alexandri Macedonis scripsit; secundam Libyssam, cuius meminerit Euripides in Lamiae prologo; tertiam Delphida, de qua Chrysippus loquatur in eo libro quem de divinatione conposuit; quartam Cimmeriam in Italia, quam Naevius in libris belli Punici, Piso in annalibus nominet; quintam Erythraeam, quam Apollodorus Erythraeus adfirmet suam fuisse civem eamque Grais Ilium petentibus vaticinatam et perituram esse Troiam et Homerum mendacia scripturum; sextam Samiam, de qua scribat Eratosthenes in antiquis annalibus Samiorum repperisse se scriptum; septimam Cumanam nomine Amaltheam, quae ab aliis Herophile vel Demophile nominetur . . . [*the story of her meeting with Tarquin*] . . . quorum postea numerus sit auctus, Capitolio refecto, quod ex omnibus civitatibus et Italicis et Graecis praecipueque Erythraeis coacti adlatique sunt Romam cuiuscumque Sibyllae nomine fuerunt; octavam Hellespontiam in agro Troiano natam, vico Marpesso circa oppidum Gergithium, quam scribat Heraclides Ponticus Solonis et Cyri fuisse temporibus; nonam Phrygiam quae vaticinata sit Ancyrae; decimam Tiburtem nomine Albuncam, quae Tiburi colatur ut dea iuxta ripas amnis Aniensis, cuius in gurgite simulacrum eius inventum esse dicitur tenens in manu librum.'

[29] Parke, *Sibyls and Sibylline Prophecy*, pp. 37–8; see Rzach, *RE* iiA. 2096.

[30] *FGrH* 146. It is tempting to identify this man with one of the Nicanors on Alexander's staff. Reports of prophecies by a Babylonian prophet would fit best into the work of a contemporary who would have been interested, and only a contemporary is likely to have picked up material of this sort for a history of Alexander the Great that others missed. The most attractive candidate of the nine Nicanors listed by Berve (*Das Alexanderreich auf prosopographischer Grundlage* (Munich, 1926), Nos. 553–61) is Nicanor of Stagira, nephew of Aristotle, who carried the Exiles' Decree to Olympia. It is not absurd to suspect such a man of literary pretensions, nor, given Callisthenes' record of oracles and transmission of information about the east to Aristotle (*FGrH* 124 T 3), that he would be interested in such things.

Varro's knowledge of her as well. Varro does not give a source for information on the Cumaean Sibyl (who was too well known in Rome to require such annotation) but he does tell the story of her dealings with Tarquin; nor does he name his source for the Tiburtine Sibyl, presumably because she was also too well known. This list, which is representative rather than complete,[31] may reflect the growth of the doxographic tradition in the Hellenistic world.

A somewhat different picture of Sibylline texts is provided by Pausanias. The variation is the result of a difference in perspective: Varro seems to have derived his knowledge of Sibyls from the works of other learned men while Pausanias derived his from personal reading of the texts and visits to the homes of famous Sibyls. Pausanias sets forth most of his knowledge about Sibyls in a digression artfully placed at the point during his tour of Delphi where he saw the rock upon which the Sibyl was supposed to have sung her prophecies.[32] He says that the Sibyl who sang there was named Herophile. She was younger than the 'earlier Sibyl' who had been the daughter of Zeus and of Lamia, the daughter of Poseidon, and who had been given the name 'Sibylla' by the Libyans. Despite this, Herophile was still born before the Trojan War: she had foretold the birth of Helen at Sparta and the ruin that the daughter of Leda would bring to Europe and Asia. She was the same woman whom the Delians remembered as the author of a poem to Apollo. It also seemed to have been the case that she suffered from divine possession and insanity while she spoke: at times she would say that she was Artemis and the wedded wife of Apollo, at others she would say simply that she was her sister or daughter.[33] In another

---

[31] Other Sibyls mentioned in various texts include the Clarian (Rzach, *RE* iiA. 2087), the Sardian, the Rhodian (Rzach, col. 2089), the Thessalian, the Thesprotian (Rzach, cols. 2090–1), the Italian, the Sicilian, the Hebrew (Rzach, cols. 2095–7), and the Egyptian (Rzach, col. 2102).

[32] For the location see P. Amandry, *La Mantique apollinienne à Delphes: Essai sur le fonctionnement de l'oracle* (Paris, 1950), 203.

[33] Paus. 10. 12. 2–3 καλεῖ δὲ οὐχ Ἡροφίλην μόνον ἀλλὰ καὶ Ἄρτεμιν ἐν τοῖς ἔπεσιν αὐτήν, καὶ Ἀπόλλωνος γυνὴ γαμετή, τοτὲ δὲ ἀδελφὴ καὶ αὖθις θυγάτηρ φησὶν εἶναι. ταῦτα μὲν δὴ μαινομένη τε καὶ ἐκ τοῦ θεοῦ κάτοχος πεποίηκεν· ἑτέρωθι δὲ εἶπε τῶν χρησμῶν ὡς μητρὸς μὲν ἀθανάτης εἴη μιᾶς τῶν ἐν Ἴδῃ νυμφῶν, πατρὸς δὲ ἀνθρώπου . . .

place in her 'oracles' she said that she was the daughter of a mortal and a nymph on Ida.

In his account of Herophile, Pausanias is clearly conflating a number of accounts he discovered in oracles which had been attributed to her because of the autobiographical accounts they contained. He reconciled them by assuming that she was possessed and therefore not to be held responsible for any inconsistency. The story Pausanias decided was true made her the daughter of a nymph and placed her birth at Marpessus in the Troad. He had even been to visit the place and seen her tomb in the Sminthian grove near Alexandria Troas. He seems to have been impressed not only by the tomb, but also by the fact that the inhabitants of Alexandria were able to tell him that she had been an attendant at the temple when she gave 'that prophecy which we know to be true' on the occasion of Hecuba's dream.[34] He goes on to say that she spent a great deal of her life on Samos, but that she also visited Delphi and Delos. He was so convinced by the people at Alexandria that he said that the people of Erythrae, who also claimed her as their citizen, were frauds.[35]

The next Sibyl whom he mentions is Demo, the Sibyl of Cumae. He also says that when he visited Cumae he had not been impressed. All that the people there could show him was a small stone urn in which her bones had been placed. They could not even quote any of her verses.[36] He also knew of a later Sibyl named Sabbe, who was the daughter of Berosus and Erymanthe. He asserts that she lived with the 'Jews around Palestine' but that others called her Babylonian and still others called her Egyptian. He also knew of women who had given prophecies but were not called Sibyls.

---

[34] Ibid. 10. 12. 5 τὴν δὲ Ἡροφίλην οἱ ἐν τῇ Ἀλεξανδρείᾳ ταύτῃ νεωκόρον τε τοῦ Ἀπόλλωνος γενέσθαι τοῦ Σμινθέως καὶ ἐπὶ τῷ ὀνείρατι τῷ Ἑκάβης χρῆσαί φασιν αὐτὴν ἃ δὴ ἐπιτελεσθέντα ἴσμεν.

[35] C. Habicht, 'Pausanias and the Evidence of Inscriptions', *Classical Antiquity*, 3 (1984), 41–3.

[36] Paus. 10. 12. 8 χρησμὸν δὲ οἱ Κυμαῖοι τῆς γυναικὸς ταύτης οὐδένα εἶχον ἐπιδείξασθαι, λίθου δὲ ὑδρίαν ἐν Ἀπόλλωνος ἱερῷ δεικνύουσιν οὐ μεγάλην, τῆς Σιβύλλης ἐνταῦθα κεῖσθαι φάμενοι τὰ ὀστᾶ . . .

Pausanias' account is of particular interest because it shows how a pious, somewhat traditional, thinking man would react to the information about Sibyls in the oracles that he had read and at the sites that he had visited.[37] He also places these Sibyls very firmly in a local context and suggests something of the rivalry between cities that laid claim to a particularly famous Sibyl as a fellow citizen. In fact, two of the places he mentions were soon to improve the evidence for their Sibylline connections. By 161, when Lucius Verus arrived at Erythrae, he found a newly con-structed shrine to the local Sibyl, complete with a fountain and statues, one of them inscribed with a long poem giving the details of the Sibyl's life.[38] At Cumae, at about the same time, the Sibyl's bones were moved to a large bronze *phakos* and the cave where she gave her prophecies was shown to tourists. This seems to have impressed the author of the *Cohortatio ad Graecos*, who visited the spot in the third century.[39]

The evidence of Pausanias is especially important because it places the Sibyls in their proper context within the Roman world. In Pausanias, as in the works of his contemporary Lucian, we can see that she was a respected prophetess. Lucian suggests through his parodies that Sibylline verses were quoted, as were those of Bacis, to lend an air of authority to contemporary events. It seems to have been important to people that the coming of Alexander of Abonuteichos had been predicted by a Sibyl and that the Sibyl would speak on the subject of Peregrinus' self-immolation.[40] Pausanias suggests that Sibyls were venerated for their powers

[37] C. Habicht, *Pausanias' Guide to Ancient Greece* (Berkeley, 1985), 141–64.

[38] Lucius Verus is the 'New Erythros' in *Insc. Eryth. u. Klaz.* 224. 16. See S. Reinach, 'Le sanctuaire de la Sibylle d'Erythrée', *RÉG* 4 (1891), 276–86; K. Buresch, 'Die sibyllinische Quellengrotte in Erythrae', *Ath. Mitt.* 17 (1892), 16–36; P. Corssen, 'Die erythraeische Sibylle', *Ath. Mitt.* 38 (1913), 1–22. The site of the grotto, which was reported on the north-west side of the acropolis of Erythrae, could not be located when I visited it in 1981. The scene is illustrated on *BMC Ionia*, 'Erythrae', Nos. 272–3; F. Imhoof-Blümer, *Griechische Münzen* (Munich, 1890), Nos. 294–5, pl. VIII, Nos. 26–7; R. Herbig, 'Θεὰ Σίβυλλα', *Jahr. d. Deut. Arch. Inst.* 59 (1944), 144–5; for another representation see Fig. 23.

[39] *Coh. ad Graecos*, 37; Parke, *Sibyls and Sibylline Prophecy*, pp. 40–1, 84–5, for discussion of this passage and the site.

[40] Luc. *Alex.* 11; *Per.* 29, 30.

and that they were cherished members of the civic community. They were people about whom civic dignitaries cared deeply and in honour of whom they spent money. Pausanias also places the composition of Sibylline verse in its proper milieu: among the educated classes of the Greek east, among the people who thought that she increased the dignity of their city and who would have the education to compose in verse. These verses are not always eloquent (some are awful), but they do represent the sort of versification that an average educated man could produce.

Varro does not discuss (there is no reason why he should) and Pausanias only briefly alludes to the appropriation of the Sibyl as a prophet by other peoples (most notably by the Jews of Alexandria) in their efforts to claim intellectual respectability in a Greek context.[41] This process may be compared to the similar appropriation of other wise men of the classical past.[42] It is also the case that this proliferation might not have been a significant development if it were not for the existence of the *libri Sibyllini* at Rome. An effort to replace the collection after it was destroyed in 83 BC certainly caused great interest in the Greek east, and the well-advertised connection between Sibyls and the greatness of Rome may well have made her words more interesting than those of other prophets throughout the Mediterranean world. It may also help to explain why Jewish Sibylline verses which echoed Old Testament prophecy were popular among Christian apologists. In the works of these apologists the Sibyl was elevated to the position of the greatest prophetess of antiquity.

THE *LIBRI SIBYLLINI* AT ROME

The collection of Sibylline oracles at Rome appears to have been very early. It seems to have consisted of a series of predictions concerning prodigies and other events, and was consulted

---

[41] The adoption of the Sibyl into the Jewish and general Near Eastern context has been discussed at great length. For a useful summary see V. Nikiprowetzky, 'La Sibylle juive et le "Troisième Livre" des "Pseudo-Oracles Sibyllins" depuis Charles Alexandre', *ANRW* ii/ 20. 466–75, 478–528; Schürer, *Jewish People in the Age of Jesus Christ* ², iii. 617–700.

[42] West, *The Orphic Poems*, pp. 33–5, for the case of Musaeus and Orpheus.

24. Sestertius of L. Torquatus depicting
a Sibyl (65 BC). *RRC* 411. Ashmolean.

at times when the natural order was disturbed or when advice
was required about a great event. These two features of the collection are best illustrated by records of Sibylline consultations
in Livy's third, fourth, and fifth decades, for here, as at no other
period in the history of the Republic, consultation of the books
is set firmly in the context of other events. Thus, at the end of
the consular year 218/7 BC Livy records that there were a number of prodigies which he says caused great excitement and that
the rites which the Sibylline books ordained greatly eased popular concern.[43] They were consulted again when a great number
of prodigies were reported at the beginning of the next year,[44]
and there was another consultation after Cannae in 216 BC. This
was the result of the seduction of two Vestal Virgins in that
year, though under these circumstances it seems to have been
felt that the Sibyl might not be the only guide. Fabius Pictor
was sent to Delphi to inquire which rites should be observed
and whether there would ever be an end to the disasters.[45]
There seem to have been two points involved: one, to ask a god
if the rites in the Sibylline books were sufficient, the other, to
seek an answer to the question that could not be answered in
those books: Would Rome survive?

Two other responses recorded in these years show that the
contents of the books were not restricted to natural disasters. One

---

[43] Livy 21. 62. 11 'haec procurata votaque ex libris Sibyllinis magna ex parte levaverant
religione animos'.

[44] Ibid. 22. 1.

[45] Ibid. 22. 57. 4–5 'hoc nefas cum inter tot, ut fit, clades in prodigium versum esset,
decemviri libros adire iussi sunt et Q. Fabius Pictor Delphos ad oraculum missus est scisci-
tatum quibus precibus suppliciisque deos possent placare et quaenam futura finis tantis
cladibus foret.'

is a response recorded in 205 BC. Livy says that a sudden outbreak of religious emotion swept Rome when the occurrence of frequent hailstorms caused the Sibylline books to be inspected. A prophecy was discovered to the effect that whenever a foreign enemy invaded Italy it would be possible to defeat him and drive him off if the 'Idaean mother' was brought from Pessinus to Italy. Livy goes on to suggest that this was taken particularly seriously because envoys who had been sent to Delphi after the battle of the Metaurus had returned with an oracle of Apollo which promised an even greater victory than they had already won over the Carthaginians. All this may seem too good to be true, and it would be possible to reconstruct a number of scenarios to explain the fabrication of this Sibylline response—but this would obscure the point that such responses could have been found in the collection before 205 (even if this one does happen to be a forgery).[46] There was no point in fabricating an oracle whose format would have been completely eccentric in the context of the collection. Another response of this sort was reported in 187 BC, which prevented Manlius Vulso from crossing the Taurus to renew the war with Antiochus.[47] The oracle of 187 is not unlike the one produced at the insistence of C. Cato in 56 BC, which forbade the restoration of the king of Egypt 'with a multitude'.[48]

---

[46] Ibid. 29. 10. 4–6 'civitatem eo tempore repens religio invaserat invento carmine in libris Sibyllinis propter crebrius eo anno de caelo lapidatum inspectis, quandoque hostis alienigena terrae Italiae bellum intulisset eum pelli Italia vincique posse si mater Idaea a Pessinunte Romam advecta foret. Id carmen ab decemviris inventum eo magis patres movit quod et legati qui donum Delphos portaverant referebant et sacrificantibus ipsis Pythio Apolloni omnia laeta fuisse et responsum oraculo editum maiorem multo victoriam quam cuius ex spoliis dona portarent adesse populo Romano.' It is hard to imagine that this oracle had remained unnoticed in the collection up to this point. Parke's objection to this passage (*Sibyls and Sibylline Prophecy*, p. 202), that it is difficult to believe that there would have been a mention of Pessinus in oracles of the 6th cent., is vitiated, I think, by the fact that there is evidence that the senate occasionally ordered the inspection of books of prophecy which were in general circulation. Ordinarily the result may have been to take books available to the general public, such as the *carmina Marciana*, out of circulation (Livy 25. 12), but it may also have resulted in the addition of new books to the collection. See below, pp. 113–14; I suspect that this discovery was connected with Scipio's campaign in Africa.

[47] Livy 38. 45. 3 'cupientem transire Taurum aegre omnium legatorum precibus, ne carminibus Sibyllae praedictam superantibus terminos fatalis cladem experiri vellet'.

[48] Parke, *Sibyls and Sibylline Prophecy*, pp. 207–8, for details.

The oracles themselves were consulted by a board of priests who acted on the orders of the Senate. In the earliest period this was a board of two patricians, in 348 BC it was expanded to a board of ten (five patricians and five plebians), and in the first century the college was expanded to fifteen.[49] Membership of this board, the *quindecimviri sacris faciundis*, was one of the most cherished positions in the state and access to the books was tightly controlled. C. Cato's manœuvre to force the *quindecimviri* to reveal the contents of the oracle which forbade the restoration of the king of Egypt appears to have been without parallel in the political annals of the late Republic.

The three books of Sibylline oracles that were allegedly purchased in the regal period do not seem to have been the only oracles in the collection by the end of the third century. The text advising the state to acquire the Magna Mater from Pessinus certainly seems to have been a later addition, as does the oracle that forbade Vulso's intended prosecution of the war against Antiochus. But texts with overt political implications were not the only ones which seem to have been added: the response which Phlegon of Tralles preserved in his *Concerning Marvellous Events* relating to the birth of an androgynous child is another case in point.[50] It is an acrostic, a style which does not seem to have appeared in Greek poetry before the end of the fourth century. It is therefore clear that this text could not have come into the collection until much after the regal period.[51] In fact, the Roman state is known to have taken cognizance of unofficial texts, such as the *carmina Marciana* (which predicted the disaster at Cannae), to have ordered an investigation of their contents, and to have declared that they were forgeries. But this process could work both ways and it is not necessary to believe that every book investigated was declared a forgery. The most famous example of the state's admission that it did not have all authentic

---

[49] Rzach, *RE* iiA. 2106–7.   [50] *FGrH* 257 F 36X.

[51] Vogt, 'Das Akrostichon in der griechischen Literatur', *Antike und Abendland*, 13 (1967), 90–1, though he also notes that *Il.* 24. 1–5 is an acrostic (p. 82); Parke, *Sibyls and Sibylline Prophecy*, pp. 138–9.

texts comes in 76 BC, when the Senate decided to replace the collection of Sibylline oracles which had been destroyed in the fire that had burnt the temple of Capitoline Jupiter in 83 BC. In order to accomplish this task it appointed a board of *triumviri*, presumably selected from among the *quindecimviri*, to assemble the new corpus. This shows that the Senate was willing to admit that there were authentic oracles not in its possession. It would be unreasonable to assume that the state had not been aware of that fact at an earlier date.

The business of authenticating the oracles then appears to have been given to the board of *quindecimviri* as a whole. In the first century the first test of legitimacy seems to have been the presence of acrostics in the texts, but there may have been others as well: it is hard to believe that the board would admit a prophecy that Rome would be destroyed just because it contained an acrostic. The board then reported their findings to the Senate.[52] Another investigation of oracular texts was carried out by Augustus, though here the circumstances are obscure,[53] and Tacitus presents a case where a new book was added to the collection in AD 32. He reports that the tribune Quintilianus complained in the Senate when the *quindecimvir* Caninius Gallus had wrongfully caused this book to be included among the Sibylline oracles, and that the Senate wrote to Tiberius asking his advice as to the way it should handle the situation. Tiberius responded, 'moderately criticizing the tribune on the grounds that he was ignorant of ancient custom because of his youth. He rebuked Gallus because he, a man experienced in religious lore and ceremonies, had brought the matter before a badly attended meeting of the Senate, on dubious authority, without the

52 Dion. Hal. 4. 62 — Carduans F 60 οἱ δὲ νῦν ὄντες ἐκ πολλῶν εἰσι συμφορητοὶ τόπων, οἱ μὲν ἐκ τῶν ἐν Ἰταλίᾳ πόλεων κομισθέντες, οἱ δ' ἐξ Ἐρυθρῶν, τῶν ἐν Ἀσίᾳ, κατὰ δόγμα βουλῆς τριῶν ἀποσταλέντων πρεσβευτῶν ἐπὶ τὴν ἀντιγραφήν. οἱ δ' ἐξ ἄλλων πόλεων καὶ παρ' ἀνδρῶν ἰδιωτῶν μεταγραφέντες· ἐν οἷς εὑρίσκονταί τινες ἐμπεποιημένοι τοῖς Σιβυλλείοις, ἐλέγχονται δὲ ταῖς καλουμέναις ἀκροστιχίσι . . .; Tac. Ann. 6. 12. 3 'datoque sacerdotibus negotio, quantum humana ope potuissent, vera discernere'. See also Cic. De div. 2. 111–12 for another assertion of the principle that true Sibylline oracles contained acrostics.
53 Parke, *Sibyls and Sibylline Prophecy*, pp. 209–10.

approval of the college, and not, as was customary, after the oracle had been read and evaluated by the magistrates.'[54] It is clear that Tiberius believed that it was ancient custom for the *quindecimviri* to investigate such matters and to approve new books. There is no reason to believe that he was wrong.

There is no detailed description of the way in which the *quindecimviri* consulted the oracles, but the text preserved by Phlegon does suggest that the process was not completely random. It specifically states that the rites it commands are to be observed in the event of an androgynous child.[55] It is therefore likely that when the Senate ordered them to investigate the books the *quindecimviri* simply went to them, looked for an appropriate case, and, when they had found it, reported back to the Senate. The fact that consultations for similar prodigies often took place and that the rites were not always the same may further suggest that there were a number of responses for the more common sorts of prodigy (hailstorms, lightning strikes, earthquakes, and the like) and that the *quindecimviri* would be able to look for a rite that had not been used recently. It was presumably in the course of searching through the books for appropriate ways to expiate a prodigy that responses such as that about the Magna Mater could be discovered. In this way the *libri Sybillini* offered an ideal tool for the manipulation of the state religion.

READING SIBYLLINE ORACLES

It has already been seen that oracles could be put to a number of uses in antiquity. For modern scholars they are also an invaluable source of information on Roman imperial history, since they can reveal the sort of things that people knew and believed about the political life of their times. But in order to

[54] Tac. *Ann.* 6. 12. 1–2 'quo per discessionem facto misit litteras Caesar, modice tribunum increpans ignarum antiqui moris ob iuventam. Gallo exprobrabat, quod scientiae caerimoniarumque vetus incerto auctore ante sententiam collegii, non, ut adsolet, lecto per magistros aestimatoque carmine, apud infrequentem senatum egisset.'

[55] *FGrH* 257 F 36x. A. 4–6 καί τοι ποτέ φημι γυναῖκα | ἀνδρόγυνον τέξεσθαι ἐχοντά περ ἄρσενα πάντα | νηπίαχαί θ' ὅσα θηλύτεραι φαίνουσι γυναῖκες.

evaluate this information it is necessary to look a bit further into the question of their readership. It is necessary to gain some impression of the way in which their readers would interpret the information that they provided. The first question that must be addressed, therefore, is that of audience expectation and response. What did the average reader of an oracle know and expect to learn, and under what circumstances would readers believe what they read? People were conscious of the existence of frauds everywhere, and were aware that the texts were not always copied faithfully. Hesychius and the author of the *Cohortatio ad graecos* remarked that the poor quality of verse in oracular texts was the result of poor copyists (evidently they felt that the divinity ought to have been able to inspire verse which scanned properly).[56] The scope of the problem may be further illustrated by Augustine's apparent explanation of the differences between two Sibylline acrostics as being the fault of the bad translation of one of them.[57] It is interesting, in fact, that when he had two different texts which purported to be the same he thought that the explanation for this was incompetence, not fraud.[58]

The current collections of Sibylline oracles and remarks about Sibylline prophecies in various authors reveal that there was not much consistency in the way the Sibyls were thought to have been inspired in the imperial period. The growth of interest in Sibyls after Alexander had also led to great variation in the way that they were believed to have acted and the way they were thought to have prophesied. Aside from the fact that all the Sibyls are women who remained virgins and that those who give some

---

[56] *Cohort. ad Graecos*, 37; Hesych. s.v. Σίβυλλα . . . εἰ δὲ οἱ στίχοι αὐτῆς ἀτελεῖς εὑρίσκονται καὶ ἄμετροι, οὐκ αὐτῆς ἡ αἰτία, ἀλλὰ τῶν ταχυγράφων, ἀσυμφθασάντων τῇ ῥύμῃ τοῦ λόγου. For complaint about the generally poor quality of oracular verse see Plut. *De Pyth. or.* 397 c.

[57] Aug. *Civ. Dei*, 18. 23 'haec sane Erythraea Sibylla quaedam de Christo manifesta conscripsit; quod etiam nos prius in Latina lingua versibus male Latinis et non stantibus legimus per nescio cuius interpretis imperitiam, sicut post cognovimus. nam vir clarissimus Flavianus, qui etiam proconsul fuit, homo facillimae facundiae multaeque doctrinae, cum de Christo conloqueremur, Graecum nobis codicem protulit, carmen esse dicens Sibyllae Erythraeae . . .'

[58] For the problem of this acrostic see above, p. 100 n. 15.

indication of their life-span were of preternatural longevity (1,000 years or so),[59] there is no consistency in the way that they were pictured as behaving. Some, as at Delphi or Erythrae, sat on rocks,[60] others, as at Cumae, inhabited caves.[61] At other times they could simply appear from the air—the Sibyl's appearance to Aeneas in Tibullus' poem for Messala's augurate being a case in point.[62] The Erythraean Sibyl, whose words are diversely repeated by Plutarch and Phlegon, claimed that after her death her sayings would be heard blowing in the wind. Plutarch had a text which went on to add the detail that her face would appear in the moon.[63] Some Sibyls seem to have been stationary: Albunaea

---

[59] *Insc. Eryth. u. Klaz.* 224. 9 τρὶς δὲ τριηκοσίοισιν ἐ|γὼ ζώουσ᾽ ἐνιαυτοῖς . . . ; *FGrH* 257 F 37v. 2 Σίβυλλα ἡ Ἐρυθραία ἐβίωσεν ἔτη ὀλίγον ἀποδέοντα τῶν χιλίων . . . ; Stat. *Silv.* 4. 3. 114–18 'sed quam fine viae recentis imo, | qua monstrat veteres Apollo Cumas, | albam crinibus infulisque cerno! | visu fallimur? an sacris ab antris | profert Chalcidicas Sibylla laurus?'; Ov. *Met.* 14. 143–6 'tremuloque gradu venit aegra senectus, | quae patienda diu est; nam iam mihi saecula septem | acta vides superest, numeros ut pulveris aequem, | ter centum messes, ter centum musta videre'. It should, however, be noted that extreme old age may not have been a hard and fast rule. The Sibyls who appear on mid-1st-cent. Republican coins appear to be young women: M. Crawford, *Roman Republican Coinage* (Cambridge, 1974), Nos. 411. 1 (L. Torquatus, 65 BC; he was a *quindecimvir*—see *MRR* suppl., p. 136, pl. 1); 464. 1 (T. Carisius, 46 BC); 474. 3*a–b* (L. Valerius Acisculus); and Potter, 'Sibyls in the Greek and Roman World', *JRA* 3 (1990) 480; see Fig. 24. For virginity see *Orac. Sib.* 7. 153, Ov. *Met.* 14. 142, *Insc. Eryth. u. Klaz.* 224. 10, etc.

[60] For Delphi see Plut. *De Pyth. orac.* 398 C ἐπειδὴ γὰρ ἔστημεν κατὰ τὴν πέτραν γενόμενοι τὴν κατὰ τὸ βουλευτήριον, ἐφ᾽ ἧς λέγεται καθίζεσθαι τὴν πρώτην Σίβυλλαν ἐκ τοῦ Ἑλικῶνος παραγενομένη ὑπὸ τῶν Μουσῶν τραφεῖσαν (ἔνιοι δέ φασιν ἐκ Μαλιέων ἀφικέσθαι Λαμίας οὖσαν θυγατέρα τῆς Ποσειδῶνος); Paus. 10. 12. 1 πέτρα δέ ἐστιν ἀνίσχουσα ὑπὲρ τῆς γῆς· ἐπὶ ταύτῃ Δελφοὶ στᾶσαι φασιν ᾆσαι τοὺς χρησμοὺς γυναῖκα ὄνομα Ἡροφίλην, Σίβυλλαν δὲ ἐπίκλησιν . . . ; for the location of the stone see Amandry, *La Mantique apollinienne*, pp. 203–4; for Erythrae, *Insc. Eryth. u. Klaz.* 224. 11–12 αὖθις δ᾽ ἐνθάδ᾽ ἔγωγε φίλη πὰρ τῇδέ γε πέτρηι | ἧμαι καὶ νῦν ἀγνοῖς ὕδα|σι τερπομένη; the scene is illustrated on *BMC Ionia*, 'Erythrae', Nos. 272–3 (and Fig. 23 in the present volume); Imhoof-Blümer, *Griechische Münzen*, Nos. 294–5, pl. VIII. 26–7; Herbig, 'Θεὰ Σίβυλλα', pp. 144–5; P. J. Alexander, *The Oracle of Baalbek* (Washington, 1967), pl. v.

[61] [Arist.] *De mirac. ausc.* 838ᵃ5–10.

[62] Tib. 2. 5. 19–21 'haec dedit Aeneae sortes, postquam ille parentem | dicitur et raptos sustinuisse Lares | nec fore credebat Romam, cum maestus ab alto | Ilion ardentes respiceretque deos'. An epiphany on Aeneas' ship seems to be envisaged here, as shown by F. Cairns, *Tibullus: A Hellenistic Poet at Rome* (Cambridge, 1979), 75–6.

[63] *FGrH* 257 F 37v. 2. 11–13 ἔνθ᾽ ἄρα μοι ψυχὴ μὲν ἐς ἠέρα πωτηθεῖσα, | πνεύματι συγκραθεῖσα βροτῶν εἰς οὔατα πέμψει | κληδόνας ἐν πυκινοῖς αἰνίγμασι συμπλεχθεῖσας . . . ; Plut. *De Pyth. orac.* 398 C–D ὁ μὲν Σαραπίων

at Tibur and the Cumaean (when she was not being identified with the Erythraean) are perhaps the most famous of these.[64] Others, such as the ubiquitous Herophile or those in the present *Third* and *Seventh Sibylline Oracles*, could wander the earth.[65] It was also possible that a new Sibyl could appear at any time. Callisthenes reported an inspired woman at Erythrae in 331 who recalled the ancient Sibyl,[66] and a Nicanor seems to have placed a Babylonian Sibyl in the context of Alexander's conquest of the east.[67] Pausanias hoped that new prophets like those of the past might some day reappear on the earth.[68]

Under these circumstances, how could someone detect a fake? What, aside from good faith, could lead someone to believe that a book of prophecy was authentic; what, aside from the title inscribed on the scroll, was specifically Sibylline about texts identified as such? Constantine said that the Sibylline texts he cited must be authentic because they were morally improving;[69]

ἐμνήσθη τῶν ἐπῶν, ἐν οἷς ὕμνησεν ἑαυτήν, ὡς οὐδ᾽ ἀποθανοῦσα λήξει μαντικῆς, ἀλλ᾽ αὐτὴ μὲν ἐν τῇ σελήνῃ περίεισι τὸ καλούμενον φαινόμενον γενομένη πρόσωπον, τῷ δ᾽ ἀέρι τὸ πνεῦμα συγκραθὲν ἐν φήμαις ἀεὶ φορήσεται καὶ κληδόσιν. The notion that the voice of a Sibyl could be heard in the 2nd cent. AD is also illustrated in Lucian's work on the death of Peregrinus, where Theagenes says that he heard the lines he uttered on the passing of the sage from the Sibyl: Luc. *Per.* 30 ταῦτα μὲν Θεαγένης Σιβύλλης ἀκηκοέναι φησίν.

[64] On their habits see Rzach, *RE* iiA. 2091–6.

[65] For Herophile: Rzach, ibid. 2081–7; *Orac. Sib.* 3. 809–11 ταῦτά σοι Ἀσσυρίης Βαβυλώνια τείχεα μακρά, | οἰστρομανὴς προλιποῦσα, ἐς Ἑλλάδα πεμπόμενον πῦρ | πᾶσι προφητεύουσα θεοῦ μηνίματα θνητοῖς (it is possible that lines similar to these were known to Ammianus, who wrote (21. 1. 11) 'unde Sibyllae crebro se dicunt ardero torrente vi magna flammarum'); 7. 153–4 μυρία μέν μοι λέκτρα, γάμος δ᾽ οὐδεὶς ἐμελήθη· | πᾶσι δ᾽ ἐγὼ πανάπιστος ἐπήγαγον ἄγριον ὅρκον.

[66] *FGrH* 124 F 14 περὶ δὲ τῆς εὐγενείας καὶ τὴν Ἐρυθραίαν Ἀθηναΐδα φησὶν ἀνειπεῖν· καὶ γὰρ ταύτην ὁμοίαν γενέσθαι τῇ παλαιᾷ Σιβύλλῃ τῇ Ἐρυθραίᾳ.

[67] See n. 30 above.

[68] Paus. 10. 12. 11 τοσαῦται μὲν ἄχρι ἐμοῦ λέγονται γυναῖκες καὶ ἄνδρες ἐκ θεοῦ μαντεύσασθαι· ἐν δὲ τῷ χρόνῳ τῷ πολλῷ καὶ αὖθις γένοιτο ἂν ἕτερα τοιαῦτα.

[69] *Orat. ad sanctos*, 19. 1 ἀλλ᾽ οἱ πολλοὶ τῶν ἀνθρώπων, ἀπιστοῦσιν, καὶ ταῦτα ὁμολογοῦντες Ἐρυθραίαν γεγενῆσθαι Σίβυλλαν μάντιν, ὑποπτεύουσι δέ τινα τῶν τῆς ἡμετέρας θρησκείας, ποιητικῆς μούσης οὐκ ἄμοιραν τὰ ἔπη ταῦτα πεποιηκέναι νοθεύεσθαί τε αὐτὰ καὶ Σιβύλλης θεσπίσματα εἶναι λέγεσθαι, ἔχοντα βιωφελεῖς γνώμας, τὴν πολλὴν τῶν ἡδονῶν περικοπτούσας ἐξουσίαν καὶ ἐπὶ τὸν σώφρονά τε καὶ κόσμιον βίον ὁδηγούσας.

Varro thought that a specific form of composition, the use of acrostics, was a useful guide, but the question cannot be left there. Very little in the extant corpus corresponds with Constantine's method of authentication, almost nothing corresponds with that suggested by Varro, and the fact of their existence guarantees that many people thought that the texts in the surviving collections were authentic. In fact all prophets could say very similar things in terms of content, and they had a tendency to repeat not only themselves but also each other.

One illustration of the scope of the problem is provided by a group of four responses, one carved in the later third century on the eastern face of the east Hellenistic wall at Oenoanda and three preserved in works by later Christian authors.[70] In the Oenoanda text the first two lines identify the supreme god as being 'self-nourished, taught by none, unmothered, unshakeable, as having a name that cannot be known, having many names, living in fire'. Those responsible for the answer appear in the third line as being messengers who are but a small part of the great divinity. The final three lines describe a consultation of the oracle and give a cult prescription. The first and third lines are exactly parallel to the first and third lines in a text quoted by Lactantius towards the beginning of the *Divine Institutes*, and to the fourteenth and sixteenth lines of one in the *Tübingen Theosophy*. The second line in Lactantius' text and the fifteenth in the *Theosophy* oracle merely claim that the god has a name that cannot be known—possibly an alteration for the sake of Christian sensibility. The third line in the Oenoanda text (and corresponding lines in the others) also appears in a response which Malalas attributed to the Pythia at the dawn of time. While the first three parallels recall the experience of Oenomaus the Cynic at Claros (whence Lactantius says that his response came) when he received a prediction of future bliss that had also been given to a merchant from Pontus,[71] the fourth is the most important for present purposes. It suggests that Malalas (or his

---

[70] The position taken here is argued in detail in app. 1.
[71] Eus. *Praep. Ev.* 5. 22. 2 — Oenomaeus fr. 14 Hammerstaedt.

source) had written something to conform with common oracular language. Certainly these lines might not have been recognized as representing a belief that could be specifically associated with Claros, but they could be recognized as lines that were typical of inspired prophets.

Repetitions very similar to that outlined in the last paragraph occur at numerous points in the present Sibylline corpus, and it will be useful to note a few of the more outstanding cases (others will appear later). In line 361 of the current *Eighth Oracle* the Christian God claims to know the number of tne sands and the measure of the sea. This is exactly the same line that appears at the beginning of a response given by the Pythia to Croesus.[72] In lines 163–71 of the *Eleventh Oracle* the Delphic Sibyl says that her words will instruct Homer. The Jewish Sibyl makes the same claim with many of the same words in the *Third Oracle*.[73] She claims that she will be incorrectly known as the Erythraean Sibyl—and this prophecy is known to have occurred in works that were definitely attributed to the Erythraean Sibyl.[74] Varro says that Apollodorus of Erythrae said that the Erythraean Sibyl predicted that Homer would tell many lies about the Trojan war,[75] and Pausanias said that she would precede Homer and predict the Trojan War.[76] Similar predictions were attributed to the Delphic Sibyl. Diodorus says that the daughter of Teiresias, 'who had no less knowledge of prophecy than her father', was the first Pythia and that people would call her Sibyl. She predicted that Homer would take many of her verses as his own and adorn

---

[72] *Orac. Sib.* 8. 362 οἶδα δ᾽ ἐγὼ ψάμμου τ᾽ ἀριθμὸν καὶ μέτρα θαλάσσης, | οἶδα μυχοὺς γαίης καὶ Τάρταρον ἠερόεντα; 8. 373 καὶ κωφοῦ ξυνίημι καὶ οὐ λαλέοντος ἀκούω; Hdt. 1. 47 = PW 52; J. Fontenrose, *The Delphic Oracle* (Berkeley, 1978), 111–15; R. Crahay, *La Littérature oraculaire chez Hérodote* (Paris, 1956), 193–7.

[73] *Orac. Sib.* 11. 163–71, 3. 419–31. I do not find Momigliano's assertion that the figure mentioned in *Orac. Sib.* 11 is Virgil rather than Homer convincing ('Dalla Sibilla pagana', p. 416).

[74] Ibid. 3. 813–16 καὶ καλέσουσι βροτοί με καθ᾽ Ἑλλάδα πατρίδος ἄλλης, | ἐξ Ἐρυθρῆς γεγαυῖαν ἀναιδέα· οἳ δέ με Κίρκης | μητρὸς καὶ Γνωστοῖο πατρὸς φήσουσι Σίβυλλαν | μαινομένην ψεύστειραν . . .; Nikiprowetzky, *La Troisième Sibylle*, pp. 41–3.

[75] See n. 28 above and Parke, *Sibyls and Sibylline Prophecy*, pp. 4–5, 109–10.

[76] Paus. 10. 12. 2.

his work with them.[77] The same prediction about Samos and Delos—Samos will be sand, Delos obscure—occurs with slightly different wording in the *Third*, *Fourth*, and *Eighth Oracles*.[78] The *Twelfth Oracle* introduces Antoninus Pius, Marcus Aurelius, and Lucius Verus with the same words as the *Fifth*.[79] The *Thirteenth Oracle* predicts woe for Antioch in the same words as the *Fourth*; it praises death with the same words as does the *Eighth*.[80] At an even more extreme level, some lines attributed to Apollo in a Syriac collection of oracles occur also in lines 324–5 of the *First Sibylline Oracle*, and moreover are cited by the author of the *Tübingen Theosophy* as coming from the second volume of prophecy given to Noah.[81] In a similar case Zosimus confessed that he did not know if verses he cited on the foundation of Constantinople were those of Phaennis or the Erythraean Sibyl.[82] This is presumably because the same lines were ascribed to both.

The explanation for the repetition outlined in the last paragraph lies in the method of composition: the long texts that have survived are manifestly compilations of shorter passages. These passages were themselves written by people who tended to draw heavily on other oracular texts for their inspiration, taking lines or portions of lines from them in order to fill out their own prophecies. Readers do not seem to have drawn a connection

---

[77] Diod. 4. 66. 6.

[78] *Orac. Sib.* 3. 363 ἔσται καὶ Σάμος ἄμμος, ἐσεῖται Δῆλος ἄδηλος; 4. 91–2 καὶ Σάμον ἄμμος ἅπασαν ὑπ' ἠιόνεσσι καλύψει, | Δῆλος δ' οὐκέτι δῆλος, ἄδηλα δὲ πάντα τὰ Δήλου; 8. 165–6 ἔσται καὶ Ῥώμη ῥύμη καὶ Δῆλος ἄδηλος | καὶ Σάμος ἄμμος. The line was known to Tertullian, *De pal.* 2. 3 'mutat et nunc localiter habitus, cum situs laeditur, cum inter insulas nulla iam Delos, harenae Samos, et Sibulla non mendax'.

[79] *Orac. Sib.* 5. 51 — 12. 176 τὸν μέτα τρεῖς ἄρξουσιν, ὁ δὲ τρίτος ὀψὲ κρατήσει.

[80] See on ll. 115, 125.

[81] S. Brock, 'A Syriac Collection of Prophecies of the Pagan Philosophers', *Orientalia Lovaniensia Periodica*, 14 (1983), 240.

[82] Zos. 2. 36. 2 καὶ ταύτην ἐκ πολλοῦ τὴν ἔννοιαν ἔχων, πολλάς τε βίβλους ἱστορικὰς καὶ χρησμῶν συναγωγὰς ἀνελίξας, χρόνον τε ἐν τῷ περὶ τούτων ἀπορεῖν δαπανήσας, ἐνέτυχον μόλις χρησμῷ τινι Σιβύλλης εἶναι λεγομένῳ τῆς Ἐρυθραίας ἢ Φαεννοῦς τῆς Ἠπειρώτιδος (καὶ αὐτὴ γὰρ γενομένη κάτοχος ἐκδεδωκέναι χρησμοὺς λέγεται) . . . ; see H. W. Parke, 'The Attribution of the Oracle in Zosimus, *New History* 2, 37', *CQ* NS 32 (1982), 441–4, who argues that the text cited here was originally the product of Apollo Chresterios at Chalcedon.

between the hermeneutic process and the content: they seem to have preferred to believe that different prophets spoke in the same way.

There was a link between the various mantics not only in the ways in which they were inspired and in how they spoke, but also in the nature of the matter they predicted. Although only three examples have survived—one in the work of Zosimus and two in that of Phlegon—the greatest number of the Sibylline texts recorded in antiquity prescribed cult activities.[83] This, of course, was also a major function of the various oracular centres and, to judge from Philostratus' Life of Apollonius or the various activities of the Apostle Paul (not to mention those attributed to Christ in the Gospels), wandering holy men. Sibyls, the prophets at oracular centres, and other holy individuals could reveal the nature of god and could predict all manner of events. The only reason why answers to more mundane questions about life are not obtained from Sibyls is simply that there were usually none available to give them. Aeneas' visit to the Sibyl, Trimalchio's alleged sighting of the bottled Sibyl, and the Shepherd of Hermas' misidentification of the spirit of the Church as the Cumaean Sibyl indicate that there was no doubt concerning a Sibyl's capacity to give such answers.[84] The way in which Sibylline books were consulted at Rome indicates that some, at least, were recorded as answers to specific questions; the texts mentioned the prodigy or problems that would be expiated or solved by the answers that the oracle prescribed.

Given the wide variety of Sibylline activity and the inadequacy of Constantine's or Varro's methods of verifying Sibylline oracles for explaining the extant evidence, it comes as no surprise to find that many people used less demanding criteria. The main consideration was that the prophet could be found to have been right about something in the past that the reader knew about—but that

---

[83] *FGrH* 257 F 36x; Zos. 2. 6; see n. 55 above.

[84] Virg. *Aen.* 6. 9–155; *Past. vis.* 2. 4. 1 ἀπεκαλύφθη δέ μοι, ἀδελφοί, κοινωμένῳ ὑπὸ νεανίσκου εὐειδεστάτου λέγοντός μοι· τὴν πρεσβυτέραν, παρ᾽ ἧς ἔλαβες τὸ βιβλίδιον, τίνα δοκεῖς εἶναι; ἐγώ φημι· Τὴν Σίβυλλαν. Petron. *Sat.* 48.

happened after the prophet's lifetime or prediction. This is clearly what one of the magicians whose prayers for mantic powers are preserved on papyrus thought he would have to be able to do.[85] Celsus asked why it should be necessary to enumerate all the events that had been predicted by oracles, prophets, prophetesses, and other inspired persons—the legitimacy of such people was obvious from the fact that the things they had predicted had come true.[86] Plutarch twice remarked on the inspiration of the Sibyl who had predicted the eruption of Vesuvius; Pausanias mentions a famous prophecy of Herophile 'which we know came true'.[87] Constantine and Lactantius both argued that the prophecies of Christ's coming which were being found during their lifetimes in the texts of the Sibyls were not forgeries. The problem was simply that these verses had not been previously recognized for what they were.[88]

Many were willing to take oracular texts at face value—if a text read like an oracle and, even better, if it contained some reference to an event the reader knew had happened, he or she might easily accept it as genuine. Dio relates that Caracalla was so taken by the sound of one verse that he refused to believe it had been forged even after the author had admitted to it.[89] If a person was more interested in the truth than Caracalla had been on that occasion it was necessary to find out some details of the prophet's life. As Lactantius wrote in the *Divine Institutes*, the discerning

---

[85] *PGM* 5. 280–301.　　　　　　　　　　[86] Orig. *Contra Cels.* 8. 45.

[87] Plut. *De Pyth. orac.* 398 E; *De sera num. vind.* 556 E; Paus. 10. 12. 5.

[88] *Orat. ad sanctos*, 19. 2 ἐν προφανεῖ δ' ἀλήθεια, τῆς τῶν ἡμετέρων ἀνδρῶν ἐπιμελείας συλλεξάσης τοὺς χρόνους ἀκριβέστερον ὡς πρὸς τὸ μηδένα τοπάζειν μετὰ τὴν τοῦ Χριστοῦ κάθοδον καὶ κρίσιν γεγενῆσθαι τὸ ποίημα καὶ ὡς πάλαι προλεχθέντων ὑπὸ Σιβύλλης τῶν ἐπῶν ψεῦδος διαφημίζεσθαι. Cf. Lact. *DI* 4. 15. 28 'verum non dubito quin illa carmina prioribus temporibus pro deliramentis habita sint, cum ea nemo intellegeret. denuntiabant enim monstruosa quaedam miracula, quorum nec ratio nec tempus nec auctor designabatur.'

[89] Dio 77. 16. 8. In this regard, it should be noted that the Sibyl may not even have had to speak in verse. D. Flusser, 'An Early Jewish–Christian Document in the Tiburtine Sibyl', in *Paganisme, Judaïsme, Christianisme: Influences et affrontements dans le monde antique. Mélanges offerts à Marcel Simon* (Paris, 1978), 153–83, esp. pp. 167–8, 176–8, argues that two passages in the medieval oracle of the Tiburtine Sibyl go back to texts that were composed under the Flavians. This is possible, though for doubts see McGinn, *'Teste David cum Sibylla'*, pp. 27–8.

seeker after divine wisdom should find out when the prophet lived and how much of what that prophet had predicted had come true.[90] This point is not only of great importance for evaluating the historical content of some Sibylline oracles, but also recalls the problem mentioned previously: how did someone discover which prophet was which and when each lived?

The answer is provided in the first instance by Lactantius, who noted that there were many separate books produced by each Sibyl, but, because they were only inscribed with the name 'Sibyl' they were believed to be the work of one person. Only the works of the Erythraean Sibyl could be distinguished, because this woman had included some lines about herself in the poem.[91] The same answer is provided by Pausanias when he says that he found out about Herophile because of what she had written in her poems. It is provided yet again by the interpretation of the *Fourth Eclogue*, in both Lactantius' *Divine Institutes* and Constantine's *Oratio ad sanctos*, as the work of the Cumaean Sibyl.[92] The clue was provided by line 5: 'ultima Cumaei venit iam carmina aetas'. In the extant corpus there are a number of passages which are biographical. In one of these, at the end of the *Third Oracle*, the Sibyl states that people will wrongly say that she is mad and that she is the daughter of Circe and Gnostos. This text deserves quotation in full since it is an example of the sort of material that ancient scholars relied upon in their efforts to identify various Sibyls, and as it illustrates the great confusion to which the tradition as a whole was subject:

[I say] these things to you, when I left the great Babylonian walls of Assyria, in frenzied madness, sent as a fire to Greece revealing the

---

[90] Lact. *DI* 4. 5. 4 'ante omnia qui veritatem studet conprehendere, non modo intellegendis prophetarum vocibus animum debet intendere, sed etiam tempora per quae quisque illorum fuerit diligentissime requirere, ut sciat et quae futura praedixerint et post quot annos praedicta conpleta sint.'

[91] Ibid. 1. 6. 13 'harum omnium Sibyllarum carmina et feruntur et habentur, praeterquam Cymaeae, cuius libri a Romanis occultantur nec eos ab ullo nisi a quindecimviris inspici fas habent. et sunt singularum singuli libri: quos, quia Sibyllae nomine inscribuntur, unius esse credunt, suntque confusi nec discerni ac suum cuique adsignari potest nisi Erythraeae, quae et nomen suum verum carmini inseruit et Erythraeam se nominaturi praelocuta est, cum esset orta Babylone.'

[92] Ibid. 7. 24. 12 'quae poeta secundum Cymaeae Sibyllae carmina prolocutus est'.

causes of divine wrath to all mortals . . .[93] so that I should prophesy
divine riddles to men, and men in Greece shall call me shameless, born
of another land, from Erythrae, who shall say that I am Sibylla, mad
and mendacious, of Circe as a mother and Gnostos as father. Whenever all things come to pass, then you will remember and no longer
will anyone say that I am mad. I who am a prophetess of the great God.
For he did reveal to me what he had revealed before to my parents but
what happened first, these things my father told me, and God put all
of the future in my mind so that I prophesy both future and former
things and tell them to mortals. For when the world was deluged with
waters, and a certain single approved man was left floating on the
waters in a house of hewn wood with beasts, and birds, so that the
world might be filled again, I was his daughter-in-law and I was of his
blood. The first things happened to him and all the later things were
revealed, so let all these things from my mouth be accounted true.
(*Orac. Sib.* 3. 809–29, trans. Collins (adapted))

The point of these lines is to prove that poems in which the
Erythraean Sibyl described herself as coming from other parentage were fraudulent, and to identify the Sibyl as a prophetess who
spoke for the Jews. This and the other passages serve as guides to
their readers and, in at least this case, as potential guides away
from fakes. A Sibyl who spoke incorrectly about her parentage
was not to be relied upon.

    The first indications the readers had that their texts were the
genuine article were very straightforward: labels on the book
saying 'Sibyl' or lines within the poems identifying the authoress.
But this need not have been all. Since readers were concerned that
there be things in the poems which could be shown to be correct,
it would be helpful if there were past events that could be recognized. This would satisfy lingering doubts about authenticity. It is
this function of such 'historical' prophecies that gives the oracles
their greatest value as historical sources. The history that these
passages present must have convinced the majority of educated

---

[93] There is a lacuna of several lines here. Geffcken notes that Blass suggested that the
name Sambathe, the name of the Babylonian Sibyl, would have appeared here. This suggestion was adopted by Parke, *Sibyls and Sibylline Prophecy*, pp. 42–3, but I doubt that it can be
correct. The question of the Sibyl's identity is thoroughly dealt with in ll. 813–16.

readers. The fact of its survival shows that readers at the time of composition were, for example, convinced that the present *Thirteenth Sibylline Oracle* provided a faithful picture of their own times. If the arguments presented in the next chapter are accepted, it will appear that these readers would also have believed that the history of the empire which the *Twelfth Oracle* presented was an accurate picture of the first centuries of Roman rule. This shows what the 'average well-educated readers' would know about Roman history, it reveals something of the ways in which they would have learnt this history, and the poems themselves also reveal how such a person would express this learning. These are the points that must be dealt with before turning to an analysis of the contents of the *Thirteenth Oracle* itself.

COMPOSING SIBYLLINE ORACLES

A detailed study of the levels of literacy among the members of the upper classes of the Greek east is beyond the scope of this introduction. The purpose of the present section is merely to present an outline of the techniques employed by the authors of the various fragments that were incorporated in the present *Twelfth* and *Thirteenth Sibylline Oracles*. Two features will emerge. The first is that these authors do not appear to have possessed great technical skill. The hexameters surveyed reveal that they relied heavily on other oracles to provide substantial portions of their work. This is not a question of sophisticated borrowing—it is a question simply of taking sections of other verse, entire lines, individual cola or portions of cola, to fill out their own. Furthermore, the proportion of lines drawn from other oracles that can be indicated here is probably considerably smaller than it was originally: the extant sample is simply not very extensive. It must also be admitted that the figures thus obtained are impressionistic. It is impossible to know just what oracular sources the author of the extant lines had to work with. All that can be said on the basis of the observed parallels is that they clearly indicate that the authors of the extant poems must have relied heavily on what may be described as a 'common body' of oracular texts for models. The parallels that are adduced in this section should all be traced back to this body of material: they are signs that the extant texts shared common material, not that the authors of any of the passages in the present collection were necessarily familiar with any of the others in the context in which they are now preserved. One reason for these borrowings was probably technical (the authors could not do better on their own); another probably stylistic. Readers might recognize the lines as 'Sibylline' because they had seen their like in other poems. The recognition could lend these poems a greater air of authenticity.

In general terms, an appreciation of the technical skill of these authors is useful as an indication of the level at which a well-educated man might be expected to be able to work. The general lack of sophistication that the lines show was surely not the result of deliberate efforts to write badly. Hesychius believed that the Sibyl herself produced excellent verse and in some quarters it was claimed that a Sibyl had composed the Homeric poems herself.[94] In the light of claims such as these, it is fair to say that if the authors of these poems could have done better, they would have.

For the purpose of this survey I have selected eight passages, each of which is clearly the work of a single hand. Four are from the *Thirteenth Oracle* and four from the *Twelfth*. Sections in bold type are paralleled in the Homeric corpus (Homeric borrowings include epic words occurring in the same metrical position here as they do in the Homeric corpus), those which are underlined are found in other Sibylline oracles. I have included Homeric echoes to offer a point of comparison for the use of passages and phrases found in other oracles. This survey will show that while oracular authors made liberal use of other oracular texts to aid them in their compositions, they did not draw heavily from non-oracular sources. Epic phrases and vocabulary appear to have

---

[94] For Hesychius see n. 56 above; for the Sibyl's composition of the Homeric poems see pp. 119–20.

been used in places for metrical convenience, and the parallels here may be accounted for in most cases by the fact that the authors were struggling to compose hexameter verse.

καὶ τότε δὴ Περσῶν ἐπανάστασις ἀλφηστήρων
Ἰνδῶν Ἀρμενίων Ἀράβων θ᾿ ἅμα· καὶ περὶ τούτοις
Ῥωμαῖος πελάσει βασιλεὺς πολέμου ἀκόρητος   15
αἰχμητὰς ἐπάγων καὶ ἐπ᾿ Ἀσσυρίους, νέος Ἄρης
ἄχρις ἐπ᾿ Εὐφράτην τε **βαθύρροον ἀργυροδίνην**
ἐκτανύσει, πέμψας λόγχην, πολεμήϊος Ἄρης
καππέσετ᾿ ἐν τάξει, τυφθεὶς αἴθωνι σιδήρῳ
⟨ζηλοσύνης⟩ ἕνεκα καί ⟨γε⟩ προδοθεὶς ὑφ᾿ ἑταίρου.⁹⁵   20

(*Orac. Sib.* 13. 13–20)

As can readily be seen, well over half of this passage is directly paralleled elsewhere. In addition compare 18 ἐκτανύσει, πέμψας λόγχην with 14. 128 ἐκτανύσει λόγχην θυμοφθόρον Ἀρμενίοισιν.

νῦν δὲ φιλοπτολέμοισιν Ἀλεξανδρεῦσιν ἀείσω
δεινοτάτους πολέμους· πουλὺς δ᾿ ἄρα λαὸς ὀλεῖται   75
ἀστῶν ὀλλυμένων ὑπ᾿ ἀντιπάλων πολιητῶν
μαρναμένων στυγερῆς ἔριδος χάριν, ἄμφι δὲ τούτοις
ἀϊκὰς φοβερωπὸς **Ἄρης** στήσει **πολέμοιο**.
καὶ τότε δ᾿ αὖ **μεγάθυμος** ἑῷ σὺν παιδὶ κραταιῷ
καππέσεται δολίως διὰ πρεσβύτερον βασιλῆα.⁹⁶   80

(*Orac. Sib.* 13. 74–80)

Approximately half of this passage has borrowed elements, and the extremely obscure explanation for the death of Philip the Arab offered by line 80 may have been included because it

---

⁹⁵ For the text see ad loc. For parallels to ll. 13–14: 12. 277; πολέμου ἀκόρητος: 13. 92, cf. *Il.* 12. 335 πολέμου ἀκορήτω; ἐπ᾿ Ἀσσυρίους: 12. 107, cf. 3. 268 πρὸς Ἀσσυρίους; βαθύροον ἀργυροδίνην: *Il.* 21. 8; πολεμήϊος Ἄρης: 12. 252; καππέσετ᾿ . . . τάξει: 13. 101; αἴθωνι σιδήρῳ: 12. 249; προδοθεὶς . . . ἑταίρου: 14. 91.

⁹⁶ νῦν δέ: 4. 48, 12. 293, 14. 296; Ἀλεξανδρεῦσιν ἀείσω: 13. 50 (by a different hand), 14. 296; πουλὺς . . . ὀλεῖται: 14. 171; μαρναμένων: *Il.* 12. 429, 13. 579, 16. 775; Ἄρης: *Il.* 6. 203; πολέμοιο: *Il.* 1. 165, 2. 368, 3. 112, 113, etc.; καὶ τότε: *Orac. Sib. passim* (see on l. 13); μεγάθυμος: *Il.* 15. 440; καππέσεται δολίως: 12. 122.

sounded like the sort of explanation that could be found in Sibylline texts.[97]

> ἄρτι δὲ σέ, τλήμων Συρίη, κατοδύρομαι οἰκτρῶς
> ἥξει καὶ πληγή σοι ἀπ᾽ ἰοβόλων ἀνθρώπων   120
> δεινή, ἥν τοι οὔποτ᾽ ἐπήλπισας ἥξουσάν σοι.
> ἥξει καὶ Ῥώμης ὁ φυγάς, μέγα ἔγχος ἀείρας,
> Εὐφράτην διαβὰς πολλαῖς ἅμα μυριάδεσσιν,
> ὅς σε καταφλέξει καὶ πάντα κακῶς διαθήσει.
> τλήμων Ἀντιόχεια, σὲ δὲ πτόλιν οὔποτ᾽ ἐροῦσιν,   125
> ὁππόταν ἀφροσύνῃσι τεαῖς ὑπὸ δούρασι πίπτῃς·
> πάντα δὲ συλήσας καὶ γυμνώσας σε προλείψει
> ἄστεγον ἀοίκητον· ἄφνω δέ σε κλαύσεθ᾽ ὁρῶν τις.
> καὶ σὺ θρίαμβος ἔσῃ, Ἱεράπολι, καὶ σύ Βέροια·
> Χαλκίδι συγκλαύσεσθε νεοτρώτοις ἐπὶ τέκνοις.[98] 130

(*Orac. Sib.* 13. 119–30)

One of the striking features of these lines is the way that several
different prophecies, one of them concerned with the return of
Nero (the individual referred to in lines 122 and 123), have been
integrated into the context of the capture of Antioch in 252. The
total proportion that can be traced from other sources is high
(about 65 per cent).

> καὶ τότε δὴ νόθος υἱὸς ἑῇ ὑπ᾽ ἀναιδεΐ τόλμῃ
> ἐξολέσει βασιλῆα, παραυτίκα δ᾽ αὐτὸς ὀλεῖται
> δυσσεβίης ἕνεκεν· μετὰ δ᾽ αὐτ᾽ ἄρξει πάλιν ἄλλος
> ἀρχὴν οὐνομάτεσσι φέρων· ταχὺ δ᾽ αὖτε πεσεῖται   145
> Ἄρηϊ κρατερῷ βληθεὶς αἴθωνι σιδήρῳ.
> καὶ πάλι κόσμος ἄκοσμος ἀπολλυμένων ἀνθρώπων
> λοιμῷ καὶ πολέμῳ. Πέρσαι δ᾽ ἐπὶ μῶλον Ἄρηος
> αὖτις ἐφορμήσουσι μεμηνότες Αὐσονίοισιν.[99]

(*Orac. Sib.* 13. 142–9)

---

[97] See n. ad loc.

[98] ἄρτι ... οἰκτρῶς: 7. 114, cf. 5. 287, 11. 122; ἥξει ... πληγή: 3. 314;
ἀνθρώπων: *Il.* 1. 250 etc., *Orac. Sib.* 1. 64 ἀνθρώπων καὶ ἰοβόλων; δεινή: 3. 315;
οὔποτ᾽ ἐπήλπισας: 3. 315; ἥξει ... μυριάδεσσιν: see n. ad loc.; τλήμων ... πίπτης:
4. 140–1; συλήσας ... γυμνώσας: 8. 55; σε κλαύσεθ᾽: 5. 170; καί ... ἔσῃ: 8. 130.

[99] καὶ τότε δή: see on ll. 13, 21–5 below; ἀναιδεΐ τόλμῃ: 13. 166; ὀλεῖται: *Il.* 2. 325,
7. 91, *Od.* 24. 196; μετὰ δ᾽ αὐτ᾽: 5. 39, 12. 142, 178, cf. 14. 135; ἄρξει ... ἄλλος:
14. 163; Ἄρηϊ ... σιδήρῳ: 14. 51, 12. 249, 13. 19; καὶ πάλι: 1. 120, 2. 236,

There are parallels to half of this passage, and certain other phrases appear to be closely modelled on other oracular texts, if they are not in fact derived from texts that are now lost. Formulations similar to δυσσεβίης ἕνεκεν are given in the note on l. 20, for λοιμῷ καὶ πολέμῳ compare *Orac. Sib.* 2. 156 λιμοὶ λοιμοὶ πόλεμοί τε; 3. 538 πόλεμός τε βροτοῖς καὶ λοιμὸς ἐπέσται; 603 καὶ πόλεμον καὶ λιμόν . . . ; and on l. 10 below. Overall, just under 60 per cent of the text in these four passages has elements that are directly paralleled in Homer or in other oracular texts (in terms of feet, 126 out of 210). The figures obtained here may be compared with those obtained from four passages in the *Twelfth Oracle*.

> πεντήκοντ' ἀριθμῶν πάλιν ἄλλος ἐλεύσεται ἀνήρ
> δεινὸς καὶ φοβερός· πολλοὺς δ' αὐτοῖς ἀπολέσσει
> ἐκ πασῶν πόλεων ὄλβῳ γεγαῶτας ἀρίστους   80
> δεινὸς ὄφις φύσεως ὁ βραχὺς λόγος, ὅς ποτε χεῖρας
> ἡμεμόνας τανύσει καὶ ὀλεῖ καὶ πολλὰ τελέσσει
> ἀθλεύων ἐλάων κτείνων καὶ μυρία τολμῶν
> καὶ τμήξει τὸ δίκυμον ὄρος, λύθρῳ δὲ παλάξει.
> ἀλλ' ἔσται καὶ ἄιστος ὀλοίιος Ἰταλίδαισιν   85
> ἰσάζων θεῷ αὐτόν, ἐλέγξει δῆμον ἑκόντα·
> εἰρήνη δ' ἔσται βαθεῖα τούτου κρατέοντος.[100]

(*Orac. Sib.* 12. 78–87)

In this case two-thirds of the passage can be found elsewhere in the corpus. In some cases, such as line 87, it would appear that the line may have been composed by combining two metrical units found elsewhere. The fact that ἐλεύσεται in line 78 also appears in this position at *Od.* 19. 300 is probably coincidence.

> αὐτίκ' ἔπειτ' ἄλλος βασιλεὺς κρατερός τ' αἰχμητής
> ὅς τε τριηκοσίων ἀριθμῶν λάχεν ἔντυπον ἀρχήν,

279, 3. 297, 490, 11. 121, 218, 12. 155, 14. 339; κόσμος . . . ἀνθρώπων: 7. 127 (and see n. ad loc.); ἐπὶ . . . Ἄρηος: *Il.* 2. 401.

[100] πάλιν ἄλλος: 13. 144, 162, 14. 74, 163; ἐλεύσεται: *Od.* 19. 300; δεινὸς . . . φοβερός: 14. 173; δεινὸς . . . φύσεως: 5. 29; ὃς . . . χεῖρας: 5. 29; ἀθλεύων . . . ὀλοίιος: 5. 31–3; Ἰταλίδαισιν: 4. 104 Ἰταλίδησιν; ἰσάζων . . . ἐλέγξει: 5. 34 ἰσάζων θεῷ αὐτόν, ἐλέγχει δ' οὔ μιν ἐόντα; εἰρήνη . . . βαθεῖα: 11. 237; τούτου κρατέοντος: 11. 25, 14. 98.

ἄρξει καὶ Θρᾳκῶν γαίην πολυποίκιλον οὖσαν
ἐκπέρσει καὶ τοὺς ἐπὶ ἔσχατα βάρβαρα Ῥήνου   150
Γερμανοὺς ναίοντας ὀϊστοβόλους τ᾽ Ἴβηρας·
αὐτίκ᾽ Ἰουδαίοις κακὸν ἔσσεται ἄλλο μέγιστον,
Φοινίκῃ δ᾽ ἐπὶ τοῖς πίεται φόνον ὀμβρήεντα·
τείχη δ᾽ Ἀσσυρίων πέσεται πολλοῖς πολεμισταῖς.[101]

(*Orac. Sib.* 12. 147–55)

Here, though the proportion that can be directly paralleled elsewhere in the corpus is smaller (a third), there are a number of
other formulations which appear to be variations on standard
themes (if they are not in fact taken directly from verses which
are now lost). αὐτίκ᾽ ἔπειτ᾽ ἄλλος βασιλεύς is a variation on
the most common style of introducing rulers, and αὐτίκα
(l. 152) followed by the name of a people to be harmed in the
dative is also a variation on a common style of introduction: see
Orac. Sib. 11. 45 καὶ τότε Ἰουδαίοις; 53 αὐτίκα δὴ Πέρ-
σαισι; 239 καὶ τότ᾽ Ἰουδαίοις. In the same line κακὸν
ἔσσεται ἄλλο μέγιστον is similar metrically and thematically
to *Orac. Sib.* 3. 486 κακὸν ἔσχατον, ἀλλὰ μέγιστον and 8. 160
κακὸν ὕστατον, ἀλλὰ μέγιστον. The expression τείχη δ᾽
Ἀσσυρίων meaning 'the land of the Assyrians' (i.e. Persia) has
numerous parallels in the corpus: see *Orac. Sib.* 12. 191 and note
on 13. 16, 105.

οὗτος ἀνὴρ ἕξει περισσοτέρῳ τε λογισμῷ
πάντα, μάλα **μεγάθυμον ὑπέρβιον** Ἡρακλῆα   210
ζηλώσει καὶ ὅπλοισιν ἀριστεύσει κρατεροῖσιν
ἔν τε κυνηγεσίαισι καὶ ἱππείαισι μέγιστον
κῦδος ἔχων· σφαλερῶς δὲ βιώσεται οἰόθεν οἷος.
σῆμα δέ τοι ἔσται φοβερὸν τούτου κρατέοντος·
ἐν δαπέδῳ Ῥώμης ἔσται νεφέλη ὁμίχλη τε,   215
ὡς ἕτερον μὴ ὁρᾶν μερόπων τὸν πλησίον αὐτοῦ.
καὶ τότε δὴ πόλεμοί τε ὁμοῦ καὶ κήδεα λυγρά,
ὁππόταν αὐτὸς ἄναξ ἐρωτομανής, ὁ μεμηνώς

---

[101] κρατερὸς . . . αἰχμητής: 12. 36, 124; ὃς . . . ἀριθμῶν: 5. 21, 12. 39; ἄρξει:
3. 121, 290, 5. 23, 8. 135, 11. 22, 39, 81, 144, 159, 195; Ῥήνου: 12. 43; ὀϊστοβόλους . . .
Ἴβηρας: cf. 13. 62, 14. 175; πίεται . . . ὀμβρήεντα: 3. 392.

ἥξει ἐπαισχύνων τὸ ἑὸν γένος ἐν λεχέεσσιν
αἰσχρὸς ἀβουλεύτοις ἐπ᾽ οὐχ ὁσίοις ὑμεναίοις.[102]   220

(*Orac. Sib.* 12. 209–20)

The proportion of repeated elements is again smaller here (30 per cent), which is no doubt a reflection of the rather singular content of these lines—the bizarre behaviour of Commodus. Still, it is clear that where possible the author had recourse to other oracular verses. The coincidence of two Homeric adjectives, μεγάθυμον and ὑπέρβιον, to modify Ἡρακλῆα in line 210 is fortuitous, as the collocation does not appear in Homer.

καὶ τότε †κρατῆσαι† δολίως ἐπιτήδεια εἰδώς[103]
ἀνὴρ ποικιλόμητις ἀφ᾽ ἑσπερίης ἐπεγερθείς,
οὔνομα δὲ σχήσει διακοσίων ἀριθμοῖο
σημεῖον· πολὺ μᾶλλον ὑπὲρ βασιληίδος ἀρχῆς
συστήσει πόλεμον, κατὰ Ἀσσυρίων <u>ἀνθρώπων</u>   260
<u>συλλέξας</u> πᾶσαν στρατιήν, καὶ πάντ᾽ ὑποτάξει.[104]

(*Orac. Sib.* 12. 256–61)

Here half the passage is paralleled elsewhere, and in two places where there are no parallels there are metrical irregularities: 258 σχήσει διακοσίων and 260 κατὰ Ἀσσυρίων.[105] In sum, roughly 45 per cent of the text in these passages derives from identifiable sources (in terms of feet the figure is 97 out of a total of 216).

The figures shown in the previous paragraphs illustrate the

[102] μεγάθυμον: *Il.* 16. 488; ὑπέρβιον: *Il.* 17. 19, *Od.* 1. 368, 12. 379, etc.; κῦδος ἔχων: 12. 24; σῆμα . . . φοβερόν: 14. 98, see 3. 796, 14. 179, and Rzach, 'Metrische Studien', p. 64; τούτου κρατέοντος: 12. 87; ἐν . . . Ῥώμης: 12. 123; καὶ τότε: see on ll. 21–5; καὶ . . . λυγρά: 12. 69; ὁππόταν: see on ll. 21–5; αὐτὸς ἄναξ: 11. 37, 311, 12. 64, 185; ἥξει: see on l. 109.

[103] This is the reading of the MSS. Mendelssohn, followed by Rzach, proposed ἀπατήλια εἰδώς ('Metrische Studien', p. 41). Mendelssohn also proposed reading καὶ τότε δ᾽ αὖτ ἄρξει in place of καὶ τότε κρατῆσει; cf. 14. 27, 116, 224.

[104] καὶ τότε: see on ll. 13, 21–5; ἀφ᾽ ἑσπερίης: 12. 128; οὔνομα . . . σχήσει: 11. 23, cf. 12. 245–6; ἀριθμοῖο: 13. 83; ὑπὲρ . . . ἀρχῆς: see on l. 6; ἀνθρώπων: *Il.* 1. 250 etc. (it is also common in the oracles); συλλέξας . . . στρατιήν: 14. 118; καὶ . . . ὑποτάξει: 11. 86, 12. 23; cf. 5. 19, 8. 13, 11. 78.

[105] This is Alexandre's reading; Geffcken produced the metrically more difficult κατ᾽ Ἀσσυρίων.

usual method of composing oracular poetry. It produces lines
that were not only similar in tone to other oracular verses, but
also involved the integration of older work into a new composition. The way in which this was done—the use of metrically
useful fragments to fill out lines and the repetition of complete
prophecies (such as that on the return of Nero in 13. 122–3)—
suggests that the reason for this was that the average author was
uncomfortable with verse as a medium of expression. It suggests
that once an author had decided what to write, he might cull
other oracular works to find lines to help him express himself.
The use of occasional Homeric phrases may be explained either
by the fact that any person of the level of education to produce
verse would have known a fair proportion of these poems from
memory or simply by coincidence. There is clearly no concerted
effort to make any of these lines sound 'Homeric'. The process
which is evident here was not limited to the realm of oracular
verse; it appears to be very similar to that which lies behind the
production of many of the verse epitaphs which have survived on
stone. The authors, who might either be the bereaved themselves
or the stone-cutters, appear to have relied upon commonly
accepted formulae for the composition of their memorials; if the
result echoed the language of classical poets or rhetoricians, this
was because they were drawing upon the common literary background of their age, not because they were aiming at a sophisticated literary effect.[106]

IMPERIAL HISTORY IN THE SIBYLLINE ORACLES

The knowledge of contemporary events shown by the authors
of Sibylline texts is the final topic that needs to be considered as
background for an analysis of the contents of the *Thirteenth
Sibylline Oracle*. The issue is important for two reasons. The first
concerns the function which the lines containing historical
information served in the whole text: to give information about

---

[106] R. Lattimore, *Themes in Greek and Latin Epitaphs* (Illinois Studies in Language and
Literature, 28; Urbana, 1942), 17–19.

the past (but after the putative lifetime of the Sibyl) which readers could check. This was an important guide to the value of the text's essential purpose, the prediction of the future. These lines reflect the best information available both to readers and authors, and they will therefore reflect how much the well-educated man knew about Roman history, the attitudes that he brought to that history, and the way in which he learnt it.

The second point stems from the ubiquity of these texts. There has been a tendency to cull the Sibylline oracles for 'anti-Roman' sentiment.[107] This does not do justice to the range of their content, or of their readership, or of their authorship. The Sibyl was, on the whole, extremely respectable. Sibylline shrines could be important tourist attractions, as they were at Erythrae and Marpessus.[108] Sibylline rocks were on display at such notable shrines as Delos and Delphi, and Sibylline books that were not part of the official collection at Rome were thought to be good things for Christians to cite in order to impress theological antagonists.[109] The Sibyl was thought by Ammianus to be remarkable, her works were studied by Pausanias, cited as authoritative by the author of a commentary on Alcaeus, and discussed with approval by Plutarch.[110] Aelius Aristides and Dio Chrysostom also cite her with respect as a prophet whose words were to be treated deference.[111] A set of Sibylline oracles at Rome (translated into Latin) remained important well into the sixth century, when Procopius read them, and Constantine thought that her words should be repeated to an assembly of bishops.[112] This would not have been the case if the opinions she expressed

---

[107] See e.g. R. MacMullen, *Roman Government's Response to Crisis* (New Haven, 1976), 8–9.

[108] See Paus. 10. 12. 4–7 and n. 38 above.

[109] Paus. 10. 12. 1; Plut. *De Pyth. orac.* 398 c; Amandry, *La Mantique apollonienne*, pp. 203–4; Orig. *Contra Cels.* 7. 53; Lact. *DI* 1. 6; Athenag. *Leg.* 30. 1.

[110] Amm. 21. 1. 11 (a passage which suggests that he may have known some of her oracles at first hand: see above, n. 65), 23. 1. 7, 30. 4. 11; Paus. 10. 12; *P. Oxy.* 3711. 27; for Plutarch (aside from references to the collection at Rome) see *Thes.* 24. 5; *Dem.* 19. 1; *Mor.* 243 B; 285 A–B; 397 A; 398 C–E; 399 A; 401 B; 406 A; 566 D; 675 A; 870 A.

[111] Ael. Arist. 45. 12, 14; Dio Chrys. 12. 35–6, 18. 2, 20. 13.

[112] Procop. *Goth.* 5. 24. 28–35; *Orat. ad sanctos*, 19. 1.

were felt to be excessively partisan or her poems were felt to be generically subversive. She might predict disaster, but she was not thought to be an enemy of the established order. As the well-documented rivalry between Erythrae and Marpessus serves to illustrate, a Sibyl conferred distinction upon her city.[113] This dispute, as well as the writings of Plutarch, Pausanias, Celsus, and the Christian apologists, shows that Sibyls had a respected place in the world of the local aristocrats of the Greek east.

In some cases it is true that historical passages are attached to prophecies of the violent end of Rome or include overtly negative statements about individual emperors. This is not true in all cases, and it is certainly not true that lines in the present collection which are attached to eschatological predictions were necessarily composed with that end in mind. Moreover, it is also the case that even prophecies about the fall of Rome can be read in a variety of different ways. When Germanicus died in 19 and when Rome burnt in 64, lines about the fall of Rome after 900 years were circulated and caused concern. Dio remarked that this was absurd since the nine hundredth year of the city was a long way off.[114] Lines 35–49 of the *Thirteenth Oracle* predict that Rome will survive for 948 years after the conquest of Egypt, and they are inserted in such a way as to suggest that they were intended to reassure, for the point of the passage is that the Persians will not conquer until that length of time had passed, something a reader in the third century would know was in the distant future.[115] In every case, the lines inserted by a compiler into his text take their meaning from the context he provided for them, no matter what the original author may have intended them to signify. Thus, the list of emperors which opens the present *Fifth Oracle* contains a good deal of positive sentiment about some of those rulers, but it is attached to a prophecy about the ruin of the empire and is therefore part of an 'anti-Roman' text. It is very doubtful that this could have been the original purpose of the writers who com-

[113] See above, pp. 108–9.
[114] Dio 57. 18. 4–5, 62. 18. 3; see on ll. 46–9 below.
[115] See on ll. 46–9 below.

posed the very flattering pictures of Augustus and Hadrian which the final compiler took into his oracle. Because these individual passages can be read in a number of different ways, the patterns of information and interpretation that can be derived from them can be taken as representative of the way in which educated people in general tended to acquire or interpret information about events in the world around them, rather than as merely communicating the opinions of overt malcontents.

Works of art appear to have been an important source of information for these authors. There is no evidence to suggest that any of the passages which have been preserved were based upon serious works of history. Thus, when the author of some lines about the events of 193 wrote with respect to Pertinax that 'the number 80 (for π) will make clear his name and grievous old age', that he will rule for a short time, kill a great number of people, and die fighting (12.238–44), the information that he gives is no more than that which could be gleaned from one of the imperial portraits which were circulated as soon as a new emperor was proclaimed (and from the speedy arrival of that of a successor, which would accompany the news of the old emperor's death). The age given for Pertinax is wrong—he was 66 in 193—and the rest of what the author has to say reflects a belief that emperors spent a substantial portion of their time killing people.

A similar conclusion can be drawn from the description of Augustus in the *Fifth* and *Twelfth Oracles*. Here it is said that Thrace, Sicily, and Memphis will crouch before him.[116] The language suggests the image of a defeated nation prostrate before the emperor that is so common on reliefs or in statue groups connected with the dynasty. The Sebasteion at Aphrodisias, with its panels depicting the subjugation of Britain by Claudius and of Armenia by Nero, and others giving representations of the nations defeated by Augustus, is a case in point.[117] So too are the

---

[116] *Orac. Sib.* 5. 16 – 12. 20 ὃν Θρῄκη πτήξει καὶ Σικελίη, μετὰ Μέμφις.

[117] K. T. Erim, 'A New Relief Showing Claudius and Britannia from Aphrodisias', *Britannia*, 13 (1982), 277–81; J. M. Reynolds, 'New Evidence for the Imperial Cult in Julio-Claudian Aphrodisias', *ZPE* 43 (1981), 317–27; id., 'Further Information on Imperial Cult at Aphrodisias', *Studii clasice*, 24 (1986), 109–17; R. R. R. Smith, 'The Imperial Reliefs from

triumphal arches, erected in three places by decree of the Senate in 19 to honour the deceased Germanicus for his deeds from one end of the empire to the other. The arches were to include panels representing the peoples defeated by Germanicus.[118]

A contemporary work of art is also likely to be the source for the account of the rain miracle of Marcus Aurelius in the _Twelfth Oracle._ The text reads, 'then he will destroy the whole country of the Germans, when the great sign of god will appear from heaven and he will save the exhausted bronze-clad men because of the piety of the king; for the heavenly god will give ear to him and he will shower down timely rain in answer to his prayers'.[119] This version of the story is clearly of early date. Like the life of Marcus in the _Historia Augusta_, it emphasizes the role of Marcus' prayers in obtaining the miracle.[120] The attribution of the miracle to a great god is also in line with the presentation of the event on Marcus' column and the tacit admission by Tertullian that the miracle was due to the beneficence of 'the God of Gods' Jupiter.[121] It is free of contamination from the later accounts

the Sebasteion at Aphrodisias', _JRS_ 77 (1987), 88–138, for publication of the imperial reliefs; id., '_Simulacra Gentium_: The _Ethne_ from the Sebasteion at Aphrodisias', _JRS_ 78 (1988), 50–77, for a thorough discussion of the _imagines_ of various peoples, arguing for a connection between this monument and monuments at Rome, a notion previously suggested by Reynolds: see esp. _JRS_ 77 (1987), 137, where Smith observes, 'The individual reliefs with imperial scenes give us the visual conception of the divine emperors together with their helpers, real and symbolic, as seen from the Greek East.'

[118] _TS_ I. 9–11 'placere uti ianus marmoreus extrueretur in circo Flaminio pe[cunia publica posi]|tus ad eum locum in quo statuae divo Augusto domuique Augus[tae ... es]|sent ab C. Norbano Flacco cum signis devictarum gentium ...'; 28–30 'statua Germanici Cae]|saris constitueretur accipienti[s – – – Germanis et praeciperetur Gal]|lis Germanisque qui citra Rhen[um incolunt'. For the text see W. D. Lebek, 'Die drei Ehrenbögen für Germanicus: Tab. Siar. frg. I 9–34; CIL VI 31199a 2–17', _ZPE_ 67 (1987), 133; D. S. Potter, 'The _Tabula Siarensis_, Tiberius, the Senate, and the Eastern Boundary of the Roman Empire', _ZPE_ 69 (1987), 269–76, on the placement of the arches.

[119] _Orac. Sib._ 12. 195–200 χώρην δέ †μιν† ἐξαλαπάξει | πᾶσαν Γερμανῶν, ὁπόταν μέγα σῆμα θεοῖο | οὐρανόθεν προφανῇ καί τ᾽ ἄνδρας χαλκοκορυστάς | τρυχομένους σώσει δι᾽ εὐσεβίην βασιλῆος· | αὐτῷ γὰρ θεὸς οὐράνιος μάλα πάνθ᾽ ὑπακούσει· | εὐξαμένῳ βρέξει παρακαίριον ὄμβριον ὕδωρ.

[120] _HA V. Marci_, 24. 4 'fulmen de caelo precibus suis contra hostium machinamentum extorsit su(i)s pluvia impetrata, cum siti laborent.'

[121] Tert. _Ad Scap._ 4. 6 'tunc et populus acclamans Deo deorum, qui solus potens. In Iovis nomine Deo nostro testimonium reddidit.' The effort of W. Jobst, _11. Juni n. Chr.: Der Tag_

which variously attribute the storm to the Egyptian magician Arnouphis, Julianus the Theurgist, or Christian prayers.[122] Although Marcus is not himself shown in prayer on his column, the fact that this is mentioned in the *Historia Augusta* (depending here on Marius Maximus) shows that it did feature in an early version of the story.

The discussion of Septimius Severus in the same oracle may reflect the information that could be gleaned by a resident of the Greek east from a less spectacular source: gossip. The movements of Niger in 193 are reflected with good accuracy: he is said to go as far as Thrace and then to be defeated in Bithynia and Cilicia.[123] Severus is then described as waging a great war on the 'Assyrian men'.[124] There is no reference to Clodius Albinus, and this suggests that all the facts noted in this text might be picked up in the course of conversation. Niger's movements would have been a matter of concern, as would Severus' Persian wars. The struggle in the west would have been less interesting to inhabitants of the east, and few, if any, might have thought that the omission was serious. The same source may also account for the strange account at 12. 185–6 of Avidius Cassius' death as the result of the intervention of a crafty beast. Marcus does not appear to have advertised this event and Cassius' sudden disappearance, as it would have seemed to most contemporaries, could best be explained in mysterious ways.[125] Gossip may also lie behind the

---

des Blitz- und Regenwunders im Quadenlande (SAWW 355: Vienna, 1978), to connect the role of Jupiter in the miracle with the shrine of Jupiter at Pfaffenburg and the celebration of the festival there on 11 June with the rain miracle, though intriguing, is not necessarily convincing; see also A. R. Birley, *Marcus Aurelius: A Biography* (New Haven, 1987), 252, who points out that the festival seems to have had rather too much significance in a Pannonian context to be connected with this one event.

[122] For the development of this tradition see J. Geffcken, 'Das Regenwunder im Quadenlande: Eine antike-moderne Streitfrage', *NJA* 2 (1899), 253–69; G. Fowden, 'Pagan Versions of the Rain Miracle', *Historia*, 36 (1987), 83–95 (though the latter does not discuss this passage); see Jobst, *11. Juni*, p. 8 n. 2, for a complete bibliography down to 1978.

[123] *Orac. Sib.* 12. 250–5.

[124] Ibid. 12. 256–61; the eastern perspective is made especially plain by the description of Severus as ἀνὴρ ποικιλόμητις ἀφ' ἑσπερίης ἐπεγερθείς (l. 257).

[125] Ibid. 12. 185–6 καὶ τότε δ' αὐτὸς ἄναξ πέσεται δολίου ὑπὸ θηρός | γυμνάζων παλάμας. . . .

description of Commodus dressed as Herakles and participating in the great games of 192: these also seem to have been items which were not illustrated in the empire as a whole.[126] This is also true of Nero's sundry artistic accomplishments in Greece— though it would also appear that such personal aberrations made an impression.[127] The false Neros all knew that they should have a lyre.[128] The same sources, artwork and gossip, lie behind the information provided by the *Thirteenth Sibylline Oracle*.

The overall impression these texts give of the imperial government is that the emperors spent most of their time at war. This is not in fact an accurate picture, but it is an accurate reflection of the public image with which their subjects would have been familiar through coins, the plastic arts, and even imperial titulature, inflated as it came to be with military titles and names commemorating the defeat of foreign peoples. It would be hard to read a dedication of the 'imperator Caesar M. Aurelius Antoninus Augustus Commodus Germanicus, Sarmaticus maximus, holder of the tribunician power, proclaimed imperator seven times, consul four times'[129] and not come away with the impression that he was a great warrior. The same impression could be obtained from a glance at his cuirassed form on a coin or a statue depicting him in military garb. It could even be obtained at a festival of the imperial cult where a panegyric on the emperor would be recited. Menander Rhetor suggested that military themes were most appropriate for such performances: 'put war first, if the subject of your praise has distinction in this. Actions of courage should come into consideration first in such subjects: courage reveals an emperor more than do other virtues. If, however, he has never fought a war (a rare circumstance), you have no choice but to proceed to peaceful topics.'[130] Hippolytus put it less politely in his commentary on Daniel when he

---

[126] *Orac. Sib.* 12. 209–13.
[127] Ibid. 12. 84–92, 5. 30–1.
[128] Tac. *Hist.* 2. 8–9, with Chilver on 2. 9.
[129] *ILS* 394.
[130] Men. Rhet. 372. 27–373. 1 (trans. Russell and Wilson).

identified the fourth beast, the one with the iron teeth, as the Roman empire. It destroyed everything, just as the Romans did.[131]

Thus it is in the oracles. The emperors Caligula, Claudius, Vespasian, Hadrian, Maximinus Thrax, Gordian III, and Gallus are identified with Ares.[132] There is stress on warfare in lines describing Tiberius, Claudius, and Trajan,[133] and much extraneous bloodshed is attributed to the reigns of Pertinax and Didius Julianus.[134] When not fighting, emperors tend to be shown collecting money. Caligula gathered it in from all over the world, as did Hadrian, Nero, Caracalla, and Marcus Aurelius: a heterogeneous collection indeed.[135] The main features that tend to set emperors apart are personal quirks such as Nero's performances or those of Commodus, Elagabalus' religious obsession and Hadrian's passion for Antinous.[136] To judge from the evidence of papyri which refer to 'Antoninus the queer' (Elagabalus) or to the influence of the court ladies upon Claudius, these were the sorts of things that could distinguish one emperor from another in the popular imagination.[137]

Death was another feature of imperial biography that attracted speculation. A number of emperors are said to have died in rather more dramatic fashions than was in fact the case. Tiberius was 'smitten with burning steel', Vespasian fell before the rage of his army, Titus was killed by 'double-edged bronze' in the plain of Rome.[138] Nerva is also said to have been murdered.[139]

---

[131] Hippol. *Comm. in Dan.* 4. 5; cited on ll. 28–30 below.

[132] *Orac. Sib.* 12. 53 (Caligula), 68–70 (Claudius), 99–100 (Vespasian), 163–5 (Hadrian), 275 (Maximinus), 13. 16 (Gordian), 105 (Gallus).

[133] Ibid. 5. 20–3, 12. 40–4 (Tiberius), 12. 69–70 (Claudius, emphasizing the Illyrian campaigns but not mentioning Britain), 120. 150–4 (Trajan). [134] Ibid. 12. 236–49.

[135] Ibid. 12. 50–2 (Caligula), 8. 53–5 (Hadrian), 12. 79–81 (Nero), 266 (Caracalla?), 8. 69–70 (Marcus Aurelius).

[136] Ibid. 5. 30–1, 12. 84–92 (Nero), 12. 210–12 (Commodus), 12. 274 ὁ νεωκόρος (Elagabalus), 8. 56–8 (Hadrian and Antinous).

[137] *P. Oxy.* 3298. i. 2 β (ἔτους) Ἀντωνείνου τοῦ κορύφου with Rea's note ad loc.; ibid. 3299. ε. 1] ἀνοσίου Ἀντωνίνου μικροῦ (Elagabalus); Musurillo, *Acta Alexandrinorum*, 4. 2. 8–9 πα[ρουσῶν δὲ καί] | τῶν ματρωνῶν (Claudius). I am grateful to Mr J. P. Walker for advice on these matters.

[138] *Orac. Sib.* 12. 47 (Tiberius), 116 (Vespasian), 123 (Titus).

[139] *Orac. Sib.* 12. 146.

The tale of the death of Gordian III as well as the deaths of Decius and Gallus in the *Thirteenth Sibylline Oracle* also seems to have been influenced by unpleasant contemporary gossip.[140] This form of speculation illustrates the tendency of people to believe the worst of their rulers, a tendency that both Tacitus and Dio say was typical. The tales which were accepted by the readers of these texts as being divinely inspired truth stand as a testament to the imperial government's failure to win the understanding affection of its subjects.[141] In this these texts do not reflect sentiment that can be regarded as anti-Roman; rather, they reflect sentiment that may be regarded as typically Roman.

[140] See on ll. 104, 141–4 below.
[141] Tac. *Ann.* 4. 11; Dio 53. 19.

4

The *Thirteenth Sibylline Oracle*

COMPOSITION

Like the other oracles which deal with historical events, the *Thirteenth Sibylline Oracle* consists of a number of texts composed at various times in the period it covers. The evaluation of its information on any given point must therefore begin with a consideration of two separate issues: the learning of the final compiler and the learning of those authors whose texts were selected for inclusion. Closely connected to these questions are broader issues of the relation of this text to other extant oracles, the purpose of the person who compiled it, and the vision of the events shared by that writer with the contemporaries who appreciated this work as being one of divine inspiration.

The first eighty-eight lines present a rather difficult mixture of material from divers hands. Lines 89 to 154 read as a reasonably coherent whole, and to judge from two extremely obscure allusions to a person called the 'bastard son' (lines 105 and 142), as well as the extreme interest they evince in the brigand Mariades, they are the product of a single hand. This man's primary concern appears to have been with the fate of Syria between the accession of Decius and Uranius Antoninus' victory in 253. Lines 155 to 171 describe the reign and ruin of Valerian, the subsequent successes of Macrianus, and the ultimate victory of Odaenathus.[1] As there is no suggestion in the passage that Uranius ever stopped acting as a bulwark against the Persians—which the cessation of his coinage suggests happened in 253[2]—it is likely that the passage describing him was written before his

[1] See on ll. 161, 162–4, 165–6, 169.
[2] See on ll. 150–4.

downfall. He is the only figure, aside from Odaenathus, who is not said to die.

Lines 155 to 171 are very different in character from the rest of the poem. They treat the events of at least nine years in fourteen lines (the last two being concerned with the future glory of Odaenathus), while the previous one hundred and fifty-four lines (including the six-line introduction) deal with events of no more than ten. The difference in the scope of coverage they allow suggests that they were written after the rest of the oracle was compiled, by someone who wanted to bring a pre-existing book of prophecy up to date by including some lines on the latest person of interest. The bulk of the poem was thus probably compiled by the author of lines 89–154 in the summer of 253. It was put into its present form by the addition of the few final lines after 261. Since he wrote the great part of the extant text, it is the first compiler's view of history that is important for understanding the poem, and in this respect the most significant thing about the final author is that he found the work of his predecessor congenial.

The first line (which is seriously corrupted) is followed by a description both of the divinity who inspires the oracle and of the things he wants to be said. This divinity is the rather ubiquitous, pure, deathless, and imperishable god who gives power to kings and takes it away, and who desires his unwilling prophetess to speak to kings about the Roman empire. The lack of a specific theological statement here is of some interest. It suggests that the author was not interested in such matters and is one indication that this text should not be read as having a specific Jewish or Christian bias, contrary to the assumption of critics such as Rzach and Geffcken that the author must be one or the other.[3]

There is a substantial lacuna between lines 6 and 7. The Sibyl's programmatic introduction ends in line 6; line 7 begins with καί and concludes with a *non sequitur*, 'and swift Ares with a spear (?), many will be destroyed by him'. The next few lines (down to line

---

[3] Geffcken, *Comp. u. Ent.*, p. 59, argued that the author was a Christian; Rzach, *RE* iiA. 2160–1, thought that he was a Jew.

12) predict horrendous disasters in the reign of Gordian III. It is therefore clear that more than one line has been lost. The nature of the context provided by line 7 indicates that Gordian III could not have received the sort of introduction in this solitary line that rulers ordinarily receive in this and other Sibylline oracles; it also leaves no other place for him to be identified. The uniformity of practice elsewhere in introducing rulers makes it very unlikely that the author would have omitted an introduction for Gordian III here, while other considerations make it rather unlikely that the author would in any case have started with Gordian. It likewise seems improbable that the present *Twelfth Oracle* would have taken anything like its present form without some further oracle to follow it. The *Twelfth Oracle* runs from the victory of Caesar to the death of Alexander Severus, and the latter event is rather an anticlimax by comparison with other oracles that give lists of rulers. The *Fourteenth* concluded with the end of Roman rule, the list in the *Fifth* closes with a vision of eschatological ruin, and the emperors included in the *Eighth* appear in the context of the world's end. It is rather absurd, therefore, to believe that someone would have compiled two hundred and ninety-nine lines about the lives and deaths of Roman emperors, when there was nothing more important to predict at the end of it all than the death of one more Roman emperor.

The *Thirteenth* introduces both Uranius Antoninus and Odaenathus as active agents of divine salvation, and, if the *Twelfth Oracle* is read with it, all imperial history ends with the emergence of a great man from Syria. This development is rather more exciting, and the death of Severus Alexander indicates clearly that the *Twelfth Oracle* exists in its present form because it was intended to be read with the *Thirteenth*. If the author of the *Thirteenth* knew that he was writing about events after 235 (as it is obvious he does) and he wanted to be as complete as possible (which the scope of his compilation also makes obvious) then it would be strange if Maximinus Thrax were omitted. It is therefore probable that he was once included and that the story of his rule has been lost in the lacuna between lines 6 and 7.[4] The only event that survives for the reign of Gordian is the campaign against Persia in lines 13–20. It is neither a very detailed nor a very accurate account: it presents the war as a sudden uprising of barbarians who are driven back by the emperor, which in fact it was not. In truth, the final campaign seems to have lasted for several years and to have ended in a serious Roman defeat at Peroz-Sapor. It was fought by the Romans when they decided, and were able, to try to wipe out Persian gains made during the great civil war of 238.[5] This being the case, the information the oracle provides is clearly deficient, less sound than that in some of the passages that follow.

Lines 21 to 34 cannot have been composed any later than the summer of 247. They describe Philip's son as *Caesar* (which he ceased to be in 247), and the numerological equivalents for their names are based on the fact that one is called *Caesar* and the other *Augustus* (ll. 24–5): upon the first (letter) and twentieth five hundreds must be placed, i.e. five hundred (= Φ for Philip) must be placed on alpha (for *Augustus*) and kappa (for $K\alpha\hat{\imath}\sigma\alpha\rho$) to arrive at their names.[6] Once he has identified the rulers, the author goes on to say that there will be a treaty between the Romans and Persians but that it will be short; the Persians will break it and the Syrians will be destroyed (the treaty in question must be that made by Philip with Sapor just after his accession). The observation that it will not last long confirms a note in Zonaras to the effect that the treaty was broken soon after Philip's return to Rome because people were angry with him for giving up territory to the Persians.[7] The fact that the oracular author attributes the trouble to barbarian treachery rather than to Roman aggression may show no more than that he was not party to whatever diplomatic activity preceded. The interest he takes in the events should indicate that he was a Syrian.

An Egyptian perspective on events is evident in lines 35–49 in a prophecy that Rome will be safe so long as Egypt sends grain to Rome. The interesting element in these lines is that the author

---

[4] See on l. 7.   [5] See on ll. 13–20.
[6] See on ll. 24–5.   [7] Zon. 12. 19; see on ll. 25–7, 27.

gives what to contemporaries must have been a reasonably clear chronological context for his prediction. When the Romans defeat the Germans there will be a war with the Persians which the Persians will not win; Rome's rule will be preserved until it has ruled Egypt for 948 years, a comfortably long time away. Rome was at war with the trans-Danubian barbarians (who qualified as Germans) from 245 until the end of Philip's reign, while also fighting the Persians (to judge from this oracle, the only source). War on more than one frontier was not a novel phenomenon and there seems little reason why anyone should question Rome's survival in such circumstances. There must have been some other reason why it should be in question. Philip himself provided such a reason when he celebrated the foundation of Rome in 248, and the uncertainty that this caused may be reflected in the compiler's inclusion of a passage concerned with the duration of Rome's rule before describing events of 249.

Anniversaries could be a time for reflection, hope, or fear. One of the great anniversaries was Rome's foundation, and one of the most portentous was the thousandth.[8] Philip clearly made a great deal of it when he celebrated Rome's millennium, while Pacatianus made something of it when he rebelled against Philip later in 248. It is not difficult to believe that others might have been disturbed or excited by the new *saeculum.* Such people may have been reassured to learn from the Sibyl that the Roman empire had a long time left, and this may be why the compiler placed this text in Philip's reign.[9]

The next nine lines (50–8) are of diverse content. Four predict otherwise unattested trouble in Alexandria, three mention a flood which (they say) will do damage to an area which should probably be identified as Phoenicia, two with a flood at Mopsuestia in Cilicia and a riot at Aigeai. They are most interesting for structural reasons. The author was evidently concerned with chronology and possibly with incorporating material—such as the prophecy about Rome's existence—at points in his chronicle corresponding to the time when he knew they had been current. Their placement may indicate that he knew these things happened before Philip's death, and it is thus of some interest that he includes a second prophecy of an Alexandrian riot at lines 74–8 before describing the end of the reign (79–80). There seems little reason to predict the same thing twice within such a short space unless it is to help indicate the passage of time; the pattern of description is regular enough to suggest that this was indeed the way the author worked. That is to say, the author notes that something will happen to some group, whereupon other things happen to other people; in the ensuing lines the first group suffers the same fate that had just been predicted for it: cf. ll. 50–4, 74–8 (Alexandrians); 28–34, 56–63, 108–35, 147–50 (Syria). That the author envisages time passing between two such passages is clear from the use of clauses introduced by ἀλλ᾽ ὁπόταν or καὶ τότε or some other temporal expression.

In lines 59–60 there is a further reference to the war with Persia and to Julius Priscus, the brother of Philip the Arab, at Antioch.[10] This is followed by a prophecy of destruction for the cities of Arabia (ll. 64–73), whose introduction is most curious: it is νῦν followed by a verb in the present. Although the Sibyl is supposed to have lived centuries before the event, as seems to have been the case with the lines about Rome and the number 948, it may be supposed that the author included these lines because he knew that they were connected with a specific event. This may have been the revolt of Jotapianus, but the final line is hopelessly corrupt and it cannot be proved that what seems to be a reference to a man coming against the cities in question definitely belongs here.[11] What is certain, however, is that these lines reflect the preferential treatment of the cities in *Provincia Arabia* under Philip.[12] All the notable construction at Philippopolis (which is singled out with Bostra here) took place in Philip's reign, and these lines could not have been written before it received its name in *c.*245.

[10] See on ll. 21, 62–3.   [11] See on l. 64–73.   [12] See on l. 68.

Trouble in Alexandria is again predicted in lines 74–8, and its placement in Philip's reign, just before his death, suggests that this is the same trouble described by Dionysius of Alexandria in 249 following a persecution of the Christians.[13] The two lines that follow Philip's death add nothing to the tale of that event in other authors.

Decius is introduced in lines 81–3 and his reign is described in lines 84–8 as a time of murder, rape, and destruction. This may seem reasonable and straightforward at first sight, but the manuscript reading in line 87 αὐτίκα δ᾽ αὖ πίπτων τε λεηλασίαι τε φόνοι τε does not make sense in the context, and the next line says that this trouble will come about because of 'the previous reign'. Various attempts have been made to make sense here, but none are as attractive as Wilamowitz's alteration of πίπτων to πιστῶν (Christians).[14] This correction has been accepted by all subsequent writers on the oracle (myself included), but it does raise one difficulty: it is the only overtly Christian remark in an oracle that is otherwise manifestly pagan, in which the god Ares or the Hypsistos or 'the Great God' are seen as the prime movers of actions that affect mortals.[15] Geffcken, Kurfess, and, with some sensible reservation, Rzach all assume that this was the addition of a later interpolator. Only Rzach noticed that it was odd to have a late Christian interpolation for Decius (whose identification as a man appearing from the Dacians, of the number three hundred, would have been totally obscure to anyone not a contemporary) but not one for the equally vicious Valerian.[16] This is a very real problem, and it is most easily resolved by assuming that there was no late interpolator—that these lines were known to and included by the principal compiler because he thought they gave a reasonable view of Decius. Given what else he has to say about that emperor, this is not difficult to believe.

The tale of Mariades' raids follows right after the mention of

---

[13] Eus. *HE* 6. 41; see on ll. 74–8.   [14] See on l. 87.

[15] Theos Hypsistos: l. 109; Great God: l. 54; Ares: ll. 7 (?), 78, 138, 140.

[16] Rzach, *RE* iiA. 2161.

the persecution. This man is the best attested of the numerous rebels against imperial authority in this area during the second quarter of the third century. To judge from the space he receives and the way he is joined to various usurpers in a rabbinic commentary on Daniel, his success in wreaking havoc on the urban areas of the eastern provinces made a deep impression upon the imaginations of his contemporaries.[17] The compiler of this text, it would appear, even went so far as to identify Mariades with the returning Nero when he described the fall of Antioch in 252. While he was still acting on his own, the imperial authorities appear to have been incapable of putting a halt to his activities even though he operated in the most important regions of northern Syria and Cappadocia, and many who desired revolution are said to have joined with his friends in welcoming him when he returned with Sapor.

After describing the flight of Mariades across the Euphrates, the author devotes two lines to the unparalleled catastrophe at Abrittus in 251, where Decius died in battle with the Goths. The scope of this narration is one of the most striking illustrations of the author's lack of interest in and ignorance of western affairs. While Mariades receives twelve lines of detailed discussion, the destruction of an emperor rates only two, and there is no suggestion here that the author actually knew what Decius was doing when he died. A pair of usurpers, a major military disaster in the field before the one at Abrittus, and the fall of a major Thracian city (Philippopolis) are all ignored.[18]

Lines 103–5 introduce Trebonianus Gallus along with someone who is obscurely referred to as the 'bastard son'. The identity of this person is not entirely clear, and the notion that he would end up by killing Gallus (which bears no relationship to what is known to have happened) suggests that he may be the product of some confusion and rumour.[19] To the ill-informed the sudden disappearance of Decius' youngest son Hostilianus and the sudden promotion of Gallus' son Volusianus, as well as the fact that Gallus had no wife, may have led people to make up bizarre

[17] See on ll. 89–100.   [18] See on ll. 101–2, 104.   [19] See on ll. 105, 141–4.

stories about this imperial family. All that can be said for certain is that whatever the story was, it must have been reasonably well known in Syria for the author to allude to it here, in a context where he is otherwise extremely clear about events.

The fall of Antioch fills the next thirty-one lines. The destruction is said to be according to the divine plan of the great Hypsistos; the agent of destruction is the fugitive of Rome. The fugitive is a well-known figure in the prophetic literature of the imperial period. He is the emperor who fled to the east and will return at the head of its armies.[20] In adopting a prophecy that was by his time centuries old the author reveals the profound fatalism that lies at the heart of his understanding of the world in which he lived. He had earlier adopted a prophecy of woe for Antioch because fierce Ares would not leave it alone, and another in which the cities of Arabia were warned that, though they might devote themselves to the gods, they were none the less doomed to destruction. He had taken up verses that told of Rome's end centuries hence and would write of ruin for other places at the hand of Ares. All things had been decreed by the gods, and men could do nothing when a god chose to act. All one could do was lament for the victims, which this author duly does.

The outlook of the oracle is profoundly fatalistic. Everything was in the hands of the gods, who had chosen to inflict great harm on Syria. In the third century, as in any other, all that a person could do was hope that the gods would be kind. Preservation under these circumstances was a sign of divine favour. This spirit is shown clearly in an inscription that was scratched roughly on rocks overlooking the desert at Qual'at al Ḥalwâys in 252–3. It reports that some people were saved when 'the Hero' called upon Kronos to protect them from the barbarians.[21]

---

[20] See on ll. 122–8.

[21] *IGLS* 1799 ἔτους | δξφ´ | ὅτε οἱ | ἄνθρω||ποι εἰς νέ|⟨μ⟩εσιν ἔστ|αντο. ὁ δὲ | ἥρως τὸν | Κρόνον ἐκάλεσε | καὶ ἐδόθη | [α]ὐτῷ νείκη. | ο[ὕ]τε βάρβαροι οὔ||[τ]ε ⟨τ⟩ις ἐν τῇ γε⟨ι⟩τονίᾳ | ἐβλάθη ⟨ὅ⟩τ⟨ι⟩ τ⟨ά⟩ξαν δι|κῶν εἴσην διδεῖν. For the cult of Kronos in this area see R. Mouterde, 'Antiquités de l'Hermon et de la Beqâ'', *MUSJ* 29 (1951–2), 79–82. For the incident (which is not otherwise recorded) see Baldus, *Uranius Antoninus*, pp. 250–2.

Another text, carved next to it, urges people to read what is written on this stone and believe.[22] At roughly the same period Clodius Celsinus thanked Mars Gradivus for helping his men at the decisive moment against the enemies of the state.[23] Epigrams at Didyma tell how Apollo chose to save his people from Ares the barbarian,[24] a text from Syedra says that he advised the people to avert ruin by binding a statue of the war-god,[25] the people of Stratonicia in Caria asked their god if they would be safe for a year and inscribed his response (that he would not send the barbarians) on the wall of their bouleuterion;[26] not even the emperors of Rome could accomplish much unless the gods were willing. Zosimus later wrote that he would receive various oracles that foretold the downfall of the Roman state in their proper place.[27] This oracle, if it does nothing else, reveals the helplessness of someone living in Syria. He could do little but believe that this was the will of the gods and pray that the gods would send him a saviour.

This saviour appears, according to the oracle at lines 150–4, after the bastard son slew his father and was himself destroyed and after yet another Persian invasion. He is the priest sent from the sun who struck fear into barbarian hearts. He is Uranius Antoninus of Emesa, and it is with him that the principal author's work ends. In this author's compilation the history of Rome had moved from Caesar to the culmination of the design ordained by heaven: the Persian attack of 252, the great Persian victory at Barbalissos, the burning of Antioch, and the ravaging of Syria.

[22] *IGLS* 1800 ἀνάγνωθι | τὰ γεγραμ|μένα καὶ | πίστευσον.

[23] A. Alföldi, 'Epigraphica I', *Pannonia Konyutár*, 14 (1935), 6–10, esp. p. 7 on Mars Gradivus.

[24] *Insc. Did.* 159. I, II.

[25] L. Robert, *Documents de l'Asie mineure méridionale* (Paris, 1966), 97.

[26] *Insc. Strat.* 1103; see in general the magnificent treatment of divine protectors by P. Roussel, 'Le miracle de Zeus Panamoros', *BCH* 55 (1931), 70–116. For the outlook of people at this period in general see G. Alföldy, 'The Crisis of the Third Century as Seen by Contemporaries', *GRBS* 15 (1974), 89–111; MacMullen, *Roman Government's Response to Crisis*, pp. 1–23.

[27] Zos. 1. 58. 4; the fact that he does not fulfil the promise might suggest that he copied the remark out of an earlier source.

This author's history came to an end when a dynast at Emesa was able to defend his people from the invader. There can be little doubt that this person lived in northern Syria, or that he wrote in 253. There is little by way of sophistication of thought or breadth of vision, but this vision and his expression of it are more eloquent testimony to the impact of Rome upon her subjects and of the Persian King upon his enemies than a triumphal arch or the *Res Gestae Divi Saporis.*

Uranius Antoninus did not endure long, and no record is preserved of his end. That there is no mention of it in this oracle suggests that the text's first redaction comes precisely in 253, when he was still exercising influence over the affairs of the area. The emperor Valerian came east and set the frontier to rights in 254.

A second compiler seems to have been responsible for the final nineteen lines. The absence of any discussion of events between 253 and 260 is in stark contrast to the thorough treatment of the previous twenty years, which suggests that the person who added these lines decided to bring this book of prophecy up to date rather quickly after the victory of Odaenathus. Valerian appears in the guise of a bull to fight the venomous serpent, but his defeat is left without comment and there is nothing in the text concerning the fate of those who suffered in Sapor's invasion. Macrianus comes upon the scene as a well-horned stag: the identification is a play on the meaning of his name in Aramaic, and it may also recall the belief that stags were particularly hostile to serpents. He roams the mountains devouring them until the appearance of the great fire-breathing lion sent from the sun, who destroys him, along with the bow-footed goat (a play on Callistus' other name, Ballista) and the serpent. In his perfection the lion will rule over the Romans and the Persians will be weak.[28] The identity of the lion in this context is obvious. It is Odaenathus of Palmyra, and it is clear from the absence of any editorial remark or break in the narrative that his triumph was what the author was interested in. Once again the story of Roman history ends with the vision of rule by a Syrian.

[28] See on l. 169.

The material that is included in this oracle must reflect the vision of two different compilers, for the style of the final sections is markedly different from that of the rest of the oracle in terms of both content and coverage. But there does not seem to have been a real difference in outlook: the second compiler must have found the content of the existing oracle congenial. They must therefore have shared the same heroes and villains. The first and most obvious point is that the heroes are both Syrians, Uranius and Odaenathus, who were able to keep the Persians at bay. This reflects the deep antipathy towards the Persian state that must have been characteristic of people in the area. Culturally the region around Antioch, Emesa, and Palmyra was closer to that of Mesopotamia than it was to Rome. Aramaic was the language of the lower classes, but it was also the first language of the Palmyrene aristocracy. The way in which Roman terms are rendered in Palmyrene suggests that Roman institutions remained somewhat foreign in the eyes of even the most important Palmyrenes, the men who were responsible for the inscription of the bilingual texts that provide our evidence.[29] In the fourth century it was considered miraculous if a Roman officer could actually speak the native language,[30] and when a Uranius Antoninus or Odaenathus chose Roman symbols of power to represent their position, they did so in a way which suggests that they did not understand what these symbols might mean in a Roman context. Indeed, the dress and ceremonial of Odaenathus were very much those of a Near Eastern dynast, for all that he held the distinguished Roman title of *corrector totius orientis*.[31] The area between Antioch and Ctesiphon was still very much a cultural whole.[32] But this did not seem to have made much

---

[29] See app. IV.   [30] Jer. *v. Hil.* 13. 2–7.   [31] See app. IV.

[32] See M. Gawlikowski, 'Some Directions and Perspectives of Research', *Mesopotamia*, 22 (1987), pp. 11–17; Millar, 'Paul of Samosata', pp. 5–8. J. Gagé, 'Les Perses à Antioche et les courses de l'hippodrome au milieu du IIIe siècle, à propos du transfuge syrien Mariades', *Bulletin de la Faculté des Lettres de Strasbourg*, 31 (1953), 301–24, discussed the evidence for appreciation of Persian art at Antioch and suggested that this could be translated into a 'pro-Persian' party there; this conclusion has been shown to be unjustified: see A. Cameron, *Circus Factions: Blues and Greens at Rome and Byzantium* (Oxford, 1976), 200–1; H. Seyrig, 'Palmyra and the East', *JRS* 40 (1950), 1–7 = *Scripta Varia: Mélanges d'archéologie et*

difference to people's politics. A Palmyrene was principally concerned with the security of the city of Palmyra, and the Sassanids
were a threat to it. An Antiochene or an Emesene would have
thought first of the safety of his own city; he would have been
proud of its native traditions but this would not have made him
think any better of Sapor: personal security was far more important than a sense of cultural identity. This was no doubt the
attitude of the vast majority of provincial aristocrats.

The oracle in its present form is the work of two people who
lived in Syria and could write Greek verse. They hated the
Persians, whose appearance calls forth extreme oracular vitriol:
they are 'evil' (ll. 10, 110) and arrogant (ll. 37, 124), they are the
wolf who will ravage the Syrian flock (ll. 29–30), and are likened
to a fierce venom-spitting serpent (ll. 160–1, 168). Equally, they
despised Mariades, the ally of the Persians, and they admired
Uranius and Odaenathus. The fact that they should express
themselves in this oracular form shows that they were at home
with features of the western classical tradition. Unlike the Jewish
authors of Sibylline oracles and other pseudepigrapha they were
not trying to make a cultural or religious point. They did not
need to, since they were pagans, members of the upper class, and
in the majority. The form may have been chosen because of piety
and because it was traditional. It placed the events of the third
century in a traditional context, that of an oracular tradition
which stretched back as far as anyone could remember. The
authors of the *Thirteenth Sibylline Oracle* admired the men who
could protect them. Roman emperors were distant figures.
Gordian was admired because he invaded Persia. The attitude
towards Philip was ambivalent. The treaty that he made was
resented, and so was the wealth that poured into the cities of
Provincia Arabia. Decius did nothing for them, and his reign was
primarily notable as the time when Mariades ravaged the land.

d'histoire (Paris, 1985), 249–57 (note esp. p. 7 — p. 255, 'They copied the Temples of
Antioch and Damascus, they began to build long colonnaded streets as they saw them in the
towns of Syria. Yet in all probability these changes did not deeply affect their minds'.) F. G.
Millar, 'Empire, Community and Culture in the Roman Near East: Greeks, Syrians, Jews
and Arabs', *JJS* 38 (1987), 143–64, provides an excellent recent summary of the issues.

Gallus was a disaster and he is presented in an unfavourable light. Aemilianus was no more than a name, and he was far less important than Uranius. The most important thing to these men would be that they should have someone to protect them from Persia, and the final redactor of the oracle found the fact that Odaenathus was a Palmyrene no more objectionable than did the intellectuals who flocked to Palmyra to enjoy Odaenathus' patronage.

THE SURVIVAL OF THE *THIRTEENTH SIBYLLINE ORACLE*

The *Twelfth* and *Thirteenth Sibylline Oracles* present the history of Rome from the foundation of the principate to the 260s and were circulated together in the mid-third century AD. In the manuscripts they follow upon another text of historical content—the *Eleventh Sibylline Oracle*—and there is some question as to whether or not it too was joined to the *Twelfth* and *Thirteenth* when they were given to the world in something like their present condition, or whether this other text was added to them somewhat later or perhaps not at all, before the collection that preserves them was assembled after the Arab conquest.[33]

Of the three possibilities outlined in the last paragraph the third is the least likely. While prophecies of Egypt's enslavement such as that which concludes the *Eleventh Oracle* might be relevant to any period in the first six centuries of the Christian era, there is no reason why this statement of the obvious, which holds out little hope of better things to come and which by the seventh century would be of no relevance to past or future circumstances, should have been preserved at length until or beyond the end of Roman rule. All the other extant oracles (if the *Twelfth* is taken with the *Thirteenth*) either conclude with eschatological visions or are primarily theological. The *Thirteenth*, finishing as it does

---

[33] This problem (to which the answers are admittedly somewhat speculative) has not been discussed at length. For what there is see Geffcken, *Comp. u. Ent.*, pp. 54–5; his assumption that *Orac. Sib.* 11 must have been composed after 226 on the basis of 11. 161, which refers to the Parthians as destroyed, is not convincing (*Comp. u. Ent.*, p. 66); Rzach, *RE* iiA. 2154–5, 2165.

with a man who will defeat the Persians and rule the Romans, would clearly be of interest after the Arab conquest, when the collection that preserves it was made; in the intervening years men might well have thought this conclusion to contemporary affairs a possibility. Unless it was being circulated with the *Thirteenth* by the time of the Arab invasions there is no reason why anyone should be particularly interested in the *Eleventh*. If it was being circulated with the *Twelfth* and *Thirteenth* by that time, it is clearly of interest, for it gives a history of the world from the flood down to the point where the *Twelfth* begins. All human history could then be read as a Sibylline prophecy up to the Arab conquest.

There is another point which reinforces the inference that the three oracles were circulated together. Though it may not be decisive in the light of Lactantius' observation about Sibyls,[34] it should be noted that there is no identification of the prophetess in the *Twelfth* or *Thirteenth Oracles*. There is one such at the end of the *Eleventh* that could serve for all three, identifying them as the work of the Delphic Sibyl. There is also a statement of method in the *Eleventh* (unparalleled elsewhere) to help with the interpretation of all the poems. Here the Sibyl says that she will give the numerical value of a person's name, name her subjects in acrostics according to the first initial, and thus reveal who they are.[35] When taken separately none of the points outlined in this or the previous paragraph is decisive, but their cumulative force should be.

The hypothesis that the current *Eleventh*, *Twelfth*, and *Thirteenth Sibylline Oracles* were circulated together as three books of the Delphic Sibyl before they came into the present collection is a reasonably secure one. But the proposition that they were circulated in this way when the prophecy about Odaenathus was written in the third century is not. The *Twelfth* is not centred on any specific area of the empire—though there is much more on

---

[34] Lact. *DI* 1. 6. 13; see ch. 3 n. 13.
[35] *Orac. Sib.* 11. 17–18 ὧν ἀριθμοὺς λέξω καὶ ἀκροστιχίοις ὀνομήσω | γράμματος ἀρχομένου καὶ τοὔνομα δηλώσαιμι.

Asia Minor than areas west of it, and some of the prophecies in
that oracle were clearly written by people whose information was
quite good for the more easterly regions and virtually non-
existent for the western. Most significant in this regard are those
prophecies about Vespasian, Trajan, Avidius Cassius, and Pescennius Niger.[36] The *Thirteenth*, as has been seen, is very clearly a
Syrian composition. The *Eleventh* is patently concerned with
Egypt and a good deal of it is manifestly Jewish. Before the
Eleventh Oracle reaches the founding of Rome by Aeneas (*sic*), the
existence of Homer, the conquests of Alexander, the behaviou
of the Diadochoi, Cleopatra, Caesar, and the Roman conquest,
there are the tales of the tower of Babel, the ten plagues, the
parting of the Red Sea, and the reign of Solomon.[37] This does not
seem to be the sort of history that would have particularly
interested the author who compiled the *Twelfth* and *Thirteenth
Sibylline Oracles*. His purpose is well enough served without it,
and this sort of doctrinal assertion is at odds with his own
practice. It may therefore be assumed that this poem was attached
to the *Twelfth* and *Thirteenth Oracles* at some point after the time
of Odaenathus.

The notion of a second edition that brings together the
Eleventh with the *Twelfth* and *Thirteenth Oracles* may explain not
only why one is so different from the other two but might also
elucidate an anomaly.in the *Twelfth*. This is the presence of
overtly Christian prophecy. The birth of Christ is put in the reign
of Augustus at *Orac. Sib.* 12. 28–34, and there is a peculiar statement that the world of the great deathless god will be incarnate
on earth, included after a mention of Caesar (who seems to have
been misidentified with Augustus) in line 232.[38] A Jewish version
of pre-Christian history such as that provided by the *Eleventh
Oracle* would be extremely attractive to a Christian, and it is not
difficult to believe that the person who included the two overtly

---

[36] *Orac. Sib.* 12. 99–112 (Vespasian), 147–55 (Trajan), 182–5 (Avidius Cassius), 250–5
(Niger).

[37] Geffcken, *Comp. u. Ent.*, pp. 65–6; Rzach, *RE* iiA. 2151–5.

[38] A. Kurfess, 'Die Oracula Sibyllina XI (IX)–XIV (XII): Nicht christlich sondern
jüdisch', *ZRGG* 7 (1955), 270–2; cf. Geffcken, *Comp. u. Ent.*, p. 58; Rzach, *RE* iiA. 2158.

Christian passages in the *Twelfth* thought of circulating the three poems together, and he may have made an additional change by removing any passage that identified the Sibyl in 12 and 13 which would conflict with the passage now at the end of 11 (or simply have moved that passage from its original location in one of those two texts). This would provide a reasonable history of the world from the flood to the coming (or second coming) of the saviour.

TEXT, TRANSLATION, AND COMMENTARY

The manuscript tradition for the *Sibylline Oracles* has been the subject of several excellent studies, so it will not be necessary to treat it at great length here.[1] There are two collections. One of them (A) is represented by eight extant manuscripts which may be divided into two classes and whose readings can be supplemented by the reports of three other codices known to the editors of early printed editions. The collection contains the *Sibylline Preface* and oracles numbered 1–8 (a numeration that is retained in modern editions). There is no way to date the archetype—though the connection between the *Preface* and the *Sibylline Theosophy* suggests that it cannot be dated much before the end of the fifth century AD—and the earliest manuscripts are of the fifteenth century.[2]

The second collection (B in modern editions) is represented by four manuscripts which contain four oracles numbered 11–14 (the numeration is retained by their editors) and three others numbered 9, 10, and 15. These are not printed in the modern editions as 9 contains 6, 7. 1, 8. 218–428 from collection A; 10 parallels 4 in A, and 15 parallels 8. 1–9. As B is not the same collection as A, the texts should not have been combined and it is to be hoped that a future edition of the oracles will print them separately. Since the *Fourteenth Oracle* predicts the Arab conquest, the present collection cannot have been made before the mid-seventh century.[3]

As A is irrelevant to the *Thirteenth Oracle*, there is no need here to give details of its constituent manuscripts.[4] The manuscripts in B are as follows:

1. *Codex Vaticanus gr.* 1120 (Q): Copied in the fourteenth century, it contains 9–14. It is damaged and difficult to read

---

[1] Rzach, pp. v–xvi; Geffcken, pp. xxi–liii.
[2] See above, pp. 95–6.
[3] See above, pp. 154–7, for a discussion of the connections between these texts.
[4] For descriptions see Rzach, pp. vii–xii; Geffcken, pp. xxii–xxv.

in many places. 12. 259–13. 6 and 14. 147–67 are missing altogether.
2. *Codex Ambrosianus gr.* E 64 (M): Copied in the fifteenth century, it contains only 9 and 14.
3. *Codex Vaticanus gr.* 743 (V): Copied in the fourteenth century, it contains 9–15. Its readings are generally inferior to those of Q and the scribe seems to have been copying a manuscript he had difficulty reading; he left many lacunae where he knew that something was missing.
4. *Codex Monacensis gr.* 312 (H): This is an apograph of V copied in January 1541 by Michael Rosaitos.

EDITIONS

The earliest printed edition of the *Sibylline Oracles* is that of Sixtus Birken, published at Basle in 1545, which was based on Codex Monacensis gr. 351 (in Collection A).[5] It contained 1–7. 485, and all subsequent editions down to the nineteenth century likewise contain only collection A. Collection B was not suspected until Cardinal Mai discovered M in 1817, and it was only published after Mai discovered QV in the Vatican Library in 1828. His edition, which has no critical apparatus and few alterations in the manuscript readings, is in *Scriptorum veterum nova collectio e Vaticanis codicibus*, iii/3 (Rome, 1828), 206–15 (11–14 only). The first edition to include both collections was J. H. Friedlieb's in 1852. It has an extensive introduction, a text, a German translation, and 102 pages of somewhat dubious textual notes at the end.[6] Friedlieb's edition was completely superseded the next year by the completion of one by Charles Alexandre.[7] Alexandre, a member of the Académie des Inscriptions et Belles Lettres and editor of *Dictionnaire grec-français*, was one of the foremost Hellenists of his age and his work remains the founda-

---

[5] For a history of the early editions see Geffcken, pp. xi–xii.

[6] F. H. Friedlieb, *Die sibyllinische Weissagungen, vollständig gesammelt nach neuer Handschriftenvergleichung, mit kritischem Kommentare und metrischer deutscher Übersetzung* (Leipzig, 1852).

[7] C. Alexandre, Χρησμοὶ Σιβυλλακοὶ *Oracula Sibyllina*, i (Paris, 1841–43), ii (Paris, 1856); i² (Paris, 1869).

tion of all future study. The first edition (which includes a verse translation in Latin) was supplemented in 1856 by a volume in Latin containing seven studies of various problems connected with the oracles. In 1869, two years before his death at the age of 74, Alexandre produced a second edition of the text and transla- tion. In 1891 Alois Rzach published his edition with an important discussion of the manuscript tradition, an extremely speculative text, full apparatus, and a limited but convenient collection of *loci similes*.[8] J. Geffcken's edition in 1902 is the only subsequent one containing all the oracles (though like previous editors he did not print 9, 10, and 15 separately).[9] It provides an extensive dis- cussion of the manuscripts, an extremely conservative text, and some useful notes. There are two translations of the complete corpus into English. One, by M. S. Terry, in blank verse, appeared in 1890;[10] the other, by J. J. Collins, in prose, was published in 1983.[11] Both include introductions discussing the texts (that by Collins is quite extensive) and some critical notes.

The present edition of the *Thirteenth Sibylline Oracle* is based upon a fresh collation of Q and V. Throughout the preparation of this edition and commentary, I have been fully conscious of the tremendous debt that I owe to the labour of Alexandre, Rzach, and Geffcken. If it had not been for their superb scholar- ship and penetrating insights, my own work would not have been possible.

---

[8] A. Rzach, *Oracula Sibyllina* (Leipzig, 1891).

[9] J. Geffcken, *Die Oracula Sibyllina* (GCS 8, Leipzig, 1902).

[10] M. S. Terry, *The Sibylline Oracles* (New York, 1890).

[11] J. J. Collins, 'The Sibylline Oracles', in J. H. Charlesworth (ed.), *Old Testament Pseudepigrapha* (London, 1983), 317–472. I have not seen the recent German translation of the Sibylline Oracles by R. Clemens.

Sigla

Codices e Ω derivati

Q = Vaticanus gr. 1120   saec. xiv
V = Vaticanus gr. 743   saec. xiv

Editiones praecipuae

Friedlieb   Lipsiae, 1852
Alexandre   Lutetiae, 1869
Rzach   Lipsiae, 1891
Geffcken   Lipsiae, 1902

Σιβύλλης λόγος ιγ´

⟨ἔν⟩θεον ἀείδειν με λόγον κέλεται †μέγαν†
ἅγιος ἀθάνατος θεὸς ἄφθιτος, ὃς βασιλεῦσιν
δῶκε κράτος καὶ ἀφείλατ᾽ ἰδὲ χρόνον ὥρισεν αὐτοῖς
ἀμφοτέρων, ζωῆς τε καὶ οὐλομένου θανάτοιο.
καὶ τὰ μὲν οὐράνιός με θεὸς ἀέκουσαν ἐπάγει   5
ἀγγέλλειν βασιλεῦσιν ὑπὲρ βασιληΐδος ἀρχῆς.
* * * * *
καὶ δόρυ θοῦρος Ἄρης· ὑπὸ δ᾽ αὐτοῦ πάντες ὀλοῦνται,
νηπίαχος γεραός τε θεμιστεύσει ἀγοραῖσιν.
πολλοὶ γὰρ πόλεμοί τε μάχαι τ᾽ ἀνδροκτασίαι τε
λιμοὶ καὶ λοιμοὶ σεισμοὶ μαλεροί τε κεραυνοὶ   10
ἀστεροπῶν τε φοραὶ πολλαὶ κατὰ κόσμον ἅπαντα
ἠδὲ λεηλασίη τε καὶ ἱεροσυλία ναῶν.
καὶ τότε δὴ Περσῶν ἐπανάστασις ἀλφηστήρων
Ἰνδῶν Ἀρμενίων Ἀράβων θ᾽ ἅμα· καὶ περὶ τούτοις
Ῥωμαῖος πελάσει βασιλεὺς πολέμου ἀκόρητος   15
αἰχμητὰς ἐπάγων καὶ ἐπ᾽ Ἀσσυρίους, νέος Ἄρης·
ἄχρις ἐπ᾽ Εὐφράτην τε βαθύρροον ἀργυροδίνην
ἐκτανύσει, πέμψας λόγχην πολεμήϊος Ἄρης,
καππέσετ᾽ ἐν τάξει τυφθεὶς αἴθωνι σιδήρῳ   20
⟨ζηλοσύνης⟩ ἕνεκα, καί ⟨γε⟩ προδοθεὶς ὑφ᾽ ἑταίρου.   19
αὐτίκα δ᾽ αὖτ᾽ ἄρξει φιλοπόρφυρος αἰχμητής τε
ἐκ Συρίης προφανείς, Ἄρεος φόβος, ἔν τε καὶ υἱῷ
Καίσαρι καὶ πείσει πᾶσαν χθόνα. τοὔνομα δ᾽ αὐτοῖς
ἐν πέλετ᾽ ἀμφοτέροισιν· ἐπὶ πρώτου κεικοστοῦ
πένθ᾽ ἑκατοντάδες εἰσὶ τεθειμέναι. ἡνίκα δ᾽ οὗτοι   25

Title σιβύλλης λόγος ιγ´ V: deest in Q   1–6 desunt in Q   1 θεσπέσιόν με λόγον κέλεται μέγαν αὖτις ἀείδειν temptavit Rzach   ἔνθεον Hartel:
θεόν V: Alexandre omisit θεόν et post μέγαν proposuit ἀνθρώποισιν   †μέγαν†]
μέγαρ αὖθις Hartel (αὖτις Friedlieb): μεγαλακὴς cogitavit Geffcken
3 ἀφείλατ᾽ ἰδὲ Alexandre: ἀφείλατο δὴ V   4 ἀμφοτέρων V: ἀμφότερον
Meineke   5 με Alexandre: τε V   6 post hunc versum lacuna plurimorum
versuum manifesta   7 hic versus 12. 258 sequitur in Q, omissis omnibus qui quon-

The Thirteenth Sibylline Oracle

The pure deathless imperishable god who gives power to kings and takes it away, and he has ordained the time both of life and of ruinous death for them, commands me to sing an inspired song. The heavenly God commands me on the one hand, against my will, to announce these things to kings about the empire of Rome. . . .

. . . and a spear, swift Ares, all will be destroyed by him, childish and old he will give justice in the market-places; for there will be many wars and battles and killings of men and famines and plagues and terrible earthquakes and lightning strikes and lightning bolts throughout the entire world, and robbery and the desecration of temples.

Then there will be an uprising of the evil Persians, Indians, Armenians, and Arabs at the same time; the Roman king, insatiate of war, will draw near to them, driving warriors against the Assyrians, a new Ares; this warlike Ares will go as far as the deep-flowing, silver-eddied Euphrates, hurling his spear, he will fall in the ranks, smitten by gleaming iron because of jealousy and moreover betrayed by a companion.

Then straight away will rule a lover of purple and a warrior, appearing from Syria, the dread of Ares, together with Caesar his son, and he will pacify the entire earth: one name will attach to both of them: upon the first and twentieth five hundreds will be

dam interiacebant   8 γεραός τε θεμιστεύσει Potter (θεμιστεύσει iam Bowie): γεγαώς τε θεμιστεύει Q: γεγαῶτες θεμιστεύει V: γεραός τε θεμιστεύων Alexandre   11 ἀστεροπῶν τε φοραὶ πολλαὶ Geffcken: ἀσσυρίων τε πόροι πολλοὶ Ω: ἀστεροπαί τ᾽ ὄμβροι τ᾽ ὀλοοὶ Rzach   14 Ἰνδῶν Ἀρμενίων Ἀράβων] Ω Ἰνδῶν τ᾽ Ἀρμενίων τ᾽ Ἀράβων Rzach   18 πέμψας λόγχην Geffcken: πέμψας ὀλόγην Ω: λόγχην ὀλοὴν Rzach   πολεμήϊος Rzach: πολέμιος Ω   19–20 versus transposuit Potter   19 ⟨ζηλοσύνης⟩ Geffcken: ἰδετέως Q: ἴδετε ὡς V: δυσσεβίης Alexandre   ⟨γε⟩ Potter: γὰρ Ω   20 αἴθωνι Mai: αἴθονι Ω   22 ἔν τε καὶ υἱῷ] ἠδὲ καὶ υἱὸς Rzach   23 Καίσαρι] Καίσαρ Rzach   πείσει] πέρσει Alexandre   24 ἔν πέλετ᾽ Alexandre: ἐκ πέλετ᾽ Ω

168 Σιβύλλης Λόγος ιγ'

ἐν πολέμοις ἄρξουσι θεμιστονόμοι δὲ γένωνται,
ἄμπαυσις πολέμου βαιὸν ἔσσεται, οὐκ ἐπὶ δηρόν·
ἀλλ' ὁπόταν ποίμνῃ λύκος ὅρκια πιστώσηται
πρὸς κύνας ἀργιόδοντας, ἔπειτα δὲ δηλήσηται
βλάψας εἰροπόκους ὄιας, περὶ δ' ὅρκια ῥίψει,   30
καὶ τότε δῆρις ἄθεσμος ὑπερφιάλων βασιλήων
ἔσσεται ἐν πολέμοισι, Σύροι δ' ἔκπαγλ' ἀπολοῦνται,
Ἰνδοί τ' Ἀρμένιοί τ' Ἄραβες Πέρσαι Βαβυλῶνες,
ἀλλήλους ὀλέσουσι διὰ κρατερὰς ὑσμίνας.
ἀλλ' ὁπόταν Ῥωμαῖος Ἄρης Γερμανὸν ὀλέσσῃ   35
Ἄρεα νικήσας θυμοφθόρον ὠκεανοῖο,
δὴ τότε καὶ Πέρσῃσιν, ὑπερφιάλοις ἀνθρώποις,
πουλυετὴς πόλεμος, νίκη δ' οὐκ ἔσσεται αὐτοῖς·
ὡς γὰρ ἐφ' ὑψηλῆς πολυδειράδος ἠνεμοέσσης
ἠλιβάτου πέτρης ἰχθὺς οὐ νήχετ' ἐπ' ἄκρης,   40
οὐδὲ χέλυς πέταται, αἰετὸς δ' οὐ νήχετ' ἐς ὕδωρ
οὕτω καὶ Πέρσαι μακρόθεν νίκης γεγάωσιν
ἤματι τῷ, ἐφ' ὅσον τε φίλη τροφὸς Ἰταλιήων
κειμένη ἐν πεδίῳ Νείλου παρὰ θέσφατον ὕδωρ
ἑπταλόφῳ Ῥώμῃ ὥρης ἀπόμοιραν ἰάλλοι.   45
ταῦτα δὲ πέπρωται· ὅσσον δέ τοι οὔνομα, Ῥώμη,
εἰν ἀριθμοῖς ἔσχεν ψηφιζομένοιο χρόνοιο,
τοσσούτους λυκάβαντας ἑκοῦσά σε σιτομετρήσει
δῖα πόλις μεγάλη Μακηδονίοιο ἄνακτος.
ἄλλο δ' ἄχος πολύμοχθον Ἀλεξανδρεῦσιν ἀείσω   50
ὀλλυμένοις διὰ δῆριν ἀεικελίων ἀνθρώπων.
ἄρσενες οἱ πρότερον δεινοὶ τότ' ἀνάλκιδες ὄντες
εἰρήνην στέρξουσι δι' ἡγεμόνων κακότητα.
καὶ χόλος Ἀσσυρίοις ἥξει μεγάλοιο θεοῖο
αὐτούς τ' ἐξολέσει ποταμοῦ χείμαρρος, ὃς ἐλθὼν   55
Καίσαρος ἐς πτολίεθρα Χαναναίους ἀδικήσει.

27 ἄμπαυσις Alexandre: ἀνάπαυσις Ω   29 ἀργιόδοντας Alexandre:
ἀργειόδοντας Ω   δηλήσηται Alexandre: δηλήσεται Ω   30 ὄιας
Alexandre: οἷς Ω   31 ἄθεσμος Alexandre: ἀθέσμων Ω   33 Ἀρμένιοί
Alexandre: ἀρμενίοις Ω   38 πουλυετὴς Alexandre: πολυετὴς Ω
40 νήχετ' Alexandre: νήχεται Ω   42 γεγάωσιν Geffcken: γεγαῶσιν Ω:

placed. When they will rule in wars and become lawgivers, there will briefly be an end to war, not for long: when the wolf shall swear oaths to the dogs of gleaming teeth against the flock he will ravage, harming the wool-fleeced sheep, and he will break the oaths and then there will be the lawless strife of arrogant kings, in wars the Syrians will perish terribly, Indians, Armenians, Arabs, Persians, and Babylonians will ruin each other in mighty battles.

When the Roman Ares destroys the German, defeating the life-destroying Ares of Ocean, then there will be long war for the Persians, arrogant men, and victory will not be with them; for just as a fish does not swim on the top of the cliff of lofty, many-ridged, wind-blown, sun-beaten rock, nor a turtle fly nor an eagle swim in water, even so shall the Persians be very far from victory at that time, as long as the dear nurse of the Italians situated in the plain by the renowned stream of the Nile shall bear the portion of harvest to seven-hilled Rome. The limit for this has been set. For your name contains in numbers the expanse of time allotted to you, Rome, and for that number of years will the great god-like city of the Macedonian king willingly provide you with grain.

I will sing of another much-suffering grief for the Alexandrians destroyed through the strife of evil men. Men who were once dreadful then, becoming feeble, will long for peace because of the evil of their leaders.

The wrath of the great god will smite the Assyrians and the flood of the river will destroy them, coming into the land of Caesar to injure the Canaanites.

γεγάασιν Alexandre   45 ὥρης Mendelssohn: μοίραν Ω: μοίρην ἀπόμοιραν Rzach   46 δὲ πέπρωται Mendelssohn: τε πέταται Ω: δέ τοι πέλεται Rzach   47 εἰν ἀριθμοῖς Friedlieb: ἐναρίθμοις Ω: εἰναρίθμως Alexandre   ἔσχεν ψηφιζομένοιο Geffcken: ἔσχεν ψηφιζόμενοι Ω   48 σε Mendelssohn: τε Ω   50 ἄλλο δ' ἄχος Alexandre: ἄλλο ἄλλος Ω   52 δεινοὶ τότ' Alexandre: δεινοὶ καὶ Ω: δειλοὶ καὶ Geffcken   54 Ἀσσυρίοις Alexandre: ἀσσυρίους Ω   55 ποταμοῦ Alexandre: ποταμοῖο Ω   56 ἐς πτολίεθρα Alexandre: ἐμπτολίεθρα Ω   Χαναναίους Q: Σαταnναίους V

Πύραμος ἀρδεύσει Μόψου πόλιν, ἔνθα πεσοῦνται
Αἰγαῖοι διὰ δῆριν ὑπερμενέων ἀνθρώπων.
τλήμων Ἀντιόχεια, σὲ δ' οὐ λείψει βαρὺς Ἄρης
Ἀσσυρίου πολέμοιο ἐπειγομένου περὶ σεῖο·   60
σοῖς γὰρ ἐνὶ μελάθροισι κατοικήσει πρόμος ἀνδρῶν,
ὃς Πέρσας μὲν ἅπαντας ὀϊστοβόλους πολεμήσει,
αὐτὸς ὁ Ῥωμαίων γεγαὼς βασιληΐδος ἀρχῆς.
νῦν κοσμεῖσθε, πόλεις Ἀράβων, ναοῖς σταδίοις τε
ἠδ' ἀγοραῖς πλατείαις τε καὶ ἀγλαοφεγγέϊ πλούτῳ   65
καὶ ξοάνοις χρυσῷ τε καὶ ἀργύρῳ ἠδ' ἐλέφαντι·
ἐκ πάντων δὲ μάλιστα μαθηματική περ ἐοῦσα
Βόστρα Φιλιππόπολίς ⟨τε⟩, ἵν' ἔλθητ' εἰς μέγα πένθος.
οὐδέ σ' ὀνήσειεν σφαιρώματα καγχαλόωντα
ζῳδιακοῦ κύκλου, Κριὸς Ταῦρος Δίδυμοί τε,   70
ἠδ' ὁπόσοι σὺν τοῖσιν ἐν οὐρανῷ ἰνδάλλονται
ἀστέρες ὡρονόμοι, τλήμων, πόλλ' οἷς σὺ πέποιθας,
ὁππόταν ἦμαρ ἐκεῖνο τὸ σὸν μετόπισθε πελάσσῃ.
νῦν δὲ φιλοπτολέμοισιν Ἀλεξανδρεῦσιν ἀείσω
δεινοτάτους πολέμους· πουλὺς δ' ἄρα λαὸς ὀλεῖται   75
ἀστῶν ὀλλυμένων ὑπ' ἀντιπάλων πολιητῶν
μαρναμένων στυγερῆς ἔριδος χάριν, ἀμφὶ δὲ τούτοις
ἀϊκὰς φοβερωπὸς Ἄρης στήσει πολέμοιο.
καὶ τότε δ' αὖ μεγάθυμος ἑῷ σὺν παιδὶ κραταιῷ
καππέσεται δολίως διὰ πρεσβύτερον βασιλῆα.   80
τὸν μέτα δ' αὐτ' ἄρξει κρατερᾶς Ῥώμης ἐριθήλου
ἄλλος ἄναξ μεγάθυμος ἐπιστάμενος πολεμίζειν,
Δακῶν ἐξαναδύς, τριηκοσίων ἀριθμοῖο·
ἔσσεται ἐκ τετράδος γενεῆς, πολλοὺς δ' ἀπολέσσει,
καὶ τότε δὴ μάλα πάντας ἀδελφειούς τε φίλους τε   85
ἐξολέσει βασιλεὺς καὶ ἀποφθιμένων βασιλήων·
αὐτίκα δ' αὖ πιστῶν τε ληλασίαι τε φόνοι τε
ἔσσοντ' ἐξαπίνης γε διὰ πρότερον βασιλῆα.

---

58 Αἰγαῖοι Alexandre: αἴγαιοι Ω   62 ὀϊστοβόλους Alexandre: οἰστρο-
βούλους Q: οἰστροβύλους V   63 ὁ Ῥωμαίων γεγαὼς] ὁ Ῥωμαίων
λελαχών Rzach   64 σταδίοις τε Alexandre: τε διοίσει Ω   65–6 ἀγλαοφεγγέϊ . . . τε καὶ deest in Q   68 Βόστρα Φιλιππόπολίς ⟨τε⟩ Alexandre:
Βάστρα Φιλιππόπολις V: Βόστρα Φιλιππόπολι Q   ἔλθητ' Rzach: ἔλθῃς Ω

The Pyramus will flood the city of Mopsus, then the Aigeans
will fall through the violence of overbearing men.
Wretched Antioch, harsh Ares will not leave you with the
Assyrian war raging around you; the foremost of men, who will do
battle against all the arrow-shooting Persians, will dwell among
your houses, he himself coming from the royal house of the
Romans.
Now be adorned, cities of Arabia, with temples and stadia and
market-places and fora and splendidly shining wealth and images
in gold, silver, and ivory; and most of all Bostra, though you be pre-
eminent among them all in astrology, and Philippopolis, so that
you will come to great grief. The resounding spheres of the zodiac
circle will not profit you, not the Ram, the Bull, the Gemini, nor as
many other ascendant stars as appear with them in heaven; alas,
you will have placed great trust in them by the time your day shall
finally come.
Now I sing of dreadful wars to the war-loving Alexandrians; a
great multitude will be destroyed, cities ruined by the rivalry of
citizens fighting for the sake of hateful envy, and Ares, dreadful of
aspect, will place the swift flights of war among them. Then the
great-hearted man with his mighty son will fall treacherously
because of the elder king.
After him another great-hearted king will rule mighty, flour-
ishing Rome, skilled in war, emerging from the Dacians, of the
number three hundred; he will be of the fourth race and destroy
many, then indeed the king will destroy all the brothers and
friends of the slaughtered kings, and immediately there will be
spoliation and murder of the faithful because of the former king.

69 οὐδέ σ᾽ ὀνήσειεν Rzach: οὐ γάρ σ᾽ ὀνήσει Ω: οὐ γὰρ ὀνήσει σε Alexandre: οὐ γὰρ
ὀνήσειεν Mendelssohn   70 ζῳδιακοῦ Alexandre: ζωδιακοῦ Ω   Δίδυμοί
Mai: Δίδυμός Ω   72 πόλλ᾽ οἷς σὺ Geffcken: πολλοῖσιν Ω   73 ὁππόταν
ἦμαρ Buresch: ὁππότ᾽ ἀνὴρ Ω   τὸ σὸν V: τοσὸν Q   μετόπισθε πελάσσῃ Alexandre: μετόπισθε παλάσσῃ Ω (μετόπισθεν Q)   76 ὑπ᾽] ὑπὸ Alexandre: περ
ὑπ᾽ Rzach   πολιητῶν Mendelssohn, Rzach: τε πολήων Ω   77 ἔριδος Alexandre: ἔδοις Q   ἔδους V   78 ἀϊκὰς Potter: ἀΐξας Ω   80 βασιλῆα
Friedlieb: βασιλείαν Ω   81 τὸν μέτα δ᾽ αὖτ᾽ Friedlieb: τὸν μετὰ ταῦτ᾽ Ω
84 γενεῆς] κεραίης Alexandre   85 ἀδελφειούς Alexandre: ἀδελφιούς Ω
87 δ᾽ αὖ πιστῶν Wilamowitz: δ᾽ αὖ πίπτων Ω   88 ἔσσοντ᾽ ἐξαπίνης γε Alexandre: ἔσσοντ᾽ ἐξαπίνης γε V: τε Q

ἔνθ' ὁπόταν δολόμητις ἀνὴρ ⟨καὶ ἐπίκλοπος⟩ ἔλθῃ
λῃστὴς ἐκ Συρίης προφανείς, Ῥωμαῖος ἄδηλος,   90
καὶ πελάσει δολίως ἐς Καππαδόκων γένος ἀνδρῶν
καὶ πολιορκήσας πιέσει πολέμου ἀκόρητος,
δὴ τότε σοι, Τύανα καὶ Μάζακα, ἔσσεθ' ἅλωσις·
λατρεύσεις ⟨θ' οὕτω τε⟩ ὑπὸ ζυγὸν αὐχένα θήσεις·
καὶ Συρίη κλαύσειεν ἀπολλυμένων ἀνθρώπων   95
οὐδὲ Σεληναίη τότε ῥύσεται ἱερὸν ἄστυ.
ἡνίκ' ἂν ἐκ Συρίης φθάμενος περιφεύξ' ἀνὰ Σούρην
Ῥωμαίους προφυγὼν διὰ Εὐφράταο ῥοάων
οὐκέτι Ῥωμαίοις ἐναλίγκιος ἀλλ' ἀγερώχοις
ἰοβόλοις Πέρσαις, τότε κοίρανος Ἰταλιητῶν   100
καππέσετ' ἐν τάξει, τυφθεὶς αἴθωνι σιδήρῳ
ὃν κόσμον ἐάσας· ἐπὶ δ' αὐτῷ παῖδες ὀλοῦνται.
ἀλλ' ὁπόταν γ' ἄλλος βασιλεὺς Ῥώμης βασιλεύσῃ,
καὶ τότε Ῥωμαίοις ἀκατάστατα ἔθνεα ἕλξῃ
οὖλος Ἄρης σὺν παιδὶ νόθῳ ἐπὶ τείχεα Ῥώμης,   105
καὶ τότε δὴ λιμοὶ λοιμοί μαλεροί τε κεραυνοὶ
καὶ πόλεμοι δεινοὶ ἀκαταστασίαι τε πολήων
ἔσσοντ' ἐξαπίνης· Σύροι δ' ἔκπαγλ' ἀπολοῦνται·
ἥξει γὰρ τούτοις μέγας χόλος Ὑψίστοιο·
αὐτίκα δὴ Περσῶν ἐπανάστασις ἀλφηστήρων,   110
Ῥωμαίους δ' ὀλέσουσι Σύροι Πέρσῃσι μιγέντες·
ἀλλ' οὐ νικήσουσι νόμους θεοκράντορι βουλῇ.
αἳ ὁπόσοι φεύξονται ἀπ' ἀντολίης γεγαῶτες
σὺν κτεάτεσσιν ἐοῖσιν ἐς ἀλλοθρόους ἀνθρώπους·
αἳ ὁπόσων ἀνδρῶν πίεται χθὼν αἷμα κελαινόν·   115
ἔσται γὰρ χρόνος οὗτος, ἐν ᾧ ποτε τοῖς τεθνεῶσιν
οἱ ζῶντες μακαρισμὸν ἀπὸ στομάτων ἐνέποντες
φθέγξονται καλὸν τὸ θανεῖν καὶ φεύξετ' ἀπ' αὐτῶν.

89 ἔνθ' ὁπόταν Alexandre: ἦν δ' ὁπόταν Q: ἦν δ' ὁποίαν V   δολόμητις Alexandre: δολιομήτις V: δολιόμητιν Q   ⟨καὶ ἐπίκλοπος⟩ Fehr: ἐπὶ κλίνης Ω
91 πελάσει] περάσει Rzach   ἐς Alexandre: ἐκ Ω   92 πιέσει Rzach:
πέσεται Ω   93 σοι Alexandre: σου Ω   ἔσσεθ' ἅλωσις Alexandre: ἔσσετ'
ἅλωσις Ω   94 θ' οὕτω τε Potter (τε iam Waś): τούτῳ δὲ Ω: δεινὸν δὲ Rzach
ὑπὸ ζυγὸν Geffcken: πολύζυγον Ω: πάλιν ζυγὸν Rzach   θήσεις Gutschmidt:
θήσει Ω   97 ἡνίκ' ἂν Alexandre: ἡνίκα ἂν Ω   περιφεύξ' ἀνὰ Σούρην

Then a crafty and deceitful man will come, a brigand appearing from Syria, an obscure Roman, and he will move treacherously against the race of Cappadocian men and, insatiable of war, besiege and beset them; then for you, Tyana and Mazaka, there will be capture and thus you will be enslaved and will place your neck under the yoke; and Syria will mourn for dead men and Selene will not save the holy city. When the swift-moving man flees from Syria through Soura, escaping the Romans across the flood of the Euphrates, no longer like to the Romans, but to the arrogant arrow-shooting Persians, then the king of the Italians will fall in battle, smitten by gleaming iron, in a state of disarray; and his sons will be destroyed with him.

When another king of Rome will rule, then ruinous Ares with his bastard son will bring the disorderly races against the Romans, against the walls of Rome. And then suddenly there will be famine, plague, dreadful lightning bolts, horrible wars, and destruction of cities. The Syrians will be terribly destroyed, for the great wrath of the lord on high will arise against them. There will be an uprising of the evil Persians, and Syrians joined with Persians will destroy the Romans; but they will not master the things ordained in the divinely wrought plan.

Alas, how many will flee, coming from the east with all their goods to men speaking other tongues. Alas for the many men whose dark blood the earth will drink; this will be the time when the living will call the dead blessed from their mouths, they will say it is a beautiful thing to die, but death will flee from them.

Potter: περιφυξανασέλγειν V: περιφυξανασέλγην Q: περιφύσαν ἀνάγκην Alexandre: προφύγῃσιν ἀσελγὴς Rzach: περὶ φύξιν ἀσελγῆ Hartel: περιφεύξ᾽ ἀνὰ Σέλγην Geffcken   98 προφυγὼν διὰ Geffcken: προφυγὼν διὰ δ᾽ Ω: περάσῃ δὲ δι᾽ Rzach   99 ἀγερώχοις Alexandre: ἀγέρωχος Ω 100 Ἰταλιητῶν Alexandre: ἰταλίη χθών Ω   101 καππέσετ᾽ ἐν τάξει Nauk: καππέσεται πατάξει Ω   τυφθεὶς αἴθωνι σιδήρῳ Mai: αἴθονι σιδήρῳ τυφθείς Ω   102 ὃν Geffcken: οὐ Ω   103 γ᾽ ἄλλος Q: γάλλος V 104 ἔθνεα ἔλξῃ Geffcken: ἔθνεα ἔλθῃ Q: ἔθνη ἔλθῃ V: ἔθνε᾽ ἐπέλθῃ Rzach 110 ἀλφηστήρων Alexandre: ἀμφίστησιν Ω   112 νόμους] ὅμως Gutschmidt   θεοκράντορι βουλῇ Alexandre: θεοκράτορι βουλῇ Ω: θεοκράντορα βουλὴν Mendelssohn

ἄρτι δὲ σέ, τλήμων Συρίη, κατοδύρομαι οἰκτρῶς·
ἥξει καὶ πληγή σοι ἀπ' ἰοβόλων ἀνθρώπων   120
δεινή, ἥν τοι οὔποτ' ἐπήλπισας ἥξουσάν σοι.
ἥξει καὶ Ῥώμης ὁ φυγάς, μέγα ἔγχος ἀείρας,
Εὐφράτην διαβὰς πολλαῖς ἅμα μυριάδεσσιν,
ὅς σε καταφλέξει καὶ πάντα κακῶς διαθήσει,
τλήμων Ἀντιόχεια, σὲ δὲ πτόλιν οὔποτ' ἐροῦσιν,   125
ὁπόταν ἀφροσύνῃσι τεαῖς ὑπὸ δούρασι πίπτῃς·
πάντα δὲ συλήσας καὶ γυμνώσας σε προλείψει
ἄστεγον ἀοίκητον· ἄφνω δέ σε κλαύσεθ' ὁρῶν τις·
καὶ σὺ θρίαμβος ἔσῃ, Ἱεράπολι, καὶ σύ, Βέροια·
Χαλκίδι συγκλαύσεσθε νεοτρώτοις ἐπὶ τέκνοις.   130
αἳ ὁπόσοι ναίουσι κατὰ Κασίου ὄρος αἰπύ,
ἠδ' ὁπόσοι κατ' Ἀμανόν, ὅσους δὲ Λύκος παρακλύζει
Μαρσύας δὲ ὅσους καὶ Πύραμος ἀργυροδίνης·
ἄχρι τε γὰρ Ἀσίης περάτων θήσουσι λάφυρα,
ἄστεα γυμνώσαντες, ὅλων δ' εἴδωλ' ἀφελοῦνται   135
καὶ ναοὺς ῥίψουσιν ἐπὶ χθονὶ πουλυβοτείρῃ.
καί ποτε Γαλλίῃ καὶ Παννονίῃ μέγα πῆμα
Μυσοῖς Βιθυνοῖς θ', ὁπόταν ἥξει πολεμιστής.
ὦ Λύκιοι, Λύκιοι, λύκος ἔρχεται αἷμα λιχμῆσαι,
Σάννοι ὅταν ἔλθωσι σὺν Ἄρηϊ πτολιπόρθῳ,   140
καὶ Κάρποι πελάσωσιν ἐπ' Αὐσονίοισι μάχεσθαι.
καὶ τότε δὴ νόθος υἱὸς ἐῇ ὑπ' ἀναιδέϊ τόλμῃ
ἐξολέσει βασιλῆα, παραυτίκα δ' αὐτὸς ὀλεῖται
δυσσεβίης ἕνεκεν· μετὰ δ' αὐτ' ἄρξει πάλιν ἄλλος
ἀρχὴν οὐνομάτεσσι φέρων· ταχὺ δ' αὖτε πεσεῖται   145
Ἄρηϊ κρατερῷ βληθεὶς αἴθωνι σιδήρῳ.
καὶ πάλι κόσμος ἄκοσμος ἀπολλυμένων ἀνθρώπων

---

120 πληγή Q: πληγῇ V   ἀπ' ἰοβόλων Alexandre: ἀμφιοβόλων Ω
122 μέγα Mai: μέγας Q: μέγε V   125 δὲ Rzach: δ' ἐς Ω   127 συλήσας
Alexandre: συλλήσας Ω   προλείψει Alexandre: προλήψει Ω   128 κλαύσεθ' Alexandre: κλαύσετ' Ω   129 Ἱεράπολι Alexandre: ἱερὰ πόλις Ω
Βέροια Mai: Βέρροια Ω   130 συγκλαύσεσθε Alexandre: συγκλαύσητε
Rzach: συγκλαύσαιτε Buresch: συγκλαύσεται Ω   131 αἳ ὁπόσοι Alexandre:
αἳ αἳ ὁπόσοι Ω: αἳ αἳ ὅσοι Meineke   ναίουσι κατὰ Κασίου Rzach: ναίουσι
κάσιον Ω: ναίουσι ὑπὸ (aut περὶ) Κάσιον Alexandre: ναίουσι κατὰ Κασίου

Now for you, wretched Syria, I have lately been piteously lamenting; a blow will befall you from the arrow-shooting men, terrible, which you never thought would come to you. The fugitive of Rome will come, waving a great spear; crossing the Euphrates with many myriads, he will burn you, he will dispose all things evilly. Alas, Antioch, they will never call you a city when you have fallen under the spear in your folly; he will leave you entirely ruined and naked, houseless, uninhabited; anyone seeing you will suddenly break out weeping; and you will be the prize of war, Hieropolis, and you, Beroia; you will join with Chalcis mourning for your recently wounded children. Alas for as many as live by the steep peak of Casius and by Amanus, as many as the Lycus and Marsyas, as many as the silver-eddied Pyramus washes: they will leave ruin as far as the borders of Asia, stripping the cities, taking the statues of all and razing the temples down to the all-nourishing earth.

And then great evil will befall Gaul and Pannonia, the Mysians and Bithynians, when the warrior shall come.

O Lycia, Lycia, the wolf comes to lick blood, when the Sannoi shall come together with city-destroying Ares, and the Carpi shall come to do battle with the Ausonians.

Then the bastard son will destroy his king in his brazen shamelessness, and he will himself be destroyed immediately because of his impiety. After him again another man will rule bearing the first letter in his names; but swiftly in his turn he will fall before powerful Ares, smitten by gleaming iron.

Again the world will be no world with men destroyed in

Meineke   132 κατ᾽ Rzach: καὶ Ω   Ἀμανόν Mai: ἄμωνον Q: ὤμωνον V
134 Ἀσίης Alexandre: ἀσίη Q: ἀσίησι V   περάτων Alexandre: τεράτων Ω
135 ὅλων Wilamowitz: ὅλα Ω   139 λιχμῆσαι Mai: λικμῆσαι Ω
140 Σάννοι Mai: σάννοι Ω   ἔλθωσι Q: ἔλθωσιν V   πτολιπόρθῳ Rzach:
πολυπάρθῳ Ω   142 ἀναιδέϊ Alexandre: ἀναιδίη Ω   145 οὐνομάτεσσι φέρων Wilamowitz: ἀρχὴν οὐνόματος φέρων Ω: οὐνόματος προφέρων
Alexandre: στοιχείου προφέρων Herwerden: ἐκ μονάδος προφέρων Buresch
αὖτε πεσεῖται V: αὖτε ἄρξει πάλιν ἄλλος πεσεῖται Q   146 Ἄρηϊ Alexandre: Ἄρῃ Ω   147 πάλι Alexandre: πάλιν Ω

λοιμῷ καὶ πολέμῳ. Πέρσαι δ' ἐπὶ μῶλον Ἄρηος
αὖτις ἐφορμήσουσι μεμηνότες Αὐσονίοισιν.
καὶ τότε Ῥωμαίων φυγὴ ἔσσεται· αὐτὰρ ἔπειτα   150
ἀρητὴρ ἥξει ὁ πανύστατος ἡλιόπεμπτος
ἐκ Συρίης προφανεὶς καὶ πάντα δόλῳ διαπράξει.
καὶ τότε δ' ἠελίου πόλις ἔσσεται, ἀμφὶ δ' ἄρ' αὐτῇ
Πέρσαι Φοινίκων φοβερὰς τλήσονται ἀπειλάς.
ἡνίκα δ' αὖτ' ἄρξουσιν ὑπερμενέων Ῥωμαίων   155
ἄνδρες ἀρηίθοοι δύο κοίρανοι, ὃς μὲν ἐφέξει
ἑβδομήκοντ' ἀριθμόν, ὁ δὲ τριτάτου ἀριθμοῖο·
καὶ τότε δ' ὑψαύχην ταῦρος σκάπτων ὀνύχεσσιν
γαῖαν καὶ κέρασιν κονίην δισσοῖσιν ἐγείρων,
ἑρπυστὴν κυανόχρωον δράσει κακὰ πολλὰ   160
ὁλκὸν σύροντα φολίσιν· ἐπὶ δ' αὐτὸς ὀλεῖται.
ἠυκέρως δ' ἔλαφος μετὰ τόνδ' ἥξει πάλιν ἄλλος
πεινάων κατ' ὄρη μεμαὼς ἐν γαστρὶ πάσασθαι
ἰοβόλους θῆρας· τότ' ἐλεύσεται ἡλιόπεμπτος
δεινός τε φοβερός τε λέων πνείων φλόγα πολλήν.   165
δὴ τόθ' ὅ γ' αὖτ' ὀλέσει πολλῇ καὶ ἀναιδέϊ τόλμῃ
εὐκεράωτ' ἔλαφόν τε θοὸν καὶ θῆρα μέγιστον
ἰοβόλον φοβερὸν συρίγματα πόλλ' ἀφιέντα
τοξοβάτην τε τράγον, ἐπὶ δ' αὐτῷ κῦδος ὀπηδεῖ.
αὐτὸς δὴ ὁλόκληρος ἀλώβητος καὶ ἄπλητος   170
ἄρξει Ῥωμαίων, Πέρσαι δ' ἔσσοντ' ἀλαπαδνοί.
ἀλλὰ ἄναξ, βασιλεῦ κόσμου, θεέ, παῦσον ἀοιδὴν
ἡμετέρων ἐπέων, δὸς δ' ἱμερόεσσαν ἀοιδήν.

149 ἐφορμήσουσι Mendelssohn, Buresch: ἐσορμήσουσι Ω   153 ἔσσεται]
ἄρξεται Buresch   154 Πέρσαι Alexandre: πᾶσαι Ω   159 κέρασιν
κονίην Rzach: κέρασι κόνιν Ω: κεράεσσι κόνιν Alexandre   160 δράσει
Alexandre: καὶ δράσει Ω   161 φολίσιν Alexandre: φολήσιν Q: φολ'ήσιν V
ἐπὶ Alexandre: ἐπεὶ Ω   162 ἠυκέρως Friedlieb: ἤνκερως Ω: εὐκέραος

plague and war. The Persians will again rush to the moil of Ares raging against the Ausonians.

Then there will be a rout of the Romans; but immediately thereafter a priest will come, the last of all, sent from the sun, appearing from Syria, and he will do everything by craft; the city of the sun will arise, and around her the Persians will endure the terrible threats of Phoenicians.

When two war-swift lordly men will rule the mighty Romans, one will show forth the number seventy, while the other will be of the third number; and the high-necked bull digging the earth with his hoofs and rousing the dust on his double horns will do much harm to the dark-hued serpent cutting a furrow with its scales; then he will be destroyed. After him again another will come, a well-horned hungry stag in the mountains desiring to feed his stomach with the venom-spitting beasts; then will come the sun-sent, dreadful, fearful lion, breathing much fire. With great and reckless courage he will destroy the well-horned swift stag and the great, venom-spitting, fearsome beast discharging many shafts and the bow-footed goat; fame will attend him; perfect, unblemished, and awesome, he will rule the Romans and the Persians will be feeble.

But king, lord of the world, god, put an end to the song of my words, give them a charming song.

Alexandre   165 δεινός τε Wilamowitz: δεινὸς καὶ Ω   166 δὴ τόθ᾽ ὅ αὖτ᾽ Wilamowitz: δὴ τότ᾽ αὖτ᾽ Ω: καὶ τότε δ᾽ αὖτ᾽ Rzach   167 εὐκεράωτ᾽ Alexandre: εὐκεραώτ᾽ V: ἠυκέρωτ᾽ Rzach   168 συρίγματα πόλλ᾽ ἀφιέντα Mendelssohn: ἀφιέντα συρίγματα πόλλα V: ἀμφιέντα συρίγγατα π. Q 169 τοξοβάτην τε τράγον] λοξοβάτην τε τ. Geffcken: τοξόβολον τ᾽ ὄναγρον Rzach   170 ἄπλητος Mendelssohn (et ἄπληκτος suspicatus): ἄπληστος Ω 171 δ᾽ ἔσσοντ᾽ Alexandre: δ᾽ ἔσονται Ω   172 ἀλλὰ Alexandre: ἀλλ᾽ Ω 173 ἱμερόεσσαν Alexandre: ἡμέραν πᾶσιν Ω

Commentary

Title. V identifies this text as σιβύλλης λόγος ιγ´. There is no super-scription in Q, probably because it was lost at the same time as lines 259–99 of *Orac. Sib.* 12 and lines 1–6 of this text: although there are superscriptions in this manuscript for *Orac. Sib.* 12 and 14 (identify-ing them as such), no break at all is indicated between *Orac. Sib.* 12. 258 and 13. 7. The text would not, however, have been identified as the *Thirteenth Sibylline Oracle* in antiquity.

No Sibyl is mentioned by name in either the *Twelfth* or *Thir-teenth* oracles, and if they were circulated with the present *Orac. Sib.* 11 before their inclusion in the present collection (as argued above, pp. 154–7), these texts would have taken their name from the Sibyl who identifies herself in that oracle. This Sibyl, who gives her biography at 11. 315–24, says that she will operate around Delphi. Thus, as there are clear breaks in the chronicle which these texts provide at 11. 322–4, 1, 296–9, and 13. 1–6, which indicate that they would have been circulated as separate books, this oracle would have been identified as the third book of the prophecies of the Delphic Sibyl: λόγος ὁ τρίτος τῆς Δελφικῆς Σιβύλλης or, more simply: τόμος ὁ τρίτος τοῦ τῆς Δελφικῆς λόγου. See above, pp. 123, 155–6, on the titles of oracles; for a parallel to the suggestions made here cf. *Sib. Theos.* 191 εἶτα τῶν ἐπῶν τοῦ δευτέρου αὐτῆς τόμου ἐπαῖμεν. . . .

1–6 Proem

1–6. ⟨ἔν⟩θεον ἀείδειν ... ὑπὲρ βασιληΐδος ἀρχῆς: as is true of most of the oracles preserved in the present collection, this text opens with a proem which sets forth its theme and gives some indication of the nature of the Sibyl's contact with the divinity; see *Orac. Sib.* 1. 1–5, 3. 1–7, 295–300, 489–91, 4. 1–23, 5. 1, 52–3, 179, 286–8, 6. 1–5, 8. 1–3, 11. 1–5, 12. 1, 14. 1–11.

1. ⟨ἔν⟩θεον ἀείδειν με λόγον κέλεται †μέγαν†: V gives θεὸν ἀείδειν με λόγον κέλεται μέγαν. θεόν is metrically impossible at the beginning of the line, μέγαν is very difficult at the end (though not impossible in view of the author's treatment of μέγας in 109), and the scribe of V indicated a lacuna in both places. Alexandre suspected that θεόν was a gloss to describe λόγον and proposed ἀείδειν με λόγον κέλεται μέγαν ⟨ἀνθρώποισιν⟩. Rzach felt that an adjective modifying λόγον was necessary and rewrote the line to read: θεσπέσιόν με λόγον κέλεται μέγαν αὖτις ἀείδειν, an effort which, though eloquent, requires the assumption of a more extreme degree of corruption in this line than the manuscript justifies. Geffcken obelized the line as it stands, though he did propose: ⟨ἔν⟩θεον ἀείδειν με λόγον κέλεται μεγαλαλκής in his apparatus.

Although I agree with Geffcken that a convincing restoration of the line is not readily apparent, I am more confident than he was concerning the restoration of the first foot. The scribe did recognize a lacuna here, and θεόν can readily be altered to ⟨ἔν⟩θεον (a proposal first made by Hartel). The word connotes an action or object which is in some way marvellous or in contact with the supernatural, and is therefore an apt description of an oracle; compare *PGM* 13. 144 (the glow in stars), 1. 20 (sunrise), 160 (the special name of a demon); Jos. *AJ* 4. 388, 6. 56 (prophets), 8. 346, *BJ* 4. 33 (violent physical activity); *AJ* 6. 76 (wisdom).

The end of the line presents more difficulties. It is not at all clear what is needed, but either a temporal adverb—these are common in this context (cf. *Orac. Sib.* 2. 2, 3. 4, 297, 490, 5. 179 πάλιν; 5. 288 ἄρτι)—or an adjective describing the inspiring divinity would do. Hartel proposed αὖθις (αὖτις Friedlieb), which would fit. The other option, that V preserves part of another adjective modifying θεός in l. 2, is also possible; but here too there is a problem. It is not easy to find a suitable word which would permit the retention of any part of the manuscript reading: Geffcken suggested μεγαλαλκής, a rare equivalent for μεγαλοσθενής, which seems rather too corporeal in the context of the epithets which follow. It is best to obelize.

ἀείδειν: oracles, like other poems, were chanted or sung in performance. This is reflected in the words used here and elsewhere to describe the Sibyl's activity: see *Orac. Sib.* 13. 50, 74, 14. 296, 2. 1 ἦμος δὴ κατέπαυσε θεὸς πολυπάνσοφον ᾠδήν, 346–7 ἥδε δ' ἐγὼ λίτομαί σε βαιὸν παῦσαι μὲν ἀοιδῆς, | ἅγιε μαννοδότα, βασιλεῦ μεγάλης βασιλείης. The word also appears in the Sibyl's autobiography at Erythrae (*Insc. Eryth. u. Klaz.* 224. 7–8): τῆιδε δ᾽ ἐφεζομένη πέτρηι θνητοῖσιν ἄεισα | μαντοσύνας παθέων αὖθις ἐπεσσομένων, and Paus. 10. 12. 1 πέτρα δέ ἐστιν ἀνίσχουσα ὑπὲρ τῆς γῆς· ἐπὶ ταύτῃ Δελφοὶ στᾶσάν φασιν ᾆσαι τοὺς χρησμοὺς γυναῖκα ὄνομα Ἡροφίλην . . . καὶ χρησμούς τε αὐτὴν γυναικῶν πρώτην ᾆσαι; Ar. *Eq.* 61 ᾄδει δὲ χρησμούς· ὁ δὲ γέρων σιβυλλιᾷ; Plut. *Mor.* 398 E καὶ ᾀδόμενα διὰ τῶν Σιβυλλείων ὁ χρόνος ὥσπερ ὀφείλων ἀποδέδωκεν. Sibyls are also envisaged as singing or chanting their works at *Orac. Sib.* 1. 35, 3. 295, 489, 11. 324; *Insc. Eryth. u. Klaz.* 224. 5–6; Plut. *Mor.* 398 D; Lact. *DI* 4. 15. 15, 18.

με . . . κέλεται: the Sibyl's description of her contact with the divinity here and in ll. 172–3, as well as her statements at l. 50, 74, and 119, suggest that although she is under the control of the god she still retains a certain degree of self-awareness (as in *Orac. Sib.* 1. 5, 3. 6–7, 165, 297–300; see also J. Reiling, *Hermas and Christian Prophecy* (Leiden, 1973), 19. For the use of κέλομαι to describe the god's action compare *Orac. Sib.* 1. 5, 133, 2. 5, 3. 7, 631. The notion that the prophetess is the victim of undesired physical compulsion is repeated at l. 5 below.

λόγον: there is no one word in Sibylline texts to describe the oracles. Various alternatives include ἀοιδή (*Orac. Sib.* 2. 1, 11. 324); αὐδή (*Orac. Sib.* 3. 5, 11. 322; cf. Eur. *IT* 976); θέσφατος (*FGrH* 257 F 37 v2); ὕμνος (*Orac. Sib.* 3. 295, 489; see *Orac. Sib.* 5. 52–3 τείρομαι ἡ τριτάλαινα κακὴν φάτιν ἐν φρεσὶ θέσθαι· | †Ἴσιδος ἡ γνωστὴ† καὶ χρησμῶν ἔνθεον ὕμνον). For λόγος cf. *Orac. Sib.* 12. 295. This variation is typical in antiquity. With the possible exceptions of Proclus and a scholiast on Thucydides, no extant author seems to have tried to draw rigid distinctions between oracular statements in terms of their form. For Proclus see H. Lewy, *The Chaldaean Oracles and Theurgy*, ed. M. Tardieu (Paris, 1978), 443–7; see also Σ Thuc. 2. 8. 2 λόγιά ἐστι τὰ παρὰ τοῦ θεοῦ λεγόμενα καταλογάδην· χρησμοὶ δέ, οἵτινες ἐμμέτρως λέγονται, θεοφορουμένων τῶν λεγόντων, and A. W. Gomme, *A Historical Commentary on Thucydides*, ii (Oxford, 1956), 9: 'this is doubtless roughly correct, though λόγια were not necessarily in prose'. Gomme's remark is considerably understated. The distinction is utterly artificial, as is indicated by the use of the word in the Sibylline oracles, and the variation is evident much earlier, e.g. at

Ar. *Eq.* 119–22 *ΔΗ*. φέρ᾽ ἴδω τί ἄρ᾽ ἔνεστιν αὐτόθι; | ὦ λόγια.
δός μοι δὸς τὸ ποτήριον ταχύ. | *ΝΙ*. ἰδού. τί φησ᾽ ὁ
χρησμός; *ΔΗ*. ἑτέραν ἔγχεον. | *ΝΙ*. ἐν τοῖς λογίοις ἔνεστιν
ἑτέραν ἔγχεον; Plut. *Mor.* 397 D καὶ τὰς νῦν καταλογάδην καὶ
διὰ τῶν ἐπιτυχόντων ὀνομάτων τοὺς χρησμοὺς λεγούσας,
ὅπως ὑμῖν ἀκεφάλων καὶ λαγαρῶν μέτρων καὶ μειούρων
εὐθύνας μὴ ὑπέχωσι.

2–6. ἅγιος ἀθάνατος θεὸς ... ὑπὲρ βασιληΐδος ἀρχῆς:
the technique of describing a god with a list of his various attributes
in the nominative followed by a relative clause or clauses is a commonplace feature of religious language; see further E. Norden,
Agnostos Theos: Untersuchungen zur Formengeschichte religiöser Rede
(Berlin, 1913), 177–201; A. J. Festugière, *La Révélation d'Hermes
Trismégiste*, 4 vols. (Paris, 1950–4), iv. 65. For the practice of using
positive and negative aspects in such a list (e.g. ἅγιος as opposed to
ἀθάνατος and ἄφθιτος) see West, ed. Hes. *The.*, p. 288, ed. Hes.
Op., p. 139; Nisbet and Hubbard, ed. Hor. *Odes 1*, p. 383.
   The most striking feature of the description of the god in these
lines is the lack of serious theological content. This is paralleled at
Orac. Sib. 11. 1–5, 14. 1–11 (see nn. following) and may be
contrasted with *Orac. Sib.* 2. 214–347, 3. 11–45, 629, 760, 4. 4–23,
8. 360–500.

2. ἅγιος: the word is not used in classical Greek as an epithet for a
divinity; such a use would have been most inappropriate as its essential meaning and implication was 'taboo' (LSJ s.v.). It is only in the
Hellenistic and Roman periods, under the influence of the influx of
oriental ideas and cults (presumably), that it came to be used as an
epithet for a god; cf. *IG* vii. 3426. 6–8 τὴν | ἁγνοτάτην
ἱεραφόρον τῆς ἁγιᾶς Εἴσιδος (Lebadea, early 3rd cent. AD);
OGIS 590. 1–2 θεῷ ἁγίῳ Βὰλ | καὶ θεᾷ Ἥρᾳ (Palmyra, 3rd
cent. AD); ibid. 620. 2 Διὶ ἁγίωι Βεε(λβ)ωσώρι (near Gerasa, 1st
cent. AD). Its use is particularly common as a cult title in Syria and
Arabia: D. Sourdel, *Les Cultes du Hauran à l'époque romaine* (Paris,
1952), 48 n. 2. This might stem from the difficulty of translating
alien notions into Greek. Thus also in LXX Isa. 5: 16 ὁ θεὸς ὁ
ἅγιος δοξασθήσεται ἐν δικαιοσύνῃ translates (rendered literally) 'the exalted one being exalted in righteousness' and ibid. 14: 27
ὁ θεὸς ὁ ἅγιος appears as a translation of 'he who is the lord of

hosts'. By the third century, however, the use of ἅγιος need not be taken to imply that the author came from a Semitic background. In general see E. Williger, *Hagios: Untersuchungen zur Terminologie des Heiligen in den hellenisch-hellenistischen Religionem* (Gießen, 1922), 80–108.

ἄφθιτος: the use of this adjective to describe gods is rare outside of the *Sibylline Oracles*, though cf. *PGM* ii. 186 (Apollo), iv. 445, 461, 1966 (Helios); Soph. *Ant.* 339 (Ge); Pind. *Pyth.* 4. 518 (Zeus). For the *Sibylline Oracles* see *Orac. Sib.* ʹ4. 10 θήσει θεὸς ἄφθιτος αἰθέρι ναίων; 2. 330 ὁ παντοκράτωρ θεὸς ἄφθιτος; 2. 214 ἡνίκα δ' ἀθανάτου θεοῦ ἄφθιτοι ἀγγελτῆρες.

For alliteration such as that manifested here as a feature of religious language see Nisbet and Hubbard, ed. Hor. *Odes 1*, pp. 260–1; G. Appel, *De Romanorum precationibus* (Gießen, 1909), 160.

2–4. ὃς βασιλεῦσιν | δῶκε κράτος καὶ ἀφείλατ' ἰδὲ ... θανάτοιο: emphasis of a god's power by description of that divinity's ability to perform opposite actions at will is a common feature of religious expression; thus LXX Job 1: 21 αὐτὸς γυμνὸς ἐξῆλθον ἐκ κοιλίας μητρός μου, | γυμνὸς καὶ ἀπελεύσομαι ἐκεῖ· | ὁ κύριος ἔδωκεν, ὁ κύριος ἀφείλατο· | ὡς τῷ κυρίῳ ἔδοξεν, οὕτως καὶ ἐγένετο· | εἴη τὸ ὄνομα κυρίου εὐλογημένον; Hes. *Op.* 5–8 ῥέα μὲν γὰρ βριάει, ῥέα δὲ βριάοντα χαλέπτει, | ῥεῖα δ' ἀρίζηλον μινύθει καὶ ἄδηλον ἀέξει, | ῥεῖα δέ τ' ἰθύνει σκολιὸν καὶ ἀγήνορα κάρφει | Ζεὺς ὑψιβρεμέτης, ὃς ὑπέρτατα δώματα ναίει; Hor. *Odes*, 1. 34. 12–14 'valet ima summis | mutare et insignem attenuat deus | obscure promens'. See further West, ed. Hes. *Op.*, pp. 139–40, ed. Hes. *The.*, p. 288; Nisbet and Hubbard, ed. Hor. *Odes 1*, pp. 383–5.

3. ἀφείλατ' ἰδέ: V reads ἀφείλατο δή, which Alexandre retained in his text, though he suggested the present reading in his note on the line. This proposal was accepted by Rzach and Geffcken. δή, when used as a connective, does not introduce clauses (see the examples collected in J. D. Denniston, *The Greek Particles* ² (Oxford, 1954), 236–40, and ἰδέ has the recourse of oracular authors to epic diction in its favour.

ὥρισεν: for the use of ὁρίζω to describe supernatural ordinances cf. Soph. *Ant.* 451–2 οὐδ' ἡ ξύνοικος τῶν κάτω θεῶν Δίκη | τοιούσδ' ἐν ἀνθρώποισιν ὥρισεν νόμους; Eur. fr. 218 φεῦ φεῦ, τὸ δοῦλον ὡς ἁπανταχῇ γένος | πρὸς τὴν ἐλάσσω μοῖραν ὥρισεν θεός, and examples in Sophocles, *Greek Lexicon*, s.v.

5. οὐράνιος ... ἐπάγει: for the idea expressed here see on l. 1. **ἐπάγει:** this is the reading of V. Nauck persuaded Rzach to alter it to ἐπείγει, and Geffcken accepted this. This is not necessary; for the lengthening of the penultimate syllable in this position see *Orac. Sib.* 8. 325 αὐτός σου βασιλεὺς ἐπιβὰς ἐπὶ πῶλον ἐσάγει.

6. βασιληΐδος: the genitive singular in this case indicates that the author can be thinking of only one empire—the Roman. For the use of the word in this sense cf. *Orac. Sib.* 12. 299; for other examples of the Roman empire referred to in this way see M. Wörrle, 'Ägyptisches Getreide für Ephesos', *Chiron*, 1 (1970), 330–1 and 330 n. 23.

7-20 The Reign of Gordian III (AD 238-244)

7. καὶ δόρυ θοῦρος Ἄρης: there are two problems here. The first is the relationship between δόρυ and θοῦρος Ἄρης. Alexandre followed the manuscripts and printed δορυθοῦρος Ἄρης. Rzach and Geffcken printed δόρυ θοῦρος Ἄρης. This is probably to be preferred, for while θοῦρος is a well-attested epithet for Ares, δορυθοῦρος does not appear (see Roscher, s.v. Ἄρης). But this still leaves a problem with respect to the relationship between Ἄρης and αὐτοῦ (καί indicates that Ares may conclude a list of some sort, either of attributes of Ares or, more generally, of woes; and there remains a still more serious problem. This is that there is no introduction to the reign of Gordian III in this poem; one line would not be enough to provide this in the standard form, which would include a reference to the ruler's name as well as, in this case, a verb for Ἄρης. It is also possible that more than an introduction to this reign has disappeared.

The chronicle of imperial history from Caesar to the triumph of Odaenathus provided by the *Twelfth* and *Thirteenth Sibylline Oracles* omits no monarch but Julius Maximinus Thrax and his ephemeral rivals in the year 238. The *Twelfth Oracle* concludes with the rise of Ardashir and the disaster of Alexander Severus. The first emperor identified in this text is Philip the Arab (see on l. 23) and the events predicted in lines 13–20 are manifestly those of Gordian III's Persian war. This oracle is 138 lines below the average for *Orac. Sib.*

11–12 (11 has 324 lines, 12 has 299), and it is attractive to imagine that it could originally have been closer in length to those texts. As it stands, there are sixty-one lines for the events of 244–9 and seventy-four for 249–252/3. It is reasonable to believe that somewhat similar scope would have been given to events before Gordian's final campaign: there would have been plenty of material for significant discourse in the troubles with Persia during 235–41 (see on ll. 13–20 below), not to mention the civil war of 238 (which may have attracted rather less space—western events tended to be given rather short shrift; see on ll. 78–80, 101–2). The manuscripts which now contain *Orac. Sib.* 11–14 allow about forty lines per page (twenty each for verso and recto), and it seems quite possible that one or two pages might have dropped out of a similar manuscript at an earlier stage. Forty to eighty lines for the period 235–41 would be roughly in line with the economy of the work as a whole.

Ἄρης: Ares appears in the nominative in this poem with various implications. He may be used as a substitute for a king or nation (see on ll. 16, 35) or as a synonym for war (see l. 78).

8. **νηπίαχος γεραός τε θεμιστεύσει ἀγοραῖσιν:** V gives νηπίαχος γεγαώς τε θεμιστεύει; Q has νηπίαχος γεγαῶτες θεμιστεύει. Alexandre proposes γεραός τε θεμιστεύων and noted 'agitur vero de duobus Gordianis, patre et filio, qui a Maximini legatis in Africa oppressi sunt'. His reading was accepted by Rzach. Friedlieb suggested νηπίαχος γεγαώς τε θεμιστεύει, by which one may presume that, like Alexandre, he envisaged 'infans in palateis regnabit', and proposed reading a lacuna between lines 7 and 8. This is not a bad idea and would fit Gordian III, were it not that τε in line 8 suggests that this person is not to be identified with the Ares in line 7, and that Ares is most probably to be identified with Gordian (who is also to be identified with Ares in lines 16 and 18). The solution proposed here, which involves only the slight change of γεγαώς (V) to γεραός—'many will be destroyed under him, childish and old he will give justice in the market-places'—is based on the assumption that the reference in these lines is not to Gordian at all, but to C. Furius Sabinius Aquila Timesitheus (*PIR*² F 581; Pflaum, *Carrières équestres*, No. 317; Dietz, *Senatus contra principem*, p. 294), father-in-law and praetorian prefect of Gordian III, and this passage reflects the way that an imperial official would appear before Rome's subjects.

Timesitheus was a man who would merit reference in oracular verses concerned with Gordian, both on account of his prominence and because of his long career as an administrator in the eastern provinces. In the years 218–22 he served a double term as *procurator provinciae Syriae Palaestinae* and *exactor reliquorum annonae sacrae expeditionis*, in 235/6 he was *procurator provinciae Bithyniae Ponti Paphlagoniae tam patrimoni quam rationis privatae* and *vice procuratoris quadragesimae*, then *procurator provinciae Asiae vice procuratoris vicesimae et quadrigesimae item vice proconsulis*. The introduction of prominent figures who were not emperors may be paralleled in this oracle at ll. 61, 89, 162 (see ad locc.) and *Orac. Sib.* 12. 182–4 (Avidius Cassius, on which see J. Geffcken, 'Römische Kaiser im Volksmunde der Provinz', *NGG* (1901), 191).

νηπίαχος γεραός: oxymoron of this sort is a feature of oracular language; see *Insc. Mag.* 228. 5 θηλοπρεποῦς Φωτὸς μελάθροις Ἥραν προσεβάζου; *Orac. Sib.* 3. 363 ἔσται καὶ Σάμος ἄμμος, ἐσεῖται Δῆλος ἄδηλος; see also l. 147 below and n. ad loc.

θεμιστεύσει: as E. L. Bowie points out to me, the future makes more sense in this context than the present θεμιστεύει of Ω. This is appropriate indeed if the person referred to here is in fact a praetorian prefect. The judicial competence of the office had much expanded in the late Severan period; thus *CJ* 1. 26. 1 'libellus praefecto praetorio datus pro contestatione haberi non potest' (230); ibid. 2 'formam a praefecto praetorio datam, et si generalis sit, minime legibus vel constitutionibus contrariam, si nihil postea ex auctoritate mea innovatum est, servari aequum est' (235). For the competence of Timesitheus (or his successors: see on l. 21) see *CJ* 9. 2. 6 'absentem capitali crimine accusari non posse, sed requirendum tantummodo adnotari solere, si desit, vetus ius est. et ideo cum absentem te et ignorantem, cui numquam ullum crimen denuntiatum esset, per iniuriam a praeside provinciae in metellum datum dicas, quo magis in praesenti te agente, ut adservas iam nunc fides veri possit illuminari, praefectos praetorio adire cura, qui, quiquid novo more et contra formam constitutionum gestum deprehenderint, pro sua iustitia reformabunt' (243); the last of these texts is particularly significant as both the praetorian prefects in question at the time it was written were in Mesopotamia with Gordian III. In general see L. L. Howe, *The Praetorian Prefect from Commodus to*

Diocletian (Chicago, 1942), 32–64; A. M. Honoré, *Emperors and Lawyers* (Oxford, 1981), 54–103; id., *Ulpian*, pp. 35–9 (for the position of Ulpian).

9–12. πολλοὶ γὰρ πόλεμοι . . . ἱεροσυλία ναῶν: such lists of catastrophes are a common feature of Sibylline prophecies; cf. *Orac. Sib.* 2. 6–11, 4. 68–9, 14. 121–3; and ll. 106–7 below. See Comm. *Carm. de duobus populis*, 899–900 'hinc lues, hinc bella, hinc fames, hinc nuntia dura | miscenturque simul, quo fiat turbatio mentis'; Lact. *Epit.* 66. 4 'civitates et oppida interibunt modo ferro et igni, modo terrae motibus crebris, modo aquarum inundatione, modo pestilentia et fame'; Matt. 24: 7 καὶ ἔσονται λιμοὶ καὶ σεισμοὶ κατὰ τόπους; Hippol. *De Antichristo*, 8. For general ruin as an eschatological motif see W. Bousset, *Der Antichrist in der Überlieferung des Judentums, des Neuen Testament und der alten Kirche* (Göttingen, 1895), 129–32. This sort of motif was also employed by more conventional prose authors: Thuc. 1. 23. 2–3; Tac. *Hist.* 1. 2–3, esp. 3. 2 'praeter multiplices rerum humanarum casus caelo terraque prodigia et fulminum monitus et futurorum praesagia, laeta tristia, ambigua manifesta'; Pol. 6. 5. 5 ὅταν ἢ διὰ κατακλυσμοὺς ἢ διὰ λοιμικὰς περιστάσεις ἢ δι᾽ ἀφορίας καρπῶν ἢ δι᾽ ἄλλας τοιαύτας αἰτίας φθορὰ γένηται τοῦ τῶν ἀνθρώπων γένους, with F. W. Walbank, *Commentary on Polybius*, i (Oxford, 1957), 650–1. From the earliest period catastrophes of this sort were believed to be related, which is the implication of Hes. *The.* 226–30 αὐτὰρ Ἔρις στυγερὴ τέκε μὲν Πόνον ἀλγινόεντα | Λήθην τε Λιμόν τε καὶ Ἄλγεα δακρυόεντα | Ὑσμίνας τε Μάχας τε Φόνους τ᾽ Ἀνδροκτασίας τε | Νείκεά τε Ψεύδεά τε Λόγους τ᾽ Ἀμφιλλογίας τε | Δυσνομίην τ᾽ Ἄτην τε, συνήθεας ἀλλήλησιν; see West, ed. Hes. *The.* pp. 230–2; P. D. Garnsey, *Famine and Food Supply in the Greco-Roman World: Responses to Risk and Crisis* (Cambridge, 1988), 25–6.

10. λιμοὶ καὶ λοιμοί: a common collocation: cf. l. 106 below; *Orac. Sib.* 2. 23, 3. 332, 8. 175, 11. 46, 240, 12. 114; Hes. *Op.* 242–3 τοῖσιν δ᾽ οὐρανόθεν μέγ᾽ ἐπήγαγε πῆμα Κρονίων, | λιμὸν ὁμοῦ καὶ λοιμόν· ἀποφθινύθουσι δὲ λαοί; see West, ed. Hes. *Op.*, p. 218; Hor. *Odes* 1. 21. 12–16 'hic bellum lacrimosum, hic miseram famem | pestemque a populo et principe Caesare in | Persas atque Britannos | vestra motus aget prece', with Nisbet and Hubbard, ed. Hor. *Odes 1*, pp. 260–1.

σεισμοί: earthquakes are a very popular element in eschatological visions of catastrophe, see _Orac. Sib._ 2. 6; Matt. 8: 24, 24: 7, 27: 54, 28: 2; Mark 13: 8; Luke 21: 11; Rev. 6: 12, 8: 5, 11: 13, 16: 18. A particularly large earthquake might be taken to presage great ills for the human race or as a sign of great divine displeasure: see the passages collected on l. 54 below and Hdt. 6. 98. 1–2 μετὰ δὲ τοῦτον ἐνθεῦτεν ἐξαναχθέντα Δῆλος ἐκινήθη, ὡς ἔλεγον οἱ Δήλιοι, καὶ πρῶτα καὶ ὕστατα μέχρι ἐμεῦ σεισθεῖσα. καὶ τοῦτο μέν κου τέρας ἀνθρώποισι τῶν μελλόντων ἔσεσθαι κακῶν ἔφηνε ὁ θεός. ἐπὶ γὰρ Δαρείου τοῦ Ὑστάσπεος καὶ Ξέρξεω τοῦ Δαρείου καὶ Ἀρτοξέρξεω τοῦ Ξέρξεω, τρίων τουτέων ἐπεξῆς γενεέων, ἐγένετο πλέω κακὰ τῇ Ἑλλάδι ἢ ἐπὶ εἴκοσι ἄλλας γενεὰς τὰς πρὸ Δαρείου γενομένας; Thuc. 1. 23. 2–3. It has been plausibly suggested that the great earthquake of 115 at Antioch had a role in spreading the Jewish revolt of 115–17; see further F. A. Lepper, _Trajan's Parthian War_ (Oxford, 1948), 28–96; this is quite likely in the light of the eschatological interests of the rebels, on which see S. Applebaum, _Jews and Greeks in Ancient Cyrene_ (Leiden, 1979), 251–60, 265–9.

11. ἀστεροπῶν τε φοραὶ πολλαί: ἀστεροπῶν τε φοραί is Geffcken's suggestion (which he did not admit in his text) to replace Ω's Ἀσσυρίων τε πόροι πολλοί. Rzach, who, like Alexandre, accepted V's reading without demur in his edition, was later inspired by Geffcken's proposal to suggest ἀστεροπαί τ' ὄμβροι τ' ὀλοοί (A. Rzach, 'Neue kritische Versuche zu den sibyllinischen Orakeln', _WS_ 33 (1911), 246). He felt that the genitive ἀστεροπῶν was objectionable in the context of other disasters in the nominative, and, since he could not retain anything like the manuscript readings if he read ἀστεροπαί, he was moved to alter the rest of the line as well. He concluded by suggesting that l. 12 was an interpolation. All this is accepted, with some further remarks on 'Sibylline doctrine' by A. Kurfess, 'Zu den _Oracula Sibyllina_', _Hermes_, 74 (1939), 223.

Rzach's massive alteration is not really necessary, and his notion that l. 12 is a late (how late?) inclusion is unacceptable (see ad loc. for parallels). But Rzach's conviction that reference to another natural catastrophe is preferable to a reference to Assyrians is surely proper. Assyrians seem very much out of place in such a list, especially as τε indicates that the disaster mentioned here is of a sort that fits closely

with those that precede it. This is also the implication of the statement that these difficulties will occur 'throughout the world'—
κατὰ κόσμον ἄπαντα. For parallels see *Orac. Sib.* 2. 6–7 ἀλλ᾽
ὁπόταν ἐπὶ γῆς σεισμοὶ μαλεροί τε κεραυνοί | βρονταί τ᾽
ἀστεροπαί; Rev. 8: 12 καὶ ὁ τέταρτος ἄγγελος ἐσάλπισε καὶ
ἐπλήγη τὸ τρίτον τοῦ ἡλίου καὶ τὸ τρίτον τῆς σελήνης καὶ
τὸ τρίτον τῶν ἀστέρων, ἵνα σκοτισθῇ τὸ τρίτον αὐτῶν, καὶ
ἡ ἡμέρα μὴ φάνῃ τὸ τρίτον αὐτῆς, καὶ ἡ νὺξ ὁμοίως; Lact.
Epit. 66. 5 'his malis accedent etiam prodigia de caelo, ne quid desit
hominibus ad timorem. cometae crebro apparebunt, sol perpetuo
pallore fuscabitur, luna sanguine inficietur nec amissae lucis damna
reparabit, stellae omnes decident nec temporibus sua ratio constabit, hieme atque aestate confusis'; Comm. *Carm. de duobus populis*,
1111–12 'stellae cadunt caeli, iudicantur astra nobiscum:|turbantur
caelicolae, agitur dum saecli ruina'.

κατὰ κόσμον ἄπαντα: cf. *Orac. Sib.* 2. 25, 8. 180, 11. 237,
12. 127.

12. ἠδὲ λεηλασίη ... ναῶν: cf. *Orac. Sib.* 2. 14, 169–70; l. 87
below. As noted above (on l. 11), I see no reason to regard this line as
a late insertion.

13–20 (19). καὶ τότε δὴ Περσῶν ... προδοθεὶς ὑφ᾽
ἑταίρου: this war, which ends after the death of the reigning
monarch and the accession of Philip the Arab (clearly identified at
ll. 23–5—see ad loc.), was fought between Rome and Sassanid Persia
during the time of Gordian III. The course of the struggle, which
culminated in a disastrous Roman invasion of Mesopotamia in the
winter of 244, is very inadequately indicated by the author of these
lines. They offer a truncated summary of the events and thus stand
in stark contrast with the general economy of the work. This is the
only place where the narration of important events, lasting several
years, on the eastern frontier appears to have been composed by an
author who did not know a great deal about them. The picture is so
jejune that it is likely that the author was familiar with the events he
narrated only through imperial missives (reflected in the picture of
Gordian's role in the struggle) and rumour (reflected in the tale of
Gordian's death). In order to appreciate these features of the
account it will be necessary to review the evidence for Gordian's
war with Persia in some detail.

According to the *Historia Augusta* biography of the Gordians, the

Persian war began during the year that Gordian III shared the consulship with Clodius Pompeianus.[1] It was in the same year that the Emperor married the daughter of Timesitheus and founded the Roman games of Athena Promachos.[2] It was also a year that corresponded in part to the twenty-fourth year in the life of the prophet Mani. According to the record of that holy man's life, this year was notable for being the one in which Ardashir captured Hatra, Sapor received the great diadem, and the Great Lord sent Mani on his first mission.[3]

The *Historia Augusta* placed the beginning of the Persian war in 241 and the biography of Mani placed the fall of Hatra in the year that ran from Apr. 240 to Mar. 241. Line 14 of this oracle attributes the presence of the emperor in the east to a Persian uprising, and it might therefore appear a safe thing to connect the fall of Hatra with the beginning of the war. As this was also the year in which Gordian married the praetorian prefect's daughter, it might even be tempting to associate the offensive with the emergence of Timesitheus as the great power behind the throne.[4] But, while this may sound reasonable at first, it does not retain much appeal on reflection. The war had already been going on for years.

According to the tradition preserved by George and Zonaras,

---

[1] *HA V. Gord.* 23. 5–6 'Gordiano iam iterum et Pompeiano conss. bellum Persicum natum est. quando et adulescens Gordianus, priusquam ad bellum proficisceretur, [et] duxit uxorem filiam Misithei'. For Pompeianus see *PIR* [2] C 1177; Dietz, *Senatus contra principem*, No. 25; he was a descendant of Lucius Verus and thus, perhaps, an appropriate person to select for an auspicious beginning to a Persian war.

[2] Robert, 'Deux concours grecs à Rome', *CRAI* (1970), 11–14.

[3] L. Koenen and C. Römer, *Der kölner Mani-Kodex: Über das Werden seines Leibes* (Papyrologica Coloniensia, 14; 1988), 10–11 [ὅτε δὲ τεσσάρων καὶ εἴ]κοσι ἐτῶν ὑπῆρξα [ἐν] | τῶι ἔτει ὧι ὑπέταξεν Ἄ|τραν τὴν πόλιν Δαριάρ|δαξαρ ὁ βασιλεὺς τῆς Περ|σίδος, ἐν ὧι καὶ Σαπώρης | ὁ βασιλεὺς ὁ υἱὸς αὐτοῦ | διάδημα μέγιστον ἀγε|δήσατο, κατὰ τὸν μῆνα | τὸν Φαρμοῦθι ἐν τῇ ἦ ἡ|μέραι τῆς σελήνης ὁ μα|καριώτατος κ(ύ)ρ(ιο)ς ἐσπλ[αγ]|χνίσθη ἐπ᾽ ἐμέ; see A. Henrichs and L. Koenen, 'Ein griechischer Mani-Codex (P. Colon. inv. nr. 4780)', *ZPE* 5 (1970), 125–32; M.-L. Chaumont, 'Corégence et avènement de Shahpuhr Ier', in P. Gignoux and A. Tafazzoli (eds.), *Mémorial Jean de Menasce* (Louvain, 1974), 133–46; K. Mosig-Walburg, 'Bisher nicht beachtete Münzen Sapurs I.', *Boreas*, 3 (1980), 117–26; A. Henrichs, 'The Timing of Supernatural Events in the Cologne Mani Codex', in L. Cirillo and A. Roselli (eds.), *Codex Manichaicus Coloniensis: Atti del simposio internazionale (Rende-Amantea 3–7 settembre 1984), Università degli Studi della Calabria, Centro interdipartimentale di scienze religiose*, 201–3.

[4] Loriot, 'De Maximin le Thrace', pp. 762–3.

Carrhae and Nisibis fell to Ardashir before the death of Maximinus in 238, and the *Historia Augusta* says that both places had to be recaptured in 242.[5] A raid is recorded around Dura in 239.[6] At the same time, although Gordian appears to have been detained in the west, some moves may have been made around Edessa and Hatra. This may have been the occasion for the brief restoration of Abgar IX to the throne,[7] and Q. Petronius Quintianus, tribune of *Legio I Parthica Gordiana* and *Cohors IX Maurorum*, dedicated two statues at Hatra between 238 and 240.[8] It is from these disparate facts that a search after the circumstances of the Roman offensive of 241–4 must begin. The question is not why Rome went to war with Persia in 241, but why it waited so long to do so.

[5] Zon. 12. 18 ὃς ἐκστρατεύσας εἰς Πέρσας, καὶ πολεμήσας αὐτοῖς, Σαπώρου τοῦ υἱοῦ Ἀρταξέρξου τοῦ ἔθνους ἡγεμονεύοντος, ἥττησέ τε τοὺς ἐναντίους, καὶ Νίσιβιν καὶ Κάρας Ῥωμαίοις αὖθις ἐπανεσώσατο, ὑπὸ Περσῶν ἐπὶ Μαξιμίνου ὑφαρπασθείσας; George, p. 681 (= Mosshammer, p. 443) οὗτος ἐξ Ἰταλίας εἰς Πάρθους ἐλθὼν καὶ Σαπώρην τὸν Ἀρταξέρξου υἱὸν Περσῶν βασιλέα πολεμήσας ἐτρέψατο καὶ Νίσιβιν καὶ Κάρρας ἀρθείσας ὑπὸ Περσῶν ἐπὶ Μαξιμίνου τοῦ Μυσοῦ Ῥωμαίοις ὑπέταξεν; *HA V. Gord.* 26. 5–6 'illic frequentibus procliis pugnavit et vicit ac, Sapore Persarum rege summoto vi, post ⟨ea⟩ Artaxiam et Antiochiam recepit et Carras et Nisibin, quae omnia sub Persarum imperio erant' (vicit ac, Sapore Persarum rege summoto vi *Forrest*: et vicit ea sapore presarum rege summoto vi post artaxansen *MSS*; post⟨ea⟩ *Potter*); see Herod. 6. 6. 6 δεῖγμα δὲ τοῦτο οὐ μικρὸν τῆς τῶν βαρβάρων κακώσεως· ἐτῶν γοῦν τριῶν ἢ τεττάρων ἡσύχασαν οὐδ᾽ ἐν ὅπλοις ἐγένετο. Herodian's remark came in the wake of his tale of events in 233/4; see Loriot, 'De Maximin le Thrace', p. 716 and n. 470, p. 759.

[6] *SEG* viii. 743b; C. B. Welles, 'The Epitaph of Julius Terentius', *HTR* 34 (1941), 101–2.

[7] X. Loriot, 'Itinera Gordiani Augusti, I: Une voyage de Gordian III à Antioche en 238 après J.-C.', *Bulletin de la Société Française de Numismatique*, 26 (1971), 18–21, adduced G. Haenel, *Corpus Legum*, p. 166 'Imp. Gordianus A. rationibus. Manifestum est nuptiis contra mandata contractis datum, quae data illo tempore cum traducta est fuerat, iuxta sententiam divi Severi fieri caducam nec si consensu postea coepisse videatur matrimonium, Antiochae Gordiano A. et Aviola coss.'; *AÉ* 1915, No. 102, for Gordian and the *Acta Arvalium* of 240 (see also Loriot, 'De Maximin le Thrace', p. 760) to argue that Gordian visited Antioch in 239. H. Halfmann, *Itinera principum: Geschichte und Typologie der Kaiserreisen im römischen Reich* (Stuttgart, 1986), 234, has shown that this is not likely and that 'Antiochae' may mean only that the rescript was received at Antioch, not that it was given there. For the brief restoration of the kingdom of Edessa under Aelius Septimius Abgar see J. Teixidor, 'Les derniers rois d'Édesse d'après deux nouveaux documents syriaques', *ZPE* 76 (1989), 221, whose point is not affected by Halfmann's demonstration (of which he was not aware).

[8] D. Oates, 'A Note on Three Latin Inscriptions from Hatra', *Sumer*, 11 (1955), 39–40; A. Maricq, 'Les dernières années de Hatra: L'alliance romaine', *Syria*, 34 (1957), 289; Drijvers, 'Hatra, Palmyra und Edessa', p. 826.

By the end of 238 the frontier region would have presented a strange picture. Persian garrisons were at Carrhae and Nisibis and thus in some sort of control of the road between them. This was the main road from the Euphrates to the northern Tigris and, perhaps more significantly, the southern section of the eastern route through the anti-Taurus to the Arsamias basin.[9] Hatra and Singara were cut off behind the Khabur and Djebel Sindjar, and thus retained only a tenuous link with Rome along the road from Dura. The loss of Hatra in 240/1 was not a sudden catastrophe, it had been a *fait accompli* for several years and the final siege does not appear to have been long. The Arab tradition, for what it is worth, tells a well-worn tale of romantic treason.[10] The ruins do not tell a tale of sudden violence and fire.[11]

There were various reasons which suggest why nothing was done in any effective way against the Persians before 241. One of these was a revolt in Africa under the governor Sabinianus, another may have been a barbarian invasion across the Danube.[12] None of this seems to have made much of an impression upon the author of these lines, who seems to have thought that the war was the result of fresh Persian aggression.

The movement of Roman armies to the east was a complicated matter. In this case it seems that various forces took various routes at different times. The *Historia Augusta* records the recovery of Carrhae and Nisibis under 242. The ultimate source for this notice was the contemporary chronographer Dexippus[13] and this date should be accepted, particularly as there is other evidence which might suggest that serious military operations were undertaken in this year, though it also seems to be the case that Gordian himself

[9] For details of the route see L. Dilleman, *Haute Mésopotamie orientale et pays adjacents: Contribution à la géographie historique de la région du ve s. avant l'ère chrétienne au vi^e s. de cette ère* (Paris, 1962), 162–5.

[10] Nöldeke, *Geschichte der Perser und Araber zur Zeit der Sasaniden: Aus der arabischen Chronik der Tabari übersetzt und mit ausführlichen Erläuterungen versehen* (Leiden, 1879), 33–40; J. Gagé, *La Montée des Sassanides à l'heure de Palmyre* (Paris, 1964), 221–6, for translations of Tabari's account.

[11] Milik, *Dédicaces faites par les dieux*, p. 355: 'les fouilles ne semblent pas avoir montré de traces de la prise par assaut et de la destruction violente de la ville. C'est aussi l'impression que laissent les légendes arabes et syriaques sur la fin de Hatra.'

[12] Loriot, 'De Maximin le Thrace', pp. 734–5, 754–7; Dietz, *Senatus contra principem*, No. 81; and above, pp. 34–5 for details.

[13] See app. II on the author of the *Historia Augusta*'s knowledge of Dexippus.

did not reach the theatre of operations until the very end of that year at the earliest. One set of indications comes from Egypt, where Cn. Domitius Philippus appears with the extraordinary, but not unparalleled, position of *Dux* in 240 and disappears after Apr. 242.[14] He seems to have been employed with broad powers to arrange sufficient logistical support for the Persian campaign. It was the sort of command that M. Aurelius Januarius Zeno evidently held a decade earlier under Alexander Severus,[15] and his departure might be connected with the arrival of the main army in the east. His appearance in this position certainly suggests that Roman preparations for the war were under way well before Gordian left Rome.

There is no evidence for naval operations in this context. Two officers of the fleets from Misenum and Ravenna appear on inscriptions which attest their presence during the oriental expedition of the 240s, one at Antioch, the other at Ephesus.[16] This is of particular interest as Gordian himself did not sail to the east. According to the *Historia Augusta*, he defeated some barbarians on the Danube while heading for the Hellespont.[17] Coins attest his presence at Beroia in Macedonia at the time of the Olympic Alexandrian games there in the summer of 242.[18] The rest of his journey has been traced overland—though there is some question as to which road he actually followed through Asia Minor[19]—and it

[14] J. Rea, 'Gn. Domitius Philippus, *Praefectus vigilum, Dux*', in D. Samuel (ed.), *Proceedings of the Twelfth International Congress of Papyrology* (Toronto, 1970), 427—9.

[15] P. J. Parsons, 'M. Aurelius Zeno Januarius', in D. Samuel (ed.), *Proceedings of the Twelfth International Congress of Papyrology* (Toronto, 1970), 395—6.

[16] *AÉ* 1910, No. 36: *ILS* 9221, C. Julius C. f. Alexander; *AÉ* 1956, No. 10, Vibius Seneca; see J. Keil, 'Ephesos und der Etappendienst zwischen der Nord- und Ostfront des Imperium Romanum', *AAWW* 12 (1955), 159–70; D. Kienast, *Untersuchungen zu den Kriegsflotten der römischen Kaiserzeit* (Bonn, 1966), 95.

[17] *HA V. Gord.* 26. 4 'fecit iter Moesiam atque in ipso procinctu quidquid hostium in Thraciis fuit, delevit, fugavit, expulit atque summovit'; see Loriot, 'De Maximin le Thrace', pp. 739, 756–7.

[18] L. Moretti, *Iscrizione agnostiche greche* (Rome, 1953), 265; see app. III.

[19] A. Krzyzanowska, *Monnaies coloniales d'Antioche de Pisidie* (Warsaw, 1970), 62, asserts that Gordian travelled through central Anatolia; Loriot, 'De Maximin le Thrace', pp. 766–7; E. Kettenhofen, 'The Persian Campaign of Gordian III and the Inscription of Šāhpuhr I at the Kaʿbe-ye Zartošt', in S. Mitchell (ed.), *Armies and Frontiers in Roman and Byzantine Anatolia* (*BAR* International Series, 156; Oxford, 1983), 152–3; H. Hommel, '*Adventus sive Profectio Gordiani III*', in *Congresso internazionale di numismatico 1961* (Rome, 1965), 330–1, proposes that he took the route south through Ephesus and Tralles. In the light of the *adventus* coinage at Synnada (*BMC Phrygia*, 'Synnada', p. 403 n. 56), Hommel's proposal is probably correct.

does not seem possible that he reached the frontier region much before the end of the year.[20]

It would thus appear that the fleet, at least, went east without Gordian and that someone cleared the Persians out of northern Mesopotamia before he got near the front line. A much-ignored apocalypse of Elijah records (with the aid of some judicious emendation) that Timesitheus the Prefect and Philip the Prefect will lead in the second war—the first being that of Severus Alexander. They would have 100,000 horse, 100,000 foot, and 30,000 men from the ships.[21]

The Persians were expelled from Roman territory—perhaps this was the result of the battle at Resaina alluded to by Ammianus—in the course of 242.[22] The emperor joined the army for the invasion of Persia a year later, after a reorganization of the reconquered territory.[23] The verses preserved in this oracle show no knowledge of these events, and the fact that the imperial expedition to the Euphrates is attributed to a Persian uprising suggests that this is not because something more has dropped out of the text in the long lacuna that has been postulated between lines 6 and 7. This is all that the compiler of the oracle had; it seems that he had access only to lines composed by someone whose own knowledge was based on an official tale which gave little of the truth. This would not be surprising if the original author lived at some distance from the Euphrates. A concerted effort had been made in the course of the

---

[20] Loriot, 'De Maximin le Thrace', pp. 766–7.

[21] S. Krauss, 'Der römisch-persische Krieg in der judischen Elia-Apocalypse', *JQR* 14 (1902), 366; id., 'Neue Aufschlüsse über Timesitheus und den Perserkrieg', *RM*, NS 58 (1903), 627–33; F. H. Lehman, *Kaiser Gordian III.* (Berlin, 1911), 77–8. A. Stein, *RE* vii. 366–7, objected to the use of this document as evidence for the period on the grounds that turning Anpolipos son of Panpos into Philip son of Philip (as Krauss suggested, 'Der römisch-persische Krieg', p. 366) did not create a historical figure. What he wanted was Philip son of Marinus. Stein's argument has no real force. The case of Ben Nazor, as Odaenathus of Palmyra is known in Jewish sources, stands as a useful parallel. Not enough is known of the family of Philip to be able to assert that he did not have an ancestor named Philip, or even Panpos. Stein's other objection, that the list of cities taken by the Persians in this piece is not in line with those known to have been taken by Sapor, also assumes that more is known about this period than is the case. For further bibliography see A.-M. Denis, *Introduction aux pseudépigraphes grecs d'ancien testament* (Leiden, 1970), 167–8.

[22] Amm. 23. 5. 17.

[23] For Gordian and Edessa see Drijvers, 'Hatra, Palmyra und Edessa', pp. 878–81.

campaign to reassure the inhabitants of the empire that their teenage emperor was acting in the finest tradition of his ancestors.[24] A rare denarius from Antioch dated to these years has a laureate bust of Trajan on the obverse and the inscription 'Imp. Traiano Pio Fel. Aug. p.p.'.[25] The reverse shows a reclining female figure holding a whip in her right hand and her foot resting on a wheel with the legend 'Via Traiana'. The symbolism is obvious at a time when Roman armies were (in theory) once again on Trajan's road to Ctesiphon. An aureus, also from Antioch, has a bust of Gordian on the obverse, and a reverse showing *Felicitas* standing with long caduceus and cornucopiae in hand, with the inscription 'Divus Pater Traianus'.[26]

Coins such as those described in the last paragraph were only one, and probably the least obvious, way of commemorating the emperor's connection with past heroes of the struggle against eastern barbarians. Various public events might be sponsored to make the point more vividly. The Capitoline games celebrated at Rome for Athena Promachos seem to have been devised to recall past triumphs against Persia.[27] Coins from Beroia, the centre of the '*Koinon* of the Macedonians', attest the foundation of the Olympic/ Alexandrian/Pythian games there in 242.[28] Other coins from the same place show Alexander the Great on the obverse and suggest his *adventus* on the reverse.[29] A coin from Aspendos shows Gordian on the obverse, the river Eurymedon on the reverse. The god reclines to the left wearing a crown of reeds and a chiton about his lower limbs. His left hand rests upon an agonistic urn.[30] The celebration of

---

[24] For his portrait see Fig. 4.   [25] *RIC* iv/3. 37.   [26] Ibid. 38.

[27] Robert, 'Deux concours grecs', pp. 15–17; R. J. Lane Fox, *Pagans and Christians* (New York, 1986), 11–14.

[28] Moretti, *Iscrizione agonistiche*, p. 265; *AÉ* 1971, No. 431; *BÉ* 1971, No. 400. L. Robert points out that the proper restoration of l. 7, which records the games of 239, is τοῦ κοινοῦ τῶν Μακεδόνων ἀγῶνος Ἀλεξανδρείου ἱεροῦ ἰσελαστικοῦ ἰσ[ακτίου, which means that the change in the style of the games must be connected with Gordian's Persian war.

[29] H. Gaebler, *Die antiken Münzen von Macedonia und Paionia*, iii (Berlin, 1906), p. 20, 140 and n. on No. 574, n. on No. 705.

[30] *BMC Pamphylia*, 'Aspendos', p. 107, No. 97. The foundation of the Isopythian games by Gordian III at Side, which has attracted some attention of late, does not seem to fit into the pattern of anti-Persian agonistic demonstration described here; see *BÉ* 1972, No. 500, for details; it may be connected with the union of Side and Perge at this time attested in *BMC Pamphylia*, 'Perge', p. 141, Nos. 105–7. More attention in the context of Gordian's

games here might have recalled accomplishments of Cimon against the barbarians. A coin from Smyrna has Gordian on the obverse, the vision of Alexander the Great that led to the city's refoundation on the reverse.[31] Someone might have wanted people to think that there was a connection between the two.

In the light of the tradition that the author has accepted about Gordian III's personal participation in what he pictures as a highly successful war with Persia, perhaps the most significant feature of this passage is that he also accepts the most negative tradition about Gordian's death: that he was murdered by his own men (ll. 19–20 with n. ad loc.). This illustrates the importance of rumour in forming public opinion.

13. **καὶ τότε δή:** a standard phrase to introduce a new event or a new member into a series of events in Sibylline verse: see *Orac. Sib.* 11. 61, 68, 80, 239, 12. 245, 256, etc. The sense is merely connective in these cases. For the use of the phrase in the apodosis of constructions beginning with ἀλλ᾽ ὁπόταν see on ll. 21–5.

13–14. **Περσῶν . . . Ἀράβων:** lists of this sort should not be taken, as some have (e.g. A. T. Olmstead, 'The Mid-Third Century of the Christian Era', *CP* 37 (1942), 258), to indicate something specific about the composition of forces attacking the empire. It is a literary commonplace meaning, in this case, no more than the peoples of the east. In other cases (cf. *Orac. Sib.* 12. 180–1 αὐτοὶ δ᾽ αὐτ᾽ ὀλέσουσι πολυστίκτους ἀνθρώπους | Βρεττανοὺς Μαύρους, μεγάλους Δάκας Ἄραβάς τε) it can imply, more generally, the peoples beyond the bounds of the empire. For parallels to this passage within the present corpus of *Sibylline Oracles* cf. *Orac. Sib.* 11. 53–5, 5. 116–17, 13. 33, 14. 173–6; cf. on ll. 137–8

campaign should perhaps be paid to G. Bean and T. B. Mitford, *Journeys in Rough Cilicia* (Vienna, 1970), No. 19; *AÉ* 1972, No. 626; *BÉ* 1972, No. 498 (from Cibyra minor), recording honours for Aurelius Mandrianus Longinus in these years. Among his good deeds was (10–11) παραπέμψαντα ἱερέας ἀννώνας εἰς | τὸ Σύρων ἔθνος τρίς. Bean and Mitford, followed by S. Mitchell, 'The Balkans, Anatolia, and Roman Armies across Asia Minor', in S. Mitchell (ed.), *Armies and Frontiers in Roman and Byzantine Anatolia* (*BAR* International Series, 156; Oxford, 1983), 142, think that this refers to three separate wars (Caracalla, Elagabalus (*sic*), and Alexander Severus). One war lasting three years would be better (e.g. 242, 243, 244), a suggestion that has been adopted by Lane Fox, *Pagans and Christians*, p. 13. Cf. Bean and Mitford, *Journeys in Rough Cilicia*, No. 20; *AÉ* 1972, No. 627; *BÉ* 1972, No. 499, referring to two shipments of grain to Syria under Gordian III.

[31] *BMC Ionia*, 'Smyrna', p. 294, No. 442. For a discussion of this type see D. A. O. Klose, *Die Münzprägung von Smyrna in der römischen Kaiserzeit* (Berlin, 1987), 29.

below. It is a common literary device: cf. P. Opt. Porph. 5. 13–15 'Indus, Arabs iam vota ferunt et Media dives, | Aethiopes gnari rapido cum lumine surgit | Tetyos ex gremio Titan', ibid. 14. 14–26; Luc. 1. 19–20; Hor. *Od.* 2. 9. 23, 4. 15. 21–4, 14. 41–4 'te Cantaber non ante domabilis | Medusque et Indus, te profugus Scythes | miratur, o tutela praesens | Italiae dominaeque Romae'; Stat. *Silv.* 4. 1. 39–43; Verg. *Aen.* 8. 705–6 'omnis eo terrore Aegyptus et Indi, | omnis Arabs, omnes vertebant terga Sabaei'.

13. ἐπανάστασις: for parallels to this usage see *Orac. Sib.* 12. 277, 11. 175, 14. 141; Zon. 12. 21 (possibly retaining the language of his source) ἤρξατο δ' αὖθις ἐπὶ τούτου ἡ κίνησις τῶν Περσῶν; Zos. 1. 29. 2 Σκυθῶν δὲ ἐξ ἠθῶν ἀναστάντων καὶ Μαρκο-μαννῶν πρὸς τούτοις; Fest. *Brev.* 22 'sub Gordiano, acri ex iuventutis fiducia principe, rebellantes Parthi ingentibus proeliis contusi sunt'; *ILS* 1327. 8–11 'pra[ep.] vexillationis per Achaiam et Macedoniam et in Hispanias adversus Castabocas et Mauros rebelles'; ibid. 638. 6–7 'municipium Rapidense ante plurima tempora rebellium incursione captum ac dirutum' (referring to events in the late third or early fourth century; the rebels are clearly tribesmen of Mauretania Caesarensis); and from a much earlier period Sen. *Apoc.* 12. 21–2 'ille rebelles fundere Parthos'. The use of the word in this context is a significant indication of the attitude of Rome's subjects to their neighbours.

14. Ἰνδῶν Ἀρμενίων Ἀράβων: this is the reading of Ω. Geffcken and Rzach inserted τ' between these words, which, though more eloquent, does not seem to be necessary; for a list such as that in the manuscripts (without connectives) see *Orac. Sib.* 12. 181.

16. ἐπ' Ἀσσυρίους: the words 'Assyria' and 'Assyrian' are used to describe a variety of people and places in the Sibylline oracles. At *Orac. Sib.* 12. 107–9 the Assyrians are either eastern peoples in general or Jews who fall victim to Vespasian. The Assyrians at *Orac. Sib.* 11. 80 are Jews, and at *Orac. Sib.* 3. 268–70 the Babylonian captivity is described as Assyrian. At *Orac. Sib.* 3. 809–10 there is reference to the Ἀσσυρίης Βαβυλώνια τείχεα μακρὰ | οἰστρομανής, and at *Orac. Sib.* 3. 99 the tower of Babel is placed in the Assyrian land. In the *Eleventh Oracle* (ll. 159–61) it is predicted that the descendants of Aeneas will rule all the races of men as far as the Tigris and Euphrates: ἄρξει γὰρ γενεὴ τούτου μετόπισθεν

ἀπάντων | ἄχρις ἐπ' Εὐφράτου Τίγριος ποταμῶν ἀνὰ
μέσσον | χώρης Ἀσσυρίων, ὅππη μηκύνετο Πάρθος. The
Assyrian land is the scene of Trajan's Parthian war in *Orac. Sib.* 12.
154. Assyrians are among the people harassed by Tiberius in *Orac.
Sib.* 12. 42–4. Roman wars with Persia are described as Assyrian at
Orac. Sib. 12. 260 and at l. 60 below. At *Orac. Sib.* 12. 135 the people
of Antioch are called Assyrian, and at *Orac. Sib.* 12. 255 Pescennius
Niger is said to have perished in the Assyrian plain. Xerxes is twice
called Assyrian (*Orac. Sib.* 5. 336, 11. 179), and the word is included
in various lists of eastern peoples (*Orac. Sib.* 3. 160, 207, 303, 8. 7, 11.
53, 174; see Procop. 5. 24. 35–6 (describing the Sibylline oracles at
Rome) εὐθὺς ἐς τὰ Πέρσων, ἤθη ἐνθένδε τε Ῥωμαίων ἐς
μνήμην ἐλθοῦσα μεταβιβάζει ἐς τοὺς Ἀσσυρίους τὸν
λόγον. Only at *Orac. Sib.* 2. 172, 4. 49 (a prediction of the canonical
four kingdoms), and 11. 210–11 καὶ τότε δὴ Κιλίκων καὶ
Ἀσσυρίων μέσον ἕξει | λιμὸς καὶ πόλεμος where the refer-
ence is to Alexander the Great's campaigns, does the word refer to
the ancient region ruled by the kings of Assur and Nineveh.

The variation within the Sibylline corpus is in line with the
broadest usage that appears in classical authors: i.e. Aramaic
speakers within the area between the Zagros and the Mediterranean; see Str. 16. 1. 1 τῇ δὲ Περσίδι καὶ τῇ Σουσιανῇ
συνάπτουσιν οἱ Ἀσσύριοι· καλοῦσι δ' οὕτω τὴν Βαβυ-
λωνίαν καὶ πολλὴν τῆς κύκλῳ γῆς, ἧς ἐν μέρει καὶ ἡ
Ἀτουρία ἐστιν, ἐν ᾗπερ ἡ Νίνος καὶ ἡ Ἀπολλωνιᾶτις καὶ
Ἐλυμαῖοι καὶ Παραιτάκαι καὶ ἡ περὶ τὸ Ζάγρον ὄρος
Χαλωνῖτις καὶ τὰ περὶ τὴν Νίνον πεδία, Δολομηνή τε καὶ
Καλαχηνὴ καὶ Χαζηνὴ καὶ Ἀδιαβηνή, καὶ τὰ τῆς Μεσοποταμίας ἔθνη τὰ περὶ Γορδυαίους καὶ τοὺς περὶ Νίσιβιν
Μυγδόνας μέχρι τοῦ Ζεύγματος τοῦ κατὰ τὸν Εὐφράτην
καὶ τῆς πέραν τοῦ Εὐφράτου πολλή, ἣν Ἄραβες κατέ-
χουσι, καὶ οἱ ἰδίως ὑπὸ τῶν νῦν λεγόμενοι Σύροι μέχρι
Κιλίκων καὶ Φοινίκων καὶ Ἰουδαίων καὶ τῆς θαλάττης τῆς
κατὰ τὸ Αἰγύπτιον πέλαγος καὶ τὸν Ἰσσικὸν κόλπον; Ptol.
6. 1 ἡ Ἀσσυρία περιορίζεται ἀπὸ μὲν ἄρκτων τῷ εἰρήμενῳ
τῆς Μεγάλης Ἀρμενίας μέρει παρὰ τὸν Νιφάτην τὸ ὄρος,
ἀπὸ δὲ δύσεως Μεσοποταμίᾳ κατὰ τὸ ἐκτεθειμένον τοῦ
Τίγριδος ποταμοῦ μέρος, ἀπὸ δὲ μεσημβρίας Σουσιανῇ
κατὰ τὴν ἀπὸ τοῦ Τίγριδος γραμμὴν μέχρι πέρατος; see

further Amm. 23. 6. 15, 23. The use of the word 'Assyrian' to mean 'Aramaic-speaker' is perhaps best illustrated by an opinion of Ulpian, *D.* 45. 1. 1. 6 'eadem an alia lingua respondeatur nihil interest. proinde si quis Latine interrogaverit, respondeatur ei Graece, dummodo congruentur respondeatur, obligatio constituta est: idem per contrarium, sed utrum hoc usque ad Graecum sermonem tantum. protrahimus an vero et ad alium, Poenum forte vel Assyrium vel cuius alterius linguae, dubitari potest' (see Honoré, *Ulpian*, pp. 4, 20, 28). For the use of the word to refer specifically to the Persian empire see Str. 16. 16 πάλαι μὲν οὖν ἡ Βαβυλὼν ἦν μητρόπολις τῆς Ἀσσυρίας, νῦν δὲ Σελεύκεια, ἡ ἐπὶ τῷ Τίγρει λεγομένη. For a thorough discussion of these points see T. Nöldeke, '*ΑΣΣΥΡΙΟΣ ΣΥΡΙΟΣ ΣΥΡΟΣ*', *Hermes*, 5 (1871), 443–68.

If this passage were all that was known about Gordian's final campaign it would only be possible to say that the Sibyl indicates a campaign against people who lived to the east of the author (see also on l. 17); for more on Near Eastern conceptions of ethnography cf. on l. 21.

νέος Ἄρης: the identification of a ruler as a 'new divinity' is a regular feature of Hellenistic and Roman eulogy, though the implications are not always clear. It might mean that the person so addressed was thought to share some attribute of the god with whom he or she was identified, or it might merely be used as a polite way of suggesting that someone was engaged in the same activity as a divinity. As far as the Sibylline oracles are concerned, it is of some significance in terms of popular perceptions of the imperial office that Roman emperors are often identified with Ares, even when they are not actually described as fighting: cf. above, pp. 134–40; in general see P. Riewald, *De imperatorum Romanorum cum certis dis comparatione et aequatione* (Halle, 1912); A. D. Nock, 'Notes on Ruler Cult, I–IV', *JHS* 48 (1928), 30–7 = *Essays*, pp. 144–52; S. Weinstock, *Divus Julius* (Oxford, 1971), 381–4.

17–20 (19). ἄχρις ἐπ᾽ Εὐφράτην ... προδοθεὶς ὑφ᾽ ἑταίρου: although the meaning of this passage is quite clear—someone of whom the author had a favourable view will reach the Euphrates and be killed there by a companion—the manuscript tradition is extremely corrupt in several places, and sense can only be made of these lines with the aid of some substantial alteration. The manuscripts give:

17 ἄχρις ἐπ᾽ Εὐφράτην τε βαθύρροον ἀργυροδίνην
18 ἐκτανύσει πέμψας ὀλόγην πολέμιος Ἄρης
19 ιδετεως (Q)/ἴδετε ὡς (V) ἕνεκα καὶ γὰρ προδοθεὶς ὑφ᾽ ἑταίρου
20 καππέσετ᾽ ἐν τάξει τυφθεὶς αἴθονι σιδήρῳ

Lines 15 and 16, in which the Roman king is shown driving out the Persians and acting like a new Ares, imply that the author was favourably impressed by Gordian. The πολεμήϊος Ἄρης (I adopt here Rzach's metrically necessary alteration for the πολέμιος of the manuscripts) in line 18 is clearly meant to be the same impressive person as the 'new Ares'. Thus, if line 19 is to occupy the position it has in the manuscripts the word governed by ἕνεκα must explain the action of Ares in a sympathetic way. In company with other editors of this text I am unable to think of a word that is suitable and will scan.

If no decent restoration for the beginning of line 19 can be discovered, two other options must be considered. One of these is to assume that a line has dropped out between 18 and 19 which referred to someone else. But this would not solve anything. The subject of the sentence remains the Ares who is killed, and ἕνεκα should then still be referring to something which Ares does in a way that implies a negative judgement on his activity up to this point, which is unlikely given the positive tone of this passage. The second option, which I have adopted here, is to assume an inversion of lines 19 and 20. In this case the word governed by ἕνεκα may be understood as expressing a judgement upon the murder of Ares. Various possibilities have been suggested: νεμέσεως (Wilamowitz); φυλόπεως (Gutschmid); δυσσεβίης (Alexandre); ζηλοσύνης (Geffcken); the most appealing is Geffcken's notion that the killer was motivated by jealousy, for which *Orac. Sib.* 12. 224–5 ἴσθι τότε Ῥώμης ὀλοὸν χρόνον ἐγγὺς ἐόντα | ζήλου κοιρανίης ἕνεκεν serves as a parallel. I have accepted his proposal here. The proposals of Wilamowitz and Alexandre imply that the judgement on Ares, rather than on his killer, is negative (νεμέσεως has the implication of divine retribution), and Gutschmid's seems somewhat banal in this context.

17. ἄχρις ἐπ' Εὐφράτην: the movements of the Roman army during the final campaign of Gordian may be reconstructed from the Naqsh-i-Rustam inscription of Sapor and Ammianus' account of Julian's campaign in 363. The dating of Gordian's campaign to the early months of 244 is secured by two rescripts. The last extant rescript of Gordian was issued on 13 Jan. 244, the earliest extant rescript of Philip was issued on 14 Mar. 244 (*CJ* 6. 10. 1 (Gordian), 3. 42. 6 (Philip)).[32] The time of year chosen for the campaign is curious. Chesney observed in 1835–7 that 'even here the cold winds of the desert are felt during the winter, and especially at the beginning of the year, at which time rain is frequent and even snow falls occasionally'.[33] It is Dilleman's opinion that there has been no climatic shift in this area for at least the last two millennia.[34]

The *Res Gestae* of Sapor record that 'the Caesar Gordian raised throughout the entire Roman empire an army of Goths and Germans and marched against Asorestan, against the empire of Iran, and against our person. On the borders of Asorestan at Misiche a great battle was fought, the Caesar Gordian perished, and we captured the Roman army, and the Romans proclaimed Philip Caesar; and the Caesar Philip made a treaty and payed 500,000 aurei to save their lives, and became our tributary. We have for this reason renamed Misiche Peroz-Sapor' (*RGDS* 6–9).

Honigmann and Maricq have shown that the city of Peroz-Sapor should be identified with the Pirisabora captured by Julian in 363 at the north-western end of the northerly channel of the Naarmalcha, the modern Al Anbar.[35] It would therefore appear that Gordian tried to follow the route down the Euphrates that had once been taken by the armies of Trajan and Septimius Severus and would later be followed by Julian the Apostate.[36]

The *Res Gestae* of Sapor indicate that the battle of Misiche/

---

[32] There is no fixed *dies imperii* for Philip; see X. Loriot, 'Chronologie du règne de Philippe l'Arabe', *ANRW* ii/2. 789. In Egypt Gordian was still believed to be alive on 25 Feb. 244: *IGR* i. 1330, 5006.

[33] F. R. Chesney, *The Expedition for the Survey of the Rivers Tigris and Euphrates* (London, 1850), 105.

[34] Dilleman, *Haute Mésopotamie*, pp. 65–7.

[35] E. Honigmann and A. Maricq, *Recherches sur les Res Gestae Divi Saporis* (Brussels, 1953), 111–18.

[36] A. Musil, *The Middle Euphrates* (New York, 1927), 337–40; Lepper, *Trajan's Parthian War*, p. 133.

Peroz-Sapor was fought before Gordian's death, and the reliefs of
Sapor represent that emperor as dead beneath the feet of Sapor's
horse.[37] The Romans commemorated Gordian's death by erecting a
large tumulus near a place called Zaitha, and according to the
speech which Ammianus gives to Julian, the tumulus was erected in
the place he died (Amm. 23. 5. 17): 'in hoc ubi sepultus est loco, vulnere impio cecidisset'. The fact that Gordian's body was taken to
Rome does not mean that Ammianus was wrong about Zaitha being
the place of Gordian's death. There must have been some compelling reason to build what was evidently a massive monument in the
desert on the Persian side of the Euphrates. The location of this
mound is thus of some importance for understanding the circumstances of the emperor's death. It is clear, despite the claims of
Sapor, that Gordian did not die on the battlefield, and it is fortunate
that sufficient indications are provided by a number of authors to
allow its position to be determined with reasonable accuracy.

At the end of his description of Gordian's life Eutropius records
'miles ei tumulum vicesimo miliario a Circesio, quod castrum nunc
Romanorum est Euphratae inminens, aedificavit' (*Brev.* 9. 2. 3).[38] In
the course of his extremely contorted account of Julian's crossing of
the Khabur Ammianus recorded 'profecti exinde Zaithan venimus
locum, qui olea arbor interpretatur. hic Gordiani imperatoris longe
conspicuum vidimus tumulum . . . (8) ubi cum pro ingenita pietate
consecrato principi parentasset pergeretque ad Duram desertum
oppidum' (23. 5. 7–8).[39] Zosimus also mentions the tomb in the

---

[37] B. C. MacDermot, 'Roman Emperors in the Sassanian Reliefs', *JRS* 44 (1954), 76–80.

[38] Cf. Fest. *Brev.* 22. 5 'milites ei tumulum in vicensimo miliario a Circensio quod nunc
exstat aedificaverunt atque exequias eius Romam cum maxima venerationis reverentia
deduxerunt'; Oros. *Hist. contra Pag.* 7. 19. 4–5 'sicut Eutropius scribit . . . (5) igitur Gordianum ingentibus procliis adversum Parthos prospere gestis suorum fraude haud longe a
Circesio super Euphraten interfectus est'. For the connection of Florus, Eutropius, and
Orosius with the Latin chronographic tradition see on l. 20.

[39] See K. Rosen, *Studien zur Darstellungskunst und Glaubwürdigkeit des Ammian Marcellinus*
(Meisenheim am Glan, 1968), 154–5, on the tragic colouring of this passage, suggesting
that Ammianus deliberately distorted the order of events to emphasize the fate that would
befall Julian. This is better than the notion that he confused his notes and did not notice
that he put this story in the wrong place, as proposed by E. A. Thompson, *The Historical
Work of Ammianus Marcellinus* (London, 1947), 29. As it appears from Amm. 23. 5. 15 that
Julian was the last member of the army to cross the Khabur, the otherwise attractive suggestion of W. R. Chalmers, 'An Alleged Doublet in Ammianus Marcellinus', *RM* 102
(1959), 183–9, that Julian visited Zaitha on an earlier reconnaissance, cannot be accepted.
See also Matthews, *The Roman World of Ammianus*, pp. 175–9.

context of Julian's march to Dura: ἐξήκοντα δὲ προελθὼν σταδίους εἴς τι χωρίον Ζαυθὰ προσαγορευόμενον ἦλθε, καὶ ἐντεῦθεν εἰς Δοῦρα, ἴχνος μὲν ὡς ἄρα ποτὲ πόλις ἦν φέρουσαν, τότε δὲ ἔρημον· οὗ Γορδιανοῦ τοῦ βασιλέως ἐδείκνυτο τάφος (3. 14. 2). The difficulty in reconciling Zosimus' statement with those of Eutropius and Ammianus is not great. If Zosimus' sixty stades are measured from the Khabur, he cannot have Julian's army very near to Dura. Dura is thirty-one English miles south of Circesium, and sixty stades are only 7.6 miles. Ammianus' use of 'locum' to qualify Zaitha suggests that he was indicating a territory rather than a specific town.[40] The fact that he says that the monument was 'longe conspicuum' from the place where the army entered Zaitha further suggests that it was well within this area, though somewhat to the north of Dura, which the army drew level with after visiting the tumulus.[41] There need be no contradiction here with Zosimus' statement that the area of Zaitha was *c.*7.6 miles from Circesium. Zaitha was a region on the east bank of the Euphrates which began about eight miles south of Circesium and extended at least as far south as the level of Dura, and the monument itself may have been about ten miles from the northern boundary.

The location of Gordian's death in the place of his monument, some seventeen to twenty miles south of Circesium, is not very much at variance with the imprecise third-century tradition as reflected by Zonaras and Zosimus (on which more below), which placed the emperor around Carrhae and Nisibis at the time of his death. More important, the erection of the tumulus at Zaitha is certainly enough to indicate that the Roman army withdrew after the battle of Misiche/Peroz-Sapor and that King Sapor was not lying when he claimed a victory.

There is no suggestion of a Roman defeat in the western sources for Gordian's campaign. The fact that Julian would go out of his way to visit the monument, and that Ammianus would recall Gordian as a hero of the wars with Persia, suggests a serious and

---

[40] See *TLL*, s.v. *locus*, cols. 1581–2, for this meaning.
[41] Musil, *The Middle Euphrates*, pp. 237–8, wishes to identify Zaitha with the modern Al-Merwanijje, 17.5 m. south of Circesium; this is quite plausible and might suggest that Eutropius' figure is for the distance between Zaitha and Circesium rather than the distance between Circesium and the monument.

long-standing distortion in the historiographic tradition. The fact that both the author of these lines on Gordian and the final compiler did not seem to know of the defeat suggests that ignorance of this mishap was widespread even among immediate contemporaries. The effect of imperial control over such information is admirably illustrated by this lapse.

βαθύρροον ἀργυροδίνην: cf. *Il.* 21. 8 ἐς ποταμὸν εἰλεῦντο βαθύρροον ἀργυροδίνην; *Orac. Sib.* 14. 66 ἰοβόλους Πάρθους τε βαθυρρόου Εὐφράταο. For epic phrases in the oracles see above, pp. 126–32. The τε following Εὐφράτην is difficult and may be a sign of the trouble that the author had in controlling his metre.

18. **ἐκτανύσει, πέμψας λόγχην πολεμήϊος Ἄρης:** λόγχην is Geffcken's suggestion in place of Ω's ὀλόγην (ὀλίγην H). *Orac. Sib.* 14. 128–9 ἐκτανύσει λόγχην θυμοφθόρον Ἀρμενίοισιν | Πάρθοις Ἀσσυρίοισι μενεπτολέμοισί τε Πέρσαις provides a good parallel to this notion, and the change from λόγχην to ολογην would not be a difficult one (H's ὀλίγην has no independent authority: it is a scribal correction for V's reading). This is certainly preferable to Rzach's extreme alteration of the line to read ἐκτανύσει λόγχην ὀλοὴν πολεμήϊος Ἄρης, which, although more eloquent, assumes too complex a process of corruption in the manuscripts—there is no easy way to see how πέμψας could have been introduced into the text by accident. Alexandre attempted to retain H's ὀλιγήν, but his ἄχρις ἐπʼ Εὐφράτην τε βαθύρροον ἀργυροδίνην | ἐκτανύσει, πέμψας ὀλίγην πολεμήϊος ἄρης is not convincing.

20 (19). **προδοθεὶς ὑφʼ ἑταίρου:** there are at least two and possibly three separate traditions represented in the extant sources about the death of Gordian III—the event to which this refers—and several indications in other texts which cast some light on the circumstances. It is worth reviewing the content of these various traditions before attempting to establish their relative merits. Once these latter have been determined it may be possible to perceive something of the workings of power within the imperial regime and the way in which those workings were understood by Rome's subjects.

The most poorly attested version appears as part of a chronographic notice in Zonaras, George Monachus, George Cedrenus, and the *Synopsis Sathas*.[42] It states that Gordian III succeeded his father Gordian I and died in a Persian war after his horse fell on him and broke his leg. The fact that Gordian III was the maternal grandson, not the son, of the Gordian I who hanged himself after hearing of the defeat and death of his son Gordian II near Carthage during their abortive uprising in 238 is as serious an indictment of this tradition as the fact that a very similar story is told about Philip the Arab. The *Chronicon Paschale* (p. 503) records that Φίλιππος ὁ Ἰουνίωρ πολλοὺς συμβαλὼν πολέμους εὐτυχῶς ἔπραξεν. καὶ ὡς πολεμεῖ τοῖς Γήπεσιν, ἐκονδύλησεν ὁ ἵππος αὐτοῦ, καὶ συμπεσὼν αὐτῷ μηρόκλαστος ἐγένετο· καὶ ἐλθὼν ἐν τῇ Ῥώμῃ ἐξ αὐτοῦ τοῦ κλάσματος τελευτᾷ, ὢν ἐτῶν με΄. The fact that the emperor here is said to be 45 indicates that the author (if he was thinking of anyone who actually existed) was thinking of Philip the Arab rather than his son. The content suggests that this writer knew little more about Philip than the author of the similar tale about Gordian III knew about the Gordians (for the circumstances of Philip's death see on ll. 78–80 below). The parallel suggests that the story was attached to both rulers by accident or through ignorance at some later date.

The second tradition is most fully reported by Eutropius: 'Gordianus admodum puer, cum Tranquillinam Romae duxisset uxorem, Ianum Geminum aperuit et ad Orientem profectus Parthis bellum intulit, qui iam moliebantur erumpere, quod quidem feliciter gessit proeliisque ingentibus Persas adflixit. rediens haude longe a Romanis finibus interfectus est fraude Philippi, qui post eum

---

[42] Zon. 12. 17 οἱ δὲ τῷ υἱῷ ἐκείνου τῷ νέῳ Γορδιανῷ τὴν τῶν Ῥωμαίων ἡγεμονίαν μετὰ τὸν ἐκ νόσου θάνατον τοῦ πρεσβυτέρου Γορδιανοῦ προσκληροῦντες, κατὰ Περσῶν αὐτὸν γεγράφασιν ἐκστρατεύσαντα καὶ συμβαλόντα αὐτοῖς κἂν τῇ μάχῃ τὸν ἵππον ἐλαύνοντα καὶ τοὺς οἰκείους παραθαρρύνοντα καὶ πρὸς ἀλκὴν ἐπαλείφοντα, ὀλισθήσαντος δὲ τοῦ ἵππου καὶ συμπεσόντος αὐτῷ, τὸν μηρὸν κατεαγῆναι, καὶ οὕτως ἀνακομισθῆναι εἰς Ῥώμην, καὶ ἐκ τοῦ κατάγματος τελευτῆσαι; *Syn. Sath.* 36. 10 Γορδιανὸς υἱὸς αὐτοῦ ἔτη ζ΄· οὗτος ἐν τῷ πρὸς Πέρσας πολέμῳ κατενεχθεὶς τοῦ ἵππου καὶ τὸν μηρὸν συνθλασθεὶς ἐπανελθὼν ἐν τῇ Ῥώμῃ ἐξ αὐτοῦ ἐτελεύτησεν, ὢν ἐτῶν πεντήκοντα. The age given here (Gordian III was 19 when he died) makes attractive the notion that this tale has been confused with the unfounded tale about Philip quoted in the text—unless Gordian III has been confused with Gordian II, as in George Mon., p. 358, and Cedr., p. 257. This story has been accepted as true by M. Sprengling, *Third Century Iran: Sapor and Kartir* (Chicago, 1953), 84; D. J. MacDonald, 'The Death of Gordian III: Another Tradition', *Historia*, 30 (1981), 502–8.

imperavit' (*Brev.* 9. 2. 2–3). This version also appears in Festus' *Breviarum*,[43] Jordanes' *Romana*,[44] the Latin chronographic tradition of the fifth and later centuries,[45] Jerome's translation of Eusebius' *Chronicle*,[46] and, with a curious variation, Orosius.[47] The reference to the gates of Janus appears in only one work by a Greek author, John of Antioch, and it is just possible that it got there through a Greek translation of a Latin work.[48]

The third version is the most fully reported, appearing in Zosimus, Zonaras, and, with fanciful additions, the *Historia Augusta* biography of the Gordians. Zosimus tells that the ambitious Philip, a disagreeable Arab, thought that he could become emperor after he had been promoted to the praetorian prefecture.[49] He decided to

[43] Fest. *Brev.* 22 'isque rediens victor de Perside fraude Philippi, qui praefectus praetorio eius erat'. The information that Philip was praetorian prefect indicates that Festus was not using Eutropius directly, but a source common to both.

[44] Jord. *Rom.* 36 'Ianumque geminum aperiens ad Orientem profectus Parthis intulit bellum indeque cum victoria revertens fraude Philippi praefecti praetorio haud longe a Romano solo interfectus est.'

[45] Cass., pp. 146–7 'his coss. Gordianus admodum adulescens Parthorum natione superata cum victor reverteretur ad patriam fraude Philippi p.p. haud longe a Romano solo interfectus est. Gordiano milites tumulum aedificant supra Euphraten ossibus eius Romam revectis'. *Chron. Is. Minor*, p. 462 'rediens victor de Persis fraude suorum interfecit'. *Chron. Prosper Tiro*, p. 438 'Gordianus cum Parthorum natione superata victor reverteretur ad patriam, fraude Philippi praefecti praetorio haud longe a Romano solo interfectus est', *Chron. Gallica*, p. 401 'hic [Gordian] adulescens victis Parthis fraude Philippi praefecti occiditur'.

[46] Jer. *Chron.*, p. 299 'Gordianus admodum adulescens Parthorum natione superata, cum victor reverteretur ad patriam, fraude Phillipi praefecti praetorio haud longe a Romano solo interfectus est. Gordiano milites tumulum aedificant qui Eufrate imminet, ossibus eius Romam revectis'. Jerome would appear to be the source for the later chronographers (previous n.). If he is in fact translating the contents of Eusebius' *Chronicle* here, it would appear that he used the Greek source which inspired Eutropius and Festus.

[47] Oros. *Hist. contra pag.* 7. 19. 4 'Gordianus admodum puer in orientem ad bellum Parthicum profecturus, sicut Eutropius scribit, Iani portus aperuit . . . igitur Gordianus ingentibus proeliis adversum Parthos prospere gestis suorum fraude haud longe a Circesso super Euphraten interfectus est.' Here he has clearly omitted Philip's role because he thought he was a Christian; see his remarks at 7. 20.

[48] John Ant. fr. 147 (*FHG* iv. 597). For his sources, which are confused and confusing, see in this case Krumbacher, *Geschichte der byzantinischen Literatur*, pp. 334–5.

[49] Zos. 1. 18. 3 ὁρμώμενος γὰρ ἐξ Ἀραβίας, ἔθνους χειρίστου, καὶ οὐδὲ ἐκ τοῦ βελτίονος εἰς τύχης ἐπίδοσιν προελθών; cf. Aur. Vict. *De Caes.* 28. 1 'igitur Marcus Iulius Philippus, Arabs Trachonites'; *Epit. de Caes.* 28. 4 'Is Philippus humillimo ortus loco fuit, patre nobilissimo latronum ductore'; *HA V. Gord.* 29. 1 'in eius locum [Timesitheus] praefectus praetorii factus est Philippus Arabs, humili genere natus'; for the truth see on l. 21. Aurelius Victor and the *Epitome de Caesaribus* do not have much to add, though it is

cause a mutiny in the Roman army as it was encamped in the region of Carrhae and Nisibis by cutting off its supplies. The plan worked and the outcome of the ensuing revolt was that Gordian died and Philip took the throne.

Zonaras, who had already told one story of Gordian's death (see above), is more circumspect.[50] He also says that Philip was inspired by his promotion to the praetorian prefecture after the death of Timesitheus (whose name he gives as Timesokles), and that he decided to cause a rebellion by cutting off the army's supply of food, and then—Zonaras adds οἱ δέ φασι—that this took place and Philip became emperor. It is of some interest that Philip is not actually with the army in the versions of Zonaras and Zosimus. He is with them in the *Historia Augusta* biography of Gordian, but this is most probably the result of the author's imagination.

The *Historia Augusta* account begins with the tale that Philip cut off supplies of food to the army.[51] This was presumably derived from the same original source that lies behind Zosimus and Zonaras, but it concludes with a great deal that is found nowhere else. There is a mutiny which results in Gordian's appointment of Philip as his colleague in the purple, a relative of Gordian who does not seem to have existed,[52] and an extremely fanciful description of

clear that they were not using the same source as that which lies behind Eutropius, Festus, and Jerome: see Aur. Vict. *De Caes.* 27. 7 'eoque anno lustri certamine, quod Nero Romam induxerat, aucto firmatoque in Persas profectus est, cum prius Iani aedes, quas Marcus clauserat, patentes more veterum fecisset. Ibi gesto insigniter bello Marci Philippi praefecti praetorio insidiis periit sexennio imperii.' The games instituted by Nero were probably those of Athena Promachos also mentioned in the Chronicle of 354. The *Epitome de Caesaribus* is more interesting, possibly betraying the influence of a Greek source: 'apud Ctesiphontem a Philippo praefecto praetorio accensis in seditionem militibus anno vitae undevicesimo. corpus eius prope fines Romani Persicique imperii positum nomen loco dedit sepulcrum Gordiani' (27. 2–3). See also George, p. 681 (= Mosshammer, p. 443). The view of C. Wagener, 'Eutropius', *Philologus*, 45 (1886), 551, and A. Enmann, 'Eine verlorene Geschichte der römischen Kaiser', *Philologus*, suppl. 4 (1884), 340–56, that Eutropius and Aurelius Victor derive here from the same source, is shown to be false by Wagener's own comparison of passages on pp. 533–45; see further J. W. Eadie, *The Breviarium of Festus: A Critical Edition with Historical Commentary* (London, 1967), 88–96, though he ignores the evidence of Greek authors. [50] Zon. 12. 18.

[51] *HA V. Gord.* 29. 2 'verum artibus Philippi primum naves frumentariae sunt adversae, deinde in ea loca deducti sunt milites, in quibus annonari non potest'.

[52] Ibid. 30. 1 'suscepto igitur imperio, cum et Philippus se contra Gordianum superbissime ageret et ille se imperatorem atque imperatorum prolem et virum nobilissime familiae recognosceret nec ferre posset improbitatem hominis ignobilis, apud duces et milites adstante praefecto Maecio Gordiano, adfini suo, in tribunali conquestus esset,

the monument at Zaitha.[53] All of this is without parallel elsewhere, and none of it need be believed.

Evidence other than that in the main narrative and chronographic sources for the third century was alluded to at the beginning of this note. The most important items are provided by Ammianus. In the speech which he gives to Julian at the crossing of the Khabur in 363, Ammianus has the emperor remind his army of the glories attained by the former Roman invaders of Persia 'redissetque pari splendore iunior Gordianus, cuius monumentum nunc vidimus honorate, apud Resainan superato fugatoque rege Persarum, ni factione Philippi praefecti praetorio sceleste iuvantibus paucis in hoc, ubi sepultus est, loco vulnere impio cecidisset' (23. 5. 17). Three points emerge from these lines (aside from the fact that Ammianus does not seem to know that Gordian III was not the son of Gordian I).[54] One is that Ammianus thought that Gordian was a hero. The second is that he did not know about the battle of Misiche/Peroz-Sapor. The third is that he thought Gordian was killed at or near Zaitha by people set up to do the job by Philip rather than by Philip himself. This may reflect the tradition known otherwise from Greek sources, though the fact that he knew that there was an invasion of Persia (as is clear from his use of *redeo*) shows that he knew something more about these years than Zonaras and Zosimus.

The artificial improvement of Gordian's military reputation and the emphasis on Philip's seminal role in his death point toward two separate but related developments in the historiographic tradition about the third century. It is unlikely that the authors responsible for the traditions who have been discussed so far, authors who did not know the details of Gordian's final campaign, could have been very well informed about the details of Philip's plot. The lines dealing with Gordian in this oracle show that ignorance concerning Gordian's defeat was fairly widespread, and it is not likely that

sperans posse imperium Philippo abrogari'. For the Maecii and Gordian see Syme, *Emperors and Biography*, p. 4.

[53] *HA V. Gord.* 34. 2–5; J. F.Gilliam, 'Three Passages in the *Historia Augusta*', in *BHAC 1968–9* (Bonn, 1970), 103–7.

[54] This is evident from his description of him as 'iunior Gordianus'; cf. Eutr. *Brev.* 9. 2. 1–2. See also *HA V. Gord.* 2. 1 'Gordiani non, ut quidam inperiti scriptores locuntur, duo sed tres fuerunt'. For other instances of Ammianus' ignorance of the history of the 3rd cent. see nn. 244, 295 below. I hope to treat this feature of his work more fully elsewhere.

Philip advertised murder as the way he took the throne—Zosimus actually records a letter from him to the Senate saying that Gordian had died of disease.[55] The story about the murder here and in other places merely serves to illustrate what people wanted to believe both at the time and subsequently. As Philip's successor, Decius, waged a campaign against Philip's memory (see on l. 88 below), the story may even have received a certain amount of official encouragement—and this would have helped Gordian's reputation even more. If Philip was a disaster, it was perhaps not good to remember that his murdered predecessor was a failure.

The considerations outlined above may explain why third-century authors handled (or mishandled) the death of Gordian as they did. But Ammianus' interest is different: for him the fate of Gordian might foreshadow that of Julian, and he contorted his narrative to bring this out, which may make the force of his testimony that Philip himself did not kill Gordian all the greater. If he had thought Philip personally responsible he would certainly have said so. The reason for his interest in these two as exemplars is not far to seek. Orosius provides the answer most easily. Although he claimed Eutropius as his source, he omitted to mention the role of Philip as Gordian's killer (see n. 47 above). In the next chapter he breaks completely with that source and observes that Philip 'primus imperatorum omnium Christianus fuit'. He goes on to reflect, concerning the millennial games, that 'magnificis ludis augustissimus omnium praeteritorum hic natalis annus a Christiano imperatore celebratus est' (*Hist. contra pag.* 7. 20. 2). The truth behind this assertion that Philip was a Christian is difficult to ascertain (see on l. 88 below), but it is not really relevant here. Orosius was not being original—the notion was already in Eusebius' *Ecclesiastical History*. For men who lived in the fourth century Philip was a Christian. Like Gordian, Julian would fall victim to a sudden and mysterious death in the midst of a glorious struggle against the Persians, to be succeeded by a Christian.

To sum up so far: there are three traditions, of which two tell that Philip organized the murder of Gordian, one of them making it clear that he was not in the camp when the killing took place. The

---

[55] Zos. 1. 19. 1 εἰς δὲ τὴν Ῥώμην ἐκπέμπων τοὺς ὅτι νόσῳ τετελεύτηκεν Γορδιανὸς ἀγγελοῦντας.

third, which has Gordian dying from a broken leg after falling off his horse, cannot be isolated in any early source. The same story is told about Philip—in error—and there is the strongest possibility that it is the product of late confusion or invention. The two other traditions are not free from difficulty either. Philip was the object of execration for different reasons in various literary circles of the third and fourth centuries. The history of Gordian was altered to obscure his failure, and there should be a strong suspicion that Philip's part in his destruction was enhanced. It is perhaps best to be content with the view that the extant traditions which can be traced to the third century agree that Gordian was murdered.

The philosopher Plotinus joined Gordian's expedition against the Persians so as to be able to study the doctrines propounded by eastern peoples.[56] When the emperor was killed he returned to Antioch only with some difficulty: Porph. *V. Plot.* 3 τοῦ δὲ Γορδιανοῦ περὶ τὴν Μεσοποταμίαν ἀναιρεθέντος μόλις φεύγων εἰς τὴν Ἀντιόχειαν διεσώθη. He was 39 at the time. He went to Rome when he was 40.[57] This suggests that there was trouble in the camp when Gordian died for people like Plotinus, but that Philip did not have much, if anything, to do with it. If Philip was involved with the trouble it would be very strange that Plotinus, who had been incommoded by it, should go to Rome, where Philip was at the time he arrived.

It is easier to understand the career of Plotinus in the context of the veneration of Gordian's memory promoted by Philip.[58] The fact that Philip honoured, rather than damned (as the facts of the final campaign might justify), the memory of Gordian and that men who had been associated with the previous regime could continue to

---

[56] Porph. *V. Plot.* 3 ὡς καὶ τῆς παρὰ τοῖς Πέρσαις ἐπιτηδευομένης πεῖραν λαβεῖν σπεῦσαι καὶ τῆς παρ᾽ Ἰνδοῖς κατορθουμένης. Γορδιανοῦ δὲ τοῦ βασιλέως ἐπὶ τοὺς Πέρσας παριέναι μέλλοντος δοὺς ἑαυτὸν τῷ στρατοπέδῳ συνεισήει ἔτος ἤδη τριακοστὸν ἄγων καὶ ἔννατον. See further S. I. Oost, 'The Death of the Emperor Gordian III', *CP* 53 (1958), 106–7.

[57] Porph. *V. Plot.* 3 καὶ Φιλίππου τὴν βασιλείαν κρατήσαντος τεσσαράκοντα γεγονὼς ἔτη εἰς τὴν Ῥώμην ἄνεισιν.

[58] *HA V. Gord.* 31. 3; Eut. *Brev.* 9. 2. 3; *ILS* 1331 (a dedication by Julius Priscus), 6–7 'item a divo] Gordiano'; the restoration 'divo' may now be confirmed from *AÉ* 1964, No. 231: *BÉ* 1963, No. 223. 23 τοῦτο καὶ θεοῦ Γο[ρδιανοῦ; see MacDonald, 'The Death of Gordian III', p. 507.

prosper suggests that Philip did not have a direct role in bringing that reign to an end.[59]

Three things may now be held to be certain. There was a mutiny in which Gordian was killed. Philip became emperor as a result, and Gordian did not suffer a *damnatio memoriae*—he was deified and his failures were obscured. The first two certainties may have been enough to inspire the charge that Gordian was killed *factione Philippi*, but they are not enough to prove it. In addition to those things which may be held to be certain, there is the very real possibility—suggested by Philip's evident absence from the camp on the fatal day in Zonaras and Zosimus, as well as the fact that Julian does not actually call Philip the killer—that Philip was not with the main army when Gordian died. It is also worth noting that Philip was not the most important man in imperial service at the time of his elevation. His brother Julius Priscus may have been, but even this is not certain (see on l. 21).

It is best to believe that Gordian was killed in a mutiny after a mismanaged attempt to invade Persia at the wrong time of year. The rank and file of the Roman army, as the fates of Elagabalus, Alexander Severus, Maximinus Thrax, Pupienus, and Balbinus serve to illustrate, had little patience in these years with commanders who seemed unmilitary or could not win.[60] The death of Gordian in a sudden uprising by his defeated and perhaps sodden and hungry men may be seen in the same way as those of his immediate predecessors and previous colleagues—the result of the same military emotion.

The elevation of Philip serves to illustrate an important *arcanum imperii*. At moments of crisis, when none of their number was pre-eminent, the men who held most power were not inclined to select a ruler from among themselves. Thus, Claudius Tacitus became emperor at an advanced age in December 275 after the assassination of Aurelian.[61] Diocles, commander of the *protectores*, was chosen on 20 November 284,[62] Flavius Jovianus was elevated from a similar

---

[59] R. W. Davies, 'M. Aurelius Atho Marcellus', *JRS* 57 (1967), 20–2, though some of the conclusions he draws are a bit extreme.

[60] For relations between emperors and their soldiers see Campbell, *The Emperor and the Roman Army*, 384–5, and above, pp. 15–16.

[61] Syme, *Emperors and Biography*, pp. 237–47.

[62] *PLRE*, pp. 253–4; T. D. Barnes, *Constantine and Eusebius* (Cambridge, 1981), 4–5; the selection of L. Caesonius Bassus, a man of some importance, as Diocletian's consular

post on 27 June 363,[63] and the previously junior Flavius Valentinianus became emperor in February 364.[64] As the Sibyl's observation on the death of Gordian reveals, the intricacies of power were lost on educated men who had no role in government. In this case the author was probably following the *communis opinio* of his contemporaries, and the ultimate compiler of the poem probably had no reason to believe that this version was anything but the truth. This is all the more interesting as this person does not seem to have been overtly hostile to Rome; he seems only to have thought that murder was a common practice in imperial circles (above, pp. 139–40).

21–80   The Reign of Philip the Arab (AD 244–249)

21–5. αὐτίκα δ᾽ αὖτ᾽ ἄρξει ... τεθειμέναι: these lines, which present Philip the Arab and his son (see on ll. 22–5),[65] though similar in format to other introductions of human characters in the *Sibylline Oracles*, are somewhat more extensive than normal. The more ordinary introduction consists simply of a clause introduced either with an adverb or with a preposition, such as αὐτίκα (*Orac. Sib.* 11. 53, 12. 147); τὸν μέτα (l. 81 below; *Orac. Sib.* 5. 51, 12. 95, 176, 187, 14. 44, 58, 126, 163, 244); καὶ τότε (*Orac. Sib.* 11. 61, 68, 80, 239, 12. 245, 256, 277, 297, 14. 18, 27, 52, 74, 80, 94, etc.); ἀλλ᾽ ὁπόταν (ll. 28, 103 below; 14. 12, 185, etc.); ἡνίκα (l. 155 below; *Orac. Sib.* 11. 104); or by a verb in the future (*Orac. Sib.* 11. 21, 24, 12. 47, 14. 21, 130) or, infrequently, with the numerological equivalent for the person being introduced followed by the verb (*Orac. Sib.* 12. 68, 78, 250). The various forms of introduction are paralleled in the recorded verse responses from oracular centres: see Fontenrose, *The Delphic Oracle*, pp. 166–74.

21. αἰχμητής: the word is also used to describe Tiberius (*Orac. Sib.* 12. 37), Domitian (12. 124), and Trajan (12. 147). Philip's career before his selection as emperor is obscure,[66] but neither the little

colleague may be more significant than Barnes allows. It should indicate that he was with the army at the time.

[63] *PLRE*, p. 461.
[64] Ibid. 993–4. This list may be extended backwards to include the likes of Galba and Trajan.
[65] See Figs. 6–7 for their portraits.
[66] For the untenable view that Philip is the ']Itius Philippus Praefectus Vigilum' on *CIL* vi. 1092 cf. Stein, *RE* vii. 367, x. 755; A. Passerini, *Le coorti pretorie* (Rome, 1939), 338. For

that is known about that period of his life or the little more that is known about his reign suggests that this is a particularly accurate description. It is more likely to be a reflection of the common belief that the Roman emperor was *eo ipso* a warrior.

The problems surrounding Philip's rise to power are inextricably bound up with the problematic career of his brother, Julius Priscus.[67] Philip is known to have become praetorian prefect in 243 after the death of Timesitheus (Zos. 1. 18. 2; Zon. 12. 19; *HA V. Gord.* 29. 1), and a rescript reveals that there were two praetorian prefects in office on 2 April 243 (*CJ* 9. 2. 6, cited on l. 8 above). Since the precise date of Timesitheus' death is not known, this is of no direct help for determining the date of Philip's rise to the prefecture. It is of some help for Priscus.

An inscription on a column at the western end of the grand colonnade at Palmyra (*CIS* ii. 3932: *IGR* iii. 1933) reveals that Priscus was praetorian prefect in the 554th year of the Seleucid era. This year ran from October 242 to September 243. Since the text was carved in honour of Julius Aurelius Zenobius, whose services to Rome had been commemorated by Priscus as praetorian prefect, it may be assumed that he had become prefect some months (at least) before the end of the Palmyrene year.

The surviving portion of an acephalous dedication at Rome gives the career of a man who was praetorian prefect, prefect of Mesopotamia, *iuridicus Alexandrinae vice praefecti Aegypti*, procurator of Macedonia, procurator of an unknown province *vice praesidis,*

the equally untenable view that he was some sort of subpraetorian prefect before becoming praetorian prefect see n. 71 below.

[67] I see no point in discussing the often, and always inconclusively, debated εἰς βασιλέα of ps.-Aelius Aristides. The attempt of C. P. Jones, 'Aelius Aristides, εἰς βασιλέα', *JRS* 62 (1972), 134–52, to show that this work is in truth one by Aristides has been called into serious question by L. Robert, *BÉ* 1974, No. 74; see also S. A. Stertz, 'Pseudo Aelius Aristeides, εἰς βασιλέα', *CQ* ns 29 (1979), 172–97; L. De Blois, 'The Εἰς Βασιλέα of Ps.-Aelius Aristides', *GRBS* 27 (1984), 279–88. It remains valuable evidence for the theoretical virtues of an emperor and social problems, on which see Rostovtzeff, *Social and Economic History*, pp. 454–9. The discussion of Priscus' career in the present commentary reaches the same conclusion as that of Stein, *RE* x. 781–2; Passerini, *Le coorti*, pp. 338–9; Howe, *The Praetorian Prefect*, pp. 106–11. It seems necessary to reargue the case in the light of Pflaum's reasoned rejection of those conclusions (*Carrières équestres*, Nos. 324, 324a), which has been accepted by *PIR* i². 488 and by Loriot, 'De Maximin le Thrace', pp. 740–3, because of the appearance of *AÉ* 1969, No. 107, on which see R. Duncan-Jones, 'Praefectus Mesopotamiae et Osrhoeniae', *CP* 64 (1969), 229–33; id., 'Praefectus Mesopotamiae et Osrhoeniae: A Postscript', *CP* 65 (1970), 107–9.

praepositus vexillationum indigenarum and of a legionary vexillation.[68] The last of these offices is said to have been at the behest of the divine Gordian, and other posts, presumably from earlier rulers, come after it. The fact that Gordian is mentioned only for one of this man's offices does not mean that he did not have a hand in bestowing any of those which follow, and the mention of the province of Mesopotamia may be taken as a positive indication that he did. The province of Mesopotamia was ordinarily described in the third century as *provincia Mesopotamiae et Osrhoenae*. The only attested instance of it as Mesopotamia (*ILS* 1388 — Pflaum, *Carrières équestres*, No. 281) occurs before the end of the kingdom of Osrhoene in 214. Osrhoene appears with a procurator who is not associated with Mesopotamia in the same period (*ILS* 1353 = Pflaum, *Carrières équestres*, No. 342). The joint province, with a senior equestrian official as *praefectus*, appears afterwards.[69] The kingdom of Osrhoene was restored for two years under Abgar IX in 240–2, and then returned to direct imperial control.[70]

The senior equestrian official on the inscription from Rome who went on from being *praefectus Mesopotamiae* to praetorian prefect must have been in the area in 240–2. Since he does not record that

---

[68] *ILS* 1331 — Pflaum, *Carrières équestres*, No. 324a 'praef. pra[etorio] | praef. Mesop. iu[rid. Alexandreae,] | vice praef. Ae[gypti, proc. prov.] | Maced., proc. pro[v. . . . . . .] | ubiq. vic. praes[idis, praeposito] | vexillation. indig . [. . . . . [item a divo] | Gordiano leg. I . . . . ., [item] | [v]exill. class. pr . . . ., | [. . . . . proc. prov.] | His]p. cit., proc. pr[ov. . . . .|. . . . . . proc. p]rov. . . . .|. . . . v . . . For the restoration of 1. 6 see n. 58 above.

[69] *AÉ* 1969–70, No. 109 'Ḍardanius. Carui avaritia, metu sollicitudine hominum. | L. Valerio Valeriano, v.p. praefecto Mesopotaniae et Hosroenae [*sic*]'; ibid. 1971, No. 476 'L. Valerio Valeriano [proc. provin.] | Syriae Palaest. provinc . [. . . .] | praeposito summ(a)e [rationis priv. (?)] Mesopotamenae [*sic*] ad [centena (?)] | praepos. vexil. felicis[simae exped.] | urbic. itemque Asiana[e adversus] | hostes publicos p. R. [et cohortium] | peregrinarum adv[ersus Parthos] proc. Cypri praef. a[lae I Hispan.] | Campagonum in Dac[ia trib. coh. I] | miliarae Hemese[norum c. R. in] | Pan(n)onia praef. c(o)ho(rtis) [V Callaecor. Lucen. in] Pannonia [. . | . .] M. (?)] | Mevius Romanus (centurio) [leg. VI Ferra]l[tae f. c. Antoninianae [ex cornicula]r. eius viro [egregio pat]l[[rono incompara]bili'.

[70] Drijvers, 'Hatra, Palmyra und Edessa', pp. 878–9. This point, which was previously based on numismatic evidence, is now confirmed by the recently discovered dossier of papyri from Mesopotamia. One document is dated to the second year of Abgar IX on 18 Dec. 240 (the second year would have commenced in the autumn of 240); a second document is dated without reference to Abgar to 1 Sept. 242, showing that his reign had come to an end at that point (Teixidor, 'Les derniers rois d'Édesse d'après deux nouveaux documents syriaques', pp. 220–1). It is possible that Abgar's reign was brought to an end in the wake of Timesitheus' victories in 242.

he was *praefectus Mesopotamiae et Osrhoenae*, he was probably advanced to the praetorian prefecture before Roman control over Osrhoene was fully restored. He must therefore have become prefect during the lifetime of Timesitheus and must therefore be either Julius Priscus or someone who is otherwise unknown and held the prefecture for a very short time. The speed at which the honorand of this text was advanced suggests that he was a man of considerable ability and importance, while the number of offices (two of them—Egypt and Macedonia—in places connected with the eastern expedition) he held after the accession of Gordian suggests that he could not have reached the prefecture much earlier than the end of 242.

It is unlikely that a man would have been raised to the prefecture only to be removed a few months later to make room for Priscus (who must be in office by 243 so that he could deal with Zenobius the Palmyrene), especially as he would have been sole prefect when Timesitheus died and there is no suggestion in the hostile tradition that Philip murdered the man who raised him to office as well as his emperor. The power of the prefect at this period was such that it is very unlikely that someone would have been promoted to this position and removed in the course of the Persian war. It is possible that this person, if not Priscus, may have been a man who had been raised to the position and then died almost immediately afterwards, but it is easier to believe that it was Julius Priscus himself, and in any event it was Julius Priscus who made Philip prefect after the death of Timesitheus.

The other document relevant to Philip's career before he became emperor dates from his tenure of the praetorian prefecture and is of some interest as an illustration of the wide-ranging power of the prefects. It is an inscription found at Yapuljan recording an appeal made to Philip as emperor from several communities in Phrygia through the agency of a soldier named Didymus. In the course of the tale of their suffering at the hands of various imperial officials, the petitioners mention an earlier plea for redress; though the text is fragmentary at this point, the sense is clear: περὶ ὧν ἀπά[ντων ἐγράφη πρὸς τὸ σόν,] | Σεβαστέ, μέγεθος, ὁπότε τὴν ἔξαρχον διεῖπε[ς ἐξουσίαν . . .]|νος, καὶ ὅπως περὶ τούτων ἐκειν⟨ή⟩θη σοῦ ἡ θε[ιότης, ἡ ἀντιγραφὴ δηλοῖ ἡ ἐνταῦθα] | ἐντεταγμένη: 'quae libello complexi esti[s ut examinet praesidi mandavi,] qui da⟨b⟩it operam ne d[iu]tiu{i}s querell[is locus sit.]'

(*OGIS* 519; *IGR* iv. 598. 23–7).[71] The most interesting feature of this is that the prefect may be seen exercising the general authority over provincial governors that had been accruing to his office (the restoration 'mandavi' being clearly justified by what follows in l. 27). In terms of the career of Philip it reveals nothing that was not already known from other sources, and it is only possible to speculate on the circumstances which led to the unparalleled tenure of such a high office by two brothers at this time.

22. ἐκ Συρίης προφανείς: for the phrase see ll. 90 and 152 below; for the construction cf. *Orac. Sib.* 14. 19, 164, 186.

The description of Philip as a Syrian exemplifies a common type of geographical confusion. The rationale for this confusion is perhaps best illustrated by the abuse of Philip for being an Arab from the Trachonitis (he was in fact born there in the village of Chahba, the later Philippopolis: see on l. 68), the essence of the argument being that 'Philip . . . was an Arab by birth and consequently, in the earlier part of his life, a robber by profession' (Gibbon, *Decline and Fall*, ch. vii). The origin of Philip is never mentioned in accounts which are favourable or neutral to him (viz. Porph. *V. Plot.* 3; Eus. *HE* 6. 34–9; Oros. *Hist. contra Pagan.* 7. 19–20.

The confusion which led to residents of the Roman province of *Arabia Petraea* being called 'Syrians' appears in a number of texts. Throughout the period in which they minted, Philadelphia, Dium, Gadara, Nysa/Scythopolis, and Pella, all cities in the so-called Decapolis (an area which seems to have been informally defined by its inhabitants as being one of predominantly Greek culture)[72] and officially part of *Provincia Arabia*, identified themselves as being in Coele Syria.[73] Coele Syria did not exist as an administrative division

---

[71] The circumlocution employed to describe Philip's office has led some (e.g. Stein, *RE* vii. 367; Passerini, *Le coorti*, p. 338; Howe, *The Praetorian Prefect*, pp. 110–11) to suppose that Philip was not praetorian prefect but rather a subprefect. Given the ornate language of this text (see esp. ll. 14–17, 28–30), circumlocution of this sort should cause neither surprise nor difficulty. Great difficulty would arise if it were allowed that Philip was a subprefect while in the east as it would necessitate the belief in a number of other such officials—at least two, if not four, if there were two prefects (it would make no sense for there to be one subprefect for two full prefects). For the text given here see Pflaum, *Carrières équestres*, p. 836; *IGR* iv. 598. Dittenberger read διεῖπε[ν in l. 24.

[72] S. T. Parker, 'The Decapolis Reviewed', *JBL* 94 (1975), 437–41.

[73] A. Spijkerman, *The Coins of the Decapolis and Provincia Arabia*, ed. M. Picirillo (Jerusalem, 1978), 118–23: Dium, pp. 126–55; Gadara, pp. 186–209; Nysa/Scythopolis, pp. 210–17; Pella, pp. 242–57; Philadelphia, pp. 259–64.

of the Roman empire until Septimius Severus' settlement of the east after his victory over Pescennius Niger in the 190s.[74] When the province was created, the simultaneously created Syria Phoenice lay between it and the Decapolis.[75] In the reign of Antoninus Pius the geographer Ptolemy, relying (it seems) on oral reports,[76] not only placed the Decapolis in Syria, but also (5. 15. 26) *Βαταναίας χώρας, ἧς ἀπ' ἀνατολῶν ἡ Σακκαία, καὶ ταύτης ὑπὸ τὸ Ἀλσάδαμον ὄρος οἱ Τραχωνῖται Ἄραβες*. He put Adraa in both Syria and Arabia—another indication of the sloppiness of his method. The most revealing document of all comes from the time of Gallienus. It is a deed of sale for a slave (*P. Oxy.* 3054) which states (ll. 5–6) *ἀπεγράψατο τῇ ἐνεστώσῃ ἡμέρᾳ Αὐρηλία . . . τις | Σίμωνος ἀπὸ Βόστρης τῆς Συρίας*.[77] The fact that Bostra, which was raised to metropolitan status by Philip, should appear as being Syrian on an official document, like Ptolemy's misplacement of cities and regions which were well within the boundaries of the provinces of Arabia, shows how eager people were not to be said to have come from Arabia and hence possibly to be called Arabs.

The word 'Arab' had unpleasant implications for a civilized man. The name *Arabs* was common for slaves (*CIL* ii. 3183, vi. 8869, viii. 15558, 18086a, 18794, x. 2935, xi. 6361, 5624, xii. 4872, xiv. 461, xv. 4534, 631), and the term 'Arab' does not seem to have been one that people might readily apply to inhabitants of the Roman empire. Thus Publius Optatianus Porphyrius wrote to Constantine that 'Indus Arabs iam vota ferunt et Media dives (5. 13) and 'Arabs mox omnis ovat laudare sereni | oris lustra tui' (14. 16–17); and they are included by authors of Sibylline verse among the outsiders who fight against the empire (see further ll. 14 above, 33 below; *Orac. Sib.* 12. 181).[78]

The word 'Arab' also had unpleasant implications for a Semite. In inscriptions from the cities of South Arabia the word is used only to

---

[74] J. F. Gilliam, 'The Governors of Syria Coele from Severus to Diocletian', *AJP* 79 (1958), 225–42; Birley, *The African Emperor*, p. 114; Rey-Coquais, 'Syrie romaine', p. 66.

[75] Bowersock, *Roman Arabia*, pp. 91–4, 115–16.

[76] Cf. A. H. M. Jones, *Cities of the Eastern Roman Provinces* [2] (Oxford, 1971), 512. See also G. W. Bowersock, 'Three Arabias in Ptolemy's Geography', in *Géographie historique au proche-orient* (Notes et Monographies Techniques, 23; Édition du CNRS; Paris, 1988), 47–53, showing how Ptolemy's geography was influenced by the attitudes of his time.

[77] Bowersock, *Roman Arabia*, p. 116 and n. 28.

[78] Ibid. 123–4 for other instances of prejudice against Arabs.

describe nomads—the distinction between the urbanized and nomadic inhabitants of the area was in fact so great that a special vocabulary developed to characterize sedentarized nomads and their descendants.[79] The Prophet Muhammad later used the word only of bedouins,[80] and it would appear from an inscription at al-Namara marking the grave of Imru'l-qais ben Amr, the King of the ʿArab, that this was the word they used to describe themselves.[81] The word derives from the root ʿrb 'desert or desert-dweller', and various Old Testament texts (Isa. 21: 13, 13: 21; Jer. 3: 2), as well as 2. Macc. 12: 10, use it as a generic term for nomad.[82] For a Syrian or city-dweller in the province of Arabia the word 'Arab' would imply a barbarous nomad. It should come as no surprise that the inhabitants of the more civilized parts of *Provincia Arabia* should refer to themselves as Syrians in common usage. As the various local coinages, the information of Ptolemy, and the Oxyrhynchus papyrus indicate, the ways in which people perceived their cultural superiority were more important to them than the administrative divisions of the Roman empire. The description of Philip in this passage is a good reflection of that attitude.

22–3. ἔν τε καὶ υἱῷ | Καίσαρι: this reading of Ω is a classic example of the associative dative with ἐν that is common in New Testament Greek, and I retain it rather than Rzach's ἠδὲ καὶ υἱὸς | Καῖσαρ. For parallels see Matt. 16: 28; Mark 1: 23, 7: 25; Luke 14: 31, 23: 42; Acts 7: 14; 1 Cor. 4: 21; and in general Moulton, *Grammar of New Testament Greek*, iii. 241.

The younger Philip, who is the person referred to here, became Caesar in the summer of 244, the earliest attestation being a rescript of 15 August (*CJ* iv. 24. 10). He became Augustus in July or August 247 (Loriot, 'Chronologie du règne de Philippe', pp. 791–2). Since

---

[79] A. F. L. Beeston, *Warfare in Ancient South Arabia, Qahtan* (Studies in Old South Arabian Epigraphy, 3; London, 1976), 2–3.

[80] *Encyclopedia of Islam*, s.v. 'Badw', pp. 884–5.

[81] For discussion of this text see I. Shahîd, *Byzantium and the Arabs in the Fourth Century* (Washington, 1984), 35–7, with the corrections offered by G. W. Bowersock, *CR* 36 (1986), 113–14. For the later use of the word 'saracen' to describe the bedouin see D. F. Graf and M. O'Connor, 'The Origin of the Term Saracen and the Ruwwāfa Inscriptions', *Byz. Stud.* 4 (1977), 52–66. Shahid's attempt to dispute the etymology they propose (from srkt 'confederation'), *Rome and the Arabs: Prolegomenon to the Study of Rome and the Arabs* (Washington, 1984), 123–41 does not convince: see Bowersock, op. cit. 113.

[82] D. S. Margoliath, *The Relations between Arabs and Israelites prior to the Rise of Islam* (London, 1924), 3.

this passage envisages Philip ruling with his son as Caesar rather than Augustus it must have been composed before the younger Philip became an Augustus, and it may therefore be assumed that lines 21–34 were written before 247.

23. καὶ πείσει πᾶσαν χθόνα: πείσει is the reading of Ω. In his note on this passage Alexandre proposed emending to πέρσει, but retained the manuscript reading in his text. Rzach and Geffcken quite wrongly adopted the suggestion. Lines 25–7 concern the brief establishment of peace with Persia and the treatment of Philip here is generally favourable. This is in keeping with the manuscripts' πείσει, and not at all in keeping with Alexandre's suggestion. For the use of πείθω to mean 'pacify' or 'conciliate' (which is manifestly its implication here) see Matt. 28: 14; 2 Macc. 10: 20; Jos. *AJ* 14. 281; *Orac. Sib.* 11. 81, 86.

24–5. ἐπὶ πρώτου . . . . τεθειμέναι: the use of numerical equivalents for the first letter of a ruler's cognomen ($\Phi = 500$) is the usual way of identifying Roman emperors in the *Sibylline Oracles* which contain prophecies about rulers; cf. *Orac. Sib.* 5. 12–15, 21, 24–5, 28, 37–42, 12. 13, 16, 39, 48, 68, 78, 95–7, 101, 121, 125, 148, 165, 176–9, 189, 238, 245, 250, 258, 271, 13. 83, 156, 14. 19, 22, 28, 44, 54, 58–60, 74, 126, 137, 149, 163, 183, 186, 227, 287–8. For another way of introducing emperors see on l. 103 below. For an explication of this system when it is based upon the numerical value of the syllables in an individual's name (see Luc. *Alex.* 11 and ll. 46–7 below for a system using the numerical value of each letter) cf. *Sib. Theos.*, p. 191 ἐννεαγράμματον ⟨οὖν⟩ ὄνομα τετρα-σύλλαβον, οὗ αἱ πρῶται τρεῖς συλλαβαὶ ἀπὸ δύο στοιχείων εἰσίν, ἡ δὲ τελευταία τριῶν "μονογενής" ἐστιν· εἰ δὲ τὰ ἐννέα ταῦτα στοιχεῖα, ἔστιν ἄφωνα πέντε μ ῦ γ ῦ ϛ· τοῦ παν-τὸς δ' ἀριθμοῦ τῶν γραμμάτων, τούτεστιν τοῦ "μονογενὴς υἱὸς θεοῦ", συνάγονται ψῆφοι, ͵αχ΄ξ΄. καὶ Ἐμμανουὴλ δὲ τοσαύτας ἔχει συλλαβὰς καὶ γράμματα; *Orac. Sib.* 11. 15–18 μερίζετο γαῖα δ' ἅπασα | ἀλλοδαπῶν ἀνδρῶν καὶ παν-τοδαπῶν διαλέκτων, | ὧν ἀριθμοὺς λέξω καὶ ἀκροστιχίοις ὀνομήσω | γράμματος ἀρχομένου καὶ τοὔνομα δηλώσαιμι; Rev. 13: 18 ὧδε ἡ σοφία ἐστίν. ὁ ἔχων νοῦν ψηφισάτω τὸν ἀριθμὸν τοῦ θηρίου, ἀριθμὸς γὰρ ἀνθρώπου ἐστὶν· καὶ ὁ ἀριθμὸς αὐτοῦ ἑξακόσιοι ἑξήκοντα ἕξ.

24. ἐπὶ πρώτου κεικοστοῦ: the reference here to the numbers one and twenty (*A* and *K*) is another indication that these lines were written before the elevation of Philip II to Augustus in the late summer of 247 (see on l. 23): the author is saying that to arrive at the names of the rulers one must add five hundred to either the first letter (*A* for Augustus) or the number twenty (*K* for Caesar). The use of Αὔγουστος rather than Σεβαστός to refer to a Roman emperor is rare in Greek before the early third century. It became quite common thereafter: see H. J. Mason, *Greek Terms for Roman Institutions: A Lexicon* (American Studies in Papyrology, 13; Toronto, 1974), 12.

25-27. ἡνίκα δ' οὗτοι … οὐκ ἐπὶ δηρόν: as these lines wert written before the summer of 247 and, to judge from the emphasis on the fate of the Syrians in l. 33, by a man living in the area of the eastern frontier, they are of great importance for understanding Rome's relations with Persia in the early years of Philip's reign. The author divided the events following Philip's accession into three sections: (1) he and his son will rule during wars (25–6 ἡνίκα δ' οὗτοι | ἐν πολέμοις ἄρξουσι); (2) they will become lawgivers (θεμιστόνομοι δὲ γένωνται); (3) there will only be a short pause in the war with Persia (27 ἄμπαυσις πολέμου βαιὸν ἔσσεται, οὐκ ἐπὶ δηρόν).

The interval which the author included between the accession of Philip and the treaty with Sapor is more likely to be the result of literary form than memory of a significant military action on Philip's part (see next n.). A dedication to him, Otacilia Severa, and Victoria Redux by soldiers of *Legio III Parthica Philippiana* on 23 July 244 suggests that he had already returned to Rome by that date (*ILS* 505). More significant is the statement that the treaty will not last long. It is clear that this author was writing after the event: otherwise he would not have bothered to predict it at such length and could not have known that the treaty would be followed by a Persian attack. Lines 35–6 (see n. ad loc.) appear to refer to events of 245/6, and they precede a further Persian invasion (ll. 37–8). It would therefore be reasonable to put the resumption of hostilities in either the campaigning season of 245 or that of 246. This is in keeping with the only other relevant piece of chronological information for the period, that of Zon. 12. 19 ἐπανελθὼν οὖν ὁ Φίλιππος ἐγκρατὴς ἐγένετο τῆς τῶν Ῥωμαίων ἀρχῆς. ἐν δὲ τῷ ἐπανιέναι τὸν υἱὸν Φίλιππον κοινωνὸν τῆς βασιλείας

προσείλετο. σπονδὰς δὲ πρὸς Σαπώρην θέμενος τὸν τῶν
Περσῶν βασιλεύοντα, τὸν πρὸς Πέρσας κατέλυσε
πόλεμον, παραχωρήσας αὐτοῖς Μεσοποταμίας καὶ Ἀρμενίας. γνοὺς δὲ Ῥωμαίους ἀχθομένους διὰ τὴν τῶν χωρῶν
τούτων παραχώρησιν, μετ᾽ ὀλίγον ἠθέτησε τὰς συνθήκας
καὶ τῶν χωρῶν ἐπελάβετο.

25–6. ἡνίκα . . . θεμιστόμενοι δὲ γένωνται: The opposition
between the rulers as warriors and lawgivers is of some interest for
an understanding of the general picture of Roman rulers in the
oracles (see above, pp. 138–9). The translation 'When they will rule
in wars and become lawgivers' does not overstress the contrast.

27. ἄμπαυσις . . . οὐκ ἐπὶ δηρόν: the terms of the treaty which
Philip made with Sapor in 244 have been much debated.[83] Aside
from Zon. 12. 19 (cited on ll. 25–7 above) and the author of these
lines, who believes that the treaty was such that it would do no harm
to people who lived in the Roman empire (see on ll. 28–30 below),
information is provided by Evagrius, Zosimus, and the Armenian
historian Moses of Khorene.[84]

Evagrius discussed Philip's treaty with Sapor when he described
the background for the Lazic War of 526. He says that Greater
Armenia, the area later known as Persarmenia, was once subject to
the Romans; but that Philip handed her over to Sapor and retained
only the so-called Lesser Armenia for Rome.[85] The authority for
this statement may be an author named Nicostratus of Trebizond.
Nicostratus wrote a history running from the reign of Gordian III,

[83] For various views see Stein, *RE* x. 759–60; W. Ensslin, *Zu den Kriegen des Sassaniden
Schapur I.* (SBAW 1947, 5; Munich, 1949), 17; id., *CAH* xii. 88; A. Christiansen, *L'Iran sous
les Sassanides* (Copenhagen, 1944), 219; Olmstead, 'The Mid-Third Century', pp. 256–8;
Sprengling, *Third Century Iran*, pp. 84–8; Loriot, 'De Maximin le Thrace', pp. 774–5; M. L.
Chaumont, *Recherches sur l'histoire d'Arminie de l'avènement des Sassanides à la conversion du
royaume* (Paris, 1969), 44–6; L. De Blois, 'The Reign of Philip the Arabian', *Τάλαντα*, 10–
11 (1978–9), 14; E. Winter, *Die sāsānidisch-römischen Friedensverträge des 3. Jahrhunderts
n. Chr.: Ein Beitrag zum Verständnis der außenpolitischen Beziehungen zwischen den beiden
Großmächten* (Frankfurt, 1988), 80–123.

[84] For an English translation see R. W. Thompson, *Moses Khorenata'i: History of the
Armenians* (Cambridge, 1978), 218–20.

[85] Evag. *HE* 5. 7 οἱ τῆς πάλαι μὲν μεγάλης Ἀρμενίας, ὕστερον δὲ Περσαρ-
μενίας ἐπονομασθείσης—ἣ πρώην Ῥωμαίοις κατήκοος ἦν, Φιλίππου δὲ τοῦ
μετὰ Γορδιανὸν καταπροδόντος αὐτὴν τῷ Σαπώρῃ, ἡ μὲν κληθεῖσα μικρὰ
Ἀρμενία πρὸς Ῥωμαίων ἐκρατήθη, ἡ δέ γε λοιπὴ πᾶσα πρὸς Περσῶν.

where Evagrius says Herodian left off, to the capture of Valerian and the victory of Odaenathus.[86] The scope of his subject is such that he should be nearly contemporary with the events he described (why else should be stop with the short-lived pre-eminence of Odaenathus?), and if this is the case it is quite possible that he knew what he was talking about.[87]

One author who seems not to have known what he was talking about was Moses of Khorene.[88] He reported that when Chosroes of Armenia wrote to Philip asking for help against the Persians, Philip replied that he would not be able to come in person, but that he had sent a letter to all the provinces from Egypt to the Black Sea ordering them to send help for the war that Chosroes was fighting against Ardashir (*sic*). This war was successful and led to the Armenian conquest of Asorestan.[89]

In his narrative of Philip's reign Zosimus tells us only that Philip made the treaty with Sapor.[90] In his discussion of the treaty of 363 between Jovian and Sapor II he says that this agreement was worse even than the disgraceful one made by Philip, for, unlike the treaty of Philip, the treaty of 363 handed Roman territory over to the Persians.[91] In view of the fact that Resaina continued to mint under Philip,[92] and that Edessa did so under Decius,[93] it has been maintained that Zosimus gave an accurate description of Philip's treaty here, and that either Zonaras and Evagrius were wrong or else their statements conceal the fact that what Philip actually did was to renounce no more than the 'Roman protectorate' over Armenia.[94] This is too sceptical.

---

[86] *FGrH* 98 T 1; Ensslin, *Zu den Kriegen*, p. 17.

[87] See above, p. 71. [88] Chaumont, *Recherches*, p. 47.

[89] For the meaning of 'Asorestan' (i.e. northern Mesopotamia) in Armenian texts see Honigmann and Maricq, *Recherches*, p. 49.

[90] Zos. 1. 19. 1 ὃ δὲ πρὸς μὲν Σαπώρην ἔθετο φιλίαν ἐνώμοτον, λύσας δὲ τὸν πόλεμον ἐπὶ τὴν Ῥώμην ἐξώρμα.

[91] Ibid. 3. 32. 4 χρόνοις δὲ πολλοῖς ὕστερον Γορδιανοῦ τοῦ βασιλέως Πέρσαις ἐπιστρατεύσαντος καὶ ἐν μέσῃ τῇ πολεμίᾳ πεσόντος, οὐδὲ μετὰ ταύτην τὴν νίκην οἱ Πέρσαι παρεσπάσαντό τι τῶν ἤδη Ῥωμαίοις ὑπηκόων γεγενημένων, καὶ ταῦτα Φιλίππου διαδεξαμένου τὴν ἀρχὴν καὶ εἰρήνην αἰσχίστην πρὸς Πέρσας θεμένου.

[92] *BMC Mesopotamia*, 'Resaina', p. 127, No. 10–p. 133, No. 41.

[93] Ibid., 'Edessa', p. 117, No. 166–p. 118, No. 172.

[94] Stein, *RE* x. 759–60; Ensslin, *Zu den Kriegen*, p. 17; Sprengling, *Third Century Iran*, pp. 84–8; Loriot, 'De Maximin le Thrace', pp. 744–5; Chaumont, *Recherches*, pp. 44–6

The evidence of Zos. 3. 32. 4 probably derived from Eunapius.[95] The point of the passage is to illustrate the enormity of Jovian's disgrace, and for this reason a certain amount of caution should be exercised in its evaluation. It is not likely that either Zosimus or his source would have taken the trouble to consult a text of the original document—or, even if one of them had wanted to take the trouble, that he would have been able to discover it. Given the short duration of the agreement, an accurate knowledge of its terms is not likely to have greatly concerned anyone but a close contemporary. Certainly, in the context of Zosimus' discourse it would seem that they were less important than the notion that Julian and Gordian were similar figures—as were their successors.

Far more important evidence for the treaty may be derived from the statements of Sapor and Philip. In lines 9–10 of the *Res Gestae* it is recorded that 'The Caesar Philip made a treaty to save their lives, he gave us 500,000 aurei[96] and he became our tributary. For this reason we renamed Misiche Peroz-Sapor. And when the Caesar lied in the next instance and did wrong with respect to Armenia we attacked the Roman Empire.' Sapor's claims only make sense if Philip had agreed to pay a subsidy and not to interfere in Armenia.

Philip himself does not seem to have been eager to advertise his dealings with Persia. Coins from Antioch do not claim a *Victoria Parthica* (*Persica*) or illustrate a Roman triumph. They merely claim 'Pax Fundata cum Persis', and provide an innocuous picture of *Pax* holding an olive-branch on the reverse.[97] The event was not, as far as can be determined from the present evidence, commemorated by other imperial mints, and the title *Parthicus/Persicus Maximus* which occurs on three inscriptions from Pannonia, one from Moesia, and one from Italy in 244/5 was not a regular feature of Philip's

(though she none the less considers this the decisive moment in Rome's relations with Armenia).

[95] See, most recently, Paschoud, ed. *Zosime*, vol. ii, pp. xii–xix; Phot. *Bibl.* 98 εἴποι δ᾿ ἄν τις οὐ γράψαι αὐτὸν ἱστορίαν, ἀλλὰ μετάγραψαι τὴν Εὐναπίου; for the interests of Eunapius and Zosimus see W. Kaegi, *Byzantium and the Decline of Rome* (Princeton, 1968), 76–86, 119; R. T. Ridley, 'Zosimus and Eunapius', *Helicon*, 9–10 (1969–70), 574–92. For a cogent assessment of Eunapius' skill as a historian see R. C. Blockley, *The Fragmentary Classicising Historians of the Later Roman Empire*, i (Trowbridge, 1981), 1–26.

[96] For the identification of the denarioi of *RGDS* 9 as aurei see J. Guey, 'Deniers (d'or) et deniers d'or (de compte anciens)', *Syria*, 38 (1961), 261–74; T. Pékary, 'Le "Tribut" aux Perses et les finances de Philippe l'Arab', ibid. 275–83.

[97] *RIC* Philip, Nos. 69, 72.

titulature.[98] It would appear that the emperor was not eager to remind people of events in Mesopotamia at the beginning of his reign. This suggests that he had made concessions which he would rather forget.

In a study of northern Iraq, D. Oates argued from the permanent destruction of a Roman fort at Ain Sinu (30 km east of Singara) around the time of Alexander Severus and Maximinus that Rome abandoned the region between Singara and the Tigris after the peace of 244.[99] This acute suggestion has since received considerable support from Italian excavations on the lower Euphrates. At Kifrin the Italian excavators discovered a fort which seems to have been constructed in the reign of Septimius Severus and to have been occupied only down to the reign of Gordian III. The coins are primarily those of Septimius, Alexander, and Gordian III. No coin so far recorded there is later than 244.[100] The results of these excavations should explain Zonaras' mention of the surrender of Mesopotamia. The reference to the treaty in this oracle as being in some way harmful to the inhabitants of the Roman empire might also support this, especially as Sapor's advance up the lower Euphrates in his campaign of 252 must have been greatly facilitated by the elimination of Roman defences in that area. It is also possible that Sapor's description of Philip as his tributary indicates that Philip agreed to the payment of a yearly subsidy after the payment of an initial 500,000 aurei,[101] an expense that would have to have been borne primarily by people who lived in the eastern provinces. This is the sort of imposition that might have provoked the response to the treaty which appears in these lines. Priscus' regime

---

[98] *CIL* iii. 4634 (Pannonia, 244), 10619 = *ILS* 507 (Pannonia, 245), 14354 (Pannonia, 245), vi. 1097 = *ILS* 506 (Rome, 244); *AÉ* 1984, No. 758 (Moesia); Loriot, 'De Maximin le Thrace', p. 775 n. 861. For a different view of the significance of these texts see Winter, *Die sāsānidisch-römischen Friedensverträge*, pp. 107–10.

[99] D. Oates, *Studies in the Ancient History of Northern Iraq* (Oxford, 1968), 82–9.

[100] E. Valtz, 'Kifrin, La Fortezza del Limes', in *La terra tra i due fiumi* (Turin, 1985), 112, 120; id., 'Kifrin, A Fortress of the *Limes* on the Euphrates', *Mesopotamia*, 22 (1987), 88–9. Recent excavations at Ana, slightly up-river from Kifrin, should yield further information; for preliminary observations see D. L. Kennedy, 'Ana on the Euphrates in the Roman Period', *Iraq*, 48 (1986), 103–4.

[101] In addition to the studies of J. Guey and T. Pékary (n. 96 above) see H. R. Baldus, *MON(eta) URB(is) ANTIOXIA: Rom und Antiochia als Prägestatten syrischer Tetradrachmen des Philippus Arabs* (Frankfurt, 1969), 38–40, who would connect what seems to be the heavy minting at Antioch in 245 with this treaty; see also De Blois, 'Philip the Arabian', p. 14.

after the departure of Philip is said to have been outstanding for its fiscal stringency (see on ll. 61–3 below).

In the light of the considerations outlined in the last paragraph it is possible to suggest the following terms for the treaty between Rome and Persia which was made in 244 and broken in the summer of 245 or 246:

1. payment of 500,000 aurei at once and an annual subsidy thereafter;
2. abandonment of the claim to the area between Singara and the Euphrates, or to any territory that had been taken by Sapor before Gordian's arrival in the east and had not been recovered;
3. agreement not to help the king of Armenia against Sapor.

The last of these terms suggests that Sassanid concern with the continuing Arsacid presence in Armenia and elsewhere was a major feature in Persia's dealings with Rome at this time (see app. III).

28–30. ἀλλ᾽ ὁπόταν ποίμνῃ ... περὶ δ᾽ ὅρκια ῥίψει: these lines have caused commentators a great deal of difficulty. Geffcken interpreted them to mean that 'unter dem Bilde des Wolfes, der mit der Herde einen Vertrag gegen die Hunde schließt, um nachher die Schafe desto gründlicher heimzusuchen, scheint er uns von einem Versuche des Großkönigs zu berichten' (*Comp. u. Enst.*, p. 60). Olmstead offered 'But when the wolf makes faithful oath against the white toothed dogs, but then deceives, tearing the woolly sheep but oaths casts off' ('The Mid-Third Century', p. 257). Terry gave 'but when unto a flock a wolf makes oath against the white-toothed dogs, then he will spoil and hurt the woolly sheep, and cast them down in spite of all his oaths'. Collins followed along the same lines with 'But when the wolf pledges oaths to the flock against the white-fanged dogs, then it will do mischief, hurting the woolfleeced sheep, and will cast off the oaths.' None of these versions can be accepted, for none of them is connected to the realities of the situation following Philip's treaty. A reasonable understanding must be based upon the belief that the author of these lines was trying to produce something that could be understood by contemporaries who were familiar with the use of animal symbolism in oracular texts. An analysis of this symbolism will show that this passage only makes sense in terms of events in the 240s if the flock is understood as the victim of the actions of the wolf and the dog. Ω's ὁπόταν ποίμνῃ is at first sight a difficult reading; but I suspect that a reader who was familiar with the symbols employed here could not have much doubt about the relationship between ποίμνῃ and λύκος. Such a reader would also be used to the style of these poems and would not be surprised to find the victim of the action coming in the dative ('of disadvantage') at the beginning of a prophecy, e.g. 'Then for the X there will be ruin': cf. ll. 37, 74, 104, 137; 12. 42, 135, 153, 262; 14. 80.

Animals could be used in place of either individuals or nations and were thought to have been selected by the prophet or his source of inspiration because they shared some characteristic of the person or people for whom they were substituted. Thus, in his commentary on Isa. 34: 7 Jerome wrote 'repletusque est sanguine et incrassatus adipe agnorum et hircorum, medullatorumque arietum atque taurorum ut et principes et populum pariter significet puniendos' (PL 24. 371). The duration of this principle of interpretation may be judged from parallels provided by works composed in the fifth century BC. Herodotus recorded that when Croesus sent to Delphi and inquired as to why the god had misled him, the priests pointed out that the god's prophecy—that he must beware when an ass became king of the Medes—had in fact come true: καὶ τὸ τελευταῖον χρηστηριαζομένῳ εἶπε Λοξίης περὶ ἡμιόνου, οὐδὲ τοῦτο συνέλαβε. ἦν γὰρ δὴ ὁ Κῦρος οὗτος ἡμίονος· ἐκ γάρ δυῶν οὐκ ὁμοεθνέων ἐγεγόνεε, μητρὸς ἀμείνονος, πατρὸς δὲ ὑποδεεστέρου (1. 91. 5). Cf. Eur. *Suppl.* 140–65; Ar. *Eq.* 1066–77.

If a text contained an animal whose features were somewhat out of the ordinary, exegesis could begin from the salient peculiarities. In interpreting the fourth beast in the first vision of Daniel (Dan. 7: 7), 'after this I saw visions in the night and beheld the fourth beast, terrible and dreadful and exceedingly strong; and it had great iron teeth and broke things in pieces and stamped on the residue', Hippolytus wrote ὅτι μὲν οὖν μετὰ τὴν τῶν Ἑλλήνων βασιλείαν ἑτέρα ἄλλη οὐκ ἐγήγερται βασιλεία, εἰ μὴ ἡ κρατοῦσα νῦν, ἢ καὶ συνέστηκεν, καὶ τοῦτο πᾶσιν πρόδηλόν ἐστιν. (2) ἥτις ὀδόντας μὲν ἔχει σιδηροῦς διὰ τὸ πάντας δαμάζειν καὶ λεπτύνειν τῇ ἰδίᾳ ἰσχύϊ ὥσπερ ὁ σίδηρος (*Comm. in Dan.* 4. 5. 1–2). In his discussion of Daniel's vision of the ram and the goat (Dan. 8: 3) Jerome observed 'et ecce aries unus stabat ante paludem habens cornua excelsa, et unum excelsius altero atque succrescens. Arietem, Darium vocat avunculum Cyri, qui post Astyagen patrem regnavit in Medis. Cornu autem unum excelsius altero atque succrescens, ipsum Cyrum significat, qui post Astyagen avum maternum cum avunculo Dario, quem Graeci κυάξαρεν vocant, Medis imperavit et Persis' (PL 25. 535). Cf. Nahum 2: 12 with Qumran comm. ad loc. (trans. G. Vermes): '[*Where is the lions' den and the cave of the lions*] [Interpreted, this concerns] . . . a dwelling-place for the ungodly of the nations. *Whither the lion goes, there is the lion's cub,* [*with none to disturb it*] [Interpreted, this concerns Deme]trius king of Greece who sought, on the counsel of those who seek smooth things, to enter Jerusalem. [But God did not permit the city to be delivered] into the hands of the kings of Greece, from the time of Antiochus to the coming of the rulers of the Kittim. But then she shall be trampled under their feet. . . . *The lion tears enough for its cubs and it chokes prey for its lionesses.* [Interpreted, this] concerns the furious young lion who strikes by means of his great men, and by means of the men of his councils. [*And chokes prey for its lionesses; and fills*] *its caves* [*with prey*] *and its dens with victims.* Interpreted, this concerns the furious young lion [who executes revenge] on those who speak smooth things and hangs men alive, [a thing never done] formerly in Israel. Because of a man hanged alive on [the] tree, He proclaims, *Behold I am against* [*you, says the Lord of Hosts*].' See also Hab. 1: 8–9 with Qumran comm. ad loc. (trans. G. Vermes): '*Their horses are swifter than leopards and fleeter than evening wolves. Their horses step forward proudly and spread their wings; they fly from afar like an eagle avid to devour. All of them come for violence; the look on their faces is like the east wind.* [Interpreted, this] concerns the Kittim who trample the earth with their horses and beasts. They come *from afar*, from the islands of the sea, to devour all the peoples *like an eagle* which cannot be satisfied, and they address [all the peoples] with anger and [wrath and fury] and indignation. For it is as He said, *the look on their faces is like the east wind.*'

The activities of animals in these lines of the oracle and in lines 158–69 below should be interpreted in the light of the conventions that have been outlined in the previous paragraphs. Since they appear in the context of Philip's treaty with Persia their dealings with each other should be taken as a commentary upon the treaty from the point of view of their author and his likely audience: the inhabitants of one of the provinces along or near the frontier with Persia.

The natural interpretation of these lines is that the wolves, whom a reader would think of as dangerous outsiders and natural predators upon the flock, made an arrangement with their natural enemies, the guardians of the flock (the dogs). The wolves may therefore be identified with the Persians, the dogs with the Romans, and the reference is clearly to an agreement between the two which hurt the subjects of Rome.

28. ποίμνη: flocks, particularly flocks of sheep, ordinarily represent people with whom the author of a prophetic text identifies in a sympathetic way; cf. Enoch 89–90; Zech. 12: 7; Matt. 26: 31; Mark 6: 34, 14: 27.

λύκος: wolves are generally portrayed as violent animals and a menace to flocks (for obvious reasons). Their appearance in oracular or pseudo-oracular texts and elsewhere is generally with hostile implications; cf. Lyc. *Alex.* 102, 147, 248, 349, 871, 901, 938, 990, 1039, 1293, 1309; *Orac. Sib.* 14. 49; *Il.* 4. 471, 11. 72, 16. 156–60, 352–5 ὡς δὲ λύκοι ἄρνεσσιν ἐπέχραον ἢ ἐρίφοισι | σίνται ὑπὲκ μήλων αἱρεύμενοι, αἵ τ' ὄρεσσι | ποιμένος ἀφραδίῃσι διέτμαγεν· οἱ δὲ ἰδόντες | αἶψα διαρπάζουσιν ἀνάλκιδα θυμὸν ἐχούσας; Tib. 1. 1. 33–4 'at vos exiguo pecori, furesque lupique,|parcite: de magno praeda petenda grege'. In texts such as Isa. 65: 25 and *Orac. Sib.* 3. 788 the pairing of wolves and sheep in miraculous circumstances emphasizes the belief that they were naturally opposites; see further Matt. 10: 6 = Luke 10: 3. Jerome's comment on Isa. 65: 25 is particularly revealing in this connection 'tunc lupus et agnus pascebantur simul, persecutor Paulus, et Ananias discipulus' (PL 24. 650).

29. κύνας ἀργιόδοντας: cf. *Il.* 1. 292; *Orac. Sib.* 14. 348 ἀλλ' ὅταν αὖτε λύκοι κυσὶν ὅρκια πιστώσωνται, where the wolves are evidently the Arabs of Amr in 637 and the dogs are the expeditionary force from Constantinople which temporarily recovered Alexandria in that year (Scott, 'The Last Sibylline Oracle', *CQ* 9, p. 226, understood the wolves to be Romans and the dogs to be Arabs). Dogs were particularly valued as guardians (cf. Hes. *Op.* 604 with West ad loc.; to the passages collected there add Solon fr. 36. 26–7 (West) τῶν οὕνεκ' ἀλκὴν πάντοθεν ποιεόμενος | ὡς ἐν κυσὶν πολλῇσιν ἐστράφην λύκος).

31. δῆρις ἄθεσμος: the author of the oracle implies that the Persians started this new war. Zon. 12. 19 (cited on ll. 25–7 above) suggests that the cause was Philip's effort to recover the territory which Zonaras says he gave up in 244. Other sources do not help to resolve the contradiction.

Moses of Khorene, as was noted in another context (on l. 27), provides a story about a letter from Philip to the eastern provinces ordering them to help the Armenians in their war with Persia. This does not inspire much confidence: both the protagonists in his story—Chosroes and Ardashir—were dead by the time of Philip (for the difficulties in reconstructing the Arsacid house in Armenia see C. Toumanoff, 'The Third Century Armenian Arsacids: A Chronological and Genealogical Commentary', *RÉ Arm.* 6 (1969), 251; the king of Armenia at this time was Tiridates II). The initially attractive statement of *RGDS* 10 καὶ ὁ Καῖσαρ πάλιν ἐψεύσατο καὶ εἰς τὴν Ἀ[ρμηνία]ν ἀδικίαν ἐποίησεν, which might indicate Roman involvement in Armenia before the reign of Trebonianus Gallus (see on l. 111 below for the dates)—not that this could be firmly dated on the basis of the statement in question anyway—is actually a somewhat misleading translation of the Persian text, which implies 'in the next instance' (Sprengling, *Third Century Iran*, p. 85, *contra* M. I. Rostovtzeff, 'Res Gestae Divi Saporis and Dura', *Berytus*, 8 (1943–4), 21–2). The epigraphic evidence from Cappadocia is quite negative. All that survives is a record of work done on the bridge at Sabrina by Julius Valerius Nepotianus in 250 (*CIL* iii. 14184. 25; *PIR* J 844), which shows only that this bridge was in bad repair—something that might suggest little activity by Roman forces in the area under Philip or that the weather had recently been harsh. It is not the sort of thing that helps much with the political history of an earlier era.

It is perhaps most likely that Zonaras' story was roughly true; certainly the oracle confirms his statement that trouble started up again soon after the treaty of 244, and there is no evidence elsewhere to contradict it. It is possible that Philip broke the agreement or part of it in 245/6 and that the oracle records only the official story to the effect that the Persians were responsible for the new outbreak.

ὑπερφιάλων βασιλήων: for arrogance as a characteristic of people engaged in a war see l. 37 below. The word appears in other contexts: *Orac. Sib.* 1. 105, 3. 73, 739—and is common in Homer without overtly hostile implication (LSJ, s.v.).

32. Σύροι δ' ἔκπαγλ' ἀπολοῦνται: cf. l. 108 below. The reference to the destruction of Syrians in this context may suggest that the author was one—certainly they are presented as the victims of the peace. This use of the neuter plural accusative of *ἔκπαγλος* as an adverb is Homeric: *Il.* 3. 415, 5. 423. For the scansion of *Σύροι* with a long first syllable see on l. 108.

33. Ἰνδοί . . . Βαβυλῶνες: for lists of people like this, implying the peoples of the east, see on l. 14 above.

34. διὰ κρατερὰς ὑσμίνας: cf. *Orac. Sib.* 11. 52, 70, 124. The collocation is common in the *Iliad*: see 2. 345, 5. 200, 330, 12. 347, 360, 17. 543.

35–49. ἀλλ' ὁπόταν Ῥωμαῖος . . . δῖα πόλις μεγάλη Μακηδονίοιο ἄνακτος: the structure of these lines is rather complex and the course of the argument they present is not developed in a manner designed to make comprehension easy. For this reason it seems best to outline their contents in some detail before dealing with two problems which concern the passage as a whole: unity and relevance to the lines which precede and follow them.

Lines 35–8 tell us that there will be a war on the Danube (see on l. 35) followed by one on the eastern frontier. The use of a temporal clause introduced with ἀλλ' ὁπόταν matched with καὶ τότε indicates that the author thought they were closely connected in time (Fontenrose, *The Delphic Oracle*, pp. 166–70, 177).

Line 38 concludes with a prediction that the Persians will not defeat the Romans. Lines 39–43 ἤματι τῷ amplify this with *adynata* which might be thought comparable to the prospect of a Persian victory (thus οὕτω introducing the notion in line 42) co-ordinated with a conditional clause asserting that the Persians will not go forth to victory at that time (for the meaning of ἤματι τῳ see ad loc.).

Lines 43 ἐφ' ὅσον–45 elaborate upon the preceding clause with another statement about the Persians' chance of winning: Persia will not conquer Rome at the time of Rome's wars on the Danube; just as fish do not swim on the cliffs, turtles do not fly, and eagles do not swim, neither will the Persians win at any time that Egypt is subject to Rome.

Lines 46–9 refine and amplify the message in the foregoing lines. Persia cannot conquer Rome so long as Egypt remains subject, and Egypt will in fact remain that way for as many years as are in the number that can be computed from the name of Rome. This comes to 948 (P (= 100) + Ω (= 800) + M (= 40) + H (= 8)).

The unity of thought in lines 35–45 indicates that they are the product of a single author, and as lines 46–9 complement their argument I am inclined to believe that the whole passage is the product of one hand. A case against this was developed by W. Scott in the third of his articles on the *Fourteenth Oracle* and it won Rzach's approval; but it is not one that can be supported in the light of the relevance of this passage to a third-century context.

Lines 21–34 were written by someone who lived in Syria or northern Mesopotamia (see on ll. 25–7 above), as were lines 54–6 (see ad loc.); so too lines 59–63 and 64–73 (see nn. ad loc.). Lines 78–80 clearly allude to an event in 249 (the death of Philip), lines 21–34 clearly refer to events before the midsummer of 247 (see on l. 24). As the prophecy in the present lines is cast in terms of Egypt (whereas all those just mentioned refer primarily to Syria), it is best to believe that they were written there. A Syrian would probably have been less obsessed with Egypt's importance to Rome and could surely have produced a similar text which emphasized Syria's loyalty to Rome, rather than Egypt's, as the determining factor in Roman fortunes *vis-à-vis* Persia.

As these lines were included by the compiler of the present oracle between two clearly dated events (the outbreak of war with Persia and Philip's death), it is reasonable to believe that they were so placed because the compiler thought they were particularly relevant to this part of the reign of Philip. It does in fact seem that lines 35–6 refer to an event datable to the years after 245 (see ad loc.), and apparently the compiler saw a progression from the lines which come before those predicting the end of Philip's peace with Persia to the war with German Ares and the subsequent war with the Persians. This prophecy is separated by a considerable interval from another prophecy of war with the Persians before Philip's death (line 59). Prophecy of the same event repeated in several places separated by passages which tell of other events appears to be a technique employed by the author for dating and to indicate the passage of time—there is no point to repeated prediction of this sort unless it is to provide points of reference. It would therefore appear that these lines were included here because the compiler knew they were relevant to a datable event in the reign of Philip. Inclusion of passages for similar reasons appears to have been the author's practice elsewhere in the text as well (see above, pp. 144–6).

As the main elements of this vaticination are the wars, which also serve roughly to indicate the date, and the duration of Rome's resistance to Persia, it is likely that these were prominent in the compiler's mind when he considered the middle years of Philip's reign. The Persian war has already been discussed (see on ll. 25–7, 31), and the reason why it should figure so strongly in a Syrian's mind is obvious: he would have been affected by it directly. Interest in the duration of Rome's rule at this point may have been stimulated by something else. This passage is included at a point in Philip's reign that corresponds to the time of the millennial games of 248. This is an event which is known to have caused significant stir elsewhere in the empire (see on ll. 46–9, 78–80), and the author may have thought of this prophecy in connection with that moment; this is not something that can be proved, but the length of the passage and the author's evident concern for chronology make it likely. The use of an Egyptian text in this way by a Syrian is testimony to the link between Egypt and Syria evident from papyri which reflect the military organization of the period (above, p. 193).

35–6. Ἄρης ... Ἄρεα νικήσας θυμοφθόρον: the use of Ares in conjunction with the name of a people to indicate that the group in question is at war is quite common. The fact that this is the implication here is clear from its use in connection with Γερμανός (It is not likely that the author would have known of a barbarian leader whom he would be describing in this way—for his possible source of information see on l. 36 ὠκεανοῖο below). In general, see *Orac. Sib.* 3. 464, 7. 46, 12. 276 (?); *Insc. Did.* 159. 1. 1–4 τὸ θαῦμα τοῦτο πρόσθε μὲν τοῦ Πυθίου, | πηγὴ βλύσασα νάμασιν χρυσορρύτοις | αὐτοῦ ταγαῖσιν, ἡνίκ' Ἄρης βάρβαρος | συνέκλησεν ἀστούς; ibid. III. 1–4 εἰμὶ μὲν Ἀπόλλωνος ὕδωρ, ναέταισι δὲ δῶρον | δῶκέ με χρυσολύρης ἐν Σκυθικῷ πολέμῳ | ἡνίκα δὴ περὶ νηὸν ἐπιβρείσαντος Ἄρηος | αὐτὸς ὁ Λητοΐδης σῷζεν ἑοὺς ἱκέτας; Robert, 'Épitaphe de provenance inconnue', 119–29. The usage would seem to be connected with the belief that war could be prevented through binding or burying statues of Ares: the figurative link between Ares and some nation engaged in war reflects the belief that war could be prevented by physically tying up the war-god. For instances of this see Olympiodorus fr. 27 (Blockley), where the tale is told of three gold statues being unearthed in Thrace just before the invasion of the Huns in 422 (on this see B. Croke, 'Evidence for the Hun Invasion of Thrace in A.D. 422', *GRBS* 18 (1977), 358–9; K. G. Holum, *Theodosian Empresses* (Berkeley, 1982), 118–19); and *Anth. Graec.* 9. 805, which may reflect a similar instance: εἰσόκε θούριος οὗτος ἐπὶ χθονὶ κέκλιται Ἄρης, | οὔποτε Θρηϊκίης ἐπιβήσεται ἔθνεα Γότθων. For the binding of Ares at Syedra upon the instructions of an oracle in the first century BC (?) and similar behaviour there in the third, see L. Robert, *Documents de l'Asie mineure méridionale* (Paris, 1966), 92–100. As the implications of this usage are quintessentially pagan it is unlikely that these lines were written by a Christian or Jew (above, pp. 148–50), for, although the sort of magic implicit in the expression certainly had a home among Christians and Jews, they would employ symbols appropriate to their faiths to express it.

35. Γερμανόν: Philip appears as *Germanicus* on an inscription of 246 from Dioscome in Phrygia (*IGR* iv. 635) and as *Germanicus Maximus Carpicus Maximus* on a medallion of 248 (A. Alföldi, *Die mönarchische Repräsentation im römischen Kaisereide* (Darmstadt, 1970), 95–6). In both cases the reference is probably to campaigns along the Danube (see on l. 36) as no activity is recorded on other European frontiers during the reign of Philip. This serves to illustrate Dio's remark upon Marcus Aurelius' acquisition of the title *Germanicus* after the defeat of the Marcomanni in 172: Γερμανοὺς γὰρ τοὺς ἐν τοῖς ἄνω χωρίοις οἰκοῦντας ὀνομάζομεν (71. 3. 5). Since the Dioscome inscription is dated to the tenth month in the year 330 of the Sullan era, the campaign which Philip's subjects commemorated by the inclusion of this title probably took place in the summer of 245.

36. θυμοφθόρον: a rare epithet; see Roscher, s.v. Ἄρης, citing only this passage. In Homer the word is ordinarily applied to physical objects or concepts, but not to divinities: see Cunliffe, s.v.

ὠκεανοῖο: Zosimus records an invasion by the Carpi in the reign of Philip at 1. 20, and Jordanes tells of one in this period which took place because Philip withdrew a subsidy from the Goths (*Get.* 89). The date for the beginning of this trouble is provided by the description of Philip as *Germanicus* on the Dioscome inscription (see on 35 Γερμανόν) and in a coin-hoard from Pons Aluti containing 152 antoniniani, none of which is dated after 245 (D. Tudor, 'Nouvelles recherches archéologiques sur le *limes Alutanus* et le *limes Transalutanus*', in *Actes du IXe congrès international d'études sur les frontières romaines* (Bucharest, Cologne, and Vienna, 1974), 245; id., 'La fortificazione delle città romane della Dacia nel sec. III dell'e. n.', *Historia*, 14 (1965), 375). The evident abandonment of the *limes transalutanus* at about this time (Tudor, 'Recherches', pp. 245–6) suggests that the area around the valley of the Olt was the centre of the Gothic activity. But this does not mean that this was the only area of difficulty. The description of German Ares here as being from the ocean suggests that there was trouble at sea as well.

The reference to Goths sailing at this period is of some importance for the history of Rome's wars with those people. Despite the fact that nautical raids by tribes living on the coast of the Black Sea are attested by Tacitus (*Hist.* 3. 47. 3), it was once seriously argued as the basis for the chronological reconstruction of the mid-third century that the Goths did not take to raiding by sea until the mid-250s and that any reference to their doing so before this point must be either fabrication or the result of confusion in the sources (Demougeot, *La Formation*, pp. 417–21; see on l. 141). Zosimus says that they first received their ships from the people of the Bosporus when their dynasty came to an end in *c.*255 (Zos. 1. 31. 3). As it stands this must be wrong—the dynasty continued for centuries thereafter—but it once appeared that there might none the less have been some substance to it as a Pharsanzes appears on Bosporan coins in 253–4. It could be argued (and was) that he had overthrown Rhescouporis IV, who was otherwise on the throne from 242 to 276 and brought in the Goths (Brandis, *RE* iii. 785). In fact, as Frolova has argued in an excellent study of Bosporan coinage, there is no reason to believe that there was a break in Rhescouporis' administration, and it seems that Pharsanzes, far from being a usurper, had been elevated by the king to help him (N. A. Frolova, *The Coinage of the Kingdom of the Bosporus A.D. 242–341/342*, trans. H. B. Wells (*BAR* International Series, 166; Oxford, 1983), 13–17). There is no certain explanation as to why he only minted for a year, but this is not important for present purposes. If there was any break in the Bosporan dynasty at all, it may have been in the years before the emergence of Rhescouporis IV as king, and Zosimus' story, if it must be believed at all, must apply to circumstances in the reign of Gordian. The Sibylline oracle may be taken as evidence for Gothic activity on the sea in the years after Gordian's death.

The fact that the author should include such detail is curious: perhaps he had seen a picture which showed the defeat of some barbarians in boats, with a caption such as 'The emperor crushes the barbarians at sea' (for the use of pictures as sources of information see above, pp. 135–7); for captions of the sort suggested here see Eunapius fr. 68 Blockley. This seems a more likely explanation than that he is trying to make a specific geographical allusion.

37–8. Πέρσῃσιν, ὑπερφιάλοις ἀνθρώποις ... αὐτοῖς: the view of the role of the Persians in this war implicit in the use of the dative here suggests that the author envisaged them (rather as he envisaged the invading barbarians in the previous two lines) as passive victims of the event. This is a rather different perception from that of the author of ll. 28–34, and may well reflect the view of Rome's foes commonly held by Rome's subjects in areas removed from the scene of action. If this writer lived in Egypt (see above, p. 231) he would probably not have had access to any more detailed information for a Persian war than he did for the war with the German Ares.

39–41. ὡς γὰρ ἐφ᾽ ὑψηλῆς ... οὐ νήχετ᾽ ἐς ὕδωρ: the use of an *adynaton* in the form of an expression to the effect that things or conditions believed impossible will come true sooner than the situation mentioned in conjunction with them is commonplace in classical and post-classical poetry. Such expressions are also characteristic of proverbs and (sometimes with significant variation in form) oracles. For other instances of *adynata* in which sea and land animals change place see *Anth. Pal.* 5. 19. 6–7; Lucr. 1. 161–6, 3. 784–6; Virg. *Ec.* 1. 59–63; Prop. 2. 3. 5–8; see H. V. Canter, 'The Figure *ΑΔΥΝΑΤΟΝ* in Greek and Latin Poetry', *AJP* 51 (1930), 33–4; for the connection between *adynata* and proverbs see G. O. Rowe, 'The *Adynaton* as a Stylistic Device', *AJP* 86 (1965), 386–96; for a collection of *adynata* with commentary see E. Dutoit, *Le Thème de l'adynaton dans la poésie antique* (Paris, 1936).

42. γεγάωσιν: although there are no parallels to this form in the *TLG* data-base, there is nothing in principle wrong with it as a form of the subjunctive and I follow Geffcken in reading it here in place of Ω's *γεγαῶσιν*. Alexandre and Rzach had emended to the common—though in the context of a prophecy rather difficult to understand—future perfect γεγάασιν, which does not have the necessary sense of futurity.

43. ἤματι τῷ: for the use of ἦμαρ to mean 'time' generally—a meaning guaranteed by ἐφ' ὅσον, see Bauer, s.v.

43–5. ἐφ' ὅσον ... ἰάλλοι: statements of this sort are often employed as adynata; cf. Virg. Aen. 1. 607–9, 9. 466–9; Hor. Od. 3. 30. 7–9; Ov. Am. 1. 15. 9–30; Stat. Silv. 1. 1. 91–4, 6. 98–102, 3. 3. 160–3; Mart. 9. 1. They are common in oracles: see Zos. 2. 6; FGrH 257 F 37. 5. 2; PW 54, 73, 366, 440.

45. ἑπταλόφῳ Ῥώμῃ: cf. Orac. Sib. 2. 18, 14. 108; this seems to have been a common way of referring to Rome: cf. Cic. Ad Att. 6. 5. 2 ἐξ ἀστέως ἑπταλόφου; Anth. Pal. 14. 121. 1 ἑπτάλοφον ποτὶ ἄστυ Γαδειρόθεν.

46–9. ὅσσον δέ τοι οὔνομα ... Μακηδονίοιο ἄνακτος: W. Scott noted that if one assumed, 'as a Sibyllist would naturally assume', that the export of grain from Alexandria to the capital of the Roman empire had gone on ever since the foundation of Alexandria in 332 BC (no matter that the description of the place in l. 49 as δῖα πόλις μεγάλη Μακηδονίοιο ἄνακτος indicates that the author knew a bit more about the history of Egypt than this), one could add 948 (the sum of the name of Rome) to it and arrive at AD 617. This was the year that Chosroes conquered Egypt, and thus these lines must refer to that event. Rzach also believed this.[102] Although this interpretation may have occurred to someone in the seventh century (and may help explain the preservation of this oracle), I do not believe that this coincidence is at all relevant to the problem of the inclusion of this prophecy at this point in the oracle.

Prophecies concerning Rome's existence or domination were quite common, and the one feature that is consistent in their citation (with one highly dubious exception) is that the people who circulated them had no clear idea of the proper starting-point for their calculation. Thus, the author of a passage in the Twelfth Oracle wrote that the time from when one man would first give law to the Romans to the end of the nineteenth such person would be 244 years and six months.[103] The first ruler in this string was Julius

---

[102] Scott, 'The Last Sibylline Oracle', CQ 10: 15–16; Rzach, RE iiA. 2158.

[103] Orac. Sib. 12. 233–5 ἐννεακαιδεκάτης βασιληίδος ἄχρι τελευτῆς | δὶς ἑκατὸν δὶς εἴκοσι δὶς δύο πληρωθείη | πρὸς τοῖς ἐξ μησὶν ἐτέων χρόνος. As the count

Caesar, the nineteenth from Caesar was Commodus.[104] This emperor died on the evening of 31 December 192, and counting backwards from 192 or 193 by 244 years gives a date of 52 or 51 BC for the beginning of Caesar's domination.[105] In another case, this one being the death of Germanicus in AD 19, an oracle was circulated at Rome, seemingly a Sibylline one, in which it was said that the city would be destroyed in the nine-hundredth year. People were very disturbed, despite the fact, as Dio says, that this bore no relationship to any known method of reckoning the years of Rome, and Tiberius decided that it was time to examine the contents of prophetic books.[106] The same verses resurfaced, with the same effect, after the great fire in 64.[107] Here too there is no connection with the date which had by that time been accepted as correct for Rome's foundation, that of Varro (753). The date which the oracle looked back to would be 881 BC in the time of Tiberius and 836 BC in the reign of Nero. Similar problems arose whenever it was decided to hold the Secular Games, and there were several ways of determining the appropriate interval.[108] It does not seem reasonable

begins with Caesar (see next n.), to reach the nineteenth king I cannot accept the suggestion of A. Kurfess, 'Zu den *Oracula Sibyllina*', in *Colligere Fragmenta: Festschrift Alban Dold* (Beuron im Hohenzollern, 1952), 75–6, that line 234 should be emended to read δὶς ἑκατὸν καὶ εἴκοσι καὶ δύο πληρωθείν, which he thinks would give 'die richtige "sibyllinische" Zahl 222 (Zeit Actium)'.

[104] J. Schwartz, 'L'historiographie impériale des *Oracula Sibyllina*', *Dial. d'hist. anc.* 2 (1970), 413.

[105] For a similar error see Theoph. *Ad Aut.* 3. 27; he counts backwards 225 years from the death of Lucius Verus to the beginning of Caesar's reign (i.e. 56 BC).

[106] Dio 57. 18. 4–5 λόγιόν τε τι ὡς καὶ Σιβύλλειον, ἄλλως μὲν οὐδὲν τῷ τῆς πόλεως χρόνῳ προσῆκον, πρὸς δὲ τὰ παρόντα ἀδόμενον, οὐχ ἡσυχῇ σφας ἐκίνει· ἔλεγε γὰρ ὅτι· τρὶς δὲ τριηκοσίων περιτελλομένων ἐνιαυτῶν | Ῥωμαίους ἔμφυλος ὀλεῖ στάσις, χἀ Συβαρῖτις | ἀφροσύνα.

[107] Dio 62. 18. 3; R. Syme, *Tacitus* (Oxford, 1958), 722. Despite Dio's statement, it is possible that there was some notional connection between the span of 900 years and the arrival of Aeneas in Cumae; for the connection between Sibylline prophecy and that event see R. Merkelbach, 'Aeneas in Cumae', *MH* 18 (1961), 90–7. In this case, however, I suspect that it was simply the number 900 that was of interest: see on ll. 46–7.

[108] For the various celebrations see E. Diehl, 'Das *saeculum*: Seine Riten und Gebete', *RM* 83 (1934), 255–72, 348–72; and see on ll. 46–7. The issue was a long-standing one: for detailed discussion of problems connected with the alleged approach of new *saecula* in the 2nd and 1st cents. BC see A. Alföldi, '*Redeunt Saturnia regna*, II: An Iconographical Pattern Heralding the Return of the Golden Age in or around 139 BC', *Chiron*, 3 (1973), 134–6; id., '*Redeunt Saturnia regna*, III: Jupiter-Apollo und Veiovis', ibid. 2 (1972), 225–8 (in the 80s); id., '*Redeunt Saturnia regna*, IV: Apollo und die Sibylle in der Epoche der Bürgerkriege', ibid.

to believe, in the face of all this, that a learned author at the time of the Bar Kochba revolt (if this is the proper context) composed the prophecy that Rome would fall 948 years after her foundation because he knew that AD 134/5 was the nine hundred and forty-eighth year from Rome's foundation as reckoned by Timaeus.[109] In the case of the present passage the number 948 is not even used with reference to the foundation of Rome, and this serves as an excellent illustration of the various uses to which these numbers could be put.

The author of this text is clearly interested in emphasizing the idea that Rome's defeat by the Persians was a long way off, and he certainly would have been knowledgeable enough to know that nothing like 900 years had passed since Egypt fell under Roman rule. What he is saying is that his audience need not fear—Rome will continue to maintain herself for centuries to come. In the light of the fact that the thousandth anniversary of any event was liable to excite people, and that if the end of the millennium might herald the birth of a new and glorious age, it might also be associated with violent destruction and the arrival of a king from the east to finish the Romans off for good (oracles of this sort seem to have been quite well known—see on ll. 122–8), people may have found this reassuring. Philip celebrated the millennium of Rome on the Parilia (21 April) of 248, while fighting a war with Persia: if the coincidence between the arrival of the year 1000 and war with an eastern king disturbed anyone, the present text might comfort such a person, and—to judge from its contents—this was its purpose.[110]

5 (1975), 180–9 (in the 60s); J. B. Pighi, *De ludis saecularibus populi Romani Quiritium*[2] (Amsterdam, 1965); 15–16, 20–1.

[109] *Orac. Sib.* 8. 148–50; *FGrH* 566 F 60—the date is 814/3; see also Jacoby ad loc. I make this suggestion *exempli gratia*. These lines are attached to a prophecy about the return of Nero and a reckoning from the Varronian date for Rome's foundation would give 195; see Rzach, *RE* iiA. 2143; Geffcken, *Comp. u. Ent.*, p. 40 (who regards this as 'christliche halb-historische, eschatologische Poesie'—he might have omitted the first adjective).

[110] The same purpose may be served by dating the renewal of the world 900 years after Boccharis in the prophecy of the lamb, as noted by Koenen, 'Prophecies of a Potter', p. 253. That text may therefore provide a useful parallel to the use of the number 948 here; see further on ll. 46–7. Nothing is known about the rites which Philip celebrated on this occasion, though his coins make it clear that there were lavish games in the amphitheatre (the *ludi honorarii* which concluded the proceedings): see Pighi, *De ludis saecularibus*, pp. 28–9. It may be suspected, however, that they were not greatly different from the *ludi saeculares* of Severus in 204: Pighi, pp. 136–94 (see also the eloquent evocation in Birley, *Septimius Severus*[2], pp. 156–60). The celebrations would include a *lustratio et frugum acceptio*, the *sacrificium saeculare et ludi sollemnes*, and then the *ludi honorarii* (Pighi, pp. 358–65).

46-7. ὅσσον δέ τοι οὔνομα, ʿΡώμη, | εἰν ἀριθμοῖς: the use of the number 948, the sum of the letters in ʿΡώμη, is not common in Egyptian prophecies. In these texts, as well as in several other texts reported in the first/second centuries AD, 900 was a more significant figure. It appears in the Sibylline text that was circulated in 19 and 48, and apparently Lucan refers to a similar text at 1. 564 'diraque per populum Cumanae carmina vatis | volgantur'.[111] The scholiast on this line observes that 'quoniam exitiosum est versus Sibyllina publice dicere, aut certe quoniam nuncentesimum exitio Romanis cecineret'.[112] Juvenal seems to allude to similar prophecy at 13. 28–30 'nona aetas agitur peioraque saecula ferri | temporibus, quorum sceleri non invenit ipsa | nomen et a nullo posuit natura metallo', though here the allusion to ages identified with metals may reflect the influence of Etruscan prophecies about the succession of *saecula*. According to their definition (though a number of others were also in use), a *saeculum* was fixed as the span of human life: it began with the foundation of a city and ended with the death of the oldest man whose birth coincided with the foundation. It was also believed that their domination would last for ten *saecula*, and, later, that the world would end after ten *saecula*.[113]

The Egyptian prophecy *The Lamb of Boccharis*, which was written in demotic in the thirty-third year of Augustus, predicts the renewal of Egypt after a period of 900 years.[114] L. Koenen points out that this number in the context of the lamb's prophecy (notionally delivered *c.* 715–709 BC) has a symbolic value as thirty times thirty years (thirty years was the regular *hebsed* period, the period of time that had to elapse after his accession before a king could celebrate this festival) and that it means that the Egyptians will have a very long time to wait for the coming of their own, strong, king. But he also points out that, in this case, it may also reflect some rather complicated calculations. If the 900 years are added to a 'Phoenix period' (the 540 years between appearances of the phoenix, according to some sources), the result

---

[111] I have benefited here from L. Koenen's unpublished *Habilitationsschrift*, 'Die Prophezeiungen des Töpfers'. The material in this work was not fully incorporated in his article of that title in *ZPE* 2 (1968).

[112] For a further reference to the prophecy of 900 years in Lucan's poem see L. Koenen, 'Lucan, VII, 378–389', *RM*, NS 107 (1964), 190–2.

[113] Weinstock, *Divus Julius*, pp. 192–3; Pighi, *De ludis saecularibus*, pp. 13–19, 23–5.

[114] *P. Rain. Cent.* No. 3, col. II, lines 19–22; L. Koenen, 'A Supplementary Note on the Date of the Oracle of the Potter', *ZPE* 54 (1984), 10–11.

almost equals a Sothis period of 1,461 years. The Sothis period arises from the fact that the Egyptian year of 365 days was a quarter of a day too short. It would therefore take 1,461 years from the beginning of one Sothis period, when the calendar was perfectly aligned at the beginning of the year, to the next. The beginning of a new Sothis period was taken to indicate the arrival of a new, better time, and the lamb's prophecy could be interpreted as indicating that the world would return to its proper order and that foreigners would leave Egypt when the next Sothis period opened, as it would do in AD 139.[115] This text could clearly be read in either way, depending on the context, and these possible interpretations serve to illustrate the wide variety of meanings which different readers could ascribe to such calculations. In the case of these lines in the *Thirteenth Sibylline Oracle* it is of some interest that the author chose a prophetic scheme which did not have an obvious connection to a specific chronological pattern (i.e. the series of *saecula* or a Sothis period).

50–3. ἄλλο δ᾽ ἄχος ... δι᾽ ἡγεμόνων κακότητα: S. I. Oost ('The Alexandrian Seditions under Philip and Gallienus', *CP* 56 (1951), 2–3), took this passage together with ll. 43–9 as evidence that there had been some attempt in the middle years of Philip's reign to halt the grain-ships from Alexandria to Rome. He went on to suggest that the issue of sending grain-ships to Rome divided the city into pro- and anti-Roman factions whose struggles did great damage. There is nothing in these lines to justify such an interpretation, and there is really no reason to believe that they were written together with ll. 35–49, which form a coherent, self-contained prophecy which need have nothing to do with any riot at Alexandria (see on ll. 39–45). These lines reflect only the internal difficulties endemic in many Greek cities of the Roman empire, difficulties which could readily lead to riot if local politicians chose to exploit them for their own purposes. The responsibility for this trouble attributed vaguely to the evils of leaders in line 53, recalls much in Plutarch and Dio Chrysostom's writing on the subject, and indeed Greek political writing as far back as the time of Solon and

[115] L. Koenen, 'Manichaean Apocalypticism at the Crossroads of Iranian, Egyptian, Jewish and Christian Thought', in Cirillo and Roselli (eds.), *Codex Manichaicus Colonensis*, pp. 315–17. See also K.-Th. Zauzich's commentary on the Lamb of Bocchoris, in *Festschrift zum 100-jährigen Bestehen der Papyrussammlung der Österreichischen Nationalbibliothek: Papyrus Erzherzog Rainer (P. Rainer Cent.)* (Vienna, 1983), 165–74, esp. p. 173; and *Lexikon der Ägyptologie*, s.v. 'Sedfest', esp. col. 789.

Theognis (see ad loc.). The fact that no individual or individuals are singled out for especial blame suggests that the author may not have been very well informed, that he knew only that there was trouble in Alexandria—a person did not need to live in Egypt to be able to predict that with reasonable certainty. In this respect these lines are very much like the prophecy of Alexandrian riot in ll. 74–8 below, and, like them, they could easily have been written in Syria or anywhere else where people had some contact with Egypt (see ad loc.). Ammianus notes that oracles showed Alexandria to be a place often subject to damage from the violent behaviour of its inhabitants: 'in civitate [Alexandria] quae suopte motu et ubi causae non suppetunt seditionibus crebris agitur et turbulentis, ut oraculorum quoque loquitur fides' (22. 11. 4).

50. ἄλλο ... ἀείσω: for programmatic statements of this sort within an oracle cf. ll. 64, 74 below and *Orac. Sib.* 3. 55, 295–302, 489–91, 698–701, 5. 286–7, 8. 151, 14. 296.

52. ἄρσενες οἱ πρότερον δεινοὶ τότ᾽ ἀνάλκιδες ὄντες: τότ᾽ is Alexandre's admirable conjecture in place of Ω's δεινοὶ καὶ ἀνάλκιδες. Geffcken followed a suggestion which he found in Alexandre's note on the line and printed δειλοὶ καὶ ἀνάλκιδες instead, which is much less attractive. The sense of this line and the next are that men who were previously something will beg for peace because of the evil of their leaders. Their desire for peace is clearly something new, i.e. it is the result of the action of their leaders (δι᾽ ἡγεμόνων κακότητα), and thus they should be seen as having manifested some trait which was rather different from their current longing for peace. Thus Alexandre's τότ᾽, which emphasizes the difference between their past and future conditions, is the best reading. For these sentiments cf. Theog. 57–8 καὶ νῦν εἰσ᾽ ἀγαθοὶ Πολυπαΐδη· οἱ δὲ πρὶν ἐσθλοὶ | νῦν δειλοί.

ἄρσενες οἱ πρότερον δεινοί: the Egyptians, especially the Alexandrians, were renowned for their violence: M. Reinhold, 'Roman Attitudes towards Egyptians', *AW* 3 (1980), 97–103.

53. δι᾽ ἡγεμόνων κακότητα: cf. Theog. 855–6 πολλάκις ἡ πόλις ἥδε δι᾽ ἡγεμόνων κακότητα | ὥσπερ κεκλιμένη ναῦς παρὰ γῆν ἔδραμεν. The theme of the ruin of a city through the folly of its leaders has a long history in Greek political thought. For the imperial period see Plut. *Praec. ger. reip.* 805 A–D, 806 B, 807 C–808 C, 809 B, 813 A–814 E, 818 C, 825 A–D, *An seni sit ger. resp.* 787 C;

Dio Chrys. *Or.* 32–4, 46 *passim*; Jones, *Plutarch and Rome*, pp. 110–21; id., *The Roman World of Dio Chrysostom* (Cambridge, 1978), 37, 39, 41–2, 75–8, 83, 95–103.

54–6. καὶ χόλος ... ἀδικήσει: the focus shifts back to Syria and to an event of such ephemeral interest—a flood which does some harm to the cities of Syria Phoenice (see on l. 57)—that these lines can safely be attributed to a local contemporary. The event itself is not otherwise attested.

54. χόλος ... μεγάλοιο θεοῖο: the notion of the great god's wrath manifesting itself in a catastrophe also appears in l. 109, which is the product of another author (probably) and another time (certainly). There is no reason (despite Rzach, *RE* iiA. 2160–1) either in that case or here to believe that such a statement marks the author as a Christian or a Jew. For contemporary reactions to natural disasters which might be taken as signs of divine displeasure see Tert. *Apol.* 40. 2 'si Tiberis ascendit in moenia, si Nilus non ascendit in rura, si caelum stetit, si terra movit, si fames, si lues, statim Christianos ad leonem. Tantos ad unum?' Orig. *Comm. Ser.* 39 'cum haec ergo contigerint mundo, consequens est, quasi derelinquentibus hominibus deorum culturam, ut propter multitudinem Christianorum dicant fieri bella et fames et pestilentias. frequenter enim famis causa Christianos culpaverunt gentiles et quiscumque sapiebant quae gentium sunt, sed et pestilentiarum causas ad Christi ecclesiam rettulerunt. scimus autem et apud nos terraemotum factum in locis quibusdam et factas fuisse quasdam ruinas, ita ut qui erant impii extra fidem causam terraemotus dicerent Christanos—propter quod et persecutiones passae sunt ecclesiae et incensae sunt' (this section of Origen's commentary on Matthew is known only through the Latin translation quoted above; for details see E. Klostermann's introduction to the GCS edition, *Origenes Werke*, xi. *Origenes Matthäuserklärung*, 2. *Die lateinische Übersetzung der commentariorum series* (Berlin, 1976), pp. vii–x); Cypr. *Epp.* 75. 10 'terrae etiam motus plurimi et frequentes extiterunt, ut et per Cappadociam et per Pontum multa subruerent, quaedam etiam civitates in profundum receptae dirupti soli hiatu devorarentur, ut ex hoc persecutio quoque gravis adversum nos nominis fieret'.

Ἀσσυρίοις ἥξει: Alexandre's correction for Ω's ἀσσυρίους ἥξει makes better grammatical sense and should be adopted. For the meaning of Ἀσσυρίοις here see on l. 16; for parallels to this use of ἥξει with the dative see *Orac. Sib.* 1. 325, 2. 170, 3. 207, 213, 486, 4. 101, 115, 8. 160, 11. 126, 217, 12. 70, 13. 109, 14. 326.

56. Καίσαρος ἐς πτολίεθρα: for the use of the genitive here compare Mark 12: 17; Luke 20: 25; Matt. 22: 21 ἀπόδοτε οὖν τὰ Καίσαρος Καίσαρι. Here Καίσαρος means only 'Roman' and serves to specify that the 'Assyrians' who will suffer will be within the empire. The further description of the inhabitants as 'Canaanites' suggests that the cities affected were in Syria Phoenice.

Χαναναίους: this is the reading of Q, which is infinitely preferable to V's Σατανναίους (wrongly reported by Mai, Alexandre, Rzach, and Geffcken as Σαταναίους), as it can be associated with a specific group of people. Although the word is used exclusively by authors such as Josephus (cf. *BJ* 4. 459, 6. 438, 439; *Ant.* 7. 61, 68, 8. 160, 162, 9. 243, and A. Schalit, *A Complete Concordance to Flavius Josephus*, suppl. 1 (Leiden, 1968), s.v. Χαναναίοι) and Philo (*De sacrif.* 89, 90; *De congr.* 81, 83, 85, 88, 121; *De fuga* 87; *De vit. Mos.* 1. 163) to refer to the biblical inhabitants of Palestine, it is used in the Gospel of Matthew to describe a woman from the area of Tyre and Sidon: (Matt. 15: 21–2 καὶ ἐξελθὼν ἐκεῖθεν ὁ Ἰησοῦς ἀνεχώρησεν εἰς τὰ μέρη Τύρου καὶ Σιδῶνος. καὶ ἰδοὺ γυνὴ Χαναναία ἀπὸ τῶν ὁρίων ἐκείνων ἐξελθοῦσα ἐκραύγασε λέγουσα; cf. Mark 7: 26, where she is described as Συροφοίνισσα τῷ γένει. For people of Punic extraction calling themselves Canaanites in North Africa in the fourth century see F. G. Millar, 'The Phoenician Cities: A Case Study of Hellenisation', *PCPS* NS 29 (1983), 58.

57–8. These lines predict disasters which will befall the two great cities of the eastern Cilician plain. Nothing is otherwise known of these events.

57. Πύραμος ἀρδεύσει: here, presumably, ἀρδεύω means flood rather than water or irrigate, the meanings offered by LSJ. It would scarcely be worth predicting the event otherwise: Mopsuestia was on the banks of the Pyramos.

Μόψου πόλιν: the tale that Mopsus (son of the prophetess Manto and grandson of Teiresias), the founder of the oracle at Claros, crossed the Taurus into Cilicia first appears in the fourth century BC. Theopompus told of his foundation of Mopsuestia and Callisthenes included an account of his journey as far as Syria in his history of Alexander the Great (*FGrH* 115 F 103; cf. F 346, 351; the fragment was once attributed to Callinus—cf. Callinus fr. 8 West). Ammianus knew that he was buried in this city after his death during the Argonautic expedition in Africa. His remains, covered in Punic soil, were said to have been of significant curative capacity (Amm. 14. 8. 3). For the description of this place as the city of Mopsus see *Anth. Pal.* 9. 698–9 Μόψου τήνδ' ἐσορᾷς κλεινὴν πόλιν, ἥν ποτε μάντις | δείματο, τῷ ποταμῷ κάλλος ὑπερκρεμάσας. See also Kruse, *RE* xvi. 242–2; Ruge, ibid. 243–50; A. H. M. Jones *et al.*, *Cities of the Eastern Roman Provinces* [2] (Oxford, 1971), 192, 197, 200, 202, 206–7. On the poem from the *Palatine Anthology* see K. Hartigan, *The Poets and the Cities* (Meisenheim am Glan, 1979), 84–5. G. Dagron and D. Feissel, *Inscriptions de Cilicie* 'Travaux et mémoires du Centre de Recherche d'Histoire et Civilisation de Byzance, Collège de France' Monographies, 4 (Paris, 1987), 129–31, provide a useful summary of epigraphic publications connected with the city.

58. **Αἰγαῖοι:** Aigeai (modern Ayas near Yamutalik) on the Cilician coast was chiefly famous in antiquity for a shrine of Asclepius, though its excellent harbour made it an important base for the *classis Syriaca* by the third century and therefore an important point for the movement of troops to the eastern frontier: see Kienast, *Untersuchungen zu den Kriegsflotten der romischen Kaiserzeit*, pp. 90–3; R. Ziegler, *Städtisches Prestige und kaiserliche Politik: Studien zum Festwesen in Ostkililien im 2. und 3. Jahrhundert n. Chr.* (Düsseldorf, 1985); J.-C. Balty, 'Apamea in Syria in the Second and Third Centuries A.D.', *JRS* 78 (1988), 98–9. For the history of the city in the late Republic and empire see L. Robert, 'De Cilicie à Messine et à Plymouth avec deux inscriptions grecques errantes', *Journal des savants* (1973), 161–211; Dagron and Feissel, *Inscriptions de Cilicie*, pp. 117–18, for a summary of the publication of inscriptions from the site.

διὰ δῆριν ὑπερμενέων ἀνθρώπων: the men referred to here are presumably Aigeians. For the theme of people bringing destruction upon themselves through their own folly see on l. 53. The implication of this line is that there was some sort of riot.

59–63. The action shifts from Cilicia to Syria and the author's attention focuses on Julius Priscus. The content of these lines ostensibly provides no significant insight into the events of his rule, but their banality is somewhat surprising in the light of the hostile tradition about this administration preserved elsewhere (see on ll. 61–3). It is also at variance with the tone of ll. 64–73, which seem to reflect the hostility aroused by the building programme undertaken at imperial expense in *Provincia Arabia* (see on l. 68).

59. τλήμων Ἀντιόχεια: cf. *Orac. Sib.* 4. 140, 7. 60; and l. 125 below; Malalas, p. 443 ἐν αὐτῷ δὲ τῷ χρόνῳ (AD 528: see G. Downey, *A History of Antioch in Syria* (Princeton, 1961), 528–30) μετεκλήθη Ἀντιόχεια Θεούπολις κατὰ κέλευσιν τοῦ ἁγίου Συμεὼν τοῦ θαυματουργοῦ. εὑρέθη δὲ καὶ ἐν τῇ αὐτῇ Ἀντιοχείᾳ χρησμὸς ἀναγεγραμμένος, περιέχων οὕτως· καὶ σύ, τάλαινα πόλις Ἀντιόχου οὐ κληθήσῃ; John Lydus, *De mens.* 4. 47 ταύτης δὲ τῆς Ἑβραίας Σιβύλλης βίβλῳ ἐνέτυχον ἐν Κύπρῳ, ἐν ᾗ πολλὰ καὶ τῶν ⟨ἑλληνικῶν⟩ προφετεύσασα διαλαμβάνει ... καὶ μέντοι καὶ περὶ τῶν γενησόμενων ἕως τῆς συντελείας, ἐν οἷς καὶ περὶ Κύπρου καὶ Ἀντιοχείας παλίμφημά τινα προφητεύει, τῆς μὲν ὡς πολέμῳ πεσουμένης καὶ μηκέτ' ἀναστησομένης, τῆς δὲ νήσου ὑποβρυχίου γενησομένης· φησὶ γὰρ· Τλήμων Ἀντιόχεια, σὲ δὲ πτόλιν οὕποτ' ἐροῦσιν. The line quoted by John here also appears in l. 125 of this oracle.

The form of direct address employed in this line is typical both of oracular responses and lament (see Fontenrose, *Delphic Oracle*, p. 177). The suggestion in these lines, as at ll. 125 ff., is that the sad fate of these people is not the result of their own misbehaviour, but of the uncontrollable action of outsiders. Here the agent is the god Ares, who refuses to leave them alone. There it is the great god.

60. Ἀσσυρίου πολέμοιο ἐπειγομένου: the direct mention of the Persians in l. 62 indicates that the little-known Persian war of Philip's reign is the subject of this prophecy. For the circumstances see on l. 31.

61–3. πρόμος ἀνδρῶν ... γεγαὼς βασιληΐδος: the foremost of men who is at Antioch can only be Julius Priscus, the older brother of Philip the Arab (see on l. 21). He remained in the east after Philip departed for the west and was subsequently given the title *rector orientis*.[116] Geffcken thought—relying on Aurelius

---

[116] Precise information which would permit a detailed evaluation of what this title implied is lacking. By analogy with the title *corrector*, it can be taken to imply a special and superior authority over the area in question: see A. Stein, ''Ἐπανορθώτης'', *Aegyptus*, 18 (1938), 234–43; id., *RE* x. 782. Pflaum, *Carrières équestres*, p. 835, wisely refrains from

Victor's description of him as a descendant of Alexander (presumably Alexander Severus)—that this could be the obscure rebel Jotapianus; but this is indefensible.[117] Jotapianus fought against the imperial authorities and this figure fights for them. As noted in the introduction to these lines, the reference to Priscus is surprisingly neutral. Priscus' fiscal exactions are said to have been the cause of Jotapianus' revolt. That statement, which is in Zosimus, is not absurd.[118] The reign of Philip was a time of massive public expenditure. The short-lived peace with Persia had cost at least 500,000 aurei (see on l. 27), the millennial games of 248 were evidently an occasion for vast imperial largess.[119] Much work seems to have been done on the road-systems in the Balkans, north Africa, and Cappadocia (most, if not all, of it at the expense of local communities).[120] There is evidence of a change in the administration of Egypt which seems to have involved a change in both the level of taxation and the efficiency of tax collection.[121] A great deal of money was spent, very probably by the imperial family, on a

speculation. The evidence that we have shows that his titulature was very fluid. He was honoured as the ἐξοχώτατος ἔπαρχος τοῦ ἱεροῦ Πραιτωρίου on an equal footing with Philip and Otacilia Severa in a text at Philippopolis in the summer of 247 (*AÉ* 1908, No. 274), and a few months later, after the promotion of Philip II to Augustus, Priscus appears as *rector orientis* on a Latin inscription from the same site (*ILS* 9005). This might suggest that he was promoted from one post to the other at the same time as the younger Philip was promoted. This could be reconciled with Zosimus' statements that he was left in charge of Syrian armies (1. 19. 2 καὶ Πρίσκον μὲν ἀδελφὸν ὄντα τῶν κατὰ Συρίαν προεστήσατο στρατοπέδων) and later that he was ruler of the east (1. 20. 2 ἄρχειν τῶν ἐκεῖσε καθεσταμένον ἐθνῶν). However, a recently published papyrus from Syria, a document subscribed by Priscus himself at Antioch, describes him as 'governor of Mesopotamia exercising the highest power', which may suggest that the changes that can be read into the sources were less clear-cut than they appear to be, and that *IGR* iii. 1201, 1202, also from Philippopolis, where he is described as ἐξοχώτατος ἔξαρχος Μεσοποταμίας, date to this period. It is probably best to be content with the point that he was the chief administrator of the eastern provinces throughout the reign of Philip, no matter what title he held.

[117] Geffcken, *Comp.u. Ent.*, p. 62 n. 2.

[118] Zos. 1. 20. 2 τὰ μὲν κατὰ τὴν ἑῴαν ταῖς τῶν φόρων εἰσπράξεσι καὶ τῷ Πρίσκον, ἄρχειν τῶν ἐκεῖσε καθεσταμένον ἐθνῶν, ἀφόρητον ἅπασιν εἶναι βαρυνόμενα, καὶ διὰ τοῦτο πρὸς τὸ νεωτερίζειν τραπέντα, Ἰωταπιανὸν παρήγαγον εἰς τὴν τῶν ὅλων ἀρχήν.

[119] Pékary, 'Le "tribut" aux perses et les finances de Philippe l'Arabe', p. 279.

[120] Ibid.; Stein, *RE* x. 766. For local expenditure on road-works see R. Cagnat, *Cours d'épigraphie latine* (Paris, 1914), 272–3; Mitchell, 'Imperial Building', pp. 336–7, with references to further discussion. [121] See ch. 1 n. 114.

massive building project in Arabia (see on l. 68). To all of this must be added the cost of war with Persia and the evidently less than successful effort to repel barbarian attacks from across the Danube (see on l. 35). The combined expense of war and imperial construction would have fallen especially upon the Danubian provinces and those of the eastern frontier, and it was precisely in these areas that revolts broke out in 248/9 (see on l. 74 for the eastern uprising; and on ll. 79–80 for those on the Danube).[122]

64–73. νῦν κοσμεῖσθε . . . μετόπισθε πελάσσῃ: these lines provide an excellent example of the way in which verses of several kinds were stitched together in the composition of this text. They may also shed some light on events removed from each other by two decades. Their inclusion would be relevant both to the late 240s and to the late 260s. This may be why they were retained by the person who completed the text as it now stands.

The notion that these lines might have been considered relevant to circumstances at two separate points in time is supported by several considerations. Most important is the use of the temporal νῦν (see also on l. 64). This should indicate that the prospect of destruction for these cities was anticipated after 244/5 (the year in which Philippopolis was refounded—see on l. 68) but before the death of Philip, where these lines are included, as well as at the time when the poem reached roughly its present form. The second consideration is that the ruin of these places is still in prospect at the later time. Had they been destroyed a more fulsome discourse on their destruction would be expected. In the context of *c.* 261–7 action by the Palmyrenes against *Provincia Arabia* might easily be foreseen. In 269/70 it did in fact take place and the temple of Jupiter Ammon (at least) is known to have been destroyed at Bostra by the 'Palmyrene enemy'[123] as the province was overrun by Zenobia's army on its way to Egypt.[124] It is time now to reflect further on the possible earlier context.

[122] See above, pp. 39–40; Callu, *Politique monétaire*, pp. 238–46. There was a sharp decline in the weight and quality of the coinage in 245–7 (though it recovered somewhat in 248–9: for figures see Walker, *Metrology*, pp. 40–1). It is also of some interest to note that the coinage which was issued from the mint of Antioch was of less quality than that at other mints. The silver content at Antioch was *c.* 39.4% in 244 and only increased to *c.* 42.5% by the end of the reign. At Rome the silver content varied between *c.* 43% and 47%.

[123] IGLS 9107 'templum Iovis Hammonis a Pal[l]myrenis hostibu[s dirutum] | quem refec[i]t cum statua argentea et ostea ferra'.

[124] Rey-Coquais, 'Syrie romaine', pp. 59–60.

25. Antoninianus of Jotapianus. *RIC*
Jotapianus, 2*b*. British Museum

As has already been noted, these lines must reflect events after
244/5, the foundation date of Philippopolis. They are included
between a prophecy that may be connected with the millennial
games of 248 (see on ll. 46–9) and the death of Philip in 249 (see on
ll. 74, 79). The precise location of the passage suggests that the
author had some specific event in mind, or that he knew that these
lines might apply to something that happened in 248/9. This is
exactly the point at which the revolt of Jotapianus broke out, and it
is therefore likely that these lines reflect attitudes and hopes then
current. To judge from his name, Jotapianus was related to the
Sampsigeramid house[125]—and Victor claims that he was descended
from the line of Alexander.[126] His activities are said to have ranged
throughout Syria and Cappadocia;[127] they are also said to have been
brought on by Priscus' financial exactions,[128] and to have come to an
end with his decapitation in the time of Decius.[129] If he was a

[125] For the family in general see R. D. Sullivan, 'The Dynasty of Emesa', *ANRW* ii/8.
198–219; for Iotapianus see Stein, *RE* ix. 2004–5; Barbieri, *Albo PIR* ² i. 49.

[126] *De Caes.* 29. 2 'et interea [under Decius] ad eum Iotapiani, qui Alexandri tumens
stirpe per Syriam tentans nova militum arbitrio occubuerat, ora ut mos inopinato
deferuntur'. A reference to the revolt of Jotapianus may also be concealed in Eutr. *Brev.* 9. 4
'bellum civile quod in Gallia motum fuerat oppressit'. J. P. Callu, 'L'empire gaulois selon
J. F. Drinkwater', *JRA* 2 (1989), 363, suggests that 'Galatia' could be read in place of 'Gallia'
here, as there is no other evidence for a revolt in Gaul. This is an extremely attractive
suggestion. For an effort to explain this passage in a Gallic context see Drinkwater, *The
Gallic Empire*, p. 21. In the light of the chronology of Decius' reign, it is very difficult
indeed to find time for Decius to have suppressed a Gallic revolt.

[127] Aur. Vic. (cited in the previous n.) gives only Syria; for Cappadocia see Pol. Silv. 37–8
'Philippus cum Philippo qui primus factus est Christianus sub quo Iotobianus tyrannus in
Cappadocia fuit'.

[128] Zos. 1. 20. 2 (cited in n. 118 above).

[129] Aur. Vict. *De Caes.* 29. 2 (cited in n. 126 above).

Sampsigeramid it may be assumed that he began his operations around Emesa, and it is possible that this caused people to think (or hope) that he might attack the cities of the Arabian province which were profiting under the new regime while the cities of Syria seem to have been paying more than usual.

64. νῦν: the use of *νῦν* with reference to a specific event has only one parallel in the extant corpus—in a section of the *Third Oracle* which seems to have been composed around the time of Actium—and even that parallel is not exact: 3. 57–9 ἄρτι δ' ἔτι κτίζεσθε, πόλεις, κοσμεῖσθέ τε πᾶσαι | ναοῖς καὶ σταδίοις ἀγοραῖς χρυσοῖς ξοάνοις τε | ἀργυρέοις λιθίνοις τε, ἵν' ἔλθητ' εἰς πικρὸν ἦμαρ (for discussion of the date, see Collins, *The Sibylline Oracles of Egyptian Judaism*, p. 65). It is somewhat inappropriate for a prophetess who is envisaged as living well before the events she predicted to speak as if in the present using the present passive *κοσμεῖσθε*. The language is more appropriate to Sibylline epitaphs (cf. Paus. 10. 12. 2).

64–8. ναοῖς σταδίοις τε … Φιλιππόπολίς ⟨τε⟩: for other instances where the conduct of people in the present is meant to justify their destruction in the future cf. Isa. 23: 1–8; Ezek. 27, 28: 1–10; Zech. 9: 1–8; *Orac. Sib.* 3. 57–9, 350–80, 5. 162–78, 397–413, 7. 40–7.

67. ἐκ πάντων … μαθηματική: Geffcken regarded the attack on astrology here as characteristically Christian; Rzach thought that Jewish dislike of that practice was evident.[130] While it is indeed possible that a Christian would express himself in this way—and, as these lines are an attack on his administration, this would be an interesting insight into Philip's relations with the Christian Church (cf. on l. 88)—there is no reason to believe that Jews would be particularly hostile.[131] Although mention of the practices of its inhabitants is a common way of describing some place, there is no other evidence to prove or disprove the suggestion here that these people were particularly keen on astrological speculation. G. Amer and M. Gawlikowski suggest that the reference here is best taken as a reflection of an imperial building

---

[130] *Comp. u. Enst.*, pp. 59–60; *RE* iiA. 2161.
[131] J. H. Charlesworth, 'Jewish Astrology in the Talmud, Pseudepigraphia, Dead Sea Scrolls and Early Palestinian Synagogues', *HTR* 70 (1977), 183–200.

programme at Philippopolis in which astral imagery may have played a major part.[132] There seems to be some support for this attractive proposal in a complex mosaic from that city which depicts Aion and the four Graces on the left, Ge and the four Karpoi to the front in the centre, with Georgia and Triptolemus leading an ox behind her (Georgia is reclining on a hill) and Prometheus creating Protoplastos on the left. Cupid and Psyche stand behind Prometheus while the four winds blow from the top corners and the Drosoi water the earth from urns over the centre.[133] The figure of Aion resembles Philip, and it has been suggested that the mosaic might imply the assimilation of the emperor with *Aeternitas* at the time of the Secular Games.[134] It might also suggest that similar imagery was associated with Philip elsewhere in the artistic programme of Philippopolis.

68. **Βόστρα Φιλιππόπολίς ⟨τε⟩ ἵν':** there are two ways to deal with the transmitted readings (*Βόστρα Φιλοππόπολι* Q; *Βάστρα Φιλοππόπολις* V). One is to assume that the final syllable of *Φιλοππόπολι(ς)* is long, an assumption that can be supported by the extremely loose prosody of this poem (see the examples collected in the n. on l. 108). This reading would have the further advantage that it would sit easily with Ω's ἔλθῃς. The disadvantage of this reading is that it would mean that the author did not know that Bostra and Philippopolis were different places. This would be an extraordinary error, since this author, and other authors whose work was adopted by the compiler, do not appear to make mistakes like this when dealing with the eastern part of the empire. Therefore, as this line can make historical sense with two small changes (in addition to correcting the orthography of the place-names), I have elected to emend, at the risk of removing what could be regarded as an interesting error on the author's part. I take some comfort in this from the evidence adduced in the previous note, which suggests that the author may in fact have been familiar with Philippopolis.

τε is Alexandre's supplement; the resulting hiatus is not uncommon in the *Sibylline Oracles* (A. Rzach, *Metrische Studien zu*

---

[132] G. Amer and M. Gawlikowski, 'Le sanctuaire impérial de Philippopolis', *Damaszener Mitteilungen*, 2 (1985), 15.

[133] E. Will, 'Une nouvelle mosaïque de Chahba Philippopolis', *AAS* 3 (1953), 27–48.

[134] J. Charbonneaux, 'Aiôn et Philippe l'Arabe', *MÉFR* 72 (1960), 253–72.

den sibyllinischen Orakeln (SAWW 126. 9; 1892), 48–9). For the difficulty caused by μαθηματική περ έοῦσα in l. 67 see on ἔλθητ᾽ εἰς below. Both Bostra and Philippopolis benefited from the reign of Philip.

While there is no evidence for any extensive building at Bostra in these years, it is clear that the city received some significant increase in its dignity. It had been given colonial status under Alexander Severus, and Philip elevated it to the rank of metropolis.[135] Coins and an inscription from Ostia also reveal Actian games in honour of the local god Dusares which were founded at this time.[136]

The city of Philippopolis was raised from obscurity to colonial status by Philip[137] and little has survived at the site (modern Chahba, 28 km north of Suweidah in the Jebel Hauran) save the evidence for a short-lived but massive building programme.[138] The great majority of the extant buildings—a palace, a temple to the family of Philip, baths, and a theatre (all but the last of these marble-faced)— are the work of western architects and may be dated to the mid-third century.[139] As it is most unlikely that much if any money from outside sources was forthcoming for such projects after 249, and as the insignificant early remains suggest that the place was not particularly wealthy,[140] it may be assumed that all these buildings were

[135] Spijkerman, *Coins of the Decapolis and Provincia Arabia*, 'Bostra', Nos. 59–60; A. Kindler, *The Coinage of Bostra* (Warminster, 1983), Nos. 43–4.

[136] Spijkerman, *Coins of the Decapolis and Provincia Arabia*, 'Bostra' Nos. 59–60; Kindler, *The Coinage of Bostra* No. 46; see also *ILS* 5233; C. Clermont-Ganneau, 'Le droit des pauvres et le cycle pentactérique chez les Nabatéens', in *Recueil d'archéologie orientale*, iv (Paris, 1901), 297–309. Aside from the usual forms of entertainment, Actian games may have included some sort of boating exhibition: see Reisch, *RE* i. 1214; P. Gardner, 'Boat-Races among the Greeks', *JHS* 2 (1882), 93–7; for Dusares see Kindler, *The Coinage of Bostra*, pp. 79–87.

[137] Spijkerman, *The Coinage of the Decapolis and Provincial Arabia*, pp. 260–1.

[138] Amer and Gawlikowski, 'Le sanctuaire impérial', p. 1, for the possibility that the original name of the site was Σαβα. They point to a number of modern place-names in the area which similarly preserve the vestige of ancient names: Chaqqa (Σακκαία); Mardouk (Μαρδέχων); Rimet el-Lohf (Ῥειμεα); Bourciké (Βορίχαθι Σαβαῶν).

[139] For the palace see H. C. Butler, *Architecture and other Arts* (Publications of the American Archeological Expedition to Syria in 1899–1900, 2; New York, 1903), 382–4; R. E. Brünnow and A. v. Domaszewski, *Die Provincia Arabia*, iii (Strasburg, 1909), 164–7; the Philippeion: Amer and Gawlikowski, 'Le sanctuaire impérial', pp. 1–14; the baths: Butler, *Architecture and Other Arts*, pp. 384–90; Brünnow and v. Domaszewski, *Provincia Arabia*, iii. 155–60; the theatre: P. Coupel and E. Frézouls, *Le Théâtre de Philippopolis en Arabie* (Paris, 1956).

[140] Butler, *Architecture and Other Arts*, pp. 377–8, for the history of the site.

constructed in the reign of Philip and that they were paid for by the emperor. The same argument may be used to date the extremely well-constructed paved streets and the great tetrapylon at the city's centre.[141] The quality of the building—Butler went so far as to claim that the construction of these baths was superior to those at Rome[142]—the expense of the building materials, and the distance of the place from anywhere that they might be readily obtained, as well as the speed with which they must have been constructed, combine to suggest an enormous outlay. Neighbouring areas most probably bore the burden of the expense.

ἔλθητ᾽ εἰς: cf. *Orac. Sib.* 3. 59, 8. 124; Ω has ἵν᾽ ἔλθῃς. Alexandre retained the manuscript reading because of μαθηματική περ ἐοῦσα in l. 67 and argued that ἔλθῃς referred to the region as a whole. But, τε can attach μαθηματική περ ἐοῦσα to Philippopolis as well, and the corruption of ἔλθητ᾽ to ἔλθῃς can be explained as a scribal correction after τε dropped out of the tradition.

69. σφαιρώματα καγχαλόωντα: cf. *Orac. Sib.* 3. 88 καγχαλάωντα in both these cases should not, I think, be translated 'laughing' (Terry) or 'joyful' (Collins) but 'resounding'. Mention of noise in the heavenly spheres is plainly a reference to the belief that music could be heard among the stars. It is a belief that was familiar to Eratosthenes in the third century BC and may go back to the early Pythagoreans in the sixth: see West, *The Orphic Poems*, pp. 31–3; A. J. Festugière, 'L'âme et la musique, d'après Aristide Quintilien', *TAPA* 85 (1954), 65, 76–8; E. des Places, 'Jamblique et les *Oracles chaldaïques*', *CRAI* (1964), 181, for the later period.

73. ὁππόταν ἦμαρ ἐκεῖνο τὸ σὸν μετόπισθε πελάσσῃ: this is Buresch's eloquent improvement on Q's ὁππότ᾽ ἀνὴρ ἄρ᾽ ἐκεῖνο τοσὸν μετόπισθεν παλάσσῃ and V's ὁππότ᾽ ἀνὴρ ἄρ᾽ ἐκεῖνο τὸ σὸν μετόπισθε παλάσσῃ. I would prefer to have some more explicit reference to the person who would destroy these places—their position suggests that there should be one. But there is no way to retain ἀνήρ in this line as it stands, and Buresch's effort restores it to what may very well be its original form.

74–8. The troubles in Alexandria mentioned here are those which

---

[141] Butler, *Architecture and Other Arts*, p. 393; Brünnow and v. Domaszewski, *Provincia Arabia*, iii. 147–51, 160–1.

[142] Butler, *Architecture and Other Arts*, p. 388.

began in the summer of 249 as a riot against the Christians and then turned into a general uprising against Roman authority. The earlier phase of the trouble is described at length by Bishop Dionysius of Alexandria in a letter to Bishop Fabian at Antioch; the later phase— which is only alluded to at the end of Dionysius' letter—is obscure.[143] The motivation for the initial riot, which the local authorities did nothing to suppress, seems to have been provided by an Egyptian holy man who fanned anew the flame of native superstition and persuaded his people that they should show their piety by killing Christians.[144] There is no way of knowing exactly what he had to say, but, as the prefect did not quickly intervene to put an end to the disorder, it is not likely to have been notably antagonistic to the rule of Philip. There is no reason to believe, as has been argued, that the Christians were singled out because Philip's interest in Christianity was well known (for that interest see on l. 88 below).[145] More probably it was connected with the interest in eschatological catastrophe that seems to have been a feature of these years, an interest which may have been heightened by Philip's proclamation of the millennium (see on ll. 46, 79–80). In the light of the close connection between Antioch and Alexandria at this period (see above, p. 193) there is no compelling reason to suppose that these lines must have been composed in Egypt. The broad outline of events, the mere fact that there was serious trouble, could have been known in Syria. Knowledge of such a general kind is all that would have been needed to produce these lines.

74. νῦν: for the programmatic use of νῦν in this context compare *Orac. Sib.* 4. 48, 8. 267, 12. 293, 14. 296.

78. ἀϊκάς: the manuscripts give ἀΐξας here, which clearly will not do: στήσει requires an object and πολέμοιο needs some governing noun. Both requirements are met by the simple alteration to ἀϊκάς, a rare word which means 'swift motion' or 'flights', as in *Il.* 15. 708–9 οὐδ᾽ ἄρα τοί γε | τόξων ἀϊκὰς ἀμφὶς μένον οὐδ᾽ ἔτ᾽ ἀκόντων. For parallel formations with στήσει cf. Hom. *Od.* 11.

---

[143] Eus. *HE* 6. 41. 9 διαδεξαμένη δὲ τοὺς ἀθλίους ἡ στάσις καὶ πόλεμος ἐμφύλιος τὴν καθ᾽ ἡμῶν ὠμότητα πρὸς ἀλλήλους αὐτῶν ἔτρεψεν, καὶ σμικρὸν μὲν προσανεπνεύσαμεν; Oost, 'The Alexandrian Seditions', pp. 4–6.

[144] Eus. *HE* 6. 41. 1 καὶ φθάσας ὁ κακῶν τῇ πόλει ταύτῃ μάντις καὶ ποιητής, ὅστις ἐκεῖνος ἦν, ἐκίνησεν καὶ παρώρμησεν καθ᾽ ἡμῶν τὰ πλήθη τῶν ἐθνῶν, εἰς τὴν ἐπιχώριον αὐτοῦ δεισιδαιμονίαν ἀναρριπίσας.

[145] Oost, 'Alexandrian Seditions', p. 5.

313–14 οἵ ῥα καὶ ἀθανάτοισιν ἀπειλήτην ἐν Ὀλύμπῳ |
φυλόπιδα στήσειν πολυάϊκος πολέμοιο; [Hes.] *Scut.* 113–14
λιλαιόμενοι πολέμοιο | φυλόπιδα στήσειν. For the imagery
cf. *Orac. Sib.* 4. 115–16 ἥξει καὶ Σολύμοισι κακὴ πολέμοιο
θύελλα | Ἰταλόθεν. The phrase may then be translated 'Ares,
dreadful of aspect, will place the swift flights of war among them.'
Alexandre, Rzach, and Geffcken (who obelized στήσει) construed
the ἀΐξας of Ω with Ares, and Wilamowitz thought that a lacuna
might be posited between this line and the one preceding to explain
why there is no object. This misled Terry, who renders 'around
these will horrid Mars rush and stir up wars', and Collins: 'ranting
around these, Ares, terrible of aspect, will stir up (the strife) of war'.

79–80. καὶ τότε δ᾽ αὖ μεγάθυμος . . . βασιλῆα: the circumstances surrounding the death of Philip are difficult to reconstruct
in more than broad outline, and these lines do not help to clarify the
picture at all. They offer no details and the motivation they provide
for the action—διὰ πρεσβύτερον βασιλῆα—is utterly obscure.
This is unfortunate: the other sources contain stories that are at best
oblique.

One of these appears in Zosimus and Zonaras.[146] It is that Philip
was shocked when he received news of Marinus' revolt. He asked
the senate what he should do about it and, while all others were
silent, Decius advised that he should do nothing at all, that the
revolt was not well supported, and that it would soon collapse of its
own accord. This was what transpired, but Philip was not satisfied;
he wanted Decius to go to the Danubian provinces and uncover the
reasons for the outbreak of the trouble in the first place. Decius
suggested that this was a bad idea, but could not refuse. It was soon
apparent that his hesitation was justified, for when he arrived in
Pannonia the legions proclaimed him emperor. Zonaras (but not
Zosimus) then records a letter from Decius to Philip in which
Decius offered to resign; but the offer was turned down and Decius
was compelled to continue as leader of the rebellion. The story for
both Zonaras and Zosimus ends with the defeat of Philip at some
unspecified spot.

The Latin tradition is less informative. Aurelius Victor, Eutro-

---

[146] Zos. 1. 21–2; Zon. 12. 19; for the connection between the two accounts (which is
obvious) see L. Fronza, 'Studi sull'imperatore Decio', *Annali triestini*, 21 (1951), 228–9; F. S.
Salisbury and H. B. Mattingly, 'The Reign of Trajan Decius', *JRS* 14 (1924), 2–3.

pius, and the Epitomator tell only that Philip was killed at Verona—
though the Epitomator adds a rather grisly, if not entirely believ-
able, detail about his decapitation.[147] Orosius says only that he
perished 'fraude Decii' in a military insurrection.[148] There is clearly
nothing here to prove or disprove any of the detail (if it may be
called that) in Zonaras and Zosimus.

John of Antioch is another matter. His story, mutilated and self-
contradictory as it is, clearly has nothing to do with those already
described.[149] It is that Philip fought the Scythians and then marched
on towards Byzantium. When he had gone as far as Perinthus he
received letters telling him of an insurrection at Rome in which
Decius, a consular and *praefectus urbi*, had been proclaimed
emperor. He then sent important men to suppress the revolt and
said that he would come with his sons (*sic*) to put an end to the
trouble.[150] As soon as his men reached Rome they were seduced by
the bribes and flattery of the *senatus populusque Romanus*. They
joined in proclaiming Decius emperor, and when Philip learnt of
this he fled to Beroia.[151] Here (it seems: there is a lacuna of uncertain
length at this point) he was killed. His son (*sic*) died at Rome.

Despite an ingenious effort to make sense of this tale in terms of
some of the odder coinage in 249 (which does not bear the weight
put on it), there seems no reason to believe a word of what John the

---

[147] Aur. Vict. *De Caes*. 28. 10 'his actis filio urbi relicto ipse quamquam debili per
aetatem corpore adversum Decium profectus Veronae cadit pulso amissoque exercitu';
Epit. de Caes. 28. 2 'Veronae ab exercitu interfectus est medio capite supra ordines dentium
praeciso'; Eutr. *Brev*. 9. 3 'ambo deinde ab exercitu interfecti sunt, senior Philippus
Veronae, Romae iunior'.

[148] Oros. *Hist. contra pag*. 7. 20 'ambo tamen quamvis diversis locis tumultu militari et
Decii fraude interfecti sunt'.

[149] *FHG* iv. 597–8, fr. 148 = de Boor, ed., *Excerpta de insidiis*, 59.

[150] *FHG* iv. 598, fr. 148 τοὺς δυναμένους ἐπισχεῖν τὰ πραττόμενα στέλλει καὶ
τὴν Δεκίου προκαταληψομένους ἐπανάστασιν· αὐτός τε σὺν τοῖς παισὶν
ἐπακολουθεῖν ἐπηγγείλατο. This passage has caused some confusion. J. M. York, 'The
Image of Philip the Arab', *Historia*, 21 (1972), 332 n. 53, translated, 'He [Philip] made ready
his men of power to hold these mischiefs in check and to frustrate the revolution. He made
a proclamation with his sons to carry this out.' S. Dušanić, 'The End of the Philippi',
Chiron, 6 (1976), 432, states that αὐτός refers to Decius and that the reference is to the
message of Decius in Zonaras. This is clearly impossible: see H. A. Pohlsander, 'Did Decius
Kill the Philippi?', *Historia*, 31 (1982), 221.

[151] This may be a confusion with Verona: cf. Matthews, *Western Aristocracies*, p. 312 n. 1.
For the same error, the confusion of Verona for Beroia at *C. Th*. 12. 1. 107, see T. D.
Barnes, 'Emperors on the Move', *JRA* 2 (1989), 257.

Antiochene has to say.[152] There is clearly something wrong with Philip making an announcement with his sons (*sic*) and then, when he never reaches Rome, having a son there.[153] It is also problematic that the existence of Marinus, which is undeniable, is omitted altogether. It looks very much as if the whole thing has been invented by someone who knew nothing about these events. Given the stories that John tells of the Persian war under Gordian III or that of Aemilianus' dealings with Gallus (*FHG* iv. 598, fr. 150), this is not difficult to believe. Neither of those accounts bears much connection with reality, and there is no reason to believe that this one should be taken any more seriously.

John of Antioch's account may be dismissed as useless, but this leaves another, very separate, question. Is there anything in the story of Decius' unwilling accession, as told by Zosimus and Zonaras, that should be believed? Zosimus was clearly impressed by Decius. He writes that the Pannonian legions thought him a far better man than Philip with respect to both his civil and his military qualities, and concludes his tale of Decius' reign with the note that he had been a most excellent emperor.[154] These remarks may go back to Zosimus' source, and there is little to justify them on any objective analysis of Decius' reign (see also above, pp. 41–5; and on ll. 100–2 below). But they are not singular: other authors seem to have thought that Decius was something of a hero, a man who bravely gave his life for the empire.[155] Heroes are not supposed to engineer their illegal election to the purple—as is clear from the panegyric of

---

[152] Dušanić, 'The End of the Philippi', *passim*. On the numismatic evidence see Pohlsander, 'Did Decius Kill the Philippi?', pp. 218–19; *AÉ* 1935, No. 164, upon which Dušanić places a good deal of stress, may now be datable to these events. The inscription is a dedication by Clodius Celsinus to Mars Gradivus in return for assistance in battle against 'hostes publici'. It is just possible that this man is to be identified as the Decian governor of Caria-Phrygia in 249–50, and therefore that these 'hostes publici' may indeed be, as Dušanić wishes, Philip and his son: see Frei-Korsunsky, 'Meilensteine', pp. 94–5.

[153] Loriot, 'Chronologie du règne de Philippe l'Arabe', p. 795; for an equally absurd tale—of Philip's death at the hands of the troops when a civil war broke out in Rome 'because of the seduction of the Brutides'—in a fragment attributed to Malalas see app. II.

[154] Zos. I. 21. 3 ὃς καὶ τῶν κοινῶν ἂν ἐπιμεληθείη κρεῖσσον καὶ οὐ σὺν πόνῳ περιέσται Φιλίππου, πολιτικῇ τε ἀρετῇ καὶ πολεμικῇ πείρᾳ προήκων; I. 23. 3 Δεκίῳ μὲν οὖν ἄριστα βεβασιλευκότι τέλος τοιόνδε συνέβη.

[155] For the posthumous reputation of Decius see R. Syme, 'Fiction in the Epitomators', *BHAC 1977/8* (Bonn, 1980), 270 = Historia Augusta *Papers*, p. 159; id., 'Emperors from Etruria', *BHAC 1979/81* (Bonn, 1983), 351–2 = Historia Augusta *Papers*, pp. 202–3.

312 on Constantine or Ammianus' account of Julian's accession (not to mention Julian's own tales about that event).[156] It is probable that the story of his letter to Philip and his advice to him before that are fantasy—but this does not mean that the circumstances these fantasies serve to obscure may not be to some degree recoverable: these are the revolt on the Danube, Decius' suppression of that revolt, and his subsequent march on Rome.

Coins, inscriptions, and papyri provide a chronological framework which tends to confirm the basic story in Zosimus and Zonaras.[157] It appears from the coins of Viminacium that T. Claudius Marinus Pacatianus[158] began his revolt against Philip in late 248 or early 249.[159] As Viminacium minted again for Philip after April 249, it would appear that his revolt was either suppressed or, more certainly, that Viminacium was recovered by that date. The first document which would suggest that Decius himself had rebelled is an inscription from Vienna on which *legio X Gemina* is described (if the restoration is correct) as 'D]ec(iana)' on 28 May 249.[160] Decius' first year in Egypt was 249/50, and the earliest dated document from his reign is a rescript of 16 October 249 (*CJ* 10. 16. 3). This suggests that he dealt with Pacatianus in the spring of 249 and that at some point after the recovery of Viminacium in April, but before the end of May, he was proclaimed emperor. The defeat of Philip came after 29 August 249 and before 16 October.[161]

Though the sources for these events are poor and the chronology is very loose, it is none the less possible to arrive at some more general conclusions. One is that Philip was deeply disliked by the soldiers of the Danubian legions: otherwise they would not have

---

[156] For the panegyric of 312 see J. Béranger, *Recherches sur l'aspect idéologique du principat* (Basle, 1953), 140; for Julian see G. W. Bowersock, *Julian the Apostate* (Cambridge, 1978), 46–54.

[157] Loriot, 'Chronologie de règne de Philippe l'Arabe', pp. 794–5.

[158] *PIR* ² C 930; Barbieri, *Albo*, 1522; see also Fig. 8.

[159] Loriot, 'Chronologie du règne de Philippe l'Arabe', pp. 794–5.

[160] *CIL* iii. 4558. It is otherwise possible to arrive at a date of 6 July from the Chronographer of 354: Loriot, 'Chronologie de règne de Philippe l'Arabe', p. 794.

[161] For the attempt by J. Schwartz to arrive at a date of 7 Sept. 249 on the basis of the Chronographer of 354, which is based on his misconceived date for Decius' death, see below, p. 278; J. Lafaurie, 'Chronologie impériale de 249 à 285', *Bulletin de la Société Nationale de France*, 48 (1965), 143, opts for 29 Aug. 249 as the date of the battle of Verona on the same evidence. For an attempt to draw rather more from these facts than is done here see Fronza, 'Studi sull' imperatore Decio' (1951), pp. 235–44.

proclaimed two rival emperors in the course of a year. The coins of
Pacatianus which proclaim the year 1001 suggest that the action of
the Danubian army may in part have been motivated by the millennial games.[162] Their celebration, the proclamation of a new millennium, may have inspired hopes for better things in the new age:
better things that could be more readily obtained without Philip.
The fact that the games were not celebrated at the other possible
dates for their celebration (288 and 304/5) suggests that Diocletian
later felt that it would be a bad idea to make too much of this
epochal moment. Fear of what might happen at such a juncture
may also explain Decius' evident obsession with ritual propriety in
the months after his accession (see on l. 87).

80. **δολίως διὰ πρεσβύτερον βασιλῆα:** the meaning of this
is obscure. δολίως ordinarily implies that the activity in question is
not very admirable (LSJ, s.v., and l. 91; *Orac. Sib.* 12. 122–3
*καππέσεται δολίως [καὶ] ἐνὶ στρατιῇσι τανυσθεὶς |
βληθεὶς δ᾽ ἐν δαπέδῳ Ῥώμης ἀμφήκεϊ χαλκῷ*; though at
l. 152 below crafty behaviour is associated with a person the author
admired), and the suggestion that Philip was badly done by because
of some predecessor is less than clear. This has nothing to do with
anything known to have been said by Decius—though it might be
guessed that the story of Philip's role in the death of Gordian III was
given currency at the time to justify Decius' action. If this is not a
reference to the tale of Gordian's death, it may be that the author,
who does not seem to have known much about what happened
beyond the confines of Syria, thought it was a reasonable explanation. In any event, the inconsistency in the picture of Philip that is
evident in these lines is paralleled by the extremely inconsistent
treatment of Decius in ll. 81–8, though in that case the problem
may be explained as the result of the less than skilful stitching
together of two passages. Here it may simply be that the author was
trying to sound oracular.

81–102   The Reign of Decius (AD 249–251)

81–8. These lines are difficult to interpret. Lines 84–8 provide a very
different view of the ruler introduced here from that given in lines
81–3. This makes it extremely likely that those five lines are either,

---

[162] *RIC* Pacatianus n. 6.

as many have argued, a later interpolation or, as I believe, by a different, but still contemporary, person from the author of 81–3.[163] The acceptance of Wilamowitz's attractive suggestion πιστῶν in l. 87 for Ω's πίπτων (see ad loc.) gives more weight to the notion that they were written by a Christian (see on ll. 87–8).

81. Ῥώμης ἐριθήλου: cf. *Orac. Sib.* 11. 261. In classical Greek ἐριθήλης is not ordinarily used to describe cities; usually it characterizes plant-life: see *Il.* 5. 90, 10. 467; 17. 53; and LSJ, s.v.

82–3. ἐπιστάμενος πολεμίζειν . . . τριηκοσίων ἀριθμοῖο: the introduction of C. Messius Quintus Decius Valerianus is extraordinarily full: Δακῶν ἐξαναδύς refers to his well-advertised Dacian origin (he was born around Sirmium *c.*190), τριηκοσίων ἀριθμοῖο 'of the number 300' alludes to the name Traianus (*T* = 300), which he seems to have assumed when he arrived in Rome after the death of Philip.[164] The name appears on coins, inscriptions, papyri, here, and in the dating formula used in recording the end of the blessed Pionius, but in no other literary work.[165] Its appearance most probably indicates that the author had read some public document employing it, and is thus perhaps a good example of the importance of that medium for spreading basic information about an emperor.

Before becoming emperor Decius had been *consul suffectus* (before 234), had governed *Moesia Inferior* in 234 under the name Q. Decius, and had held Hispania Tarraconensis for Maximinus Thrax under the name Q. Decius Valerianus in 238.[166] The statement in

[163] Geffcken, *Comp. u. Enst.*, p. 59, found ll. 87–8 particularly Christian; Rzach, *RE* iiA. 2161, thought that the couplet might have been included by the same person who (he thought) interpolated *Orac. Sib.* 12. 30–5, 232. He was properly concerned by the absence of any comparable description of Valerian. Kurfess, 'Zu den *Oracular Sibyllina*', p. 80, and '*Oracula Sibyllina* XI (IX)–XIV (XII)', p. 272, also marks ll. 87–8 as an interpolation and would punctuate with a full stop after βασιλήων in l. 86. Although these lines are not necessary to complete the sense of ll. 84–6, and thus could be an interpolation, Rzach's observation about Valerian appears to me to be a decisive argument against it. A person who wanted to include lines at a later date could not have resisted a chance to include a similar passage about Valerian, whose persecution edict was a more serious matter than the Decian edict on sacrifices.

[164] Wittig, *RE* xv. 1247; Syme, *Emperors and Biography*, p. 220.

[165] Syme, *Emperors and Biography*, p. 220. For the importance of the dating formula in the *Passio Pionii*, see T. D. Barnes, 'Pre-Decian *Acta Martyrum*', *JTS*, NS 19 (1968), 529–31; see also *AÉ* 1984, No. 448 (a milestone from Sardinia) 'nobilissimis [Caesaribus] | principibus iuve[ntutis] | fili(i)s d.n. Traia[ni Aug.]'.

[166] Syme, *Emperors and Biography*, p. 196.

John of Antioch that he was *praefectus urbi* in 249 cannot be supported by any other evidence.[167] Nothing else is known, but his marriage to Herennia Cupressenia Etruscilla, very probably a descendant of Cupressenus Gallus, consul of 147,[168] as well as his distinguished early career—he seems to have held his several offices at, or nearly at, the earliest possible age—suggests that he came from a family of distinction around Sirmium. His failures as emperor suggest that he was not a man of great personal ability. For the problems connected with his sons see on ll. 105, 142. For portraits of Decius and his sons see Figs. 9–11.

84. ἔσσεται ἐκ τετράδος γενεῆς: this is the reading of Ω, which I retain in place of Alexandre's ἐκ τετράδος κεραίης (supported by parallels at *Orac. Sib.* 12. 124–5, 5. 39–40) with some reluctance. Although Alexandre's proposal has the attraction of providing a direct reference to the name Decius (Δ = 4), there are two good reasons for rejecting it. The first is that after Δακῶν ἐξαναδύς, τριηκοσίων ἀριθμοῖο a further identification is redundant, and there is in fact no parallel for such an extended reference to an emperor's name anywhere else in the extant corpus: one clue is ordinarily enough. The second reason is that the manuscript reading makes sense as it stands. It is quite possible to see this as a reference to the theory (current among Christians) that Decius was the forerunner of the Antichrist, whose appearance was imminently expected by people like Cyprian (see Cyp. *Epp.* 67. 7, 22. 1, where Decius is referred to as the 'metator antichristi'; for further parallels see on ll. 121–2 below). There could be four kingdoms before the end of the world, as in the vision of Daniel (see on ll. 28–30 for instances of Rome's identification with the fourth kingdom), and this may be what is meant by describing the person introduced here as being of the fourth race. On the other hand, a reader familiar with Hesiod might think of the fourth Hesiodic race, the race of iron. (I owe this point to A. E. Hanson.)

86. ἀποφθιμένων βασιλήων: it is difficult to be certain to whom this could be referring: possibly the several usurpers (Jotapianus, Valens, and Priscus—for the latter two see on ll. 101–2) who perished in Decius' reign, possibly to the family of Philip, or possibly to all the above. There is no parallel in extant oracles which refer to Rome.

[167] It is accepted as genuine by Wittig, *RE* xv. 1250; Syme, *Emperors and Biography*, p. 197.　　[168] Syme, *Emperors and Biography*, pp. 197–8.

87. αὖ πιστῶν: this is Wilamowitz's correction for Ω's δ᾽ αὖ πίπτων. The simplicity of the alteration makes it extremely appealing, far more so than Alexandre's πόλεμοι, Gutschmidt's ἐν Αἰγύπτῳ, or Rzach's αὖτε μάχαι. The reference—as is the case when πιστοί are mentioned at *Orac. Sib.* 2. 169—is to Christians, here to those who suffered as a result of Decius' edict ordering all of his subjects to sacrifice in the autumn of 249.[169]

Decius' action was unprecedented, and the precise terms of his edict can be recovered only with difficulty from various sources. It is necessary to examine these with some care in order to be able to interpret the perception of this author, namely, that the edict was motivated by Decius' hatred of Philip. The points of most importance for this inquiry are the edict's date, the provision for sacrifice, and its relevance to Christians.

There is no direct evidence for the date upon which Decius promulgated the decree, and it may only be guessed at—though with a certain degree of precision—from the dates given for various martyrdoms and some remarks in the correspondence of two bishops. One of these, Cyprian, wrote to several confessors before the end of 250 congratulating them on their endurance of the suffering that he had avoided through his timely removal from Carthage. He implies that this suffering had lasted for nearly a year.[170] The other bishop, Dionysius of Alexandria, whose testimony is far more important, wrote that news of Decius' edict reached Egypt shortly after that of Philip's death.[171] The news of Philip's death must have reached Egypt between early September

---

[169] For the scope of the edict see G. W. Clarke, *The Letters of St. Cyprian of Carthage*, i (New York, 1984), 27–8.

[170] Cyp. *Epp.* 37. 2. 1 'eant nunc magistratus et consules sive proconsules, annuae dignitatis insignibus et duodecim fascibus glorientur. Ecce dignitas caelestis in vobis honoris annui claritate signata est et iam revertentis anni volubilem circulum victricis gloriae diuturnitate transgressa est'. Were this the only evidence, the objection of G. W. Clarke, 'Some Observations on the Persecution of Decius', *Antichthon*, 3 (1967), 67, and *The Letters of St. Cyprian of Carthage*, ii (New York, 1984), 174–5, to its use for dating purposes would be valid, but it is not the only evidence (see next n.).

[171] Eus. *HE* 6. 41. 9–10 εὐθέως δὲ ἡ τῆς βασιλείας ἐκείνης τῆς εὐμενεστέρας ἡμῖν μεταβολὴ διήγγελται, καὶ πολὺς ὁ τῆς ἐφ᾽ ἡμᾶς ἀπειλῆς φόβος ἀνετείνετο. καὶ δὴ καὶ παρῆν τὸ πρόσταγμα, αὐτὸ σχεδὸν ἐκεῖνο οἷον τὸ προρρηθὲν ὑπὸ τοῦ κυρίου ἡμῶν παρὰ βραχὺ τὸ φοβερώτατον. See Salisbury and Mattingly, 'The Reign of Trajan Decius', p. 8; J. Molthagen, *Der römische Staat und die Christen im zweiten und dritten Jahrhundert* (Göttingen, 1970), 66.

and 27 November 249.[172] The fact that a date for the edict in the autumn of 249 seems a bit early in view of the dates of extant Egyptian *libelli* which attest performance of the sacrifice in obedience to the edict (all the extant texts are from June or July 250) is obviously irrelevant to the question of the date when the edict was issued.[173] These *libelli* may reflect either the sloth of the local officials, or the fact that they had set a generous time-limit for the performance of the sacrifice.[174] A date in the autumn of 249 is perfectly in keeping with the dates for the earliest martyrdoms: Babylas in Antioch (24 January 250), Nestor in Pamphylia (28 February 250), Pionius in Smyrna (24 March 250), Fabian in Rome (20 January 250).[175] To judge from evidence for the speed at which an edict might travel, it would be some months, particularly if the edict was issued late in the year, before the imperial order was known in Syria or Pamphylia.[176] Four or five months would be reasonable, and this (counting back from the death of Babylas and Nestor) would suggest a

---

[172] *P. Oxy.* 1638, of 27 Nov. 249; Stein, 'Zur Chronologie der römischen Kaiser', p. 40 (where the date is wrongly given as 27 Sept. 249).

[173] For these see J. Knipfing, 'The *Libelli* of the Decian Persecution', *HTR* 16 (1923), 345–90. Since his article two more *libelli* have come to light: *PSI* 778; J. Schwartz, 'Une déclaration de sacrifice du temps de Dèce', *RB* 54 (1947), 365–7.

[174] For the problem of the date of the sacrifices and the *libelli* see P. Keresztes, 'The Decian *Libelli* and Contemporary Literature', *Latomus*, 34 (1975), 761–81; G. W. Clarke, 'Two Measures in the Persecution of Decius', *BICS* 20 (1973), 118–23; id., 'Prosopographical Notes on the Epistles of Cyprian, II: The Proconsul of Africa in 250 A.D.', *Latomus*, 31 (1972), 1053–7. Throughout my discussion I take it as proven (by Clarke) that there was only one Decian edict. The notion that the *libelli* reflect a later phase of activity under the edict and were demanded only of suspected Christians has been eloquently restated by Lane Fox, *Pagans and Christians*, pp. 455–7. I cannot accept this for two reasons. Firstly, the fact that the *libelli* only appear around June in Egypt means no more than that it took time for the ordinance to take effect in outlying areas (Clarke, *Letters of St. Cyprian*, i. 29)—as Lane Fox rightly observes, the requirement for everyone to obtain a certificate would be a 'bureaucratic nightmare', but no more so than the issuing of tax receipts, and possibly less difficult than had been the keeping of records of practising Jews who paid taxes to the *fiscus Judaicus* (for this see now M. Goodman, 'Nerva, the *Fiscus Judaicus*, and Jewish Identity', *JRS* 79 (1989), 41–2). It may well have been the practical problem of setting up the issue of the certificates which put off the day by which sacrifice had to be made for so long. The second reason is that I find it hard to believe that the priestess of the crocodile god at Theadelphia was a Christian suspect (Knipfing, 'The *Libelli* of the Decian Persecution', n. 3).

[175] For these dates see W. H. C. Frend, *Martyrdom and Persecution in the Early Church* (New York, 1967), 301; Knipfing, 'The *Libelli* of the Decian Persecution', p. 353; M. M. Sage, *Saint Cyprian* (Cambridge, 1975), 174–206.

[176] Millar, 'Emperors, Frontiers and Foreign Relations', p. 10, for the speed at which edicts were communicated.

date in line with that which can be obtained from Dionysius' letter. It may therefore be assumed that the edict was issued very shortly after the death of Philip.[177] What did Decius tell people to do? Here the best evidence is provided by Egyptian *libelli* that relate to the sacrifice, by the letter of Dionysius preserved in Eusebius' history, by the *Passio Pionii*, and by Cyprian's *De lapsis*. The form of the *libelli* is reasonably consistent. They consist of an application that the appellants' sacrifice before the superintending officials be registered by them, the signature or signatures of those who witnessed the sacrifice, and possibly that of an additional observer. The sacrificant testified his or her loyalty to the ancestral gods and to his or her consumption of sacrificial food and drink.[178] That this format was widespread and therefore likely to have been so prescribed in the edict itself is suggested by the form of Pionius' interrogation—he was asked whom he worshipped and then instructed to offer sacrifice to some acceptable divinity—or Cyprian's complaints about the behaviour of various bishops before magistrates.[179] The possession of a *libellus* was sufficient proof that a person had performed these acts, just as a tax receipt was sufficient proof that a person had paid his taxes: if it were not, then the issue of what penance, if any, should be imposed upon those who had fraudulently obtained *libelli* without sacrificing, before they could be readmitted to communion, would not have arisen.

It is clear from the Egyptian *libelli* and Cyprian's discourse on the lapsed that the sacrificants were supposed to show up of their own accord. Thus the *libelli* are couched in the form of applications, and Cyprian wrote that on the day by which the sacrifice had to be offered Christians filled the Capitolium at Carthage in such numbers that those administering the sacrifice had to be asked to allow more time so that all those who had appeared could perform the required acts.[180] If people did not appear they might be subject

---

[177] Clarke, *Letters of St. Cyprian*, i. 23, favours Jan. 250, but this seems rather late for the news to reach Antioch by 24 Jan.

[178] Knipfing, 'The *Libelli* of the Decian Persecution', pp. 346–7.

[179] *Pass. Pion.* 8; Cyp. *Epp.* 67. 6.

[180] Cyp. *De lapsis*, 8 'nec hoc sibi reliquerunt ut sacrificare idolis viderentur inviti: ultro ad forum currere, ad mortem sponte properare, quasi hoc olim cuperent, quasi amplecterentur occasionem datam quam libenter optassent. Quot illic a magistratibus vespera urgente dilati sunt, quot ne eorum differretur interitus et rogaverunt.'

to loss of property.[181] If they appeared (either willingly or un-
willingly) and refused to make the sacrifice, they could be treated in
accordance with existing laws pertaining to civil disobedience.[182] In
the case of Christians (if not other potential troublemakers as well)
these had been catalogued by Ulpian in his *De officiis proconsulis*.[183]
The relevance of the edict on sacrifices to Christians was tangen-
tial. It was not directed against them in specific terms. Indeed, when
he describes the edict, Dionysius gives no indication that it had
language in it singling out the Christians for special attention. He
alludes to it with a line adapted from Christ's warning to his followers at Matt. 24: 24, that false Christs and prophets would try to
lead even the faithful astray. The implication was that the Church
was threatened by the failings of its members in the face of tempta-
tion rather than by direct assault. Certainly, the debate on the
lapsed—what to do about *libellatici* and *sacrificati*—indicates that
the decree presented a serious problem. It could be readily agreed
that ordinary sacrifice was wrong, but was just one sacrifice for the
good of the empire all that bad? No arguments for the lapsed are
preserved, but the priests and bishops who performed the act clearly
thought—in some cases quite rightly—that their flocks would
forgive them.[184] The burden of Cyprian's case in the *De lapsis*, that
this sacrifice was like any other, surely comes in response to an
argument that it was not. But still, the sacrifice was a special case
because of the imperial order, and even Cyprian had to admit that
there were different degrees of wrongdoing.[185]

---

[181] Cyp. *De lapsis*, 10 'nec est, pro dolor, iusta aliqua et gravis causa quae tantum facinus
excuset: relinquenda erat patria et patrimonii facienda iactura'. See Molthagen, *Der römische
Staat und die Christen*, p. 69.

[182] T. D. Barnes, 'Legislation against the Christians', *JRS* 58 (1968), 32–50, for the
principles by which Christians were tried.

[183] Honoré, *Ulpian*, pp. 32, 154–6.

[184] Cyp. *Epp.* 14. 1 (lapsed clergy), 55. 2. 1 (Trofomius at Rome), 55. 10. 2 (other Italian
bishops who were *libellatici* or *sacrificati*), 65 (Fortunatianus, still bishop of Assuras after
sacrificing), 67 (Basilides and Martialis, both *libellatici* with some suggestion that they were
also blasphemers and *sacrificati*, and both still bishops); *Pass. Pion.* 15. 2 (sacrifice of
Euctemon, ὁ προεστὼς ὑμῶν (i.e. the Christians), for a further demonstration of piety
(bringing a lamb to sacrifice in the temple of Nemesis and proceeding in garland through
the streets); 18. 12 his future in the faith is unknown). In fact it is possible that the issue was
never seriously raised. See further n. 189 below.

[185] Cyp. *Epp.* 55. 13. 2 'nec tu existimes, frater carissime, sicut quibusdam videtur,
libellaticos cum sacrificatis aequari oportere, quando inter ipsos etiam qui sacrificaverint et
condicio frequenter et causa diversa sit'.

The Decian edict was only coincidentally concerned with coercing or annihilating recalcitrants and fanatics. The emperor's subjects were asked to sacrifice, pour a libation, and partake of the victim in honour of the ancestral gods. In some places, if the potential sacrificant, like Pionius, refused to acknowledge a divinity other than 'the God we know through Christ his word', and did not wish to sacrifice, it was possible to fulfil the requirements of the edict by making sacrifice to the emperor.[186] The problem of the lapsed reveals that people could claim that this sacrifice did not constitute a serious act of apostasy. There is no suggestion that Decius required people to sacrifice more than once—if someone had a *libellus* there was presumably no question that he or she would be called on by the authorities to make another pious demonstration. There is also no suggestion that Decius was trying to make Christians apostasize, or that he was sufficiently knowledgeable to think that his order would cause people great doctrinal difficulty. The edict was issued very soon after his accession and was no doubt intended to please the gods. As the year 1000 had just passed this might have seemed a very important and useful thing to do.[187] In any event, the emperor does not seem to have followed up his first edict with any direct action against the Church, and even before his death some governors may have been releasing Christians under the terms of amnesty decrees which they issued upon entry into their provinces. Certainly Cyprian was planning his return to Carthage in March

---

[186] *Pass. Pion.* 8. 3–4 Πολέμων εἶπεν· Ποῖον θεὸν σέβῃ; Πιόνιος εἶπεν· Τὸν Θεὸν τὸν παντοκράτορα τὸν ποιήσαντα τὸν οὐρανὸν καὶ τὴν γῆν καὶ πάντα τὰ ἐν αὐτοῖς καὶ πάντας ἡμᾶς, ὃς παρέχει ἡμῖν πάντα πλουσίως, ὃν ἐγνώκαμεν διὰ τοῦ Λόγου αὐτοῦ Χριστοῦ. (4) Πολέμων εἶπεν· Ἐπίθυσον οὖν κἂν τῷ αὐτοκράτορι. Πιόνιος εἶπεν· Ἐγὼ ἀνθρώπῳ οὐκ ἐπιθύω· Χριστιανὸς γάρ εἰμι.

[187] Molthagen, *Der römische Staat und die Christen*, pp. 71–80, and A. Alföldi, 'Zu den Christenverfolgungen in der Mitte des 3. Jahrhunderts', *Klio*, 31 (1938), 323–37 = *Studien*, pp. 285–300, take positions similar to the one adopted here, though they go a good deal further in creating a theoretical basis and ignore the millennium. The millennium is properly emphasized by Clarke, *Letters of St. Cyprian*, i. 23; J. Geffcken, *The Last Days of Greco-Roman Paganism*, trans. S. MacCormack (New York, 1978), 14; Lane Fox, *Pagans and Christians*, pp. 452–3. L. Fronza, 'Studi sull'imperatore Decio', *Annali triestini*, 23 (1953), 317, 320–2, and M. Sordi, 'La data dell'editto di Decio e il significato della chiesa in Italia', *RSCI* 34 (1980), 457–60, both take the view that the measure was directed against Philip, though the former pays excessive attention to the constitutional aspects and the latter dates it to May 250. See also the sensible discussion of N. H. Baynes, *CAH* xii. 646–7, and the useful summary by H. A. Pohlsander, 'The Religious Policy of Decius', *ANRW* ii/16. 1826–42.

251, and the problem of what to do about the lapsed was already beginning to plague the Church.[188]

It is against this background that these lines must be interpreted. Two options are open. One is to assert that the persecution may not have seemed a very serious issue everywhere—and it does seem that the matter of what to do about *libellatici* and *sacrificati* was never an important one in the east, even though the Roman Church was split by the Novatian controversy and Cyprian faced great difficulties arising from his own conduct, as well as his variably strict attitude towards the lapsed.[189] It could then be argued, on the basis of this assumption, that the picture which these lines present of Decius is likely to have developed some time later, as the Christian tradition concerning persecuting emperors solidified along the lines which had been proposed by Melito of Sardis and Tertullian. The explanation given for the attack on the faithful, διὰ πρότερον βασιλῆα, may then be taken as a reference to Philip's alleged Christianity (see on l. 88). Outside of this oracle, the first extant appearance of the tradition that the edict was a reaction against Philip is in Eusebius' *Ecclesiastical History* (see on l. 88; Eusebius has it from a letter of Dionysius). It could then be asserted that the insertion of these lines took place well after the completion of the rest of the poem, perhaps at the time of Eusebius. One problem would then be to explain why the later interpolator should pick on Decius and not Valerian.[190] It is also possible to object that the absence of such an explanation in the letters of Cyprian or Dionysius proves nothing about what other contemporaries might think. The second option is to believe that these lines were in the poem or tradition known to

---

[188] Clarke, *The Letters of St. Cyprian*, i. 31, with n. 137 (on amnesties issued by governors).

[189] For the Church in the east see Clarke, *The Letters of St. Cyprian*, i. 36–8 (though for a refinement of his treatment of the *Passio Pionii* cf. D. S. Potter, 'Martyrdom as Spectacle', forthcoming), ii. 11–13; G. E. M. de Ste Croix, 'The Persecutions: Christianity's Encounter with the Roman Imperial Government', in A. J. Toynbee (ed.), *The Crucible of Christianity* (New York, 1969), 349, points out that in Peter of Alexandria's canonical letter of 306 people who purchased their safety would not be thought to have lapsed. Although Peter's stand on the persecutions was the subject of vigorous debate, it is possible that this does reflect a policy that had developed in the 3rd cent. as a result of the Decian edict, when in general flight from persecution appears to have become a respectable option: for this see O. Nicholson, 'Flight from Persecution as Imitation of Christ', *JTS*, NS 40 (1989), 48–65. For the Novatian controversy see Clarke, *Letters of St. Cyprian*, ii. 5–11, iii. 14–28; Sage, *Saint Cyprian*, pp. 248–65.

[190] Rzach, *RE* iiA. 2161.

the author of lines 155–71. This would involve the hypothesis that the passage was written by a Christian during or shortly after the reign of Decius who believed (perhaps on the quite reasonable basis of personal experience) that the edict was directed against himself and his correligionists and that it was issued because Decius despised the memory of Philip (see on l. 88). This seems more plausible, and the reason why such a passage might be included or retained by the person who produced the oracle in its present form is quite simple: whether or not he recognized the reference to the faithful, he still thought that these lines presented a reasonable picture of the reign of Decius.

88. διὰ πρότερον βασιλῆα: this may be explained in two ways, which are not mutually exclusive. Most obviously, if the reference in these lines is to Decius' edict on sacrifices, the allusion is to Philip's alleged Christianity. The question of his interest in that faith, an interest which was believed by contemporaries of Dionysius of Alexandria to have involved his conversion,[191] is a difficult one. On the one hand, it is very difficult to believe that he was ever a practising Christian. He deified his father Marinus and publicized his own involvement in state cult at the time of the millennial games. On the other hand, Eusebius tells us that he sought to attend a Christian service but was refused admittance until he confessed. John Chrysostom adds the detail that Babylas of Antioch refused an emperor entrance to his church, and the *Chronicon Paschale* identifies that emperor as Philip.[192] Eusebius knew of letters from Origen to Philip and to Otacilia Severa,[193] and—while it would be difficult to believe that the more extreme stories about Philip's Christianity were contained in those letters—this should indicate that Origen thought they would be interested in what he had to say. In this context the fact that the most extreme story about Philip's

---

[191] Eus. *HE* 7. 10. 3 οὐδὲ γὰρ ἄλλος τις οὕτω τῶν πρὸ αὐτοῦ βασιλέων εὐμενῶς καὶ δεξιῶς πρὸς αὐτοὺς διετέθη, οὐδ' οἱ λεχθέντες ἀναφανδὸν Χριστιανοὶ γεγονέναι. On the question of Philip's dealings with Christians see Stein, *RE* x. 768–9; H. Crouzel, 'Le christianisme de l'empereur Philippe l'Arabe', *Gregorianum*, 56 (1975), 545–50; H. A. Pohlsander, 'Philip the Arab and the Christians', *Historia*, 29 (1980), 463–73; Bowersock, *Roman Arabia*, pp. 125–6; Lane Fox, *Pagans and Christians*, pp. 452–3; Shahîd, *Rome and the Arabs*, pp. 65–93.

[192] Eus. *HE* 6. 34; John Chrys. PG 50. 529, 62. 71; Downey, *History of Antioch*, pp. 306–7; Stein, *RE* x. 768.

[193] *HE* 6. 36. 3.

involvement with Christians is set at Antioch, the likely place of this oracle's compilation, may be significant. The story that he dealt with Babylas may in fact be confirmed by these lines—for it would seem that Antiochenes might have been impressed by the fact, and even have passed the news on. When Philip died Dionysius wrote from Alexandria (a city closely linked with Antioch throughout these years) that he had been kind to Christians.[194] In the light of this and the date of Decius' edict (see on l. 87), it is not difficult to believe that a Christian would have interpreted Decius' action as a reaction against Philip's decency.[195]

It is also possible that Philip's Christianity (invented though it may have been by his subjects) has nothing to do with this line. Commodus' name was taken off inscriptions because people such as those at Bubon (who later saw fit to reinscribe it) believed it would be a good idea after his death, the attitude of his successors being uncertain.[196] They may have thought that Niger would be hostile to his memory. In the context of the 240s, there certainly had been cases in the recent past (Maximinus and Severus Alexander, Gordian III and Maximinus) where hostility towards a predecessor had been publicly displayed, and such hostility was also displayed by Decius towards Philip. Decius' edict, along with the *damnatio* of Philip, may have been perceived as measures to correct previous actions. At Cosa Decius was called *restitutor sacrorum*,[197] which would suggest that people thought or had been told that Decius was correcting abuses of the past. It is certain that Pacatianus felt that the celebration of the year 1000 was significant; others may have felt it disturbing, and any public religious activity on Decius' part could be associated with the religious acts of his predecessor. This may even have been what Decius intended.

89–100. Alexandre first identified the character introduced in these lines as the Mariades who was involved in Sapor's capture of

---

[194] Eus. *HE* 6. 41. 9.

[195] For the notion that the edict was motivated by hatred of Philip see ibid. 39. 1 ἀλλὰ γὰρ Φίλιππον ἔτεσιν ἑπτὰ βασιλεύσαντα διαδέχεται Δέκιος· ὃς δὴ τοῦ πρὸς Φίλιππον ἔχθους ἕνεκα διωγμὸν κατὰ τῶν ἐκκλησιῶν ἐγείρει.

[196] F. Schindler, *Die Inschriften von Bubon (Nordlykien)* (SAWW 278. 3; 1973, 12; BÉ 1973, No. 451; for similar erasures cf. BÉ 1972, No. 520; 1976, Nos. 476, 751; see also D. S. Potter, 'Recent Inscriptions from Flat Cilicia', *JRA* 2 (1989), 308.

[197] *AÉ* 1973, No. 235; see also *Aphrodisias and Rome*, No. 25, for others who thought (correctly, as far as they were told) that Decius had an interest in sacrifice.

Antioch (for the date see on l. 110). Objections have been raised on various counts, and a review of his career is necessary in order to vindicate Alexandre's suggestion.[198] The sources for Mariades' life may be divided into four categories.[199] The first is a local Antiochene tradition represented by Malalas, Libanius, and Ammianus Marcellinus. The second appears in the *Historia Augusta*, the third in the Continuator of Dio, and the fourth in a rabbinic commentary on Daniel.

According to Malalas, Mariades fled to Persia after he was expelled from the Antiochene Boule for embezzling funds placed in his care for the purchase of race-horses.[200] There he persuaded Sapor to invade Roman territory: καὶ ἦλθεν ὁ αὐτὸς Σαπώρης βασιλεὺς Περσῶν μετὰ δυνάμεως στρατοῦ πολλοῦ διὰ

---

[198] Rostovtzeff, '*Res Gestae* and Dura', pp. 32–3, considered the ravages recorded here 'a repetition of the military activity of Jotapianus, the robber being a Roman and not a Syrian, perhaps another ephemeral pretender to the Roman throne'; Sprengling, *Third Century Iran*, p. 87, asked, 'Why not Iotapianus himself?'; Kzach, *RE* iiA. 2139, felt that the identification with Mariades was secure, but that the oracle was not valuable as a historical source because he had become confused with the returning Nero (see on ll. 122–8); L. de Blois, 'Odaenathus and the Roman–Persian War of 252–264 A.D.', *Talanta*, 6 (1975), 13–14, thinks that these lines refer to Odaenathus; for the other side see Geffcken, *Comp. u. Enst.*, pp. 59–60; Olmstead, 'The Mid-Third Century', pp. 398–400; Stein, *RE* xiv. 1745. Since Jotapianus was not active in the reign of Gallus, as this person was, Sprengling's suggestion will not do; neither will that of de Blois: Odaenathus never led a Persian attack on Antioch; it is clear that this person must be identified with the fugitive in l. 122. As there is only one person who fits, the scepticism of Rostovtzeff is also unwarranted.

[199] The name Mariades is produced by the combination of the fairly common name Marea (*IGLS* vii. 60 n. 2 for a survey of its occurrences) with the Greek ending -αδης (this explanation was suggested in conversation by Prof. G. W. Bowersock; for another view see Stein, *RE* xiv. 1744). As Marea derives from the root *mr* 'lord', Cyriades is simply a translation of the Semitic part of the name. For a similar phenomenon compare the activity of the tax-agent at Karanis who provided Greek equivalents or translations of Egyptian names from the text of Callimachus (H. C. Youtie, 'Callimachus on the Tax Rolls', in D. Samuel (ed.), *Proceedings of the Twelfth International Congress of Papyrology*, pp. 545–51 = *Scriptiunculae* (Amsterdam, 1973), 1035–41). It appears in a Hebrew text (see p. 271) as *Qrydws*, which suggests that he might have been better known to contemporaries by that name; I use Mariades throughout as it is the most common form in modern works; the form 'Mariadnes' which appears in a fragment of the Continuator of Dio (below, n. 203) is a mistake.

[200] This version inspired the fanciful reconstruction of J. Gagé, 'Les Perses à Antioche', pp. 301–24. His attempt to connect the circus faction of Mariades with the 'Greens' and develop it on the basis of evidence from Chosroes' invasion of 540 as evidence for an anti-Roman Syrian nationalist faction with a natural leaning towards Persia is well treated by A. Cameron, *Circus Factions* (Oxford, 1976), 200–1.

τοῦ λιμίτου Χάλκιδος, καὶ παραλαμβάνει τὴν Συρίαν πᾶσαν
καὶ πραιδεύει αὐτήν. καὶ παραλαμβάνει Ἀντιόχειαν τὴν
μεγάλην πόλιν ἐν ἑσπέρᾳ καὶ πραιδεύει αὐτὴν καὶ στρέφει
καὶ καίει αὐτήν, χρηματιζούσης τότε τῆς μεγάλης Ἀντιοχείας τιδ'. ἀπεκεφάλισε δὲ καὶ τὸν πολιτευόμενον ὡς
προδότην ὄντα πατρίδος ἰδίας (12. 26, p. 296). The date and the
last sentence quoted here reveal the link between Malalas' story and
that told by Ammianus, who records that the city was taken while the
citizens were at the theatre and even that (23. 5. 3) 'Mareade vivo
exusto, qui eos ad suorum interitum civium duxerat inconsulte. et
haec quidem Gallieni temporibus evenerunt.' Malalas had begun his
account by placing these events in the reign of Valerian, but the date
he gives (which the corrupt manuscript gives as δτι') seems to have
been the 314th (reading τιδ') of the era of Antioch, which is 266/7
and thus in the reign of Gallienus.[201] Libanius alludes to the story in
two of his orations,[202] which suggests that it was current in late
fourth-century Antioch. The absence of allusion to it outside of
Antiochene authors suggests that it was not widely known elsewhere.

A fragment of the Continuator of Dio tells a very different
tale.[203] In this version Sapor encamped twenty stades from the city
with Mariades beside him. The wiser citizens fled, but the great
majority remained, friends of Mariades and those hoping for
revolution among them. There is no date, but in the Excerpta de
sententiis, the source for this fragment, it is placed immediately
before a fragment mentioning a letter which Aemilianus is alleged
to have sent to the Senate immediately after his accession in 253.
This should indicate that the author placed the fall of Antioch
before the reign of Aemilianus, and shows that he placed the
activity of Mariades in the early 250s.

[201] D. Magie, Roman Rule in Asia Minor (Princeton, 1950), 1568 n. 29; Downey, History of
Antioch, p. 590, for other attempts at emendation. None of them yields a proper date (for
which see on l. 110).

[202] Lib. 24. 38 οὔτε φόβῳ συνοικοῦμεν οὔτε μή τι σύμβῃ τοιοῦτον οἷον καὶ ἐπὶ
τῶν προγόνων δεδοίκαμεν, οἷς ἐν τῷ θεάτρῳ συγκαθημένοις ἐφειστήκεσαν οἱ
τοξόται τὸ ὄρος κατειληφότες; 60. 2 τόν τοι βασιλέα Περσῶν τοῦ νῦν τούτου
πολεμοῦντος πρόγονον προδοσίᾳ τὸ ἄστυ λαβόντα.

[203] FHG iv. 192 = Boissevain, cd. Excerpta de sententiis, fr. 157 ὅτι ὁ τῶν Περσῶν
βασιλεὺς μετὰ Μαριάδου πρὸ τῆς πόλεως Ἀντιοχείας ὡς εἴκοσι σταδίους
στρατοπεδεύεται. καὶ οἱ μὲν φρόνιμοι ἔφυγον τῆς πόλεως, τὸ δὲ πολὺ πλῆθος
ἔμεινεν, τοῦτο μὲν φίλοι φιλοῦντες τὸν Μαριάδην, τοῦτο δὲ καὶ τοῖς
καινισμοῖς χαίροντες, ὅπερ ὑπὸ ἀνοίας πάσχειν εἰώθασι.

In the *Historia Augusta* biography of Cyriades it appears that, after a degenerate youth, he stole a large sum of money from his father, fled to Persia, and 'deinde Saporem ad Romanum solum traxit; Antiochia etiam capta et Caesarea Caesareanum nomen meruit' (*v. Tyr. trig.* 2. 2). His death is placed before the coming of Valerian to the east. A final relevant text is a Jewish commentary on Dan. 7: 6;[204] 'and behold there will come up among them another horn, a little one: this refers to Ben Nazor; before which three of the first were uprooted: this refers to Macr[ian]us, Quietus, and Cyriades'. Though the placement of Mariades in the company of Macrianus and Quietus is a bit disturbing, the fact that he should be thought of in the same light as these two usurpers is testimony to his impact on the imagination of his contemporaries.

There are two options for the reconstruction of Mariades' career. He can be placed, as he was by Gibbon and subsequently by others, at the end of the 250s[205] and associated with the events surrounding the capture of Valerian, or his activity can be dated to the first part of the decade and associated with the second of Sapor's successful campaigns against Rome (for the date see on l. 110). The first option is superficially the more attractive. It would explain why he was placed in the reign of Valerian or Gallienus by the Antiochene chronicle as well as the collocation with Macrianus and Quietus in the commentary on Daniel. It might also explain why he was associated with the fall of Caesarea and thus satisfy those who would argue that it could only have fallen once (see on l. 93).

The problems with the dating outlined above are serious. Despite the date that he gives, Malalas was clearly recording a tradition which was relevant to the early 250s. He went on from the story of Sapor's capture of Antioch to describe (albeit in a rather fanciful fashion) the resistance mounted against the Persians by Lucius Julius Aurelius Sulpicius (Uranius) Antoninus (see on ll. 150–4). After this he further confused his story with an account of the deeds

---

[204] The translation used here is that of S. Lieberman, 'Palestine in the Third and Fourth Centuries', *JQR* 37 (1947), 37–8.

[205] Gibbon, *Decline and Fall*, ch. x, preferring 'a probable course of events to the doubtful chronology of a most inaccurate writer', with reference to the *Historia Augusta*; see also A. Alföldi, 'Die Hauptereignisse der Jahre 253–261 n. Chr. im Orient im Spiegel der Münzprägung', *Berytus*, 4 (1937), 58–60 = *Studien*, pp. 144–6; Ensslin, *Zu den Kriegen*, pp. 57–8.

of Odaenathus the Palmyrene that appears to have been derived from the work of another historian, Philostratus.[206] Despite his confusion, Malalas gave the impression that Mariades' activity culminated before Valerian arrived in the east. This impression is also given by the *Historia Augusta* biography of Cyriades, which records 'ipse per insidias suorum, cum Valerianus iam ad bellum Persicum veniret' (*v. Tyr. trig.* 2. 3), and the fragment in the *Excerpta* which placed him before Aemilianus. Finally, there is the question of the number of times that Sapor captured Antioch. It has been argued that he took the city twice. This is wrong. There was only one capture of the city and it took place in 252 (see on ll. 110, 161–3). If Mariades was involved in this, as all the sources say he was, his activity can only be dated to the early 250s, and it may even be true, as the *Historia Augusta* says, that he was killed shortly after the accession of Valerian.

The commentary on Daniel and the Continuator of Dio both suggest that Mariades was a man of considerable importance. The one placed him on a level with usurpers who challenged the supremacy of Gallienus, according to the other he had a considerable following at Antioch. The inclusion of a biography for him by the author of the *Historia Augusta* in the early section of the *vitae Tyrannorum triginta*, before he was reduced to invention to fill out the number, similarly indicates that there was a tradition which made him out to be an important aid to the Persians. This is not at all impossible. Mariades was a more substantial figure than the brigand Claudius who once rode out of the desert to meet Septimius Severus, or the fourth-century deserters Antoninus and Craugasius, and he must have operated with the same, or possibly even greater, forces as did the Uranius who maintained himself for some time in the reign of Severus Alexander, or Jotapianus in the reigns of Philip and Decius.[207]

Lines 97–100 of this text describe the flight of the man in question across the Euphrates. This rules out Jotapianus as the

---

[206] A. Schenk Graf von Stauffenberg, *Die römische Kaisergeschichte bei Malalas: Griechischer Texte der Bücher IX–XII und Untersuchungen* (Stuttgart, 1931), 374–5, who observes that Domninus appears to have been the source for the early history of Valerian's war with Persia and Philostratus (*FGrH* 99) for later events.

[207] For a general survey of the role of traitors in wars on the eastern frontiers see V. Chapot, *La Frontière de l'Euphrate de Pompée à la conquête arabe* (Paris, 1907), 199–205.

person mentioned here, and the prominence accorded the fugitive is in accord with that of Mariades in other sources. As there is universal agreement that Mariades played a role in Sapor's one and only capture of Antioch, and as this person should be identified with the 'fugitive of Rome' who appears in l. 122, Alexandre's identification should be maintained.

89. ⟨καὶ ἐπίκλοπος⟩ ἔλθῃ: Ω gives ἐπὶ κλίνης ἔλθῃ. Fehr's proposal is the easiest solution to the problem of this hemistich, which either identified the person, or included a further adjective or adjectives to describe him, or described the effect of his coming. Alexandre contemplated the first two options in his note on this line, proposing: ἐπικαίριος or ἀπὸ εἰκάδος. Rzach produced ἐπίκλητος ἐπέλθη in his text; Geffcken, while obelizing ἐπὶ κλίνης, recorded καὶ ἐπίκλοπος and ἐπὶ Κλίμακος. ἐπικαίριος does not make sense and ἀπὸ εἰκάδος, although it does have the attraction of yielding a numerical equivalent for the name Kyriades (*K* = 20), is odd without κεραία or ἀριθμός (though cf. *Orac. Sib.* 12. 176–9 τὸν μέτα τρεῖς ἄρξουσιν, ὁ δὲ τρίτος ὀψὲ κρατήσει | τρεῖς δεκάδας κατέχων· αὐτὰρ μονάδος πάλι πρώτης | ἄλλος ἄναξ ἄρξει· μετὰ δ᾽ αὐτὸν κοίρανος ἄλλος | ἐκ δεκάδων ἑπτά; 14. 137–8 ἄρξει δ᾽ ἄλλος ἀνὴρ τριάδων δέκα θηρὶ ἐοικὼς | εὐχαίτῃ βλοσυρῷ; 14. 185–6 ἀλλ᾽ ὁπόταν ἄρχῃ τούτου παῖς ἐν χθονὶ 'Ρώμης | ἐκ μονάδος προφανείς). ἐπίκλητος ἐπέλθῃ makes no sense in this context; ἐπὶ Κλίμακος, referring to the mountain above Beirut, is more appealing, but it would place Mariades well to the south of his other area of operation, which appears to have been Cappadocia. Fehr's reading also appealed to Rzach, who approved it in his *RE* article (iiA. 2159), and Kurfess, 'Zu den *Oracula Sibyllina*', p. 80. For parallels cf. 5. 362 πόλεμος καὶ ἐπίκλοπος ἐν δολότητι; Hes. *Op.* 67 ἐν δὲ θέμεν κύνεόν τε νόον καὶ ἐπίκλοπον ἦθος; *Od.* 13. 291 κερδαλέος κ᾽ εἴη καὶ ἐπίκλοπος ὅς σε παρέλθοι. For the use of the word see West on *Op.* 67. Because Mariades was so well known, it appears that the author did not feel that he needed to include any further reference to his name here, as was also the case with Priscus in l. 61, Uranius Antoninus in l. 151;, and Odaenathus in l. 165. For this reason I see no need to assume a lacuna after l. 90, as Kurfess suggested ('Zu den *Oracula Sibyllina*', p. 80: he filled it with ὅντινα δισδεκάτη κεραίη δείκνυσι πρόδηλον). Such a postponement would also be out of keeping with the style of these texts.

90. ἐκ Συρίης προφανείς: cf. on l. 22.

ʿΡωμαῖος ἄδηλος: since we may not know Mariades' full name, it is impossible to determine what the point of this is, but the reference may only be to the fact that he had a Roman nomen and thus (as Malalas, Ammianus, and the *Historia Augusta* suggest) that he was born within the empire.

91–4. καὶ πελάσει δολίως ... θήσεις: as the author of the *Cohortatio ad Graecos* and Hesychius of Miletus reminded his readers (ch. 3 n. 56), the poems of the Sibyl were not always perfect and did not always conform well to the rules of the metre. When they came across such a passage they should not blame the Sibyl, but the scribes who had transmitted her utterances throughout the ages. The textual problems with these lines are serious and attempts to solve them do not always yield a reading that is entirely satisfactory. The least that can be said is that the style of the text here would be of the sort known to Hesychius.

91. πελάσει ... ἐς: ἐς is Alexandre's necessary correction for the ἐκ of Ω. Rzach's additional alteration of πελάσει to περάσῃ, though superficially attractive, as it might enhance the suggestion of Mariades' geographical progress, is unnecessary. It would also require the assumption that περάσει be scanned πἔρᾰσεῖ rather than πἔρᾱσεῖ, though this is certainly not a fatal objection in view of the author's other metrical liberties.

δολίως: cf. on l. 80.

93. Τύανα καὶ Μάζακα: the fate of Tyana and Caesarea-Mazaka in these years is obscure.[208] They are both known to have fallen to Sapor in 260 (*RGDS* 32), Caesarea after a stubborn resistance (Zon. 12. 23). In describing the fall of the city Zonaras included the note τὴν Καισάρειαν δὲ πολυάνθρωπον οὖσαν, περὶ τεσσαράκοντα γὰρ μυριάδας ἀνθρώπων ἐν αὐτῇ λέγεται κατοικεῖν, οὐ πρότερον εἷλον. This detail has caused a great deal of difficulty in the light of the (admittedly scant) supplementary evidence.

There are two relevant texts aside from this oracle. The first is a somewhat obscure note in the Babylonian Talmud:[209] 'when they

---

[208] J. Neusner, *A History of the Jews in Babylonia*, ii (Leiden, 1966), 45 n. 1, for a summary of the problems.

[209] Translated by Neusner, *History of the Jews*, ii. 45.

informed Samuel that King Sapor had slain 12,000 Jews in Caesarea Mazaka he did not rend his clothes . . . "And is it a fact that King Sapor killed Jews?" For King Sapor said to Samuel, May evil befall me if I have ever slain a Jew! For it was they who had brought it upon themselves, for R. Ammi said the noise of the harpstrings of Caesarea-Mazaka burst the walls of Laodicea.' The traditional date for Rabbi Sherira's death was 254/5, and this text might be taken as evidence for Persian participation in a sack of the city in the early 250s. Neusner has, however, cast serious doubt on the principles through which this date was obtained, and nothing can really be built upon it.[210] The second text is the *Historia Augusta*, which has been seen to contain some reasonable information, including the proper date for Mariades' death and the otherwise unattested (in western sources) though correct alternative form for Mariades' name, and can be made, with the aid of a simple correction, to yield the name of Sapor's eldest son.[211] Its information is therefore not to be rejected out of hand, particularly as it places a fall of Caesarea in a chronological context similar to that provided in this oracle. In view of this it would be unwise to give too much emphasis to Zonaras' statement; it is better to believe that Caesarea had been raided by Mariades in the reign of Decius.

The fact that Mariades was active in Cappadocia and Syria, as Rostovtzeff and Sprengling realized (see n. 198), makes his career appear curiously similar to that of Jotapianus as it emerges from Polemius Silvanus (see n. 127). It is impossible to judge the severity of Priscus' exactions, which Zosimus gives as the reason for the revolt (see on ll. 61–3), but oppression of this sort was scarcely a novelty, and it is difficult to see how it alone could have caused so much unrest.

The failures which preceded Alexander Severus' Persian war seem to have been followed by the emergence of Uranius (ch. 1 n. 55). It may well be that this failure, along with that of Gordian III's effort, considerably diminished the prestige of Rome in the eyes of her subjects. This is the first time since the end of Bar Kochba's revolt (given the peculiar circumstances involved with

---

[210] Ibid. 47–8.
[211] *Trig. Tyr.* 2. 2: 'Odomastem primum' is the reading of the manuscripts; Nöldeke, *Geschichte der Perser und Araber*, p. 43 n. 2, proposed 'Oromastem', the Latinized form of Horimizd.

that outbreak, the revolt of 116/17 might be a better point to take)[212] that Rome's subjects were willing to engage in serious revolt against her authority; they were willing to do so in the same part of the empire four times within four decades.

93. **πιέσει πολέμου ἀκόρητος:** this is Rzach's proposal for Ω's *πέσεται πολέμου ἀκόρητος*. Alexandre accepted Ω's reading as it stood, Geffcken obelized because it is clear from the fate suffered by Tyana and Mazaka in lines 93–4 that the subject of these lines— Mariades—did not fall, and because it makes no grammatical sense after *πολιορκήσας*. This is perfectly reasonable, but he would have done better to print Rzach's admirably simple alteration of *πέσεται* to *πιέσει* as it certainly achieves the appropriate sense— that the Cappadocians will come to some harm.

94. **λατρεύσεις ⟨θ᾽ οὕτω τε⟩ ὑπὸ ζυγὸν αὐχένα θήσεις:** Ω has *λατρεύσεις τούτῳ δὲ πολύζυγον αὐχένα θήσει*. Alexandre printed the text almost as it stands in the manuscripts (he read *θήσῃ* for *θήσει*), though he observed in a note that *ὑπὸ ζυγὸν αὐχένα* (cf. 8. 126; 11. 67, 76; 14. 308) could be read at the end of the line and translated 'victor iura dabit, colloque iugum accipietis herile'. Rzach proposed *λατρεύσεις, δεινὸν δὲ πάλιν ζυγὸν αὐχένι θήσῃ*, and Geffcken printed *λατρεύσεις, τούτῳ δὲ ὑπὸ ζυγὸν αὐχένα θήσεις*. All of these avoid the main problem, that of reading *λατρεύσεις* after *ἔσσεθ᾽ ἅλωσις* without a full stop or a connective. This may be solved by the simple alteration of *τούτῳ* to *θ᾽ οὕτω* and by emending *δὲ* to *τε*, which produces the sense required in the line.

96. **Σεληναίη ... ἱερὸν ἄστυ:** Alexandre was uncertain which city was being referred to here, though he considered Seleucia on the Tigris a possibility. This was taken up by Terry in his note on the passage and the matter has been left at that since. This is unfortunate. The person involved in the ruin which Selene will not prevent is clearly to the west of the Euphrates (l. 95), while *ἱερὸν ἄστυ* suggests that the city in question was of religious significance. The location to the west of the Euphrates rules out Carrhae, the most obvious candidate for special lunar protection, but Selene does

not evoke the famous moon-god of that city, Sin, and the description of the city itself suggests an obvious alternative. It looks like a play on Hierapolis, and Hierapolis lay on the main route to the Euphrates from Antioch (see on ll. 97, 129–30). According to Lucian (*D. Syr.* 34), statues of the sun and moon stood on the left side of the entrance to the temple of Atargetis at Hierapolis. The goddess herself could be identified with the moon—as seems to have been the case when Antiochus IV simulated a marriage between himself and Diana there—and was often represented with a variety of astral images, including a crescent, which assisted the identification: Gran. Licin. 28. 6 'Asturcone pompam agebat' [Antiochus IV] et se simulabat Hieropoli Dianam ducere uxorem'; see further Luc. *D. Syr.* 4; G. Goossens, *Hierapolis de Syrie: Essai de monographie historique* (Leuven, 1943), 66; R. A. Oden, *Studies in Lucian's* De Dea Syria (Missoula, 1977), 47–108, 146. This may explain why Selene was picked out as the city's defender. For the form of the prophecy here see on ll. 67–72.

97. περιφεύξ᾿ ἀνὰ Σούρην: Q has περιφυξανασέλγην, V has περιφυξανασέλγειν. Various attempts have been made to render this line sensible. Both a main verb and then either the name of a place through which the fugitive can pass on his way out of Syria or some phrase to describe the flight in more general terms should be restored here. Alexandre offered περιφῦσαν ἀνάγκην; Rzach had προφύγῃσιν ἀσελγής; Hartel had περὶ φύσιν ἀσελγῆ; and Geffcken canvassed the geographically impossible περιφεύξ᾿ ἀνὰ Σέλγην.

Soura was the junction between the road south along the Euphrates from Samosata (through Zeugma, Aroudia, Europos, Caecilia, Bethmaria, Gere, Dpara, Ourima, Eraginza, Barbalissos, Athis, and Alalis) with the road north from Damascus through Palmyra. At Caecilia the northern road was joined by that from Antioch through Chalkis, Beroia, Batna, and Hierapolis (details in Honigmann, *RE* iiiA. 1657–8, 1663–8). It is therefore the natural place for someone to pass through who was heading from Cappadocia or western Syria to Persia. Unlike the solutions proposed by editors other than Geffcken, it requires only a slight palaeographic alteration.

100. ἰοβόλοις: this word is used to describe the Persians and Parthians more often than any other adjective in the oracles: see ll. 120, 164, 168 below; *Orac. Sib.* 12. 40, 14. 66, 81; cf. 14. 68.

100–2. τότε κοίρανος Ἰταλιητῶν . . . ἐάσας: the absence of
detail about the campaigns leading up to Decius' final defeat near
Abrittus, possibly the modern Abtat Kalessi in Rumania, and the
revolts against him in the first few months of 251 is striking after
the extended treatment given to Mariades.[213] A review of the rather
confused evidence for these events will be useful for an assessment
of the author's ignorance; it will also be useful in more general
terms to re-examine the connections between the various disasters
which beset a significant area of the Roman empire at this period.[214]

The literary evidence for the last few months of Decius' life, provided by Aurelius Victor, Ammianus, Jordanes, George, Zonaras,
Zosimus, and a letter of Cyprian, does not yield a lucid chronological account, and any attempt at chronology can have only one
roughly fixed point. This is the date of the battle on the Abrittus, in
which Decius died—though even here there has been some dispute.

J. Schwartz attempted to arrange the imperial chronology for the
years between the death of Philip and the murder of Gallienus on
the basis of dates given by the chronographer of 354 (slightly
emended when it suited his purpose), so that Decius' *dies imperii* is
7 September 249, and the date of his death 24 March 251; so that
Gallus ruled from 24 March 251 until 1 August 253; Aemilianus
from 1 August 253 until 27 October of the same year; and Gallienus from 27 October 253 until 23 September 268.[215] This does
not conform with the other evidence for Decius' death, and if one
of his dates falls they all do.

The most important evidence for the time of Decius' death is
provided by two Italian inscriptions. The first of these (*CIL* vi.
31129) reads 'COL : V : ID : IUN | DD : NN : DECIO : AUG : III : ET | DECIO .
AUG : COS' showing that Decius' death was unknown at Rome on
9 June. The second text (*CIL* vi. 36760) runs 'DEDIC : VIII : KAL : IUL |
DIVO DECIO : III : ET | DIVO : HERENNIO : COS . . .', showing that his
death was known in Rome by 24 June. The date of the Abrittus is
thus not likely to have been as early as March, and more probably, as

---

[213] For the location of the battle see Demougeot, *La Formation*, p. 412.

[214] The basic treatments of these years remain those of Wittig, *RE* xv. 1269–76, and
Demougeot, *La Formation*, pp. 404–13; both date the fall of Philippopolis to 250.

[215] J. Schwartz, 'Chronologie du IIIe s. p.c.', *ZPE* 24 (1977), 170–3; Lafaurie, 'Chronologie impériale', pp. 142–3, also based his chronology on the Chronographer and obtained
a date of 28 August for Decius' death.

Stein realized, in late May or early June.[216] This date has some important implications, for much befell in the context of Decius' last campaign, and three winter months would be a short and improbable span to allow. The addition of May and April makes it just conceivable.

Wittig wished to find a second fixed point in a letter of Cyprian.[217] After the death of Decius, Cyprian wrote a long tract to Antonianus about the Novatian heresy in which he had occasion to reflect upon the courage of Cornelius, who had become bishop of Rome during March 251: 'cum multo patientius et tolerabilius audiret levari adversus se aemulum principem quam constitui Romae Dei sacerdotem' (*Epp.* 55. 9). Wittig saw a reference here to Julius Valens Licinianus.[218] This is possible, but the use of the imperfect subjunctive 'audiret' does not make it a very attractive criterion for dating the revolt. It is best not to press the point, even though the other evidence for Valens' revolt does suggest that it occurred at about this time.

So much for the date. It is time now to turn to the events. First and foremost there is the evidence provided by George, citing Dexippus as follows (pp. 705–6 = Mosshammer, p. 459 = *FGrH* 100, fr. 22; for another problem with this passage see on ll. 141–4):

Σκύθαι περαιωθέντες οἱ λεγόμενοι Γότθοι τὸν Ἴστρον ποταμὸν ἐπὶ Δεκίου πλεῖστοι τὴν Ῥωμαίων ἐπικράτειαν κατενέμοντο. οὗτοι τοὺς Μυσοὺς φεύγοντας εἰς Νικόπολιν περιέσχον· Δέκιος δὲ ἐπελθὼν αὐτοῖς ὡς Δέξιππος ἱστορεῖ, καὶ τρισμυρίους κτείνας ἐλαττοῦται κατὰ μάχην, ὡς καὶ τὴν Φιλιππόπολιν ἀπολέσαι ληφθεῖσαν ὑπ᾽ αὐτῶν καὶ Θρᾷκας πολλοὺς ἀναιρεθῆναι. ἐπανιοῦσι δὲ Σκύθαις ἐπὶ τὰ σφέτερα ὁ αὐτὸς Δέκιος ἐπιθέμενος ἀναιρεῖται ἐν Ἀβρύτῳ, τῷ λεγομένῳ φόρῳ Θεμβρωνίῳ, σὺν τῷ παιδὶ λίαν

---

[216] 'Zur Chronologie der römischen Kaiser', pp. 42–3, 50.

[217] *RE* xv. 1272; for a reasonable doubt see *PIR* ² J 610.

[218] *PIR* ² J 610; Barbieri, *Albo*, pp. 406–7 n. 19; Stein, *RE* x. 845, canvassing the notion that he has in fact been confused with Decius' younger son C. Valens Hostilianus Messius Quintus—though the fact that the main sources for his revolt (if Victor and the epitomator can be called that) are both aware that Hostilianus reigned briefly with Gallus (see on l. 104) makes this less likely, as does the fact that these authors give elements of his name which have no connection with Hostilianus. For a full discussion of the possibilities (oddly including Uranius Antoninus, who is impossible) see Clarke, *Letters of St. Cyprian*, iii. 178–80.

οἰκτρῶς ὁ θεόμαχος. Useful though it is as a summary which can be traced directly to a third-century author, this passage is not without its difficulties. The passive ἐλαττοῦται suggests that τρισμυρίους κτείνας, which has bothered a number of scholars,[219] is an excessively abbreviated summary of the action: it may preserve a figure for total losses, or mean 'despite killing thirty thousand of the enemy', or conceal a statement to the effect that he killed thirty thousand of his own men.[220] The justification for reading the passage as an abbreviated reference to a Roman defeat is that the battle mentioned here is manifestly the same as one described by Jordanes (who had a source that knew Dexippus)[221] in which a great part of Decius' army is said to have been slaughtered in a surprise attack at Beroia.[222] This defeat was followed by the revolt of T. Iulius Priscus[223] and the destruction of Philippopolis. The rough

---

[219] B. Rappaport, *Die Enfälle der Goten in das römische Reich* (Leipzig, 1899), 40 (he does not give a firm date for the event). Wittig, *RE* xv. 1271; Demougeot, *La Formation*, p. 411. Müller translated as follows: 'impressione in eos facta, etsi triginta millia occidit, nihilominus proelio inferior discessit' (*FHG* iii. 674, fr. 16).

[220] For problems of this sort see in general Brunt, 'On Historical Fragments and Epitomes'. Not only has the argument been altered here. The epitomator has clearly added the description of Decius as ὁ θεόμαχος. On the other hand, Dexippus does seem to be responsible for the error which made Volusianus a son of Decius rather than of Gallus; see on l. 142.

[221] *FGrH* 100 F 30.

[222] Jord. *Get.* 102–3 'cuius secessu Decius imperator cognoscens et ipsius urbis ferre subsidium gestiens iugum Hemi montis transacto ad Beroam venit. ibique dum equos exercitumque lassum refoveret, ilico Cniva cum Gothis in modum fulminis ruit, vastatoque Romano exercitu imperatorem cum pauculis, qui fugere quiverant, ad Eusciam rursus trans Alpes in Mysia proturbavit, ubi tunc Gallus dux limitis cum plurima manu bellantium morabatur; collectoque tam exinde quam de Usco exercitu, futuri belli se parat in acie. (103) Cniva vero diu obsessam invadit Philoppopolim praedaque potitus Prisco duce qui inerat sibi foederavit quasi cum Decio pugnaturum.'

[223] *PIR*² i. 489; Barbiera, *Albo*, Nos. 1610, 1706, seems excessively cautious in distinguishing the governor of Macedonia in 250, T. Iulius Priscus (attested on *IGrB* 2009), from the usurper in Macedonia in 251 merely because the praenomen Lucius appears in Aurelius Victor. It is more likely that either the manuscripts or Victor were wrong. T. Iulius Priscus is likely to be the addressee of the letter of Decius in Dexippus' *Skythika* (*FGrH* 100 F 26. 3), which is datable to either 250 or 251. G. Walser, in his otherwise valuable essay on the problems faced by the empire in the 3rd cent., asserts that Priscus was the 'advocate' of Gothic confederates and that he 'based his usurpation against Decius on the power of the barbarian confederates' ('The Crisis of the Third Century A.D.: A Re-Interpretation', *Bucknell Review*, 13 (1965), 5–6). There is no evidence for this in the sources, which make it quite clear that a Gothic invasion preceded the elevation of Priscus by some time. For discussion of the letter of Decius in Dexippus see ch. 2 n. 58 above.

date for the fall of the city is provided by Zosimus' statement that Gallus allowed the Goths to take the prisoners captured at Philippopolis back across the Danube with them after his accession.[224] It is not likely that they would have been waiting around with their prisoners in Roman territory for long, and the site of the final battle in the Dobrudja suggests that they were in fact heading home when Decius caught up with them; this is also in line with Dexippus' statement that Decius attacked the Goths when they were 'returning to their own territory' after the capture of the city.

The fall of Philippopolis, the battle of Beroia, and the revolt of Priscus all belong in the context of the same campaign, that of 251. Aurelius Victor adds another problem: 'simulque per eos dies Lucio Prisco, qui Macedonas praesidatu regebat, delata dominatio, Gothorum concursu postquam direptis Thraciae plerisque illo pervenerant. qua causa Decio quam potuit maturrime Roma digresso Julius Valens cupientissimo vulgo imperium capit. verum utrique mox caesi, cum Priscum nobilitas hostem patriae censuisset' (*De Caes*. 29. 2–3). This Valens also appears in Polemius Silvanus' note on the usurpers of the period: 'sub quo [Decius] Priscus in Macedonia et Valens Romae tyranni fuerunt' (40); in the *Epitome de Caesaribus* 'huius temporibus Valens Licinianus imperator effectus est' (29. 5); and, obliquely, in the *Historia Augusta*.[225]

The sack of Philippopolis should not be placed at too great an interval before the battle of Abrittus—April or May at the latest—and it was coincidental with the revolt of Priscus, which in turn suggests that the obscure Valens attempted to seize power in the same months. The initial defeat at Beroia may fall in February or March 251, as Decius will have needed some time to recoup his losses before engaging the Goths again in May or June.

[224] Zos. 1. 24. 2 καὶ τοὺς αἰχμαλώτους, οἳ μάλιστα τῶν εὐπατριδῶν ἦσαν, ἐνεδίδου κατ᾽ ἐξουσίαν ἀπάγειν, ὧν οἱ πλείους ἐκ τῆς ἐν Θρᾴκῃ Φιλιππουπόλεως ἁλούσης ἔτυχον εἰλημμένοι.

[225] *v. Tyr. trig*. 20 'et bene venit in mentem, ut, cum de hoc Valente loquimur, etiam de illo Valente, qui superiorum principum temporibus interemptus est, aliquid diceremus. nam huius Valentis, qui sub Gallieno imperavit, avunculus magnus fuisse perhibetur, alii tantum avunculum dicunt'. The reference is to a Valens (*PLRE*, s.v. Valens 2; *PIR* V 7) who is alleged to have rebelled against Gallienus *c*. 260–2. Not everyone believes that he existed: thus H. Peter, 'Die römischen sogennanten Dreissig Tyrannen', *Königliche sächsische Gesellschaft der Wissenschaften*, 27 (1909), 215; J. F. Gilliam, 'Ammianus and the *Historia Augusta*: The Lost Books and the Period 117–285', *BHAC 1970* (Bonn, 1972), 141; contrast R. Syme, *Ammianus and the* Historia Augusta (Oxford, 1968), 54; Clarke, *Letters of St. Cyprian*, iii. 179.

The string of disasters which befell Decius and the Roman empire in short succession may be taken as evidence for his supreme bad luck or his supreme incompetence. Certainly the attack on the Goths at Abrittus appears to have been the result of a terrible miscalculation.[226] Neither of these possibilities made much impression on later tradition, which was more interested in his persecution of the Christians; an interest which may in great measure be due to these catastrophes: as a 'persecutor' Decius was getting what he deserved, yet another illustration of the power of God. As Lactantius put it, 'protinus contra deum coepit, ut protinus caderet' (*DMP* 4. 3), and when he died his body 'exutus ac nudus, ut hostem dei oportebat, pabulum feris ac volucribus iacuit'. More significant for present purposes is that the various events outlined in this note did not stir the author of these lines to comment upon them.

102. ὃν κόσμον ἐάσας: this is printed by Geffcken, as it is a simple correction for Ω's οὐ κόσμον ἐάσας. Rzach felt the need to provide some sort of explanation for the action in the previous line, and came up with πότμον ἀναπλήσας. It is a nice idea, but palaeographically difficult and unnecessary as the text (with Geffcken's slight change) makes sense as it stands.

The brevity of this description of Decius' end is somewhat unusual. Ordinarily some space is given to explaining the reasons for a ruler's death (cf. ll. 14, 80, 144; *Orac. Sib.* 12. 145–6, 175, 185–6, 204–5), though it is not an absolute rule (see *Orac. Sib.* 14. 125). The brevity of the treatment of this event reflects the author's fundamental lack of interest in matters beyond his immediate area.

ἐπὶ δ' αὐτῷ παῖδες ὀλοῦνται: Decius had two sons, Q. Herennius Etruscus Messius Decius[227] and C. Valens Hostilianus Messius Quintus.[228] The former appears to have become Caesar by 8 June 250, the latter was Caesar along with his brother by 1 December of the same year.[229] Both received grants of the tribunician power with their enhanced status. In the next year Herennius Etruscus was consul with his father and elevated to Augustus; his brother reigned briefly after the battle of Abrittus (see

---

[226] See above, p. 13.   [227] Wittig, *RE* xv. 1284–5; *PIR*² H 106.

[228] Wittig, *RE* xv. 1285; *PIR* V 8.

[229] The dates are secured by *CJ* 7. 32. 3 headed merely 'Imp. Decius A.' on 28 Mar. 250; ibid. 5. 12. 9, headed 'Imp. Decius A. et Decius C.' on 8 June; and ibid. 3. 22. 2, headed 'Imp. Decius A. et Decius et Quintus CC.' See also Wittig, *RE* xv. 1261.

on l. 104). To judge from the way they were depicted on coins, both were under twenty (see Figs. 10–11). There is some confusion as to when Herennius Etruscus died. Ammianus recorded simply 'ceciderunt dimicando cum barbaris imperatores Decii pater et filius' (31. 5. 16). The same information is provided by George (*FGrH* 100 F 22, cited above on ll. 100–2) and Zonaras,[230] but not by Zosimus. Aurelius Victor and Jordanes tell us that he was killed in an earlier engagement.[231] This provided an occasion to reflect upon the noble, almost Republican, virtue of the elder emperor, and there is not likely to have been much more to it than that. It is of interest merely as an illustration of the sort of distortion to which the tradition about Decius was prone.

If these lines are taken literally, it would appear once again that their author, though well informed about events in the eastern part of the empire, was very seriously ignorant of events elsewhere. This is even more odd as Hostilianus (see on ll. 105, 142) was briefly recognized in the east along with Gallus, and the plural παῖδες is therefore clearly wrong.

103–144 The Reign of Gallus (AD 251–253)

103. γ' ἄλλος: V gives γάλλος, Q has γ' ἄλλος. Rzach was the first to print Q's reading. Geffcken accepted this, but it has been challenged by Olmstead, Manni, and Baldus.[232] The challenge should be ignored. ἄλλος often appears with an adversative particle in passages where a new ruler is introduced: cf. *Orac. Sib.* 5. 46 μετ' αὐτὸν δ' ἄλλος; 12. 48 ἄρξει δ' αὖ μετέπειτ' ἄλλος; 12. 187 (a parallel to this passage) μετά γ' ἄλλος; 14. 149 ἄλλος δ' αὖτ' ἄρξει; 14. 195 ἄλλοι δ' αὖ μετέπειτα πάλιν κρατεροὶ

---

[230] Zon. 12. 20.

[231] Aur. Vict. *De Caes.* 29. 5 'sed Deciorum mortem plerique illustrem ferunt; namque filium audacius congredientem cecidisse in acie; patrem autem, cum perculsi milites ad solandum imperatorem multa praefarentur, strenue dixisse detrimentum unius militis parum videri sibi'; Jord. *Get.* 103 'venientesque ad conflictum ilico Decii filium sagitta saucium crudeli funere confodiunt. quod pater animadvertens licet ad confortandos animos militum fertur dixisse: "nemo tristetur: perditio unius militis non est rei publicae deminutio", tamen, paterno affectu non ferens, hostes invadit, aut mortem aut ultionem fili exposcens, veniensque ad Abritto Moesiae civitatem circumseptus a Gothis et ipse extinguitur.'

[232] Olmstead, 'The Mid-Third Century', p. 400; Baldus, *Uranius Antoninus*, p. 240 (with hesitation); E. Manni, 'Note valeriane', *Epigraphica*, 11 (1947), 14.

πολεμισταί (contrast *Orac. Sib.* 11. 224, 12. 78, 117, 147, 14. 21, 163). The reading of Q is additionally attractive as the use of the standard form of introduction provides a play on the name of the emperor C. Vibius Trebonianus Gallus in the oblique way that is common in oracular texts: cf. *Orac. Sib.* 5. 46–7 μετ᾽ αὐτὸν δ᾽ ἄλλος ἀνάξει | ἀργυρόκρανος ἀνήρ· τῷ δ᾽ ἔσσεται οὔνομα πόντου = 12. 163–4 (Hadrian); 12. 269–70 ἔνθ᾽ ὅτε νηπίαχος Καῖσαρ σὺν τῷ βασιλεύσῃ | τοὔνομ᾽ ἔχων βριαροῖο Μακηδονίοιο ἄνακτος (Alexander Severus); Luc. *Alex.* 11 ἀνδρὸς ἀλεξητῆρος ὁμωνυμίην τετράκυκλον; Heliod *Aeth.* 2. 35. 5 τὴν χάριν ἐν πρώτοις αὐτὰρ κλέος ὕστατ᾽ ἔχουσαν | φράζεσθ᾽, ὦ Δελφοί, τόν τε θεᾶς γενέτην (playing on Theogenes and Charis); Robert, *Documents de l'Asie mineure méridionale*, 92. 1–2 Πάμφυλοι Συεδρῆες ἐπίξυν[ον πάτριόν τ]ε | ναίοντες χθόνα παμμιγέων; see further K. Buresch, 'Pseudosibyllinisches', *RM* NS 47 (1892), 341.

Little is known of Trebonianus Gallus before he became emperor in June 251 (for the date see on ll. 100–2), at which point he was probably legate of *Moesia Inferior*.[233] He has been born of a family which obtained curial status at Perusia by the time of Antoninus Pius at the latest[234] and had married Afinia Gemina Baebina, who died or was divorced before his proclamation.[235] For the story that he betrayed Decius at the battle of Abrittus see next n.

The play on Gallus' name can also be read as a suggestion that he was a gallus (a eunuch priest of Cybele). Geffcken used this point, along with the generally negative picture of his reign in the lines that follow, to argue that the author was a Christian. He noted that

[233] Barbieri, *Albo*, No. 1759; A. Stein, *Die Legaten von Moesien* (Budapest, 1950), 103; Hanslik, *RE* viiiA. 1985; J. Fitz, 'Die Vereinigung der Donauprovinzen in der Mitte des 3. Jahrhunderts', *Studien zu den Militärgrenzen Roms* (Cologne, 1967), 113–21; id., *Les Syriens à Intercisa* (Brussels, 1972), 119, suggested that the Danubian provinces were united under a single official from the reign of Philip through that of Valerian. While the evidence from Philip's reign supports this notion, the other cases for such appointments that he adduces do not. Odaenathus (see on l. 171 below) was exceptional, and Postumus, who he suggests commanded the legions in all the Rhine provinces before his revolt, did not (*PIR*² C 466; *PLRE*, p. 720; Barbieri, *Albo* No. 1504; König, *Die gallischen Usurpatoren*, p. 53). Fitz's assumptions about Aemilianus (see on l. 143), Ingenuus, and Regalianus are not supported by any evidence.

[234] *CIL* xi. 1930, 1931, show that Perusia became Colonia Vibia Augusta under Gallus; for the family see *CIL* xi. 1926; Hanslik, *RE* viiiA. 1985. For a good summary of the reign see Clarke, *The Letters of St. Cyprian*, iii. 1–4.   [235] *PIR*² A 439.

Zonaras records that Gallus was a persecutor and suggested on the basis of this that the author's attitude was a reflection of that persecution (*Comp. u. Ent.*, p. 59). Zonaras' statement is not supported by third-century evidence, and Clarke has shown, on the basis of a careful analysis of the relevant texts, that there was no imperial edict proclaiming such a persecution (*Letters of St. Cyprian*, iii. 4–17).

104. ἀκατάστατα ἔθνεα ἔλξῃ: Q has ἀκατάστατα ἔθνεα ἔλθῃ; V has ἀκατάστατ᾽ ἔθνη ἔλθῃ. Alexandre understood ἀκατάστατα ἔθνεα as a nominative and punctuated with a comma after ἔλθῃ, thus giving καὶ τότε Ῥωμαίοις ἀκατάστατα ἔθνεα ἔλθῃ, | οὖλος Ἄρης σὺν παιδὶ νόθῳ ἐπὶ τείχεα Ῥώμης, which is not very attractive because it leaves οὖλος Ἄρης without a verb, and he was forced to offer 'surgent infestae Romanis undique gentes, | Marte fero cum prole notha Romana petente | moenia' as a translation. Rzach proposed ἔθνε᾽ ἐπέλθῃ, which is liable to the same criticism as Alexandre's proposal. Geffcken proposed ἔλξῃ in a note though he left it out of his text and obelized ἔλθῃ. He should have had more confidence in his idea as it yields reasonable sense (that οὖλος Ἄρης is responsible for bringing the disorderly races against Rome), and it should be adopted. Although in classical Greek ἕλκω has the sense of forceful and hostile dragging or simply that of mechanical hauling (LSJ, s.v.), it can have the more neutral sense of 'bringing' in the Septuagint, Gospels, and later imperial writers (Bauer, s.v.).

The association of the Ares in l. 105 with the 'bastard son' shows up again in l. 142 in a context that ensures that he must be identified as Gallus' son Volusianus. The action that is alluded to here as 'bringing the disorderly races' against the empire (for the meaning of τείχεα Ῥώμης see ad loc.) is not likely to be the treaty which Gallus made after Abrittus, in which he allowed the Goths to leave Roman territory with their booty and with the promise of an annual subsidy.[236] It is hard to see how this would have appeared to be 'bringing' these people against Rome. On the other hand, it makes a good deal of sense as an allusion to the story that Gallus betrayed Decius at the battle of Abrittus.

[236] The terms are given by Zon. 12. 21 κρατήσας τοίνυν τῆς τῶν Ῥωμαίων ὁ Γάλλος ἀρχῆς, σπένδεται τοῖς βαρβάροις ἐπὶ συνθήκαις τοῦ λαμβάνειν ἐκείνους παρὰ Ῥωμαίων δασμὸν ἐνιαύσιον καὶ μὴ τὰ Ῥωμαίων ληΐζεσθαι.

The tradition concerning the disaster in which Decius died is confused in the extreme. Dexippus (*FGrH* 100 F 22, cited on ll. 101–2) did not mention Gallus' treason (or at least not as he is preserved by George). Neither did Jordanes, Eutropius,[237] the Epitomator,[238] or Ammianus.[239] Lactantius merely says that he was killed by the Goths and his body was devoured by animals as just retribution for his persecution of the Christians. Aurelius Victor places the battle across the Danube and attributes the defeat to the treachery of Brutus.[240] Zosimus puts the battle on the Tanais, which he seems to have confused with the Danube, as he appears to have thought that it was the border of Roman territory when he records that the Goths crossed that river and ravaged Thrace.[241] He tells us that Decius gave Gallus a force with which to guard the crossing of the Tanais while he himself attacked the Goths. Gallus made a deal with those barbarians, suggesting that they divide themselves into three groups by a marsh and await the emperor. After Decius had defeated the first two sections and was in the swamp, Gallus gave a signal to the third section of the Goths and they destroyed the Roman army.[242] Zonaras merely says

---

[237] *Brev.* 9. 4 'cum biennio imperassent ipse et filius, uterque in barbarico interfecti sunt.'

[238] *Epit. de Caes.* 29. 3 'in solo barbarico inter confusas turbas gurgite paludis submersus est, ita ut nec cadaver eius potuerit inveniri. Filius vero eius bello exstinctus est.'

[239] 31. 5. 16.

[240] *De Caes.* 29. 4 'Decii barbaros trans Danubium persectantes Bruti fraude cecidere exacto regni biennio.'

[241] 1. 23. 1 τῶν δὲ πραγμάτων διὰ τὴν Φιλίππου περὶ πάντα ἐκμέλειαν ταραχῆς πληρωθέντων, Σκύθαι τὸν Τάναϊν διαβάντες ἐλήϊζοντο τὰ περὶ τὴν Θρᾴκην χωρία.

[242] 1. 23. 2–3 Γάλλον δὴ ἐπιστήσας τῇ τοῦ Τανάϊδος ὄχθῃ μετὰ δυνάμεως ἀρκούσης αὐτὸς τοῖς λειπομένοις ἐπῄει· χωρούντων δὲ τῶν πραγμάτων αὐτῷ κατὰ νοῦν, εἰς τὸ νεωτερίζειν ὁ Γάλλος τραπεὶς ἐπικηρυκεύεται πρὸς τοὺς βαρβάρους, κοινωνῆσαι τῆς ἐπιβουλῆς τῆς κατὰ Δεκίου παρακαλῶν· ἀσμενέστατα δὲ τὸ προταθὲν δεξαμένων, ὁ Γάλλος μὲν τῆς ἐπὶ ⟨τῇ⟩ τοῦ Τανάϊδος ὄχθῃ φυλακῆς εἴχετο, οἱ δὲ βάρβαροι διελόντες αὑτοὺς τριχῇ διέταξαν ἔν τινι τόπῳ τὴν πρώτην μοῖραν, οὗ προβέβλητο τέλμα. (3) τοῦ Δεκίου δὲ τοὺς πολλοὺς αὐτῶν διαφθείραντος, τὸ δεύτερον ἐπεγένετο τάγμα· τραπέντος δὲ καὶ τούτου, ἐκ τοῦ τρίτου τάγματος ὀλίγοι πλησίον τοῦ τέλματος ἐπεφάνησαν· τοῦ δὲ Γάλλου διὰ τοῦ τέλματος ἐπ' αὐτοὺς ὁρμῆσαι τῷ Δεκίῳ σημήναντος, ἀγνοίᾳ τῶν τόπων ἀπερισκέπτως ἐπελθών, ἐμπαγείς τε ἅμα τῇ σὺν αὐτῷ δυνάμει τῷ πηλῷ καὶ πανταχόθεν ὑπὸ τῶν βαρβάρων ἀκοντιζόμενος μετὰ τῶν συνόντων αὐτῷ διεφθάρη, διαφυγεῖν οὐδενὸς δυνηθέντος.

that Gallus advised the Goths to draw up their army in a swamp, and when Decius entered he, his son, and his army were destroyed.[243] The summary of Dexippus in George is too brief to allow us to ascertain just what Dexippus had written about the battle, and it was not in Jordanes' interest to play down the valour of the Goths by suggesting that Roman treason was responsible for their greatest triumph in the third century (if he even had the story in his sources). Ammianus, for what he is worth on these matters, does not seem to have known about Gallus' alleged treason. But all of this is less significant than the divergence between Aurelius Victor and the two Greek authors who tell a tale of treachery. The variation— Brutus rather than Gallus is the traitor, and a battle placed 'trans Danubium' (the Epitomator (*Epit. de Caes.* 29) offered 'in solo barbarico', but no traitor)—indicates that more than one version was available, and on the basis of what survives it cannot be proved that Zosimus and Zonaras were using a common tradition. This may be illustrated by the fate of Herennius Etruscus (see also on l. 102 ἐπὶ δ' αὐτῷ παῖδες ὀλοῦνται), for Zosimus, unlike Zonaras, has no record of his death. The fact that there could be so much confusion in the tradition—two sites for the battle (at least), two possible traitors, and two possible places for Herennius to die (when he is even remembered)—suggests that no one who wrote a history of the event was in a position to provide an authoritative account.[244] This should not be surprising.

It is highly unlikely that, if he had betrayed Decius, Gallus would have advertised the fact. It is also rather unlikely that he would have bothered to send a detailed account around the provinces or that there was any kind of official record which a historian could have used. The fact that Gallus did deal briefly with Decius' surviving

[243] 12. 20 ὁ δὲ Γάλλος ὑπέθετο τοῖς βαρβάροις, ἐπιβουλεύων Δεκίῳ, πλησίον τέλματος βαθέος ὄντος, ἐκεῖ παρατάξασθαι. οὕτω δὲ παραταξαμένων τῶν βαρβάρων καὶ τὰ νῶτα τρεψάντων ὁ Δέκιος ἐπεδίωκε· καὶ αὐτός τε σὺν τῷ υἱῷ καὶ πλῆθος τῶν Ῥωμαίων ἐνεπέπτωκε τῷ τέλματι, καὶ πάντες ἐκεῖσε ἀπώλοντο, ὡς μηδὲ τὰ σώματα αὐτῶν εὑρεθῆναι, καταχωσθέντα τῇ ἰλύϊ τοῦ τέλματος

[244] In addition to the sources discussed here and elsewhere see Amm. 31. 5. 17 'post clades acceptas illatasque multas et saevas excisa est Philippopolis, centum hominum milibus, nisi fingunt annales, intra moenia iugulatis'. The *Annales* referred to here are unknowable, but the context they provided him for the sack of Philippopolis was the reign of Gallus—or perhaps even that of Gallienus, as the Decii died in the previous section and Claudius Gothicus is the next emperor mentioned.

son, Hostilianus (see next n.), and that Decius was deified, and then that Gallus broke with Hostilianus and removed Decius' name from the *fasti* of the year,[245] as well as his treaty with the Goths, may have given rise to the story. It is a tale which should be seen as another example of the tendency described by Dio (see ch. 3 n. 141) for people who did not know what had happened to believe the worst about those in power. It is particularly striking in this case that Gallus did not suffer an official *damnatio* under Valerian, which suggests that there was no official motive for the story—the detail into which Zosimus enters in the telling of it, as was also the case with his account of Gordian III's murder, merely illustrates the range of a historian's imagination. The reference to the story in this oracle merely suggests that the story goes back to a contemporary rumour.

105. **σὺν παιδὶ νόθῳ:** Olmstead ('The Mid-Third Century', p. 400) and Geffcken (*Comp. u. Enst.*, p. 59) assume that this is a reference to C. Vibius Veldumnianus Volusianus, the son of Gallus who became Caesar at the time of his father's selection as Augustus, who appears as *princeps iuventutis* on coins and inscriptions from the summer of 251 and who became Augustus in October of the same year.[246] This may be true, but it is curious that he should be called a bastard, and the fact that he should later (l. 142) be said to have killed Gallus suggests that the author was somewhat confused as to who he was and what he did. Various explanations for this are canvassed in the n. on l. 142.

ἐπὶ τείχεα Ῥώμης: see *Orac. Sib.* 14. 165, 247, where no actual attack on the city of Rome is implied in either case; it is likely (since such an attack did not take place under Gallus' command) that the phrase should be taken figuratively here as well. For this usage cf. *Orac. Sib.* 12. 154–5 τείχη δ' Ἀσσυρίων πέσεται πολλοῖς πολεμισταῖς | καὶ πάλιν ἐξολέσει τούτους θυμοφθόρος ἀνήρ.

The reference here to the *limes* may be compared with the description of Rome as a military camp that begins to appear with the extant authors of the Antonine age: cf. App. *Praef.* 28 τήν τε ἀρχὴν ἐν κύκλῳ περικάθηνται μεγάλοις στρατοπέδοις καὶ

[245] J. F. Gilliam, 'Trebonianus Gallus and the Decii: III et I cos', in *Studi in onore di Aristide Calderini e Roberto Paribeni* i (Milan, 1956), 308–11.
[246] Hanslik, *RE* viiiA. 1996.

φυλάσσουσι τὴν τοσήνδε γῆν καὶ θάλασσαν ὥσπερ χωρίον; Arist. 26. 29, 82–4, 35. 36; Herod. 2. 11. 5 φρούρια δὲ καὶ στρατόπεδα τῆς ἀρχῆς προυβάλετο, μισθοφόρους ἐπὶ ῥητοῖς σιτηρεσίοις στρατιώτας καταστησάμενος ἀντὶ τείχους τῆς Ῥωμαίων ἀρχῆς (the person involved here is Severus). The *limes* in the imperial period came to represent the physical embodiment of the division between the 'civilized world' of the Roman empire and the 'barbarian world'. For the development of this theme in imperial literature see J. Palm, *Rom, Römertum und Imperium in der griechischen Literatur der Kaiserzeit* (Lund, 1959), 56–62 (Aelius Aristides), 76 (Appian), 83 (Herodian).

The view of the empire as an area existing within the confines provided by a line of fortifications is a radical change from earlier notions that there were *termini imperii* which it was possible to pass beyond. Cf. e.g. Tac. *Ann.* 2. 61. 2 'Exim ventum Elephantinen ac Syenen, claustra olim Romani imperii, quod nunc rubrum ad mare patescit'; 1. 11. 4 'quae cuncta sua manu perscripserat Augustus addideratque consilium coercendi intra terminos imperii, incertum metu an per invidiam'; E&J² 69. 9–11 'post consulatum quem ultra finis extremas popu|li [Ro]mani bellum gerens feliciter peregerat, bene gesta re publica, devicteis aut | in fidem receptis bellicosissimis ac maxsimis gentibus'. It is even further from earlier notions, current in the last century of the free Republic, to the effect that the potential boundary of Roman power was heaven: cf. Virg. *Aen.* 1. 278–9 'his ego non metas rerum nec tempora pono:|imperium sine fine dedi'; 286–8 'nascetur pulchra Troianus origine Caesar, | imperium Oceano, famam qui terminet astres, | Iulius, a magno demissum nomen Iulo'; for Republican views in general see P. A. Brunt, 'Laus Imperii', in P. Garnsey and C. R. Whittaker (eds.), *Imperialism in the Ancient World* (Cambridge, 1978), 168–172; W. Harris, *War and Imperialism in Republican Rome* (Oxford, 1979), 105–30. For developments in the imperial period see F. G. Millar, 'Emperors, Frontiers and Foreign Relations, 31 B.C. to A.D. 378', *Britannia*, 13 (1982), 19; D. S. Potter, 'The *Tabula Siarensis*, Tiberius, the Senate, and the Eastern Boundary of the Roman Empire', *ZPE* 69 (1987), 269–76.

106–8. καὶ τότε δὴ λιμοὶ ... ἐξαπίνης: for passages of this sort, inserted, it seems, to enhance the impression of catastrophe, see on ll. 9–12 above, and the oracles collected by Phlegon of Tralles, *FGrH* 257 F 36. ii. 8. 11–16, iii. 10. 8–16, 13. 6–9.

108. **Σύροι:** for the scansion of this word with a long first syllable see A. Rzach, *Analekta zur Kritik und Exegese der sibyllinischen Orakel* (SAWW 156; 1907), 49–50, who points out that the *Sibylline Oracles* provide a significant number of parallels for this sort of variation in the scansion of place-names. Cf. 7. 62 *Τῦρε* ~ 4. 90, 5. 455 *Τῦρος*, 4. 90, 14. 87 *Τῦρῖοι*; 14. 312 *Σῖκελῶν* ~ 5. 16, 7. 6, 12. 20 *Σῖκελιη*, 4. 80 *Σῖκελιην*; 3. 597, 14. 40, 187 *Λᾶτῖνοι* ~ 12. 34 *Λᾶτῖνων*, 8. 152, 12. 190 *Λᾶτῖνοις* ~ 3. 51, 8. 131, 14. 244, 280 *Λᾶτῖνων*, 12. 183 *Παρθῖα*. For other examples within this poem see 22, 90, 152 *Σύριης*, 119 *Σύριη*, 111 *Σύροι* but 32, 108 *Σύροι*; 49 *Μᾱκηδονιοιο*; 137 *Γαλλῖη*; note also 35, 78, 105 *Ἄρης* vs. 59 *Ἄρης*, 36 *Ἄρεα*, 146 *Ἀρηΐ*; 76 *ὑπ'*; 102 *κοσμὸν*; 157 *ἐβδόμηκοντ'*. See also Nikiprowetsky, *La Troisième Sibylle*, p. 276.

109. **ἥξει:** the third-person singular future of *ἥκω* for the first foot is quite common in oracular verse: see *Orac. Sib.* 2. 182, 183, 241, 3. 49, 60, 314, 742, 4. 76, 115, 138, 145, 5. 93, 107, 147, 157, 306, 363, 6. 11, 7. 86, 8. 37, 140, 160, 218, 310, 11. 123, 126, 146, 278, 12. 70, 103, 219; *FGrH* 257 F 36 iii. 7. 5, 10. 9, 13. 5.

μέγας χόλος Ὑψίστοιο: Rzach adduced this passage to support his belief that the author of the oracle was a Jewish monotheist (*RE* iiA. 2160–1); cf. ll. 54, 112, and above, pp. 149–50, for this problem in general. Despite the fact that *ὕψιστος* is common in the Septuagint, the Gospels, and elsewhere for Yahweh, Rzach's assumption is unnecessary. The worship of Zeus Hypsistos or merely Theos Hypsistos was widespread throughout the Greek (and if *Jupiter Exsuperantissimus* is an equivalent, the Latin) world from at least the second century BC onwards. The title had the advantage, in Nock's words, of being 'vague enough to suit any God treated as the supreme being' ('The Gild of Zeus Hypsistos', *HTR* 29 (1936), 66 = *Essays*, p. 425). His worship was as common in Syria and Palestine as it was elsewhere, and it should be no surprise that he would be invoked by an author living in that part of the world, whatever his religious sympathy. See in general Nock, 'The Gild of Zeus Hypsistos', pp. 55–71 = *Essays*, pp. 416–30.

110. **αὐτίκα . . . ἀλφηστήρων:** the prophecy concerning the destruction of Antioch in lines 125–36 indicates that the events

predicted here are those which are narrated in the events predicted here are those which are narrated in the *Res Gestae* of Sapor as his second campaign against Rome. It was a Roman defeat without parallel in the east since the invasion of Pacorus.

For chronological purposes the most important feature of this text is the care taken to put Uranius Antoninus after the accession of Aemilianus (see on ll. 150–4) in a context different from that surrounding the fall of Antioch. This would suggest that the author was thinking of a disaster that occurred before the summer of 253, and this conforms with some of the other evidence for the second invasion of Sapor.

No western source is as helpful for the reconstruction of the events of this year as this oracle. Zosimus merely records that the Persians invaded Mesopotamia (which is not strictly true: see on ll. 128–30) in the reign of Gallus and advanced as far as Antioch.[247] They captured the city, slaughtering or enslaving the inhabitants, and returned home without meeting any opposition. They could have conquered the entire east if they had not already been satisfied with the amount of their booty. Zonaras says only that there was a Persian invasion brought about by what appears to have been a civil war in Armenia and the flight of King Tiridates.[248] The *Res Gestae* of Sapor give no firm chronological data, while the information provided by the Antiochene tradition of Malalas and Ammianus has already been seen to be useless (see on ll. 89–100).

In 1937 Alföldi argued forcefully that the key to the chronology of the period lay not with the literary sources, which he rightly found to be of a rather low quality, but with the coinage.[249] He

---

[247] Zos. 1. 27. 2 Πέρσαι δὲ τὴν Ἀσίαν ἐπήεσαν, τήν τε μέσην καταστρεφόμενοι τῶν ποταμῶν καὶ ἐπὶ Συρίαν προϊόντες ἄχρι καὶ Ἀντιοχείας αὐτῆς, ἕως εἷλον καὶ ταύτην τῆς ἑῴας πάσης μητρόπολιν οὖσαν, καὶ τοὺς μὲν κατασφάξαντες τῶν οἰκητόρων τοὺς δὲ αἰχμαλώτους ἀπαγαγόντες ἅμα λείας ἀναριθμήτῳ πλήθει οἴκαδε ἀπήεσαν, πᾶν ὁτιοῦν ἴδιον ἢ δημόσιον τῆς πόλεως οἰκοδόμημα διαφθείραντες, οὐδενὸς παντάπασιν ἀντιστάντος· Πέρσαις μὲν οὖν ἐξεγένετο ῥᾳδίως τὴν Ἀσίαν κατακτήσασθαι πᾶσαν, εἰ μὴ τῇ τῶν λαφύρων ὑπερβολῇ περιχαρεῖς γεγονότες ἀσμένως ταῦτα περισῶσαι καὶ ἀπαγαγεῖν οἴκοι διενοήθησαν. The suggestion that there was no serious resistance is also false (see on ll. 150–4, 164) and is indicative of the poor quality of Zosimus' source for these events.

[248] Zon. 12. 21 ἤρξατο δ' αὖθις ἐπὶ τούτου ἡ κίνησις τῶν Περσῶν, καὶ κατεσχέθη παρ' αὐτῶν ἡ Ἀρμενία, τοῦ ταύτης βασιλέως Τιριδάτου φυγόντος, τῶν δὲ παίδων ἐκείνου προσρυέντων τοῖς Πέρσαις.

[249] Alföldi, 'Die Hauptereignisse der Jahre 253–261'.

observed that the mint of Antioch struck for Gallus (whose Antiochene issues he forbore to discuss), but not for Aemilianus or for
Valerian until his second year.[250] This phenomenon suggested to
him that there was something terribly wrong (though when the
Antiochene mint ceased to function while Valerian was still alive in
258/9 he found another solution[251]) which could only be explained
by the Persian capture of the city. His was a form of negative argument that has not been to everyone's taste, particularly not to that of
Ensslin or Honigmann and Maricq, who preferred to base their
chronologies on emendations of Malalas which could yield a date of
256, thus conforming with what they believed was the evidence for
the destruction of Dura.[252] This is obviously not acceptable and
dodges the issue raised by Alföldi's refusal to put undue weight on a
corrupt or incompetent text. As the coinage of Gallus at Antioch is
undated, it is impossible to tell when it stopped—252 is as possible
as 253—and during 253 there were two civil wars in the west as well
as a usurper at Emesa, all of which might have inhibited the striking
of imperial coinage; nor is enough known about the working of the
Antiochene mint to make a firm case to explain any break in its
operation.

It is fortunate that further evidence can be adduced from three
other sources. One of them is the thirteenth-century Arabic
chronicle of Seert.[253] Here it is stated that Sapor the son of Ardashir
invaded the country of the Romans in his eleventh year, stayed
there for some time, and destroyed many cities. In the course of

---

[250] Alföldi, 'Die Hauptereignisse der Jahre 253–261', p. 42 = *Studien*, p. 125.

[251] This being the opening of a mint at Samosata under the care of the elder Macrianus: ibid. 53, 61 = *Studien*, pp. 138, 148.

[252] Ensslin, *Zu den Kriegen*, p. 33; Honigmann and Maricq, *Recherches*, pp. 132–42; for a summary of the problem, which was found disturbing even in the time of Tillemont, see Alföldi, 'Die Hauptereignisse', p. 54 n. 23 = *Studien*, p. 138 n. 23; Downey, *History of Antioch*, pp. 587–95. The evidence from Dura has since been re-evaluated in two studies, which, though independent of each other, reach the same conclusions: that there is no firm evidence for the date of Dura's capture. It can be as early as 254 or as late as 257, though 255 and 256 are preferable conjectures. The one thing that is clear is that no conclusions about the overall chronology of the period can be based on the coin-hoards found by the Dura excavators: S. James, 'Dura-Europos and the Chronology of Syria in the 250s A.D.', *Chiron*, 15 (1985), 111–24 (esp. p. 122); D. J. MacDonald, 'Dating the Fall of Dura-Europos', *Historia*, 35 (1986), 45–68 (though he does assert that 257 was the date of the final capture and would base the chronology of the period on this conclusion).

[253] *PO* iv. (1908), 220–1; Ensslin, *Zu den Kriegen*, pp. 19–29.

these depredations he captured Valerian in the country of the
Nabataeans. Valerian fell ill from grief and died; other prisoners,
including Demetrianus—whose name the chronicle gives as Deme-
trius—the bishop of Antioch, were taken back to Persia. The
eleventh year is now known to be 252 (see above, n. 3, on the Mani
codex), but Valerian was captured in 260 (see on l. 161) and there is
no way to remove Demetrianus from Antioch before the same year.
Eusebius recorded his death after the consecration of Dionysius at
Rome on 22 July 260,[254] and the chronicle of Jerome placed the
election of Demetrianus' successor, the infamous Paul of Samosata,
in 261.[255]

Clearly two events were conflated—a serious flaw, but not one
that is without parallel (Malalas did the same thing) or one that
necessarily invalidates the date for the first invasion. This is significant, for the same date is given in the other two sources. One of
these is the so-called *Liber Caliphorum*, an eighth-century Syriac
chronicle which placed Sapor's invasion in the 563rd year of the
Seleucid era: October 251 to October 252.[256] The Arab historian
Tabari recorded that Sapor failed to take Nisibis in his eleventh
year, 252 (Nisibis notably does not figure in the list of cities taken in
the second campaign according to Sapor's *Res Gestae*, but neither
does any other place in northern Mesopotamia).[257] After his failure,
according to Tabari, Sapor had to campaign in Chorasan, something that would not be in keeping with a campaign against Syria in
his twelfth year (253).

Zonaras records that the war with Persia under Gallus began
when Tiridates II fled Armenia (cited in n. 248). It is impossible to
date this event firmly, but, as Rostovtzeff observed, it appears at the
beginning of Zonaras' account of Gallus reign, which would
suggest a date of 251/2.[258] He might also have observed that this

[254] For the date see now König, *Die gallischen Usurpatoren*, pp. 19–29.

[255] Millar, 'Paul of Samosata, Zenobia and Aurelian', pp. 5–17, for his career and dates.

[256] Ed. J. P. N. Land, *Anecdota Syriaca*, i (Leiden, 1862), 117: 'in year 563 Sapor the king
of the Persians devastated Syria and Cappadocia. In the same year the barbarians crossed the
Danube and devastated the islands' (my translation based on Land's Latin).

[257] Nöldeke, *Geschichte der Perser und Araber*, pp. 31–2; Gagé, *Montée des Sassanides*,
p. 220, gives a translation in which year 15 appears in place of year 11; the reason for this is
not given. E. Kettenhoffen, *Die römisch-persischen Kriege des 3. Jahrhunderts n. Chr. nach der
Inschrift Sahpuhrs I. an des Ka'be-ye Zartost (skz)* (Wiesbaden, 1982), 38–43.

[258] Rostovtzeff, '*Res Gestae* and Dura', p. 33. See also Toumanoff, 'The Third Century
Arsacids', p. 18; Kettenhoffen, *Die römisch-persischen Kriege*, pp. 44–6.

yields a date in line with that given by the other sources which provide one. Nor is this all.

The *Res Gestae* of Sapor explained that the King's second campaign against the Roman empire was brought about by Caesar's 'lie' concerning Armenia.[259] The great event of the campaign was the battle at Barbalissos in which 60,000 Romans were said to have been among those destroyed. The question of whether or not the number is correct is less important than the mere fact that there was a significant concentration of Roman troops on the middle Euphrates at the time of the invasion. As far as can be determined—the evidence gives reasonable grounds for inference, but nothing more—the legions on the eastern frontier of the Roman empire in the mid-third century were *IV Scythica* at Zeugma or Cyrrhus or Oresa,[260] *XVI Flavia Firma* at Samosata or Soura,[261] *III Gallica* at Danaba,[262] *XV Apollinaris* at Satala,[263] *I Parthica* at Singara,[264] and *III Parthica* at Rhesaena.[265] The muster of a substantial force drawn from these legions would take a good deal of time, and the very existence of such a force does not suggest that the Romans were taken off guard by the Persian attack. Nor, of course, can it be proved that a force of this size did not include elements drawn from other parts of the empire.

The gathering of the army which was defeated at Barbalissos suggests that Gallus had planned to undertake some sort of offensive operation. This conforms with the claim of the *Res Gestae* and the statement of Zonaras that earlier trouble in Armenia lay behind the Persian invasion.

Offensive operatïons of the sort evidently contemplated by Gallus did not usually take place without some kind of imperial presence. One antoninianus type of Antioch celebrated the *adventus*

[259] For the translation of this passage see on l. 31.

[260] Ritterling, *RE* xii. 1560–1; E. van Berchem, *L'armée de Dioclétien et la réforme constantinienne* (Paris, 1952), 27. It is impossible to trace the movements of this legion in detail.

[261] Ritterling, *RE* xii. 1560–1; van Berchem, *L'armée*, p. 27. The date at which this legion was transferred is unknown; it is last attested at Samosata under Severus Alexander and appears at Soura under Diocletian.

[262] Ritterling, *RE* xii. 1528.   [263] Ibid. 1754–5.

[264] Ibid. 1436.

[265] Ibid. 1539. A *Legio IV Parthica* appears in the *Notitia* at Circesium, but the date of its formation is unknown: Ritterling, *RE* xii. 1556; for Diocletian's activity at Circesium, which might be connected, see Amm. 23. 5. 2. A portion at least of *Legio II Parthica* was also based at Apamea: see Balty, 'Apamea in Syria', pp. 97–104.

of Gallus and four that of Volusianus.[266] None of them is dated, but the imperial titles for Volusianus indicate a date between late 251 and mid-253. An aureus type was also issued for the Caesar from the same mint, which should also be taken as a sign that his arrival was expected.[267] Both emperors were in Italy in 253 when they were killed by Aemilianus, and the Gothic invasion over the Danube in 252/3 (see on l. 137) suggests that a major campaign would not have been contemplated after 252. As Herodian observed, Roman emperors were ever more concerned to protect those provinces which bordered Italy by land than those separated from it by sea.[268] Whether or not they ever actually reached the east, and the fact that neither of them seems to have been depicted on the reliefs of Sapor suggests that the intent advertised on the coins of Antioch was never fulfilled,[269] the year 252 appears the most promising for Gallus to have contemplated action against Persia. This is convenient, as it is precisely the year 252 which is given by three sources which do not manifestly depend upon each other for Sapor's second campaign.

The evidence of these texts may receive further support from a series of ten funerary monuments discovered in the area of Apamea in Syria. J.-C. Balty has pointed out that they should all date to 252 (though only one contains a date, 21 April 252) and associates them

---

[266] *RIC* 'Gallus', Nos. 79, 214, 224*a*, *b*, *c*. It should be noted that Volusianus appears on these coins to be in his twenties or older (see Fig. 13). It may be significant that the recently discovered hoard found near Antioch, which has the characteristics of an emergency deposit (all coins are in mint condition), can be dated to 252. For details (though he contemplates a date of 253 on the basis of the literary evidence) see W. E. Metcalf, 'The Antioch Hoard of Antoniniani and the Eastern Coinage of Trebonianus Gallus and Volusian', *The American Numismatic Society Museum Notes*, 22 (1977), 71–94; id., and P. M. Walker, 'The Antioch Hoard: A Supplement', ibid. 23 (1978), 129–32.

[267] *RIC* 'Gallus', No. 227; R. Ziegler, *Städtisches Prestige und kaiserliche Politik: Studien zum Festwesen in Ostkilikien im. 2. und 3. Jahrhundert n. Chr.* (Düsseldorf, 1985), 110. Zeigler also shows that coinage for Volusianus was minted at Nicomedia, Pisidian Antioch, Anazarbus, and Augusta in Cilicia. The coins of Augusta are dated to the year 233 – 252 (summer)/253 (autumn), and he favours a date of 252 for the other issues (pp. 111–13).

[268] Herod. 6. 7. 4 οὐ γὰρ ὅμοιον ἡγοῦντο τὸν ἐκ Περσῶν κίνδυνον οἷον τὸν ἐκ Γερμανῶν· οἱ μὲν γὰρ ὑπὸ ταῖς ἀνατολαῖς κατοικοῦντες, μακρᾷ γῇ καὶ θαλάττῃ πολλῇ διῃρημένοι, τὴν Ἰταλῶν χώραν μόλις ἀκούουσι, τὰ Ἰλλυρικὰ δὲ ἔθνη στενὰ ὄντα καὶ οὐ πολλὴν ἔχοντα τὴν ὑπὸ Ῥωμαίοις γῆν, παρὰ τοσοῦτον ὁμόρους καὶ γείτονας ποιεῖ Γερμανοὺς Ἰταλιώταις.

[269] For those represented see McDermot, 'Roman Emperors in the Sassanian Reliefs', pp. 76–82.

26. Antoninianus of Volusianus, mint of Antioch (*reverse*). 'Adventus Aug.'; Volusian on horseback l., raising r. hand and holding spear. *RIC* Gallus, 214. Private collection in the Ashmolean.

with Roman preparations to fight Sapor in that year.[270] The case is extremely attractive.

A date for Sapor's invasion in 252 is most satisfactory from the point of view of the oracle. Lines 148–50 indicate a new rout of the Romans in 253. This would be unnecessary if the author meant to give the impression that the rise of Uranius Antoninus was synchronous with the sack of Antioch, and a reasonably decent command of chronology—at least by contemporary standards—was an important consideration for an author of oracular verse. The scanty supplementary evidence from Dura for this period is non-existent for 252 and indicates that life was carrying on as normal in 253.[271] Dura appears in the list of cities captured by Sapor in the second campaign.[272]

There is one other story, aside from Zonaras' statement that the dispute between Rome and Armenia was the cause for this invasion (which the *Res Gestae* of Sapor supports), to explain the Persian

[270] J.-C. Balty, 'Nouvelles données sur l'armée romaine d'orient et les raids sassanides du milieu du iiiᵉ siècle', *CRAI* (1987), 213–42, esp. pp. 229–31. The inscription reads as follows: 'Aur(elio) Basso qu⟨o⟩|dam sig(nifero) al(a)e I | Ulp(iae) ⟨C⟩ontariorum | stipendiorum | VIII vixit annos | XXVIIII (ante diem) XI kal(endas) M|aias Gallo et V|olusiano cons⟨u⟩|libus titulus p⟨o⟩|situs a Marc(o) Cot|um [*sic*] ⟨d⟩ec(urio) al(a)e c(ivium) R(omanorum?.' His analysis of the literary evidence on pp. 232–9 agrees with that offered here.

[271] Rostovtzeff, '*Res Gestae* and Dura', p. 17; although this may not be significant, as both James and MacDermot have pointed out, the evidence is not sufficient to prove much if anything and the paintings at Dura upon which Rostovtzeff based his conclusions will not bear the weight he placed on them: James, 'Dura-Europus', pp. 115–16; MacDonald, 'Dating the Fall of Dura-Europus', pp. 45–63 (his remarks, pp. 54–7, on the 'cultural mix' at Dura and the connection between this 'mix' and the Iranian style of art found there are particularly apposite).

[272] *RGDS* 17.

attack. That given with various details by Malalas, Ammianus, and the *Historia Augusta* is that Mariades persuaded Sapor that he should invade (see on ll. 89–100, 131–3). There is a parallel to this story in John of Antioch's tale that the war of Gordian III began when a governor of Syria invited the Persians to invade.[273] The tendency to emphasize personal factors also appears to lie behind Ammianus' belief that the wars of Constantius II on the eastern frontier were caused by the lies told to Constantine by Metrodorus.[274] Such views are indicative of the poor capacity for the analysis of historical causation which is typical of the later empire.

111. Σύροι Πέρσῃσι μιγέντες: a reference to Mariades' band (see on ll. 89, 122–3). The Continuator of Dio (*FHG* iv. 192 F 1 = Boissevain, *Excerpta de sententiis*, 'Petrus', fr. 157, cited in n. 203 above) mentions 'friends of Mariades' in Antioch in such a way as to suggest that he had a considerable local following and that this contributed to the fall of the city.

The route up the Euphrates taken by Sapor on this occasion (see on ll. 129–30) was highly unusual for a Persian army, though (in reverse) it was the normal route to Ctesiphon for a Roman force. In 238/9 (see above, pp. 191–2), 296, 343, 346, 348, 350, and 359 Persian armies invaded northern Mesopotamia and, with the evident exception of the campaign in 238/9 and the certain exception of that in 260, they accomplished little that was significant. On other expeditions they were prevented from accomplishing any useful objective by the punishing waste of time spent in besieging fortified cities.[275] The weakness of Roman defences on the middle Euphrates in the third century is suggested by Ammianus[276] and the ravages of Mariades attested in this oracle imply that he was right.

---

[273] *FHG* iv. 597 F 147 = De Boor, *Excerpta de insidiis*, 'John', No. 58 ὅτι ἐπειδὴ καὶ Γορδιανὸν ἔμελλε τὸ κοινὸν τοῦ βίου καταλαβεῖν τέλος, ὁ τῆς Συρίας ἡγούμενος ἐπιστέλλει τὸν Περσῶν βασιλέα τοὺς ἰδίους ὅρους ὑπερβάντα τὴν τῶν Ῥωμαίων γῆν κατατρέχειν· καὶ δεῖσθαι τῆς αὐτοῦ παρουσίας τὸν πόλεμον. Olmstead, 'The Mid-Third Century', p. 399 n. 75, understood this as a reference to Mariades.

[274] Amm. 25. 4. 3; *PLRE*, p. 601, s.v. Metrodoros 1. See further Matthews, *The Roman World of Ammianus*, pp. 135–6.

[275] Amm. 18. 5. 7; 6. 3 (Antoninus to Sapor II) 'posthabitis civitatum perniciosis obsidiis perrumperetur Euphrates ireturque prorsus, ut occupari possint provinciae fama celeritate praeventa, omnibus ante bellis, nisi temporibus Gallieni, intactae pacequae longissima locupletes'.   [276] 23. 5. 2.

The tradition that Mariades persuaded Sapor to go to war has been dismissed as ill-founded fantasy (see on l. 110), but it is not impossible that his knowledge of the region contributed to Sapor's choice of route in 252. The role of Antoninus in 359 could be adduced as a parallel, and the prominence given to the Syrians in Persian service here might be taken as evidence for their importance in Sapor's success. Another factor may have been the destruction of Roman fortifications on the middle Euphrates in the wake of Philip's treaty in 244 (see on ll. 25–7 above).

112. ἀλλ' οὐ νικήσουσι νόμους θεοκράντορι βουλῇ: this line, which is important as an indication of the author's outlook, has caused interpreters of the oracle a good deal of trouble. Alexandre translated 'sed non magna Dei dabitur convellere fata'; Terry offered 'but, controlled by the decree of power they shall not conquer laws'; and Collins gives 'but nevertheless they will not conquer by the divine decreed plan'. Geffcken adopted a suggestion by Gutschmidt and printed ἀλλ' οὐ νικήσουσιν ὅμως θεοκράντορι βουλῇ, which Olmstead ('The Mid-Third Century', p. 402) translated 'but, they will not conquer nevertheless by the almighty divine will'. Gutschmidt's proposal (even if translated rather more eloquently) is difficult to understand in this context. It would imply that although the Persians will inflict great destruction as part of a divine plan, they will not destroy the Roman empire. In view of the fact that these lines predict a major Persian victory in Syria, this would then have to imply that, although the Persians were inflicting great damage upon the Romans as part of a divine plan (the μέγας χόλος Ὑψίστοιο of 109), this same divine plan is preventing them from destroying the whole empire. This seems to me to force the sense very badly indeed. The retention of the manuscript reading allows for a somewhat easier interpretation. As it stands, the text reads in a way that is roughly parallel to the construction at Eur. *Hec.* 659–60 ἡ πάντα νικῶσ' ἄνδρα καὶ θῆλυν σποράν | κακοῖσιν. νικῶσα in this case has the same sense as νικήσουσι in the line of the oracle in question: 'surpass'. νόμους is best translated as 'things ordained', thus giving 'but they will not surpass the things ordained in the divinely wrought plan', i.e. the god did a lot worse for the Syrians than the Persians on their own could have.

θεοκράντορι βουλῇ: θεοκράντορι βουλῇ is Alexandre's improvement on the θεοκράτορι βουλῇ of Ω. Rzach (*RE* iiA.

2160–1) adduced the phrase as further evidence for the 'Jewish monotheist' he believed wrote this oracle (see on ll. 54, 109). This is clearly unnecessary, as there is nothing peculiarly monotheistic or Jewish about the notion of a divine plan; cf. A. *Ag.* 1487–8 τί γὰρ βροτοῖς ἄνευ Διὸς τέλεται; | τί τῶνδ᾽ οὐ θεόκραντόν ἐστιν;

113–18. αἲ ὁπόσοι . . . ἀπ᾽ αὐτῶν: these lines exhibit two of the more striking topoi in laments for cities or nations: the exile of a population and unfavourable comparison between the lot of the living and that of the dead. For the uses of lament forms cf. on ll. 59, 125, 131. The extensive exploitation of language appropriate to a lament throughout the description of the campaign of 252 suggests that the author was deeply and, very probably, personally affected by the events he narrates.

The amount of space given to lament for Syria and Antioch is also notable because it is without parallel in the context of the dynastic-style prophecies preserved in the present collection. Nor is this all. The structure of lines 113–36 is remarkably skilful for verse of this sort. The action moves from Syria as a whole (ll. 113–21) to Antioch in particular (ll. 122–8) and then back to Syria as a whole (ll. 129–36). Aside from the placement of the capture of Hierapolis, Beroia, and Chalkis after that of Antioch, this also corresponds very closely to the actual campaign of Sapor (cf. on ll. 131–3).

113. αἲ: the use of an exclamation at the beginning of a line is typical of laments in oracular verse and elsewhere; cf. *Orac. Sib.* 3. 303, 323, 492, 504, 4. 143, 7. 64, 13. 115, 131; M. Alexiou, *The Ritual Lament in Greek Tradition* (Cambridge, 1974), 135.

115–18. ὁπόσων . . . αὐτῶν: the notion that the living will envy the dead is a commonplace; cf. *Orac. Sib.* 2. 307; Job 3: 21; Rev. 9: 6; Lact. *DI* 7. 16. 12 'tunc orabunt deum et non exaudiet, optabitur mors et non veniet'; *Asclep.* 3. 25 'nam et tenebrae praeponentur lumini et mors vita utilior iudicabitur'. *Apoc. Elijah* 2. 32 'those who are in Egypt will weep together. They will desire death, [but] death will flee from them' (trans. Wintermute). Comparison between the living and the dead (albeit more often to the advantage of the former) is a standard feature of lament: see Alexiou, *Ritual Lament*, pp. 171–7.

119. ἄρτι δὲ σέ: for direct address of this sort in laments see on l. 59.

120. ἥξει καὶ πληγή . . . ἀνθρώπων: cf. *Orac. Sib.* 3. 314.

Spondees of this sort in the fifth foot are common, see ll. 13, 21, 28, 29, 37, 51, 58, 65, 71, 95, 110, 114, 147, 155.

122–8. ἥξει καὶ Ῥώμης ... σε κλαύσεθ᾽ ὁρῶν τις: the use of the third-person singular προλείψει in l. 127 indicates that these seven lines should be taken together and that the responsibility for the destruction of Antioch is being attributed to the φυγάς of l. 122. The problem then is with the identity of the fugitive. It is a question of some complexity, and the solution is of some significance for understanding the way in which the author interpreted the events of his own time.

In *Orac. Sib.* 4. 138–9 there is a prophecy of war coming to the west at the time of a great volcanic eruption (ll. 130–7). The prediction runs as follows: ἥξει καὶ Ῥώμης ὁ φυγάς, μέγα ἔγχος ἀείρας, | Εὐφρήτην διαβὰς πολλαῖς ἅμα μυριάδεσσιν. The fugitive in this case is Nero, who was described as being in flight across the Euphrates in lines 119–23. The volcanic eruption may readily be taken as that of Vesuvius, and the return of Nero predicted here corresponds with the appearance of the false Nero Terentius Maximus, who was reported in Asia Minor during the reign of Titus.[277] Lines 140–1 of *Orac. Sib.* 4 continue: τλήμων Ἀντιόχεια, σὲ δὲ πτόλιν οὔποτ᾽ ἐροῦσιν, | ἡνίκ᾽ ἂν ἀφροσύνῃσι τεαῖς ὑπὸ δούρασι πίπτῃς (a verbatim parallel—with the substitution of ἡνίκ᾽ ἂν for ὁππόταν—to these lines in the *Thirteenth Oracle*; similar lines were included in an oracle known to John Lydus: see on l. 59). As Antioch would be on the way to Italy from Parthia it is reasonable to see these lines in *Orac. Sib.* 4 as having been part of the prophecy about the return of Nero. The parallel between the lines in an oracle of AD 71 and lines 122–8 in this oracle is such that it seems likely that the author of the third-century text, struck by the similarity between events in his own time and those in the prophecy about Nero, incorporated into his own composition an earlier text which told of Nero's return. The tendency to reinterpret old prophecies in the light of current events is well known (nor was the tendency limited to antiquity).[278] The fact that the author should pick up a prophecy which featured a

---

[277] Syme, *Tacitus*, p. 773; J. Geffcken, 'Studien zur älteren Nerosage', *NGG* (1899), 446; E. M. Sanford, 'Nero and the East', *HSCP* 48 (1937), 99–100.

[278] See in general the exemplary study by N. Cohn, *The Pursuit of the Millennium* (London, 1957).

fugitive from Rome as the agent of Antioch's destruction, rather than a Persian, indicates that he had Mariades in mind, and that it was his activity which provided the author's inspiration.[279]

The use of a prophecy about Nero to describe activity on the part of Mariades is paralleled by the equation of individuals with those mentioned in eschatological prophecies of many sorts. The Jewish commentary on Daniel which identified Mariades, Quietus, Macrianus, and Odaenathus as horns on the second beast is an immediately contemporary case (see on ll. 89–100). A few years earlier the African Christian Lucian described Decius as 'ipsam anguem maiorem, metatorem antichristi' (Cypr. *Epp.* 22. 1).[280] A few years later Dionysius of Alexandria analysed the career of Macrianus in terms of some less than pleasant biblical prophecy: he wrote that God visited the sins of the fathers upon the children until the third or fourth generation 'in those that hate me' (Exod. 20: 5).[281] The emperor Constantine was later to write to the heretic Arius and explain to him that he was the figure who the Sibyl had predicted would cause ruin in 'Libya'.[282] During the second century the Rabbi Akhiva had helped to fan the flames of the Bar Kochba revolt by identifying that leader with the star in Num. 22: 17.[283] The legend of Nero's return itself seems to have been promoted by the uncertainty surrounding that emperor's death, which led people to believe that there might be some truth to the prophecies circulating during his reign that he would be the last emperor of Rome.[284] The

---

[279] Rzach, *RE* iiA. 2159; the notion had once been rejected by Geffcken (*Comp. u. Enst.*, p. 60 n. 2) as absurd.

[280] J. Gagé, 'Commodien et le moment millénnairiste du iiie siècle', *Rev. d'hist. et de philos. relig.* 41 (1961), 355–78, esp. pp. 357–60, for interest in Decius as the seventh persecutor and interpretation of events in 260 in the light of this—interpretations which involved the return of Nero. Cf. Bousset, *Antichrist*, p. 85, for the notion that Nero is to be identified as the Antichrist in a work of Clement.

[281] Eus. *HE* 7. 10. 7–8. The prophecy is particularly apposite in this case as Macrianus ruled through his sons, Macrianus and Quietus.

[282] Gelasius, *HE* 3. 19.

[283] Schürer, *History of the Jewish People in the Age of Jesus Christ* [2], i. 544–5; P. Schäfer, 'Rabbi Aquiva and Bar Kochba', in W. S. Green (ed.), *Approaches to Judaism*, ii (Chico, 1978), 117–19; Isaac and Oppenheimer, 'The Revolt of Bar Kokhba', pp. 57–8. Bar Kochba is said to have increased belief in his identification as a Messiah by breathing fire (Jer. *Contra Ruf.* 3. 31)—it was a trick with a long history (e.g. Diod. 34. 2, on Eunus).

[284] Dio 62. 18; Suet. *Nero*, 40. 2 'spoponderant tamen quidam destituto Orientis dominationem, nonnulli nominatim regnum Hierosolymorum, plures omnis pristinae fortunae restitutionem'; Sanford, 'Nero and the East', 83–5.

Jewish revolt of 66 and the career of Vespasian in 69 appear to have caught the imagination of contemporaries because of prophecies that a ruler for Rome would come from Judaea, which were widely known,[285] while the great revolt of 116 may have received some impetus from the severe earthquake which levelled Antioch in 115. It was an event which could have led people to believe that better things (of a supernatural sort) were soon to come and confirm various eschatological fantasies (see on l. 10 σεισμοί). The commencement of the Parthian war in 161 with various Persian successes seems to have inspired another author to predict the imminent return of Nero,[286] and in 249 Pacatianus seems to have tried to exploit the belief that something special was meant to happen at the achievement of a millennium (see on ll. 79–80).

The author's use of a prophecy about Nero to describe the activity of Mariades is not surprising, but the lack of theological subtlety in the way he did it would be if he were a Christian. For him it seems that Nero comes to life in Mariades. Christian theologians from the time of John through Commodian to Lactantius, Jerome, and Sulpicius Severus were all sure that Nero would appear *in propria persona* (or as a dragon) to provide a prelude to the second coming of Christ.[287] In this case the author seems to have

---

[285] Tac. *Hist.* 5. 13. 2 'pluribus persuasio inerat antiquis sacerdotum litteris contineri eo ipso tempore fore ut valesceret Oriens profectique Iudaea rerum potirentur'; Suet. *Vesp.* 4. 5 'percrebruerat Oriente toto vetus et constans opinio esse in fatis ut eo tempore Iudaea profecti rerum potirentur. id de imperatore Romano, quantum postea eventu paruit, praedictum Iudaei ad se trahentes rebellarunt'; Jos. *BJ* 6. 312. For further discussion see Sanford, 'Nero and the East', p. 85; R. Lattimore, 'Portents and Prophecies in Connection with the Emperor Vespasian', *CJ* 29 (1934), 445; E. Norden, 'Josephus und Tacitus über Jesus Christus und eine messianische Prophetie', *NJA* 31 (1913), 654–62.

[286] *Orac. Sib.* 8. 70–2 ὅταν γ᾽ ἐπανέλθῃ | ἐκ περάτων γαίης ὁ φυγὰς μητροκτόνος αἴθων, | ταῦτα ἅπασι διδοὺς πλοῦτον μέγαν Ἀσίδι θήσει; see Geffcken, 'Studien zur älteren Nerosage', pp. 456–7; id., *Comp. u. Enst.*, pp. 42–4. He does not attempt to date these verses as precisely as I attempt here. My reason for doing so is that the lines occur just after the introduction of Marcus Aurelius. The early events of the Persian war in 161 were decidedly unfavourable to Rome, and the invasion of Armenia by the Persian king might inspire thoughts of eschatological events. I do not agree with Geffcken that this is a specifically Christian prophecy.

[287] Rev. 13: 11–18; Lact. *DMP* 2. 7–8; Commod. *Carm. de duobus populis* 5–14, 823–36; Jer. *Epp.* 121. 12 = CSEL 56. 54, *Comm. in Dan.* 29. 30; Ser. Sulp. *Dial.* 2. 14; Bousset, *Antichrist*, pp. 79–86; Geffcken, 'Studien zur älteren Nerosage', *passim*; E. Renoir, 'Chiffre de la Bête', in *Dictionnaire d'archéologie chrétienne et de liturgie*, c. 1341–52; H. Fuchs, *Der geistige Widerstand, gegen Rom in der antiken Welt* (Berlin, 1938), 31–5; G. Walter, *Nero*, trans. E. Crawford (London, 1957), 206–2.

been content to see the fulfilment of a prophecy about Nero in the person of someone he knew was not Nero, and the only saviour he seems to have been interested in was not Christ—it was Uranius Antoninus.

122. μέγα: Mai's correction for Q's μέγας, V's μέγε. The resulting hiatus should not cause concern: the authors of such verse were themselves not adverse to it (see Rzach, 'Metrische Studien', p. 58, adducing *Orac. Sib.* 4. 138; *Od.* 22. 408 ἐπεὶ μέγα ἔσιδεν ἔργον).

129–130. καὶ σὺ θρίαμβος ... ἐπὶ τέκνοις: Chalkis, Beroia, and Hierapolis are the principal cities on the road from Antioch to the Euphrates at Barbalissos, and all three appear in the *Res Gestae* of Sapor as having been taken before the fall of Antioch in the summer of 252 (for further details see on l. 133).

καὶ σὺ θρίαμβος: cf. *Orac. Sib.* 8. 130 καὶ σὺ θρίαμβος ἔσῃ κόσμῳ καὶ ὄνειδος ἁπάντων. The meaning of θρίαμβος in both these cases seems to be 'spoil of war', which is common in later, but not classical, Greek. For the use of anaphora in laments see Alexiou, *Ritual Lament*, pp. 161–78.

130. Χαλκίδι συγκλαύσεσθε: the future middle which Alexandre printed here makes more sense than the aorist optative συγκλαύσαιτε printed by Geffcken (following a suggestion by Buresch). A lament by a city for its dead or ruined citizens is a feature of both Greek and Semitic literature, the book of Lamentation being the most extensive example. For examples in the classical tradition see Ant. Thess. 113 Gow and Page; *AP* 9. 425; Honestus 6 Gow and Page; Antonius 1 Gow and Page; Mundus 1 Gow and Page; Pompeius 2 Gow and Page; and Hartigen, *Poets and Cities*, pp. 23–30, 71–5.

131–3. αἱ ὁπόσοι ναίουσι ... καὶ Πύραμος ἀργυρο-δίνης: the geographical spread here indicates that the author was thinking of all Syria; Amanus and Casius are the two principal peaks in northern Syria, the Pyramos is in south-eastern Cilicia, the Lycus runs from Casius to the sea, and the Marsyas flows from Casius into the middle Orontes.[288] The event narrated is manifestly the campaign of 252, and the range of territory indicated by these lines is appropriate to that disaster.

The circumstances surrounding the capture of Antioch and other events after the battle of Barbalissos are difficult to establish,

---

[288] The exact stream is not now ascertainable: see Honigmann, *RE* xiv. 1985–6.

and a picture of them may only be obtained in broad outline through close examination of the *Res Gestae* of Sapor. In that text the cities taken by the Persians during 252 and 260 (for the date see on l. 155 below) are arranged by order of capture within an area of operation.[289] As one group of cities is often followed in the list by another group in a distant area, it appears that the Persian army split into a number of detachments, and that although the lists suggest consecutive actions, they in fact record a number of simultaneous operations. Thus, the cities in lines 13–15 are Soura, Barbalissos, Hierapolis, Beroia, Chalkis, Apamea, Raphanaea, Zeugma, Ourima, Gindaros, Armenaza, Seleucia, Antioch, Cyrrhus, another Seleucia, and Alexandria. Hierapolis was the junction at which the major road to south-western Syria split off from the main north–south road along the Euphrates. Beroia, Chalkis, and Apamea are all along that road as it ran down towards Raphanea, where it split to Antarados on the coast and Emesa. Zeugma and Ourima are the next two towns north of Hierapolis on the Euphrates road, while Gindaros and Arzemena are on the road south-west from Zeugma to Antioch. The first Seleucia is presumably Seleucia πρὸς Βήλῳ (Seleucobelos) in the Orontes valley on the route through Apamea from Raphanaea to Antioch.[290]

[289] Sprengling, *Third Century Iran*, p. 89; Rostovtzeff, '*Res Gestae* and Dura', p. 25; Baldus, *Uranius Antoninus*, p. 232; Kettenhoffen, *Die römisch-persischen Kriege*, p. 58.

[290] Rostovtzeff ('*Res Gestae* and Dura', p. 25) identified this first Seleucia as Seleucia Pieria. He was followed by Baldus (*Uranius Antoninus*, p. 232) and Kettenhoffen (*Die römisch-persischen Kriege*, pp. 59–61). Olmstead ('The Mid-Third Century', p. 406) identified the second Seleucia as Seleucobelos. He has been supported by Maricq and Honigmann (*Recherches*, p. 158), Baldus (*Uranius Antoninus*, p. 233), and Kettenhoffen (*Die römisch-persischen Kriege*, p. 67). This is not tenable. In order to get to Antioch, a Persian force at Raphanaea would have taken the road to the coast through Antarados and from there through Laodicea to Seleucia Pieria and Antioch or the road back through Apamea and from there up the Orontes valley. Antarados and Laodicea are not mentioned in the *Res Gestae*, which suggests that the Persians did not take the road through them. The first Seleucia is on the list before Antioch and the second is on the list before Alexandria ad Issum and Nicopolis—which precede three other cities which are south of Seleucobolos in the Orontes valley (Larissa, Epiphania, and Arethusa). Therefore, neither Seleucia was taken at the same time as the three cities on the road south from Apamea. It thus makes more sense to believe that the first Seleucia is one taken by the Persian force moving towards Antioch on the road from Apamea. Seleucia πρὸς Βήλῳ was surely the first one taken (there is even literary evidence of a sort which says so: see n. 298 below for Malalas' statement that Sapor advanced along the road from Chalcis), and the second is Seleucia Pieria, which was thus captured after the fall of Antioch (the Persians could not get there very easily anyway until Antioch had fallen).

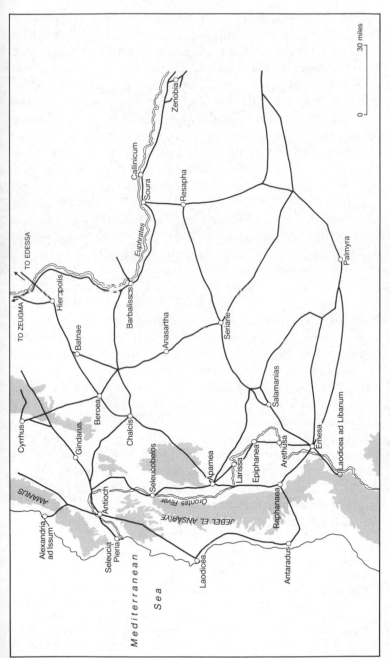

MAP 2. Central Syria in the third century AD.

In the light of the distribution of cities in the *Res Gestae* it is clear that the Persian army divided into two sections after the battle of Barbalissos. One column moved on up the Euphrates to Zeugma and then down the road from there to Antioch. This should have taken it through Cyrrhus, but Cyrrhus does not appear on the list until after Antioch. When it is listed, however, it is in isolation from other places in the vicinity, and its position may be explained by the presumption that it was besieged by a passing column but not taken until after the fall of Antioch. The other column moved south to Raphanaea after Barbalissos, initially bypassing the road from Apamea to Antioch. This is probably because Apamea was an important base at this time, like Zeugma and Cyrrhus,[291] and the initial purpose of the division of the Persian forces seems to have been to eliminate both of these Roman bases before any attempt was to be made on the provincial capital.[292] Raphanaea was an easy target after the capture of Apamea, and a post of some significance on the route which led towards the coast. The two columns seem to have rejoined at Antioch, which fell to them along with Seleucia Pieria (the 'other Seleucia' in the *Res Gestae*).

After ravaging the region around Antioch the Persian army split up once again. One group moved through Alexandria ad Issum to Nicopolis and then over Amanus to Dichor, Doliche, and Germanicia. Another group went back down the Orontes valley taking Larisa, Epiphania, and Arethusa. It is impossible to say in detail what happened next, only that other attacks resulted in the capture of Circesium and Dura as well as heavy destruction in Cappadocia.[293]

Apart from this oracle, the western sources for the events of the campaign may be divided into two categories, the useless and the obscure. Among the useless are the stories that Antioch was surprised while the citizens were at the theatre: given the extent of the campaign leading up to the fall of the city, this is incon-

---

[291] See on l. 110 above for the distribution of legions in Syria at this time.

[292] Rostovtzeff, '*Res Gestae* and Dura', pp. 25–6.

[293] Kettenhoffen, *Die römisch-persischen Kriege*, pp. 83–7, for details; though it should be noted here that the evidence for Dura is notoriously complex. The Sassanid *dipinti* from the synagogue may show that the city was occupied before March 253, but even this is not certain: R. Altheim-Stiehl, 'Die Zeitangaben der mittelpersischen Dipinti in der einstigen Synagoge zu Dura-Europos', *Boreas*, 5 (1982), 152–9; MacDonald, 'Dating the Fall of Dura-Europos', pp. 57–62.

ceivable.[294] Among the obscure are a passing remark in Ammianus (perhaps this should be relegated to the former category) and a fragment of the Continuator of Dio. Ammianus reports that for the siege of Bezabde in 360 Constantius used the head of a battering ram employed by Sapor to capture Antioch, which had been left behind at Carrhae in 252.[295] Since the Persians do not seem to have been in Carrhae in 252, this may actually be a ram used by the Persians to capture that place in 260: certainty is impossible.[296] It is impossible to tell what further tales the source used by Malalas for Mariades' career might have told[297]—all that remains is that the Persians took the city towards evening after having advanced διὰ τοῦ λιμίτου Χαλκίδος, which would seem to mean 'along the road from Chalkis'.[298]

The Continuator described a delay before the walls of Antioch by Sapor and Mariades during which the sensible citizens fled, while the friends of Mariades and the generally revolutionary made trouble.[299] It is unfortunate that his account breaks off here; but it does seem a safe assumption that the 'friends of Mariades' had a hand in the fall of the city in his account. In view of the fact that the Continuator was able to put this campaign in the right place, it might also be the case that there is some truth in what he had to say. This may be confirmed by the *Thirteenth Sibylline Oracle*. Although it does not add anything in detail to what is known from other sources, the author did hold Mariades very much responsible for what happened, and the lines which he adopted from the prophecy about Nero attribute the disaster, in part, to the 'thoughtlessness' of the Antiochenes. This may suggest that the unrest which the Continuator records was indeed serious.

The main point that appears from all of the evidence is the totality of the Roman defeat. Nowhere in the western sources is there any suggestion of Roman resistance, and the capture of the camps of the Syrian legions suggests that effective Roman control

---

[294] Amm. 23. 5. 3; Lib. *Or.* 24. 38; see on ll. 89–100.

[295] Amm. 20. 11. 11 'transferri placuerat molem arietis magnam, quam Persae quondam Antiochia pulsibus eius excisa relatam reliquerant apud Carrhas'.

[296] The city is not in the *Res Gestae* of Sapor for the second campaign; it is for the third.

[297] See on ll. 89–100 above.

[298] For the meaning of this phrase see B. Isaac, 'The Meaning of the Terms *Limes* and *Limitanei*', *JRS* 78 (1988), 136.

[299] *FHG* iv. 192, cited in n. 203 above.

was temporarily destroyed. This may explain the emergence of the ephemeral Uranius Antoninus in the next year (see on ll. 151–4 below).

131. αἱ ὁπόσοι ναίουσι κατὰ Κασίου ὄρος αἰπύ: this is Rzach's conjecture for Ω's αἱ αἱ ὁπόσοι ναίουσι κάσιον ὄρος αἰπύ. The insertion of κατά is metrically defensible as an instance of the lengthening of a syllable before a proper name, a phenomenon in later Greek hexameter: see A. Rzach, 'Neue Beiträge zur Technik des nachhomerischen Hexameter', SAWW 100 (1882), 325–6 (ibid. 321–30 for other similar instances of lengthening). In view of αἰπύ, modifying ὄρος, the alteration Κασίου for Κασίον seems necessary: cf. *Il.* 2. 603 οἳ δ᾽ ἔχον Ἀρκαδίην ὑπὸ Κυλλήνης ὄρος αἰπύ. Alexandre had proposed αἱ ὁπόσοι ναίουσι ⟨ὑπὸ⟩ Κάσιον ὄρος αἰπύ (or even ⟨περὶ⟩ Κάσιον ὄρος αἰπύ); Meineke tried αἱ αἱ ὅσοι ναίουσι κατὰ Κάσιον ὄρος αἰπύ.

133. Μαρσύας δὲ ὅσους: this is the reading of Ω, which I retain in place of Rzach's smoother Μαρσύας δ᾽ ὁπόσους. Rzach's proposal has the advantage of eliminating the strong hiatus of δὲ ὅσους, but I am not convinced that this is a necessary change in a text such as this. The manuscript reading was retained by Alexandre and Geffcken.

134. λάφυρα: the use of τίθημι indicates that the word must be taken here to mean 'ruin' or 'destruction' rather than the 'spoils of war' (neither of the alternatives proposed here is listed in LSJ, but see Pol. 4. 26. 7).

135. ὅλων: Wilamowitz's emendation here for Ω's ὅλα is secured by the fact that πᾶς and ὅλος became interchangeable in later Greek: see Bauer, s.v. ὅλος; Moulton, *Grammar of New Testament Greek*, iii. 199; J. H. Moulton and G. Milligan, *The Vocabulary of the Greek New Testament Illustrated from the Papyri and Other Non-Literary Sources*, s.v. ὅλος.

137–8. καὶ τότε Γαλλίη … ὁπόταν ἥξει πολεμιστής: the wide-ranging list of places to be affected by the great disaster may be compared with the similarly expansive lists at *Orac. Sib.* 3. 205–10, 484–8 (470–88 in general), 512–18, 598–600, 5. 115–25, 11. 53–5. In none of these cases is the reference to a specific historical event or historical events: 3. 205–6, for example, refers to the Trojan War; 3. 207–10 to woe that will befall Persians, Assyrians,

Egyptians, Libyans, Ethiopians, Carians, and Pamphylians; 3. 470–88 to Italy, Laodicea on the Lycus, Thracians, Campanians, Sardis, Mysians, Galatians, Carthaginians, Tenedos, Sicyon, and Corinth. It is a stylistic feature which was remarked upon with some irritation by Procopius: ἡ Σίβυλλα οὐχ ἅπαντα ἑξῆς τὰ πράγματα λέγει οὐδὲ ἁρμονίαν τινὰ ποιουμένη τοῦ λόγου, ἀλλ' ἔπος εἰποῦσα ὅ τι δὴ ἀμφὶ τοῖς Λιβύης κακοῖς ἀπεπήδησεν εὐθὺς ἐς τὰ Περσῶν ἤθη. ἐνθένδε τε Ῥωμαίων ἐς μνήμην ἐλθοῦσα μεταβιβάζει ἐς τοὺς Ἀσσυρίους τὸν λόγον. καὶ πάλιν ἀμφὶ Ῥωμαίοις μαντευομένη προλέγει τὰ Βρέττανων πάθη (5. 24. 35–6). The implication of this passage, then, is merely that there will be widespread ruin. Despite the fact that all the places mentioned here did indeed suffer barbarian raids in the 250s (see on l. 140 for Asia Minor), this should not be taken to imply that their author knew that they were all attacked in the winter of 252/3.

The most significant feature of these lines and the eleven that follow them is their position in the narrative. They serve to separate the sack of Antioch in 252 from the appearance of Uranius Antoninus, and the prime reason for their inclusion at this point would seem to have been as an indication of the passage of time. This technique also appears to have been employed by the author in the tale of Philip's reign (see on ll. 35–49), where a reference to war with 'German Ares' interrupts the tale of Philip's war with Persia.

138. πολεμιστής: the extent of the destruction which the arrival of the warrior occasioned suggests that he is an individual whose power could be exercised over a great area. This would seem to rule out an identification with a specific enemy, whose activity would be more localized, and suggests that the warrior might be either a Roman emperor or a god. Of these two options only the latter makes sense in the context of these lines. The territory which the warrior will harm corresponds with what we know to have been the extent of barbarian activity in 252/3, therefore the warrior may be identified as a god, more specifically as the god Ares, who alone of the divinities for whom cult-titles are listed by Roscher is referred to as πολεμιστής (see *Il.* 5. 289, 20. 78, 22. 267). The appearance of Ares as an active agent tells strongly against the notion that the author of these lines was either a Christian or a Jew (see on ll. 54, 109, 112).

310   Commentary

139. ὦ Λύκιοι Λύκιοι, λύκος: both the play on Λύκιος/λύκος
and the initial vocative are standard features of oracular verse (the
latter also of lament: see on l. 113). For ὦ Λύκιοι see FGrH 257 F 1.
6. 1, 36II. 8. 1, 36III. 7. 1; PW 94, 96, 487; Eus. Praep. Ev. 6. 3 = Porph.
Philos. ex orac. 170 Wolff; see Fontenrose, Delphic Oracle, p. 177. For
word-plays comparable to Λύκιος/λύκος cf. examples cited on
l. 103 and Orac. Sib. 3. 363–4, 4. 91–2, 8. 165–6.

140. Σάννοι: Olmstead ('The Mid-Third Century', p. 405 n. 1) was
surely correct to identify these people with the tribe on the Black
Sea also known as the Makrones (on whom see A. Herrmann, RE
xiv. 815, without reference to this passage). They were still causing
trouble in the reign of Claudius Tacitus in 275 (Malalas, 12. 301—
also not in Herrmann's article).

σὺν Ἄρηϊ πτολιπόρθῳ: while it is possible that the author
would have been thinking of some specific leader of the Sannoi or
their possible associates, it seems more likely that this Ares should
simply be taken to be the god of war. The implication of his appearance here for the question of the author's religious convictions is
the same as that noted for πολεμιστής in l. 138.

πτολιπόρθῳ: the epic form is Rzach's improvement on
πολιπόρθῳ, proposed by Alexandre for Ω's πολυπαρθῳ; cf. Hes.
The. 936–7; A. Rzach, 'Zur Verstechnick der Sibyllisten', WS 14
(1892), 22.

141. καὶ Κάρποι ... μάχεσθαι: the evidence for the various
Gothic invasions of the Balkans and Asia Minor during the 250s is
extremely confused, and it will be useful to set it forth at some
length. These lines have not been suitably exploited in previous
discussions.

The most important source is Zosimus. He describes various
barbarian invasions under Gallus from the twenty-sixth to the
twenty-eighth chapter in the first book of his history. The first of
these chapters serves as a sort of general introduction: Gallus ruled
in a slothful way and the Scythians began to attack the provinces
which were on their borders. No province was spared: all cities
without walls and many of those which had them were destroyed.[300]

300 Zos. 1. 26. 1 ἐκμελῶς δὲ τοῦ Γάλλου τὴν ἀρχὴν μεταχειριζομένου, Σκύθαι
πρῶτον μὲν τὰ πλησιόχωρα σφίσι συνετάραττον ἔθνη, προϊόντες δὲ ὁδῷ καὶ τὰ
μέχρι θαλάττης αὐτῆς ἐλῄζοντο, ὥστε μηδὲ ἓν ἔθνος Ῥωμαίοις ὑπήκοον
ἀπόρθητον ὑπὸ τούτων καταλειφθῆναι, πᾶσαν δὲ ὡς εἰπεῖν ἀτείχιστον πόλιν

The second chapter in the group is rather more specific. The generally bad situation of the empire in the previous chapter came about when the Goths, Boranoi, Burgundians, and Carpi seized the cities of Europe while the Persians captured Antioch.[301] The synchronism here parallels that in the *Liber Caliphorum* (see on l. 110 above), which also provides the year 252 as a date. Since Zosimus records another barbarian invasion in the next chapter, one aimed at areas which had escaped destruction in the previous year, an attack which failed to accomplish anything because of the valour of Aemilius Aemilianus, it would appear that the date given by the *Liber Caliphorum* is sound.[302] Aemilianus' victory preceded his rebellion, which is securely dated to 253.

Despite the evident simplicity of Zosimus' arrangement, and despite the confirmation of its essential content from other sources, these three chapters have caused interpreters a great deal of difficulty. Mommsen did not want to believe that the Goths could launch naval raids as early as the 250s, and so suggested that Zosimus' mention of an attack on Cappadocia, Pessinus, and Ephesus in chapter 28 was the result of some conflation or confusion of events in that decade with those in the 260s.[303] Rappaport went on from there to argue that the final expedition mentioned by Zosimus was the result of the whole-sale telescoping of events, and that the several Gothic invasions over a course of twenty years had been run together in two chapters.[304] He

καὶ τῶν ὠχυρωμένων τείχεσι τὰς πλείους ἁλῶναι. The essential quality of this chapter was recognized by Rappaport, *Die Einfälle der Goten*, p. 43.

[301] Zos. 1. 27. 1 ἐν τούτοις δὲ τῶν πραγμάτων ὄντων, καὶ τῶν κρατούντων οὐδαμῶς οἵων τε ὄντων ἀμῦναι τῷ πολιτεύματι, πάντα δὲ τὰ τῆς Ῥώμης ἔξω περιορώντων, αὖθις Γότθοι καὶ Βορανοὶ καὶ Οὐρουγοῦνδοι καὶ Κάρποι τὰς κατὰ τὴν Εὐρώπην ἐλήζοντο πόλεις, εἴ τι περιλελειμμένον ἦν οἰκειούμενοι. The Οὐρουγοῦνδοι are presumably the Burgundians.

[302] Zos. 1. 28. 1 τῶν δὲ Σκυθῶν ὅσον ἦν τῆς Εὐρώπης ἐν ἀδείᾳ πολλῇ νεμομένων, ἤδη δὲ καὶ διαβάντων εἰς τὴν Ἀσίαν καὶ τὰ μέχρι Καππαδοκίας καὶ Πεσσινοῦντος καὶ Ἐφέσου λησαμένων, Αἰμιλιανὸς Παιονικῶν ἡγούμενος τάξεων, ἀτόλμους ὄντας τοὺς ὑφ' ἑαυτὸν στρατιώτας ἀντιστῆναι τῇ τῶν βαρβάρων εὐημερίᾳ παραθαρσύνας ὡς οἷός τε ἦν, καὶ τοῦ Ῥωμαίων ἀξιώματος ἀναμνήσας, ἐπῄει τοῖς εὑρεθεῖσιν ἐκεῖσε βαρβάροις ἀπροσδο-κήτοις.

[303] T. Mommsen, *The Provinces of the Roman Empire from Caesar to Diocletian*, trans. W. P. Dickson (London, 1909), i. 243 n. 1.

[304] Rappaport, *Die Einfälle der Goten*, pp. 44–5. For an account which, quite properly, takes Zosimus more seriously see Alföldi, 'Die Hauptereignisse der Jahre 253–261', pp. 55–6 = *Studien*, pp. 140–1.

noted that the Artemision at Ephesus was destroyed during the
reign of Gallienus and assumed that the record of the sack of
Ephesus in chapter twenty-eight of Zosimus proved his point.
He believed that the city could not have fallen in both 253 and 262.[305]
The views of Mommsen and Rappaport on Zosimus' chronology
have been further supported by the novel and ingenious (although
unnecessary) observation that the order of the regimes of Gallus and
Volusianus, Valerian and Gallienus could be confused by medieval
scribes, who might reverse their putative abbreviations: Γαλλ. –
Οὐολ. and Οὐαλ. –Γαλλ. [306]
The problem with the suggestions reported in the last paragraph
is that they ignore the point that Zosimus did actually know the
difference between Gallus and Valerian; and it is rather bizarre to
assume that just because a city was sacked in 262 it could not have
been sacked in 253 (especially when the two sources used to reconstruct these events are quite clear about it), or that barbarians could
not sail before 260 (see on l. 36). The Sannoi (see on l. 140) were a
tribe ordinarily domiciled in the area of Trebizond, and the oracle
connects them with trouble in Lycia. They could have gone there to
cause this trouble in one of two ways: they could have walked or
they could have sailed. The latter is rather easier and the route
would have taken them past Ephesus. Zonaras tells us that some of
the barbarians who attacked the empire after an invasion across the
Danube (an invasion which he placed after the beginning of the
Persian war) arrived at the Black Sea and ravaged many lands.[307] It is
not difficult to see that there may be a link between these people,
the raiders at Ephesus, trouble among peoples on the Black Sea, and
the Sannoi in Lycia. There is little reason to believe that Zosimus
was wrong when he wrote that there was a general movement of
barbarians through the Bosporus and along the coast of Asia Minor
in 252/3.

---

[305] For the raid in 262 see Robert, 'Épitaphe de provenance inconnue' confirming the
date given by HA V. Gall. 6. 2.

[306] M. Salmon, 'The Chronology of the Gothic Incursions into Asia Minor in the IIIrd
Century A.D.', Eos, 49 (1971), 116–17.

[307] Zon. 12. 21 καὶ Σκύθαι δὲ εἰς τὴν Ἰταλίαν εἰσέβαλον, πλῆθος ὄντες σχεδὸν
ὑπερβαῖνον καὶ ἀριθμόν, καὶ Μακεδονίαν καὶ Θεσσαλίαν καὶ Ἑλλάδα
κατέδραμον. λέγεται δὲ τούτων μοῖράν τινα διὰ Βοσπόρου παρελθοῦσαν καὶ
τὴν Μαιῶτιδα λίμνην ὑπερβᾶσαν ἐπὶ τὸν Εὔξεινον γενέσθαι πόντον καὶ χώρας
πορθῆσαι πολλάς.

Evidence for widespread destruction and fear of war appears in a
number of places and a number of ways throughout Asia Minor
from the middle years of the third century. Ancyra was fortified
anew and a man was honoured there for his actions during a time of
barbarian invasion.[308] The walls of Dorylaeum may have been
rebuilt, and much further south the people of Stratonicea consulted
Zeus Panormus about the possibility of barbarian attack.[309] They
appear to have been preserved from danger (hence the inscription
of the god's response on the wall of the Bouleuterion), but others
were not. The experiences reported by Gregory Thaumatourgos
when he oversaw recovery from a raid (probably the one in 252)
through Pontus—the rape of virgins (and of some women who
were not), forced consumption of sacrificial meats, and association
with the enemy against one's neighbours—may have been common
to many communities.[310]

Between the invasion of 253 and that of 262 there was another
serious barbarian incursion into Asia. The removal of an officer
named Successianus from a command at Pittys by Valerian led to
what Zosimus called the second invasion by the Goths, Borani,
Carpi, and Burgundians.[311] No date is given, and Alföldi's effort to
provide one on the basis of Valerian's coinage is not convincing.[312]

[308] *IGR* iii. 206 κ(αὶ) σύμπαν τὸ τ[ε]ῖχος | ἐν σειτοδεί[ᾳ] κ(αὶ) βαρ-
βαρικα[ῖς] | ἐφόδοις ἐκ θεμελίων εἰς | τέλος ἀναγόν[τ]α. A. Korte, rev. of
G. Radet, *En Phrygie*, in *GGA* (1897), 392; *MAMA*, vol. v, p. xii; for further discussion see
Mitchell, 'Imperial Building', p. 341.
[309] For Dorylaeum see Magie, *Roman Rule*, ii. 1567; Salmon, 'Chronology', p. 128; for
Stratonicaea see *Insc. Strat.* 1103.
[310] Greg. Neocaes. *Can. Ep.* (ed. Routh, *Reliquiae Sacrae*) 1 (7 for the instances mentioned
here). The barbarians are identified (*Can. Ep.* 5) as Goths and Boradoi; the latter presumably are identical to the Boranoi of Zos. 1. 27. 1, 31. 1, under the years 253 and 259. As they
are specifically attested in Pontus in 259, that date is marginally preferable, but there is no
way to prove that they were not there on another, earlier occasion. For a general discussion
of this text see Lane Fox, *Pagans and Christians*, pp. 539–41.
[311] Zos. 1. 31–5; see esp. 35. 2 τοῦτο τῆς δευτέρας ἐφόδου ποιησάμενοι τέλος.
This was probably the raid in which the family of Ulfilas was captured, a raid which Philo-
storgius described as follows: Βασιλεύοντος Οὐαλλεριανοῦ καὶ Γαλλιήνου, μοῖρα
Σκυθῶν βαρεῖα τῶν πέραν τοῦ Ἴστρου διέβησαν εἰς τὴν Ῥωμαίων, καὶ πολλὴν
μὲν κατέδραμον τῆς Εὐρώπης· διαβάντες δὲ καὶ εἰς τὴν Ἀσίαν, τήν τε Γαλα-
τίαν καὶ τὴν Καππαδοκίαν ἐπῆλθον, καὶ πολλοὺς ἔλαβον αἰχμαλώτους ἄλλους
τε καὶ τῶν κατειλεγμένων τῷ κλήρῳ, καὶ μετὰ πολλῆς λείας ἀπεκομίσθησαν
οἴκαδε (2. 5).
[312] Alföldi, 'Die Hauptereignisse der Jahre 253–61', p. 57 — *Studien*, pp. 142–3; on
which see Salmon, 'Chronology', p. 121 n. 54.

He argued that the issue at Antioch in 257 commemorating a *Victoria Germanica* commemorated a victory by Valerian over the Goths, who had invaded Asia Minor and ravaged territory as far east as Cappadocia. But it is more likely that it refers to a victory gained under the auspices of Gallienus in Gaul and that the barbarian raid into Asia actually occurred in 259.[313] The narrative of Zosimus places Valerian's attempt to catch the raiders in close conjunction with his final campaign against Sapor in 260: λοιμοῦ δὲ τοῖς στρατοπέδοις ἐμπεσόντος καὶ τὴν πλείω μοῖραν αὐτῶν διαφθείραντος, Σαπώρης ἐπιὼν τὴν ἑῴαν ἅπαντα κατεστρέφετο (1. 36. 1). As a plague also appears in an account of Valerian's capture preserved by Petrus Patricius (see on l. 161) it is very tempting to place his attempt to catch the Goths and the infection of his army with disease where the narrative of Zosimus clearly has it: just before Sapor's invasion in 260.

So much, then, for Asia Minor. Two major raids were launched by various barbarians coming out of the area around the Black Sea before 262. One of these, the one alluded to in this oracle, took place during 252/3. The other, which immediately preceded the capture of Valerian, occurred in 259/60. More cannot be said without further evidence.

Perhaps the most curious feature of these lines is that the author did not bother to say what would happen when the Carpi will do battle with the Ausonians. Perhaps, unlike the author of lines 35–6, this writer did not know. Battle between the Carpi and the Romans could be expected at just about any time during these years, and perhaps that is all the detail about them that this writer commanded. The deeds of Aemilianus on the Danube during 253 do not seem to have impinged upon the author's consciousness—the account that he gives of Aemilianus' accession shows that he knew nothing about the details of the civil war in 253.

142–4. καὶ τότε δὴ νόθος υἱὸς ... δυσσεβίης ἕνεκεν: the description of Gallus' end which appears here allows of several interpretations, which fall into four general categories. One of these involves the belief that the bastard son is meant to be Hostilianus, that his death has been misplaced, and that its circumstances have been embellished for literary purposes, or through ignorance, or

---

[313] For the campaigns in these years in the west see Drinkwater, *The Gallic Empire*, pp. 21–2.

through ill will. Another possibility is that this son is Volusianus and that one can make what one will of the story about his rebellion. The third possibility—which does not a priori exclude the second or even the first—is that Hostilianus and Volusianus were conflated in the author's mind so that a tradition of hostility between Hostilianus and Gallus was transferred to Volusianus. If Dio could be wrong about the reign of Diadumenianus and the ancestry of Elagabalus,[314] if an oracular author on Severus' civil wars could omit Clodius Albinus (*Orac. Sib.* 12. 250–63), and if the author of Revelation could omit sundry emperors in the year 69, this sort of confusion is not at all unbelievable. The fourth option is that this passage is meaningless nonsense which somehow passed for divine revelation—a possibility which is only to be taken seriously if there was a great deal of confusion about the people involved.

Hostilianus' brief association with Gallus caused a great deal of difficulty for the writers whose accounts of these years survive. In a sentence for which Dexippus is cited as an authority (though the citation is otherwise slightly problematic: see on l. 100) George noted καὶ τὰ στρατόπεδα βασιλέα πάλαι τινὰ γενόμενον ὕπατον Γάλλον ἀναγορεύουσιν ἅμα Βουλουσιανῷ τῷ Δεκίου παιδί· οἳ καὶ βασιλεύουσι κατὰ Δέξιππον μῆνας ιη′ (p. 705 = Mosshammer, p. 459 = *FGrH* 100 F 22). A later reference, in the context of Valerian's succession, reveals the unfortunate fact that the text here is not likely to be corrupt; the notice opens μετὰ Γάλλον καὶ Βουλουσιανὸν τὸν Δεκίου παιδά (p. 715 = Mosshammer, p. 465). This is enough to prove that it was possible to confuse Volusianus and Hostilianus and enough to suggest very strongly that such confusion was possible for a man who was regarded in antiquity as a well-informed third-century historian.

The most extensive discussion of Gallus' reign is preserved by Zosimus, but even it is not very helpful. He does not mention Volusianus at all, but does say that Decius was survived by a son. He says that Gallus spoke kindly of his predecessor at first, and adopted the child. Subsequently he began to fear that revolutionaries might recall the virtues of Decius and hand the empire over to that son. He began to plot against this lad and it is implied that the boy fell

---

[314] Dio 78. 17. 1; Millar, *Cassius Dio*, p. 163 (Diadumenianus); Dio 78. 30. 2; Bowersock, 'Herodian and Elagabalus', pp. 231–4 (Elagabalus).

316   *Commentary*

victim to his schemes.[315] Unfortunately, there is no way to know
what name Zosimus had for the boy (if he actually did know one);
but this is certainly not the same story as that known to George.
Tremendous confusion is also evident in other sources. Eutropius is extreme, introducing 'Gallus Hostilianus et Galli filius
Volusianus' (*Brev.* 9. 5). Orosius did the same.[316] Zonaras observes
that there was a great deal of trouble in his sources on this point—
some writers thought that Volusianus was a cognomen of Gallus.
He got them sorted out correctly, but makes no mention of Hostilianus.[317] The Epitomator puts Gallus and Volusianus in the right
relationship and notes that Hostilianus Perpenna, who soon died of
the plague, was elected by the Senate (the cognomen is surely
wrong—it appears on no document).[318] Aurelius Victor says that the
Senate elected Gallus and Hostilianus upon learning that Decius
had died, that Volusianus was Gallus' son, and that Hostilianus soon
died of the plague.[319] This rates higher marks than any other author
for prosopography (though it leaves some doubt as to whether he
knew that Decius was Hostilianus' father) and is particularly
impressive alongside some of the rubbish in other authors. Cedrenus is the worst. He places the reign of Gallus between that of
Valerian and Gallienus and that of Valerian and Gallienus (*sic*). He
tells us that Gallus was killed by his wife and Volusianus by his
soldiers. A Hostilianus is given a reign of two years before that of
Philip. (Philip is given a reign of seven years which ends in battle for
the Christians against Decius—Valerian then appears (not Decius)

[315] Zos. 1. 25. 2 χρόνου δὲ προϊόντος εἰς δέος καταστὰς μή ποτέ τινες τῶν εἰς τὰ
πράγματα νεωτερίζειν εἰωθότων εἰς μνήμην τῶν Δεκίου βασιλικῶν ἀρετῶν
ἀνατρέχοντες τῷ τούτου παιδὶ τὴν τῶν ὅλων ἀρχὴν παραδοῖεν, ἐπιβουλεύει
θάνατον αὐτῷ οὔτε τῆς ποιήσεως οὔτε τοῦ καλῶς ἔχοντος λόγον τινὰ
ποιησάμενος.

[316] Oros. *Hist. Contra pag.* 7. 21. 4.

[317] Zon. 12. 21 κρατεῖ οὖν ὁ Γάλλος, ὃν τινὲς μὲν τῶν συγγραφέων καὶ
Βολουσιανὸν κεκλῆσθαί φασιν ὡς διώνυμον, ἄλλοι δὲ τὸν Βουλουσιανὸν υἱὸν
αὐτοῦ εἶναι γεγράφασι καὶ συνάρχειν αὐτῷ.

[318] *Epit. de Caes.* 30 'Vibius Gallus cum Volusiano filio imperaverunt annos duos. horum
temporibus Hostilianus Perpenna a senatu imperator creatus, nec multo post pestilentia
consumptus est.' For Stein's suggestion that he is to be identified with the usurper Valens
see n. 218 above.

[319] Aur. Vict. *De Caes.* 30 'haec ubi patres comperere, Gallo Hostilianoque Augusta
imperia, Volusianum Gallo editum Caesarem decernunt. dein pestilentia oritur; qua
atrocius saeviente Hostilianus interiit'.

as his successor: Cedr., pp. 451–4). A slightly more confused section in the *Synopsis Sathas* places Hostilianus, along with a Severus, after Marcus; possibly this man is only Marcus Philippus, Philip the Arab, without his cognomen) (*Syn. Sath.* 37. 10).

Leaving aside Cedrenus and the *Synopsis Sathas*, whose ignorance is too great to allow for reasoned contemplation—though they do raise a rather interesting question about the way in which these stories could have developed—it is clear that there was not a great deal that can be said to have been written very well about Hostilianus and Volusianus. Eutropius and Orosius show that Gallus and Hostilianus could be conflated in the fourth century. Zonaras knew sources that did the same for Gallus and his son in the twelfth. George shows that Gallus and Hostilianus could be confused in the ninth century, and does so in such a way as to suggest that this might have been done in the third.

The documentary evidence for Hostilianus suggests both why contemporaries could have been confused and, perhaps, why the version of Gallus' death presented in this oracle might have had some appeal to his contemporaries. There is not much, and it was only in 1950 that J. F. Gilliam published what he properly pointed out was to become the most important text relating to the problem. It is a list of horses in the *Cohors XX Palmyrenorum* at Dura.[320]

The list, preserved on a papyrus written some time after 31 August 251, gives the members of the cohort followed by details of the horse that was then in their possession.[321] The description of the horses included their age at the time, then distinctive marking and the year in which the horse was purchased. It is with this last entry that a significant peculiarity in the unit's bookkeeping appears. In line 5 a horse is listed as having been purchased 'Tittiano cos.' and being two years old. Tittianus was consul in 245 with Philip. Five years seem to have disappeared from its life. In line 24 the date of a horse's purchase is given as 'III et II cos.' and in lines 4, 9, 14, 17, 22, and 24 as 'III et I cos.'. The dating formula 'III et II cos.'

---

[320] *P. Dura* 97 = Fink, *Roman Military Records*, No. 83; J. F. Gilliam, 'Some Latin Military Records from Papyri', *YCS* 14 (1950), 189–209. For other documentary evidence see C. Préaux, 'Trébonien Gallus et Hostilianus', *Aegyptus*, 32 (1952), 152–7. What follows here is based on J. F. Gilliam, 'Trebonianus Gallus and the Decii'.

[321] *P. Dura* 97. 1–3, 6–7, 13, 22.

also appears on an inscription from Mainz;[322] 'III et I cos.' appears on
one other papyrus from Dura and three inscriptions from Italy.[323]

The formulae clearly indicate people who held repeated consul-
ships in the mid-third century, people who must therefore be
wearers of the imperial purple, and the date 'Tittiano cos.' reveals
the principle behind this numbering. Tittianus is otherwise known
only as the consular colleague of Philip in 245, who did not, unlike
Philip, suffer a *damnatio memoriae*.[324] Philip and his son both
suffered this fate and had their name struck from the *fasti*; hence
the year 'III et II cos.' referring to 248, when they were last consuls
together. 'III et I cos.' can thus only refer to Decius and Herennius
Etruscus. Since there would be no other reason to date a dedication
(like the three from Italy) 'III et I cos.' in a year other than 251, this
proves that their memories had been officially damned before the
end of the year. Hostilianus, who had earlier appeared on documents with Gallus, disappeared for good and Volusianus took his
place as *Augustus*.[325]

The brief career of Hostilianus, as Zosimus' account shows, gave
rise to various stories, and the thrust of some of these (they may
even have been true) was that Gallus killed him in secret. But this is
not all. As emperor, Gallus had no wife or, at least, did not advertise
one, and this may well have confused people for whom the
prescripts of decrees and imperial *imagines* were main sources of
information about Volusianus (see above, pp. 135–8, for people of
this sort). Hence he might be conflated with a son of Decius who
had been on the throne when Gallus became emperor. This confusion might also have led people to believe that Volusianus was the
prince whom Gallus had evidently murdered.

The lack of evidence in these lines about what happened in the
summer of 253 between Gallus and Aemilianus is not difficult to
understand. Detailed news about civil war and insurrection in
distant areas tended not to travel far among the sort of men who
read or wrote works such as the *Oracula Sibyllina*. But the story told
here and the peculiar interest in the bastard son suggest a good deal

---

[322] *ILS* 7091; Gilliam, 'Trebonianus Gallus and the Decii', p. 306.

[323] *ILS* 4174, 6149; *CIL* xi. 4086; *P. Dura* 29.   [324] *PIR* T 186.

[325] Gilliam, 'Trebonianus Gallus and the Decii', pp. 308–11. See now *P. Oxy.* 3610 and
commentary in *P. Oxy.* li. 19–20. It appears that Gallus may have ruled alone for a short
time between the death of Hostilianus and the elevation of Volusianus.

about what this ill-informed author and his audience felt when they turned their minds to Gallus. This author is as clear as the genre allows about the identity of the emperor described in ll. 103–43. Thus, when he wrote about the bastard son, he presumably thought that this person would be readily recognizable. In both places where the pair appear, they are presented in a very unpleasant light: in the first case they bring enemies against the empire, in the second one murders the other. It is a good illustration of the emotional response that might be elicited by an emperor from people for whom his reign had been an unmitigated disaster.

The Reign of Aemilianus (AD 253)

144. μετὰ δ' αὖτ' ἄρξει: the use of this standard introductory formula (cf. on ll. 21, 103, for others) completely obscures Aemilianus' role in bringing the reign of Gallus to an end. In view of the role given to the 'bastard son' in the previous two lines, this is perhaps not surprising. The author seems to have known very little, if anything, about these events.

144–5. ἄλλος | ἀρχὴν οὐνομάτεσσι φέρων: 'obscurissime natus obscurius imperavit' (Eutr. *Brev.* 9. 6). This may be Eutropius' most apposite remark on the history of the third century. Almost nothing is known of Aemilius Aemilianus save (possibly) his place of birth and something of the circumstances under which he was recognized as emperor in Italy, Africa, Sardinia, Asia, Syria, Egypt, and along the Danube for a few months in the late summer of 253.[326]

According to the Epitomator and Zonaras, he was an African: he is called 'Maurus' by the former, *Λίβυς* by the latter.[327] In the summer of 253 he was in command of one of the provinces of Moesia—probably, but not certainly, *Moesia Inferior*.[328] In this

---

[326] *PIR* ² A 330; Barbieri, *Albo*, No. 1419; not much has come to light since: *AÉ* 1954, No. 129 (a milestone from Libya); ibid. 1983, No. 901 (a milestone from Asia). See Fig. 14.

[327] *Epit. de Caes.* 31; Zon. 12. 21. He may have been from the isle of Girga, as argued by Syme, 'Emperors from Etruria', p. 348 – Historia Augusta *Papers*, p. 200.

[328] A. Stein, *Die Reichsbeamten von Dazien* (Budapest, 1944), 104–5. Although the evidence is not totally convincing, this is the most likely place in view of the amount of time involved (though von Rhodhen, *RE* i. 545–6, does not venture a solution). *AÉ* 1935, No. 164, which Stein thought (following Alföldi) could refer to these events, is now, I think, reasonably securely dated to the reign of Decius (see on ll. 79–80). Whatever

capacity he is said by Zosimus and Zonaras to have won a great victory over some barbarians, and to have ravaged their lands.[329] His troops, glad at their victory and enamoured of their leader (Aurelius Victor said he corrupted them, Zonaras says that he promised them all the booty taken from the barbarians),[330] proclaimed him emperor and marched on Italy.

When he heard about the march of Aemilianus, Gallus sent Valerian to bring the Rhine legions to his rescue and marched against the usurper with whatever forces were at his disposal.[331] The armies met at Interamna on the *via Flaminia*.[332] It was there that the soldiers of Gallus recognized the inferiority of their numbers, perhaps of their leader as well, and went over to Aemilianus. Soon afterwards Valerian returned to Italy and Aemilianus was murdered by his own men at Spoletium.[333]

The dates for the events narrated in the last paragraph may be roughly fixed with the aid of an inscription and papyri. The inscription is a dedication by the officers of the *vexillatio millaria* from *legio III Augusta*, found at Gemellae in the far corner of Numidia, and records the devotion of its dedicants to Valerian and Gallienus on 22 October 253.[334] This vexillation had come from Rhaetia, and the officers responsible for the dedication were no doubt participants in the campaign which culminated in the death of Aemilianus. Given

province Aemilianus governed, the descriptions by John Ant, fr. 150 as ὁ τῆς Μυσιᾶς ἔπαρχος, Zon. 12. 21 as ἄρχων τοῦ ἐν Μυσίᾳ στρατεύματος, Zos. 1. 28. 1 as Παιονικῶν ἡγούμενος τάξεων, and Eutr. *Brev.* 9. 5. 1 'sub his [Gallus and Volusianus] Aemilianus in Moesia res novas molitus est', Jord. *Get.* 105 'Emilianus quidam tyrannidem in Moesia arripuit', do not support the contention of Fitz, 'Die Vereinigung der Donauprovinzen', pp. 114–15, that Aemilianus had a general command over all the Danubian provinces.

[329] Zos. 1. 28. 1–2; Zon. 12. 21.
[330] Aur. Vict. *De Caes.* 31. 1 'Aemilius Aemilianus summam potestatem corruptis militibus arripuit'; Zon. 12. 21.
[331] Zos. 1. 28. 3.
[332] Aur. Vict. *De Caes.* 31. 2 'ad quem [Aemilianus] expugnandum profecti [Gallus and Volusianus] Interamnae ab suis caeduntur spe praemii maioris ab Aemilio'; Zos. 1. 28. 3; Zon. 12. 21.
[333] *Epit. de Caes.* 31. 2 'Aemilianus vero mense quarto dominatus apud Spoletium, sive pontem, quem ab eius caede Sanguinarium accepisse nomen ferunt, inter Ocriculum Narniamque, Spoletium et urbem Romam regione media positum'; Zos. 1. 29. 1.
[334] *ILS* 531 'Vic(toriae) Aug(ustae) | pro sal(ute) dd. nn. | Valeriani et Gall|ieni [Augg., vexi]llat(io) mill|iaria leg. III Aug. re]stitu|tae, e Raet(ia) Geme|ll(as) regressi, [die | XI kal. Nove. Volusiano II et Maximo cos.'; Stein, 'Chronologie', p. 44.

the distance they had come, their victory could not have occurred much later than the early part of September. Nor could it have occurred much earlier than that. The count of Valerian's regnal years in Egypt opened during 253/4, in the year which began on 30 August.[335] Gallus was still mentioned as emperor in a report to the στρατηγός of Oxyrhynchus as late as 22 August 253,[336] and an account relating to pitch, also from Oxyrhyncus, mentions Aemilianus' second year;[337] news of his accession must therefore have reached Egypt some time between 22 and 29 August. News of his death could not have arrived too much after this. These texts suggest that the three or four months given in various sources for the reign of Aemilianus must be dated from the time of his proclamation, rather than the death of Gallus.[338] The papyri show that his death could not have been much earlier than the end of July or the beginning of August. For the circumstances of Valerian's revolt see on ll. 145–6.

145. **ἀρχήν:** the use of ἀρχή to mean alpha here appears to be a development of a formula which is used in other oracles to introduce emperors whose name began with A; cf. *Orac. Sib.* 5. 15 στοιχείων ὅστις λάχε γράμματος ἀρχήν (referring to Augustus); 12. 16 ἀρχὴν στοιχείων ὅστις λάχε (Augustus); 12. 165 ἀρχὴν στοιχείου προφέρων (Hadrian). This meaning is not listed in LSJ.

ἀρχὴν οὐνομάτεσσι φέρων: the reading adopted here is registered by Geffcken as the suggestion of Wilamowitz in place of Ω's οὐνόματος. Alexandre, who was followed by Rzach, had offered ἀρχὴν οὐνόματος προφέρων. Despite the fact that it was his idea, Alexandre seems to have realized that the proposition was obscure: he translated 'insignis primo numero' (cf. Terry, 'whose name presents the first of letters'). Wilamowitz's suggestion not only has the advantage of being completely comprehensible, but also of yielding an attractive play upon two meanings of ἀρχή ('to rule' and 'the first letter of the alphabet') as well as upon the name of Aemilius Aemilianus.

145–6: ταχὺ δ' αὖτε ... αἴθωνι σιδήρῳ: the Ares introduced here is to be identified with P. Licinius Valerianus.[339] According to

---

[335] Stein, 'Chronologie', p. 32.   [336] *P. Oxy.* 1119.   [337] Ibid. 1286.
[338] For the various statements as to how long he ruled see *PIR*² A 330.
[339] Ibid. L 258; see on l. 157. For an illustration see Fig. 15.

Zosimus, Gallus sent him to bring troops from the northern frontier into Italy after he had received the news of Aemilianus' revolt. Other sources omit the notion that his activity against Aemilianus was consistent with his loyalty to Gallus. In view of the time involved they were probably wrong to do so. The roughly three months attributed to Aemilianus date from the time of his accession in Moesia. This is clear from the fact that little more than a month intervened between his death and that of his predecessors (see on l. 145). Since it took the army of Vitellius (albeit in winter) something like four months to reach Cremona in 69,[340] it seems unlikely that Valerian could have reached central Italy to meet Aemilianus at Spoletium within a month of Gallus' death if he had not started his march soon after the Moesian legions rebelled. The march of Aemilianus' army, to judge from the speed of Severus' campaign in 193, would have taken about two months.[341]

The force which Valerian commanded was described by Zosimus as 'the army north of the Alps', and Aurelius Victor describes these men as 'milites, qui contracti undique apud Raetias ob instans bellum morabantur' (*Caes.* 32. 1).[342] As *ILS* 531 describes the men at Gemellae as the 'vexillatio millaria e Raetia', it is possible that Victor's words here reflect the official designation of this army. M. Christol has suggested that the concentration of troops in this area might have begun under Gallus to form an expeditionary force against the Persians, as a response to the invasion of 252, and that Victor's 'instans bellum' was in fact the war with Sapor.[343] These are both extremely attractive suggestions and may explain why Valerian was able to mobilize a large army against Aemilianus with such speed.

[340] For the chronology of Vitellius' march see Chilver on Tac. *Hist.* 1–2, appendix, pp. 264–7.

[341] Birley, *Septimius Severus* [2], pp. 97–106. Somewhat different views on various aspects of the problem appear in G. M. Bersanetti, 'Valeriano ed Emiliano', *Rivista di filologia*, 26 (1948), 257–79; E. Manni, 'L'accazione di Valeriano', ibid. 25 (1947), 106–17; H. B. Mattingly, 'Tribunicia Potestate', *JRS* 20 (1930), 88–9; id., 'The Reign of Aemilian: A Chronological Note', *JRS* 25 (1935), 55–8.

[342] Cf. Zos. 1. 29. 1 Βαλεριανοῦ δὲ μετὰ τῶν ὑπὲρ τὰς Ἄλπεις δυνάμεων ἐπὶ τὴν Ἰταλίαν ἐλαύνοντος.

[343] Christol, 'Politique extérieure de Trébonien Galle', p. 73, though he dates the invasion to 253; the new date makes his suggestion more attractive.

Uranius Antoninus (AD 253)

147. **καὶ πάλι:** the use of πάλι suggests that this is not the same Persian attack as that described in ll. 108–36 (see on l. 110). A Persian invasion during 253 is hinted at in a letter which Aemilianus is alleged to have sent to the Senate, recorded at Zon. 12. 22 ἀναρρηθεὶς δὲ οὕτως αὐτοκράτωρ ὁ Αἰμιλιανὸς ἐπέστειλε τῇ συγκλήτῳ, ἐπαγγελλόμενος ὡς καὶ τὴν Θρᾴκην ἀπαλλάξει βαρβάρων καὶ κατὰ Περσῶν ἐκστρατεύσεται καὶ πάντα πράξει καὶ ἀγωνίσεται ὡς στρατηγὸς αὐτῶν (cf. *Anon. post Dionem*, fr. 2 (*FHG* iv. 193 = Boissevain, *Excerpta de sententiis*, 'Petrus', 158); Christol, 'Politique extérieure de Trébonien Galle', pp. 73–4.

κόσμος ἄκοσμος: cf. *Orac. Sib.* 7. 123 ἔσται κόσμος ἄκοσμος ἀπολλυμένων ἀνθρώπων and Lact. *DI* 7. 16. 13, where this line also appears. Oxymoron of this sort is also common in tragic and other forms of lament: see A. *Pers.* 680 (with Broadhead ad loc.); *Ag.* 1142 (with Fraenkel ad loc.); *PV* 69 (with Griffiths ad loc.). For the antithetical form of lament in which this figures see Alexiou, *Ritual Lament*, pp. 150–60 and above on ll. 115–18.

150–4. **αὐτὰρ ... ἀπειλάς:** the identity of the individual introduced in these lines has occasioned some debate. Earlier commentators believed that it was Odaenathus of Palmyra,[344] but since Olmstead's article[345] there has been fairly general agreement that this is in fact Lucius Julius Aurelius Sulpicius Uranius Severus Antoninus of Emesa (I know of only one subsequent objection, but it is supported by no convincing argument).[346] It was a brilliant conjecture. At the time it was made, this man was known only from an obscure passage in Malalas' *Chronicle*, and it was only six years after Olmstead's article that Delbrück finally elucidated his coinage.[347] Perhaps as a result of these circumstances the reasons why this identification should be accepted have never been fully exposed, and it will be worth doing so before discussing the value of the *Sibylline Oracle* for knowledge of Uranius' career.

---

[344] Alexandre on l. 150; Geffcken, *Comp. u. Enst.*, p. 61; Rzach, *RE* iiA. 2159.
[345] 'The Mid-Third Century', pp. 407–8.
[346] De Blois, 'Odaenathus and the Roman–Persian War', pp. 16–17.
[347] R. Delbrück, 'Uranius of Emesa', *Num. Chron.*⁶ 8 (1948), 11–29.

Obverse   *Reverse*

27. Antoninianus of Uranius Antoninus; *reverse*: conical stone representing the god Elagabal, draped and ornamented, parasol to r. and l. *RIC* Uranius Antoninus, 1. British Museum.

1. The description of the new arrival in l. 151 as ἀρητήρ. In so far as can be determined, the male heir to the family descended from the old line of the Sampsigeramids was priest of the god Elagabal.[348]

2. The description of the city that will emerge as powerful in l. 153 as ἠελίου πόλις. Elagabal was identified with Helios, and it is entirely appropriate that his city, Emesa, should be referred to in this way. The description of Hierapolis as a place particularly protected by the moon provides a useful parallel in l. 96 (see ad loc.).[349]

3. The people who it is said will strike great fear into the Persians are described as Phoenicians (l. 154). This is appropriate for Emesa, which was in Syria Phoenice (cf. *Orac. Sib.* 7. 64, where people from this region are also called Phoenicians). It would be a very odd way to describe the Palmyrenes, which would be the case with Odaenathus, the other candidate for identification with the character introduced here.[350]

[348] For the history of the family see R. D. Sullivan, 'The Dynasty of Emesa', pp. 198–219; for the connection with Elagabalus, see Herod. 5. 3. 6.

[349] For the character of Elagabal see on l. 151 ἠλιόπεμπτος.

[350] For various Emesenes being called Phoenician see Millar, 'The Phoenician Cities', p. 59, and *HA V. Macr.* 9. 2; Herod. 5. 3. 4. Despite the fact that Palmyra was also in the province of Syria Phoenice, Palmyrenes were not considered Phoenicians. This distinction may be reflected in *D.* 50. 15. 1. 4–5 'sed et Emisenae civitati Phoenices imperator noster ius coloniae dedit iurisque Italici eam fecit. (5) Est et Palmyrena civitas in provincia Phoenice prope barbaras gentes et nationes collocata.' The Palmyrenes appear to have been thought of as Arabs by their contemporaries (quite properly so).

Aside from this passage and his coins, which seem to date from 252/3 to 254, the only evidence for Uranius is the passage in Malalas alluded to above. According to this a priest of Aphrodite named Sampsigeramus, aided by farmers and some stone-slingers, went out in his hieratic garb to meet Sapor after the capture of Antioch. In the course of their discussion, one of Sampsigeramus' slingers hit Sapor with a stone. Sapor died and the Persians ran away.[351]

There is obviously no reason to believe much of what Malalas has to say about Sampsigeramus—save that the Persians did not capture Emesa in the wake of the fall of Antioch during 252. This is indirectly confirmed by the absence of that city from the list of cities taken in the *Res Gestae* of Sapor. Beyond this, nothing is known,[352] save only the fact that the mint of Antioch issued for Valerian in 254, which suggests that Uranius' activity had come to an end.

Here the main interest of the passage in question is the evidence it provides for the date of Uranius' activity. It places him firmly after the fall of Antioch in 252 and the accession of Aemilianus in 253, in the context of further troubles on the eastern frontier. That trouble should continue on that frontier is scarcely surprising; it may even suggest that there is some truth to the story of Aemilianus' desire to fight the Persians (see on l. 147).

The essential question that this oracle may help to solve by clarifying the chronology of Uranius' uprising is that of what he thought he was doing. He has been described as an eminent Arab rising up to meet the Persian threat, and one who 'will have seen a suitable occasion for proclaiming himself emperor and . . . restoring the Arab domination of the central government'.[353] In view of the

[351] Mal., p. 296 παρέλαβε δὲ καὶ πάντα τὰ ἀνατολικὰ μέρη, καὶ στρέφει καὶ καίει καὶ πραιδεύει αὐτά, καὶ ἐφόνευσεν πάντας ἕως πόλεως Ἐμίσης, τῆς τοῦ Λιβάνου Φοινίκης. καὶ ἐξελθὼν ὁ ἱερεὺς τῆς Ἀφροδίτης ὀνόματι Σαμψιγέρα-μος μετὰ βοηθείας ἀγροικικῆς καὶ σφενδόβολων ὑπήντησεν αὐτῷ· καὶ προσεσχηκὼς ὁ Σαπώρης βασιλεὺς Περσῶν ἱερατικὸν σχῆμα, παρήγγειλεν τῷ στρατῷ τῷ ἰδίῳ μὴ τοξεῦσαι κατ᾽ αὐτῶν μήτε ἐπελθεῖν αὐτοῖς μήτε πολεμῆσαι αὐτοῖς, εἰς πρεσβείαν δεχόμενος τὸν ἱερέα. προεδήλωσεν γὰρ αὐτῷ ὁ ἱερεὺς δέξασθαι αὐτὸν πρεσβεύοντα ὑπὲρ τῆς ἰδίας χώρας. ἐν τῷ δὲ διαλέγεσθαι αὐτὸν τῷ ἱερεῖ, ἐν ὑψηλῷ βωμῷ καθημένου τοῦ αὐτοῦ βασιλέως Σαπώρη ἔρριψεν εἰς τῶν ἀγροίκων σφενδοβόλῳ λίθον καὶ ἔδωκε τῷ αὐτῷ Σαπώρῃ βασιλεῖ κατὰ τοῦ μετώπου· καὶ εὐθέως ἀπέθανεν ἐπὶ τόπον.
[352] For a more optimistic appraisal of the evidence see Baldus, *Uranius Antoninus*, pp. 246–50.
[353] Bowersock, *Roman Arabia*, p. 128.

fact that he did not rise up to meet the threat until the year after the capture of Antioch, it can be suggested instead that he seized an opportunity to strike out on his own while the imperial administration was in confusion. The fact that he presented himself as an emperor on his coins does not necessarily mean that he wanted to restore Arab domination of the central government. Study of the coin-types has shown that his mint-workers do not seem to have been able to read Latin, and that the forms which they adopted to represent his authority were used without great consistency.[354] It seems that he merely wanted to express his importance in terms that were familiar to his neighbours and contemporaries (see ch. 1 n. 139).

151. πανύστατος: I retain this obscure reading of the manuscripts with much hesitation. It may possibly mean that Uranius was the last of all the lines of the Sampsigeramids. Otherwise, in view of the connection between this person and the sun, it is tempting to emend to *πανύκρατος*. For the description of the sun as all-powerful see O. Neugebauer and H. D. van Hoesen, *Greek Horoscopes* (Philadelphia, 1959), No. 46. 1 *εὑρίσκομεν τὸν ἥλιον τὸν κοσμοκράτωρα*; cf. ibid., No. 81. 48–51 *ὅθεν ὁ | μὲν μεγιστότατος | ἥλιος καὶ τῶν ὅλων | δυνάστης*; cf. also the story told of Elagabalus at *HA V. Heliog.* 7. 4 'omnes sane deos sui dei ministros esse aiebat'. Rzach's *ἀνυπόστατος* (*RE* iiA. 2159) is attractive for the same reasons as *πανύκρατος*. Less good, because it lacks the connection with the sun, is *περίκλυτος*, which Rzach prints in his text.

ἡλιόπεμπτος: for a saviour being sent from the sun see *Orac. Sib.* 3. 652–4; ll. ‾164–5 below; Lact. *DI* 7. 18. 7 (where *Orac. Sib.* 3. 652–4 are cited); *Orac. Pott.* P₂ 39–41 *ἐπὰν ὁ τὰ πεντήκοντα πέγ‿τ‿ε ἔτη εὐμενὴς | ὑπάρχων ἀπὸ Ἡλίου παραγένηται βασιλεύς, ἀγαθῶν δοτήρ, καθιστά|μενος ὑπὸ θεᾶς μεγίστης {Ἴσιδος}*; cf. *Orac. Pott.* P₃. 64–7.[355] Although the appearance of a 'sun-sent' hero is a theme in oracular verse (but in the *Apocalypse of Elijah*, 2. 46, a villain appears from 'the city of the sun', Heliopolis in Egypt), it is an entirely appropriate description for a person from the city of Elagabal, and Starkey is surely correct

---

[354] J. D. Breckenridge, rev. of Baldus, *Uranius Antoninus*, in *AJA* 79 (1975), 396–7.
[355] See also A. D. Nock, 'Greeks and Magi', *JRS* 30 (1940), 196 n. 32 = *Essays*, p. 522 n. 32; id., 'The Emperor's Divine *Comes*', ibid. 37 (1947), 114–15 = *Essays*, pp. 672–3.

to connect it as well with the name of Sampsigeramus, derived from *šmš-grm* 'Shamash [the sun] has decided'.[356] Bowersock's observation, 'another possibility is an allusion to Urania (Aphrodite) whose priest Sampsigeramus was' (*Roman Arabia*, p. 128 n. 24), does not seem to be correct as Urania would more obviously be identified with Astarte and thus with the moon (see on l. 96). In fact the inscriptions of the Syrian cohort stationed at Intercisa suggest that Astarte was worshipped with Elagabal in the guise of Diana (Fitz, *Les Syriens à Intercisa*, pp. 26–7, 192–3; see also the other entries s.v. 'Diane' in his index). Malalas' statement that Sampsigeramus was a priest of Aphrodite is therefore most likely to be based upon an incorrect identification of the local Astarte.

The process by which the god Elagabal came to be equated with the heavens is of some interest, especially as the Semitic name for Elagabal, *'lh' gbl*, means 'god mountain' (see Starkey, 'Stele d'Elahagabal', p. 504, for correction of the erroneous 'god of the mountain'). The first phase appears to have involved the identification of the meteorite which represented the god as the agent of a sky-god (hence the regular representation of the stone with an eagle on Emesene coins).[357] The identification is explicitly made by Herodian,[358] and on inscriptions which have been found both in the area of Emesa and in areas where Syrians settled; thus, from Emesa, Θεῷ Ἡλίῳ | Ἐλαγαβάλ|ῳ Μαιδου|ας Γαλασου | εὐχαρ-ιστία|ς ἀνέθηκεν (see M. Moussli, 'Griechische Inschriften aus Emesa und Laodicea ad Libanum', *Philologus*, NS 127 (1983), 257–9 n. 2); *AÉ* 1962, No. 229 'Deo P[atrio] | Soli Ela[gabalo] | G. Iul. Av[itus] | Alexi[anus] | Soda[lis?] | Titia [. . . .] | Lega[tus aug. pr. pr.] | prov[inciae raetiae]'; see also Fitz, *Les Syriens à Intercisa*, pp. 26–7, 90, 101 (and his index, s.v. 'Deus Sol Elagabalus'). It thus appears that the inhabitants of Emesa identified the sky-god with whom they had earlier identified their mountain-god, *'lh'gbl*, as Helios.[359]

152. ἐκ Συρίης προφανείς: see on l. 22.

---

[356] Starkey, 'Stele d'Elahagabal', *MUSJ* 49 (1975–6), 511, *contra* Baldus, *Uranius Antoninus*, p. 248, who gives the name as 'sun-sent'.

[357] Starkey, 'Stele d'Elahagabal', pp. 503–20, for discussion of the early history of the cult; J. Teixidor, *Bulletin d'épigraphie sémitique* (1964–80), 459.

[358] Herod. 5. 3. 4 ἱερῶντο δὲ αὐτοὶ θεῷ ἡμίῳ· τοῦτον γὰρ οἱ ἐπιχώριοι σέβουσι, τῇ Φοινίκων φωνῇ Ἐλαιαγάβαλον καλοῦντες. Cf. Barnes, '*Ultimus Antoninorum*', *BHAC 1970* (Bonn, 1970), 60–2, for literary references to the cult.

[359] See also Millar, 'Empire, Community and Culture', pp. 157–8.

153. ἔσσεται: this form, here as elsewhere when it is used to introduce a new character, should be understood to mean 'shall arise'; see *Orac. Sib.* 3. 76, 175, 419, 11. 80, 14. 277. For this reason Buresch's suggestion (registered by Geffcken) that it should be changed to ἄρξεται is unnecessary.

155–171 The Reigns of Valerian and Gallienus, and the Victory of Oedaenathus (AD 253–?267)

155–71. These lines, which describe the war between Valerian and Sapor, the fall of Valerian, the subsequent victories under Macrianus, and the triumph of Odaenathus in 261–5, are almost certainly by a different author from the one who wrote the passage which concludes in l. 154 with the emergence of Uranius Antoninus. This is clear from the fact that no mention is made of Uranius' ultimate fate, information that the author would have supplied if he had written after the event. These lines do not really pick up from those which precede them and must have been written at some point between the defeat of Macrianus in 261 and the death of Odaenathus in 267/8.

156. ἀρηίθοοι: the word is rare outside of epic. For the emphasis upon the warlike qualities of an emperor see ll. 16, 22, 82; and above, pp. 138–9.

157. ἑβδομήκοντ' ἀριθμόν: the emperor whose name begins with the number seventy (omicron) must be Valerian, whose name was ordinarily spelt Οὐαλεριανός in Greek. The man of the number three (gamma) is thus Gallienus. Valerian was a man of distinguished connections,[360] a consul before 238 and married to a woman from the house of the Egnatii Victores, which produced three consuls under the Severans.[361] In 238 he played a role—somewhat obscure now because of the incompetence of Zosimus and the *Historia Augusta*, and the ignorance of Herodian—in organizing resistance to Maximinus Thrax as an agent of Gordian I.[362] Rumour

[360] *PIR* ² L 258; Barbieri, *Albo*, No. 1629; Dietz, *Senatus contra principem*, No. 49, pp. 177–81; Syme, 'Emperors from Etruria', p. 343 — *Historia Augusta Papers*, p. 197 (he may have been from Etruria).
[361] Egnatia Mariniana (*PIR* E 39).
[362] *HA V. Gord.* 9. 7 (where he is rather dubiously styled 'princeps senatus'); Zos. 1. 14. 1; Dietz, *Senatus contra principem*, p. 180.

had it that he had been a close associate of the Emperor Decius,[363] and at the end of Gallus' reign he appears to have been given a senior command along the Rhine, and thus to have been one of Gallus' most trusted officers. For the circumstances surrounding his accession see on ll. 144–5.

ὁ δὲ τριτάτου ἀριθμοῖο: P. Licinius Egnatius Gallienus, the eldest son of Valerian, became emperor at the same time as his father and survived him to rule the much-truncated empire until 268.[364] For the events of his reign, which fall outside the scope of this poem, see above, pp. 51–5. I suspect that the judgement of Gibbon on this emperor, that 'he was a master of several curious but useless sciences, a ready orator and elegant poet, a skillful gardener, an excellent cook and a most contemptible prince', was justified.[365]

Gallienus had two sons by Cornelia Salonina[366] who were at times associated with his father and himself in the imperial dignity. The eldest of these was P. Licinius Valerianus,[367] *Caesar* in 254, *Augustus* in 256. He died on the Danube (probably) in 258. The younger, P. Licinius Cornelius Saloninus Valerianus, became *Caesar* during 258 and was murdered at Moguntiacum at the beginning of Postumus' revolt in 260.[368] Other known members of the family are Gallienus' brother, who was consul for the second time in 265[369] and who was killed after Gallienus' death in 268; and another son of Gallienus, Licinius Egnatius Marinianus, consul in 268, who was killed after the accession of Claudius.[370]

158–61. καὶ τότε δ᾽ ὑψαύχην ... φολίσιν: for the use of animal imagery of this sort see on ll. 28–30.

The action alluded to in these lines is manifestly Valerian's war with Persia. It is a war for which there is very little evidence and for which the chronology can only be established in the most basic outline. Valerian had certainly reached Antioch to take up command in

[363] Zon. 12. 20 ἀποσκοπήσας δὲ πρὸς τὸν τῆς ἐξουσίας ὄγκον καὶ τὴν τῶν πραγμάτων οἰκονομίαν, ὡς ἔνιοι λέγουσι, τὸν Βαλεριανὸν ἐπὶ τῇ τῶν πραγμάτων διοικήσει προσείλετο.
[364] PIR² L 197; Barbieri, *Albo*, No. 1630; *PLRE*, pp. 383–4.
[365] Gibbon, *Decline and Fall*, ch. x.
[366] PIR² C 1499. [367] Ibid. L 184.
[368] Ibid. L 183; for the circumstances of his death see König, *Die gallischen Usurpatoren*, pp. 43–51; Drinkwater, *The Gallic Empire*, pp. 23–6.
[369] (Licinius) Valerianus: PIR² L 257; *PLRE* i. 939; see Figs. 15–18.
[370] PIR² L 198; *PLRE* i. 559.

person by 18 January 255. On that day he wrote to the city of Philadelphia in Lydia confirming its rights against its metropolis.[371] The date of the document suggests that he may have arrived some months earlier—winter was not the best time to travel—but it is not possible to trace his movements more precisely than this. The imperial coinage of Antioch, which some have pressed into service to prove that he arrived in the early part of the year, does not seem to me actually to be that informative.[372] We do not have enough information about the operation of this mint to draw precise conclusions about imperial movements. The other evidence, a papyrus from Oxyrhynchus recording a shipment of oxen to Syria at some point between 253 and 256, may be connected with the military operations, but it is not certain: the fact that they were wanted as plough-oxen suggests that it is not relevant, though it may reflect efforts to repair the damage that had been done by Sapor.[373]

If Valerian arrived in the mid-summer of 254, he seems to have been reasonably satisfied with the situation as he found it. He did not stay long. An inscription found near Sirmium, at the confluence of the Danube and the Tisa,[374] reveals that he was on the Danube at some point in 255. A rescript on inheritance dated 10 October 256 shows that he eventually returned to Rome.[375]

It is certain that Valerian left Rome before early 258. Cyprian says that his orders concerning Christians who had been imprisoned under an earlier edict arrived at Rome from abroad.[376] This was in the spring or early summer. Two rescripts, both received at Antioch on the same day, 1 May 258, may show that Valerian had returned

---

[371] J. Keil and F. Gschnitzer, 'Neue Inschriften aus Lydien', *AAWW* (*phil.-hist. Klasse*) 93 (1956), No. 8; *AÉ* 1957, No. 19; *BÉ* 1958, No. 438; *SEG* 17 (1960), No. 528; T. Pékary, 'Bemerkungen zur Chronologie des Jahrzehnts 250–260', *Historia*, 11 (1962), 124.

[372] For more serious consideration of the coinage see Alföldi, 'Die Hauptereignisse der Jahre 253–261', p. 57 = *Studien*, p. 142; Baldus, *Uranius Antoninus*, pp. 259–61; nothing, save bibliography, is added by K. Harl, *Civic Coins and Civic Politics in the Roman East* (Berkeley, 1986), 109–13.

[373] *P. Oxy.* 3109, with Rea's note ad loc. suggesting that this had something to do with the war.

[374] *AÉ* 1965, No. 304 'Imp. Caes. P. Lic. | Valeriano p.f. | Aug. p.m. trib. | pot. III cos. p.p. | procos. ordo | col. pr. appar[a]t(u) d[cv]o|tus numini | corum'. There is no reason to assume that 'trib. pot. III' is an engraver's error, as is stated in *AÉ*.

[375] *CJ* 6. 42. 15. [376] Cyp. *Epp.* 80. 2 'rescripsisse Valerianum ad senatum'.

to Antioch in the spring of that year, and coins proclaiming a 'Victoria Parthica' in 257 might suggest that he had already reached Antioch before the end of that year. He was at Antioch before the Gothic invasion of Cappadocia in 259.[377] The return of Valerian to the east may be connected with a Persian offensive in 256 or 257 which had culminated in the capture of Dura Europos.[378] A few years later, probably in 259—as its fall opened the route across northern Mesopotamia that Sapor took in 260—the Persians captured Nisibis.[379] It is tempting to see this as a result of Valerian's distraction by the Goths in Cappadocia (see on l. 141). For the date and circumstances of the final campaign see on l. 161.

160. ἑρπυστὴν κυανόχρωον: the identification of the Persians with serpents may be particularly appropriate in view of their famous dragon banners and the play in lines 164 and 168 upon two meanings of ἰοβόλος: 'arrow-shooting' (see l. 120) and 'venom-spitting'.

161. ἐπὶ δ' αὐτὸς ὀλεῖται: as αὐτός in this line must be the bull

---

[377] *CJ* 5. 3. 5; 9. 9. 18 (not two copies of the same edict, but two edicts on the same topic); Pekary, 'Bemerkungen', pp. 125–7. There has been some objection to this: Millar, *The Emperor*, p. 570 n. 24, argues that they indicate only that the recipients of the responses were at Antioch on the grounds that the *CJ* only records that they were *accepta* there rather than *data*, though he does acknowledge the probability that Valerian was in the area on the basis of Cyp. *Epp.* 80 (on the subject of the persecution edict). Rouché, *Aphrodisias in Late Antiquity*, No. 1, publishes a letter of Valerian and Gallienus from Cologne which is dated 23 Aug. in a year that is now lost, though it is probably 256 (an easier proposition than 254, the only other option: see J. Reynolds's note ad loc.). It is unfortunate that more is not known of the movements of Macrianus, for the persecution edict must have been issued at a time when he was in Valerian's company: see Eus. *HE* 7. 10. 4 (quoting Dionysius of Alexandria on Macrianus' responsibility for the edict); Alföldi, 'Die Hauptereignisse der Jahre 253–261', p. 59 = *Studien*, p. 145.

[378] Rostovtzeff, '*Res Gestae* and Dura', p. 48; A. R. Bellinger, 'The Numismatic Evidence from Dura', *Berytus*, 8 (1943), 65–71; for further bibliography see Kettenhoffen, *Die römisch-persischen Kriege*, pp. 77–8, all assuming that the city fell in 256. The value of the numismatic evidence upon which these earlier papers were based has very properly been questioned by James and MacDonald ('Dura-Europos', p. 122; 'Dating the Fall of Dura-Europos', pp. 63–4, respectively); though 257 does remain the latest possible date.

[379] Nisibis was clearly in Persian hands in 262, as Zos. 1. 39. 1 and *HA V. Gall.* 10. 3, 12. 2, *Tyr. Trig.* 15. 3 note that Odaenathus recovered it. Tabari (Nöldeke, *Geschichte der Perser und Araber*, p. 32) records that Sapor captured the city before he captured Valerian. Nisibis is not mentioned in the *Res Gestae* under the campaign of 252 or that of 260, and is known to have been in Roman hands after 243. It therefore follows that the city fell between 252 and 260 (with either 256 or 257 being ruled out because the Persians were then at Dura), and, as noted in the text, its capture fits most readily into the context of 259.

of l. 158, the event which these lines predict must be Sapor's third great campaign against Rome and the capture of Valerian. I. König has finally and firmly fixed the date of this event to 260. He points out that Valerian and Gallienus were replaced in the prescripts (or postscripts) to papyri in Egypt between 28 August 260 and 17 September of the same year.[380] He also observes that Bishop Dionysius was elected at Rome on 22 July of the same year and makes the extremely attractive suggestion that this was shortly after the arrival at Rome of news about the campaign of Valerian. There had not been a bishop since the execution of Xystus on 6 August 258, and it appears that no Christian was willing to take up the see at a time when important Christians were attracting the particular attention of the imperial authorities.[381]

J. F. Drinkwater, who has doubts about the value of the evidence from Egypt which I do not share, has added further arguments in favour of 260.[382] He observes that the alternative date for the capture of Valerian, 259, was maintained on the basis of numismatic evidence for the revolt of Postumus and the mint of Viminacium. It once appeared that the coins of Postumus began in 259/60, and the mint of Viminacium was replaced by the mint at Milan as one of the principal mints in the west during 259. It could therefore be argued that the coinage of Postumus began as early as 259, and that the closure of the mint at Viminacium was associated with the revolts of Ingenuus and Regalianus. Literary sources indicate that these revolts occurred after the capture of Valerian. It was also argued that the large number of coin-hoards that have come to light from 259/60 suggests that there was a serious barbarian invasion, which would have precluded a civil war. Drinkwater has shown that this numismatic evidence will not bear the weight that is placed on it. The mint at Milan opened at the very end

---

[380] König suggested 29 Sept. This may now be somewhat further refined by *P. Oxy.* 3476, which is dated in the reign of Macrianus and Quietus on 17 Sept. 260: J. Rea, 'The Date of P. Strassb. I 32', *ZPE* 46 (1982), 210–11.

[381] König, *Die gallischen Usurpatoren*, pp. 20–31.

[382] Drinkwater, *The Gallic Empire*, p. 97, quite properly observes that the appearance of a ruler's name on an Egyptian document does not prove that he was alive. But I think that it is quite incredible that, however eccentric they may have been (and they were not particularly eccentric), people would have regularly dated by an emperor who had been dead for a year. Rea's exemplary study of the Oxyrhyncus corn archive shows that third-century documents are quite reliable guides to imperial chronology (*P. Oxy.* lx).

of 259, and its opening does not coincide exactly with the closure of the mint at Viminacium. The Milan mint issued coins of Valerian which are found in the Danubian hoards, which means that they must have had some time in which to circulate in that area. Hence Valerian could not have been captured before the beginning of 260.[383]

The evidence of papyri seems to me to support the notion that the capture of Valerian occurred in the early summer of 260. The earliest date for Macrianus and Quietus is 17 September 260, and the last date for Valerian is 28 August,[384] which suggests that they were recognized in Egypt in early September. It must have taken some time for their authority to be recognized there, and the literary sources show that they were not proclaimed until Sapor had withdrawn. Therefore several months must have intervened between Valerian's fall and the earliest Egyptian evidence for the usurpers.

While the date of the disaster has now been established, its circumstances remain extremely obscure. The reasons for this are of some interest, and it is worth reviewing the various accounts in detail. Zosimus tells us that Sapor attacked the eastern provinces while Valerian's army was suffering from the plague it had picked up in Cappadocia. Valerian realized that he could not hope to win with his troops in such bad shape, and tried to buy a peace. Sapor dismissed his ambassadors and requested that he appear in person. When he did, the perfidious Persians threw him into chains.[385] Aurelius Victor seems to have known a similar story, and wrote 'dolo circumventus foede laniatus interiit' (De Caes. 32. 5).

Petrus Patricius' account of the capture does not survive, but a fragment from his history and a fragment of the Continuator of

---

[383] Ibid. 101–2.   [384] P. Oxy. 2186.

[385] Zos. 1. 36. 2 Οὐαλεριανοῦ δὲ διά τε μαλακίαν καὶ βίου χαυνότητα βοηθῆσαι μὲν εἰς ἔσχατον ἐλθοῦσι τοῖς πράγμασιν ἀπογνόντος, χρημάτων δὲ δόσει καταλῦσαι τὸν πόλεμον βουλομένου, τοὺς μὲν ἐπὶ τούτῳ σταλέντας πρέσβεις ἀπράκτους ὁ Σαπώρης ἀπέπεμψεν, αὐτὸν δὲ ᾔτει τὸν βασιλέα περὶ τῶν ἀναγκαίων αὐτῷ νομιζομένων εἰς λόγους ἐλθεῖν· ὃ δὲ σὺν οὐδεμιᾷ φρονήσει κατανεύσας τοῖς αἰτουμένοις, ἀπερισκέπτως μετ' ὀλίγων ὁρμήσας ἐπὶ Σαπώρην ὡς δὴ περὶ σπονδῶν αὐτῷ διαλεξόμενος, ἄφνω συλλαμβάνεται παρὰ τῶν πολεμίων· καὶ ἐν αἰχμαλώτου τάξει καταστὰς παρὰ Πέρσαις τὸν βίον ἀπέλιπεν, μεγίστην αἰσχύνην ἐν τοῖς μετὰ ταῦτα τῷ Ῥωμαίων ὀνόματι καταλελοιπώς.

Dio describe events on either side of the disaster; a second fragment of Petrus alludes to it indirectly. In the first fragment of Petrus it is said that Valerian, fearing the invasion of the Persians (for his army, especially the Moorish contingent, was suffering from the plague), gathered together a great deal of money and sent ambassadors to Sapor, asking to end the war in return for the money that he had collected.[386] This looks rather like the story known to Zosimus. The fragment concludes with the note that Sapor detained the messengers for some time while the Roman plight worsened and then sent them back empty-handed. The Continuator of Dio says that after the capture of Valerian, Sapor wrote to Macrianus, who οὐχ εὑρέθη ἐν τῷ πολέμῳ ἀλλ' ἐν Σαμοσάτοις, καὶ ἀπεδέχετο τοὺς στρατιώτας καὶ ἀνεκτᾶτο. He offered to return the captured emperor for a large ransom and Macrianus refused him (Anon. *Post Dion.* F 3, *FHG* iv. 193 = Boissevain, *Excerpta de sententiis.*, 'Petrus', fr. 159). The second fragment from Petrus comes from a later section, one that contains a speech of Galerius to Narses in which the *Caesar* rebukes him for Sapor's treacherous capture of Valerian and posthumous stuffing of his skin.[387]

The fact that there was a battle which led directly to the capture of Valerian appears in a number of sources. Both the *Epitome de Caesaribus* and Eutropius report the event with almost the same words: 'Valerianus in Mesopotamia bellum gerens a Sapore, Persarum rege, superatus est, mox etiam captus apud Parthos ignobili servitute consenuit' (*Brev.* 9. 7, *Epit. de Caes.* 32. 5). Zonaras, in one of his two accounts of the capture, also admits a battle. When Valerian was unwilling to engage the enemy, some of his troops sortied from Edessa and defeated the Persians. Encouraged by this

---

[386] Pet. Patric. fr. 9 (*FHG* iv. 187 = De Boor, *Excerpta de legat. Romanorum*, Petrus, fr. 1)
ὅτι Βαλλεριανὸς εὐλαβηθεὶς τὴν ἔφοδον τῶν Περσῶν (ἐλοίμωξε γὰρ τὸ στράτευμα αὐτοῦ, καὶ μᾶλλον οἱ Μαυρούσιοι), χρυσίον ἄφατον συναγαγὼν ἔπεμψε πρέσβεις πρὸς Σαπώρην, ἐπὶ μεγάλαις δόσεσι τὸν πόλεμον καταλῦσαι βουλόμενος. ὁ δὲ τά τε περὶ τοῦ λοιμοῦ μαθὼν τῇ τε παρακλήσει Βαλλεριανοῦ πλέον ἐπαρθείς, τοὺς πρέσβεις παρελκύσας ἀπράκτους αὐτοὺς ἀπολύσας εὐθὺς ἐπηκολούθησεν. (The readings ἐλοίμωξε and λοιμοῦ are Müller's proposals in place of the MSS' ἐλίμωξε and λιμοῦ and are open to question.)

[387] Pet. Patric. fr. 13 (*FHG* iv. 188) = De Boor, *Excerpta de legat. gentium*, Petrus, fr. 12
καλῶς γὰρ καὶ ἐπὶ Βαλεριανοῦ τὸ μέτρον τῆς νίκης ἐφυλάξατε, οἵτινες δόλοις αὐτὸν ἀπατήσαντες κατέσχετε καὶ μέχρι γήρως ἐσχάτου καὶ τελευτῆς ἀτίμου οὐκ ἀπελύσατε. εἶτα μετὰ θάνατον μυσαρᾷ τινι τέχνῃ τὸ δέρμα αὐτοῦ φυλάξαντες θνητῷ σώματι ἀθάνατον ὕβριν ἐπηγάγετε.

success, Valerian led the whole army out and was utterly defeated. He himself was captured and taken before Sapor.[388] In the *Res Gestae* Sapor asserted that 'between Carrhae and Edessa we fought a battle with the Caesar Valerianus. We made the Caesar Valerianus our prisoner with our own hand' (*RGDS* 24). He then went on to list all the nations which provided soldiers who were captured at the same time. The notion that Valerian's reign ended after a defeat in battle also suits the brief description in this oracle; as it is reported by several and diverse sources, some of them derived from a contemporary account, it is very probably true.

A version that is very probably not anything like true appears in the text in George, and is mentioned as a story believed by some in Zonaras' work. It is that Valerian surrendered himself to escape his own troops, who were suffering from the famine and angry with him (unless λοιμός should be read rather than λιμός in both cases).[389] Although there is little reason to believe that this story goes back to a close contemporary, it is none the less worth while to explore what lay behind it.

Falsification of history can occur for a number of reasons:

---

[388] Zon. 12. 23 Οὐαλεριανὸς δὲ ὤκνει προσμῖξαι τοῖς πολεμίοις. μαθὼν δὲ ὡς οἱ ἐν Ἐδέσῃ στρατιῶται ἐξιόντες τῆς πόλεως καὶ συμπλεκόμενοι τοῖς βαρβάροις πολλοὺς ἀναιροῦσι καὶ πλεῖστα σκῦλα λαμβάνουσιν, ἀνεθάρσησε, καὶ ἀπελθὼν μετὰ τῆς συνούσης αὐτῷ στρατιᾶς συνεπλάκη τοῖς Πέρσαις. οἱ δὲ πολυπλασίους ὄντες τοὺς Ῥωμαίους ἐκύκλωσαν, καὶ οἱ πλείους μὲν ἔπεσον, ἔνιοι δὲ καὶ διέφυγον, Οὐαλεριανὸς δὲ σὺν τοῖς περὶ αὐτὸν συνελήφθη τοῖς πολεμίοις καὶ πρὸς τὸν Σαπώρην ἀπήχθη.

[389] Pet. Patric. fr. 9 (*FHG* iv. 187) = De Boor, *Excerpta de legat. Romanorum*, Petrus, fr. 1 (cited n. 386 above); Zon. 12. 23 εἰσὶ δ᾽ οἳ ἑκόντα φασὶ τὸν Οὐαλεριανὸν προσχωρῆσαι τοῖς Πέρσαις, ὅτι ἐν Ἐδέσῃ διάγοντος αὐτοῦ λιμὸς ἐπῆκτο τοῖς στρατιώταις, κἀντεῦθεν εἰς στάσιν κεκίνηντο καὶ ἀνελεῖν ἐζήτουν τὸν αὐτοκράτορα. ὁ δὲ τὴν τῶν στρατιωτῶν δεδοικὼς ἐπανάστασιν πρὸς τὸν Σαπώρην κατέφυγεν, ἵνα μὴ ὑπὸ τῶν οἰκείων ἀπόληται, τῷ πολεμίῳ προδεδωκὼς ἑαυτόν, ἀλλὰ μέντοι, ὅσον τὸ ἐπ᾽ αὐτῷ, καὶ τὰ Ῥωμαίων στρατεύματα. I suspect that λοιμός should be read in this passage and that λοιμώξαντος should probably be read in George, as Müller thought was the case with Petrus (on the basis of the plague mentioned by Zosimus at 1. 36. 1); but Petrus does not seem to have taken the completely negative view of Valerian implicit in these accounts, and it may be better to retain the manuscript readings of Zonaras and George, and not to assume that there must be a direct connection between their accounts and that of Petrus. See also George, p. 715 (= Mosshammer, p. 466) τοῦ δὲ Ῥωμαϊκοῦ στρατοῦ λιμώξαντος ἐν Ἐδέσσῃ καὶ διὰ τοῦτο ταραχθέντος Οὐαλεριανὸς πτοηθεὶς καὶ σχηματισάμενος ἐπὶ δευτέραν ἰέναι μάχην ἑαυτὸν προῦδωκε τῷ Περῶν βασιλεῖ Σαπώρῃ. George's account may conflate the two accounts known to Zonaras.

ignorance, the desire to edify, or the desire to deceive being three among them. Lactantius saw Valerian's defeat as just retribution for his persecution of the Christians[390] and added the lurid detail that the imperial hide was stuffed and hung in a temple to impress Roman ambassadors.[391] Constantine adopted the story to warn Sapor of what could happen if he persecuted Christians (or, if the document is not genuine, someone thought that he could have).[392] But the tale was not only useful in a Christian context. Galerius used it to assail the cruel pride of Persia when he had Narses at a disadvantage.[393]

Valerian as the victim of divine indignation was a useful paradigm for the education of infidels—so he appears in the works of Lactantius, Orosius, and Jerome.[394] Dionysius of Alexandria, contemporary with the events, said only that his end illustrated the truth of Isa. 66: 3–4 'And those who have chosen their own ways and abominations, in which their soul delights, and I will choose their mockings, and I will avenge their sins'.[395] In none of these cases (though it must be admitted that Dionysius' presentation is incomplete) is the treacherous capture of the emperor a factor, and there is no reason why it should be: it would detract from the main point. Galerius, however, could be portrayed as including the treachery of Sapor. There is every reason why he should: that helped his point, and the notion that Valerian was not the victim of defeat in war might salvage something out of that ruler's reputation. In fact it does actually seem to have done so. He was quite a hero in some circles.

---

[390] Lact. *DMP* 5. 1 'non multo post Valerianus quoque non dissimili furore correptus impias manus in deum intentavit et multum quamvis brevi tempore iusti sanguinis fudit. at illum deus novo ac singulari poenae genere adfecit.'

[391] Ibid. 5. 6 'derepta est ei cutis et exuta visceribus pellis infecta rubro colore, ut in templo barbarorum deorum ad memoriam clarissimi triumphi poneretur legatisque nostris semper esset ostentui'.

[392] Eus. *V. Const.* 4. 11 (without reference to the stuffed skin). For discussion of the authenticity of this document (coming out in favour of it), see T. D. Barnes, 'Constantine and the Christians of Persia', *JRS* 75 (1985), 126–36, esp. pp. 130–3.

[393] See n. 387 above.

[394] Lact. *DMP* 5. 1–7; Oros. *Hist. contra pag.* 7. 22. 4 'Valerianus ilico, nefarii auctor edicti, a Sapore Persarum rege captus, imperator populi Romani ignominiosissima apud Persas servitute consenuit'; Jer. *Chron.* (Ol. 259. 3) 'Valerianus in Christianos persecutione commota statim a Sapore Persarum rege capitur ibique servitute miserabiliter consenuit.'

[395] Eus. *HE* 7. 9. 6–10. 4.

Although the main portion of Valerian's biography in the *Historia Augustus* has been lost, enough survives to indicate that it was laudatory indeed. The emperor is described as a man who lived a praiseworthy life for seventy years. He bore all his offices with distinction and was made emperor not through tumult and mutiny of plebs or army 'sed iure meritorum et quasi ex totius orbis una sententia' (*HA V. Val.* 5. 1–2). The work concludes with a forged *senatus consultum* recommending his virtues to Decius and an equally dubious letter from Decius accepting the point.[396] The message here is very different, but equally improving. As the various kings whose letters to Sapor survive in the *Vita Valeriani* remind Sapor: 'fors omnia regit'.[397] Even the best and most decent princes could fall victim to fortune.

It is not likely that the story as told in the *Historia Augusta* is a wholly imaginative development. There are signs that a source depending upon authors who wrote in the third century was used in this life, as it was in those of the other emperors after Alexander Severus,[398] and there is some reason to believe that the *Historia Augusta*'s story of Valerian's capture was one in which the emperor both suffered misfortune on the battlefield and was captured by Persian treachery.[399] A story which stressed the treacherous conduct of Sapor would not have been a bad one to concoct in order to disguise the unpleasant truth that Valerian had been fool enough to give battle to Sapor on the flat plain south of Edessa which had once been the scene of Crassus' disaster and would later be the site of Galerius' humiliation.

162–4. ἠυκέρως δ᾽ ἔλαφος ... ἰοβόλους θῆρας: events immediately after the disaster at Edessa may be constructed with some confidence with the aid of a reasonably detailed account by

---

[396] *HA V. Val.* 5. 4–6. 9.

[397] See esp. *V. Val.* 2. 2 'age igitur ut prudentem decet, nec fortuna te inflammet, quae multos decepit'; 3. 1.

[398] See esp. *HA V. Val.* 4. 2–4 'sed Valeriano apud Persas consene(s)cente Ode[o]natus Palmyrenus collecto exercitu rem Romanam prope in pristinum statum reddidit. c[o]epit regis thesauros, cepit etiam, quas thesauraris c[h]ariores habent reges Parthici, concubinas. quare magis reformidans Romanos duces Sapor timore Ballistae atque Odenati in regnum suum ocius se recepit.' This story appears to be connected with an account of the campaign of 260 which the author of the *Historia Augusta*'s source derived from Dexippus and Philostratus; see app. II.

[399] *HA V. Val.* 1. 2 'ne, quod senem imperatorem cepisti, et id quidem fraude, male tibi cedat posteris(ve) tuis'.

Zonaras and the _Res Gestae_ of Sapor. But there is a great deal of difficulty with the accounts of the subsequent Roman resistance to Sapor, and it will be best to discuss these in detail where the people concerned are introduced in this oracle (see on ll. 164–5, 169). After the capture of Valerian the _Res Gestae_ record that the Persians burnt, devastated, and pillaged Syria, Cilicia, and Cappadocia (_RGDS_ 26–34). The cities destroyed are then listed in the order in which they were taken—this presumption is based (as is also the case with events in 252) upon the fact that while cities which were in the same area are listed together, they are not always listed in the order in which an army would encounter them (see on ll. 131–3). Once this is recognized, two assumptions may be made. The first of these is based upon the fact that the first places mentioned are Samosata, Alexandria (ad Issum), Katabala, Aigeai, Mopsuestia, Mallos, Adana, and Tarsus. It may therefore be concluded that after attacking the main Roman stronghold from whence troops might come to threaten its march (Samosata), the Persian army crossed Amanus along or near what is now the Marash route to the gulf of Issus, and then turned north into Cilicia.[400] No city south of Alexandria ad Issum is mentioned in the _Res Gestae_. The second point is that, as the cities are once again listed in a sequence by which it would have been impossible for a single force to have taken them, it seems that Sapor split his army into a number of groups after it entered Cilicia. This may explain both the form and success of Roman countermeasures.

There is, it must be admitted, one problem with the basic outline offered on the basis of the _Res Gestae_ in the last paragraph: various literary sources record that Antioch on the Orontes was captured. One of these, Philostratus (as quoted by Malalas), says that Sapor captured Antioch the Great, Rhosus, Anazarbos, Aigeai, and Nicopolis.[401] Zonaras, whose source here was probably Dexippus or

---

[400] Since no city is mentioned between Samosata and Alexandria certainty as to his route is impossible, but the present state of knowledge about the Roman road system in the Amanus region does not leave much room for conjecture. The route from Samosata through Doliche, Hieracome, and Pagaris to Alexandria seems the most plausible one for the Persian army: it is the easiest.

[401] _FGrH_ 99 F 2 ὁ δὲ σοφώτατος Φιλόστρατος ἄλλως συνεγράψατο τὰ περὶ Σάπωρος, βασιλέως Περσῶν, εἰπὼν ὅτι καὶ τὴν Συρίην παρέλαβε καὶ ἔκαυσε σὺν τῇ μεγάλῃ Ἀντιοχείᾳ καὶ ἄλλας πόλεις πολλάς. ὁμοίως δὲ καὶ τὴν Κιλικίαν παρέλαβε, καύσας Ἀλεξάνδρειαν τὴν μικρὰν καὶ Ῥωσσὸν καὶ

someone who used his work, mentions Antioch, Tarsus, and Caesarea as places taken by the Persians.[402] The same three places also appear in George's account of the event.[403]

Antioch on the Orontes does not appear in the *Res Gestae* of Sapor and, since every other place mentioned after the capture of Alexandria ad Issum was either in Cilicia or Cappadocia, there is no reason to think that it should have been. The Persians did not go anywhere south of Alexandria and their most likely route after the battle of Edessa would have taken them to the coast on the wrong side of Amanus, well to the north of Antioch.[404] But they did capture Antioch ad Cragum (*RGDS* 31), and it is not impossible that the two cities were confused in the transmission of the tale. It is also possible that people believed that a disaster in the east must involve the destruction of Antioch on the Orontes and so included it for that reason—or, in the case of Malalas, that the traditions about the two campaigns (those of 252 and 260) were conflated. The capture or death of the bishop Demetrianus of Antioch, which is associated by the author of the *Chronicle of Seert* with the fall of the city, seems indeed to have been the result of both these sorts of confusion—the author dated the event to 252 and placed the deaths of both Valerian and Demetrianus in that context.[405] The rather better-informed Eusebius knew nothing of it and wrote that Demetrianus died of natural causes.[406] This sort of explanation is reasonably straightforward and is not, to my mind, vitiated as an explanation by Philostratus' reference to Rhosos in the same context. This is not anywhere in the *Res Gestae*, either for 252 or for 260, and it may be simply a mistake on the part of either Philostratus or Malalas. The important point remains that Sapor took the northern route over Amanus and did

Ἀνάζαρβον καὶ Αἰγὰς καὶ Νικόπολιν καὶ ἄλλας πολλὰς πόλεις τῆς Κιλικίας, καὶ διὰ τῆς Καππαδοκίας κατῆλθεν ἐπὶ τὰ Περσικὰ μέρη.

[402] Zon. 12. 23 οἱ Πέρσαι δὲ κατὰ πᾶσαν ἄδειαν ταῖς πόλεσιν ἐπιόντες τήν τε πρὸς τῷ Ὀρόντῃ αἱροῦσιν Ἀντιόχειαν καὶ τὴν περιφανεστέραν τῶν τῆς Κιλικίας πόλεων τὴν Ταρσὸν καὶ τὴν ἐν Καππαδοκίᾳ Καισάρειαν.

[403] George, p. 716 (= Mosshammer, p. 466) ὁ Περσῶν βασιλεὺς Σαπώρης τήν τε μεγάλην Ἀντιόχειαν αἱρεῖ καὶ τὴν Κιλίκων Ταρσὸν καὶ τὴν Καππαδόκων Καισάρειαν.

[404] For discussion of the routes over Amanus see Potter, 'The *Tabula Siarensis*', pp. 271–2.

[405] *Chron. Seert*, pp. 220–1.

[406] Eus. *HE* 7. 27; cf. ibid. 5, where he is said to be alive after Gallienus' edict of toleration; see Millar, 'Paul of Samosata', pp. 10–11.

not afterwards cross the southern 'Amanic gates' which led from Cilicia to Syria. When he reached the Cilician plain, Sapor seems to have divided his force into three sections. One of these moved along the main road to Aigeai and then up to Adana, Tarsus, through the Cilician gates, and into Cappadocia.[407] Another group travelled along the coast road as far as Selinus.[408] The third seems to have moved against the cities of eastern Cilicia: Kastabala, Neronias, Flavias, Nicopolis, and Epiphaneia.[409]

It is against the background of the Persian movements described in the last paragraph that the Roman response must be understood. It came initially from two separate places under two separate leaders. One of these was Fulvius Macrianus (see on ll. 164–5). He is attested at Samosata before Sapor's crossing of Amanus, and this oracle describes the well-horned stag (with whom he is to be identified: see n. 413) as keeping to the hills when destroying the serpents.[410] This would suggest that he followed long behind Sapor's army from Commagene and (possibly) that he dealt with that part of the Persian army attacking eastern Cilicia—which would explain why it took so few cities.

The second actor was a naval officer whose name is variously given as Callistus or Ballista (see on l. 169). He is said to have attacked the Persians at Soli and Korykos, and to have seized the gold and the harem of Sapor.[411] In the wake of this disaster the

---

[407] Kettenhoffen, *Die römisch-persischen Kriege*, pp. 117–22, for details.

[408] Ibid. 106–11.

[409] For another view, according to which these places were taken on the return of the Persians from Cappadocia, see Ensslin, *Zu den Kriegen*, pp. 69–70; Kettenhoffen, *Die römisch-persischen Kriege*, pp. 111–13. My reason for identifying the destruction of these cities as the work of a separate group is that they precede mention of the destruction of the cities in western Cilicia and Cappadocia in the *Res Gestae*, while the order in which they are listed suggests a force moving from west to east. As for the return of the group that invaded Cappadocia to Persia, the implication of Malalas, p. 297, is that it was directly from Cappadocia.

[410] *FHG* iv. 193; see on l. 161.

[411] George, p. 716 (= Mosshammer, p. 466) τότε Πέρσαι διασπαρέντες ὑπὸ πλεονεξίας ἄλλοι ἀλλαχοῦ καὶ τὴν πρὸς θάλασσαν Πομπηιούπολιν αἱρεῖν μέλλοντες, Λυκαονίαν τε πορθοῦντες, ἀναιροῦνται πλεῖστοι Καλλίστου τούτοις ἐπελθόντος ἀδοκήτως ναυσὶ μετὰ δυνάμεως τοῦ Ῥωμαίων στρατηγοῦ, ὃν φυγόντες προεστήσαντο ἑαυτοῖς. οὗτος καὶ τὰς Σαπώρου παλλακίδας σὺν πολλῷ πλουτῷ λαβὼν εἰς Σεβαστὴν καὶ Κώρυκον μετέστη σὺν τῷ στολῷ, ἔνθα τρισχιλίους Περσῶν ἀνεῖλε. I adopt A's reading Καλλίστου in place of C's

Persian king began his return to Persia and encountered his third enemy: Odaenathus of Palmyra.

In the section of his history that seems to have been based upon the work of the same Philostratus who provided information for Malalas, the Continuator of Dio tells us that Odaenathus sent gifts to Sapor and sought a separate peace.[412] He was refused and went to war. The story may be false, or somewhat distorted—there is no obvious reason why Odaenathus should have sought to negotiate with Sapor after his defeat by Callistus, and it is possible that he actually joined the Romans while they were fighting in Cilicia. Certainty is impossible.

164–5. τότ᾽ ἐλεύσεται ἡλιόπεμπτος ... φλόγα πολλήν: the lion who will destroy the well-horned stag (l. 167), the bow-footed goat (l. 169), and the venom-spitting beast (l. 168), must be Odaenathus of Palmyra. His rivals are Macrianus (the stag), Callistus (see on l. 169), and the Persians (see on ll. 160–5). Baldus' effort to identify the character appearing here as Uranius Antoninus (which is primarily based upon the representation of this character as ἡλιόπεμπτος, on which see on l. 169) is vitiated by the rather obvious identifications of the people with whom he is involved.[413] The position of Odaenathus at Palmyra and other problems connected with his career after 260 are discussed in Appendix IV and it will not be necessary to deal with them here. There is no firm evidence for any action on his part before this. Rostovtzeff's interesting suggestion that he can be identified as the man celebrating a triumph at Dura after its putative recapture from the Persians in 252 has been shown to rest upon insufficient evidence.[414]

Βάλλιστου, which is read by Mosshammer. George here depends on the same source as Zon. 12. 23 οἱ μέντοι Ῥωμαῖοι φυγόντες, ὡς εἴρηται, στρατηγὸν ἑαυτοῖς ἐπέστησαν Κάλλιστόν τινα· ὃς σκεδαννυμένους τοὺς Πέρσας ὁρῶν καὶ ἀπερισκέπτως ἐπιόντας ταῖς χώραις τῷ μή τινα οἴεσθαι αὐτοῖς ἀντιτάξασθαι καὶ παλλακὰς εἷλε Σαπώρου σὺν πλούτῳ πολλῷ.

[412] *FHG* iv. 187 F 11; cf. *FGrH* 99 F 2 καὶ ὅτι ἀπήντησεν αὐτῷ Ἔναθος βασιλεὺς Σαρακηνῶν εἰς συμμαχίαν αὐτοῦ, φῆσιν, ἐλθών. . . . The connection between these stories is noticed by Bowersock, *Roman Arabia*, p. 130 n. 29.

[413] Baldus, *Uranius Antoninus*, pp. 252–5. He appears not to have known the important article of Lieberman, 'Palestine in the Third and Fourth Centuries', 37–8 which confirms the identification of the stag with Macrianus as the Aramaic *mqrw* − stag.

[414] MacDonald, 'Dating the Fall of Dura-Europos', pp. 45–63, and James, 'Dura-Europos and the Chronology of Syria in the 250s', pp. 111–24, show that the paintings from Dura which Rostovtzeff used to reconstruct Palmyrene intervention there *c.*253 will

Now that these paintings can no longer be used as the basis for speculation about Odaenathus' life before Valerian's capture, there are only the slight indications offered by inscriptions to suggest that he had come to occupy an important position in Valerian's plans for the defence of the eastern frontier before 260.

The relevant texts include five inscriptions dating to the years 252–8 which describe Odaenathus as ὁ λαμπρότατος ὑπατικός (four at Palmyra, one from Tyre), and a number of other inscriptions from Palmyra referring to Odaenathus simply as a senator and 'lord of Palmyra'.[415] It may be presumed that he did something for Rome to earn this dignity and it is possible that this had something to do with the war of 252–3. For his subsequent relations with Macrianus and Gallienus see on ll. 162, 169.

164. ἡλιόπεμπτος: see on l. 152.

165. λέων: for the lion as symbol of various Palmyrene gods, including (though rarely) Bel, see R. comte du Mesnil du Buisson, _Les Tessères et monnaies de Palmyre_ (Paris, 1962), 433–4. For the character of Bel at Palmyra—he was supreme divinity in the cosmic triad—see H. Seyrig, 'Bêl de Palmyre', _Syria_, 48 (1971), 85–114; J. Teixidor, _The Pagan God: Popular Religion in the Greco-Roman Near East_ (Princeton, 1977), 113–21; id., _The Pantheon of Palmyra_ (Leiden, 1979), 1–28.

166. ⟨δὴ τόθ᾿ ὅ γ᾿ αὖτ᾿⟩ ὀλέσει: this is Wilamowitz's eloquent correction of Ω's δὴ τότ᾿ αὖτ᾿. Alexandre had offered δὴ τότε αὖτ᾿; Rzach printed καὶ τότε δ᾿ αὖτ᾿. The sense of these lines suggests that there should be a strong break after πολλήν and therefore that an expressed subject for ὀλέσει would be preferable here, as Wilamowitz saw.

167–9. εὐκεράωτ᾿ ἔλαφον ... τράγον: the victims of Odaenathus are mingled together here without regard to the chronology of his campaigns. The order of their appearance in these lines is Macrianus (the stag), Sapor (the serpent—the use of the singular

not bear the weight he placed on them in 'Res Gestae and Dura', pp. 56–9, and in 'Dura and the Problem of Parthian Art', _YCS_ 5 (1935), 249–52, 283–7.

[415] _Inv._ iii, No. 17; H. Seyrig, 'Les fils du roi Odainath', _AAS_ 13 (1963), 161 = _Scripta Varia_, p. 267; C. Dunant, _Le Sanctuaire du Baalshamin_ (Rome, 1971), 66, No. 52 and n. 2; M. Chéhab, 'Tyr à l'époque romaine', _MUSJ_ 38 (1962), 11, for the title ὁ λαμπρότατος ὑπατικός. See also M. Gawlikowski, 'Les princes de Palmyre', _Syria_, 62 (1985), 254–5, for a fundamental analysis of the family, and app. iv on the problem of the title 'lord of Palmyra'.

suggests that this should be taken as a reference to him personally), and Callistus (the goat). The final campaign against Macrianus and Callistus took place in 261, wars against Persia seem to have continued until at least 265 (*HA V. Gall.* 12. 1). For the fall of Callistus and Macrianus see on l. 169.

As the lion is presented as coming from the sun, the use of the serpent for the Persian army may take on an added significance. A lion coming from on high might be seen as especially connected with Bel, and Bel was often represented as conquering a snake-footed demon: the imagery is particularly appropriate. The struggle between Bel and this demon recalled the cosmogonic myth in which the sky-god defeated the forces of Chaos, represented by a sea monster; see comte du Mesnil du Buisson, *Les Tesséres*, pp. 191–5; H. Seyrig, 'Antiquités syriennes', *Syria*, 15 (1934), 165–73.

169. τοξοβάτην τε τράγον: this is the reading of Ω. In his note on this line Alexandre conjectured that λοξοβάτην might be read instead; Geffcken and Rzach—though he later changed his mind when he saw that there might be a play on the name Ballista here—both printed it in their texts.[416] Emendation is not necessary: τοξοβάτην is easily understood as a play on the name of Ballista, an additional cognomen for Callistus.[417]

The deeds of Macrianus and Callistus in 260 have already been discussed at length (see on ll. 162–5), and in the context of this passage it will be necessary only to review the events which led to their downfall in the summer of 261. It was in this summer that Macrianus set out with his homonymous son to overthrow Gallienus.[418] Brought to battle in Thrace by Aureolus, the future usurper,[419] who was then in command of Gallienus' troops on the Danube, they were decisively defeated.

[416] Rzach, *RE* iiA. 2160 contemplated τοξοβόλον τ' ὄναγρον, noting 'mit Anspielung auf den artilleristischen Namen Ballista, da das Onager-Geschütz in der Kaiserzeit häufige Verwendung fand: dabei bliebe das Tierbild—der wilde Esel—festgehalten'.

[417] The reason why he should be known by these two names is beyond certain recovery. A. von Domaszewski, 'Beiträge zur Kaisergeschichte', *Philologus*, 65 (1906), 351 n. 34, noted that 'Der Name Ballista (= Kanone) der lateinischer überlieferung ist ein militärisches signum, wie ein Reiteroberst unter Augustus Sagitta heißt'. More probably the man was polynomous and Ballista was one of the cognomina. It is attested as such on inscriptions and in the *Digest*: E. Birley, 'Ballista and Trebellius Pollio', *BHAC 1984/5* (Bonn, 1987), 55–6.

[418] For the chronology see *PIR* F 546; *PLRE*, p. 528.

[419] *PIR* A 1672; *PLRE*, p. 138.

It is not likely that Macrianus would have left the east if he had not felt that he was in reasonably secure control, and it may be conjectured that he had reached some agreement with Odaenathus as well as, perhaps, with Persia. The fact that anyone could have thought of raising an army with which to fight those of Gallienus in the west (albeit even in the wake of Postumus' revolt)[420] after the disaster of 260 seems extraordinary. It is possible that the losses sustained in the previous year were not in fact terribly severe (this might also be suggested by the speed of the Roman recovery after Edessa). If, as seems a reasonable conclusion to draw from Sapor's description of Valerian's army, there were a substantial number of troops in the army of Macrianus from the Rhenish, African, and Danubian provinces, it is also possible that there may have been some pressure from the ranks of these men to be taken home.[421] Zonaras does say that Pannonian troops were an important part of his army, and this statement may go back to the third-century historian Philostratus.[422]

Whatever the reason for Macrianus' march, it was probably the news of his failure—as the sources say[423]—that led Odaenathus to reconsider his position. The two accounts of what happened next, in the *Historia Augusta* and Zonaras, complement each other—a rare occurrence and one which sheds some useful light not only upon the deeds of Odaenathus, but also upon the practice of history. It is therefore worth analysing them with some care.

The first and most significant problem is with the name Ballista. He is manifestly the same man who won the battle of Soli and captured the concubines of Sapor (see above, pp. 340–1). It is therefore of some importance that the name of Callistus is not known to the author of the *Historia Augusta* and that for Zonaras he

---

[420] For the circumstances see above, pp. 52–3.

[421] *RGDS* 20–3 'The Caesar Valerian marched against us. He had with him troops (coming from) Germany, Rhaetia, Noricum, Dacia, Pannonia, Moesia, Istria, Spain, Mauritania, Thrace, Bithynia, Asia, Pamphylia, Isauria, Lycaonia, Galatia, Lycia, Cilicia, Cappadocia, Phrygia, Syria, Phoenicia, Judaea, Arabia, Mauritania, Germany, Lydia, Asia, Mesopotamia.'

[422] Zon. 12. 24; see above, p. 91.

[423] Zon. 12. 24 ἐφ᾽ οὓς [Ballista and Quietus] ὁ Γαλιῆνος Ὠδέναθον ἔπεμψεν. Cf. *HA V. Gal.* 3. 1 'ubi Odenatus comperit Macrianum cum filio interemptum, regnare Aureolum, Gallienum remissius rem gerere, festinavit ad alterum filium Macriani cum exercitu.'

is Ballista when the author is using a source derived from Petrus Patricius (for details of Zonaras' sources see Appendix II). Petrus, as was seen in a previous note (on l. 162), used an author named Philostratus, who was of variable reliability, for some of his information on the third century.

The source of the *Historia Augusta* used some information about the third century from the *Chronika* of Dexippus. This is evident from his frequent references to that author and from his dating of third-century events by consul, a system which is in one place accompanied by material which is traceable directly to Dexippus (see ch. 2 n. 43 and Appendix II). But all the stories this historian told need not have come from that author. The author's ignorance of the name Callistus has a parallel in his treatment of the reign of Maximinus, when he twice gives the name of Titus for a usurper who is called Quartinus by Herodian (see Appendix II). This is the sort of confusion which shows that the author of the *Historia Augusta* did not know his Greek sources directly, and suggests that his Latin source was composed by an author who would ordinarily abbreviate the work of some Greek author and supplement that work, which provided the basis for his narrative, with information from other sources.

The fact that Ballista was a name by which the praetorian prefect of Macrianus was known to contemporaries is evident from the play on that name in this line of the oracle. This confirms the propriety of referring to him by this name and suggests that the authors who know it may have a source which was comparatively well informed.

According to Zonaras, Gallienus wrote to Odaenathus and asked him to attack Quietus, the son of Macrianus who had been left in the east under the care of Ballista. When news of Macrianus' defeat arrived, the cities of the east went over to Gallienus and the surviving servants of the usurpers fled to Emesa (the choice of this city suggests that they thought they were on good terms with Odaenathus). It was there that the Palmyrenes met them in battle and killed Ballista. Quietus was then killed by the people of Emesa.[424]

---

[424] Zon. 12. 24 Κύϊντός γε μὴν ὁ νεώτερος τοῦ Μακρίνου υἱὸς ἐν τῇ ἑῴᾳ ἦν σὺν Βαλλίστᾳ, πᾶσαν αὐτὴν σχεδὸν πεποιημένος ὑφ᾽ ἑαυτόν. ἐφ᾽ οὓς ὁ Γαλιηνὸς Ὠδέναθον ἔπεμψεν, ἡγεμονεύοντα τῶν Παλμυρηνῶν. τῆς ἥττης δὲ τῶν Μακρίνων τῆς κατὰ Παιονίαν συμβάσης ἀγγελθείσης τῷ Κύϊντῳ καὶ τῷ

In the *Historia Augusta* Odaenathus attacks Quietus around Emesa after the defeat of Macrianus. Ballista then has Quietus murdered in the city and his body thrown over the wall. This is followed by a general massacre of the local population: 'idem Ballista multos Emisenos, ad quos confugerant Macriani milites, cum Quieto et thesaurorum custode[m] interfecit' (*HA V. Gall.* 3. 4). While this is not identical as it stands to the story in Zonaras, it is very close, close enough in points of circumstantial detail (the timing of Odaenathus' action, the death of Quietus inside Emesa, and the use of the name Ballista) to suggest a common source. The story itself is sufficiently plausible in outline to be believed, perhaps.

Several points follow from the connection between the tales of Zonaras and those in the *Historia Augusta*. The first is that since Petrus, Zonaras' source, probably used the work of Philostratus as his source, the latter historian is also likely to have been the ultimate source for the story in the *Historia Augusta*.[425] Secondly, and more importantly, it can be maintained that something like the truth about Odaenathus' relations with Rome has been recovered. The tale of his deeds has shown how tenuous was the control of the central government when authority was not supported by overwhelming military force.

κῦδος ὀπηδεῖ: the phrase is Homeric (see *Il.* 17. 251), which may explain why the present tense is retained here (I owe this observation to E. L. Bowie).

170. ὁλόκληρος: not, as Terry translated, 'obtaining all by lot' or, as Olmstead ('The Mid-Third Century', p. 420) and Collins have it, 'intact' or 'sound'. In this context it should be understood in its meaning 'perfect'; see Pl. *Phaedr.* 205 c, *Leg.* 759 c; LSJ s.v.

ἀλώβητος: this is best understood in the sense 'unblemished' (for which see references in LSJ, s.v.). Odaenathus is being spoken of as a god; Terry's 'uninjured' and Olmstead's 'unhurt' ('The Mid-Third Century', p. 420) do not adequately convey this.

ἄπλητος: the epic form of ἄπλατος is Mendelssohn's correction of Ω's ἄπληστος, and it should not here be translated 'insati-

Βαλλίστᾳ, πολλαὶ τῶν ὑπ' αὐτοὺς ἀπέστησαν πόλεων. οἱ δ' ἐν Ἐμέσῃ διῆγον. ἔνθα γενόμενος ὁ Ὠδέναθος καὶ συμβαλὼν αὐτοῖς νικᾷ, καὶ τὸν μὲν Βαλλίσταν αὐτὸς ἀναιρεῖ, τὸν δὲ Κύϊντον οἱ τῆς πόλεως.

425 See appendix II.

able' (Terry) or 'unapproachable (in his desert home)' (Olmstead, 'The Mid-Third Century', p. 420) or even 'great' (Collins). The word conveys a sense of the monstrous and supernatural (see LSJ, s.v. ἄπλατος); hence the best translation is a word such as 'awesome'.

171. ἄρξει Ῥωμαίων: after the defeat of Quietus and Ballista, Gallienus recognized the *de facto* supremacy of Odaenathus in the provinces on the eastern frontier, giving him the title *corrector totius orientis*. The implication of the title, as far as Odaenathus was concerned, is best illustrated by his assumption of the dignity King of Kings. For details see Appendix IV.

Πέρσαι . . . ἀλαπαδνοί: it is tempting to understand this in the context of Odaenathus' campaigns during 264 and 265 in northern Mesopotamia and around Ctesiphon. If this is correct the date of this section may be fixed at 264–7/8 (the year of Odaenathus' death). If not, the limits are 261–7/8. See ch. 1 n. 147 above for questions connected with Odaenathus' administration.

172–173 Epilogue

172–3. ἀλλὰ ἄναξ . . . δὸς δ' ἱμερόεσσαν ἀοιδήν: similar sentiments conclude *Orac. Sib.* 11 and 12; cf. 11. 322–4, 12. 298–9, and also 2. 346–7, 3. 1–3, 295–6, 489. For prophets who are conscious of themselves as being under the divine impulse, as this one clearly is, see on l. 1 με . . . κέλεται.

APPENDICES

APPENDIX I
An Oracle Inscribed at Oenoanda

In 1971 G. E. Bean published a new and very much improved text for an inscription at the Lycian city of Oenoanda.[1] It is on an altar carved out of half a block on the outer face of the eastern hellenistic city-wall and, aside from one very short dedication inscribed a few yards away, it is the only text deliberately cut into the city's surviving defences.[2] This inscription is an oracle of six hexameters and runs as follows:[3]

[α]ὐτοφυής, ἀδί|δακτος, ἀμήτωρ, | ἀστυφέλικτος,
οὔνομα μὴ χω|ρῶν, πολυώνομος, | ἐν πυρὶ ναίων. |
τοῦτο θεός· μεικρὰ | δὲ θεοῦ μερὶς ἄν|γελοι ἡμεῖς.
τοῦτο πευ|θομένοισι θεοῦ πέ|ρι ὅστις ὑπάρχει, |
Αἰ[θ]ε̣[ρ]α πανδερκ[ῆ | θε]ὸν ἔννεπεν, εἰς | ὃν ὁρῶντας   5
εὔχεσθ᾽ ἠῳ|ους πρὸς ἀντολίην ἐσορῶ[ν]|τας.

Self-nourished, taught by none, unmothered, unshakeable,
having no name, many-named, dwelling in fire.
This (is) god; we messengers (are) a small part of god.
He says this to inquirers of the God about his being:
Aither is the all-seeing God, pray gazing at   5
him at sunrise while looking east.

Bean thought that this sounded Orphic,[4] but L. Robert pointed out that it could not be. He saw that the first three lines paralleled three lines at the end of a sixteen-line response in the *Tübingen Theosophy* (though there Christians—he assumed—had altered line 2 (*T. Theos.*

---

[1] G. E. Bean, *Journeys in Northern Lycia* (Vienna, 1971), 20–2.

[2] The best description of the site is that in A. S. Hall, 'The Klarian Oracle at Oenoanda', *ZPE* 32 (1978), 263–8, esp. p. 264. I benefited greatly from discussions with the late Mr Hall at Oenoanda in the summer of 1981 and am grateful to him for his kindness in lavishly entertaining an uninvited guest.

[3] This is the text published by Bean (*Journeys in Northern Lycia*, p. 21). M. Guarducci, 'Chi è Dio? L'oracolo di Apollo Klarios e un epigrafe di Enoanda', *Rend. Lincei* 27 (1972), 343, proposes to read τοῦτο⟨ν⟩ in place of τοῦτο in l. 4.

[4] Bean, *Journeys in Northern Lycia*, pp. 21–2.

13. 15) to read οὔνομα μηδὲ λόγῳ χωρούμενος, ἐν πυρὶ ναίων).[5] Exactly the same lines as those in the *Theosophy* text also appear in Lactantius' *Divine Institutes*, but there he says that they were at the beginning of a response of twenty-one lines in which Apollo identified himself.[6]

Similar wisdom to that in these three texts appears in one other place as well. This is Malalas' tale of the early history of the world, a tale that was later copied out wholesale by Cedrenus. In this case Petissonios, son of Pharaoh, asked the Pythia who had the foremost position among the gods and who was the great god of Israel. The Pythia answered as follows: 'There will have descended from great heaven a celestial, eternal, deathless flame that surpasses fire, at which all things tremble—heaven, earth, and the sea—and the demons of the pit of Tartarus fear it. This is god who is his own father, without a father, who is father and son of himself, thrice blessed; we are but a small part of his messengers. Now you have learnt, go in silence.'[7]

With the exception of A. D. Nock, who thought that the text cited by Lactantius and that contained in the *Theosophy* (where it is said to be a response given to someone named Theophilus) might be two redactions of a well-known text found in Porphyry's work on philosophy from oracles,[8] and H. Lewy, who thought that the lines might be the work of Julianus the Theurgist,[9] it has been generally believed that the

[5] L. Robert, 'Un oracle gravé a Oinoanda', *CRAI* (1971), 604–5.

[6] Lact. *DI* 1. 7 'Apollo enim, quem praeter ceteros divinum maximeque fatidicum existimant, Colophone residens, quo Delphis credo migraverat, amoenitate Asiae ductus, quaerenti cuidam, quis aut quid esset omnino Deus, respondit viginti et uno versibus quarum hoc principium est: αὐτοφυής, ἀδίδακτος, ἀμήτωρ, ἀστυφέλικτος, | οὔνομα μηδὲ λόγῳ χωρούμενος, ἐν πυρὶ ναίων. | τοῦτο θεός· μεικρὰ δὲ θεοῦ μερὶς ἄγγελοι ἡμεῖς.

[7] Malalas, pp. 65–6 καὶ ποιήσας (Petissonios son of Pharaoh) θυσίαν ἐπηρώτα τὴν Πυθίαν λέγων, Σαφήνισόν μοι τίς ἐστιν πρῶτος ὑμῶν καὶ μέγας θεὸς τοῦ Ἰσραήλ; καὶ ἐδόθη αὐτῷ χρησμὸς οὗτος· Ἔστι κατ' οὐρανοῖο μεγάλοιο βεβηκὸς φλογὸς ὑπερβάλλων αἴθριον, ἀέναον, ἀθάνατον πῦρ, ὃ τρέμει πᾶν, οὐρανός, γαῖά τε καὶ θάλασσα, ταρτάριοί τε βύθιοι δαίμονες ἐρρίγησαν. οὗτος ὁ θεὸς αὐτοπάτωρ, ἀπάτωρ, πατήρ, υἱὸς αὐτὸς ἑαυτοῦ, τρισόλβιος· εἰς μικρὸν δὲ μέρος ἀγγέλων ἡμεῖς. μαθὼν ἄπιθι σιγῶν.

[8] A. D. Nock, 'Oracles théologiques', *RÉA* 30 (1928), 280–1 = *Essays*, pp. 160–1.

[9] Lewy, *The Chaldean Oracles and Theurgy*[2], pp. 18–19. Cf. C. Gallevotti, 'Un' epigrafe teosofico ad Enoanda nel quadro della teurgia caldaica', *Philologus*, 121 (1977), 95–105, esp. p. 101 'Chi sono indicati con pronome? A mio parere, sono uomini: identici a quelli che aspirano a conoscere dio nel v. 4 πευθομένοισι.' The people who inscribed this text were therefore theurgists. But the passage in Malalas (cited in n. 7 above) proves that

text given by Lactantius and that in the *Theosophy* were one and the same response. The rationale for this was devised by Buresch, and it is that when Lactantius wrote 'querenti cuidam quis aut quid esset omnino Deus respondit viginti et uno versibus, quorum hoc principium est', he did not mean that he was giving the opening lines of the text. He meant that he was giving its 'main point'.[10] The reason that the *Theosophy* text has sixteen instead of twenty-one lines is that either something has gone wrong with the manuscript tradition or else someone deliberately omitted five lines that were embarrassing. This is, however, a difficult point to maintain, for the *Theosophy* text is concerned with Aion, while Lactantius' response is said to have been about Apollo, and *principium* does not appear to be attested anywhere in extant Latin literature as meaning the 'main point'.[11]

When the Oenoanda text was discovered Robert thought that he had seen the reason why the *Theosophy* text had only sixteen lines. He argued that the final three lines of the Oenoanda inscription were a mere summary of a longer text ordaining cult observances, that there had once been six lines in the actual response, and that they were left out of the *Theosophy* because they were of no interest in a theological discourse.[12] Bean's publication meant that there were now three independent records of the same response.

Robert's explanation of the *Theosophy* oracle is not without problems. There is no reason other than one provided by a mistranslation of Lactantius to believe that there is a lacuna that need be explained here. Lactantius presumably could read the text he was citing, and when he wrote 'quorum hoc principium': αὐτοφυής,

the phrase which interests him could be used of gods in contact with a prophet. Furthermore the theosophy texts can be linked firmly with Didyma at a time when the works of Julianus the Theurgist had not yet been given to the world: see L. Robert, 'Trois oracles de la Théosophie et un prophète d'Apollon', *CRAI* (1968), 568–99; Guarducci, 'Chi è Dio?', p. 343.

[10] K. Buresch, *Klaros: Untersuchungen zum Orakelwesen des späteren Altertums* (Leipzig, 1889), 57.

[11] The passages adduced by Buresch (*Klaros*, p. 57) to support his reading are Tert. *Contr. Hermog.* 19; Plin. *NH* 9. 106; neither of these supports him.

[12] Robert, 'Un oracle', p. 609: 'sur la muraille, ils ont fait graver "la somme" de l'oracle, le *principium*, et pour la doctrine et pour le rite, et non pas le très long et difficile texte intégral qui eût tenu beaucoup de place et demandé une grande stele que l'on ne pouvait placer dans la muraille à la porte.' The inscription is not placed by a gate (Hall, 'The Klarian Oracle', p. 264: 'the block is manifestly integral to the fabric of the Hellenistic wall'), but by the entrance to a tower.

ἀδίδακτος, ἀμήτωρ, ἀστυφέλικτος, οὔνομα μηδὲ λόγῳ
χωρούμενος, ἐν πυρὶ ναίων. | τοῦτο θεός· μικρὰ δὲ θεοῦ μερὶς
ἄγγελοι ἡμεῖς, he did not mean that these lines were the main point
of a text which opened ἔσθ᾽ ὑπερουρανίου κύτεος καθύπερθε
λελογχώς, | φλογμὸς ἀπειρέσιος, κινούμενος, ἄπλετος Αἰών·
| ἔστι δ᾽ ἐνὶ μακάρεσσιν ἀμήχανος, εἰ μὴ ἑαυτὸν | βουλὰς
βουλεύσῃσι πατὴρ μέγας, ὡς ἐσιδέσθαι (*T. Theos.* 13. 1–4). The
other texts are not the only problem with this explanation. The
Oenoanda oracle is inscribed on one half of one block of the wall. If
the response had been longer, the rest of the block could have been
used. The lettering of the text is so small that it cannot be read clearly
from the ground, and the reason that it is placed where it is on the wall
seems to be that this is the point facing the spot where the sun appears
over the eastern mountains in the morning. Anyone rich and devout
enough to go and obtain the response and to inscribe it where only the
god could see it would clearly have been able to put up a longer text if
he had one.

The first three lines of the Oenoanda text, like the parallel three
lines at the end of the *Theosophy* oracle, seem gratuitous. All the information needed about Aion is provided in the first thirteen lines there,
all the information about the consultation by the people at Oenoanda
is recorded in the last three lines. They record both the question put to
the god ('Who is he?') and the answer, that he is all-seeing Aither to
whom you should pray while looking at the rising sun; and the position of the Oenoanda inscription suggests that this is exactly what the
recipients of the response did. There seems no better reason why a text
should be carved high up on an isolated section of a wall directly opposite the spot where the sun first appears than that this was the place
where the devotee or devotees of Aither gathered in the morning to
worship him in accordance with the command of the oracle.

The Oenoanda inscription does not provide another copy of a
response already known from two other sources, but it helps to make it
clear that the two previously known responses which say the same
thing were not necessarily given at the same time. There are now three
distinct texts which describe a divinity and his contact with the beings
who give oracular responses in very much the same language. One of
these is specifically connected with Claros (the one in Lactantius), and
it is not impossible that the other two came from there as well. These
texts provide one more intance of the well-attested propensity of

oracles to repeat themselves. Oenomaus the cynic tells us that he had once been greatly excited by a response from the Clarian god. It had called him Hercules and told him that his garden lay in Trachis, where all the flowers bloom eternally, are laden with dew, are even picked and never diminish. But, when he enquired further as to whether the gods were inclined to help him reach his end, he was told by someone in the crowd that this very same answer had recently been given to Callistratus, merchant of Pontus.[13] He was therefore inclined to believe that he had been lied to; perhaps others under these circumstances were not inclined to believe this, and the preservation of the Oenoanda text shows how pleased someone was to have the god speak to him as he had done to others.

[13] Eus. *Praep. Ev.* 5. 22 (fr. 14 Hammerstaedt). For the general context see Lane Fox, *Pagans and Christians*, pp. 168–200.

APPENDIX II

Sources for the History of the Mid-Third century AD

As a great deal has been said in the commentary about the various extant accounts of Roman history in the third century AD, it may be useful to present here a somewhat broader discussion of the connections between the four most important ones and their value as sources for the period. The works in question are Zosimus' *Historia Nova*, Zonaras' chronicle, the chronicle of George Syncellus, and the *Historia Augusta*. The most useful way to proceed through them will be to look first at the Greek writers, and then at the narrative for third-century history known to the author of the *Historia Augusta*.

This examination should also cast some light on a serious problem in the history of Latin literature. This is the fact that between the death of Tacitus and the beginning of Ammianus Marcellinus' *Res Gestae* there was no major work of history (as opposed to biography) written in that language. It should serve to illustrate the way in which the fourth-century authors, who are responsible for the extant Latin tradition about the third century, made use of Greek sources to supplement the meagre information at their disposal for this period. It is an important point for the intellectual history of the empire that an educated man who lived in the Latin west during the early fourth century would have had to depend upon histories that were written in Greek in order to learn about the third century.

George cites the third-century Athenian writer Dexippus for information on the return of the Heracleidae, Alexander the Great, the Phoenix in the reign of Claudius, and the death of Decius in his chronicle of world history from Creation to the time of Diocletian.[1] The firm testimony that some things in George's work can be traced to this author is valuable. It provides a basis from which to begin the

[1] *FGrH* 100 F 9, 10, 11, 22.

search for traces of Dexippus' work in other authors. If close parallels can be shown between a passage in George and one in another author who does not (or could not) have used him, it stands to reason that this author also had access to information from Dexippus. While Dexippus was probably not a particularly great historian, it is still useful to have some assurance that a story about third-century events as told by a third-century writer can be recovered.[2] The question that must then be dealt with is that of how well it was preserved.

The clearest parallel between George and two other writers appears in the context of the Gothic invasions:

George, p. 715 (= Mosshammer, p. 466)	Zon. 12. 23.	Zos. 1. 29. 2–3
ἐπὶ Οὐαλεριανοῦ δὲ καὶ Γαλιηνοῦ πάλιν οἱ Σκύθαι διαβάντες τὸν Ἴστρον ποταμὸν τήν τε Θρᾴκην ἐδῄωσαν καὶ Θεσσαλονίκην ἐπολιόρκησαν τὴν Ἰλλυρίδα πόλιν, οὐδὲν ἄριστον ἐπ' αὐτῇ δράσαντες τῇ τῶν φυλάκων ἀνδρείᾳ. διὰ τοῦτο ταραχθέντες Ἕλληνες τὰς Θερμοπύλας ἐφρούρησαν τό τε τεῖχος Ἀθηναῖοι ἀνῳκοδόμησαν καθαιρεθὲν ἀπὸ τῶν Σύλλου χρόνων, Πελοποννήσιοι δὲ ἀπὸ θαλάσσης εἰς θάλασσαν τὸν Ἰσθμὸν διετείχισαν.	οἵ τε γὰρ Σκύθαι τὸν Ἴστρον διαβάντες καὶ αὖθις τὴν Θρακῴαν χώραν ἠνδραποδίσαντο καὶ πόλιν περιφανῆ τὴν Θεσσαλονίκην ἐπολιόρκησαν μέν, οὐ μὴν καὶ εἷλον. εἰς δέος δὲ τοσοῦτον ἅπαντας περιέστησαν ὡς Ἀθηναίους μὲν ἀνοικοδομῆσαι τὸ τεῖχος τῆς ἑαυτῶν πόλεως, καθῃρημένον ἐκ τῶν τοῦ Σύλλα χρόνων, Πελοποννησίους δὲ διατειχίσαι τὸν Ἰσθμὸν ἀπὸ θαλάσσης εἰς θάλασσαν.	εἰς ἔσχατον μὲν ἡ Θεσσαλονίκη περιέστη κινδύνου, μόλις δὲ καὶ σὺν πόνῳ πολλῷ τῆς πολιορκίας λυθείσης τῶν ἔνδον καρτερῶς ἀντισχόντων, ταραχαῖς ἡ Ἑλλὰς ἐξητάζετο πᾶσα. καὶ Ἀθηναῖοι μὲν τοῦ τείχους ἐπεμελοῦντο μηδεμιᾶς, ἐξότε Σύλλας τοῦτο διέφθειρεν, ἀξιωθέντος φροντίδος, Πελοποννήσιοι δὲ τὸν Ἰσθμὸν διετείχιζον, κοινὴ δὲ παρὰ πάσης φυλακὴ τῆς Ἑλλάδος ἐπ' ἀσφαλείᾳ τῆς χώρας ἐγίνετο.

George and Zonaras are also very close to each other at:

---

[2] See above, pp. 71–94.

George, p. 681 (= Mosshammer,
	p. 443)

οὗτος ἐξ Ἰταλίας εἰς Πάρθους
ἐλθὼν καὶ Σαπώρην τὸν
Ἀρταξέρξου υἱὸν Περσῶν
βασιλέα πολεμήσας ἐτρέψατο
καὶ Νίσιβιν καὶ Κάρρας ἀρθείσας ὑπὸ Περσῶν ἐπὶ Μαξιμίνου τοῦ Μυσοῦ Ῥωμαίοις
ὑπέταξεν. ἀλλὰ πρὸς
Κτησιφῶντα γενόμενος
ἀναιρεῖται ὑπὸ τῶν οἰκείων
στρατιωτῶν ὑπάρχου Φιλίπ-
που γνώμῃ τοῦ μετ᾽ αὐτὸν
βασιλεύσαντος ἔτη ζ΄.

Zon. 12. 18

ὃς ἐκστρατεύσας εἰς Πέρσας
καὶ πολεμήσας αὐτοῖς Σαπώρου τοῦ υἱοῦ Ἀρταξέρξου τοῦ
ἔθνους ἡγεμονεύοντος, ἥττησέ
τε τοὺς ἐναντίους, καὶ Νίσιβιν
καὶ Κάρας Ῥωμαίοις αὖθις
ἐπανεσώσατο, ὑπὸ Περσῶν
ἐπὶ Μαξιμίνου ὑφαρπασθεί-
σας, εἶτα πρὸς Κτησιφῶντα
γενόμενος ἐξ ἐπιβουλῆς
Φιλίππου τοῦ ἐξάρχου τοῦ
δοροφορικοῦ ἀνῃρέθη.

George, p. 715 (= Mosshammer,
	p. 466)

οὓς καταδιώκων ὁ Περσῶν
Βασιλεὺς Σαπώρης τήν τε
μεγάλην Ἀντιόχειαν αἱρεῖ καὶ
τὴν Κιλίκων Ταρσὸν καὶ τὴν
Καππαδόκων Καισάρειαν.

Zon. 12. 23

οἱ Πέρσαι δὲ κατὰ πᾶσαν
ἄδειαν ταῖς πόλεσιν ἐπιόντες
τήν τε πρὸς τῷ Ὀρόντῃ αἱροῦσιν Ἀντιόχειαν καὶ τὴν περιφανεστέραν τῶν τῆς Κιλικίας
πόλεων τὴν Ταρσὸν καὶ τὴν ἐν
Καππαδοκίᾳ Καισάρειαν.

George, p. 716 (= Mosshammer,
	p. 466)

τότε Πέρσαι διασπαρέντες
ὑπὸ πλεονεξίας ἄλλοι
ἀλλαχοῦ καὶ τὴν πρός θά-
λασσαν Πομπηιούπολιν
αἱρεῖν μέλλοντες, Λυκαονίαν
τε πορθοῦντες, ἀναιροῦνται
πλεῖστοι Καλλίστου τούτοις
ἐπελθόντος ἀδοκήτως ναυσὶ
μετὰ δυνάμεως, τοῦ
Ῥωμαίων στρατηγοῦ ὃν
φυγόντες προεστήσαντο ἑαυ-

Zon. 12. 23

οἱ μέντοι Ῥωμαῖοι φυγόντες,
ὡς εἴρηται, στρατηγὸν ἑαυτοῖς ἐπέστησαν Κάλλιστόν
τινα· ὃς σκεδαννυμένους τοὺς
Πέρσας ὁρῶν καὶ ἀπερισ-
κέπτως ἐπιόντας ταῖς χώραις
τῷ μή τινα οἴεσθαι αὐτοῖς
ἀντιτάξασθαι, ἐπιτίθεται
ἀθρόον αὐτοῖς, καὶ φόνον
τῶν βαρβάρων πλεῖστον
εἰργάσατο, καὶ παλλακὰς

τοῖς. οὗτος καὶ τὰς Σαπώρου   εἷλε Σαπώρου σὺν πλούτῳ
παλλακίδας σὺν πολλῷ   πολλῷ.
πλούτῳ λαβὼν εἰς Σεβαστὴν
καὶ Κώρυκον μετέστη σὺν τῷ
στόλῳ, ἔνθα τρισχιλίους
Περσῶν ἀνεῖλε.

Although the parallel passages in the works of George and Zonaras reveal that they derived information from a common original—and the fact that George cites Dexippus on several occasions suggests that this original was Dexippus—it is not clear how close in scope and detail their information is to the ultimate source. It appears from passages other than those cited above that the common source was known to both authors through an intermediary or intermediaries. Dexippus' *Chronika* came to an end in the second year of Claudius,[3] but George and Zonaras produce statements about Aurelian that are as close verbally as their parallel discussions of the Gothic invasion or Gordian III's death.[4]

The fact that there was an intermediary author who adapted Dexippus' *Chronika* and formed the tradition as it was known to the two extant chroniclers suggests the possibility that this lost author (or these lost authors) may have altered things found in the original through ignorance or malice. The latter may lie behind the tale that Valerian surrendered himself to the Persians, which is in both authors,[5] and George's description of Decius as the enemy of god.[6] The former may or may not explain why George identified Volusianus as Decius' son in two places,[7] or why both authors wrongly state that Antioch fell to the Persians in 260.[8] Another problem (this is one that appears most clearly in the passage about Callistus and the concubines of Sapor from George, p. 716 (= Mosshammer, p. 466), and Zon. 12. 23) is that the two can retail their original source with variable consistency. For these reasons the exploitation of their evidence cannot proceed from any hard and fast principles, save only that each passage must be evaluated on its own merits.

---

[3] *FGrH* 100 T 1.

[4] George, pp. 721 (= Mosshammer, p. 470); Zon. 12. 27; Schwartz, *RE* v. 290.

[5] George, p. 715 (= Mosshammer, p. 466); Zon. 12. 23; see on l. 161.

[6] *FGrH* 100 F 22.

[7] Ibid.; George, p. 706 (= Mosshammer, p. 459); see on ll. 142–4.

[8] George, p. 715 (= Mosshammer, p. 466); Zon. 12. 23; see on ll. 161–3.

Zonaras presents problems beyond those connected with his use of someone who had access to Dexippus' *Chronika*. He had a source that provided him with information which was very different from that which could be obtained from Dexippus, and was somewhat more verbose. He was able to join the disparate accounts with various degrees of competence. When writing about Gordian III's death he tells us at one point that Gordian perished after having fallen off his horse.[9] In another place he gives brief notice that Philip murdered him, and then gives a long tale of how that murder took place, a tale that he does not seem over-ready to credit,[10] though the story is one which must have convinced other people, as it also appears in Zosimus and the *Historia Augusta*. It is that Philip cut off supplies to the army until a mutiny broke out. Somewhat later, Zonaras joins a story that Valerian was captured in a battle which he fought after his troops had won an earlier engagement with one that Valerian surrendered himself to escape from his men.[11] He introduces the second story with a note of disbelief. No disbelief is evident when he writes about Decius' defeat by the Goths.[12] Unlike George, he does not mention the Abrittus and does not record that there was a battle with the Goths before this (George had his information from Dexippus).[13] He does know that Gallus betrayed his emperor by advising the Goths to draw the Romans into a swamp, and does know that there was trouble about the name of Volusianus—some thought it was a cognomen of Gallus, others that it was the name of his son.[14] He does not seem to have realized that Callistus an Ballista were one and the same person.[15] In four places where he is giving stories about events from the 250s to the 270s—these are a letter from Aemilianus to the Senate offering to undertake the war with Persia, the tale that the Goths did not burn the books of Athens lest without them the Athenians should learn how to fight, the misspelling of Quietus as Κύϊντος and of Macrianus as Μακρῖνος, and some anonymous advice on government given to Aurelian—Zonaras' information parallels that found in fragments of the Continuator of Dio.[16] It is likely that the material which the

---

[9] Zon. 12. 17; see on l. 20.   [10] Zon. 12. 18; see on l. 20.
[11] Zon. 12. 23; see on ll. 161–3.   [12] Zon. 12. 20; see on l. 104.
[13] *FGrH* 100 F 22; see Schwartz, *RE* v. 291.
[14] Zon. 12. 21; see on ll. 141–4.   [15] See on l. 169.
[16] Aemilianus: Zon. 12. 22; *FHG* iv. 193 F 2 = Boissevain, *Excerpta de sententiis*, 'Petrus', No. 158; see on l. 158; the Goths at Athens: Zon. 12. 26; *FHG* iv. 196 F 9. 1 = Boissevain, *Excerpta de sententiis*, 'Petrus', No. 169; Macrianus and Quietus: Zon. 12. 24; *FHG* iv. 193

Continuator and Zonaras have in common derives from Petrus Patricius, who was Zonaras' source elsewhere.[17] I shall therefore refer to this tradition as that of Petrus Patricius.

It is clear that Zonaras had material from Petrus as well as from Dexippus, but here there are problems: how completely was Petrus repeated and where did Petrus get his information if he was not reading Dexippus? The second question cannot be answered with complete certainty: there were several people who are known to have dealt with the third century. There was a man from Trebizond named Nicostratus (called a sophist by Evagrius) who wrote from where Herodian left off to the triumph of Odaenathus.[18] There was an Athenian named Philostratus who was said to have flourished under Aurelian,[19] a Eusebius who wrote the history of Rome from the death of Augustus to the death of Carus,[20] and an Ephorus of Cyme (called ὁ νεώτερος by the *Suda*) who wrote about Gallienus in twenty-six books.[21] Contributions to Petrus from any of these cannot be ruled out, but a point of contact can be established only with Philostratus. This is provided by a fragment of a passage preserved in the *Excerpta de legationibus Romanorum ad gentes* describing an embassy from Odaenathus to Sapor and a statement by Philostratus (preserved by Malalas) that Odaenathus sent an embassy to the Persians before attacking him.[22] All that can be said beyond this is that there were certainly people who could have provided information to Petrus who lived during the period in question, and that it is fairly certain that he used the work of one of them.

The problem of how Zonaras used or knew the account of Petrus may be put simply. It appears from fragments preserved in the Constantinian *Excerpta de legationibus* that Petrus wrote at some length and that he included conversations and speeches. The best-preserved of these incidents are an embassy from Narses to Galerius and a story about Tullus Menophilus' dealings with the Carpi in the reign of Gordian III.[23] Episodes of this sort leave some trace in the narrative of Zonaras (the letter of Aemilianus, for example) but clearly there

F 3, 195 F 8 – Boissevain, *Excerpta de sententiis*, 'Petrus', No. 159, 167; Aurelian: Zon. 12. 27; *FHG* iv. 197 F 10 – Boissevain, *Excerpta de sententiis*, 'Petrus', No. 173.

[17] For the Continuator of Dio see app. v.   [18] *FGrH* 98.
[19] Ibid. 99.   [20] Ibid. 101.   [21] Ibid. 212.
[22] Ibid. 99 F 1; *FHG* iv. 187 F 10.
[23] *FGH* iv. 186 F 8 (Tullus Menophilus); ibid. iv. 188–9 F 13 (embassy of Narses); see also above, p. 334.

is nothing like the volume of material that was once in Petrus' history of the Caesars from the death of Julius to that of Julian.[24] The same strictures which are applied to the use of Zonaras' work when he exhibits use of some material from Dexippus must be observed when dealing with his evidence from Petrus. There is information here which reflects the rumour, propaganda, and even some of the truth about events, but the content of every statement needs to be scrutinized with care.

It was noted above that a passage in Zosimus' *Historia Nova* about the Gothic incursions of the 250s parallels one in George and Zonaras. This may suggest that he had some contact with Dexippus, but it should also be noted that he had a story about the death of Decius that is paralleled in Zonaras but is certainly not from Dexippus.[25] Zosimus placed the fatal confrontation on the Tanais instead of the Abrittus. Nor is this all. Zosimus tells a story about Decius' unwilling acceptance of the purple from the Danubian legions that is also in Zonaras,[26] and gives an account of Valerian's capture that may be the same as that told by Petrus but does not seem to be connected with one told by Zonaras.[27]

Zonaras told of a minor battle which the Romans won, saying that the troops were so eager to fight again that Valerian could not restrain them. He then fought the major battle that ended in his capture. Zosimus tells of no first battle but, instead, of a plague in the Roman camp and, in the sequel, of how Valerian tried to buy Sapor off rather than fight. His first embassy failed and he went in person to negotiate: this mission ended in his capture. A fragment of Petrus tells of a famine (plague?) in the Roman camp at Edessa and an unsuccessful Roman embassy to the Persians. All this suggests (though it does not actually prove) that Zosimus and Petrus had a common source.

Other features of Zosimus' narrative suggest that he had before him a work written by someone who knew a good deal about the Gothic wars. There is a substantial amount concerning them in his history, but little on events in the east or in Gaul under Gallienus. Were it not for the fact that he disagrees with Dexippus on the placement of Decius' defeat, it would be tempting to believe that he had the *Skythika Dexippi*

---

[24] For his work see Krumbacher, *Geschichte der byzantinischen Literatur*[2], p. 238.
[25] Zon. 12. 20; Zos. 1. 23; see on l. 104.
[26] Zon. 12. 19; Zos. 1. 21; see on ll. 79–80.
[27] Zos. 1. 36; *FHG* iv. 323 F 9; see on l. 161.

as a primary guide to the period (various reasons could then be devised to explain why he bears such an affinity to parts of Zonaras from Petrus), but the disagreement between him and Dexippus on a matter of such importance appears to be fatal. The disagreement between him and Zonaras on the capture of Valerian (despite Zosimus' possible contact with the source of Petrus) shows how little point there is in further speculation. It must simply be admitted that Zosimus probably based his account on an author who was also known to Petrus and, again, a firm view must be taken as to the parameters of his use as a source for the history of these years. He writes on the basis of something written by someone who knew some things (though this knowledge may not have been very precise) about the period. When he says that one thing happened after another he should probably be believed—but the details he gives about any event (beyond the fact that it took place) are always open to question.

The *Historia Augusta* is the principal Latin source for the years covered by the *Thirteenth Sibylline Oracle*. The other extant Latin works dealing with the period, the *Epitome de Caesaribus*, Victor's *Caesares*, Eutropius' *Breviarium*, and the *Breviarium* of Festus all contain points of interest, but these points are of such a diverse nature that extended speculation on the sources of their knowledge does not seem worth while.[28] Thus Victor knows that Philip was an Arab from the Trachonitis and that Decius was born around Sirmium; but he also knows that Decius died 'trans Danubium, fraude Bruti'.[29] The Epitomator knows that Budalia

---

[28] For the sources of these people see A. Enmann, 'Eine verlorene Geschichte der römischen Kaiser', *Philologus*, suppl. 4 (1884), 337–460. Enmann produces a sufficient number of convincing parallels between the *Historia Augusta* and the Epitomator (pp. 356–96) to add force to his observation (p. 339) that the lost history of Rome from Augustus to Constantine which he postulates as the main source for Victor, Eutropius, and the Epitomator must have been known to the author of the *Historia Augusta*. For a summary of the debate over its existence see T. D. Barnes, *The Sources of the* Historia Augusta (Brussels, 1978), 92; for further remarks on its content for 3rd-cent. subjects see Syme, *Emperors and Biography*, pp. 221–36; Barnes, *Sources*, pp. 90–7. The *Kaisergeschichte* (as Enmann's creation is known) is not the lost work I postulate for the narrative sections of the *Historia Augusta*. The existence of a work like the one I argue for was advocated at great length by F. Graebner, 'Eine Zosimosquelle', *BZ* 14 (1905), 87–153, esp. pp. 142–53, though he did not advance many of the arguments employed below.

[29] Aur. Vict. *De Caes.* 28. 1 (for Philip); 29. 1 (Decius' birthplace: see Syme, *Emperors and Biography*, pp. 196–8); 29. 4 (death of Decius; see on l. 104). A Brutides appears in a fragment of Malalas as the killer of Philip: ὅτι ἐπὶ τῆς βασιλείας Φιλίππου τοῦ Ῥωμαίων βασιλέως ἐμφυλίου πολέμου γενομένου ἐν τῇ Ῥώμῃ μεταξὺ στρατιωτῶν

was Decius' birthplace, and knows about someone called Hostilianus Perpenna, which seems to be a strange variation on Decius' son Hostilianus; but he also knows about Decius' defeat 'in solo barbarico, inter confusas turbas gurgite paludis submersus', and that Gallus and Volusianus were proclaimed (*creati*) 'in insula Meninge, quae nunc Girba dicitur'.[30] Eutropius has 'Gallus Hostilianus et Galli filius Volusianus imperatores' as well as Budalia for Decius.[31] Festus seems not to know much of anything, but still there is Odaenathus, 'decurio palmyrenus', with a band of Syrian farmers which is nowhere else.[32] There are definite links between these writers in some places and definite divergences in others, but not enough on the whole to support any elaborate theory about the state of Latin historiography before they wrote. Some view of this subject can only be obtained through study of narrative passages in the *Historia Augusta*.

The author of the *Historia Augusta* has a definite penchant for asserting his knowledge of Greek authorities for the history of the third century. In the *praefatio* to the *Vita divi Aureliani* 'Flavius Vopiscus' observed that he knew of no Latin author who had treated the reign of Aurelian, but that there were several Greeks who had written on that subject. He was given access to the Ulpian library for their consultation, and Greek names abound among the sources cited in the works of 'Vopiscus'.[33] There are a Callicrates of Tyre, a Theocritus, and a Nicomachus in the life of Aurelian.[34] There is Onesimus (who may actually have existed) in the *Vita Probi* and the *Vitae quadrigae tyrannorum*.[35] Fabius Ceryllianus and Claudius Euthenius are authorities for

ἕνεκε Βρούτιδος μοιχευθείσης, καὶ πολλῶν σφαγέντων, ἐξῆλθεν ὁ Φίλιππος ἐκ τοῦ παλατίου μετὰ τῶν ἰδίων αὐτοῦ υἱῶν παῦσαι αὐτούς, καὶ ἐπῆλθον αὐτῷ οἱ τοῦ ἑνὸς μέρους στρατιῶται καὶ ἔσφαξαν αὐτὸν μετὰ τῶν ἰδίων τέκνων, καὶ ἐτελεύτησεν ὧν ἐνιαυτῶν ξγ' (de Boor, *Excerpta de insidiis*, p. 159, 'Malalas', 19). It is impossible to know how this story developed.

[30] For Decius see *Epit. de Caes.* 29; for Hostilianus Perpenna see *Epit. de Caes.* 30. 2; for the proclamation of Gallus (this is clearly what *creatus* means in this context) see *Epit. de Caes.* 31. 1; Syme, 'Emperors from Etruria', p. 348 = Historia Augusta *Papers*, p. 200.

[31] Eutr. *Brev.* 9. 4 (Decius); 9. 5 (Gallus).

[32] Fest. *Brev.* 23. He may have been aware of the role of Odaenathus in driving back the Persians because he was *consularis Syriae* in 365 or 368; cf. *PLRE*, pp. 334–5.

[33] *HA V. Aurel.* 1; see also B. Baldwin, 'Some Alleged Greek Sources of the *Historia Augusta*', *LCM* 4 (1979), 19–23, who not unreasonably casts doubt on all these characters, but does not address the problem of how any fact at all entered the *Historia Augusta*.

[34] Their fragments appear as *FGrH* 213, 214, 215.

[35] Ibid. 216; the *Suda* registers a historian and sophist of this name in the age of Constantine; see Baldwin, 'Alleged Greek Sources', p. 21.

the four tyrants as well.[36] These names may inspire doubt, but it remains true that there are signs of some link between the narrative of events in the last biographies of the *Historia Augusta* and the narrative of Zosimus. The parallels are not constant or close, but they do exist. The narrative of Claudius Tacitus' war in Pontus is similar to that in Zosimus.[37] There are some evident mistranslations, such as the Jupiter Consul in the *Quadrigae tyrannorum*, who may be Ζεὺς ὕπατος,[38] and Mnesteus appears as Aurelian's murderer, probably reflecting the description of Eros (the murderer in Zosimus) as μηνυτὴς τεταγμένος.[39] Some parallels are in the disposition of, or interest in, events: Aurelian's foundation of the temple of the sun in a sentence preceding the outbreak of the war with Tetricus in the *Vita Aureliani* parallels a passage in Zosimus; and Zosimus' discourse on Aurelian's intention to destroy Tyana, Zenobia's flight on a camel, and the fate of the philosopher Longinus are paralleled in the *Historia Augusta*; all contribute to the impression that the author had some contact with history as written at length by a Greek or Greeks.[40]

For the lives between Alexander Severus and Claudius Gothicus the ground is more solid. Once again only Greeks are cited as sources, and when narrative is provided contact with texts known in Greek appears. The fact that one of the *Historia Augusta*'s sources has survived intact makes it possible to see how Greek works came into his tradition.

The chief problem that must be faced is that of whether or not third-century Greek sources were taken into the *Historia Augusta* directly, or whether they were known through an intermediary who might have changed things at random. The easiest way to approach this question is through comparison of two passages in the history of

---

[36] *FGrH* 217, 218.

[37] *HA V. Tac.* 13. 1; Zos. 1. 63. 1; E. Hohl, 'Vopiscus und die Biographie des Kaisers Tacitus', *Klio*, 11 (1911), 307–9.

[38] *HA Quad. Tyr.* 3. 4–6; see also J. Straub, 'Juppiter Consul', *BHAC* 1971 (Bonn, 1974), 165–84.

[39] *HA V. Aurel.* 36. 1–37. 1; cf. Zos. 1. 62. 1; Hohl, 'Vopiscus und die Biographie des Kaisers Tacitus', pp. 285–8.

[40] *HA V. Aurel.* 35. 3–4; Zos. 1. 61. 2 (the temple of Sol and Tetricus); *HA V. Aurel.* 22. 5–23. 2; *FHG* iv. 197 F 10. 4 (Aurelian's desire to destroy Tyana; see Graebner, 'Eine Zosimus-quelle', p. 152); *HA V. Aurel.* 28; Zos. 1. 55. 2 (Zenobia and the camel); *HA V. Aurel.* 30; Zos. 1. 56 (Longinus).

Herodian and the life of Maximinus Thrax. The first pair is Herod.
7. 2. 2–5 and *V. Max.* 11. 8–12. 1:

μάλιστά τε οἱ ἀκοντισταὶ καὶ οἱ τοξόται πρὸς τὰς Γερμανῶν
quod nullis magis contra Germanos quam expediti sagittarii

μάχας ἐπιτήδειοι δοκοῦσιν, ἐπιτρέχοντές τε αὐτοῖς κούφως
οὐ
valent. mirandum autem adparatum belli Alexander habuit,

προσδοκῶσι καὶ ἀναχωροῦντες ῥᾳδίως. γενόμενος δὲ ἐν τῇ
cui Maximinus multa dicitur addidisse. ingressus igitur

πολεμίᾳ Μαξιμῖνος πολλὴν γῆν ἐπῆλθεν, οὐδενὸς αὐτῷ
Germaniam Transrenanam per triginta vel quadraginta milia

ἀνθεστῶτος, ἀλλὰ τῶν βαρβάρων ἀνακεχωρηκότων. ἐδῄου
τε οὖν πᾶσαν τὴν χώραν, μάλιστα τῶν ληίων ἀκμαζόντων,
τάς τε κώμας ἐμπιπρὰς διαρπάζειν ἐδίδου τῷ στρατῷ.
εὐμαρέστατα γὰρ τὸ πῦρ ἐπινέμεται τάς τε πόλεις αὐτῶν ἃς
ἔχουσι, καὶ τὰς οἰκήσεις ἁπάσας· λίθων μὲν γὰρ παρ' αὐτοῖς ἢ
πλίνθων ὀπτῶν σπάνις,
barbarici soli vicos incendit,

ὗλαι δ' εὔδενδροι, ὅθεν ξύλων οὔσης ἐκτενείας συμπηγνύντες
αὐτὰ καὶ ἁρμόζοντες σκηνοποιοῦνται. ὁ δὲ Μαξιμῖνος ἐπὶ
πολὺ μὲν προεχώρησε, πράττων τε τὰ προειρημένα
greges abegit, praedas sustulit, barbarorum plurimos

καὶ λείας ἀπελαύνων, διδούς τε τὰς ἀγέλας τῷ στρατῷ αἷς
interemit, militem divitem reduxit, cepit innumeros, et nisi

περιτύγχανον. οἱ δὲ Γερμανοὶ ἀπὸ μὲν τῶν πεδίων, καὶ εἴ
τινες
Germani a campis ad paludes et silvas confugissent, omnem

ἦσαν χῶραι ἄδενδροι, ἀνακεχωρήκεσαν, ἐν δὲ ταῖς ὕλαις
ἐκρύπτοντο περί τε τὰ ἔλη διέτριβον.
Germaniam in Romanam ditionem redegisset.

The opening reference in the passage from the *Historia Augusta* to
Alexander Severus is explained by an earlier reference to that

emperor's preparation for war on the Rhine in the text of Herodian, as is the note that Maximinus improved the fitness for war of the troops.[41] On the whole the tendency of the Latin author appears to be to provide an account based on that of Herodian, but not to translate him directly. The only significant addition in this passage is the detail 'per triginta vel quadraginta milia barbarici soli'. It is a phenomenon that was observed by Mommsen long ago,[42] and is one that is of fundamental importance for evaluating differences in fact that appear.

One major difference of fact betwen two otherwise parallel passages occurs at Herod. 7. 1. 9 and *V. Max.* 11. 1–2:

ἐγένετο δέ τις καὶ Ὀσροηνῶν τοξοτῶν ἀπόστασις, οἳ πάνυ

fuit etiam sub eodem factio desciscentibus sagittariis

ἀλγοῦντες ἐπὶ τῇ Ἀλεξάνδρου τελευτῇ, περιτυχόντες τῶν ἀπὸ

Osdroenis ab eodem ob amorem Alexandri et desiderium, quem

ὑπατείας καὶ φίλων Ἀλεξάνδρου τινί (Κουαρτῖνος δὲ ἦν ὄνομα, ὃν

Maximino apud eos occisum esse constabat, nec aliud

Μαξιμῖνος ἐκπέμψας ἦν τοῦ στρατοῦ) ἁρπάσαντες ἄκοντα καὶ οὐδὲν

persuaderi potuerat denique etiam ipsi Titum, unum ex suis,

προειδότα στρατηγὸν ἑαυτῶν κατέστησαν, πορφύρᾳ τε καὶ πυρὶ

sibi ducem atque imperatorem fecerunt, quem Maximinus

προπομπεύοντι, ὀλεθρίοις τιμαῖς, ἐκόσμησαν, ἐπί τε τὴν ἀρχὴν ἦγον οὔ τι βουλόμενον.

privatum iam dimiserat. quem quidem et purpura circumdederunt, regio adparatu ornarunt et quasi sui milites obsaepserunt, et invitum quidem.

---

[41] Herod. 7. 2. 2.

[42] T. Mommsen, 'Die Scriptores Historiae Augustae', *Hermes*, 25 (1890), 260–70 = *Gesammelte Schriften*, vii (Berlin, 1909), 332–41, esp. pp. 262–8 = 334–40. His conclusion (p. 268 = p. 340), 'Meines Erachtens ist mit der oben bezeichneten Ausnahme der gesammte Inhalt dieser Biographie entweder herodianisch oder apokryph', is unfortunate in view of the fact that the inclusion of Titus suggests an intermediary. More recent work, for which see the discussion in Barnes, *Sources*, pp. 79–89, has not improved on Mommsen.

It is difficult to believe that the author of the *Historia Augusta* would have altered the name of the conspirator from Quartinus to Titus on his own and passed over the chance for learned disquisition of the sort for which he reveals a fondness in the tale of Pupienus and Balbinus or that of Gallienus' murderer.[43] The author's belief that the man's name really was Titus, and that Herodian gave no other, is evident from the biography of him included among the Thirty Tyrants which is introduced in the words 'docet Dexippus nec Herodianus tacet omnesque, qui talia legenda posteris tradiderunt, Titum tribunum Maurorum, qui a Maximino inter privatos relictus fuerat' (*HA Tyr. Trig.* 32. 1). The author later concedes the version he had given under another name (the 'Thirty Tyrants' was the work of 'Trebellius Pollio', the life of Maximinus is by 'Julius Capitolinus'): 'alii dicunt ab Armeniis sagitariis, quos Maximinus ut Alexandrinos et oderat et offenderat, principem factum' (*HA Tyr. Trig.* 32. 3). This suggests that he believed that there was no information to expose the fantasy he indulged in for what it was,[44] and there are other places where he can be seen operating in a similar way. One of these is in his treatment of Ballista, of whose other name Callistus he is unaware,[45] another is the creation of some bogus sons of Odaenathus.[46]

Two propositions may now be advanced. The first is that the author of the *Historia Augusta* drew narrative material from a Latin work which derived information from a number of Greek sources: one of them was Dexippus, another (probably) the person whom Petrus drew

[43] *HA V. Max. et Balb.* 1. 2, 15. 3, 16. 7; *V. Gall.* 14. 4.

[44] Schwartz, *RE* v. 293, 'Aber die corrupte Namensform *Titus* erscheint auch hier, so daß dieser Bericht nur entstanden sein kann aus dem originalen in der Vita Maximins, der mit Randbemerkungen versehen war.' Thus also he explains the appearance of Arrian where he feels that the author ought to have written Herodianus (*HA V. Max.* 33. 3; *V. Gord.* 2. 1; *V. Max. et Balb.* 1. 2). I do not see how Herodianus readily becomes Arrianus in a marginal note. Since Dexippus and Arrianus are always cited as a pair and in agreement I would like to imagine that this was the result of a note in the *Historia Augusta*'s source to the effect that Dexippus modelled himself on Arrian—something that Dexippus actually did in the case of his history of the Diadochoi (*FGrH* 100 F 8). Mommsen's notion, 'Dexippus gennante Arrianus' ('Die Scriptores', p. 261 n. 2 = p. 333 n. 2), is extremely appealing in view of the parallel provided by Arrian himself: see P. Stadter, 'Flavius Arrianus: The New Xenophon', *GRBS* 8 (1967), 155–61.

[45] See on l. 169.

[46] *HA Tyr. Trig.* 27–8 (biographies of Herennianus and Timolaus, *filii Odenati*). Though Mommsen (*The Provinces of the Roman Empire*, ii. 106 n. 4) saw through this, the passage continues to deceive; cf. Seyrig, 'Les fils du roi Odainat'; Milik, *Dédicaces faites par des dieux*, pp. 316–21. See app. IV for details of Oedaenathus' family.

on when he wrote about Ballista. The author of this Latin work, though he tended to compose by adapting one source for a story, would occasionally change the received account in matters of detail. To judge from the fact that conflicting accounts are cited in the *Historia Augusta* under the names of the authors who supposedly provided them, it would appear that this was the practice of the *Historia Augusta*'s source. Citations of the memoirs of Septimius Severus in the *Vita* of that emperor provide a parallel: they appear to have been derived from Marius Maximus.[47] In the case of Herodian, the validity of the citations may be checked in the author's work and they are reasonably sound.[48] It would not be preposterous to suppose that the same is true for direct citations from Dexippus. In other places the author of this history corrected details without giving his reasons, which accounts for some odd variations in the *Historia Augusta*.

When the author of the *Historia Augusta* gives information in a narrative context—not in a letter—or cites a detail under Dexippus' name, he does so on the basis of his Latin source. This source was composed by someone who followed his Greek models closely enough to retain peculiarities of style such as the consular dates which appear in the biographies from that of Gordian III to the second year of Claudius Gothicus—the period which corresponds to that between the end of the Herodian and the conclusion of Dexippus' *Chronika*. So much is good. The bad should not be passed over. Diversion from known sources to no good end (i.e. the creation of Titus) has been shown in minor matters. Sometimes it may not be easy to sift fact from invention, and thus the conclusion must be that the unsupported narrative of the *Historia Augusta* can be used for relative chronology and a general outline of events, but nothing more specific than this. Such is the sorry state of the evidence for these years.

---

[47] The notion is touched on by Rubin, *Civil War Propaganda*, pp. 133–99. His treatment is hampered by his belief in the ephemeral Ignotus (in favour of his existence cf. Syme, *Emperors and Biography*, pp. 98–107; Barnes, *Sources*, pp. 98–107; the case against is well put by A. Cameron, 'Review of Syme, *Ammianus and the* Historia Augusta', *JRS* 61 (1971), 262–7; Birley, *Septimus Severus* ¹, pp. 308–26; and the 2nd edn., p. 205, for a summary of more recent work). If the argument of Syme and Barnes, that one man could not produce biographies which contained both valuable material and gossip, is accepted, then Suetonius could be revealed as two persons.

[48] *HA V. Clod. Alb.* 1. 2 − Herod. 2. 15. 1; *V. Clod. Alb.* 12. 4 − Herod. 3. 8. 1; *V. Diad.* 2. 5 − Herod. 5. 4. 12; *V. Alex. Sev.* 57. 3 − Herod. 6. 6. 2−3; *V. Max. et Balb.* 15. 3 − Herod. 8. 8. 4; *Tyr. Trig.* 32. 1 is discussed above.

APPENDIX III
Alexander Severus and Ardashir

There are few issues as important for students of Roman military or political history as the wars that Rome fought against Sassanid Persia. Once the two powers had come into conflict with each other, their antagonism took on a life of its own: neither side could long abide the real or fancied advantage of the other, and relations were conducted in an atmosphere of hostility and suspicion, which merely served to increase mutual antipathy. The long tale of self-perpetuating slaughter tends to obscure the problem of its origins. In order to approach this question, it is necessary first to deal with the problems caused by the western sources which present an account of Sassanian intentions for which no support can be found in Iranian documents, and then to place the events leading up to the outbreak of the first war, in the reign of Alexander Severus, in the context of Roman, Parthian, and Sassanian contacts with the states of the frontier region.[1]

Cassius Dio and Herodian both note that Persian policy underwent a radical transformation when Ardashir, son of Papak, the descendant of Sassan, became King of Kings at Ctesiphon.[2] They both say that he desired lordship over the full extent of the ancient Achaemenid empire. Dio's reasons for making such a claim, if he ever bothered to record them, have disappeared in Xiphilinus' epitome,[3] and the source

This appendix is a slightly revised version of my article of the same title that appeared in *Mesopotamia* in 1987. Now, as then, I am grateful to the participants in the conference on Roman and Sassanian frontiers at Turin in June 1985 for their advice in preparing the paper.

[1] For a summary of earlier bibliography see E. Kettenhoffen, 'Die Einforderung des Achamenidenerbes durch Ardasir: Eine Interpretatio Romana', *Orientalia Lovaniensa Periodica*, 15 (1984), 177 n. 1, 179 nn. 10–13.

[2] Christiansen, *L'Iran sous les sassanides*, pp. 84–7, remains the basic treatment of the earliest Sassanids, though see now R. N. Frye, 'The Political History of Iran under the Sassanians', *The Cambridge History of Iran*, iii/1 (Cambridge, 1983), 116–18.

[3] Dio 80. 4. 1 οὗτός τε οὖν φοβερὸς ἡμῖν ἐγένετο, στρατεύματί τε πολλῷ οὐ μόνον τῇ Μεσοποταμίᾳ ἀλλὰ καὶ τῇ Συρίᾳ ἐφεδρεύσας, καὶ ἀπειλῶν ἀνακτήσεσθαι πάντα, ὡς καὶ προσήκοντά οἱ ἐκ προγόνων, ὅσα ποτὲ οἱ πάλαι Πέρσαι μέχρι τῆς Ἑλληνικῆς θαλάσσης ἔσχον.

of his information concerning the inner cogitations of the Sassanid monarch must remain a matter for conjecture.

Herodian introduces Ardashir as a man who believed in Persia's historical claim to all Asia.[4] Somewhat later he says that the Persian, having easily subdued the neighbouring races of barbarians, plotted against the empire of the Romans.[5] The authority for this is, to say the least, somewhat obscure. Finally, he reports a letter from Ardashir to Alexander Severus ordering him to surrender Asia, as it was the ancestral possession of the Persians.[6] Here again the question of authority must be raised. Herodian was not the sort of person who was admitted to the councils of kings. He was the sort of person who might recount a tale that he had been told on less than good authority. Several of his accounts of imperial campaigns appear to be based on no more than the information that could be gleaned from pictures sent by an emperor to inform the people of his accomplishments.[7]

Dio and Herodian wrote in an age when men were apt to interpret the present danger in terms of the great events of the classical past.[8] Gordian III set out for the eastern frontier in 241 under the protection

---

[4] Herod. 6. 2. 1–2 οὐχ ἡσυχάζει οὐδ᾿ ἐντὸς Τίγριδος ποταμοῦ μένει, ἀλλὰ τὰς ὄχθας ὑπερβαίνων καὶ τοὺς Ῥωμαίων ἀρχῆς ὅρους Μεσοποταμίαν τε κατατρέχει καὶ Σύροις ἀπειλεῖ, πᾶσάν τε τὴν ἀντικειμένην ἤπειρον Εὐρώπῃ καὶ διαιρουμένην Αἰγαίῳ τε καὶ τῷ πορθμῷ τῆς Προποντίδος, Ἀσίαν τε πᾶσαν καλουμένην προγονικὸν κτῆμα ἡγούμενος τῇ Περσῶν ἀρχῇ ἀνακτήσασθαι βούλεται. The position of G. Alföldy, 'Cassius Dio und Herodian über die Anfänge des neupersischen Reiches', *RM*, NS 114 (1971), 360–6 (= *Die Krise des Römischen Reiches: Geschichte, Geschichtsschreibung und Geschichtsbetrachtung* (Stuttgart, 1988), 229–37), that Dio was Herodian's source here, is not supported by the passages that he adduces—though it is possible that they may have a common source, and even that this source was an official document. The parallel between them merely provides further evidence of how widespread the tendency to interpret current events in the light of the past was: see below. On the subject of Herodian's ignorance of Dio in all other areas see T. D. Barnes, review of F. Kolb, *Literarische Beziehungen zwischen Cassius Dio, Herodian und der Historia Augusta*, in *Gnomon*, 47 (1975), 370–3.

[5] Herod. 6. 2. 7 τά τε γειτνιῶντα ἔθνη βάρβαρα χειρωσάμενος ῥᾳδίως ἤδη καὶ τῇ Ῥωμαίων ἀρχῇ ἐπεβούλευσεν.

[6] Ibid. 6. 4. 4–5.

[7] See Dio 53. 19 on the difficulty of obtaining information; on Herodian's use of pictures as historical sources see G. Picard, 'Les reliefs de l'arc de Septime Sévère au Forum Romain', *CRAI* (1962), 13; R. Brilliant, *The Arch of Septimius Severus in the Roman Forum* (Rome, 1967), 172–4; Z. Rubin, 'Dio, Herodian and Severus' Second Parthian War', *Chiron*, 5 (1975), 428–30.

[8] See my remarks in *CR* 33 (1983), 318.

of Athena Promachos. She had championed Athens at Marathon.[9] Caracalla had created a corps of Macedonian phalangites and seems to have deliberately set himself on the path of Alexander the Great through Asia Minor in 214–15.[10] Elagabalus gave a second *neocorate* to Beroia, and the *koinon* of the Macedonians minted coins with Alexander on the obverse in his reign and in those of his successors down to Decius, as a way of recalling the glories of their ancestors.[11] Decius seems to have been less interested in Alexander than in his spiritual heir: thus he added the name Trajan to his own after his accession.[12] Similar behaviour is attested elsewhere in the empire. Nor was interest in the past manifested only through imperial eccentricities and games. Lucian complained that historians of Lucius Verus' Persian war were apt to describe the Persian war of 480 or the struggle between Athens and Sparta in place of their ostensible subject.[13] The testimony of authors who had no direct contact with Ardashir's court and worked in this milieu, a milieu in which literary reminiscence might stand in place of serious analysis without arousing too much adverse comment, should be handled with care. Unless evidence to support their claims can be discovered in Sassanid sources, it may well be that they have revealed more about the attitudes and prejudices of their contemporaries inside the empire than about the interests of the empire's neighbours. The place to search for a rationale in Persian policy is in Persia.

There is no indication in the Iranian evidence that the first two Sassanid kings had any interest in appearing as *Darii redivivi*. The most important evidence for early Sassanid propaganda comes from Naqsh-i-Rustam, a mountain between Persepolis and Sivan in the modern province of Fars. At the time that Ardashir took the throne of Persia,

[9] Robert, 'Deux concours grecs', pp. 14–17.

[10] Herod. 4. 8. 1–2; Dio 77. 7–9; *HA V. Carac.* 13. 2; see Millar, *Cassius Dio*, pp. 215–16; B. M. Levick, 'Caracalla's Path', in *Hommages à Marcel Renard* (Brussels, 1969), 426–46; the main point of Levick's piece is not altered by the criticisms in A. Johnston, 'Caracalla's Path', *Historia*, 32 (1983), 58–76.

[11] Gaebler, *Die antiken Münzen von Makedonia und Paionia*, iii. 12–17; R. Delbrück, *Die Münzbildnisse von Maximinus bis Carinus* (Berlin, 1940), 30, 73; M. Bieber, *Alexander the Great in Greek and Roman Art* (Chicago, 1964), 76–82; *BMC Lycia, Pamphylia* . . ., pp. 202 n. 1, 204 nn. 9–10. On Alexander in 2nd- and 3rd-cent. literature see E. L. Bowie, 'The Greeks and their Past in the Second Sophistic', *Past and Present*, 46 (1970), 7–10 = M. I. Finley (ed.), *Studies in Ancient Society* (London, 1974), 170–4.

[12] See on l. 82.

[13] Luc. *Quomodo hist. con.* 14–15, 18–19.

the site contained the tombs of Darius I, Xerxes, Artaxerxes I, and Darius II, a relief representing the investiture of Sapor's father by Ahura Mazda, two large fire-altars, and a tower 12.6 m. tall. It was built of black and white stone with no windows, but with a grand entrance on the north side leading to a stairway which rose to the single room at the top of the tower. At the time that it was excavated, natives called this tower the Ka'bahi Zardusht: the cube of Zoroaster.[14] In Achaemenid and Sassanian times the place seems to have become the religious centre of the kingdom. It is therefore not surprising that it was one of the places where Ardashir chose to commemorate his victory over Artabanus, and that Sapor had a long inscription, in Middle Persian, Parthian, and Greek, carved on three walls of this tower commemorating his victories over Rome. The middle Persian text is carved on the east wall, the Parthian on the west wall, and the Greek on the south wall. By the side of the inscription he founded fire-altars for himself and his children. Kartir, chief of the magi under Sapor's sons, claimed, in an inscription on the east side of the same building, that 'Sapor, king of kings, said to his heir apparent. "As you know, the gods have done well by me; and so you also ought to make this a foundation house".'[15] Whatever this means precisely—which is not quite certain—it seems at the very least to indicate that both Kartir and Sapor were more interested in the Ka'bah than in the cliffs opposite. The best explanation for this interest is that in the time of Ardashir the royal fire of the Sassanians had been lit in the room at the top. This was very probably its use in Achaemenid times as well.[16]

The god Ahura Mazda had a progressively more important place in the propaganda of Ardashir—or so it would appear from the rock-cut reliefs with which he illustrated his several triumphs. The earliest of these is carved on a cliff in the gorge leading away from Firzabad, Ardashir's first capital. It shows, from left to right, a beardless Sassanid soldier defeating a beardless Arsacid warrior, Sapor unhorsing an Arsacid notable, believed to be Darabanad, the vizier of Ardashir

---

[14] M. L. Chaumont, 'L'inscription de Kartir à la Ka'bah de Zoroastre', *JA* 248 (1960), 339. For earlier religious associations of the spot, going back to the Elamites, see E. F. Schmidt, *Persepolis*, iii. *The Royal Tombs and Other Monuments* (Chicago, 1970), 10–12; see Schmidt's pls. 1–17 for excellent photographs of the tower and the inscriptions.

[15] My translation, based on that of Chaumont, 'L'inscription', p. 348; see id., p. 352, for the problems of translation.

[16] Schmidt, *Persepolis*, iii. 41–9.

mentioned as his victim by Tabari, and Ardashir himself in the act of unhorsing Artabanus V.[17]

A second relief is somewhat further down the gorge, as one moves away from Ardashir's palace. It depicts the investiture of the king by Ahura Mazda. The god stands to the left of an altar offering a diadem with his right hand to Ardashir, who receives it with his own right hand, while making a gesture of respect with his left. The king and the god are the same size. A very much smaller figure stands behind the king holding a fan. Three somewhat larger figures stand to the right. The emblem of the crown prince is represented on the helmet of the first of these figures, and they have therefore been plausibly identified as Ardashir's sons: Sapor, Ardashir, and Peroz.[18]

There are two other reliefs illustrating the investiture of Ardashir, one at Naqsh-i-Radjab, the other at Naqsh-i-Rustam. On the Naqsh-i-Radjab relief a large figure and then a small one, presumably Sapor and a servant, stand at the left behind Ardashir, who receives a diadem with his right hand from the right hand of Ahura Mazda. Two small figures stand between the king and the God. One of them is evidently the god Bahram, the other is not readily identifiable. Two women stand behind Ahura Mazda with their faces averted. They may be of the royal household.[19] At Naqsh-i-Rustam the king is shown mounted with a servant behind him to the left and he is identified by a trilingual inscription (Greek, Middle Persian, and Parthian) carved on his horse. He receives his diadem in the usual way from a mounted Ahura Mazda. The god carries a large staff in his left hand which has been identified as a *barsom*—the staff which played a large part in Zoroastrian cult. A bilingual (Greek and Middle Persian) inscription on the god's horse identifies him. The heads of the horses are touching and they are both treading on prostrate figures. The victim of Ardashir may be identified as Artabanus V, that of Ahura Mazda as Ahriman, the spirit of evil.[20]

The trilingual inscription on the Naqsh-i-Rustam relief identifies Ardashir as 'the Mazda-worshipper . . . the king of kings of Iran of the

[17] W. Hinz, *Altiranische Funde und Forschungen* (Berlin, 1969), 115; R. Girshman, *Iran: Parthians and Sassanids* (London, 1962), 125–6.

[18] Hinz, *Funde und Forschungen*, pp. 118, 123; Girshman, *Iran*, p. 131.

[19] Hinz, *Funde und Forschungen*, pp. 123–5; for the role of women at the Sassanian court see M. L. Chaumont, 'A propos de quelques personnages féminins figurant dans l'inscription trilingue de Shapuhr I à la Kaʿbah de Zoroastre', *JNES* 22 (1963), 194–9.

[20] Hinz, *Funde und Forschungen*, p. 125; Schmidt, *Persepolis*, iii. 122–3, pls. 80–2.

race of the gods, son of Papak the king'.[21] Sapor described himself in the *Res Gestae* inscription as 'the divine Mazda-worshipper, Sapor, king of kings of the Aryans and the non-Aryans, of the race of the gods, son of the divine Mazda—worshipper Ardashir, king of kings of the Aryans, of the race of the gods, grandson of the divine Papak' (*RGDS* 1). The Achaemenids are notable throughout for their absence. The concern of these monarchs was to stress their divine right to rule Persia. This concern should not cause great surprise: they were usurpers.

Both the Achaemenids and Ahura Mazda are missing from Sapor's exposition of the reasons for his wars with Rome. In the account of the war with Gordian he says only that 'the Emperor Gordian raised an army of Goths and Germans from the entire Roman Empire and marched upon Asorestan, against the Empire of Iran and against our person' (*RGDS* 6–7). In the preamble to the second great campaign, that which resulted in the capture of Antioch in 252, Sapor says only that 'Caesar lied about Armenia' (*RGDS* 10). In both these cases it is significant that Sapor did not question the right of the Roman empire to exist on ancient Achaemenid lands: Sapor did not lay claim to it. Gordian did not revolt against his rightful lord and master but rather attacked the innocent Sapor. When Caesar lied to Sapor, the war took place in the Roman empire, not on land that was truly Persian.

In describing his third campaign, the one that resulted in the capture of Valerian during 260, Sapor gives no cause for the war but does list the provinces from which the Roman army had been raised (*RGDS* 19–23): 'in the course of our third campaign when we attacked Edessa and Carrhae and we besieged Edessa and Carrhae, the Caesar Valerian marched against us. He had with him troops (coming from) Germany, Rhaetia, Noricum, Dacia, Pannonia, Moesia, Istria, Spain, Mauritania, Thrace, Bithynia, Asia, Pamphylia, Isauria, Lycaonia, Galatia, Lycia, Cilicia, Cappadocia, Phrygia, Syria, Phoenicia, Judaea, Arabia, Mauritania, Germany, Lydia, Asia, Mesopotamia: a force of 70,000 men.' The purpose of this list, as is clear from the repetition of places, which serves to make it longer, was to emphasize the great power of the defeated emperor. The world that did not belong to Sapor was led against him (not all the world that ought to belong to him by right of inheritance). It was to that world that he took his

---

[21] Christiansen, *Iran sous les sassanides*, p. 92; E. E. Herzfeld, *Paikuli Monument and Inscription of the Early History of the Sasanian Empire* (Berlin, 1724), i. 84; Schmidt, *Persepolis*, iii. 123.

prisoners (*RGDS* 34–5), 'the men taken from the Roman empire, from the non-Iranians, we deported. And in our empire of Iran, in Persis, in Parthia, in Susiana, and in Asorestan, and in each other land that was in the domains of our father, of our grandfathers and ancestors, there we have established them.'[22]

There is no evidence here to support the claim of Dio and Herodian that Sassanid policy was dictated by a desire to restore Achaemenid hegemony. There is evidence to suggest that Ardashir was at pains to represent himself as the chosen of Ahura Mazda; he was, after all, a usurper from a backward province. His son was clearly not at pains to assert a claim over all the lands of Darius. He does not, in fact, seem to have been aware that these lands belonged by right to anyone but the Romans.

Viewing the period of Ardashir's rise from the Roman point of view, Dio records that Ardashir attacked Hatra after his victory over Artabanus, hoping to use it as a future base for attacks on the Roman empire.[23] Here again, Dio's statement of fact must be separated from his statement of opinion. There is no evidence in Dio's account of Ardashir's next moves that he had any intention of attacking the Roman empire. After he failed to take Hatra, Ardashir moved against Media and Parthia. He won these places over by force or diplomacy and moved on to Armenia. There he was defeated by what Dio describes as a combination of natives, Medes, and the sons of Artabanus.[24] One of the sons of Artabanus may have been the Artavasdes whose coinage was still circulating as far south as Khurramabad.[25] Another man who claimed the throne in these years (to judge from his coinage) was Vologaeses VI, former rival of Artabanus.[26] The royal houses of Media, Parthia, and Armenia were closely linked with the

---

[22] See Kettenhoffen, 'Die Einforderung des Achameniderbes', pp. 185–6; on the distinction between Iran as the 'land of the Iranians' and 'Non-Iran' see Chaumont, 'L'inscription', p. 359.

[23] Dio 80. 3. 2 ἐπὶ τὰ Ἄτρα ἐπεστράτευσεν, ἐπιβασίαν ἀπ' αὐτῶν ἐπὶ τοὺς Ῥωμαίους ποιούμενος.

[24] Dio 80. 3. 3 κἀνταῦθα πρός τε τῶν ἐπιχωρίων καὶ πρὸς Μήδων τινῶν τῶν τε τοῦ Ἀρταβάνου παίδων πταίσας. For the possible location of this battle see Frye, *The History of Ancient Iran*, p. 293.

[25] S. H. Taqizadeh, 'The Early Sassanians: Some Chronological Points which Possibly Call for Revision', *BSOAS* 11 (1943), 21.

[26] B. Simonetta, 'A Note on Vologaeses V, Artabanus V and Artavasdes', *Num. Chron.*[6] 16 (1956), 77–82; see A. D. H. Bivar, 'The Political History of Iran under the Arsacids', in *The Cambridge History of Iran*, iii/1 (Cambridge, 1983), 21–99.

rulers at Ctesiphon; so too seems to have been an Arab kingdom in the eastern part of the peninsula whose king, Sanatruq, was killed by Ardashir in a campaign that seems to have taken place just before the accession of Sapor.[27] Ardashir seems to have been after Arsacid survivors, and such a pursuit would lead him beyond the Trigris.

It is also worth reviewing the evidence for two other royal houses: those of Hatra and Edessa. The first man who is known to have held the position of Lord (*Maria*) of Hatra was one Worod (*c.* AD 110), then, possibly, Wologas (*c.* 150 or 200); certainly there was a Nasru there in the mid-second century, followed by Sanatruq I (*c.* 164), Barasamias, who defeated Septimius Severus (*c.* 193–200), Abdsimya (if he is not in fact to be identified with Barsamias; *c.* 200–15), and finally, Sanatruq II, whose children were Abdsimya, Mac̔na, and a daughter named Duspari.[28] The names Worod and Wologas among the highest members of the Arab aristocracy suggest a marriage connection with the Arsacid royal house at Hatra, similar to the one which may have led to the appearance of the Sanatruq who was killed in Arabia. Two kings named Ma̔nu ruled Edessa from 123 to 139 and 139–63, 165–77. A third Ma̔nu ruled from 214 to 240.[29] The congruence of names again suggests blood relationship connecting these people with the Arsacids. It has also been suggested that the Julius Aurelius (Septimius) Vorod who obtained high dignity at Palmyra in the time of Odaenathus was a survivor of the Arsacid catastrophe. Even though this does not seem probable, it is still very likely that he was descended from a house that had long and close connections with Mesopotamia in the years before Ardashir's victory.[30] The connection between an Arsacid or Arsacids

[27] Nöldeke, *Geschichte der Perser und Araber*, pp. 36 n. 1, 500.

[28] I have here tentatively accepted the conclusions of Milik, *Dédicaces faites par les dieux*, pp. 361–4. Alternative versions have been proposed by F. Safar, 'The Lords and Kings of Hatra', *Sumer*, 29 (1973), 87–97, and Drijvers, 'Hatra, Palmyra und Edessa', pp. 817–25. I am tempted to agree with Drijvers and Safar that Barsamias and Abdsimya are one and the same.

[29] See Drijvers, 'Hatra, Palmyra und Edessa', pp. 875–83; C. B. Welles and A. R. Bellinger, 'A Third Century Contract of Sale from Edessa in Osrhoene', *YCS* 5 (1935), 142–54.

[30] D. Schlumberger, 'Vorod l'agoronome', *Syria*, 49 (1972), 339–41, suggests that he is in fact to be identified with the Vorod the *agoronomos* who appears at *RGDS* 67. I find this very difficult to believe (both because Palmyra was at war with Persia at the time and because the man was a Roman citizen). To my mind Vorod is most probably descended from a family which had married into the Parthian aristocracy some time in the 2nd cent. For contacts between Palmyra and the east see most recently M. Gawlikowski, 'Palmyre et l'Euphrate', *Syria*, 60 (1983), 53–68; Matthews, 'The Tax Law of Palmyra', pp. 157–80.

and Palmyra should perhaps be considered in the light of the movement of tribes across northern Arabia that seems to have taken place at Sassanid instigation in the second quarter of the third century, and which seems to have caused considerable trouble for the Palmyrenes.[31]

When the Arsacids ruled at Ctesiphon the city of Hatra, whose rulers had Arsacid names, three times repelled the armies of otherwise victorious Roman emperors. Armenia was at best a shaky buffer between the two powers: 'situ terrarum similitudine morum Parthis propriores conubiisque permixti ac libertate ignota illuc magis ad servitium inclinantes' (Tac. *Ann.* 13. 34. 2). The alignment of both states shifted swiftly after the fall of Ctesiphon in 225.[32]

A milestone at the third mile from the camp of *legio I Parthica* at Singara was inscribed in the eleventh year of Severus Alexander's tribunician power (231), indicating some work on the road towards Callinicum and Carrhae.[33] A line of forts which runs along the road from Hatra to the eastern Singara–Nisibis road may also date from this period, and the earliest Latin dedication in the temple of Šamaš at Hatra is dated 'non(is) iunis Severo Quintiano cos' (5 June 235).[34] It

---

[31] See G. W. Bowersock, 'The Greek–Nabataean Bilingual Inscription at Ruwwāfa Saudi Arabia', in *Le Monde grec: Hommages à Claire Préaux* (Brussels, 1975), 521–2; id., *Roman Arabia*, pp. 132–7; Sartre, *Trois études*, pp. 132–6; Gawlikowski, 'Palmyre et l'Euphrate', pp. 67–8.

[32] Drijvers, 'Hatra, Palmyra und Edessa', p. 827; Oates, 'Three Latin Inscriptions', pp. 41–3; Maricq, 'Les dernières années de Hatra', pp. 288–9. Kennedy, '"European" Soldiers and the Severan Siege of Hatra', p. 404, has argued that the beginning of Hatra's shift towards Rome should be dated to the time of Septimius Severus—a result of the Roman take-over of the area around it. This may be true, and it is also true that there was no need for a Roman garrison there until the time of Alexander Severus. None the less, there is still no evidence to show that Hatra was firmly within the Roman orbit until the years after the fall of the Arsacids. Furthermore, Dio's description of Ardashir's campaigns (81. 3. 2 ἐπὶ τὰ Ἄτρα ἐπεστράτευσεν, ἐπιβασίαν ἀπ' αὐτῶν ἐπὶ τοὺς Ῥωμαίους ποιούμενος) makes it look as if he still regarded Hatra as an independent state: he says that Ardashir wanted to make Hatra a base for operations against the Romans, not that he was making an attack on Roman territory. See also J. Wiesehöfer, 'Die Anfänge sassanidischer Westpolitik und der Untergang Hatras', *Klio*, 64 (1982), 445, who sees the war between Alexander and Ardashir as an extension of the conflict between Ardashir and Hatra. His general analysis of these events, which I only became aware of as this book was going to press, is very much in line with the one offered here.

[33] Drijvers, 'Hatra Palmyra und Edessa', p. 827; Oates, 'Three Latin Inscriptions', pp. 41–3; Maricq, 'Les dernières années de Hatra', p. 294.

[34] Drijvers, 'Hatra, Palmyra und Edessa', p. 825; Oates, 'Three Latin Inscriptions', p. 39; Maricq, 'Les dernières années de Hatra', pp. 288–9. See Dilleman, *Haute Mésopotamie*,

would appear that Hatra was firmly in the Roman camp by this date, and the earlier road construction may have been connected with this new alignment.

The expedition of Alexander Severus to the east in 232/3 was not an outstanding success. A failure or a draw, the Severan effort was at best the latter; this was not the sort of thing that would ordinarily inspire an outbreak of loyal demonstration or enthusiasm for Rome on the eastern fringes of her domain.[35]

Roman power had not manifested itself to great effect even in the years before the campaign of 232/3. Herodian suggests that the inability of the eastern legions to contain Persian attack was the prime reason for Severus Alexander's personal appearance on the eastern frontier.[36] Nor might the Persians have been the only problem. Zosimus, George, and the Latin chronographic tradition record the existence of at least one usurper.[37] George connects his existence with a Persian attack on Nisibis. It is tempting to see the connection between the Persian king and this person as part of the latter's response to Roman friendship with rivals to his dynasty. The existence of coins minted for Vologaeses V at Seleuceia in 227/8 suggests that a direct threat to the new dynasty continued to be very real even after Ardashir had been crowned at Ctesiphon.[38]

Whatever the cause may be, the overwhelming strength of Rome certainly could not have been the cause for her anomalous alliances with Hatra and Armenia in the late 220s and their maintenance into the 230s or later. The rough outline of events beyond the easternmost areas where Rome's legions kept order suggests that these years were filled by the slow and difficult struggle of the Sassanian house to supremacy; the monuments of Ardashir indicate a concern to reinforce the fact of his legitimate rule over the Persians. The intransigence of recalcitrant reactionaries prolonged his fight beyond

pp. 198–210, esp. pp. 201–2, for the problem of the *limes* in this period. He is justifiably sceptical of the value of aerial photography unsupported by excavation in determining the line of the *limes* in any given period.

[35] See G. W. Bowersock, 'A New Inscription from the Syrian Desert', *Chiron*, 6 (1976), 355, on loyalty to Rome inspired by Lucius Verus' victory.

[36] Herod. 6. 2. 5.

[37] See ch. 1 n. 55 for discussions of the usurpers in the time of Alexander.

[38] Simonetta, 'A Note on Volgaeses V', pp. 81–2; for the date of Ardashir's coronation see Tagizadeh, 'The Early Sassanians', pp. 17–36; Henrichs and Koenen, 'Ein griechischer Mani-Codex', pp. 125–32. See also Chaumont, *Recherches*, pp. 35–9.

reasonable lengths, and may have enhanced a desire to eliminate those who steadfastly refused to recognize the new truth—or who might be thought to have failed to recognize the new truth. It is notable that Ardashir's campaigns were directed into areas which might contain, for reasons of blood or taste, supporters of the old regime. The beginning of Rome's wars with the Sassanids came about as a result of these campaigns and may thus be seen as the coincidental legacy of Parthian policy and the insecurity of the new regime.

APPENDIX IV
The Career of Odaenathus

The purpose of this appendix is to elucidate three problems in modern understanding of the career of Odaenathus, the ruler of Palmyra. The first two are closely connected—these are his ancestry and his family's position at Palmyra before 260; the third is his Roman title after the battle of Emesa in the summer of 261. The first two problems need to be discussed in the light of M. Gawlikowski's important preliminary publication of a bilingual Greek–Palmyrene text mentioning Odaenathus that was recently discovered at Palmyra,[1] and the preliminary publication of a papyrus which, although it concerns the royal house of Edessa, may provide a useful parallel for the position of Odaenathus.[2] The proper solution to the third problem was arrived at many years ago by C. Clermont-Ganneau through careful study of inscriptions from the time of Vaballathus.[3] His conclusions, which are of some importance for the history of the period, need to be restated in detail because subsequent scholars have tended to reject them for quite insufficient reasons.[4]

Up until 1985 our knowledge of the ancestors of Odaenathus was based upon the following texts:

I.
1. *l*[*y*]*qr 'dynt br ḥyrn whbl*[*t*]
2. [*rš*] *'dy tdmwr 'bd 'gylw b*[*r*]
3. [*m*]*qy ḥdwdn ḥd' mw*[*tb*] *'dnh*
4. [*wq*]*rb* [*mwdq'*] *wk*[*n*]*wn' wmq*[*lwt*]
5. [*'lm'*   ]

---

[1] Gawlikowski, 'Les princes de Palmyre', p. 257. The text was discovered by Khaled As'ad, and full publication is promised in the near future.

[2] Teixidor, 'Les derniers rois d'Édesse', pp. 220–1.

[3] C. Clermont-Ganneau, 'Odeinat et Vaballat: Rois de Palmyre, et leur titre romain de *corrector*', *RB* 29 (1920), 382–419.

[4] J. Cantineau, 'Un *Restitutor Orientis* dans les inscriptions de Palmyre', *JA* 222 (1933), 217; Millar, 'Paul of Samosata, Zenobia and Aurelian', pp. 9–10. Rey-Coquais, 'Syrie romaine', p. 59, and Bowersock, *Roman Arabia*, p. 130 n. 32, accept, without discussion, that the title was *corrector*.

1. In honour of Odaenathus son of Hairan [son of] Vaballathus,
2. [ruler] of Tadmor, Ogilu son of
3. [Ma]aqqai [son of] Haddûdan [son of] Haddâ has made this [throne]; he also offers
4. [a portico], and an altar and perpetual holocausts.[5]

II. τὸ μνημῖον τοῦ ταφεῶνος ἔκτισεν ἐξ ἰδίων Σεπτίμιος
Ὀδαίναθος ὁ λαμπρότατ[ος συνκλητικὸς]
Αἱράνου Οὐαβαλλάθου τοῦ Νασώρου αὐτῷ τε καὶ υἱοῖς
αὐτοῦ καὶ υἱωνοῖς εἰς τὸ παντελὲς αἰώνιον τειμήν.

[*qbr' dn*]*h bn' 'dynt sqltyq' br ḥyrn whblt nṣwr lh wlbnwh wlbn' bnwhy l'lm'*

Septimius Odaenathus the most famous senator, son of Hairan [son of] Vaballathus [son of] Nasôr, built this funerary monument at his own expense for himself and his children and grandchildren, for all time, in eternal honour.[6]

III. Σεπτίμιον Αἱράνην Ὀ-
δαινάθου τὸν λαμπρό-
τατον συγκλητικὸν
ἔξα[ρχον Παλμυ]ρηνῶν
Αὐρήλι[ος Φιλεῖνο]ς [. .]ρ. Ἡλι-   5
οδώρο[υ τοῦ Ρααίου] στρατιώ-
της λεγ[εῶνος Κυρηνα]ϊκῆς τὸν
πάτρωνα, τειμῆς καὶ εὐχα-
ριστίας χάριν, ἔτους γξφ'

1. *ṣlm' dnh dy spṭmyws ḥyrn br*
2. *'dynt snqltyq' nhyr' wrš*
3. *tdmwr dy 'qym lh 'wrlys*
4. *plynws br mry' plyn' r'g plḥ'*
5. *dblgywn' dy bṣr' lyqrh byrḥ*
6. *tšry dy šnt 563*

1. In honour of Septimius Hairan son
2. of Odaenathus, *senator clarissimus* and ruler
3. of Tadmor; Aurelius

⁵ J. Cantineau, 'Textes palmyréniens du temple de Bel', *Syria*, 12 (1931), 138 n. 17; Milik, *Dédicaces faites par les dieux*, 317; Gawlikowski, 'Les princes de Palmyre', 253.
⁶ *Inv.* viii. 55; *CIS* ii. 4202.

4. Philinus son of Marius Philinus, son of Aurelius Heliodorus, soldier
5. in the legion of Bosra, erected this in his honour, in the month of
6. Tishri, in the year 563 [October 251].[7]

On the basis of these texts, it appeared that the stemma for the family
could be reconstructed in either of the following ways:[8]

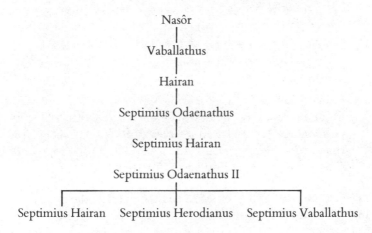

or

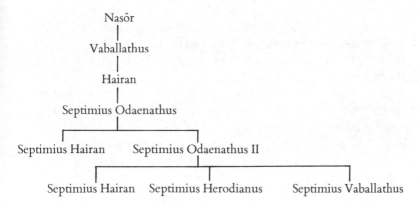

[7] *Inv.* iii. 16; *CIS* ii. 3944.

[8] M. Gawlikowski, 'A propos des reliefs du temple des Gaddê à Doura', *Berytus*, 18 (1969), 109 (I omit here Gawlikowski's speculation on the basis of texts from Dura about earlier ancestors). For an alternative view, in which the Septimius Hairan of *CIS* ii. 3944 is identified as Odaenathus' brother, see Seyrig, 'Les fils du roi Odainat', p. 167 = *Scripta Varia*, p. 273.

The newly discovered text runs as follows (Gawlikowski gives it without indication of the line-breaks):

IV. Σεπτίμιον Ὀδαίνα[θον Αἱ]ράνου Ο[ὐαβ]αλλάθ[ου τοῦ
Νασώρου] λα[μ]πρότατον [ἔξαρχον Παλμυ]ρηνῶν
Ἰούλιος Αὐρήλιος Ἀθηακά[βος Ὀ]γήλου Ζαβδιβώ[λου
. . .] τοῦ καὶ Κωρα, τὸν φίλον στοργῆς ἔνεκεν, ἔτους γξφ΄
μηνεὶ [Ξανδ]ικῷ.

ṣlm ʾspṭmyws ʾ[dynt br ḥyrn] br whblt nṣwr rš[ʾ] dy [tdmw] r nhyrʾ dʿbd lh
ʾtʿqb br ʿgylw br zbdbwl br mqymw dmqrʾ qrʾ rḥmh lyqrhwn brbnwth byrḥ
nysn šnt 563.

Julius Aurelius Ateʿaqab son of ʿOgilu son of Zabdibôl son of
Moqîmû, who is also called Qôrâ, erected this for Septimius
Odaenathus son of Hairan son of Vaballathus [son of] Nasôr, the
ruler of Tadmor, his friend, in his honour, during his presidency.
The month of Nisan in the year 563 [April 252].

The Odaenathus mentioned in text IV is clearly the same man who
appears in the first three texts. The important contribution of the
fourth text is that it shows that he was alive in April 253. Gawlikowski
has argued that this person should therefore also be identified with the
great Odaenathus, and that 'En fin de compte, aucun témoignage ne
permet d'affirmer qu'Odaenait l'Ancien ait jamais existé.'[9] Text III
should therefore reflect a coregency between Odaenathus and his son
Septimius Hairan at this time; the absence of Odaenathus from that
dedication merely illustrates the fact that it was possible to honour one
regent in a dedication that did not mention the other. This feature of
the Palmyrene epigraphy of the period had already emerged from a
text found at Palmyra in 1895 which was published from a sketch in
1898,[10] and subsequently the subject of perceptive discussions by
C. Clermont-Ganneau in 1900 and H. Seyrig in 1937;[11] it was later

---

[9] 'Les princes de Palmyre', p. 260.

[10] J.-B. Chabot, 'Notes d'épigraphie et d'archéologie orientale', *JA* 11 (1898) No. 28,
pp. 96–7; the publication was based upon a copy made by the diplomat and architect
É. Bertone in the course of a five-month visit to Palmyra in 1895.

[11] C. Clermont-Ganneau, 'La famille royal de Palmyre, d'après une nouvelle inscription', *Recueil d'archéologie orientale*, iii (Paris, 1900), 194–201, noting its importance and
suggesting that the stone was a lintel-block, but expressing the view that it referred to
events after the death of Vabalathus; H. Seyrig, 'Note sur Hérodien, prince de Palmyre',
Syria, 18 (1937), 1–4, dating the inscription to the period between 261 and 264. See also *Inv.*

revised after a re-examination of the stone by Daniel Schlumberger, who discussed it in an important article that appeared in 1942–3 (see n. 13). It is a dedication by Julius Aurelius Septimius Vorodes,[12] who appears to have been Odaenathus' most important officer, in honour of a son of Odaenathus, possibly from a building erected in commemoration of his elevation as coregent with his father at a ceremony which took place on the plain of Orontes, presumably outside Antioch after a defeat of the Persians in (probably) 262. The text runs as follows:[13]

V. [β]ασιλεῖ βασιλέων πρὸς ['Ορ]όντῃ [. . . βα]σιλείας
 τὴν κατὰ
 [Π]ε[ρ]σῶν νείκην ἀναδησαμένῳ Σεπ[τιμίῳ
 Ἡρωδι]ανῷ, Ἰούλιος Αὐρήλιος
 [Σεπτί]μιος Ο[ὐ]ρ[ρ]ώδης [καὶ Ἰούλιος Αὐρήλιος . . .
 ἐπίτροπος τῆς δ]ερ(π)
 ῥίνης κεντηνά[ριος] ἀμφότεροι στρα[τηγοὶ τῆς
 λαμ]προτάτης
 [κ]ολω[ν]είας.

On the basis of text IV Gawlikowski has proposed the following stemma:

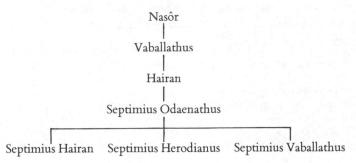

iii. 3 for a conservative text based on the sketch upon Cantineau's own study of the stone. *IGR* iii. 1032 is based on Bretone's sketch, reproduced by Chabot.

[12] See app. III n. 30 for discussion of his background, and D. Schlumberger, 'Les gentilices romains des Palmyréniens', *Bulletin d'études orientales*, 11 (1942–3), 60–1.

[13] D. Schlumberger, 'L'inscription d'Hérodien: Remarques sur l'histoire des princes de Palmyre', *Bulletin d'études orientales*, 11 (1942–3), 36–50. His text is reproduced here. For further discussion of this text see H. Ingholt, 'Varia Tadmorea', in *Palmyre: Bilan et perspectives* (Colloque de Strasbourg (18–20 Octobre 1973), Universités des sciences humaines de Strasbourg, travaux du centre de recherche sur le Proche-orient et la Grèce antiques, 3; Strasburg, 1976), 134–6.

The conclusion which Gawlikowski has drawn concerning this inscription is surely correct. The only problem with this reconstruction of Odaenathus' ancestry, as Gawlikowski himself admits, is that text I looks as if it is establishing something for someone who is dead. On the other hand, again as Gawlikowski points out, there is not really enough of this text left to be absolutely certain of its contents, and it could very well be taken as reflecting nothing more than Odaenathus' extraordinary prominence in the city. This prominence, reflected in the title 'ruler of Tadmor', is the next problem that needs to be addressed. But before passing on to this question, something should also be said about the sons of Odaenathus.

The *Historia Augusta* mentions four sons: Herodes, Vaballathus, Herennianus, and Timolaus. Herodes is mentioned three times in the *Vitae tyrannorum triginta* and once in the *Vitae Gallieni duo*,[14] Vaballathus appears in the Life of Aurelian,[15] Timolaus and Herennianus are the subjects of separate biographies in the *Tyranni triginta*, and appear to reflect the fact that the author knew, at that point, only that Odaenathus had fathered two sons, both of whom he thought survived their father, and both of whom he describes as sons of Zenobia—as opposed to Herodes, whom he calls his son by an earlier marriage.[16] In this place the author reveals that he knew nothing about Vaballathus, whose name he only seems to have come across when he wrote about Aurelian, and in the *Vita Aureliani* he explicitly corrects the earlier error.[17] His testimony

---

[14] *V. Gall.* 13. 1 'per idem tempus Odenatus insidiis consobrini sui interemptus est cum filio Herode, quem et ipsum imperatorem appellaverat', *Tyr. trig.* 15. 2 'quare adsumpto nomine primum regali cum uxore Zenobia et filio maiore, cui erat nomen Herodes, minoribus Herenniano et [a] Timolao collecto exercitu contra Persas profectus est'; *Tyr. trig.* 16 (a *Vita*), 17 'hic [Maeonius] consobrinus Odenati fuit nec ulla re alia ductus nisi damnabili invidia imperatorem optimum interemit, cum ei nihil aliud obiceret praeter filii Herodis ⟨luxuriem⟩. dicitur autem primum cum Zenobia consensisse, quae ferre non poterat, ut privignus eius Herodes priore loco quam filii eius, Herennianus et Timolaus, principes dicerentur.'

[15] *HA V. Aur.* 38. 1; see next n.

[16] *HA Tyr. trig.* 27, 28; see esp. 27. 1 'Odenatus moriens duos parvulos reliquit, Herennianum et fratrem eius Timolaum, quorum nomine Zenobia usurpato sibi imperio diutius quam feminam decuit rem p. obtinuit.'

[17] *HA V. Aur.* 38. 1 'hoc quoque ad rem pertinere arbitror, Vabalathi filii nomine Zenobia⟨m⟩, non Timolai et Herenniani, imperium tenuisse quod tenuit'. This passage appears in a biography composed by 'Flavius Vopiscus', whereas the *Tyranni triginta* was the purported work of 'Trebellius Pollio'. This is an interesting example of the author's self-correction; the point was already noted by Clermont-Ganneau, 'La famille royale de Palmyre', pp. 196–7. For other problems of this sort see app. II.

is only good, therefore, to show that he knew of two children, and that he assumed that Zenobia had taken power in both their names. Since he does not show any knowledge of the fact that Zenobia actually took power in Vaballathus' name in the *Tyranni triginta*, there is no reason to believe him when he says that she took power for her sons Herennianus and Timolaus. But this does not mean that he was wrong about two sons.

The inscriptions of Palmyra show that Odaenathus must have had at least two, and possibly four (Hairan I and II, Herodianus, and Vaballathus). The question, then, is whether or not any credence should be accorded to the *Historia Augusta*'s statement about two sons of Zenobia. H. Seyrig pointed out that both a Hairan and Vaballathus appear on a Palmyrene seal impression, and therefore that we can assume that they both existed and that they were brothers;[18] Herodianus also appears on a lead token from Antioch with Zenobia.[19] The fact that a Hairan appears on a text in 252 as a person of some eminence—he is described as a 'senator' (text III)—suggests that he may have been the oldest brother, and the fact that Herodianus, not Hairan, appears as co-regent with Odaenathus after 260 may suggest that this Hairan was dead at that point. On the other hand, it is also possible, as J. T. Milik has pointed out, that Hairan used the name Herodianus in a Greek context after 260 (it only appears on texts where his royal dignity is mentioned),[20] although it must be conceded that the use of Hairan on earlier bilingual texts and the fact that neither Vaballathus nor Odaenathus used Greek names in any context make this an unlikely assumption. It therefore appears that Odaenathus did indeed have two sons by Zenobia, as the *Historia Augusta* says, and that their names were Hairan and Vaballathus. It also appears likely, though not absolutely certain, that Odaenathus had two other sons, another Hairan (who, it

---

[18] 'Les fils du roi Odainat', pp. 171–2 = *Scripta Varia*, pp. 277–8.

[19] Seyrig, 'Note sur Hérodien', pp. 3–4, with pl. vi. 1–2, 3–4; Schlumberger, 'L'inscription d'Hérodien', p. 39; Seyrig, 'Les fils du roi Odainat', p. 168 = *Scripta Varia*, p. 274. The lead token was acquired by the museum at Damascus from a collector whose pieces otherwise appear to have come from Antioch. A second lead token in the Damascus museum, of a similar sort, but this time representing only Zenobia, certainly comes from Antioch.

[20] Milik, *Dédicaces faites par les dieux*, pp. 246 (on *Inv.* viii. 124 + 186, showing that they are two parts of the same inscription and that Herodes appears for Hairan in the Greek text), 317. The point had been made in a different fashion by Clermont-Ganneau, who suggested that the *HA*'s Herennianus was a corruption for Herodianus ('La famille royale de Palmyre', pp. 197–8).

may be assumed, died before the birth of the second Hairan) and Herodianus. The stemma can therefore be reconstructed as follows:

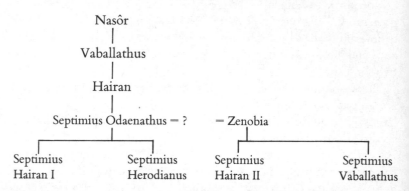

The question of Odaenathus' position at Palmyra before his victory at Emesa stems from the pairing of the title 'senator' or 'consular' with that of 'lord of Palmyra' on dedications in the 250s. Membership in the Roman senate would not a priori put Odaenathus in a position such that it would be normal for someone to call him 'ruler of Tadmor'. Furthermore, the title only appears in connection with him and his son (text III, where the Greek version gives it as ἔξαρχος Παλμυρηνῶν in l. 4). It may also be surmised that this position is what is meant when the association of gold- and silver-workers honoured Odaenathus as *mrn* 'our lord',[21] rendered as δεσπότης in the Greek version, with the following dedication:

VI. Σεπ[τίμιον 'Οδαίναθον]
τόν λαμ[πρότατον ὑπατικ]ὸν
συντέ[λεια τῶν χρυσοχ]όων
καὶ ἀργυ[ροκόπων, τ]ὸν δεσπότην
τειμῆς χάριν, [ἔτ]ους θξφ΄
μηνεὶ Ξανδικῷ.

1. ṣlm spṭmyws 'dynt
2. nhyr' hpṭyq' mrn dy
3. 'qym lh tgm' dy qyny'
4. 'bd' dhb' wksp' lyqrh
5. byrḥ nysn dy šnt 569

[21] *Inv.* iii. 17; *CIS* ii. 3945.

1. Statue of Septimius Odaenathus,
2. *clarissimus consularis*, our lord,
3-4. which the association of gold- and silver-workers erected for him, in his honour,
5. in the month of Nisan, in the year 569 [April 258].

Mr is properly used to describe reigning princes,[22] and it seems to be separate from Odaenathus' consular dignity in this dedication, as the title *senator clarissimus* (*snqlṭyq' nhyr'*) is separate from 'ruler of Tadmor' (*rš' dy tdmwr*) in text III. As only members of this family are referred to in this way at Palmyra, and as the position is entirely without parallel in the framework of Palmyra's municipal government,[23] it would appear to be a hereditary title created for that family. We do not know when this title was created, but it is possible that it was conferred when Septimius Severus granted the franchise to the family, or it may have been created for Odaenathus himself in the course of the Persian wars in the 240s. These texts therefore reveal the meaning and propriety of Malalas' description of Odaenathus as 'king of the Saracens'.[24] If faith may be placed in later Arab legends, the house of Odaenathus was vigorous in its efforts to control the tribes of the desert.[25]

There is also a problem with Odaenathus' title λαμπρότατος ὑπατικός, which appears on three inscriptions from the grand colonnade at Palmyra and one from the temple of Baalshashamîn.[26] It has also been understood to appear on a text from Tyre which reads Σεπτίμ(ιον) | 'Οδαίναθον | τὸν λαμπρότατ(ον) | Σεπτιμία | Κολ(ωνία) Τύρος | ἡ μητρόπολις.[27] This Tyrian text has been taken to show that Odaenathus' title λαμπρότατος ὑπατικός indicates that he was governor of Syria Phoenice, probably in 258. This does not seem necessary: τὸν λαμπρότατ(ον) can easily be interpreted to mean no more than ὁ λαμπρότατος συνκλητικός. Furthermore,

---

[22] See *An Aramaic Handbook*, s.v.; Brown, Driver, and Briggs, s.v.

[23] For its various ranks and offices see J. Starcky, 'Palmyre', *Dictionnaire de la Bible*, suppl. xi. 1080. See M. Gawlikowski, 'Palmyrena', *Berytus*, 19 (1970), 68.

[24] Malalas, p. 297.

[25] Bowersock, *Roman Arabia*, pp. 132–7, for the evidence on the relations between the Palmyrenes and their nomadic neighbours.

[26] Gawlikowski, 'Les princes de Palmyre', pp. 254–5; three of these texts are dated to 257/8.

[27] Chéhab, 'Tyr à l'époque romaine', pp. 19–20.

there is now an interesting parallel for Odaenathus' title of λαμπρότατος ὑπατικός from Edessa, which suggests that an altogether
different interpretation of λαμπρότατος ὑπατικός is in order in the
context of these eastern dynasts. On a papyrus that has recently been
partially published by J. Teixidor, Aelius Septimius Abgar (Abgar IX)
is described as *mlk' dmyqr bhpty' b'rhy* 'king who is honoured as
ὑπατικός at Urhaï (Edessa)'.[28] Teixidor recognized the parallel
between this formulation and Odaenathus' title 'ruler of Tadmor and
λαμπρότατος ὑπατικός', and suggested that Abgar was also a
provincial governor. Although this is possible, there is another solution
which seems more likely. The qualification *dmyqr b'rhy* 'who is
honoured at Edessa' suggests that Abgar's title had only local importance, and thus that he was given the *ornamenta consularia* rather than a
position within the imperial government. Since there is no evidence
for Odaenathus' exercise of authority outside of Palmyra before the
defeat of Macrianus and Ballista (the Tyrian inscription obviously
proves nothing other than the fact that Odaenathus was an important
man), the title ὁ λαμπρότατος ὑπατικός should also be taken to
mean that he too was given the *ornamenta*.

There are only two texts mentioning Odaenathus which date certainly
from the period after 261/2. One of them is a milestone of Vaballathus
and Zenobia, later reused under Diocletian,[29] the other is a statue-base
from the grand colonnade at Palmyra.[30] The texts are as follows:

VII. . . . . α . . . καὶ ὑπὲρ σω-
τηρίας Σεπτιμίας Ζηνο-
βίας τῆς λαμπροτάτης
βασιλίσσης· μητρὸς τοῦ
βασιλέως . . . . υ . . . .[31]

---

[28] Teixidor, 'Les derniers rois d'Édesse', pp. 220–1. Another interesting parallel, not
noted by Teixidor, appears on lead tokens from Antioch and Edessa. When he published
the token of Herodianus mentioned above, Seyrig pointed to the striking similarity
between his coiffure and that of Abgar IX (as Teixidor has shown that the last king should
be known, not Abgar X as Seyrig then supposed): see Seyrig, 'Note sur Hérodien', p. 3 and
pl. VI. 1–3. It appears therefore that the rulers of Palmyra not only imitated the titulature of
the Edessene king, but also his dress.   [29] CIS ii. 3971.

[30] *Inv.* iii. 19; CIS ii. 3946.

[31] For possible supplements to the end of this line see CIS ii. 3971. The most attractive is
Clermont-Ganneau's (θυγατρός) or θυγ. (CIS ii. 3946) τοῦ Ἀντιόχου ('Odeinat et
Vaballat', p. 396).

1. *'lh [ywh] wzkwṯh dy] sptymws*
2. *whblt 'ṯndr[ws nhy]r' mlk mlk'*
3. *w'pnrtṯ' dy mdnḥ' klh br*
4. *spt[ymy]ws ['dynṯ mlk] mlk' w'l*
5. *ḥyh dy sptymy' bṯzby nhyrt'*
6. *mlkṯ' 'mh dy mlk mlk'*
7. *bt 'ntywkws s 14*

1. For the safety and victory of Septimius
2. Vaballathus Athenodorus illustrious King of Kings,
3. who is also corrector of the entire region, son of
4. Septimius Odaenathus King of Kings, and also
5. on behalf of Septimia Bath-Zabbai illustrious
6. Queen, mother of the sovereign King,
7. daughter of Antiochus. Fourteen miles.   [32]

VIII.
    1. *ṣlm sptmyws 'dy[nt] mlk mlk'*
    2. *wmtqnn' dy mdnḥ' klh spṭmy'*
    3. *zbd' rb ḥyl' rb' wzby rb ḥyl'*
    4. *dy tdmwr qrṭṣ' 'qym lmrhwn*
    5. *byrḥ 'b dy šnt 582*

1. Statue of Septimius Odaenathus, King of Kings
2. and *corrector* of the whole east, the Septimii
3. Zabda, chief of the great army, and Zabbai, general of the army
4. of Palmyra, *potentissimi*, erected this for their lord
5. in the month of Ab, in the year 582 [August 271].

The difference between the descriptions of Odaenathus and Vaballathus in these two texts—the former is called *mtqnn' dy mdnḥ' klh* (text VIII, line 2), the latter is *'pnrtṯ' dy mdnḥ' klh* (text VII, line 3)—has caused some scholars concern.[33] While Vaballathus is clearly called *corrector totius orientis* (*'pnrtṯ'* is a transliteration of ἐπανορθωτής),[34] the fact that a different word was used to describe Odaenathus' position has been taken as proving that he had a different title. *Mtqnn'* is connected with the verb *tqn* 'to arrange', 'set right', or 'set in order',[35]

[32]   For the interpretation of this number see Clermont-Ganneau, 'Odeinat et Vaballat', p. 399.
[33]   Cantineau, 'Un *Restitutor*', p. 217; Millar, 'Paul of Samosata, Zenobia and Aurelian', p. 10.   [34]   See *CIS* ii. 3946, 3971, and notes ad loc.
[35]   Clermont-Ganneau, 'Odeinat et Vaballat', pp. 387–8; see Brown, Driver, and Briggs, s.v.

and could conceivably, as Cantineau suggested, be translated *restitutor* rather than *corrector*.[36] Thus Odaenathus would have had only the honorific, but technically vacuous, title *restitutor* while Vaballathus laid claim to the east as a subject of the emperor and as *corrector*. The title implied the power to give orders to all Roman officials in the east.[37]

There are several problems with the notion that Odaenathus had no official Roman position after 261. First of all there is the linguistic point which opponents of the notion that Odaenathus was *corrector* necessarily consider decisive in their favour. This it is not; the use of *mtqnn'* instead of *'pnrtṭ'* may equally well reflect the fact that the Palmyrenes were not consistent in the way that they translated foreign words. While it was sometimes Palmyrene practice to transliterate foreign titles, it was also their practice to translate or even omit them. Thus in *CIS* ii. 3943. 4 all that appears in place of ἱππεὺς Ῥωμαίων is *hpq'*, a transliteration of ἱππεύς. In *CIS* ii. 3932. 4 *q[r]spynws hygmwn' wbdy 'ty lk' yt lgyny'* 'Crispinus who leads the legion here' translates Ῥουτιλλίου Κρισπείνου τοῦ ἡγησαμένου καὶ ταῖς ἐπιδημησάσαις οὐηξιλλατίοσιν. The reason for this would seem to be that the Palmyrenes had no readily available term to use for *vexillatio* and were not greatly bothered about representing the precise details of Roman military organization in their own language. In the same inscription (l. 7) Julius Priscus (then praetorian prefect? is described as *dy sp '*(man) in charge of the supplies'.[38] In text II. 5 above the Palmyrene inscription has 'the legion at Bostra' in place of the *legio Cyrenaica* which appears in the Greek, and in *CIS* ii. 3962. 2 *dy mn lgywn' dy 'rb'ṭ'* 'from the-legion which is at Arbata' appears in place of 'c]oh. I Gebasis |. . . vᴘᴀᴠɪ [qui agun]t (?) Hieropoli'.[39] In the Palmyrene text honouring Odaenathus, then, *mtqnn'* is best taken as a description

---

[36] Cantineau, 'Un *Restitutor*', p. 223.

[37] See Stein, ''Επανορθωτής'. Stein's article remains the basic discussion. However, the recently discovered Mesopotamian papyri reveal a novel formula 'governor of Mesopotamia holding the highest power', which is used to describe Julius Priscus on a document subscribed by Priscus himself (or one of his staff), which should indicate that this was the way that he was described. This may indicate that such positions were very badly defined indeed in the eyes of the Roman government, or that the terminology had not yet developed to describe someone who is probably best described as 'the official in charge of protecting the frontier'.

[38] Cantineau, 'Un *Restitutor*', p. 223.

[39] C. Clermont-Ganneau, 'Épigraphie palmyrénienne', in *Recueil d'archéologie orientale*, vii (Paris, 1906), 17.

of the effective power of Odaenathus which serves to translate his title. In order for this to make sense, the Palmyrenes must have believed that this title conferred some real power—as they thought that the title King of Kings, which is paired with it, did. The meaning of the word is therefore *corrector*.

A second consideration is that the text honouring Vaballathus is clearly from the early part of his reign—certainly from before the time that he took to styling himself *imperator* and *dux Romanorum*. The first of these developments took place by 269 at the latest.[40] As Vaballathus was very young when Odaenathus was murdered, and his city was on good terms with the central government at that time, there is no reason to believe that he would either have been granted greater authority than his father or that it would have been claimed for him. The titles of Vaballathus on text VII are therefore most easily understood as being the same as those of Odaenathus at the time of his death.

This point emerges from two literary texts. One of them is this oracle, in which the narrative concludes ἄρξει Ῥωμαίων, Πέρσαι δ᾽ ἔσσοντ᾽ ἀλαπαδνοί. The second text is Zon. 12. 24 ἐφ᾽ οὓς Γαλιῆνος Ὠδέναθον ἔπεμψεν, ἡγεμονεύοντα τῶν Παλμυρηνῶν . . . Ὠδέναθον δὲ τῆς ἀνδραγαθίας ὁ βασιλεὺς ἀμειβόμενος πάσης ἀνατολῆς αὐτὸν προεχειρίσατο στρατηγόν. The clear implication of this is that Odaenathus was given an official position after the battle at Emesa—Zonaras' στρατηγός may be taken as a reference to the office *corrector* here. This also explains why Odaenathus chose the plain of Orontes, presumably outside of Antioch, to confer the title 'King of Kings' upon his son Herodian (text V above). As the centre of Roman government in Syria, Antioch was the best place for Odaenathus to advertise his triumph when he was officially recognized as ruler of the provinces on the eastern frontier. This may also help to explain the (admittedly few) lead tokens that have been found there with the images of Herodianus and Zenobia on them: they may have served as tokens for admission to games or some other public benefit. They can very well be taken to indicate a Palmyrene presence in the city.

---

[40] IGR iii. 1027 [Αὐτοκράτορι Καισάρι] | M. Ἀυρ. Κλαυδίῳ,] | [ἀρχιερεῖ μεγίστ]ῳ [ὑ]π[άτῳ] | ἀνθυπάτ[ῳ πατρὶ πατρίδος] || ἀνεικήτῳ Σεβαστῷ, | καὶ Σεπτιμίᾳ Ζενοβίᾳ | Σεβαστῇ, μητρὶ τοῦ [δεσπό]|[του ἀνηττήτου ἡμῶν Αὐτο]κράτορος Οὐαβαλλά[θου] || Ἀθηνοδώρου. For the titulature of Claudius here cf. ILS 571.

If it may be taken as certain that Odaenathus was made *corrector totius orientis*, a title which implies that he could give orders to the Roman governors of the area, the full implications of this are none the less hard to determine. What is meant by *totius orientis*? All that can be said for certain is that after Odaenathus' death the governors of Egypt and Arabia, who resisted the Palmyrenes with what force they could muster, did not think that they were bound to respect Vaballathus' authority,[41] and this led to Palmyra's fatal war with Rome.

---

[41] For the circumstances see Bowersock, *Roman Arabia*, pp. 134–7; ch. 1 n. 157 and n. 37 above.

APPENDIX V

The Continuator of Dio

Cardinal Angelo Mai published the first edition of the *Excerpta de sententiis*, which is the sole authority for the Continuator of Dio, from the palimpsest of *codex Vaticanus graecus* 73 in 1827.[1] His edition remained the basis for further work on this text until Boissevain's impressive edition appeared in 1906.[2] The manuscript is very difficult to read; the original quartos were severely disordered when the text was reused, and some were lost. None the less, Boissevain was able to reconstruct the original as follows: there were (Boissevain believed) fragments of fourteen authors (those of a fifteenth were lost) organized in sections by author. The order was as follows: Xenophon, Agathias, Menander, Theophylact, Procopius, Arrian, the lost author, Eunapius, Polybius, Dexippus, Iamblichus, Petrus Patricius, Diodorus, Dio, and Appian.[3] The reason why a section for Petrus was included is complicated. There are 161 fragments clearly attributed to Dio, extending as far as the battle of Cannae (fr. 161 stands incomplete before a lacuna of several folios). Turning to the imperial period, although the first 155 fragments manifestly derive from Dio, there are 191 concerning Roman imperial history in all and they do not conclude where Dio's history concluded: they conclude with Constantine. Furthermore, these fragments precede, rather than follow, the Republican history in the manuscript.

Before Boissevain produced his edition, the incomplete state of Dio's Republican history suggested to de Boor, in what has remained the most influential article on the subject,[4] that the author of the *excerpta* had used Dio for Republican history and Petrus for imperial history. He argued the point on the basis of 'the connection with Zonaras'. Boissevain accepted his arguments and therefore included a

---

[1] A. Mai, *Scriptorum veterum nova collatio e vaticanis codicibus edita*, ii (Rome, 1827).
[2] *Excerpta historica iussu imperatoris Constantini Porphyrogeniti confecta*, iv (Berlin, 1906).
[3] Boissevain, *Excerpta de sententiis*, pp. x–xv.
[4] C. de Boor, 'Römische Kaisergeschichte in byzantinischer Fassung', *BZ* 1 (1892), 13–33.

section for Petrus in his edition. Subsequent writers, of whom the most recent is Drinkwater,[5] have not advanced the question. Indeed, Drinkwater's hesitation about the identification, based upon the difference in the tone between the material in the excerptor and that in the fragments of Petrus, is answered by the fact that the fragments from Petrus come from the *Excerpta de legationibus Romanorum ad gentos* and the *Excerpta de legationibus gentium ad Romanos*, while the anonymous fragments are contained in the *Excerpta de sententiis*, which by definition would contain different material. There are more serious objections to de Boor's thesis.

In arguing that the fragments of the Continuator of Dio were distinct from those of any other author, K. Müller made a number of astute observations. He asked why the excerptor began his excerpts from the new history only where Dio left off. If he was trying to establish a link here, this was distinct from his practice elsewhere, as well as from that of other excerptors. He noted that the excerptor's quotations from Dio were similar to those of John of Antioch, and suggested that he was using a manuscript in which this additional material had already been added. This manuscript also represented the tradition known to John.[6] De Boor answered this with his suggestion that the excerptor began with the empire and only used Dio for the Republic. But he failed to explain why the excerptor should have ended his work with Constantine when Petrus extended his history down to the time of Julian. Furthermore, De Boor did not note that there is a serious discrepancy between Zonaras and the Continuator in one place. This is in the account of Odaenathus' death. The Continuator says that a man named Rufinus killed Odaenathus and that Odaenathus' son accused him before Gallienus; Rufinus offered to kill the son as well if Gallienus would give him the wherewithal. When Gallienus asked how he would do this, as he suffered severely from gout, he said that he would use soldiers. This is completely at variance with Zonaras' account of the murder of Odaenathus and his son at a banquet by an angry nephew who was too vigorous in the hunt (Zon. 12. 25).

It would appear therefore that Müller's notion, that the excerptor was dealing with a contaminated text of Dio, must stand. In fact it is likely that he had one text of Dio which ended with book 44 (the death of Caesar) and another which began with book 45 (the arrival of

⁵ Drinkwater, *Gallic Empire*, pp. 83–4. ⁶ *FHG* iv. 191–2.

Augustus at Rome). The first fragment in the imperial *excerpta* concerns the operations of Brutus and Cassius in the east.

The next issue that must be faced is that the assumption that the author of the *excerpta* had a corrupt manuscript requires some explanation of what sort of corruption this manuscript had suffered. Here the problem is that the fragments are generally of variable quality, and there are two places where there are close verbal correspondences between Zonaras and the Continuator;[7] and one other place where the Continuator appears to have good information which may go back to the contemporary account of the third century that Petrus used: this is the story concerning Mariades before Antioch in 252 (*FHG* iv. 192 F 1 = Boissevain, *Excerpta de sententiis*, 'Petrus', fr. 157). I would therefore suggest that Müller was essentially correct in his assumption that the excerptor was dealing with a manuscript of Dio that already contained the Continuator and would add the proposition that the Continuator's account was derived from a number of sources, including Petrus. The examples of the Byzantine Chronographic tradition concerning the third century, collected by von Stauffenberg, show that there was immense confusion of sources even by the sixth century.[8] The work of the Continuator is yet another example of that confusion.

---

[7] *FHG* iv. 193, fr. 2 (Boissevain, *Excerpta de sententiis*, 'Petrus', fr. 158 = Zon. 12. 22; *FHG* iv. 196, fr. 9. 1 (Boissevain, *Excerpta de sententiis*, 'Petrus', fr. 169 = Zon. 12. 26).

[8] Von Stauffenberg, *Die römische Kaisergeschichte bei Malalas*, pp. 61–4.

Bibliography

ALEXANDER, P. J., *The Oracle of Baalbek* (Washington, 1967).

ALEXIOU, M., *The Ritual Lament in Greek Tradition* (Cambridge, 1974).

ALFÖLDI, A., *Studien zur Geschichte der Weltkrise des 3. Jahrhunderts nach Christus* (Darmstadt, 1967).

—— *Die monarchische Repräsentation im römischen Kaiserreiche* (Darmstadt, 1970).

—— 'Zur Kenntnis der Zeit der römischen Soldatenkaiser, 1. Der Usurpator Aureolus und die Kavalleriereform des Gallienus', *ZN* 37 (1927), 198–212 = *Studien*, pp. 1–15.

—— 'Zur Kenntnis der Zeit der römischen Soldatenkaiser, 2. Das Problem des "verweiblichten" Kaisers Gallienus', *ZN* 38 (1928), 156–203 = *Studien*, pp. 16–57.

—— 'The Numbering of the Victories of the Emperor Gallienus and the Loyalty of his Legions', *Num. Chron.*⁵ 9 (1929), 218–79 = *Studien*, pp. 73–119.

—— 'Epigraphica I', *Pannonia Konyutár*, 14 (1935), 3–10.

—— 'Die Hauptereignisse der Jahre 253–261 n. Chr. im Orient im Spiegel der Münzprägung', *Berytus*, 4 (1937), 41–68 = *Studien*, pp. 123–54.

—— 'Zu den Christenverfolgungen in der Mitte des 3. Jahrhunderts', *Klio*, 31 (1938), 323–48 = *Studien*, pp. 285–311.

—— 'The Sources for the Gothic Invasions of the Years 260–270', *CAH* xii. 721–3 = *Studien*, pp. 436–9.

—— 'Über die Juthungeneinfälle unter Aurelian', *Bull. de l'Inst. Arch. Bulg.* 16 (1950), 21–4 = *Studien*, pp. 427–30.

—— 'Redeunt Saturnia regna, III: Juppiter-Apollo und Veiovis', *Chiron*, 2 (1972), 215–30.

—— 'Redeunt Saturnia regna, II: An Iconographical Pattern Heralding the Return of the Golden Age in or around 139 B.C., *Chiron*, 3 (1973), 131–40.

—— 'Redeunt Saturnia regna, IV: Apollo und die Sibylle in der Epoche der Bürgerkriege', *Chiron*, 5 (1975), 165–92.

ALFÖLDY, G., 'Cassius Dio und Herodian über die Anfänge des neupersischen Reiches', *RM*, NS 114 (1971), 360–6 = *Die Krise des*

Römischen Reiches: Geschichtsschreibung und Geschichtsbetrachtung (Stuttgart, 1988), 229–37.

ALFÖLDY, G., 'The Crisis of the Third Century as Seen by Contemporaries', *GRBS* 15 (1974), 89–111 = *Die Krise des Römischen Reiches*, pp. 319–42.

ALTHEIM-STEIHL, R., 'Die Zeitangaben der mittelpersischen Dipinti in der einstigen Synagoge zu Dura-Europos', *Boreas*, 5 (1982), 152–9.

AMANDRY, P., *La Mantique apollinienne à Delphes: Essai sur le fonctionnement de l'oracle* (Paris, 1950).

AMER, G., and GAWLIKOWSKI, M., 'Le sanctuaire impérial de Philippopolis', *Damaszener Mitteilungen*, 2 (1985), 1–15.

ANSON, E. M., 'Diodorus and the Date of Triparadeisus', *AJP* 107 (1986), 208–17.

APPEL, G., *De Romanorum precationibus* (Gießen, 1909).

APPELBAUM, S., *Jews and Greeks in Ancient Cyrene* (Leiden, 1979).

BABCOCK, C. L., 'An Inscription of Trajan Decius from Cosa', *AJP* 83 (1962), 147–58.

BALDUS, H. R., *MON(eta) URB(is) ANTIOXIA: Rom und Antiochia als Prägestatten syrischer Tetradrachmen des Philippus Arabs* (Frankfurt, 1969).

—— *Uranius Antoninus* (Bonn, 1971).

BALDWIN, B., 'Some Alleged Greek Sources of the *Historia Augusta*', *LCM* 4 (1979), 19–23.

BALTY, J.-C., 'Nouvelles données sur l'armée romaine d'orient et les raids sassanides du milieu du IIIᵉ siècle', *CRAI* (1987), 213–42.

—— 'Apamea in Syria in the Second and Third Centuries A.D.', *JRS* 78 (1988), 91–104.

BARBIERI, G., *L'albo senatorio da Settimio Severo a Carino (193–285)* (Rome, 1952).

BARNES, T. D., *The Sources of the Historia Augusta* (Brussels, 1978).

—— *Constantine and Eusebius* (Cambridge, 1981).

—— *The New Empire of Diocletian and Constantine* (Cambridge, 1982).

—— 'Pre-Decian *Acta Martyrum*', *JTS*, NS 19 (1968), 509–31.

—— 'Legislation against the Christians', *JRS* 58 (1968), 32–50.

—— 'The Lost Kaisergeschichte and the Latin Historical Tradition', *BHAC 1968/9* (Bonn, 1970), 13–43.

—— '*Ultimus Antoninorum*', *BHAC 1970* (Bonn, 1970), 53–74.

—— 'Sosianus Hierocles and the Antecedents of the Great Persecution', *HSCP* 80 (1976), 239–52.

—— 'The Composition of Cassius Dio's *Roman History*', *Phoenix*, 38 (1984), 240–55.

—— 'Constantine and the Christians of Persia', *JRS* 75 (1985), 126–36.

—— 'Emperors on the Move', *JRA* 2 (1989), 247–61.

BATOMSKY, S. J., 'The Emperor Nero in Talmudic Legend', *JQR*, NS 59 (1969), 312–17.

BAYNES, N. H., 'The Great Persecution', *CAH* xii. 646–7.

BEAN, G. E., *Journeys in Northern Lycia* (Vienna, 1971).

—— and MITFORD, T. B., *Journeys in Rough Cilicia* (Vienna, 1970).

BEESTON, A. F. L., *Warfare in Ancient South Arabia, Qahtan* (Studies in Old South Arabian Epigraphy, 3; London, 1976).

BELLINGER, A. R., 'The Numismatic Evidence from Dura', *Berytus*, 8 (1943), 65–71.

BÉRANGER, J., *Recherches sur l'aspect idéologique du principat* (Basle, 1953).

BERCHEM, D. VAN, *L'Armée de Dioclétien et la réforme constantinienne* (Paris, 1952).

BERSANETTI, G. M., 'Valeriano e Emiliano', *Rivista de filologia*, 26 (1948), 257–79.

BERVE, H., *Das Alexanderreich auf prosopographischer Grundlage*, 2 vols. (Munich, 1926).

BIEBER, M., *Alexander the Great in Greek and Roman Art* (Chicago, 1964).

BIRLEY, A. R., *Marcus Aurelius: A Biography* (London, 1987).

—— *Septimius Severus: The African Emperor* (London, 1972); 2nd edn. = *The African Emperor: Septimius Severus* (London, 1988).

—— 'The Third Century Crisis in the Roman Empire', *Bulletin of the John Rylands University Library of Manchester*, 58 (1976), 253–81.

—— 'The Economic Effects of Roman Frontier Policy', in A. King and M. Henig (eds.), *The Roman West in the Third Century* (*BAR* International Series, 109, Oxford, 1981), 39–53.

BIRLEY, E., 'Ballista and Trebellius Pollio', *BHAC 1984/5* (Bonn, 1987), 55–60.

BIVAR, A. D. H., 'The Political History of Iran under the Arsacids', in *The Cambridge History of Iran*, iii/1 (Cambridge, 1983), 21–99.

BLOCKLEY, R. C., *The Fragmentary Classicising Historians of the Later Roman Empire*, 2 vols. (Trowbridge, 1981–3).

—— 'Dexippus and Priscus and the Thucydidean Account of the Siege of Plataea', *Phoenix*, 26 (1971), 18–27.

—— 'Dexippus of Athens and Eunapius of Sardis', *Latomus*, 30 (1971), 710–15.

BLOIS, L. DE, *The Policy of the Emperor Gallienus* (Leiden, 1976).

—— 'Odaenathus and the Roman–Persian War of 252–264 A.D.', *ΤΑΛΑΝΤΑ*, 6 (1975), 7–23.

—— 'The Reign of Philip the Arabian', *ΤΑΛΑΝΤΑ*, 10–11 (1978–9), 11–43.

—— 'The *Εἰς βασιλέα* of Ps.-Aelius Aristides', *GRBS* 27 (1984), 279–88.

BONNER, C., 'A Papyrus Describing Magical Powers', *TAPA* 52 (1921), 111–18.

BOOR, C. DE, 'Römische Kaisergeschichte in byzantinischer Fassung', *BZ* 1 (1892), 1–33.

BOUCHÉ-LECLERCQ, A., *Histoire de la divination dans l'antiquité*, 4 vols. (Paris, 1872–82).

BOUSSET, W., *Der Antichrist in der Überlieferung des Judentums des Neuen Testaments und der alten Kirche* (Göttingen, 1895).

BOWERSOCK, G. W., *Greek Sophists in the Roman Empire* (Oxford, 1969).

—— *Julian the Apostate* (Cambridge, 1978).

—— *Roman Arabia* (Cambridge, 1983).

—— 'The Greek–Nabataean Bilingual Inscription at Ruwwāfa Saudi Arabia', in *Le Monde grec: Hommages à Claire Préaux* (Brussels, 1975), 513–22.

—— 'Herodian and Elagabalus', *YCS* 24 (1975), 229–36.

—— 'A New Inscription from the Syrian Desert', *Chiron*, 6 (1976), 349–55.

—— 'A Roman Perspective on the Bar Kochba War', in W. S. Green (ed.), *Approaches to Ancient Judaism*, ii (Providence, 1980), 131–41.

—— 'The Emperor Julian and his Predecessors', *YCS* 27 (1982), 159–72.

—— Review of I. Shakîd, *Rome and the Arabs*, in *CR* 36 (1986), 111–17.

—— 'Arabs and Saracens in the *Historia Augusta*', *BHAC 1984/5* (Bonn, 1987), 71–80.

—— 'The Hellenism of Zenobia', in J. T. A. Koumoulides (ed.), *Greek Connections: Essays in Culture and Diplomacy* (Notre Dame, 1987), 19–27.

—— 'Three Arabias in Ptolemy's Geography', in *Géographie historique au proche-orient* (Notes et Monographies Techniques, 23; Éditions du CNRS; Paris, 1988), 47–53.

BOWIE, E. L., 'The Greeks and their Past in the Second Sophistic', *Past and Present*, 46 (1970), 1–41 = M. I. Finley (ed.), *Studies in Ancient Society* (London, 1974), 166–209.

—— 'Apollonius of Tyana: Tradition and Reality', *ANRW* ii/16. 1652–99.

—— 'The Importance of Sophists', *YCS* 27 (1982), 29–59.

BRANDIS, P., 'Bosporos', *RE* iii. 741–89.

BRAUDEL, F., *The Structures of Everyday Life: Civilization and Capitalism, 15th–18th Century*, rev. edn. (New York, 1981).

BRECKENRIDGE, J. D., Review of H. R. Baldus, *Uranius Antoninus*, in *AJA* 79 (1975), 396–7.

BRILLIANT, R., *The Arch of Septimius Severus in the Roman Forum* (Rome, 1967).

BROCK, S., 'A Syriac Collection of Prophecies of the Pagan Philosophers', *Orientalia Lovaniensia Periodica*, 14 (1983), 203–46.

BROWN, F. E., 'Cosa, I: History and Topography', *MAAR* 20 (1951), 5–113.

BRÜNNOW, R. E., and DOMASZEWSKI, A. VON, *Die Provincia Arabia*, iii (Strasburg, 1909).

BRUNT, P. A., 'Laus Imperii', in P. Garnsey and C. R. Whittaker (eds.), *Imperialism in the Ancient World* (Cambridge, 1978), 151–91.

—— 'On Historical Fragments and Epitomes', *CQ*, NS 30 (1980), 477–94.

—— 'The Revenues of Rome', *JRS* 71 (1981), 161–72.

BUCK, D., 'A Reconstruction of Dexippus' *Chronika*', *Latomus*, 43 (1984), 596–7.

BURESCH, K., *Klaros: Untersuchungen zum Orakelwesen des späteren Altertums* (Leipzig, 1889).

—— 'Pseudosibyllinisches', *RM*, NS 47 (1892), 329–58.

—— 'Die sibyllinische Quellengrotte in Erythrae', *Ath. Mitt.* 17 (1982), 16–36.

BUTLER, H. C., *Architecture and Other Arts* (Publications of an American Archaeological Expedition to Syria in 1899–1900 ², New York, 1903).

CAGNAT, R., *Cours d'épigraphie latine* (Paris, 1914).

CAIRNS, F., *Tibullus: A Hellenistic Poet at Rome* (Cambridge, 1979).

CALLU, J.-P., *La Politique monétaire des empereurs romains de 238 à 311* (Paris, 1969).

—— 'L'empire gaulois selon J. F. Drinkwater', *JRA* 2 (1989), 362–73.

CAMERON, A., *Circus Factions: Blues and Greens at Rome and Byzantium* (Oxford, 1976).

CANTER, H. V., 'The Figure *ΑΔΥΝΑΤΟΝ* in Greek and Latin Poetry', *AJP* 51 (1930), 32–41.

CANTINEAU, J., 'Textes palmyréniens du temple de Bel', *Syria*, 12 (1931), 116–41.

—— 'Un *Restitutor Orientis* dans les inscriptions de Palmyre', *JA* 222 (1933), 219–34.

CHABOT, J.-B., 'Notes d'épigraphie et d'archéologie orientale', *JA* 11 (1898), 68–123.

CHALMERS, W. R., 'An Alleged Doublet in Ammianus Marcellinus', *RM* 102 (1959), 183–9.

CHAPOT, V., *La Frontière de l'Euphrate de Pompée à la conquête arabe* (Paris, 1907).

CHARBONNEAUX, J., 'Aiôn et Philippe l'Arabe', *MÉFR* 72 (1960), 253–72.

CHARLESWORTH, J. H., 'Jewish Astrology in the Talmud, Pseudepigraphia, Dead Sea Scrolls and Early Palestinian Synagogues', *HTR* 70 (1977), 183–200.

CHAUMONT, M. L., *Recherches sur l'histoire d'Armenie de l'avènement des Sassanides à la conversion du royaume* (Paris, 1969).

—— 'L'inscription de Kartir à la Ka'bah de Zoroastre', *JA* 248 (1960), 339–80.

—— 'A propos de quelques personnages féminins figurant dans l'inscription trilingue de Schapur I à la Ka'bah de Zoroastre', *JNES* 22 (1963), 194–9.

—— 'Corégence et avènement de Shahpuhr Ier', in P. Gignoux and A. Tafazzoli (eds.), *Mémorial Jean de Menasce* (Louvain, 1974), 133–46.

CHÉHAB, M., 'Tyr à l'époque romaine: Aspects de la cité à la lumière des textes et des fouilles', *MUSJ* 38 (1962), 13–40.

CHESNEY, F. R., *The Expedition for the Survey of the Rivers Tigris and Euphrates* (London, 1850).

CHRISTIANSEN, A., *L'Iran sous les Sassanides* (Copenhagen, 1944).

CHRISTOL, M., *Essai sur l'évolution des carrières sénatoriales dans la 2e moitié du IIIe s. ap J.-C.* (Paris, 1986).

—— 'Les règnes de Valérien et de Gallien (253–268), traveaux d'ensemble, questions chronologiques', *ANRW* ii/2. 803–27.

—— 'La carrière de Traianus Mucianus et l'origine des *protectores*', *Chiron*, 7 (1977), 393–408.

—— 'A propos de la politique extérieure de Trébonien Galle', *Rev. Num.* (1980), 68–74.

—— 'Les reformes de Gallien et la carrière sénatoriale', *Epigrafia e ordine senatorio*, i. *Tituli*, 4 (Rome, 1982), 143–66.

CLARKE, G. W., *The Letters of St. Cyprian of Carthage*, 4 vols. (New York, 1981–9).

—— 'Some Observations on the Persecution of Decius', *Antichthon*, 3 (1967), 63–76.

—— 'Prosopographical Notes on the Epistles of Cyprian, II: The Proconsul of Africa in 250 A.D.', *Latomus*, 31 (1972), 1053–7.

—— 'Two Measures in the Persecution of Decius', *BICS* 20 (1973), 118–23.

CLERMONT-GANNEAU, C., 'La famille royale de Palmyre, d'après une nouvelle inscription', in *Recueil d'archéologie orientale*, iii (Paris, 1900), 194–201.

—— 'Le droit des pauvres et le cycle pentaétérique chez les Nabatéens', in *Recueil d'archéologie orientale*, iv (Paris, 1901), 289–319.

—— 'Les cerfs mangeurs de serpents', in *Recueil d'archéologie orientale*, iv (Paris, 1901), 319–22.

—— 'Épigraphie palmyrénienne', in *Recueil d'archéologie orientale*, vii (Paris, 1906), 1–40.

—— 'Odeinat et Vaballat: Rois de Palmyre, et leur titre romain de *corrector*', *RB* 29 (1920), 382–419.

COHN, N., *The Pursuit of the Millennium* (London, 1957).

COLLINS, J. J., *The Sibylline Oracles of Egyptian Judaism* (Missoula, 1974).

—— 'The Sibylline Oracles', in J. H. Charlesworth (ed.), *Old Testament Pseudepigraphia* (London, 1983), 317–476.

—— 'The Development of the Sibylline Tradition', *ANRW* ii/20. 1. 421–53.

COOK, J. M., *The Troad* (Oxford, 1973).

—— *The Persian Empire* (London, 1983).

COPE, L. H., 'The Nadir of the Imperial Antoninianus in the Reign of Claudius II Gothicus A.D. 268–270', *Num. Chron.* [7] 9 (1969), 145–61.

CORSSEN, P., 'Die erythraeische Sibylle', *Ath. Mitt.* 38 (1913), 1–22.

COUPEL, P., and FRÉZOULS, E., *Le Théâtre de Philippopolis en Arabie* (Paris, 1956).

CRAHAY, R., *La Littérature oraculaire chez Herodote* (Paris, 1956).

CRAWFORD, M. H., *Roman Republican Coinage* (Cambridge, 1974).

CRAWFORD, M. H., 'Finance, Coinage and Money from the Severans to Constantine', *ANRW* ii/2. 560–93.

CROKE, B., 'Evidence for the Hun Invasion of Thrace in A.D. 422', *GRBS* 18 (1977), 347–67.

CROUZEL, H., 'Le christianisme de l'empereur Philippe l'Arabe', *Gregorianum*, 55 (1975), 545–50.

DAGRON, G., and FEISSEL, D., *Inscriptions de Cilicie* (Travaux et mémoires du Centre de Recherche d'Histoire et Civilisation de Byzance, Collège de France, Monographies, 4; Paris, 1987).

DAVIES, R. W., 'M. Aurelius Atho Marcellus', *JRS* 57 (1967), 20–2.

DEBEVOIS, N. C., *A Political History of Parthia* (Chicago, 1938).

DELBRÜCK, R., *Die Münzbildnisse von Maximinus bis Carinus* (Berlin, 1940).

—— 'Uranius of Emesa', *Num. Chron.*⁶ 8 (1948), 11–29.

DEMOUGEOT, E., *La Formation de l'Europe et les invasions barbares*, i. *Des origines germaniques à l'avènement de Dioclétien* (Paris, 1969).

DENIS, A.-M., *Introduction aux pseudépigraphes d'ancien testament* (Leiden, 1970).

DIEHL, E., 'Das *saeculum*: Seine Riten und Gebete', *RM* 83 (1934), 255–72, 348–72.

DIELS, H., *Sibyllinische Blätter* (Berlin, 1890).

DIETZ, K., *Senatus contra principem: Untersuchungen zur senatorischen Opposition gegen Kaiser Maximinus Thrax* (Munich, 1980).

DILLEMAN, L., *Haute Mésopotamie orientale et pays adjacents: Contribution à la géographie historique de la région du vᵉ s. avant l'ère chrétienne au viᵉ s. de cette ère* (Paris, 1962).

DOMASZEWSKI, A. VON, 'Untersuchungen zur römischen Kaisergeschichte', *RM*, NS 58 (1903), 382–90.

—— 'Beiträge zur Kaisergeschichte', *Philologus*, 65 (1906), 321–56.

DORESSE, J., *The Secret Books of the Egyptian Gnostics*, trans. P. Mairet (London, 1960).

DOWNEY, G., *A History of Antioch in Syria* (Princeton, 1961).

DRIJVERS, H. J. W., 'Hatra, Palmyra und Edessa: Die Städte der syrisch-mesopotamischen Wüste in politischer kulturgeschichtlicher Beleuchtung', *ANRW* ii/8. 799–906.

DRINKWATER, J. F., *The Gallic Empire: Separatism and Continuity in the North-Western Provinces of the Roman Empire A.D. 260–272* (Stuttgart, 1987).

DUNANT, C., *Le Sanctuaire du Baalshamin* (Rome, 1971).

Duncan-Jones, R., *The Economy of the Roman Empire: Quantitative Studies*[2] (Cambridge, 1982).

—— 'Praefectus Mesopotamiae et Osrhoeniae', *CP* 64 (1969), 229–33.

—— 'Praefectus Mesopotamiae et Osrhoeniae: A Postscript', *CP* 65 (1970), 107–9.

—— 'The Price of Wheat in Roman Egypt under the Principate', *Chiron*, 6 (1976), 241–62.

Dušanić, S., 'The End of the Philippi', *Chiron*, 6 (1976), 427–39.

Dutoit, E., *Le Thème de l'adynaton dans la poésie antique* (Paris, 1936).

Eadie, J. W., *The Breviorium of Festus: A Critical Edition with Historical Commentary* (London, 1967).

Enmann, A., 'Eine verlorene Geschichte der römischen Kaiser', *Philologus*, suppl. 4 (1884), 337–501.

Ensslin, W., *Zu den Kriegen des Sassaniden Schapur I* (SBAW 1947, 5; Munich, 1949).

Erbse, H., *Fragmente griechischer Theosophien: Herausgegeben und quellenkritisch untersucht* (Hamburg, 1941).

Erim, K. T., 'A New Relief Showing Claudius and Britannia from Aphrodisios', *Britannia*, 13 (1982).

Errington, R. M., 'From Babylon to Triparadeisos: 323–320 b.c.', *JHS* 90 (1970), 49–77.

Feissel, D. and Dagron, G., 'Documents d'archives romains inédits du moyen Euphrate (IIIe siècle après J.-C.)', *CRAI* (1989), 535–61.

Festugière, A. J., *La Révélation d'Hermès Trismégiste*, 4 vols. (Paris, 1950–4).

—— 'L'experience religieuse du médécin Thessalos', *RB* 48 (1939), 45–64.

—— 'L'âme et la musique, d'après Aristide Quintilien', *TAPA* 85 (1954), 55–78.

Fink, J., *Roman Military Records on Papyri* (Ann Arbor, 1971).

Fisher, E. A., 'Greek Translations of Latin Literature in the Fourth Century', *YCS* 27 (1982), 173–215.

Fitz, J., *Les Syriens à Intercisa* (Brussels, 1972).

—— *Ingenuus et Régalien* (Brussels, 1976).

—— 'Die Vereinigung der Donauprovinzen in der Mitte des 3. Jahrhunderts', in *Studien zu den Militärgrenzen Roms* (Cologne, 1967), 113–21.

Flusser, D., 'An Early Jewish–Christian Document in the Tiburtine Sibyl', in *Paganisme, Judaïsme, Christianisme: Influences et affrontements*

FLUSSER, D. [cont.]
    dans le monde antique. Mélanges offerts à Marcel Simon (Paris,
    1978), 153–83.
FONTENROSE, J., The Delphic Oracle (Berkeley, 1978).
FOWDEN, G., 'Pagan Versions of the Rain Miracle', Historia, 36 (1987),
    83–95.
FREI-KORSUNSKY, S., 'Meilensteine aus der Gegend von Eskişehir',
    Epigraphica Anatolica, 8 (1986), 1–5.
FREND, W. H. C., Martyrdom and Persecution in the Early Church (New
    York, 1967).
FROLOVA, N. A., The Coinage of the Kingdom of the Bosporus A.D. 242–341/
    342, trans. H. B. Wells (BAR International Series, 166; Oxford,
    1983).
FRONZA, L., 'Studi sull'imperatore Decio, I', Annali triestini, 21 (1951),
    227–45.
—— 'Studi sull'imperatore Decio, II', Annali triestini, 23 (1953), 311–
    33.
FRYE, R. N., The History of Ancient Iran (Munich, 1984).
—— 'The Political History of Iran under the Sasanians', The Cambridge
    History of Iran, iii/1 (Cambridge, 1983), 116–80.
FUCHS, H., Der geistige Widerstand gegen Rom in der antiken Welt (Berlin,
    1938).
GAEBLER, H., Die antiken Münzen von Macedonia und Paionia, iii (Berlin,
    1906).
GAGÉ, J., La Montée des Sassanides à l'heure de Palmyre (Paris, 1964).
—— 'Les Perses à Antioche et les courses de l'hippodrome au milieu du
    IIIe siècle à propos du transfuge syrien Mariades', Bulletin de la Faculté
    des Lettres de Strasbourg, 31 (1953), 301–24.
—— 'Commodien et le moment millénairiste du IIIe siècle', Rev. d'hist.
    et de philos. relig. 41 (1961), 355–78.
GAGER, J. G., 'Some Attempts to Label the Oracula Sibyllina, Book 7',
    HTR 65 (1972), 91–7.
GALLAVOTTI, C., 'Un' epigrafe teosofico ad Enoanda nel quadro della
    teurgia caldaica', Philologus, 121 (1977), 75–105.
GARDNER, P., 'Boat-Races among the Greeks', JHS 2 (1882), 90–7.
GARNSEY, P. D., Famine and Food Supply in the Greco-Roman World:
    Responses to Risk and Crisis (Cambridge, 1988).
GARZETTI, A., From Tiberius to the Antonines (London, 1974).
GAWLIKOWSKI, M., 'A propos des reliefs du temple des Gaddê a Doura',
    Berytus, 18 (1969), 105–9.

—— 'Palmyrena', *Berytus*, 19 (1970), 65–74.

—— 'Palmyre et l'Euphrate', *Syria*, 60 (1983), 53–68.

—— 'Les princes de Palmyre', *Syria*, 62 (1985), 251–61.

—— 'Some Directions and Perspectives of Research', *Mesopotamia*, 22 (1987), 11–18.

GEFFCKEN, J., *Composition und Entstehungszeit der Oracula Sibyllina* (Leipzig, 1902).

—— *The Last Days of Greco-Roman Paganism*, trans. S. MacCormack (New York, 1978).

—— 'Studien zur älteren Nerosage', *NGG* (1899), 441–62.

—— 'Das Regenwunder im Quadenlande: Eine antike-moderne Streitfrage', *NJA* 2 (1899), 253–69.

—— 'Die babylonische Sibylle', *NGG* (1900), 88–102.

—— 'Römische Kaiser im Volksmunde der Provinz', *NGG* (1901), 183–95.

GILLIAM, J. F., 'Some Latin Military Records from Papyri', *YCS* 14 (1950), 171–252.

—— 'Trebonianus Gallus and the Decii: III and I cos', in *Studi in onore di Aristide Calderini e Roberto Paribeni*, i (Milan, 1956), 305–11.

—— 'The Governors of Syria Coele from Severus to Diocletian', *AJP* 79 (1958), 225–42.

—— 'The Plague under Marcus Aurelius', *AJP* 82 (1961), 225–51 = *Roman Army Papers* (Amsterdam, 1986), 227–54.

—— 'Three Passages in the *Historia Augusta*', in *BHAC 1968–9* (Bonn, 1970), 99–110.

—— 'Ammianus and the *Historia Augusta*: The Lost Books and the Period 117–285', *BHAC 1970* (Bonn, 1972), 125–47.

GIRSHMAN, R., *Iran: Parthians and Sassanids* (London, 1962).

GOLDSMITH, R., 'An Estimate of the Size and Structure of the National Product of the Early Roman Empire', *Review of Income and Wealth*, 30 (1984), 263–88.

—— *Premodern Financial Systems: A Historical Comparative Study* (Cambridge, 1987).

GOODMAN, M., 'Nerva, the *Fiscus Judaicus*, and Jewish Identity', *JRS* 79 (1989), 40–9.

GOOSENS, G., *Hieropolis de Syrie: Essai de monographie historique* (Leuven, 1943).

GRAEBNER, F., 'Eine Zosimosquelle', *BZ* 14 (1905), 87–153.

GRAF, D. F., and O'CONNOR, M., 'The Origin of the Term Saracen and the Rūwwafa Inscriptions', *Byz. Stud.* 4 (1977), 52–66.

410   Bibliography

GRAYSON, A. K., *Babylonian Historical-Literary Texts* (Toronto, 1975).
—— and LAMBERT, W. G., 'Akkadian Prophecies', *JCS* 18 (1964), 7–3c
GUARDUCCI, M., 'Chi è Dio? L'oraculo di Apollo Karios e un epigrafe d
    Enoanda', *Rend. Lincei*, 27 (1972), 335–47.
GUEY, J., 'Deniers (d'or) et deniers d'or (de compte ancien)', *Syria*, 3&
    (1961), 261–74.
GUILLAUMIN, M.-L., 'L'exploitation des "oracles sibyllins" par Lactancc
    et par le "discours a l'assemblée des saints"', tr. J. Fontaine anc
    M. Perrin (eds.), *Lactance et son temps* (Paris, 1978), 189–200.
HABICHT, C., *Pausanias' Guide to Ancient Greece* (Berkeley, 1985).
—— 'Pausanias and the Evidence of Inscriptions', *Classical Antiquity*, 3
    (1984), 40–56.
HALFMANN, H., *Itinera principum: Geschichte und Typologie der Kaiserreiser.
    im römischen Reich* (Stuttgart, 1986).
HALL, A. S., 'The Klarian Oracle at Oenoanda', *ZPE* 32 (1978), 263–8
HALLO, W. W., 'Akkadian Apocalypses', *IEJ* 16 (1966), 231–42.
HANSEN, R. P. C., 'The *oratio ad sanctos* attributed to the Emperor Con-
    stantine and the Oracle at Daphne', *JTS* 24 (1973), 505–11.
HANSLIK, R., 'Imp. Caes. C. Vibius Trebonianus Gallus Augustus', *RE*
    viiiA, 1984–94.
HARL, K., *Civic Coins and Civic Politics in the Roman East* (Berkeley,
    1986).
HARRIS, W., *War and Imperialism in Republican Rome* (Oxford, 1979).
HARTIGAN, J., *The Poets and the Cities* (Meisenheim am Glan, 1979).
HARTMANN, F., *Herrscherwechsel und Reichskrise: Untersuchungen zu den
    Ursachen und Konsequenzen der Herrscherwechsel im Imperium Romanum
    der Soldatenkaiserzeit (3. Jahrhundert n. Chr.)* (Frankfurt am Main,
    1982).
HENDY, M., *Studies in the Byzantine Monetary Economy* (Cambridge,
    1985).
HENRICHS, A., 'Vespasian's Visit to Alexandria', *ZPE* 3 (1968), 51–80.
—— 'The Timing of Supernatural Events in the Cologne Mani
    Codex', in L. Cirillo and A. Roselli (eds.), *Codex Manichaicus Colo-
    nensis: Atti del simposio internazionale* (Cosenza, 1986), 183–204.
—— and KOENEN, L., 'Ein griechischer Mani-Codex (P. Colon. inv. nr.
    4780)', *ZPE* 5 (1970), 97–216.
HERBIG, R., '*Θεὰ Σίβυλλα*', *Jahrb. d. Deut. Arch. Inst.* 59 (1944), 141–7.
HERRMANN, A., 'Makrones', *RE* xiv. 815.

HERZFELD, E. E., *Paikuli Monument and Inscription of the Early History of the Sasanian Empire* (Berlin, 1924).

HINZ, W., *Altiranische Funde und Forschungen* (Berlin, 1969).

HOHL, E., 'Vopiscus und die Biographie des Kaisers Tacitus', *Klio*, 11 (1911), 128–229, 284–324.

HOLUM, K. G., *Theodosian Empresses* (Berkeley, 1982).

HOMMEL, H., '*Adventus sive Profectio Gordiani III*', in *Congresso internazionale di numismatico 1961* (Rome, 1965), 327–39.

HONIGMANN, E., 'Syria', in *RE* iiiA. 1549–1727.

—— 'Marsyas', *RE* xiv (1930), 1985–6.

—— and MARICQ, A., *Recherches sur les Res Gestae Divi Saporis* (Brussels, 1953).

HONORÉ, A. M., *Emperors and Lawyers* (Oxford, 1981).

—— *Ulpian* (Oxford, 1982).

HOPKINS, K., 'Taxes and Trade in the Roman Empire (200 B.C.–400 A.D.)', *JRS* 70 (1980), 101–25.

HOWE, L. L., *The Praetorian Prefect from Commodus to Diocletian* (Chicago, 1942).

HOWGEGO, C. J., *Greek Imperial Countermarks: Studies in the Provincial Coinage of the Roman Empire* (London, 1985).

HUNGER, H., *Die hochsprachliche profane Literatur der Byzantiner* (Handbuch der Altertumswissenschaft, 12/5. 1; Munich, 1978).

IMHOOF-BLÜMER, F., *Griechische Münzen* (Munich, 1890).

INGHOLT, H., 'Vario Tadmorea', in *Palmyre: Bilan et perspectives* (Colloque de Strasbourg (18–20 Octobre 1973), Universités des sciences humaines de Strasbourg, travaux du centre de recherche sur le Proche-orient et la Grèce antiques, 3; Strasburg, 1976), 101–37.

ISAAC, B., 'The Meaning of the Terms *Limes* and *Limitanei*', *JRS* 78 (1988), 125–47.

—— and OPPENHEIMER, A., 'The Revolt of Bar Kokhba: Ideology and Modern Scholarship', *JJS* 36 (1985), 33–60.

JAMES, S., 'Dura-Europos and the Chronology of Syria in the 250s A.D.', *Chiron*, 15 (1985), 111–24.

JARDÉ, A., *Études critiques sur la vie et le règne de Sévère Alexandre* (Paris, 1925).

JOBST, W., *11. Juni n. Chr.: Der Tag des Blitz- und Regenwunders im Quadenlande* (SAWW 335; Vienna, 1978).

JOHNSTON, A., 'Caracalla's Path', *Historia*, 32 (1983), 58–76.

JONES, A. H. M., *The Later Roman Empire* (Oxford, 1964).

JONES, A. H. M. *et al.*, *Cities of the Eastern Roman Provinces*² (Oxford, 1971).

JONES, C. P., *Plutarch and Rome* (Oxford, 1971).

—— *The Roman World of Dio Chrysostom* (Cambridge, 1978).

—— 'Aelius Aristides, εἰς βασιλέα', *JRS* 62 (1972), 134–52.

KAEGI, W., *Byzantium and the Decline of Rome* (Princeton, 1968).

KAYGUSUZ, I., 'Funerary Epigram of Karzane (Paphlagonia): A Girl Raped by the Goths?', *Epigraphica Anatolica*, 4 (1984), 61–2.

KEHOE, D., *The Economics of Agriculture on Roman Imperial Estates in North Africa* (Göttingen, 1988).

KEIL, J., 'Ephesos und der Etappendienst zwischen der Nord- und Ostfront des Imperium Romanum', *AAWW* 12 (1955), 159–70.

—— and GSCHNITZER, F., 'Neue Inschriften aus Lydien', *AWW* (*phil.-hist. Klasse*) 93 (1956), 219–31.

KENNEDY, D. L., 'The Frontier Policy of Septimius Severus', in *Roman Frontier Studies 1979* (*BAR* International Series, 71; Oxford, 1980), 879–87.

—— 'Ana on the Euphrates in the Roman Period', *Iraq*, 48 (1986), 103–4.

—— '"European" Soldiers and the Severan Siege of Hatra', in P. Freeman and D. L. Kennedy (eds.), *The Defence of the Roman and Byzantine East; Proceedings of a Colloquium Held at the University of Sheffield* (*BAR* International Series, 297; Oxford, 1986), 397–409.

KERESZTES, P., 'The Decian *Libelli* and Contemporary Literature', *Latomus*, 34 (1975), 761–81.

KETTENHOFFEN, E., *Die römisch-persischen Kriege des 3. Jahrhunderts n. Chr. nach der Inschrift Sahpuhrs I. an der Ka´be-ye Zartost* (*skz*) (Wiesbaden, 1982).

—— 'The Persian Campaign of Gordian III and the Inscription of Šāhpuhr I at the Ka´be-ye Zartošt', in S. Mitchell (ed.), *Armies and Frontiers in Roman and Byzantine Anatolia* (*BAR* International Series, 156; Oxford, 1983), 151–71.

—— 'Die Einforderung des Achamenidenerbes durch Ardasir: Eine Interpretatio Romana', *Orientalia Lovaniensia Periodica*, 15 (1984), 177–90.

KIENAST, D., *Untersuchungen zu den Kriegsflotten der römischen Kaiserzeit* (Bonn, 1966).

KINDLER, A., *The Coinage of Bostra* (Warminster, 1983).

KING, C. E., 'Denarii and Quinarii, A.D. 253–295', in R. A. G. Carson and C. M. Kraay (eds.), *Scripta Nummaria Romana: Essays Presented to Humphrey Sutherland* (London, 1978), 75–104.

KLOSE, D. A. O., *Die Münzprägung von Smyrna in der römischen Kaiserzeit* (Berlin, 1987).

KNIPFING, J., 'The *Libelli* of the Decian Persecution', *HTR* 16 (1923), 345–90.

KOENEN, L., 'Lucan VII, 387–389', *RM*, NS 107 (1964), 190–2.

—— 'Die Prophezeiungen des Töpfers', *ZPE* 2 (1968), 178–209.

—— 'The Prophecies of a Potter: A Prophecy of World Renewal Becomes an Apocalypse', in D. Samuel (ed.), *Proceedings of the Twelfth International Congress of Papyrology* (Toronto, 1970), 249–54.

—— 'Manichäische Mission und Kloster in Ägypten', in *Das römisch-byzantinische Ägypten* (Mainz am Rhein, 1983), 93–108.

—— 'A Supplementary Note on the Date of the Oracle of the Potter', *ZPE* 54 (1984), 9–14.

—— 'Manichaean Apocalypticism at the Crossroads of Iranian, Egyptian, Jewish and Christian Thought', in L. Cirillo and A. Roselli (eds.), *Codex Manichaicus Colonensis: Atti del simposio internazionale (Rende-Amantea 3–7 settembre 1984)*, *Università degli Studi delle Calabria, Centro interdipartimentale di scienze religiose*, Cosenza, 1986), 285–332.

—— and RÖMER, C., *Der Kölner Mani-Kodex: Über das Werden seines Leibes* (Papyrologica Colonensia, 14; Opladen, 1988).

KÖNIG, I., *Die gallischen Usurpatoren von Postumus bis Tetricus* (Munich, 1981).

KRAUSS, S., 'Der römisch-persische Krieg in der judischen Elia-Apocalypse', *JQR* 14 (1902), 359–72.

—— 'Neue Aufschlüsse über Timesitheus und den Perserkrieg', *RM*, NS 58 (1903), 627–33.

KRUMBACHER, K., *Geschichte der byzantinischen Literatur*², 2 vols. (Munich, 1896).

KRUSE, H., *Studien zur Officiellengeltung des Kaiserbildes im römischen Reiche* (Paderborn, 1934).

—— 'Mopsos', *RE* xvi (1935), 242–3.

KRYZNANOWSKA, A., *Monnaies coloniales d'Antioche de Pisidie* (Warsaw, 1970).

KÜMMEL, W., *Introduction to the New Testament*², trans. H. C. Kee (London, 1973).

KURFESS, A., *Sibyllinische Weissagen* (Nordlingen, 1951).

KURFESS, A., 'Zu den *Oracula Sibyllina*', *Hermes*, 74 (1939), 221–3.

—— 'Zu den *Oracula Sibyllina*', in *Colligere Fragmenta: Festschrift Alban Dold* (Beuron in Hohenzollern, 1952), 75–83.

—— 'Die Oracula Sibyllina XI (IX)–XIV (XII): Nicht christlich sondern jüdisch', *ZRGG* 7 (1955), 270–2.

LAFAURIE, J., 'Chronologie impériale de 249 à 285', *Bulletin de la Société Nationale de France*, 48 (1965), 139–54.

LAMBERT, W. G., *The Background of Jewish Apocalyptic* (Ethel Wood Lecture; London, 1978).

LANE FOX, R. J., *Pagans and Christians* (New York, 1986).

LATTIMORE, R., *Themes in Greek and Latin Epitaphs* (Illinois Studies in Language and Literature, 28; Urbana, 1942).

—— 'Portents and Prophecies in Connection with the Emperor Vespasian', *CJ* 29 (1934), 441–9.

LEBEK, W. D., 'Die drei Ehrenbögen für Germanicus: Tab. Siar. frg. I 9–34; CIL vi 31199a 2–17', *ZPE* 67 (1987), 129–48.

LEHMAN, F. H., *Kaiser Gordian III.* (Berlin, 1911).

LEPPER, F. A., *Trajan's Parthian War* (Oxford, 1948).

LEVICK, B. M., 'Caracalla's Path', in *Hommages à Marcel Renard* (Brussels, 1969), 426–46.

LEWY, H., *The Chaldaean Oracles and Theurgy*², ed. M. Tardieu (Paris, 1978).

LIEBERMAN, S., 'Palestine in the Third and Fourth Centuries', *JQR* 37 (1947), 31–54.

LIEBESCHUETZ, J. H. W. G., *Continuity and Change in Roman Religion* (Oxford, 1979).

LITTMAN, R. J., and LITTMAN, M. L., 'Galen and the Antonine Plague', *AJP* 94 (1973), 243–55.

LORIOT, X., 'Itinera Gordiani Augusti, I: Un voyage de Gordian III à Antioche en 232 après J.-C.', *Bulletin de la Société Française de Numismatique*, 26 (1971), 18–21.

—— 'Les premières années de la grande crise du iiiᵉ sicle: De l'avènement de Maximin le Thrace (235) à la mort de Gordian III (244)', *ANRW* ii/2. 657–787.

—— 'Chronologie du règne de Philippe l'Arabe', *ANRW* ii/2. 788–97.

LUTTWAK, E., *The Grand Strategy of the Roman Empire* (Baltimore, 1976).

MACCORMACK, S., *Art and Ceremony in Late Antiquity* (Berkeley, 1981).

MCDERMOT, B. C., 'Roman Emperors in the Sassanian Reliefs', *JRS* 44 (1954), 76–80.

MacDonald, D. J., *Greek and Roman Coins from Aphrodisias* (Oxford, 1976).

—— 'The Death of Gordian III: Another Tradition', *Historia*, 30 (1981), 502–8.

—— 'Dating the Fall of Dura-Europos', *Historia*, 35 (1986), 45–68.

McGinn, B., '*Teste David cum Sibylla*: The Significance of the Sibylline Tradition in the Middle Ages', in J. Kirshner and S. F. Wemple (eds.), *Women of the Medieval World: Essays in Honor of John H. Mundy* (Oxford, 1985), 7–35.

MacMullen, R., *Enemies of the Roman Order* (Cambridge, 1966).

—— *Roman Government's Response to Crisis* (New Haven, 1976).

—— *Paganism in the Roman Empire* (New Haven, 1981).

—— 'The Roman Emperor's Army Costs', *Latomus*, 43 (1984), 571–80.

Magie, D., *Roman Rule in Asia Minor*, 2 vols. (Princeton, 1950).

Malcus, B., 'Notes sur la révolution du système administratif romain au IIIe siècle', *Opuscula Romana*, 7 (1969), 213–37.

Mango, C., 'Who Wrote the Chronicle of Theophanes?', *ZRVI* 18 (1978), 9–18.

Manni, E., 'L'accazione di Valeriano', *Rivista di filologia*, 25 (1947), 106–17.

—— 'Note valerianee', *Epigraphica*, 11 (1949), 3–32.

Margoliath, D. S., *The Relations between Arabs and Israelites prior to the Rise of Islam* (London, 1924).

Maricq, A., 'Les dernières années de Hatra: L'alliance romaine', *Syria*, 34 (1957), 288–96.

—— 'Res Gestae Divi Saporis', *Syria*, 35 (1958), 295–360.

Marrou, H. I., *A History of Education in Antiquity*, trans. G. Lamb (London, 1956).

Martin, A., 'Le réconciliation des lapsi en Égypte de Denys à Pierre d'Alexandrie: Une querelle des clercs', *Rivista di storia e letteratura religiosa*, 22 (1986), 256–69.

Mason, H. J., *Greek Terms for Roman Institutions: A Lexicon* (American Studies in Papyrology, 13; Toronto, 1974).

Matthews, J. F., *Western Aristocracies and Imperial Court A.D. 364–425* (Oxford, 1975).

—— 'The Tax Law of Palmyra: Evidence for Economic History in a City of the Roman East', *JRS* 74 (1984), 157–80.

—— *The Roman Empire of Ammianus* (London, 1989).

Mattingly, H. B., 'Tribunicia Potestate', *JRS* 20 (1930), 78–91.

416 *Bibliography*

MATTINGLY, H. B., 'The Reign of Aemilian: A Chronological Note', *JRS* 25 (1935), 55–8.

MENDELS, D., 'The Five Empires: A Note on a Propagandist Topos', *AJP* 102 (1981), 330–7.

MENDELSSOHN, L., 'Zu den *Oracula Sibyllina*', *Philologus*, NS 3 (1890), 24–70.

MERKELBACH, R., 'Aeneas in Cumae', *MH* 18 (1961), 83–99.

MESNIL DU BUISSON, R. COMTE DU, *Les Tessères et monnaies de Palmyre* (Paris, 1962).

METCALF, W. E., 'The Antioch Hoard of Antoniniani and the Eastern Coinage of Trebonianus Gallus and Volusian', *The American Numismatic Society Museum Notes*, 22 (1977), 71–94.

—— and WALKER, P. M., 'The Antioch Hoard: A Supplement', *The American Numismatic Society Museum Notes*, 23 (1978), 129–32.

MILIK, J. T., *Dédicaces faites par les dieux* (Paris, 1972).

MILLAR, F. G., *A Study of Cassius Dio* (Oxford, 1964).

—— *The Emperor in the Roman World* (London, 1977).

—— 'P. Herennius Dexippus: The Greek World and the Third Century Invasions', *JRS* 59 (1969), 12–29.

—— 'Paul of Samosata, Zenobia and Aurelian: The Church, Local Culture and Political Allegiance in Third-Century Syria', *JRS* 61 (1971), 1–17.

—— 'Emperors, Frontiers and Foreign Relations, 31 B.C. to A.D. 378', *Britannia*, 13 (1982), 1–23.

—— 'The Phoenician Cities: A Case Study of Hellenisation', *PCPS*, NS 29 (1983), 55–71.

—— 'Empire, Community and Culture in the Roman Near East: Greeks, Syrians, Jews and Arabs', *JJS* 38 (1987), 143–69.

MITCHELL, S., 'The Balkans, Anatolia, and Roman Armies across Asia Minor', in S. Mitchell (ed.), *Armies and Frontiers in Roman and Byzantine Anatolia* (*BAR* International Series, 156; Oxford, 1983), 131–50.

—— 'Imperial Building in the Eastern Roman Provinces', *HSCP* 91 (1987), 333–65.

—— 'Maximinus and the Christians', *JRS* 78 (1988), 105–24.

MÓCSY, A., *Pannonia and Upper Moesia*, trans. S. Frere (London, 1974).

MOLTHAGEN, J., *Der römische Staat und die Christen im zweiten und dritten Jahrhundert* (Göttingen, 1970).

MOMMSEN, T., *Römisches Staatsrecht* 3, 3 vols. (Berlin, 1887–8).

—— *The Provinces of the Roman Empire from Caesar to Diocletian*, trans. W. P. Dickson, 2 vols. (London, 1909).

—— 'Die Scriptores Historiae Augustae', *Hermes*, 25 (1890), 228–92 = *Gesammelte Schriften*, vii (Berlin, 1909), 302–62.

MORETTI, L., *Iscrizione agnostiche greche* (Rome, 1953).

MOSIG-WALBURG, A., 'Bisher nicht beachtete Münzen Sapurs I.', *Boreas*, 3 (1980), 117–26.

MOUSSLI, M., 'Griechische Inschriften aus Emesa und Laodicea ad Libanum', *Philologus*, NS 127 (1983), 254–61.

MOUTERDE, R., 'Antiquités de l'Hermon et de la Beqâ', *MUSJ* 29 (1951–2), 21–89.

MUSIL, A., *The Middle Euphrates* (New York, 1927).

NEUGEBAUER, O., and VAN HOESEN, H. D., *Greek Horoscopes* (Philadelphia, 1959).

NEUSNER, J., *A History of the Jews in Babylonia*, ii (Leiden, 1966).

NICHOLSON, O., 'Flight from Persecution as Imitation of Christ', *JTS*, NS 40 (1989), 48–65.

NIKIPROWETZKY, V., *La Troisième Sibylle* (Paris, 1970).

—— 'La Sibylle juive et le "Troisième Livre" des "Pseudo-Oracles Sibyllins" depuis Charles Alexandre', *ANRW* ii/20, 460–542.

NISBET, R. G. M., and HUBBARD, M., *A Commentary on Horace: Odes I* (Oxford, 1970).

—— *A Commentary on Horace: Odes II* (Oxford, 1978).

NOCK, A. D., *Essays on Religion and the Ancient World*, ed. Z. Stewart (Oxford, 1972).

—— 'Two Notes on the *Asclepius*', *JTS* 26 (1925), 173–6.

—— 'Notes on Ruler Cult, I–IV', *JHS* 48 (1928), 21–43 = *Essays*, pp. 134–59.

—— 'Oracles théologiques', *RÉA* 30 (1928), 280–90 = *Essays*, pp. 160–8.

—— 'Greek Magical Papyri', *JEA* 15 (1929), 219–35 = *Essays*, pp. 176–94.

—— 'A Vision of Mandaulis Aion', *HTR* 27 (1934), 67–77 = *Essays*, pp. 368–77.

—— 'The Gild of Zeus Hypistos', *HTR* 29 (1936), 55–71 = *Essays*, pp. 416–30.

—— 'Greeks and Magi', *JRS* 30 (1940), 191–8 = *Essays*, pp. 516–26.

—— 'The Emperor's Divine *Comes*', *JRS* 37 (1947), 102–16 = *Essays*, pp. 653–75.

NÖLDEKE, T., *Geschichte der Perser und Araber zur Zeit der Sasaniden: Aus der arabischen Chronik des Tabari übersetzt und mit ausführlichen Erläuterungen reisehen* (Leiden, 1879).

—— '*ΑΣΣΥΡΙΟΙ ΣΥΡΙΟΣ ΣΥΡΟΣ*', *Hermes*, 5 (1871), 443–68.

NORDEN, E., *Agnostos Theos: Untersuchungen zur Formengeschichte religiöser Rede* (Berlin, 1913).

—— 'Josephus und Tacitus über Jesus Christus und eine messianische Prophetie', *NJA* 31 (1913), 637–66.

OATES, D., *Studies in the Ancient History of Northern Iraq* (Oxford, 1968).

—— 'A Note on Three Latin Inscriptions from Hatra', *Sumer*, 11 (1955), 39–43.

ODEN, R. A., *Studies in Lucian's* De Dea Syria (Missoula, 1977).

OLMSTEAD, A. T., 'The Mid-Third Century of the Christian Era', *CP* 37 (1942), 241–62, 398–420.

OOST, S. I., 'The Death of the Emperor Gordian III', *CP* 53 (1958), 106–7.

—— 'The Alexandrian Seditions under Philip and Gallienus', *CP* 56 (1961), 1–20.

PALM, J., *Rom, Römertum und Imperium in der griechischen Literatur der Kaiserzeit* (Lund, 1959).

PARKE, H. W., *Sibyls and Sibylline Prophecy in Classical Antiquity* (London, 1988).

—— 'The Attribution of the Oracle in Zosimus, *New History* 2 37', *CQ*, NS 32 (1982), 441–4.

—— and WORMELL, D. E. W., *The Delphic Oracle*, 2 vols. (Oxford, 1956).

PARKER, S. T., 'The Decapolis Reviewed', *JBL* 94 (1975), 437–41.

PARSONS, P. J., 'Philippus Arabs and Egypt', *JRS* 57 (1967), 134–41.

—— 'M. Aurelius Zeno Januarius', in D. Samuel (ed.), *Proceedings of the Twelfth International Congress of Papyrology* (Toronto, 1970), 389–97.

PASSERINI, A., *Le coorti pretorie* (Rome, 1939).

—— 'Gli aumenti del soldo militare da Commodo a Massimino', *Athenaeum*, 24 (1946), 145–59.

PÉKARY, T., 'Le "tribut" aux Perses et les finances de Philippe l'Arabe', *Syria*, 38 (1961), 275–83.

—— 'Bemerkungen zur Chronologie des Jahrzehnts 250–260', *Historia*, 11 (1962), 123–8.

PERETTI, A., *La sibilla babilonese* (Florence, 1943).

PETER, H., 'Die römischen sogennanten Dreissig Tyrannen', *Königliche sächsische Gesellschaft der Wissenschaften*, 27 (1909), 181–222.

PFLAUM, H.-G., *Le Marbre de Thorigny* (Bibliothèque de l'école des hautes études, 242; Paris, 1948).

—— *Les Carrières procuratoriennes équestres sous le haut-empire romain*, 3 vols. (Paris, 1960–1).

—— 'La fortification de la ville d'Adraha d'Arabie (259–260 à 274–275) d'après des inscriptions récemment découvertes', *Syria*, 29 (1952), 307–30.

PICARD, G., 'Les reliefs de l'arc de Septime Sévère au Forum Romain', *CRAI* (1962), 7–14.

PIGHI, J. B., *De ludis saecularibus populi Romani Quiritium* ² (Amsterdam, 1965).

PITTS, F., 'Relations between Rome and German "Kings" on the Middle Danube in the First to Fourth Centuries A.D.', *JRS* 79 (1989), 45–58.

PLACES, R. P. DES, 'Jamblique et les *Oracles Chaldaïques*', *CRAI* (1964), 178–85.

POHLSANDER, H. A., 'Philip the Arab and the Christians', *Historia*, 29 (1980), 463–73.

—— 'Did Decius Kill the Philippi?', *Historia*, 31 (1982), 214–22.

—— 'The Religious Policy of Decius', *ANRW* ii/1b. 1826–42.

POTTER, D. S., 'The *Tabula Siarensis*, Tiberius, the Senate, and the Eastern Boundary of the Roman Empire', *ZPE* 69 (1987), 269–76.

—— 'Alexander Severus and Ardashir', *Mesopotamia*, 22 (1987), 147–57.

—— 'Recent Inscriptions from Flat Cilicia', *JRA* 2 (1989), 305–12.

—— 'The Persecution of the Early Church', in *The Anchor Bible Dictionary* (forthcoming).

—— 'The Sibyl in the Greek and Roman World', *JRA* 3 (1990), 471–83.

—— 'Martyrdom as Spectacle' (forthcoming).

PRÉAUX, C., 'Trébonien Gallus et Hostilianus', *Aegyptus*, 32 (1952), 152–7.

PRICE, M. J., 'The Lost Year: Greek Light on a Problem of Roman Chronology', *Num. Chron.*⁷ 13 (1973), 75–86.

RAPPAPORT, B., *Die Einfälle der Goten in das römische Reich* (Leipzig, 1899).

REA, J., 'Gn. Domitius Philippus, *Praefectus vigilum, Dux*', in D. Samuel (ed.), *Proceedings of the Twelfth International Congress of Papyrology* (Toronto, 1970), 427–9.

REA, J., 'The Date of P. Strassb. I 32', *ZPE* 46 (1982), 210–11.

REILING, J., *Hermas and Christian Prophecy* (Leiden, 1973).

REINACH, S., 'Le sanctuaire de la Sibylle d'Erythrée', *RÉG* 4 (1891), 276–86.

REINHOLD, M., 'Roman Attitudes towards Egyptians', *AW* 3 (1980), 97–103.

REISCH, E., '*Ἄκτια*', *RE* i. 1213–14.

RENOIR, E., 'Chiffre de la Bête', in *Dictionnaire d'archéologie chrétienne et de liturgie*, iii. 1341–53.

REY-COQUAIS, J.-P., 'Syrie romaine de Pompée à Dioclétien', *JRS* 68 (1978), 44–73.

REYNOLDS, J. M., *Aphrodisias and Rome* (London, 1982).

—— 'New Evidence for the Imperial Cult in Julio-Claudian Aphrodisias', *ZPE* 43 (1981), 317–27.

—— 'Further Information on Imperial Cult at Aphrodisias', *Studii clasice*, 24 (1986), 109–17.

RHODEN, A., 'M. Aemilius Aemilianus', *RE* i. 545–6.

RICHARDSON, N. J., *The Homeric Hymn to Demeter* (Oxford, 1974).

RIDLEY, R. T., 'Zosimus and Eunapius', *Helicon*, 9–10 (1969–70), 574–92.

RIEWALD, P., *De imperatorum Romanorum cum certis dis comparatione et aequatione* (Halle, 1912).

RITTERLING, E., 'Zum römischen Heerwesen des ausgehenden dritten Jahrhunderts', in *Beiträge zur alten Geschichte und griechisch-römischen Althertumskunde: Festschrift zu Otto Hirschfelds Sechzigstem Geburtstag* (Berlin, 1903), 345–9.

—— 'Legio', *RE* xii. 1211–1829.

ROBERT, L., *Documents de l'Asie mineure méridionale* (Paris, 1966).

—— *A travers de l'Asie Mineure* (Paris, 1980).

—— 'Hellenica', *Rev. Phil.*, 3rd ser. 13 (1939), 97–217.

—— 'Épitaphe de provenance inconnue faisant mention des barbares', in *Hellenica*, vi (Paris, 1948), 117–22.

—— 'Trois oracles de la Théosophie et un prophète d'Apollon', *CRAI* (1968), 568–99.

—— 'Deux concours grecs à Rome', *CRAI* (1970), 6–27.

—— 'Un oracle gravé à Oinoanda', *CRAI* (1971), 597–619.

—— 'De Cilicie à Messine et à Plymouth avec deux inscriptions grecques errantes', *Journal des savants* (1973), 161–211.

—— 'Épitaphes de Nicomédie', *BCH* 102 (1978), 408–28.

—— 'Une épigramme d'Automédon et Athènes au début de l'empire', *RÉG* 94 (1981), 348–61.

—— 'Une vision de Pérpetue martyre', *CRAI* (1982), 228–76.

ROHDE, E., *Psyche: Seelencult und Unsterblichkeitsglaube der Griechen* [4] (Tübingen, 1907).

ROSEN, K., *Studien zur Darstellungskunst und Glaubwürdigkeit des Ammian Marcellin* (Meisenheim am Glan, 1968).

ROSTOVTZEFF, M. I., *The Social and Economic History of the Roman Empire* [2], ed. P. M. Fraser (Oxford, 1957).

—— 'Dura and the Problem of Parthian Art', *YCS* 5 (1935), 157–304.

—— '*Res Gestae Divi Saporis* and Dura', *Berytus*, 8 (1943–4), 17–60.

ROUECHÉ, C., *Aphrodisias in Late Antiquity* (*JRS* Monograph 5; London, 1989).

—— 'Rome, Asia and Aphrodisias in the Third Century', *JRS* 71 (1981), 103–120.

ROUSSEL, P., 'Le miracle de Zeus Panamoros', *BCH* 55 (1931), 70–116.

ROWE, G. O., 'The *Adynaton* as a Stylistic Device', *AJP* 86 (1965), 386–96.

RUBIN, Z., *Civil War Propaganda and Historiography* (Brussels, 1980).

—— 'Dio, Herodian and Severus' Second Parthian War', *Chiron*, 5 (1975), 419–41.

RUGE, W., 'Mopsu(h)estia', *RE* xvi (1935), 243–50.

RZACH, A., *Metrische Studien zu den sibyllinischen Orakeln* (SAWW 126. 9; 1892).

—— *Analekta zur Kritik und Exegese der sibyllinischen Orakel* (SAWW 156; 1907).

—— 'Studien zur Technik des nachhomerischen heroischen Verses', *SAWW* 95 (1880), 681–871.

—— 'Neue Beiträge zur Technik des nachhomerischen Hexameter', *SAWW* 100 (1882), 307–432.

—— 'Zur Verstechnik der Sibyllisten', *WS* 14 (1892), 18–39.

—— 'Zur Metrik der Oracula Sibyllina', *WS* 15 (1893), 77–115.

—— 'Neue kritische Versuche zu den sibyllinischen Orakeln', *WS* 33 (1911), 233–50.

—— 'Sibyllen', *RE* iiA (1923), 2073–103.

—— 'Sibyllinische Orakel', *RE* iiA (1923), 2103–83.

SACKUR, E., *Sibyllinische Texte und Forschungen* (Halle, 1898).

SAFAR, F., 'The Lords and Kings of Hatra', *Sumer*, 29 (1973), 87–97.

SAGE, M. M., *Saint Cyprian* (Cambridge, 1975).

SAGE, M. M., 'The Persecution of Valerian and the Peace of Gallienus', *WS*, NS 17 (1983), 137–486.

STE CROIX, G. E. M. DE, *The Class Struggle in the Ancient Greek World* (London, 1981).

—— 'Aspects of the Great Persecution', *HTR* 47 (1954), 73–113.

—— 'The Persecutions: Christianity's Encounter with the Roman Imperial Government', in A. J. Toynbee (ed.), *The Crucible of Christianity* (London, 1969), 331–51.

SALISBURY, F. S., and MATTINGLY, H. B., 'The Reign of Trajan Decius', *JRS* 14 (1924), 1–23.

SALMON, M., 'The Chronology of the Gothic Incursions into Asia Minor in the IIIrd Century A.D.', *Eos*, 49 (1971), 109–39.

SANFORD, E. M., 'Nero and the East', *HSCP* 48 (1937), 75–103.

SARTRE, M., *Trois études sur l'Arabie romaine et byzantine* (Brussels, 1982).

—— 'Le *Dies Imperii* de Gordien III: une inscription inédite de Syrie', *Syria*, 61 (1984), 49–61.

SAUMAGNE, C., *Saint Cyprien Évêque de Carthage 'Pape' d'Afrique* (Paris, 1975).

SCHÄFER, P., 'Rabbi Aquiva and Bar Kokhba', in W. S. Green (ed.), *Approaches to Ancient Judaism*, ii (Chico, 1978), 113–30.

SCHINDLER, F., *Die Inschriften von Bubon (Nordlykien)* (SAWW 278. 3; 1973).

SCHLUMBERGER, D., 'L'inscription d'Hérodien: Remarques sur l'histoire des princes de Palmyre', *Bulletin d'études orientales*, 11 (1942–3), 35–50.

—— 'Les gentilices romains des Palmyréniens', *Bulletin d'études orientales*, 11 (1942–3), 53–64.

—— 'Vorod l'agoronome', *Syria*, 49 (1972), 339–41.

SCHMIDT, E. F., *Persepolis*, iii. *The Royal Tombs and Other Monuments* (Chicago, 1970).

SCHÖNFELD, M., 'Iuthungi', *RE* x. 1347–8.

SCHÜRER, E., *The History of the Jewish People in the Age of Jesus Christ* ², i, ed. G. Vermes and F. G. Millar (Edinburgh, 1973); ii, ed. G. Vermes, F. G. Millar, and M. Black (Edinburgh, 1979); iii, ed. G. Vermes, F. G. Millar, and M. Goodman (Edinburgh, 1986).

SCHWARTZ, E., 'Dexippos', *RE* v. 288–93.

—— 'Diodorus', *RE* v. 663–704.

SCHWARTZ, J., 'Une déclaration de sacrifice du temps de Dèce', *RB* 54 (1947), 365–7.

—— 'L'historiographie impériale des *Oracula Sibyllina*', *Dial. d'hist. anc.* 2 (1970), 413–20.

—— 'Chronologie du IIIe s. p.c.', *ZPE* 24 (1977), 167–77.

SCOTT, W., 'The Last Sibylline Oracle of Alexandria', *CQ* 9 (1915), 144–66, 207–28; ibid. 10 (1916), 7–16.

SEYRIG, H., 'Antiquités syriennes', *Syria*, 15 (1934), 165–73.

—— 'Note sur Hérodien, prince de Palmyre', *Syria*, 18 (1937), 1–4.

—— 'Palmyra and the East', *JRS* 40 (1950), 1–7 = *Scripta Varia: Mélanges d'archéologie et d'histoire* (Paris, 1985), 249–57.

—— 'Les fils du roi Odainat', *AAS* 13 (1963), 159–72 = *Scripta Varia: Mélanges d'archéologie et d'histoire* (Paris, 1985), pp. 265–78.

—— 'Némésis et le temple de Maqam Er-Rabb', *MUSJ* 37 (1960–1), 261–70 = *Scripta Varia: Mélanges d'archéologie et d'histoire* (Paris, 1985), 145–56.

—— 'Bêl de Palmyre', *Syria*, 48 (1971), 85–114.

SHAHÎD, I., *Byzantium and the Arabs in the Fourth Century* (Washington, 1984).

—— *Rome and the Arabs: Prolegomenon to the Study of Rome and the Arabs* (Washington, 1984).

SIMONETTA, B., 'A Note on Vologaeses V., Artabanus V and Arta-vasdes', *Num. Chron.*^6 16 (1956), 77–82.

SMITH, R. R. R., 'The Imperial Reliefs from the Sebasteion at Aphro-disias', *JRS* 77 (1987), 88–138.

—— '*Simulacra Gentium*: The *Ethne* from the Sebasteion at Aphro-disias', *JRS* 78 (1988), 50–77.

SORDI, M., 'La data dell'editto di Decio e il significato della chiesa in Italia', *RSCI* 34 (1980), 451–61.

SOURDEL, D., *Les Cultes du Hauran à l'époque romaine* (Paris, 1952).

SPEIDEL, M. P., *Roman Army Studies* (Amsterdam, 1984).

—— 'The Rise of Ethnic Cavalry Units in the Roman Army', *ANRW* ii/3. 202–231 = *Studies*, pp. 117–48.

SPIJKERMAN, A., *The Coins of the Decapolis and Provincia Arabia*, ed. M. Picirillo (Jerusalem, 1978).

SPRENGLING, M., *Third Century Iran: Sapor and Kartir* (Chicago, 1953).

STADTER, P., 'Flavius Arrianus: The New Xenophon', *GRBS* 8 (1967), 155–61.

—— *Arrian of Nicomedia* (Chapel Hill, 1980).

STARCKY, J., 'Palmyre', *Dictionnaire de la Bible*, suppl. xi. 1066–103.

—— 'Stele d'Elahagabal', *MUSJ* 49 (1975–6), 503–20.

STAUFFENBERG, A. SCHENK GRAF VON, *Die römische Geschichte bei Malalas: Griechischer Text der Bücher IX–XI und Untersuchungen* (Stuttgart, 1931).

STEIN, A., *Die Legaten von Moesien* (Budapest, 1940).

—— *Die Reichsbeamten von Dazien* (Budapest, 1944).

—— 'C. Furius Sabinius Aquila Timesitheus', *RE* vii (1912), 364–7.

—— 'Iotapianus', *RE* ix (1914), 2004–5.

—— 'Julius Philippus', *RE* x (1917), 753–72.

—— 'Julius Priscus', *RE* x (1917), 781–2.

—— 'Julius Valens Licinianus', *RE* x (1917), 1845.

—— 'Mariades', *RE* xiv (1930), 1744–5.

—— 'Zur Chronologie der römischen Kaiser von Decius bis Diocletian', *Archiv für Papyrusforschung*, 7 (1924), 30–51.

—— 'Ἐπανορθώτης', *Aegyptus*, 18 (1938), 234–43.

STEIN, F. J., *Dexippus et Herodianus: Rerum scriptores quatenus Thucydidem secuti sint* (Bonn, 1957).

STERTZ, S. A., 'Pseudo Aelius Aristeides, εἰς βασιλέα', *CQ*, NS 29 (1979), 172–97.

STRAUB, J., 'Juppiter Consul', *BHAC 1971* (Bonn, 1974), 165–84.

SULLIVAN, R. D., 'The Dynasty of Emesa', *ANRW* ii/8. 198–219.

SWAIN, J. W., 'The Theory of the Four Monarchies under the Roman Empire', *CP* 35 (1940), 1–21.

SYME, R., *Tacitus*, 2 vols. (Oxford, 1958).

—— *Ammianus and the Historia Augusta* (Oxford, 1968).

—— *Emperors and Biography* (Oxford, 1971).

—— *Historia Augusta Papers* (Oxford, 1983).

—— 'History or Biography: The Case of Tiberius Caesar', *Historia*, 23 (1974), 481–96 = *Roman Papers*, iii (Oxford, 1984), 937–52.

—— 'Fiction in the Epitomators', *BHAC 1977/8* (Bonn, 1980), 267–98 = *Historia Augusta Papers*, pp. 156–67.

—— 'The Career of Arrian', *HSCP* 86 (1982), 181–211 = *Roman Papers*, iv (Oxford, 1988), 21–49.

—— 'Emperors from Etruria', *BHAC 1979/81* (Bonn, 1983), 333–60 = *Historia Augusta Papers*, pp. 189–208.

—— 'Antonine Government and the Governing Class', *Roman Papers*, v (Oxford, 1988), 668–88.

TADMOR, H., 'Addendum', *AJP* 102 (1981), 338–9.

TAQIZADEH, S. H., 'The Early Sassanians: Some Chronological Points which Possibly Call for Revision', *BSOAS* 11 (1943), 6–51.

Teixidor, J., *The Pagan God: Popular Religion in the Greco-Roman Near East* (Princeton, 1977).

—— *The Pantheon of Palmyra* (Leiden, 1979).

—— 'Les derniers rois d'Édesse d'après deux nouveaux documents syriaques', *ZPE* 76 (1989), 219–22.

Thomas, J. D., 'The Introduction of Dekaprotoi and Comarchs into Egypt in the Third Century A.D.', *ZPE* 19 (1975), 111–19.

Thompson, B., 'The Patristic Use of the Sibylline Oracles', *Review of Religion*, 16 (1952), 115–36.

Thompson, E. A., *The Historical Work of Ammianus Marcellinus* (London, 1947).

Thompson, R. W., *Moses Khorenataʻi: History of the Armenians* (Cambridge, 1978).

Togilescu, G., 'Neue Inschriften aus der Dobrudscha und Rumanien', *Arch.-epig. Mitt. aus Öst-Ungaren*, 8 (1884), 1–34.

Toumanoff, C., 'The Third Century Armenian Arsacids: A Chronological and Genealogical Commentary', *RÉ Arm.* 6 (1969), 233–81.

Townsend, P. W., 'The Revolution of 238: The Leaders and their Aims', *YCS* 14 (1955), 49–105.

Tudor, D., 'La fortificazione delle città romane della Dacia nel sec. iii dell'e. n.', *Historia*, 14 (1965), 368–80.

—— 'Nouvelles recherches archéologiques sur le *limes Alutanus* et le *limes Transalutanus*', in *Actes du IXᵉ congrès international d'études sur les frontières romaines* (Bucharest, Cologne, and Vienna, 1974), 235–46.

Valtz, E., 'Kifrin, a Fortress of the *Limes* on the Euphrates', *Mesopotamia*, 22 (1987), 81–9.

Vogt, E., 'Das Akrostichon in der griechischen Literatur', *Antike und Abendland*, 13 (1967), 80–95.

Wagener, C., 'Eutropios', *Philologus*, 45 (1886), 509–51.

Walker, D., *The Metrology of Roman Silver Coinage*, iii. *From Pertinax to Uranius Antoninus* (*BAR* International Series, 40; Oxford, 1978).

Walser, G., 'The Crisis of the Third Century A.D.: A Reinterpretation', *Bucknell Review*, 13 (1965), 1–10.

Walter, G., *Nero*, trans. E. Crawford (London, 1957).

Weinstock, S., *Divus Julius* (Oxford, 1971).

Welles, C. B., 'The Epitaph of Julius Terentius', *HTR* 34 (1941), 79–102.

—— and Bellinger, A. R., 'A Third Century Contract of Sale from Edessa in Osrhoene', *YCS* 5 (1935), 95–154.

426   *Bibliography*

WEST, M. L., *Hesiod:* Theogony (Oxford, 1966).
—— *Hesiod:* Works and Days (Oxford, 1978).
—— *The Orphic Poems* (Oxford, 1983).
WIESEHÖFER, J., 'Die Anfänge sassanidischer Westpolitik und der Untergang Hatras', *Klio*, 64 (1982), 437–47.
WILL, E., 'Une nouvelle mosaïque de Chahba Philippopolis', *AAS* 3 (1953), 27–48.
WILLIGER, E., *Hagios: Untersuchungen zur Terminologie des Heiligen in den hellenisch-hellenistischen Religionen* (Gießen, 1922).
WINTER, E., *Die sāsānidisch-römischen Friedensverträge des 3. Jahrhunderts n. Chr.: Ein Beitrag zum Verständnis der außenpolitischen Beziehungen zwischen den beiden Großmächten* (Frankfurt, 1988).
WITTIG, K., 'C. Messius Quintus Traianus Decius', *RE* xv (1932), 1244–84.
—— 'Q. Herennius Etruscus Messius Decius', *RE* xv (1932), 1284–5.
—— 'C. Valens Hostilianus Messius Quintus', *RE* xv (1932), 1285–6.
WOLFF, G., *Porphyri de philosophia ex oraculis haurienda* (Berlin, 1856).
WÖRRLE, M., 'Ägyptisches Getreide für Ephesos', *Chiron*, 1 (1971), 325–40.
—— *Stadt und Fest im kaiserzeitlichen Kleinasien* (Munich, 1988).
YORK, J. M., 'The Image of Philip the Arab', *Historia*, 21 (1972), 320–32.
YOUTIE, H. C., 'Callimachus on the Tax Rolls', in *Proceedings of the 12th International Congress of Papyrology* (Toronto, 1970), 545–51 = *Scriptiunculae* (Amsterdam, 1973), 1035–41.
ZIEGLER, R., *Städtisches Prestige und kaiserliche Politik: Studien zum Festwesen in Ostkilikien im 2. und 3. Jahrhundert n. Chr.* (Düsseldorf, 1985).

Index of Sources

INSCRIPTIONS AND PAPYRI

COINS

General Index

DATE DUE
